LIGHTING THE WAY

*Nine Women Who Changed
Modern America*

KARENNA GORE SCHIFF

miramax books

HYPERION

NEW YORK

Library of Congress Cataloging-in-Publication Data

Schiff, Karenna Gore.
   Lighting the way : nine women who changed modern America /
Karenna Gore Schiff—1st ed.
        p.   cm.
   Includes bibliographical references and index.
   ISBN 1-4013-6015-7
   1. Women—United States—Biography.   2. Social reformers—
United States—Biography.   3. Women social reformers—
United States—Biography.   4. United States—Social conditions—
20th century.   I. Title.

CT3260.S35   2006
920.720973—dc22
[B]   2005056247

First Paperback Edition
10   9   8   7   6   5   4   3   2   1

"All [the women] are covered in a serious, fascinatingly footnoted, yet warm personal style."

—*Vanity Fair*

"These are stories worth telling, and Schiff does them proud."

—*People*

"In *Lighting the Way*, Karenna Gore Schiff draws compelling portraits of nine women who helped bring about a quiet revolution in the American way of life. This book vividly shows the power of individual passions for justice."

—Arthur Schlesinger, Jr.

"Schiff has done excellent research . . . she shows her heroines as fully rounded figures."

—*PublisherWeekly*

"I am so grateful Karenna Gore Schiff has written this book and told these women's compelling stories. Read it and be inspired."

—Marian Wright Edelman,
CEO and founder, Children's Defense Fund

"Karenna Gore Schiff recaptures the lives of nine women who entered public life, even as she illuminates the practice of women's politics. In celebrating a varied group of women who changed the course of twentieth-century America, Schiff reminds us that the ultimate purpose of politics is public service, not personal gain. *Lighting the Way* pierces the gathering gloom and cynicism surrounding contemporary politics by reminding us that leaders emerge in the darkest days and that change is possible."

—Glenda E. Gilmore, Peter V. and C. Vann Woodward
Professor of History, Yale University

"Inspiring . . . a feminist-influenced sequel to a similar book of real-life portraits of activists by another famous Democrat—*Profiles in Courage* by John F. Kennedy."

—*The Seattle Post-Intelligencer*

"This lively popular history will introduce Americans to a group of courageous and influential women—women about whom too few of us have known too little. Thanks to Karenna Gore Schiff, that's about to change."

—Mary Beth Norton, author of *Liberty's Daughters:
The Revolutionary Experience of American Women*

more . . .

Dedicated with love to my husband,
Drew Schiff

and

In memory of my two grandmothers,
Margaret Ann Carlson Aitcheson (1925–2001) and
Pauline LaFon Gore (1912–2004)

Contents

Introduction

Again and again in history some people wake up. They have no ground in the crowd and they move to broader, deeper laws. They carry strange customs with them and demand room for bold and audacious action. The future speaks ruthlessly through them. They change the world.
—Rainer Maria Rilke

I grew up around politics. One of my first memories is being on a stage with my parents in 1976 when my dad narrowly won the primary of his first political race—for the U.S. House of Representatives from Tennessee. Because the district was overwhelmingly Democratic, this meant he would go on to win the general election several months later and go to Washington, following the path of my grandfather, who had served in the House and then the Senate from 1938 until 1970. My third birthday was the day after the primary so just after midnight—as the final votes were being counted—the assembled crowd sang to me. More often than not, my exposure to politics has been on this level—a privileged vantage point on conventions, debates, rallies, and nail-biting election nights.

I also, like every American of my generation, grew up in a time of pervasive cynicism about politics. The unrelenting spin, the superficiality, the scandals (real or manufactured), the cold fact that so many people do not even vote—all dampen even the most coddled patriotic spirit, especially at times when patriotism is casually equated with unquestioning support of the decisions made by those in power. After the disappointment of the 2000 election, when I was drawn to that cynicism, I found that the best antidote is stories of those who fought against it by keeping politics grounded in public service. While there are elected officials who have done this, some of the more interesting and inspiring examples come from among the many other public servants behind the scenes. The positive turns of American history have often come about through the unheralded efforts of those who took heart in dark days, guiding politics—and politicians—toward our nation's ideals.

I have always been especially intrigued by the ways in which women in circumscribed roles have done this, perhaps because of the example of someone else who was there on that election night in 1976: my grandmother, Pauline Lafon Gore. The third of six children in a poor family from West Tennessee, she resolved early on that she wanted to make something of herself. Waiting tables at local restaurants and helping her mother take in boarders in their home, she worked her way through college and then Vanderbilt law school, becoming in 1936 one of the first women to graduate. It was very difficult to find work as a

My family on August 6, 1976, shortly after learning that my father had won the Democratic primary for the Congressional seat representing Tennessee's Fourth District: l-r, my grandfather Albert Gore, Sr., my father Albert Gore Jr., me, my mother Tipper Aitcheson Gore, my grandmother Pauline LaFon Gore.

female lawyer—"they'd tell me I was taking a job away from a man, a head of a household"—and she ended up in a small office in Texarkana, Arkansas, practicing both oil and gas law and divorce law. Soon she married my grandfather, then superintendent of schools in Smith County, and helped him win election to the U.S. Congress in 1938.

For the next forty-two years (until my grandfather left the Senate), she did not have her own separate career. Even so, she was often referred to as the best politician in the Gore family. I loved watching her with people; she had a sweet but steely way of getting them to do exactly what she wanted. She brought this to Washington, where she volunteered in First Lady Eleanor Roosevelt's office and lobbied all the officials she came into contact with on issues she felt so passionately about: quality public education, equal rights, criminal justice, international cooperation, free trade, respect for the rule of law. She brought it to the campaign trail in Tennessee, where she lingered talking with my grandfather's constituents and with those who had the power to help them. She constantly turned both her charm and her sharp analytical mind to helping solve social and economic problems. She urged my grandfather to take bold stands in his career, including his refusal to sign Strom Thurmond's Southern Manifesto, which declared that the Supreme Court's decision in *Brown v. Board of Education* would not be obeyed. Many have mused about what sort of career she might have had if more opportunities had been open to her. But the "she could have been a great senator herself" conversation always leaves me thinking that she was, after all, a great public servant.

I did not profile my grandmother, but all of these women remind me of her in some way. This is a personal rather than an academic work, and the process I used for selecting the women I write about here reflects that. At first it felt like organizing a dinner party: I considered how colorful and interesting each individual was, how well they fit together, how many was too many. But as I focused on the stories that resonated most with me, I was struck by how connected their lives were. Each acted as much out of patriotism as humanitarianism, a sense that what makes this country great is the principle that anyone, no matter what his or her background, should have the opportunity to succeed.

In simple terms, Ida B. Wells-Barnett campaigned against lynching and segregation, Mother Jones organized coal miners and fought child labor, Alice Hamilton pushed for regulation of industrial chemicals and for workers' compensation, Frances Perkins worked to establish Social Security and the right to collective bargaining, Virginia Durr fought to abolish the poll tax and racism, Septima Poinsette Clark established citizenship schools that registered black voters and cultivated civic leaders, Dolores Huerta organized farm workers, Helen Rodriguez-Trias was an activist for reproductive rights, and Gretchen Buchenholz is a child advocate.

Among the many fascinating women I did not profile are three that I consider giants of the past century—Jane Addams, Eleanor Roosevelt, and Rachel Carson—preferring to observe how their influence rippled out to the women I did focus on. By profiling women who are less well-known, I hope to help broaden the spectrum of American heroines. For similar reasons I chose not to feature the champions of equal rights, from Susan B. Anthony to Gloria Steinem. All nine women were influenced by and part of the women's movement, although they expressed it in different ways.

And I obviously also left out men (although those that weave throughout the text range from familiar pillars such as Franklin Roosevelt and Martin Luther King Jr. to lesser-known heroes such as Myles Horton and Fred Ross). The reason why *Lighting the Way* features women is not only that many have been overlooked because of the traditional bias toward male leadership. It is also because I wanted to tell the story of how that bias caused some women to influence the political agenda in creative, innovative ways.

Gender is of the essence in these stories. For one thing, these women focused on human needs that were sidelined by those seeking to project a more "masculine" political agenda. Alice Hamilton explained that initially she felt a special responsibility to study the effects of chemicals on factory workers because qualified male scientists had rejected the field as "tainted with Socialism or with feminine sentimentality for the poor." This "taint" helps explain why so many issues—racial violence, the welfare of children, prejudice, illiteracy, public health—went unheeded by the establishment for so long. The genius of these individuals is that they not only addressed them, they made them part of the mainstream dialogue, effectively removing the taint and putting their causes on the political agenda.

They all keenly understood and used the power of public awareness. Mother Jones's march of the mill children forced consumers to confront the suffering of the children who produced the goods they bought. More than seventy years later, Gretchen Buchenholz snuck a crew from *60 Minutes* into one of New York City's squalid and treacherous welfare hotels to expose the plight of homeless children.

They all believed in the importance of grassroots political movements, favoring a bottom-up approach to organizations and campaigns. While King was the national voice for civil rights, Septima Clark's citizenship classes provided what historian Taylor Branch calls the "payload" of the movement. While César Chávez rose to international fame for leading the farm workers, Dolores Huerta organized the strikes and boycotts that gave them political leverage.

They all wove webs of friendships and relationships that made their own attitude, in the words of George Eliot,[1] "incalculably diffusive." Virginia Durr, a gregarious hostess in her own home in Alabama, also wrote letters to her powerful friends in Washington, D.C., urging them to enforce federal civil rights laws. Helen Rodriguez-Trias recruited so many others to the campaign against coerced sterilization that one friend described her as the center of a wheel with spokes coming out on all sides, helping it turn.

Their experiences juggling work and family, a dilemma sometimes portrayed as unique to our time, were also a source of strength and imagination. The tales are harrowing: Dolores Huerta raised eleven children while organizing farm workers; Secretary of Labor Frances Perkins was responsible for both her teenage daughter and mentally ill husband (on the morning that President Roosevelt signed the Social Security Act into law, Perkins got a call informing her that her husband had escaped from a sanitarium); Helen Rodriguez-Trias gave birth to her fourth child in between graduating at the top of her class in medical school and establishing the first neonatal clinic on the island of Puerto Rico. In part because of their comfort with conflict and confusion, these women could see clearly above the fray and recognize opportunities to recalibrate social structures. As Septima Clark said, "I

---

[1] George Eliot closes her novel *Middlemarch* by describing the heroine Dorothea: "But the effect of her being on those around her was incalculably diffusive: for the growing good of the world is partly dependent on unhistoric acts; and that things are not so ill with you and me as they might have been, is half owing to the number who lived faithfully a hidden life, and rest in unvisited tombs."

have a great belief in the fact that whenever there is chaos, it creates wonderful thinking. I consider chaos a gift."

Although I did not select them for this reason, I think it is significant that all but one were teachers at some point in their lives. During most of the twentieth century, teaching (like nursing) was one of the few professions open to women and also one that was particularly eye-opening for those interested in socioeconomic issues affecting families. Some of these heroines were drawn to political action specifically because of the needs of their students. As Dolores Huerta put it, "I thought I could do more by organizing farm workers than by teaching their hungry children." The two women who were doctors also found that their professions put them in contact with the roots of social inequality. Hamilton's care for poor immigrants in Chicago led her to investigate the toxins in their workplaces and homes. Rodriguez-Trias' work as a pediatrician—a field she originally chose because she could "identify with mothers a lot"—led her to see the need for a public health agenda that addressed diseases like AIDS well before most politicians did.

There is another reason I wrote this book: I hope these stories illustrate how valuable the right to dissent is, how often the unpopular view is prescient, and how reactionaries use the same arguments over and over to block progress. In retrospect, the messages of these women seem obvious—people shouldn't be murdered by vigilante mobs, young children shouldn't be sent into mine shafts to work—but they were shunned and attacked for delivering them, and it was not that long ago. In forging the major movements of the twentieth century—civil rights, labor, public health, equal rights, environmentalism—these women were called unpatriotic so often it becomes almost comical (not to mention the fact that almost all were doggedly tracked by the FBI).

Often their efforts were so solitary, so against the grain, that they must have felt the temptation to give in. Alice Hamilton was chastised by her Harvard colleagues for speaking out against the post–World War I Allied blockade that exacerbated the suffering and instability in Germany, but she refused to back down, lamenting the "joyous ruthlessness" around her. Virginia Durr, whose own internal transformation from a racist college student to a charismatic figure on the vanguard of the civil rights movement provides a telescoped view of the awakening that much of the nation was going through, described

her efforts to eradicate racism in Alabama in the 1950s as "trying to sweep the sea back with a broom." It is humbling to think how often all of these women must have felt this way. As someone whose life of privilege has included an insider's vantage point on the sometimes imperfect electoral process, I was heartened to learn how much real political valor—and power—you cannot see from there.

These individuals had the extraordinary vision and courage to combat injustice, and our country is the better for it. Here are nine stories of women who were not afraid to give up the ground in the crowd Rilke spoke of and, in Virginia Durr's words, "step outside the magic circle." With perseverance and compassion they lived full bore in the service of others and of truth, lighting the way.

Ida B. Wells-Barnett

We do not believe that the moral conscience of this nation—that which is highest and best among us—will always remain silent in the face of such outrages—When this conscience wakes and speaks out in thunder tones, as it must, it will need facts to use as a weapon against injustice, barbarism, and wrong. It is for this reason that I carefully compile, print, and send forth these facts.

—IDA B. WELLS

ONE EVENING IN SEPTEMBER 1883, A YOUNG SCHOOLTEACHER named Ida B. Wells bought a first-class railroad ticket in Memphis, Tennessee, and boarded the eastbound Chesapeake, Ohio, and Southwestern train to Woodstock, Tennessee. In some ways, Ida was a model of proper Southern womanhood—petite, poised, pretty, and a bit vain about her appearance.

But Wells was no Scarlett O'Hara. For one thing, she had been born a slave in 1862, six months before the Emancipation Proclamation. Her parents died in a yellow fever epidemic when she was sixteen, and after that, she'd struggled to help support her younger siblings. She was a conscientious but unenthusiastic teacher and longed for a dramatic and wide-reaching career. She had no interest in "sugaring" young men to snare a beau, but she worried that she'd never fall in love and never have a family. She was a devout Baptist with impeccably high standards of social behavior, and yet her powerful sense of justice and her refusal to tolerate abuse overrode her notions of propriety, as the conductor on that train headed to Woodstock, Tennessee, would soon discover.

Shortly after the train left Memphis, the conductor informed Wells that she would have to move to the crowded and dirty smoking car, which also served as the "Negro car." Wells refused, pointing out that she'd bought a first-class ticket and was in the only first-class car. Writing her memoirs fifty years later, Ida recalled the scene:

> He tried to drag me out of the seat, but the moment he caught hold of my arm I fastened my teeth in the back of his hand. I had braced my feet against the back of the seat in front and was holding to the back and as he had already been badly bitten he didn't try it again by himself. He went forward and got the baggage man and another man to help him and of course they succeeded in dragging me out. They were encouraged to do this by the attitude of the white ladies and gentlemen in the car; some of them even stood on the seats so that they could get a good view and continued applauding the conductor for his brave stand.

Furious and humiliated, Wells left the train at the next stop. But she was far from defeated, and she thought that Tennessee law might offer her some recourse. In 1881, the legislature had passed a law requiring railroads to provide "separate but equal" accommodations for African-American passengers. The law was passed over the objections of the four African-American members of the legislature, who'd pushed for a ban on discrimination but had been overwhelmed by the growing power of white conservatives who were regaining seats as federal support for Reconstruction waned.

Ida hired an African-American attorney named Thomas Cassells to file suit. Cassells, working with a white attorney named James Greer, argued that the treatment of Wells violated the legal standard because there was no equivalent first-class "colored" car. In May 1884, Memphis Circuit Court Judge James O. Pierce, a Union veteran from Minnesota, found in Wells's favor and awarded her $200 in damages. The railroad immediately filed an appeal.

Cassells urged Ida to settle, assuring her that the railroad had promised she wouldn't be bothered anymore. Angered by his defeatism and suspecting he'd been bought off, she promptly fired him and hired Greer to fight the appeal. Soon after, on another train trip, Wells was again asked to leave the first-class car for which she had bought a ticket. She had Greer bring another suit, this time alleging both assault and discrimination. This second case was argued in November 1884, again in Judge Pierce's court. Pierce dismissed the assault charge but ruled in Wells's favor on the discrimination charge and awarded her $500 in damages (roughly equivalent to $9,000 today). The *Memphis Daily Appeal* noted the verdict in an article headlined, A DARKY DAMSEL OBTAINS A VERDICT FOR DAMAGES AGAINST THE CHESAPEAKE & OHIO RAILROAD.

Again the railroad appealed, and in the spring of 1887, the Tennessee Supreme Court overturned the verdict. The railroad's attorneys carried the day with their argument that the accommodations offered to Wells were "alike in every respect as to comfort, convenience, and safety" and that her true purpose was "to harass with a view to this suit." Wells was even held liable for court costs, which exceeded the amount she had originally been awarded.

The ruling indicated growing changes in race relations. Ida had come of age during the relatively progressive atmosphere of Reconstruction, which had led to some successful lawsuits against the railroads. In 1880, a federal judge awarded Jane Brown $3,000 after she was excluded from a first-class train car. Two years later, the Louisville and Nashville Railroad settled with Ada Buck, paying her $750 after refusing her a seat in the first-class car despite her purchase of a first-class ticket. The reforms of Reconstruction came to a screeching halt as reactionaries claimed power in the South, enabled by a loosening of federal control that culminated in the Supreme Court's 1896 decision in *Plessy v. Ferguson*.[1]

---

[1] In 1892 a cobbler named Homer Plessy was arrested for sitting in a whites-only car on the East Louisiana Railroad. He took the case to state court, arguing violation of the Thirteenth and Fourteenth Amendments. He lost, appealed to the state supreme court and lost again, appealed to the United States Supreme Court and, in 1896, lost one final, groundbreaking time. Thirteen years after Wells filed her suit, *Plessy v. Ferguson* established that "separate but equal" accommodations were constitutional, and enabled the network of legal and social segregation that came to be called Jim Crow.

Deeply disappointed, Ida wrote about the case in her diary:

Went to see [Greer] this afternoon & he tells me that four of them cast their personal prejudices in the scale of justice. . . . I felt so disappointed because I had hoped such great things from my suit for my people generally. I have firmly believed all along that the law was on our side and would, when we appealed to it, give us justice. I feel shorn of that belief and utterly discouraged, and just now if it were possible would gather my race in my arms and fly far away with them. O God is there no redress, no peace, no justice in this land for us?

Ida B. Wells turned her sharp intellect and resolve to fighting discrimination at a time when few else dared. As she delved deeper into the many issues of racial injustice, she focused on the most horrific: lynching, the routine torture and murder of black men, women, and children. Within ten years of the Chesapeake Railroad incident, Wells had become the leading antilynching activist, forceful, controversial, and renowned throughout the United States and the United Kingdom. For decades to come, she investigated and researched lynchings, gathering facts to counter the lies told by many in the mainstream press. In a career that spanned almost forty years, she made countless speeches, published articles and essays, and built a network of clubs and community organizations for American blacks. She worked with notable activists of her time, including Susan B. Anthony, Frederick Douglass, and W. E. B. Du Bois, but always maintained her own independent voice. Writing, speaking, or organizing, she was willing to stand on the bold, unpopular edge, incurring significant personal risk in the process. For the rest of her long career, throughout innumerable battles, Wells showed the same bravery and ferocity that she found to face that conductor.

Family Roots

Ida Bell Wells was born on July 16, 1862, in Holly Springs, Mississippi, the first child of James Wells and Elizabeth Warrenton, both slaves. Jim's master had sent him to Holly Springs from the plantation in nearby Tippah County and had him apprenticed to a carpenter. While working with a builder named Bolling, Jim fell in love with

Lizzie, the Bollings' cook. Though they lived together as husband and wife, the couple (like all slaves) were legally barred from marrying until after Emancipation. The couple would have eight children in all, four girls and four boys. (Two of the boys would die in early childhood.)

Jim Wells was a relatively privileged bondsman: trained in a skill, hired out away from the isolation of the plantation, able to exercise some amount of control over his time and life. No doubt his master noticed that Jim was intelligent and industrious, but there's a more basic reason for the special attention and treatment: Jim Wells's master was also his father. The plantation owner had no children with his wife, Miss Polly, and James was born late in his life, to a slave named Peggy. (James's father is never named in *Crusade for Justice*, Wells's autobiography, or in Linda McMurry's biography of her.)

Jim never discussed the details of his parentage with his daughter, but Ida recalled one searing moment of truth:

> The only thing I remember about my father's reference to slave days was when his mother came to town on one of her annual visits. . . . On one such occasion she told about "Miss Polly," her former mistress, and said "Jim, Miss Polly wants you to come and bring the children. She wants to see them."
>
> "Mother," said he, "I never want to see that old woman as long as I live. I'll never forget how she had you stripped and whipped the day after the old man died, and I am never going to see her. I guess it is all right for you to take care of her and forgive her for what she did to you, but she could have starved to death if I'd had my say-so. She certainly would have, if it hadn't been for you."
>
> I was burning to ask what he meant, but children were seen and not heard in those days. They didn't dare break into old folks' conversation. But I have never forgotten those words. Since I have grown old enough to understand I cannot help but feel what an insight to slavery they give.

Jim Wells stayed busy with his work and his civic activities. He was a member of the Masons, a trustee of Shaw University, and active in the local Republican Party. (At the end of the Civil War, Bolling asked Wells to continue working for him, which he did. But when the younger man refused to vote a Democratic ticket, Bolling locked him out of his shop. Wells set up his own carpentry business, which prospered.) Elizabeth ran the household with a strict but loving hand: assigning chores, overseeing schoolwork, imposing the kind of discipline Ida would later use with her own children.

Neither James nor Elizabeth had ever received an education, and they were determined to do better for their children. "I do not remember when or where I started school," Ida wrote. "My earliest recollections are of reading the newspaper to my father and an admiring group of his friends." Ida and her school-age siblings attended Shaw University, which offered elementary education as well as teacher training. Elizabeth accompanied her children to school until she too had learned to read.

Thriving at school, well-loved and well-cared-for by her parents, Ida Wells had a remarkably happy childhood. Sadly, her childhood ended in the summer of 1878, when the Wells family fell victim to an epidemic of yellow fever so terrible that it had a role in reshaping the South.

Yellow Fever

In the nineteenth century, yellow fever epidemics periodically swept the region, killing thousands. The usual symptoms include fever, chills, headache, muscle aches, vomiting, backache, and jaundice, the yellowed eyes and skin characteristic of liver failure that gave the disease its name. Severe yellow fever cases result in ruptured blood vessels and both internal and external bleeding, systemic shock, and acute kidney and liver damage.[2] The disease struck the young and healthy especially hard, and whites were more susceptible than blacks. Those who had survived a previous spell of yellow fever

---

[2] The disease first appeared in Boston in the eighteenth century, and Philadelphia suffered a horrible epidemic in 1793, but in the nineteenth century, yellow fever disappeared from the Northeast and became endemic to the South. As epidemics struck various cities—Galveston in 1839, New Orleans in 1853—the disease grew more virulent over time, and became closely identified with the South as a distinctive region. Southerners complained about Northerners' exaggerations of yellow-fever terrors, while Northerners only became more convinced that the "Sickly South" was indeed a foreign and unhealthy land.

seemed immune, while those who had recently moved to the area were especially likely to contract it. (Another name for yellow fever was "stranger's disease.")

For all of its horrors, the most frightening aspect of yellow fever was that no one knew how it spread. The "fomite theory" held that the fever was transmitted by contact with infected people or with fomites—infected objects, such as clothing or bedding. Some researchers believed the fever was transmitted through miasmas or unhealthy air associated with marshy soil. Stricken cities, including Memphis in 1878, tried to ward off the disease by lighting bonfires and setting off cannons to disrupt the noxious atmosphere. In 1880 one physician theorized that yellow fever, like malaria, was spread via mosquitoes, but his experiments couldn't confirm this and his theory was largely dismissed. (Finally, in 1900, Major Walter Reed of the United States Army's Yellow Fever Commission demonstrated that the infectious agent was an "ultra-microscopic germ," or what we now call a virus. His discovery led to a vaccine that helped stamp out the last vestiges of what had been a fierce and prolific killer.)

Ships arriving from yellow-fever regions had to anchor offshore until it was clear no one on board was infected. When ships and towns were found to be infected, they were quarantined and required to post a yellow flag, or yellow jack, which reinforced the disease's name. Survivors described deserted streets, shuttered stores, dwindling supplies of food and medicine, nurses and physicians overwhelmed by the sheer numbers of the sick, entire families dying alone and untended, stacks of coffins waiting for burial. Any serious outbreak was also accompanied by reports of looting and robbery of the dead and dying. Yet the suffering also brought out the best in some people, prompting outpourings of support from Americans across the country. The Howard Association, a service organization of young men who voluntarily helped tend the sick and bury the dead, established chapters throughout the South.

The epidemic of 1878 was the most widespread and deadly outbreak in this country. The first cases appeared in New Orleans in August, and the disease spread through two hundred communities in eight states, reaching as far north as Gallipolis, Ohio, and infecting new victims until the first frost brought relief in November. Memphis was devastated, and anyone with the means to leave the city fled. By the time a quarantine was issued, there were about 20,000 people left in Memphis: 14,000 blacks and 6,000 whites, mostly poor Irish. At the end of the epidemic, blacks had suffered 946 deaths among 11,000 cases. Almost all the whites were infected and 4,204 of them died. In the wake of the disaster, the city—already struggling under a corrupt administration—went bankrupt.[3]

This was the reality that Ida B. Wells faced in the summer of 1878. She was visiting her grandmother, who'd settled on a farm outside Holly Springs, when they got word that yellow fever was spreading through Memphis, fifty miles away. A few days later came worse news: both James and Elizabeth were dead, as was their youngest boy. Ida insisted on returning home as soon as possible. In her memoir, she describes waiting for the first available train.

> It was a freight train. No passenger trains were running or needed. And the caboose in which I rode was draped in black for two previous conductors who had fallen victims to the dreaded disease. The conductor who told me this was sure I had made a mistake to go home. I asked him why he was running the train when he knew he was likely to get the fever as had those for whom the car was draped. He shrugged his shoulders and said that somebody had to do it. "That's exactly why I am going home. I am the oldest of seven living children. There's nobody but me to look after them now. Don't you think I should do my duty, too?" He said nothing but bade me goodbye as though he never expected to see me again.

Though orphaned, the Wells children weren't completely alone. They had family in the area, and Jim Wells's fellow Masons also offered

---

[3] In his book *Yellow Fever & Public Health in the New South*, historian John H. Ellis argues that the deadly 1878 epidemic rallied public opinion in support of new federal standards for public health. The hygiene movement was well under way in Northern cities but Southerners resisted outside interference. The crushing loss and misery of the 1878 outbreak created openings for organizations such as the fledgling American Public Health Association. APHA and others advocated improvements in water supply, sewage, trash disposal, and other municipal tasks that had been handled ineptly, corruptly, or both. Though there were limited outbreaks of yellow fever after 1878, there was never another attack as costly or as vicious.

help. Jim had left the family debt-free with some savings, but not nearly enough for them to live on for long. Ida insisted that the family stay together. "I took the examination for a country schoolteacher and had my dresses lengthened, and I got a school six miles out in the country." A family friend stayed at the Wells house during the week and Ida came home every Friday "on the back of a big mule" to spend the weekend cooking and cleaning before riding the mule back out to her school.

It was too much to sustain indefinitely. In 1881 a widowed aunt living in Memphis invited Ida to settle with her and her three small children. Ida took her two youngest sisters with her while the others stayed in Holly Springs with relatives. In search of a decent paycheck to help support her siblings, Ida first got a job teaching in a county school and later passed the test to teach in city schools.

Memphis

The city of Memphis had survived the Civil War with its infrastructure largely intact, but its racial makeup drastically changed. During the war, the black population surged—an astonishing 450 percent increase from 1860 (3,500 slaves and 200 freedmen) to 1865 (over 16,000 blacks)—largely because of the influx of blacks who fled their bondage on rural plantations.

White hostility grew, as reflected in a local paper's observation that "thousands of lazy Negro men and women" were now "spending most of their time sunning themselves by day and stealing at night" under the protection of federal troops. Another writer complained of the men "playing, idling, and sleeping in the sun" and the growing shantytowns, "where disease and vice in their most loathsome and revolting characters abound." One of the ironies of this blatant hostility was that the newly arrived black Memphians were competing with whites for low-wage jobs.

The inhabitants of cities, struggling with economic hardship, would have resented an influx of poor citizens of any race. But in their defeat, white Southerners could scarcely tolerate the newly freed blacks. The mere sight of them seemed to be an insult, and politicians exploited these feelings, promising to redeem the South. In August 1865 Tennessee governor William G. Brownlow proclaimed, "The Negroes, like the Indian tribes, will gradually become extinct, having no owners to care for them . . . Idleness, starvation, and disease will remove the majority of this generation."

With tensions running high, racial violence broke out in many cities throughout the South. One of the worst riots took place in Memphis in May 1866, triggered by the arrest of a black man and the subsequent confrontation between police and a group that included freedmen and demobilized soldiers. In the end forty-eight people were killed in the Memphis race riot of 1866: forty-one black men, two black women, three black children, and two white men. In the aftermath, an editorial took pleasure in the effort: "The late riots in our city have satisfied all of one thing: that the southern men will not be ruled by the negro. . . . The negroes now know, to their sorrow, that it is best not to arouse the fury of the white man."

By the time Ida arrived in Memphis, fifteen years after the race riot, the racial tensions were on a low simmer, with whites ever ready to subjugate blacks who crossed the line. As before, blacks forged a separate culture and Ida joined a well-established black middle class, with its own churches, civic groups, and cultural organizations.

Ida had a difficult social life, disdaining "frivolous inanity" in herself and others. She longed for friendships with other women but felt incapable of inspiring or sustaining them. She enjoyed engaging in highbrow repartee and pointed irony with the men she knew, but was unwilling to play the role demanded of a sweetheart: "I will not begin at this late date by doing that that my soul abhors; sugaring men, weak deceitful creatures, with flattery to retain them as escorts or to gratify a revenge." She wrote of one beau, "[he] came home with me & told me of his love for me & I reciprocated. I told him I was not conscious of an absorbing feeling for him but I thought it would grow. I feel so lonely and isolated."

Ida lived with her aunt at first but later stayed in a series of boardinghouses or rented rooms in the homes of other respectable black women in the neighborhood. Her aunt and her youngest sisters soon moved to Visalia, California. After leaving school, her brothers went back and forth between Mississippi and Tennessee, often working as carpenters' apprentices. Even after all her siblings had moved away, Ida regularly sent money to them.

Teaching was one of the few respectable, reasonably well-paying jobs open to her, and Ida pursued it. Her first job was at a county school ten miles north of Memphis, but soon she began teaching in schools inside the city. Ida was never happy as a teacher and became frustrated when the "confinement and monotony of the primary work began to grow distasteful." In her diaries, she often wrote about her fellow teachers but rarely about the work itself, and she never mentions any particular student. Perhaps this indicates both her difficulty with collaboration and her yearning to have a broader impact.

Wells had a deeply grounded sense of her own potential, an occasionally wavering but deep-seated certainty that she could, and would, influence the world around her. She pushed herself very hard because she felt that she had a responsibility to her race and nation, and the more she saw of her own potential, the more she despised Jim Crow.[4] Even while supporting her siblings, continuing her vigorous self-education, and building a career as a journalist, Wells bemoaned her "sluggish nature" and all the "wasted opportunities" in her life.

Princess of the Press

Wells's writing career really took off when she published a piece about her lawsuit in *Living Way* a few months after the Tennessee Supreme Court had overturned her victory. As she published more articles, she also channeled some self-criticism into effective evaluation of her own work. "It reads very well, but a little disconnected," she wrote of one essay. "I think sometimes I can write a readable article and then again I wonder how I could have been so mistaken in myself." "A glance at all my 'brilliant?' productions pall on my understanding; they all savor of dreary sameness, however varied the

---

[4] This term originated in the late 1820s when white entertainer Thomas Dartmouth Rice began dressing in blackface and performing a song-and-dance act called "Jump Jim Crow." (He later said he'd come up with the shambling steps after watching a crippled black man make his way through the streets.) A typical verse, from sheet music titled "Jim Crow! The Celebrated Nigger Song": "I sit upon a hornet's nest / I dance upon my head / I tie a wiper round my neck / and den I goes to bed / Wheel about and turn about and do jis so / Ebry time I wheel about I jump Jim Crow." The term was applied first to blacks themselves but later described the separate facilities set aside for them. As early as 1842, a newspaper writer referred to the "spirit that compels the colored man to ride in the Jim-Crow car."

1. T. THOMAS FORTUNE, Journalist.
2. BOOKER T. WASHINGTON, Educator.
3. HON. FREDERICK DOUGLASS, Statesman.
4. I. GARLAND PENN, Author, Orator;
Chief Commissioner, Atlanta Exposition.
5. MISS IDA B. WELLS
Lecturer, Defender of the Race.

This collage appeared in the book *The College of Life or Practical Self-Educator, A Manual of Self-Improvement for The Colored Race*, published in 1900. (courtesy Manuscripts, Archives and Rare Books Division, Schomburg Center for Research in Black Culture, The New York Public library, Astor, Lenox and Tilden Foundations).

subject, and the style is monotonous. I find a paucity of ideas that makes it a labor to write freely and yet—what is it that keeps urging me to write notwithstanding?"

As her writing career grew, Ida honed her negotiating skills to secure appropriate payment, turning down offers that paid too little and learning to pitch and parry with the editors. "The *Sun* unhesitatingly accepts my offer to go to Washington as its representative," she recorded, "but remains pointedly mum about the money question. I answered immediately to say I could not go without them paying my way but nothing has resulted but a silence blank and discreet."

By 1888 Wells was contributing to black newspapers around the country, including the *Indianapolis World*, the *Chicago Conservator*, the *A.M.E. Church Review*, the *Detroit Plain Dealer*, and the *People's Choice*, often writing under the pen name "Iola."[5] She attended National Colored Press Association meetings and networked with editors and journalists from all over the country. She also frequently wrote letters to the editor to white newspapers such as the *Memphis Scimitar*, pointing out their racism and factual errors. Soon Iola was widely cited and often praised, earning the respect of her mostly male colleagues. A correspondent for the New Orleans *Weekly Pelican* proclaimed in 1887 that "the pleasant-faced, modest Miss Ida Wells" was "the most prominent correspondent at present connected with the Negro press."

That year T. Thomas Fortune,[6] editor of the *New York Age*, wrote of Iola, "She has become famous as one of the few of our women who handles a goose quill with diamond point as handily as any man in newspaper work. She has plenty of nerve and is as sharp as a steel

---

[5] I found no clear indication of the reason (or reasons) why Wells chose this pen name. "Iola" was a relatively common girl's name in the nineteenth century and the letters themselves echo those in her own name.

[6] Fortune was a prominent black journalist and an outspoken advocate for civil rights. He was active in the Afro-American League, founded in 1887 and later called the National Afro-American Council. The group's platform included demands for equal accommodations, voting rights, and an end to lynching. Early on, Wells and Fortune established a friendly professional relationship via letter. Ida may have hoped for something more, until she saw his photograph in the *Age*. She wrote in her diary, "My curiosity is satisfied but I am disappointed in him. With his long hair, curling about his forehead and his spectacles he looks more like the dude of the period than the strong, sensible, brainy man I have pictured him. But then . . . one should not judge a person by the cut or rather uncut of his hair any more than by his clothes." The two remained friends and Thomas would later hire Ida to write for the *Age*.

trap." Another reporter called her "the Princess of the Press" and an "inspiration to the younger writers." (At the time, Ida herself was twenty-three.) The other writers marveled at her ambition to edit a paper and her belief that "there is no agency so potent as the press in reaching and elevating a people."

I find two themes in Wells's early writing particularly striking. First, she urged black Americans to do everything in their power to help themselves, as individuals and as a group. She believed that all blacks should stand up for themselves, refuse to bow to Jim Crow, and speak out against discrimination, stereotypes, and lynching. Throughout her life, she advocated fierce, even armed self-defense. Stressing the moral imperative to help those in need, she was especially critical of leading blacks who seemed to pay more attention to the elite than to the rest of the population. "What material benefit is a 'leader' if he does not, to some extent, devote his time, talent and wealth to the alleviation of the poverty and misery, and elevation of his people?" she wrote in *Living Way*. She constantly held self-styled leaders—including herself—to that high standard.

Like her parents, Wells was a strong believer in the value of education, formal and informal. While living in Memphis, she took elocution classes, attended plays, and participated in a weekly lyceum discussing literature, poetry, essays, and music. Wells wanted to extend these benefits beyond her circle: "I had an instinctive feeling that the people who had little or no school training should have something coming into their homes weekly which dealt with their problems in a simple, helpful way. So in weekly letters to the *Living Way*, I wrote in a plain, common sense way on the things which concerned our people." These letters were picked up by other black newspapers and, along with her articles about the railroad lawsuit, formed the basis of her earliest professional writing.

Wells's other focus was more controversial: exposing the unacknowledged truths regarding sex and race in the South, truths Ida knew all too well. The knowledge of the relationship between her own grandparents must have shaped the self-assured intensity with which she described and fought against the routine rape of black women by white men. The truth was no secret. As she later pointed out, "It is written in the faces of the million mulattoes in the South."

Though she never addressed this issue in her published work of the time, Wells did note in her diary at least six cases in Memphis where white women had voluntarily taken black lovers. One of her diary entries recounts the story of a white man who cut the finger of his black lover and sucked her blood so that he could claim to have some Negro blood in his veins when he procured a marriage license. "The facts were brought out in his subsequent trial as his friends knew him to be of Caucasian blood & parentage & proved it." These early, private writings prefigure her later published accounts about sexual attraction between the races, such as when she shocked readers by declaring: "The miscegenation laws of the South only operate against the legitimate union of the races; they leave the white man free to seduce all the colored girls he can, but it is death to the colored man who yields to the force and advances of a similar attraction in white women."

Ida B. Wells, increasingly sure of her own powerful mind, experienced what W. E. B. Du Bois would later describe as "double-consciousness, this sense of always looking at one's self through the eyes of others, of measuring one's soul by the tape of a world that looks on in amused contempt and pity. One ever feels his two-ness—an American, a Negro; two souls, two thoughts, two unreconciled strivings; two warring ideals in one dark body." Her attention to dispelling the stereotype of black women as amoral sluts—which was repeated in conversations, stories, and even academic texts, and which served to justify the ubiquitous sexual exploitation of black women by white men—reflects her own war against the "double-consciousness" imposed upon her. One of her many experiences of being branded with this stereotype happened right after her parents died, when a rumor circulated that she'd kept her siblings out of foster care by prostituting herself to white men.

As Wells reached her midtwenties still unmarried, the rumors intensified: she engaged in "immoral conduct" with her male colleagues, she was kept as a mistress by at least one white man, she had an illegitimate child. Wells was astute enough to recognize that she was an especially appealing target because of her outspokenness, her lack of a male relative to defend her, and her refusal to conform to the standards of the Victorian lady. The unfairness infuriated her and also fueled her sense of mission. "I have been so long misrepresented that I begin to rebel."

This rebellion took the form of an active counteroffensive. When a newspaper editor mentioned the emblematic "black harlot" in a column, Wells wrote to protest the casual slander. She also wrote essays, such as "Our Women," which defended the virtue of black women: "None [of the accusations] sting so deeply and keenly as the taunt of immorality; the jest and sneer with which our women are spoken of, and the utter incapacity or refusal to believe there are among us mothers, wives and maidens who have attained a true, noble, and refining womanhood."

Wells often attended journalism and church conferences, frequently staying with friends or colleagues. On a trip to Natchez, Mississippi, she'd boarded with the family of a respected minister who was caste-conscious and looked down on Wells. Apparently he snooped through Ida's trash, read her discarded letters, then warned others that she was not a fit partner for an upstanding young man. Once word of this accusation reached Ida, she immediately confronted him. Not only did she secure a private apology, she insisted that the preacher address his congregation from the pulpit and apologize for making false remarks that reflected on the character of Miss Ida B. Wells.

In the face of these interior conflicts and external battles, Ida's writing became more and more crucial to her self-confidence. Using surprisingly modern phrasing, Wells said in her autobiography, "The correspondence I had built up in newspaper work gave me an outlet through which to express the real 'me' and I enjoyed my work to the utmost." But for Wells, her writing meant more than self-expression. It was her vehicle for leadership, her way to devote herself to the "elevation" of her people.

In 1889, when Wells was twenty-seven, the owners of a local African-American paper, the *Free Speech and Headlight*, approached her about working for them. Ida agreed, but only if she became an equal partner. Ida took over editing duties from Reverend Taylor Nightingale, pastor of the Beale Street Baptist Church, who became the sales manager, and the third partner, J. L. Fleming, continued as the business manager. Nightingale's congregation provided a built-in audience for the paper, and having her own paper was a huge boost for Wells. Even so she kept her teaching job, handling the writing and editing in her off hours.

In 1891 Wells caused an uproar when she wrote an editorial criticizing the school system. "I felt that some protest should be made over conditions in the colored schools," she explained later. "The article was a protest against the few and utterly inadequate buildings for colored children. I also spoke of the poor teachers given us whose mental and moral character was not the best." Wells's teaching contract was not renewed. Rather than fighting to get her job back, she moved on, committing herself to her work as a truth-telling journalist. "I thought it was right to strike a blow against a glaring evil and I did not regret it."

Wells had found the meaningful work she'd been seeking and was becoming quite successful at it. She must have felt a sense of accomplishment, of hope for the future. Within a year, that hope would be replaced by fury.

The People's Grocery Lynchings

Despite her worries about her inability to make friends, Wells was part of a thriving social circle of successful black Memphians. Among her closest friends were Thomas and Betty Moss, who asked Ida to be godmother to one of their daughters, Maurine. When a group of African Americans organized to establish a store, the People's Grocery, Thomas Moss was the corporation's president. (He was also a postal worker, a position of some prestige.) Opened in a mixed neighborhood called the Curve, the new store successfully competed with the white-owned grocery that had monopolized the market. In March 1892, a trivial argument—Ida later said it was a boys' squabble

Ida B. Wells with lynching victim Thomas Moss's widow, Betty, Thomas Moss, Jr. and Maurine Moss, Wells' goddaughter. The photograph was taken ca. 1894 in Indianapolis where Mrs. Moss relocated after her husband's murder. (courtesy Special Collections Research Center, The University of Chicago Library)

over a game of marbles—escalated into violence. The fight ended when Calvin McDowell, a clerk at the People's Grocery, prevailed over W. H. Barrett, owner of the competing grocery. Barrett filed assault charges against McDowell in the Shelby County criminal court and then, following an angry meeting of the black community, Barrett convinced Judge Julius DuBose of the criminal court that an insurrection was being planned. DuBose issued bench warrants for two speakers at the meeting, and plans were made to arrest the men at the People's Grocery that weekend. Fanning the flames yet more, Barrett then spread word that a white mob was coming on Saturday night to clean out the People's Grocery.

The store owners consulted a lawyer, who told them that because the store was outside the city limits, they could expect no police protection and should defend the store themselves. Accordingly, several men armed themselves and planned to stay overnight. Around 10 P.M. someone shouted out a warning of intruders, and the defenders opened fire, wounding three. The white men turned out to be sheriff's deputies, though they wore plain clothes and didn't identify themselves. About a dozen African Americans, including McDowell and People's Grocery stockholder Will Stewart, were immediately arrested.

The shooting seemed to confirm threats of a black uprising and, in response, whites began breaking into black homes. Police arrested and jailed thirty more blacks, including Thomas Moss, who was accused of leading the People's Grocery defenders. For two nights, members of the Tennessee Rifles, an African-American militia, guarded the jail, but then, in a example of the continuing reversal of Reconstruction measures, Judge DuBose issued an order to disarm all black citizens. The jail was undefended.

Though it soon became clear that the three wounded men would live, white Memphians stayed enraged. On Wednesday night a group of men entered the jail, let in by a jailer who said he didn't notice they were masked until they'd already forced their way in. The mob seized Moss, McDowell, and Stewart. All three were taken to a pasture about a mile out of town and shot to death. As the newspaper reported, McDowell's eyes were also gouged out.

Then, as Wells later recounted, "the mob took possession of the People's Grocery Company, helping themselves to food and drink, and destroyed what they could not eat or steal." Ida seethed beneath her grief: "The only reason hundreds of Negroes were not killed that day by the mobs was because of the forbearance of the colored men [who] submitted to outrages and insults for the sake of those depending on them." No one was punished, or even arrested, for these murders. In her memoirs, Ida wrote, "This is what opened my eyes to what lynching really was. An excuse to get rid of Negroes who were acquiring wealth and property and thus keep the race terrorized and 'keep the nigger down.'"

Horrible as they were, the People's Grocery murders were not extreme by the brutal standards of lynch law.[7] While lynching is now sometimes assumed to denote hanging, the true distinguishing characteristic of lynching is its extralegal nature. Lynch mobs killed men and women in a horrific variety of ways, often calculated to inflict the most pain over the longest period of time: dismemberment, flaying, burning alive. They acted without legal authority and outside the legal system as self-appointed judges, juries, and executioners. They were also terrorists. Their violence was aimed not only at the men and women actually killed but also at thousands of others who would become more docile, afraid of attracting the same fatal attention.

Lynching became a routine business in the immediate wake of the Civil War, but the incidents went largely unrecorded except for irregular entries in the records of local Freedmen's Bureaus.[8] One Kentucky

---

[7] While there's some dispute over the origin of the term, "lynch law" was likely named for Captain William Lynch, a Revolutionary War patriot and planter near Pittsylvania, Virginia. In 1780, frustrated by the inaccessibility of civil courts, he drew up a compact with other nearby planters to punish vandals, thieves, and Tories on their own authority. The phrase "lynch law" first appeared in print in 1811, referring to William Lynch and the tribunals over which he presided.

[8] Officially known as the Bureau of Refugees, Freedmen, and Abandoned Lands, the Freedmen's Bureau was set up in 1865 as a branch of the War Department in order to handle the needs of the former slaves: arranging transportation, housing, schooling, marriage certificates, labor contracts, and medical care. In 1866 the Freedmen's Bureau also became responsible for filing claims for back pay, bounties, or pensions on behalf of blacks who had served in the military. The effectiveness of each office was largely determined by the competence and sympathies of the assistant commissioner in charge. By 1869, most of the bureau's activities had been curtailed, and the Freedmen's Bureau was officially shut down in 1872.

In 1901, W. E. B. Du Bois wrote an article about the Freedmen's Bureau for the *Atlantic Monthly* that began and ended with his famous and prophetic statement: "The problem of the twentieth century is the problem of the color line."

officer documented dozens of vicious attacks, with the victims "whipped until insensible," "assaulted and ravished," "beaten to death," "beaten and roasted," "beaten and driven from their homes." In each case, he named the perpetrators and provided sworn witness testimony to the crimes. In Mississippi an officer named the men who had murdered a freedman, leaving him "beheaded, skinned, and his skin nailed to the barn." In Alabama, a young black minister was attacked by men who feared he would begin agitating for black schools and stirring up his congregation. When a colleague saw the preacher later, he described him as "a curdled lump of blood." In each case, the local Freedmen's Bureau declined to investigate.

Although the members of the lynching party rarely bothered to conceal their identities, the prisoner's death was almost always attributed to "person or persons unknown." The police, as well as local politicians, condoned—and sometimes participated in—the ritual murders. As one relatively conscientious police officer charged with guarding a black prisoner recalled, "I went into that cell block with every intention of fulfilling my oath and protecting that man, but when the mob opened the door, the first half-a-dozen men standing there were leading citizens—businessmen, leaders of their churches and the community—I just couldn't do it." Lynch mobs were even known to hold prayer sessions at local churches before going to seize their victims. This hypocrisy enraged Ida, who was deeply religious herself and devastated by the churches' indifference: "Our American Christians are too busy saving the souls of white Christians from burning in hell-fire to save the lives of black ones from present burning in fires kindled by white Christians," she wrote.

The press often wrote up the proceedings with an air of satisfaction, as if justice had been done. Blunt, unapologetic newspaper accounts ran under headlines such as "Colored Man Roasted Alive." Victims were routinely tortured to death, with bits of clothing and even body parts sliced off and handed around as souvenirs. The advent of more portable cameras and equipment introduced a new and macabre form of documentation: photographs taken on the scene and handed out as souvenirs, even mailed out as postcards. The fact that so many lynchings were photographed—and so many photographs were circulated—reveals the extent to which these heinous murders were celebrated. The photographs themselves often depict a carnival-like atmosphere; several show men grinning at the camera, or small children perched on a grown-up's shoulders for a better view. As collected in the chilling and important book *Without Sanctuary*, they provide an unimpeachable record of the horrors of lynch law.

At the time they were taken and distributed, the photographs served to extend the violence and threats. After John H. Holmes, a Unitarian minister in New York, publicly condemned lynching, he received a postcard of an Alabama crowd posing around the body of a black man dangling from a rope. Written on the back: "This is the way we do things down here. The last lynching has not been put on card yet. Will put you on our regular mailing list. Expect one a month on the average."

The white press continually gave the same justification for lynching—to protect white women against being raped by monstrous, oversexed black men. As Ida so clearly saw, the real motivation was white Southerners' fear of "black power" in any form. The South's entire economic and cultural system was based on keeping the black population on the bottom rung socially and financially. Rape was the symbol for all of that anxiety and the justification for what became systematic racial terrorism. Of course, black women were also victimized by lynch mobs (Wells herself would be threatened) though less frequently than black men. Attacks against black women took place with immeasurable frequency, out of public view.

The following passage appeared in a newspaper owned by leading white businessmen in Memphis:

> The lynching of three Negro scoundrels reported in our dispatches from Anniston, Ala., for brutal outrage committed upon a white woman will be a text for much comment on "Southern barbarism" by Northern newspapers; but we fancy it will hardly prove effective for campaign purposes among intelligent people. The frequency of these lynchings calls attention to the frequency of the crimes which causes [sic] lynching. The "Southern barbarism"which deserves the serious attention of all people North and South, is the barbarism which preys upon weak and defenseless women. Nothing but the most prompt, speedy, and extreme punishment can hold in check the horrible and bestial propensities of the Negro race.

Iola's Crusade

Following the People's Grocery murders, Ida embarked on a fight against lynching and the lies that supported it. First, she appealed to the ideals and principles of American law and democracy. Wells, who understood that knowledge of the law was one of the only forms of power accessible to African-Americans, felt that it was within the legal system that social change would occur. She would have made a brilliant lawyer: her ability to understand statutes, to craft arguments, and to apply them to specific situations was razor sharp. As it was, she applied those skills to her writing and her growing political activism.

In forceful editorials, Wells was a brave and lonely voice among Southerners, incurring extreme personal risk. She put her head down every night, alone in her small room in Memphis, knowing that she was an obvious target for a lynch mob, and got up the next day to anger the mob more. Immediately after the murders, she bought a pistol for self-defense. "I felt that one had better die fighting against injustice than to die like a dog or a rat in a trap. I had already determined to sell my life as dearly as possible if attacked. I felt if I could take one lyncher with me, this would even up the score a little bit." While she never advocated preemptive violence, Ida described armed resistance not only as a right but as a duty.

Writing as Iola, Wells urged black Memphians to use their economic clout, to vote with their feet and move west, abandoning a city that would not protect or respect them: "The city of Memphis has demonstrated that neither character nor standing avails the Negro if he dares to protect himself against the white man or become his rival. . . . [we must] save our money and leave a town that will neither protect our lives and property, nor give us a fair trial in the courts . . . when accused by white persons."

Thousands of blacks did leave the city, depriving its economy of both workers and consumers. In a precursor to the Montgomery bus boycott, the privately owned streetcar companies suffered greatly and sent a delegation to ask Wells to retract her message. It is fascinating to track the many critical moments in the civil rights movement that took place on public transportation, a critical point of contact between oppressed and oppressors. Wells also, with this editorial, hit other points of contact: domestic servitude and consumerism. She refused the request of the delegation of white streetcar owners and stood defi-antly, delighted to watch the whites realize that they had "killed the goose that laid the golden egg," as they saw their cooks, nannies, laundresses, maids, servants, construction workers, and consumers of cheap goods leave the city in droves.

Effective as they were, Wells's editorials no doubt frustrated and infuriated her opponents. But whatever emotions she'd stirred were nothing compared to the rage unleashed on May 21, 1892. That day's *Free Speech* ran another of Iola's antilynching editorials. But this one went beyond an impassioned demand for justice or a shrewd call for a demonstration of power.

> Eight negroes lynched since the last issue of the *Free Speech* . . . five on the same old racket—the new alarm about raping white women. The same programme of hanging, then shooting bul-lets into the lifeless bodies was carried out to the letter.
>
> Nobody in this section of the country believes the old thread-bare lie that Negro men rape white women. If South-ern white men are not careful, they will overreach themselves and public sentiment will have a reaction; a conclusion will then be reached which will be very damaging to the moral reputation of their women.

Response in the white press was immediate and venomous. "The fact that a black scoundrel is allowed to live and utter such loath-some and repulsive calumnies is a volume of evidence as to the won-derful patience of Southern whites," thundered one editorial. "But we have had enough of it. There are some things the Southern white man will not tolerate." The *Evening Scimitar* editors mischaracter-ized her—intentionally or not—as a man when they threatened "to tie the wretch who utters these calumnies to a stake at the intersec-tion of Main and Madison Sts., brand him in the forehead with a hot iron and perform upon him a surgical operation with a pair of tailor's shears."

White Memphians took those words to heart. On May 24, a mob descended on the *Free Speech* office and set fire to it. Nightingale and Fleming fled to safety across the Mississippi. Ida herself was visiting the East Coast for the first time, attending the African Methodist Episcopal

Church convention in Philadelphia and then traveling on to New York City to visit her friend and colleague Thomas Fortune. He met her train in Jersey City and told her about the destruction of the *Free Speech* property. He also passed on the warning that she'd be killed if she returned to Memphis. She never set foot in the city again.

Ida even lacked the full support of her own community. A few weeks after she was driven out of Memphis, several of the "most prominent and respected" members of the city's African-American community issued this public statement: "We desire to put on record a most positive disapproval of the course pursued by Miss Ida Wells through the medium of the *New York Age*, in stirring up, from week to week, this community and wherever the paper goes, the spirit of strife over the unhappy question at issue. We see no good to come from this method of this issue on either side."

For the next three years, Ida made it her mission to create a rising tide of awareness that would sweep away lynching. She wrote countless articles for major African-American newspapers such as the *New York Age*, and she took two extended tours through England, successfully rousing antilynching sentiment.

As was common practice then, Ida self-published many of her essays and speeches. *Southern Horrors* was issued in 1892, followed a few years later by *A Red Record: Tabulated Statistics and Alleged Causes of Lynchings in the United States,* and *Mob Rule in New Orleans.* She also produced countless other uncollected essays, editorials, and speeches. Her voice made an unmistakable impact: as a prominent black clergyman put it, "she has shaken this country like an earthquake."

The rhetorical foundation of Ida's antilynching argument was her use of factual evidence to counter the lies told to justify the murders. In a brilliant stroke, Wells used the data compiled by mainstream white journalists, which was not subject to the same dismissive attitude with which whites treated her own fact gathering. Wells sifted through these published accounts to establish patterns and record details, but she also conducted her own investigations. Her reports are filled with both documented statistics and personalized accounts of the most horrible torture and murder, almost always committed with no legal consequences. She interviewed witnesses as well as poring over every news account, and she spared no detail, no matter how gruesome. "There is no word equal to it in convincing power," proclaimed Frederick Douglass,[9] the escaped slave turned Lincoln advisor who was also working to raise awareness about lynching.

Ida traveled to the communities where lynchings had occurred and conducted her own investigations, juxtaposing a full factual account with the propagandist aspects of white newspapers' versions. In one case she quoted the Associated Press account of a lynching in Tunica County, Mississippi: "The big burly brute was lynched because he had raped the seven-year-old daughter of the sheriff." Ida discovered that the sheriff's daughter was almost eighteen and her father had discovered her in the man's cabin.

These investigations were financed by a few black newspapers, including the *New York Age* and the *Chicago Inter-Ocean*. Other black newspapers often picked up her work, further broadening her reach. The *Richmond Planet* published the following article, headlined "How an Innocent Man Was Treated" and accompanied by a drawing of the murder.

The above is a rough sketch made from a photograph taken on the spot. The man suspended from a telegraph pole is C.J. Miller, the colored man who was lynched by a mob at Bardwell, Ky., Friday, July 7th, 1893.

Two hours after he was lynched it was ascertained that he was the wrong man, and was innocent of the crime alleged against him.

He was hung with a trace chain.

---

[9] In February of 1818 Frederick Bailey was born on a Maryland plantation. At around age eight he was sent to Baltimore to serve as a "houseboy" for relatives of his master. His new mistress illegally taught him the alphabet until her husband ordered her to stop. Bailey then traded his food to other boys in the neighborhood in exchange for reading lessons. As a teenager, he was brought back to the plantation as a field hand, working in brutal conditions by day and continuing his education by night. With a circle of white friends, Bailey founded the clandestine East Baltimore Mental Improvement Society, a debating club that focused on the ethics of slavery. At one point, Bailey fought a vicious "slave-breaker" to a draw, an experience that fueled his determination to escape. After one unsuccessful attempt, he managed to reach Massachusetts in early September 1838, at the age of twenty. There, he took the surname Douglass and became a lecturer for the Massachusetts Anti-Slavery Society. His powerful speeches soon led to a remarkable career as an writer, public speaker, and political strategist. Abraham Lincoln relied on his counsel and President Benjamin Harrison appointed him minister-general to the Republic of Haiti. Douglass died in Washington, D.C., on February 20, 1895.

Miss Ida B. Wells was employed by the *Chicago Inter-Ocean* to go to the scene of the outrage and write it up. She gave to that journal a most graphic account and it is to her that we are indebted for the illustration which we present our readers.

"My name is Seay J. Miller. I am from Springfield, Ill. My wife lives at 716 N. Second Street. I am among you to-day looked up on as one of the most brutal men before the people.

"I stand here surrounded by men who are excited, men who are not willing to let the law take its course, and as far as the crime is concerned, I have committed no crime and certainly no crime gross enough to deprive me of my life and liberty to walk upon the green earth. *** The day I was supposed to have committed the crime, I was at Bismark."—The last words of Seay J. Miller, the innocent man who was lynched for the murder of three white girls at Bardwell, Kentucky, July 7th, 1893

In the face of such undeniably shocking brutality, most lynching apologists continued offering the same ridiculous rationale: the barbarity of lynching, while unfortunate, was the understandable response to sexual attacks on white women. In *A Red Record*, Ida directly refuted this argument. As she documented, an accusation of actual or attempted rape prompted only one-third of all recorded lynchings. Ida's choice of titles (*Southern Horrors, Mob Rule in New Orleans, A Red Record*) is stunning, and her chapter heads hammer home the simple truth of her message: "Lynching Imbeciles," "Lynching of Innocent Men," "Lynched for Anything or Nothing." Subtitles include: "Killed for His Stepfather's Crime," "Hanged for Stealing Hogs," "Lynched because the Jury Acquitted Him," "Lynched because They Were Saucy," "Lynched for a Quarrel," "Should Have Been in an Asylum."

Ida also brought to bear her own insightful analysis and a clear call for an "awakening of the public conscience." She reached across the boundaries of geography, race, and gender so often used to evade responsibility or justify inaction, and cast lynching as an American problem: "No other civilized nation stands condemned before the world with a series of crimes so peculiarly national. It becomes a painful duty of the Negro to reproduce a record which shows that a large portion of the American people avow anarchy, condone murder, and defy the contempt of civ- ilization. . . . We plead not for the colored people alone, but for all victims of the terrible injustice which puts men and women to death without form of law." She compiled and published the details of these terrible crimes "in a plain, unvarnished, connected way" because "We do not be- lieve that the American peo- ple who have encouraged such scenes by their indiffer- ence will read unmoved these accounts of brutality, injus- tice, and oppression. . . . For God is not dead, and His spirit is not entirely driven from men's hearts."

Amazingly, she did this all on her own—a black woman in her early thirties in the turn-of-the-century American South. If she had not had the

An advertisement in the *Washington Bee* promoted a lecture by Ida B. Wells on October 30, 1892, a few months into her new career as a public speaker. The text just to the right of her image reads, "The way to Right Wrongs is to turn the Light of Truth on them." (courtesy Manuscripts, Archives and Rare Books Division, Schomburg Center for Research in Black Culture, The New York Public library, Astor, Lenox and Tilden Foundations)

courage and intellect to undertake these investigations, gather this in- formation, and write these pamphlets, the murders might have re- mained scattered incidents, eventually forgotten by everyone but the victims' families. Frederick Douglass praised her in the preface to *A Red Record*: "Brave woman! You have done your people and mine a service which can neither be weighed nor measured."

Ida's campaign was effective, as shown by the brutal threats and taunts she received. A Chicago newspaper she was affiliated with re- ceived a letter inviting her to come watch a lynching that was yet to take place. "Lee Walker, colored man, accused of raping white women, in jail here, will be taken out and burned by whites tonight. Can you send Miss Ida Wells to write it up?"

Despite the risks, Wells continued on her mission, establishing the first record of lynching and almost single-handedly raising the public awareness that would eventually eradicate it.

Dignified Agitator

Within a year of the *Free Speech* looting, the thirty-one-year-old Ida was a prominent speaker and antilynching activist, touring almost every major city in the United States (outside the South), sharing the stage with Susan B. Anthony and Frederick Douglass, and receiving favorable reviews for her presentations. One noted that she spoke "for two hours, without manuscript, holding the undivided attention of her hearers."

She gained a reputation as a powerful and effective advocate, relying on facts and logic rather than dramatic rhetorical flourishes. In November 1892 one newspaper noted that "she is spoken of as a pleasing and thrilling speaker fired with a desire for justice for her race." After another speech, an observer said, "She spoke with singular refinement, dignity and self-restraint, nor have I ever met any 'agitator' so cautious and unimpassioned in speech." The *New York Tribune* printed a largely respectful account of one of her speeches (with a bit of matter-of-fact racism).

> Miss Wells is a quiet, demure-looking . . . negro girl, who, to prove a point, quotes great writers with an ease which makes it apparent that larger questions even than the one for which she discoursed last night, have occupied her leisure hours. Her voice was not strong enough to be heard by everybody who was present, but all who did hear her simple narrative appeared to be convinced. She has not a trace of the accent that one is accustomed to associate with negroes.

Her adversaries attacked her in the press as a liar, a fraud out to profit from her fund-raising, and worse. A writer for the Memphis *Daily Commercial* worked himself into a frenzy, denouncing Ida as (among other things) a "notorious negro courtesan," a "half-cultured hater of all things Southern," "a saddle-colored Sapphira." These writers used their smearing of Ida to present the same ridiculous case for lynching: "The moment the colored criminal of the South gives up his favorite crime, that moment ninety-nine percent of the Southern lynchings will cease. Instead of defaming the white women of the South, Miss Ida B. Wells might better try to tame the brutal and bestial natures of too many men of her own color in the South."

Outside the South, Wells was attacked by white reporters, who were no doubt made uncomfortable by her direct and uncompromising message. During her tours through England, the *Washington Post* ran several editorials, with the hostility escalating over time. At first, Ida was accused of "exaggerations which she has perhaps unwittingly yet mischievously made," by focusing on lynchings of blacks rather than whites. Later the editor snidely declared that Ida "had made her tour very comfortably profitable" and dismissed her as a liar and her audience as an "assemblage of credulous and gaping Cockneys." Following Ida's second tour of Britain, in 1894, the *New York Times* ran an editorial making it clear where their sympathies lay.

> Miss Ida B. Wells, a mulatress who has been "stumping" the British Islands to set for the brutality of Southern white men and the unchastity and untruthfulness of Southern white women, has just returned to these shores. On the same day on which an interview with her was reported it was also reported that a negro had made an assault upon a white woman for purposes of lust and plunder, not in Texas or Mississippi, but in the heart of the City of New-York. The wretch is probably safe from lynching here, which is to the credit of the civilization of New-York. Thus far he seems to have escaped the clutch of the law. But the circumstances of his fiendish crime may serve to convince the mulatress missionary that the promulgation in New-York just now of her theory of negro outrages is, to say the least of it, inopportune.

Ida's Feuds

Ida B. Wells had an inflexible sense of purpose, which did not endear her to all her colleagues. She recalls that a group of African-American men met with her and pleaded that she "soft pedal on charges against white women and their relations with black men," and she "indignantly refused to do so." This incident is particularly interesting because it must have come in the wake of her mentioning publicly what she had recorded in her diary—that some white women voluntarily took black lovers. I would imagine that, at the time, some people found this point was a distraction from the main arguments against lynching, but Ida was wholly committed to telling the truth. She also instinctively bridled at being told what to do, especially in areas that had bearing on how seriously she was taken as a political voice. Told that she was unfairly seizing leadership of some issues before men of her race had a chance to do so, she simply forged ahead.

Wells's critics also felt that she picked unnecessary fights, distracting from her core cause and hampering its effectiveness. There was some truth to this, as illustrated by her feud with Frances Willard, the head of the Women's Christian Temperance Union. Willard was touring England at the same time Ida visited. As a leader of both the temperance and suffrage movements (and as a genteel woman with socialite sensibilities), Willard was widely respected in reform circles, but Ida was not one of her admirers.

Months before, Willard had toured the South and, in a newspaper interview, had drawn a connection between alcohol and black violence, using unbridled racist language in a way that Ida took to condone lynching. Willard said: "The colored race multiplies like the locusts of Egypt. The grog-shop is the center of power . . . 'Better whiskey and more of it' has been the rallying cry of great dark–faced mobs in the Southern localities where local option was snowed under by the colored vote. . . . The safety of women, of children, of the home is menaced in a thousand localities at this moment."

During her first tour of England, Ida, when asked about Willard's statements, didn't hesitate to condemn them. British reformers, otherwise inclined to support Ida, defended the better-known Willard and expressed some doubt about Ida's credibility. When Ida returned to England the next year, she brought the copy of the *New York Voice* in which Willard's comments had been reported. Willard was forced to respond, and the argument played out in the press for some time. In her biography of Ida B. Wells, Linda McMurry posits that the feud may have cooled some of British society to Wells's crusade. The incident is certainly emblematic of the kinds of confrontations that did alienate many from Wells, whose inflexible combativeness was both a virtue and an Achilles' heel.

The White City

Ida also fought with other black Americans over the proper response to the 1893 World's Columbian Exposition in Chicago. Marking the four-hundredth anniversary of Columbus's arrival in the New World, the fair's organizers and promoters conceived of the expo as a grand tribute to the splendor of Gilded Age America. The complex of new exhibition halls was called "the White City," and indeed, there were no blacks on any of the planning committees and no exhibitions that documented black Americans' contributions to American society. Until Haiti asked its former ambassador, Frederick Douglass, to preside over its pavilion at the fair, the only representations of African-Americans were ethnographic displays of "primitive" cultures and stereotypical images of happy slaves used to promote commercial products.[10]

There were deep divisions in the black community over how, or even whether, to address the situation. Ida and several others, including Douglass, settled on writing and distributing a pamphlet that would explain, as its title declared, *The Reason Why the Colored American Is Not in the World's Columbian Exposition*. Others objected to this direct and confrontational approach, and the dispute continued throughout the months Ida was trying to organize and finance the pamphlet project.

There was another debate over whether to accept the fair organizers' offer of a "Colored People's Day" at White City. A prominent black newspaper, the *Indianapolis Freedman*, ran an editorial titled "No Nigger Day." Ida wrote a cordial letter of agreement, and I imagine she was sorely disappointed when they ran another editorial, "No Nigger Day, No Nigger Pamphlet," which argued that both efforts would make the black community look foolish in the eyes of the white world.

---

[10] During the expo, a former slave named Nancy Green stood in a booth shaped like a flour barrel and wowed the crowds with lighthearted stories of plantation days and fluffy flapjacks made from a brand-new product, Aunt Jemima's Pancake Mix. Over the course of the fair, she gave away nearly a million pancakes and prompted more than 50,000 orders for the mix. R. T. Davis Milling Company was so thrilled with Green's personification of Aunt Jemima that they signed her to a lifetime contract and had her likeness printed on packages, in advertisements, and on souvenir buttons with the tagline "I's in town, honey." One hundred seven years later, the trade magazine *Advertising Age* named Aunt Jemima one of the top ten advertising icons of the twentieth century.

Douglass, believing it was better to take advantage of the offer than to hold out on principle, announced his support for Jubilee Day, as the event had been renamed. Ida remained vocally opposed. It is an impressive indication of Ida's single-mindedness and self-confidence that she was willing to openly dispute the revered Douglass, already an icon among African-Americans, a man known and respected throughout the world.

Ida left for a speaking tour in England in June of 1893, obliged to leave the final decisions to others. When she returned in early August, she discovered that her fears had been realized: Jubilee Day was on track but the pamphlet had been shelved. With her characteristic tenacity, Wells single-handedly revived the project, managing to produce a stripped-down version by the end of the month. It included a preface translated into French and German and an introduction by Douglass. Ida contributed chapters presenting and analyzing antimiscegenation laws, segregation, the convict lease system, and, of course, lynching. Educator and journalist I. Garland Penn documented the many post-Emancipation accomplishments of black Americans in arts, sciences, education, politics, and religion. The final chapter, "The Reason Why," was written by Ferdinand Barnett, a Chicago lawyer and owner of the *Conservator* newspaper. It recounted the African-American community's fruitless efforts to participate in the Columbian Expo.

In the end both Jubilee Day and the pamphlet distribution went off reasonably well. Douglass's speech at the opening ceremony was especially powerful. Heckled by a few whites in the crowd, he set aside his prepared speech. "Men talk of the Negro problem," he began. "There is no Negro problem. The problem is whether the American people have honesty enough, loyalty enough, honor enough, patriotism enough to live up to their own Constitution." Douglass described the progress made by African-Americans in the thirty years since the end of slavery, and condemned white Americans for resisting that progress. Ida had boycotted Jubilee Day, but reading accounts of Douglass's speech, she was moved to do what I imagine was very hard for such a proud woman. As she later wrote, she went "straight out to the fair and begged his pardon for presuming in my youth and inexperience to criticize him." Douglass accepted her apology and confirmed that she would hand out *The Reason Why* from the Haiti pavilion. Beginning on August 30, Wells distributed over ten thousand pamphlets. In her memoirs she expressed satisfaction that "echoes from that little volume have been received by me from Germany, France, Russia, and far-away India."

Marriage and Family

The Reason Why was a monumental project for Ida for a personal reason: she and Ferdinand Barnett fell in love, got married in 1895, and set up their household in Chicago. Barnett was an even-tempered, intellectual man, far less fiery than his wife, and McMurry describes the mean-spirited commentary the match prompted within the African-American

Ida with her firstborn, Charles Aked Barnett, in 1898. (courtesy Special Collections Research Center, The University of Chicago Library)

press: that Ida "gives Ferd her skirts and dons his trousers," that her "determination to marry a man while still married to a cause will be a topic of national interest and comment." But neither of them seemed to let the criticism get under their skin. Barnett, who served as assistant state attorney for Illinois from 1896 to 1911 and advised many national politicians on black politics, was secure enough to let Ida take the spotlight. She had no intention of being a traditional housewife, so he hired a nurse and housekeeper and delighted in doing much of the cooking himself. They had four children together—Charles, Herman, Ida, and Alfreda—and remained close to his two children by his late wife. Wells chose not to drop her maiden name and asked to be known as "Mrs. Wells-Barnett."[11]

---

[11] In referring to Ida B. Wells, I've chosen to honor her wishes at the expense of strict consistency. When describing events, I use the surname Wells-Barnett herself was using when the event took place.

One of my favorite photos of Wells-Barnett is the one of her looking at her first baby. She is wearing a particularly severe hat—obviously still in Iola mode—and looking at him with apparent trepidation
as well as obvious pride. Ida was charmingly surprised at the extent to
which motherhood changed her. She later wrote, "I had not entered
into the bonds of matrimony with the same longing for children that
so many other women have. It may be that my early entrance into
public life and the turning of my efforts, physical and mental, in that
direction had something to do with smothering the mother instinct."
Yet once she had her first child, she "realized what a wonderful place
in the scheme of things the Creator had given women."

Caught in the juggling act often wrongly portrayed as unique to
our day, Wells-Barnett did bold things to combine the roles of a wife,
mother, journalist, and activist, such as the unprecedented move (not
that anything she was doing had notable precedents) of bringing her
nursing child with her to work. "I honestly believe that I am the only
woman in the United States who ever traveled . . . with a nursing
baby to make political speeches," she wrote. Understandably, com-
bining the lynching crusade with child care took its toll, and when
her second child was born, "all this public work was given up and
I retired to the privacy of my home to . . . give my attention to my
children."

Some of her colleagues were less than supportive. Wells had become friendly with Susan B. Anthony, who was thoroughly behind
the antilynching agenda[12] but critical of Ida's choice to balance it with
marriage and motherhood. On a personal level, Anthony treated Wells

---

[12] In 1895 Anthony attended a lecture Wells gave at a church in Rochester, New
York, shortly before she married Barnett. A young man in the audience rose and
asked Ida the question, "If the Negroes don't like it in the South, why don't they leave
and go north?" Horrified, Anthony stood up and answered him herself: "It is because
they get no better treatment in the North than the South. That is why they don't come
here. I will relate an incident that occurred in our city only last week that will serve to
illustrate what I mean. A dance was to be given in No. 3 school for the benefit of children for ten cents apiece. Now it happened there was a colored girl in that grade who
wanted to go to the dance as well as the white children and so she asked her mother
for the money to buy a ticket. But when she went to her teacher, Miss Agnes M. Stewart, she was told that if she insisted on going to the dance, none of the white children
would attend and that the affair would be given up; so the poor child was turned
away. I consider that the outrage on the feelings of that colored girl was the result of
the same spirit that inspire[s] the lynchings in the South."

with utmost respect and hosted Wells in her own home at least once. (During that visit, Anthony promptly fired her own personal secretary when the woman refused to take dictation from Ida because she was black.) Yet the suffragist's own sense of priorities brought the two into conflict. After Wells-Barnett's marriage, Anthony told her, "I know of no one in this country better fitted to do the work you had in hand than yourself. Since you have gotten married, agitation seems practically to have ceased. Besides, you have a divided duty. You are here trying to help in the formation of the league, and your eleven-month-old baby needs your attention at home. You are distracted over the thought that maybe he is not being looked after as he would if you were there, and that makes for divided duty."

This exchange reminds me of the current debate that appears on magazine covers every few months, and my sympathies lie with Ida. But the conversation is also grounded in a particularly rich historical moment—the struggle to reconcile the women's movement with the black civil rights movement. Susan B. Anthony and Elizabeth Cady Stanton had objected to the passage of the Fifteenth Amendment[13] because, as Anthony put it in a riveting public debate with Frederick Douglass in 1869, "Neither [women nor black men] have a claim of precedence upon an Equal Rights platform."

After their conversation, Anthony sought ways to heal the divide, but the rift was severe and clearly rooted in the different social circumstances that black and white women lived in. I imagine that for Ida, whose own parents were not allowed to legally marry until after she was born, whose own grandmother bore her master's child, the desire to have her marriage publicly recognized and respected was profound. "I had been with [Anthony] for several days before I noticed the way

---

[13] The Fifteenth Amendment, ratified in 1870, was intended to guarantee voting rights for African-American men. It specified that race, color, or past status as a slave could not be used to bar anyone otherwise qualified from the polls. Anthony and Stanton were devastated that women were not included in this amendment, and it marked a break between them and some black leaders with whom they had been allied. The amendment did not have the full effect intended. Southern states instituted poll taxes, literacy tests, and other legal requirements to disenfranchise African-Americans and, incidentally, poor whites. In 1898, the United States Supreme Court issued a unanimous decision declaring that voting regulations with the effect of disenfranchising blacks were constitutional, as long as the legal language did not specifically refer to race.

she would bite out my married name in addressing me," Wells-Barnett later wrote.

Ida brought particular intensity to her parenting. When her children reached school age, she hovered over their schoolwork and encouraged them to reach high professionally. "Vicariously, she always wanted me to be a lawyer," recalled her daughter Alfreda Duster. "She impressed upon her children their responsibilities, one of the most important being good conduct in her absence. There was never any need to be concerned when she was present. She did not have to speak; her 'look' was enough to bring under control any mischievous youngster." Duster also recalled her mother's softer side, especially her laughing over a "humorous record called 'The Preacher and the Bear.' It told about the preacher 'who went out hunting one Sunday morn / And though it was against his religion / He took his gun along. On his way home he met a great big bear. The preacher prayed, 'Now, Lord, if you can't help me / for goodness sake, don't you help that bear.' We played it often, and every time we played it Mother laughed and laughed."

Alfreda Duster recounted an incident that illustrates Ida's determination and a bit of her sly wit. "Even when there was no segregation in Chicago, there were certain places you didn't go because you know they wouldn't treat you right. After discrimination intensified, Mother went to Marshall Fields department store. She waited and waited but no clerk would help her. Finally, she took a pair of men's underpants, put them over her arm, and walked toward the door. Immediately, a floorwalker stopped her, and so she was able to buy them. She used to tell about this as a funny incident, Ida Wells-Barnett with a pair of underpants dangling over her arm."

Ida never completely abandoned the public sphere, acknowledging that the home was not her "chosen kingdom." She hated housework, and according to Duster, "Mother was very displeased by the fact that if you swept the floor today, there'd be more dust there tomorrow. . . . She didn't feel that she was *accomplishing* anything." At different stages, Wells-Barnett eased back into her schedule, trying to maintain a balance of public and private duties. After she weaned her second son, she felt she "could safely leave him with his grandmother" to attend the meeting of the National Afro-American Council.

As her children grew older, Wells-Barnett was touched to see that they were proud of the work she had done outside the home. In 1909, she learned about a hearing in Cairo, Illinois, to consider reinstating the local sheriff, who had been fired pursuant to an Illinois state law that provided that any officer who failed to protect his prisoner from lynching would lose his job. A prisoner under the charge of Sheriff Frank Davis was lynched in a particularly brutal and excessive way: shot over five hundred times, beheaded, and "burned to a crisp." But the campaign to reinstate Davis was strong and—surprisingly—was supported by a large segment of the African-American community. Apparently they did not think Davis was to blame and, moreover, had no particular fondness for the victim. Their response is an indication of how slow the progress on lynching was and how apprehensive many African-Americans were—afraid of losing whatever status or security they'd gained, eager to demonstrate their support of powerful whites and separate themselves from disreputable blacks.

Ferdinand urged his wife to go to Cairo, investigate the case, and help prevent Davis's reinstatement, but she resisted, saying she had obligations in Chicago. Touchingly, Ida recalls this as the first time one of her children voiced a recognition of the importance of her work, even while she struggled to find the time to do it.

> It was not very convenient for me to be leaving home at that time. . . . Mr. Barnett replied that I knew it was important that somebody gather the evidence as well as he did, but if I was not willing to go, there was no more to be said. He picked up the evening paper and I picked up my baby and took her upstairs to bed. As usual, I not only sang her to sleep, but put myself to sleep lying beside her. . . . I was awakened by my oldest child, who said . . . "Mother, if you don't go nobody else will."

The next morning Ida began preparing for her trip. Doing her typical amount of exhaustive research, she became convinced that failure to uphold the law would mean "an increase of lynchings in the state of Illinois and an encouragement to mob violence." She swayed most of the community to her point of view and successfully argued the case in court. In her memoirs, she proudly noted the response: "I was quite surprised when the session adjourned that every one of those white men [on the opposing side] came over and shook my hand and con-

gratulated me on what they called the wonderful speech I had made. . . .
The state's attorney of Alexander County wanted to know if I was not
a lawyer. The United States land commissioner, a little old man, said,
'Whether you are a lawyer or not you made the best speech of the
day.'" She also noted that in the twenty years since the hearing, there
had been no lynchings in the state.

W. E. B. Du Bois and the NAACP

Ida credited Susan B. Anthony with "endeavor[ing] to make me see
that for the sake of expediency one had often to stoop to conquer on
this color question." This was not a lesson that took hold for Ida, who
acknowledged that her temper "has always been my besetting sin."
That besetting sin was on display frequently during the time Wells-
Barnett engaged in the great debate in the black community between
Booker T. Washington and W. E. B. Du Bois.

Washington, the most prominent African American since Frederick Douglass, had written a memoir called *Up From Slavery*, which
put forth a vision of industrial education for blacks, a vision he had
founded the Tuskegee Normal and Industrial Institute to implement.
Du Bois, a powerful political theorist, felt that Washington was wrong
to accommodate segregation and racism and that it was crucial for
African-Americans to develop their own elite—the "talented tenth"—
who would have access to the same opportunities for education and
employment as whites. Wells-Barnett clearly favored Du Bois.

In *Crusade for Justice*, Ida describes asking for city funding to
keep one of her projects, the Negro Fellowship League, from shutting
down. Several city officials, headed by a Mr. Sachs, visited Ida's office.

After looking us over, the committee was invited to be seated.
Mr. Sachs said that he had heard Booker T. Washington the
night before at the Standard Club. He said, "He told us a very
funny story about an old man who said his wife had left him;
that he did not mind her going so much, but that she had left
the chicken coop door open and all the chickens had gone
home, too."

He laughed very heartily as he told the story, but when he
saw I didn't laugh he asked me if the colored people accepted

Mr. Washington as their leader, and if they didn't believe in his doctrine. I said, "We have very great respect for Mr. Washington's ability to reach the influential people of this country and interest them in his theories of industrial education and secure their help for the same. We don't all agree entirely with his program.

"As to his being our leader, I will answer your question by asking one. Rabbi Hirsch is your leading Jew in Chicago. He is constantly invited to appear before representative gentile audiences, and because of his wonderful eloquence is a general favorite. But I am wondering if you Jews would acclaim him so highly if every time he appeared before a gentile audience he would amuse them by telling stories about Jews burning down their stores to get their insurance?" His face turned very red, and I said, "I am sure you would not, and a great many of us cannot approve Mr. Washington's plan of telling chicken-stealing stories on his own people in order to amuse his audiences and get money for Tuskegee." Needless to say, the conversation ended there.

This incident reveals so much about Ida—her fearlessness, her unwillingness to compromise principles, her inability to go along and get along. Unable to accept Washington's gradual, accommodationist approach, she allied herself with Du Bois, and she and Ferdinand likely considered themselves the epitome of his notion of the "talented tenth." In *Crusade for Justice*, Wells-Barnett recalled a time when they were invited to the home of Celia Parker Wooley, a white Unitarian minister who headed the Frederick Douglass Center, to discuss Du Bois's new book *The Souls of Black Folk*, published in 1903. The conversation turned to the chapter assailing Washington's methods, and most of those present, including four of the six African-Americans, united in condemning Du Bois. The Barnetts stood up for him.

We saw, as perhaps never before, that Mr. Washington's views on industrial education had become an obsession with the white people of this country. We thought it was up to us to show them the sophistry of the reasoning that any one system of education could fit the needs of an entire race; that to sneer at and discourage higher education would mean to rob the race of leaders which it so badly needed; and that all the industrial education in the world could not take the place of manhood. We had a warm session but came away with the feeling that we had given them an entirely new view of the situation.

Given this affinity, as well as her own desire to be a consequential leader, the rupture that upset Ida most had to have been her exclusion from the founding membership of the National Association for the Advancement of Colored People.

On November 9, 1909—the hundredth anniversary of Abraham Lincoln's birth—a group of prominent activists, both black and white, issued "The Call." This document proclaimed the need for an organization that would continue and strengthen "the struggle for civil and political liberty" and proposed a conference to establish such an organization. When determining who should participate, Mary White Ovington, a descendant of white abolitionists and a longtime supporter of Du Bois, insisted that Booker T. Washington be invited because "if you want to raise money in New York for anything related to the Negro, you must have Washington's endorsement." Much to the relief of many behind "The Call," Washington himself did not attend, but the organizers took pains to include some of his followers so as not to seem "anti-Washington." The conference took place in New York City's Charity Organization Hall. Ida was invited and saw it as a big opportunity to forward her cause.

On the opening night of the conference, Wells-Barnett delivered a speech entitled "Lynching: Our National Crime." She laid out the facts, statistics, and anecdotes, declaring "the only certain remedy is an appeal to law." She recommended federal antilynching legislation and a bureau devoted to the investigation of every incident of lynching. Her speech was well-received but forgotten the next day, when attention turned to resolutions and selection of the committee: forty people who would be the nucleus of the new organization, which would become the NAACP. As the committee was being chosen, there was a great deal of lobbying and horse-trading behind the scenes. Du Bois had recruited many prominent whites to his cause and wanted some to be included. Accordingly, he decided to sideline those, like Ida, who might have trouble getting along with them. In fact, Du Bois himself was the only black member of the nominating committee. As Ovington later explained, the decision was made to exclude not only Booker T. Washington but also those at the other extreme, the "powerful personalities who had gone their own ways, fitted for courageous work, but perhaps not fitted to accept the restraints of organization."

Later Ida attributed her exclusion from the committee of forty to W. E. B. Du Bois's caving in to the white activists who assisted in the founding of the NAACP. As her daughter recalled, "Mother was with W. E. B. Du Bois in his basic concepts, but she didn't mince words with anybody. She . . . [thought there] should [have] been all Black folks at the head of the NAACP. She took a violent antipathy to Mary White Ovington being secretary, and of course those who were trying to have peace and quiet would naturally try to go around Ida B. Wells."

At the conference, Ida had been assured that she would be included in the committee and assumed she would be, right up to the moment the membership was announced. Stunned, she left the hall. After supporters convinced her to return for an explanation, Du Bois

The Barnett family in 1917. (courtesy Special Collections Research Center, The University of Chicago Library)

told her that her affiliation with the Frederick Douglass Center led him to believe that Celia Parker Wooley, as head of the center, could represent her interests and perspective well. How infuriating this must have been. Had Celia Parker Wooley been dragged off a first-class train car? Had Celia Parker Wooley single-handedly investigated and exposed lynching? Ida did have supporters among the group and there was a chance that her name could have been added but, as she put it later, "I did a foolish thing. My anger at having been treated in such a fashion outweighed my judgment and again I left the building." (Wells–Barnett did become involved in the NAACP briefly. In 1910 she joined the executive committee and participated in setting the group's aims and agenda. But soon she was shut out again and severed all ties with the organization.)

Despite her failure to fit into the NAACP, Wells did start many organizations that became vital forces for the black community. On her tours of England, Ida was impressed by the effectiveness of sociopolitical clubs there and sought to implement that model in the United States. She was personally responsible for many organizations, such as the Negro Fellowship League; the National Black Women's Club movement; Ida B. Wells Clubs, which established both the first black kindergarten and the first black orchestra in Chicago; and the Alpha Suffrage Club, which was the first such organization for black women in Chicago.

In addition, from 1913 to 1915, Wells-Barnett became Chicago's first black probation officer, in charge of up to two hundred probationers who reported to her office at the Negro Fellowship League. She spent half of the day in court and the other half checking on them in their homes. Like her husband, Ida invited many indigent people into their home and took an interest in helping people get back on their feet. "All through my childhood I can remember this stream of underprivileged boys and young men who formed a part of our home life," recalled Alfreda, who noted that none of them betrayed her parents' trust by disturbing their house or family. Wells-Barnett's caseload never dropped below 150, and she began lobbying for more black probation officers. However, before she could make any progress on this, she lost her position. After supporting the loser in a mayoral race, her contract was not renewed.

Race Riots

Having already made a name for herself as an antilynching activist, Wells continued to fight racial violence in the years during and after World War I when bloody race riots broke out in cities around the country. The worst such incident took place in East Saint Louis, Illinois, in the summer of 1917.

On July 2 a car full of white men repeatedly drove through the black sections of the city, harassing and attacking residents. This was the most recent outbreak of the hatred that had been simmering since May, when white laborers clashed with members of the growing black community. While that initial conflict was quickly squelched, smaller-scale confrontations continued in what Wells-Barnett later called "efforts to terrorize Negroes, who were fast being taken on at industrial plants there."

City and state officials had shown marked indifference to protecting black citizens, so an armed self-defense group—the kind Ida had long advocated—was organized. After the drive-bys during the day, members of this group spotted a similar car that evening. They opened fire, killing the driver and passenger, who turned out to be policemen.

The full-scale attack that followed largely destroyed the black section of the city and thirty-nine African-Americans were killed. According to one white eyewitness, "'Get a nigger!' was the slogan, and it varied by the recurrent cry, 'Get another!' It was like nothing so much as the holiday crowd, with thumbs turned down, in the Roman Colosseum, except that here the shouters were their own gladiators, and their own wild beasts."

The Negro Fellowship League raised money to send Ida to East Saint Louis to investigate the situation herself. In the riot's aftermath, a black dentist named Leroy Bundy had been singled out as the ringleader. Wells-Barnett felt he was being made a scapegoat and, furthermore, "had Bundy done what they charged him with, he did no more than any red-blooded American would do in preparing for armed self-defense." She set out to gather the facts and published her findings in the pamphlet *The East Saint Louis Massacre, the Greatest Outrage of the Century*. Her documentation, as well as work done by others, was so disturbing and effectively presented that a congressional committee was formed to investigate. However, the investigation was largely ineffective and the committee chair declined to publish their findings. Eventually, five white men were arrested and prosecuted, although more than 150 blacks were also jailed for longer terms, and Bundy himself was convicted of conspiracy to murder.

The Barnetts took up Bundy's cause, raising money and assisting in his legal defense. They felt that the NAACP, which had agreed to handle Bundy's case, was not making much of an effort, so Ida went around them and approached Bundy directly, recruiting lawyers and raising money for his defense. (When the NAACP criticized the Barnetts, Bundy responded in a letter stating "that after repeated [requests] to officials of your organization which brought no response, I deemed it absolutely necessary to seek help elsewhere.")

This activity on Bundy's behalf not only further strained relationships with the NAACP, but also drew the attention of the FBI, which opened a file on both Barnetts and forwarded a copy of the East Saint Louis pamphlet to the War Department along with the warning that the material was "being used to stir up a great deal of inter-racial antagonism."

After World War I, as returning black soldiers demanded some of the freedom that they had been sent to fight for abroad, tensions increased. More race riots erupted during the "Red Summer" of 1919. By October hundreds of Americans, mostly black, had been injured or killed in more than twenty riots.[14] As the violence unfolded, Ida helped organize the Protective Association, intended to act as a watchdog group to ensure that law enforcement officers protected blacks and their property from violence.

She also investigated the final event of the Red Summer: the massacre near Elaine, Arkansas. On the night of September 30, 1919, black cotton farmers gathered at a church in Hoop Spur, Arkansas, to

---

[14] In Chicago a riot was set off when a black teenager named Eugene Williams, swimming in Lake Michigan, strayed near a section of beach claimed by whites, who began throwing rocks at him. Williams drowned trying to escape. Police refused to arrest the rock throwers, and for the next five days, violence spread through the city. Fifteen whites and twenty-three African-Americans were killed, and property damage left an estimated one thousand African-Americans homeless.

consider unionizing. As sharecroppers, they weren't allowed to sell their cotton on the open market, their accounts were charged for seed and supplies, and they were even forbidden to access their account records. Tired of the exploitation, these farmers were receptive when they were contacted by Robert Hill, representing the new Progressive Farmers and Household Union of America.

During the meeting, two sheriff's deputies and another man set out from nearby Helena. At some point their car pulled over and stopped outside the church. There are conflicting accounts of what the officers' mission was, why they pulled over, and how the shooting began, but when it stopped, one white officer and an unknown number of black farmers were dead. Immediately word of a "Negro uprising" spread, and the Helena American Legion post sent volunteers to quell the unrest. As many as a thousand armed whites poured into the Elaine area the next day. Vigilantes shot at blacks from trains and ransacked and robbed the homes of suspected insurrectionists. Governor Charles Hillman Brough asked for federal troops to help quell the violence; soldiers from Camp Pike arrived in Helena on October 2, took charge of the town and the surrounding area, and helped the white residents conduct an investigation of the supposed insurrection. During this time, hundreds of blacks were held until white employers vouched for them; many were subjected to torture. The final count of the dead: five whites and at least twenty-five blacks. (The toll among whites was well documented but there's no way to arrive at a definitive total for the number of black dead. Twenty-five can be confirmed and some estimates go into the hundreds.) At the end of October, 122 blacks were indicted on charges ranging from nightriding[15] to murder.

On November 3, as the first murder trials began, threatening mobs gathered outside the courthouse, where they remained throughout the proceedings. Witnesses offered the same narrative that had been detailed in the newspapers: the black farmers had organized an insurrection targeting specific landowners for murder. The imposition of martial law, the killings of an undetermined number of blacks, the seizure of their property—all were legitimate actions of self-defense

---

[15] "Nightriding" refers to a common tactic used by outlaws and vigilantes, including the early Klan: riding a horse at night, alone or in groups, for the purpose of violent intimidation.

against this threat. By the next afternoon, all twelve defendants had been convicted and sentenced to death. The longest any jury deliberated was eight minutes.

The NAACP became involved in the case on October 8, when assistant field secretary Walter White,[16] a blue-eyed, fair-haired black man, gained an interview with Governor Brough by passing himself off as a sympathetic white journalist. White then recruited a local lawyer, Scipio Jones, to represent the men and continued to write about the case for the NAACP's *The Crisis*.

In December Wells-Barnett wrote about the Elaine prisoners in the *Chicago Defender*. One of the prisoners sent her a letter of thanks and through him, Ida gained contacts in the area. As the legal battle continued, she began a fundraising campaign in the *Defender*. At one point during her campaign, when she submitted another piece, Ida recalled the newspaper's managing editor informing her that the NAACP objected to her efforts because it was "already doing all the work necessary in the matter." The editor suggested that she send the money raised to the NAACP.

Instead, Ida decided to use the money to conduct her own investigation. Accordingly, she boarded a train south in January 1922. At the prison, Ida joined the wives and mothers visiting the men, passing as a relative herself. As they entered, the guard looked up and, as Ida described it, "saw only a group of insignificant-looking colored women who had been there many times before, so he went on reading his newspaper." One of the women whispered to the prison-

---

[16] The NAACP hired Atlanta native Walter White in January 1916 as a field organizer. In his first few years with the organization, he investigated more than forty lynchings. White rose in the ranks, becoming the executive secretary in 1931. He focused on developing the NAACP's lobbying capacity; by the end of the 1940s, the organization had over one thousand well-organized chapters able to mobilize significant numbers of voters. White also laid the groundwork for the NAACP's fight against desegregation through a series of state and regional conventions. Thurgood Marshall, Robert L. Carter, and others involved in the legal campaign attended, explaining strategies and shoring up political and financial support. One of White's long-standing goals, never achieved, was passage of federal anti-lynching legislation. He was an advisor to both the 1945 founding conference of the United Nations and the 1948 General Assembly in Paris. Eleanor Roosevelt was a longtime friend and faithful ally, supporting him throughout internal conflicts and threats to his power. White remained executive secretary of the NAACP until his death in 1955, at the age of 62.

ers that it was "Mrs. Barnett from Chicago." Ida put her finger to her lips and cautioned them not to let on. Then she began her investigation, asking them to relate to her the details of their experiences, from the number of acres they had tilled to the way they were treated in prison.

After Ida interviewed the men for several hours, one of the women asked the men to sing for Ida. "Whereupon," Ida later wrote, "they sang a song of their own composition and many others—it was the note of hope they were voicing for the first time, because in me they seemed to see somebody who had come to help them in their trouble." The soulful singing continued for almost two hours, and the warden and his wife brought their Sunday visitors to listen. Finally, Ida stepped up close to the bars and spoke to the men.

> You have talked and sung and prayed about dying, and forgiving your enemies, and of feeling sure that you are going to be received in the New Jerusalem because your God knows that you are innocent of the offense for which you expect to be electrocuted. But why don't you pray to live and ask to be freed? The God you serve is the God of Paul and Silas who opened their prison gates, and if you have all the faith you say you have, you ought to believe that he will open your prison doors too.
>
> If you do believe that, let all of your songs and prayers hereafter be songs of faith and hope that God will set you free; that the judges who have to pass on your cases will be given the wisdom and courage to decide in your behalf. That is all I've got to say. Quit talking about dying; if you believe your God is all powerful, believe he is powerful enough to open these prison doors, and say so. Dying is the last thing you ought to even think about, much less talk about. Pray to live and believe you are going to get out.

Classic Ida—stressing resistance and action over acquiescence and passivity, refusing to let religious belief have any part in supporting the injustices against these men and so many others. It reminds me of the saying often heard from sharecropper turned civil rights leader turned statesman and congressman John Lewis: "When you pray, move your feet."

The next day Wells visited Scipio Jones, who, in her recollection, credited her with "starting this whole movement" to free the men. (I suspect she may have let her own bruised ego color her memory here.) Jones shared with her all the material he'd gathered and she visited with the local fund-raising committee to offer her help.

After returning to Chicago, Ida wrote *The Arkansas Race Riot*, in which she concluded that whites in the county "made a cool million last year off the cotton crop of the twelve men who are sentenced to death, the seventy-five who are in the Arkansas penitentiary and the one hundred whom they lynched outright on that awful October 1, 1919!" Though she had a thousand copies printed up and many circulated in Arkansas, she never received any acknowledgment from the local NAACP committee.[17]

Some time later, a young man appeared at her door. Though Ida didn't recognize him, he was one of the Elaine Twelve, now living in Chicago. She wrote:

> When my family came in to be introduced, he said, "Mrs. Barnett told us to quit talking about dying, that if we really had faith in the God we worshipped we ought to pray to him to open our prison doors, like he did for Paul and Silas. After that," he said, "we never talked about dying any more, but did as she told us, and now every last one of us is out enjoying his freedom."

---

[17] By all accounts, the NAACP served the men well, defending them through appeals, overturns, and retrials. In May 1920 the Arkansas Supreme Court issued a split decision, affirming the convictions of six defendants and overturning those of the other six. Each group was known by the name of a member, Ed Ware or Frank Moore. The Ware defendants were retried and reconvicted while the Moore cases made their way to the United States Supreme Court as *Moore v. Dempsey*. The men's lawyers argued that the extensive, biased press coverage and the hostile mob milling outside the courthouse made a fair trial impossible. On February 19, 1923, the court agreed and overturned their convictions. By now, two men who had participated in torturing the prisoners had come forward, seriously damaging the prosecution's case, and the situation had become a national embarrassment for Arkansas. On June 25, 1923, the Ware defendants were freed by order of the state supreme court. The Moore defendants were released on "indefinite furlough" on January 15, 1925.

"The Gallant Fight and Marvelous Bravery"

Though Wells-Barnett remained active, the years following the Elaine riots were relatively quiet. Her failing health and increasing marginalization reduced her effectiveness. Most of the organizations she'd founded were no longer operating, she still had trouble building alliances, and she was certain the NAACP would continue to co-opt her efforts. In 1930 she ran for state Senate and placed a humiliating third.

In the last years of her life, Wells worked on an autobiography, *Crusade for Justice*. In the preface, she explains why she took on the task:

A young woman recently asked me to tell her of my connection with the lynching agitation which was started in 1892. She said she was at a YWCA vesper service when the subject for discussion was Joan of Arc, and each person was asked to tell of someone they knew who had traits of character resembling this French heroine and martyr. She was the only colored girl present, and not wishing to lag behind the others, she named me. She was then asked to tell why she thought I deserved such mention. She said, "Mrs. Barnett, I couldn't tell why I thought so. I have heard you mentioned so often by that name, so I gave it. I was dreadfully embarrassed. Won't you please tell me what it was you did, so the next time I am asked such a question I can give an intelligent answer?"

When she told me she was twenty-five years old, I realized that one reason she did not know was because the happenings about which she inquired took place before she was born. Another was that there was no record from which she could inform herself. . . . It is therefore for the young people who have so little of our race's history recorded that I am for the first time in my life writing about myself. . . .

The gallant fight and marvelous bravery of the black men of the South fighting and dying to exercise and maintain their newborn rights as free men and citizens, with little protection from the government which gave them these rights and with no previous training in citizenship or politics, is a story which would fire the race pride of all our young people if it had only been written down.

Ida B. Wells-Barnett died on March 25, 1931, with the manuscript unfinished. At her funeral, the church was packed and it took almost an hour for the mourners to file past her coffin. Though the standards of the time called for reading telegrams and memorials, only one of each was read at Wells-Barnett's funeral. Ferdinand was determined that those who had fought or dismissed her while she was alive would have no part in the ritual following her death. More than two months later, a memorial from W. E. B. Du Bois was printed in *The Crisis* magazine. He declared that she had begun "the awakening of the conscience of the nation" and added that her "work has easily been forgotten because it was taken up on a much larger scale by the N.A.A.C.P. and carried to greater success." She left a remarkable legacy and an inspiring personal story of how one individual can consistently stand for what she believes in, face down powerful forces, and take actions that will resound throughout history as having been prescient and just.

Mother Jones

I asked the newspaper men why they didn't publish the facts about child labor in Pennsylvania. They said they couldn't because the mill owners had stock in the papers. "Well, I've got stock in these little children," said I "and I'll arrange a little publicity."

—MOTHER JONES

"Mother" Jones and her "Army" held their last campfire prior to the invasion of New York in Central Hall in Jersey Heights last evening . . . She [said she] did not approve of millionaires riding in automobiles while children worked in mills and the "teaching of French to poodle dogs." She thought the appropriation of $45,000 by Congress to entertain Prince Henry was an outrage.

—NEW YORK TIMES, JULY 23, 1903

ON AUGUST 1, 1903, FRANK BOSTOCK'S WILD ANIMAL SHOW on Coney Island was commandeered by an archetypal "little old lady," complete with gold-rimmed spectacles, a neat black dress, and snow-colored hair swept up under a pancake hat. This impromptu ring-master was the labor activist Mother Jones, best known for her organizing efforts among the coal miners in West Virginia. For the previous month, she'd led a march of underage mill workers from Philadelphia to New York. She wanted to force Americans to confront the reality of child labor, to embarrass the rich businessmen who profited from it, and, in the process, to raise funds for the textile strike in Kensington, Pennsylvania. "I am going to show Wall Street the flesh and blood from which it squeezes its wealth," she announced.

At towns along the way, Mother Jones and her band staged parades and rallies, with the children (some maimed and crippled by their work) holding signs reading, "We want time to go to school" and "55 hours or nothing." A row of tiny boys marched behind a banner that simply said, "We are Textile Workers." The group also staged skits featuring top-hatted "Mr. Capital" and bejeweled "Mrs. Mill Owner," but the star was always the charismatic Mother Jones herself. At each stop, she delivered a blistering tirade against the mill owners and the financiers who supported them. Thousands gathered in Trenton, in Princeton, in Jersey City, and they donated hundreds of dollars to support the strike fund. (The strikers had been earning as little as two dollars a week, roughly equivalent to forty dollars today.) Now the marchers were nearing their goal: President Theodore Roosevelt's summer compound in Oyster Bay, Long Island.

In *The Autobiography of Mother Jones*, she described the scene:

> There was a backdrop to the tiny stage of the Roman Colosseum with the audience painted in and two Roman emperors down in front with their thumbs down. Right in front of the emperors were the empty iron cages of the animals. I put my little children in the cages and they clung to the iron bars while I talked.
>
> I told the crowd that the scene was typical of the aristocracy of employers with their thumbs down to the little ones of the mills and factories, and people sitting dumbly by.
>
> "We want President Roosevelt to hear the wail of the children who never have a chance to go to school but work eleven and twelve hours a day in the textile mills of Pennsylvania; who weave the carpets that he and you walk upon; and the lace curtains in your windows, and the clothes of the people. Fifty years ago, there was a cry against slavery and men gave up their lives to stop the selling of black children on the block. Today the white child is sold for two dollars a week to the manufacturers. Fifty

years ago the black babies were sold C.O.D. Today the white baby is sold on the installment plan."

Mother Jones's rhetoric is as arresting as it is shrill, given its context: a time when most of the United States nonchalantly accepted the fact that poor young children worked twelve-hour days in mine shafts or factories, regularly injured and maimed on the job and left with no support. Jones's style included unapologetic, earthy showmanship, a sharp tongue, and a visceral articulation of right and wrong. She drew on elements of the stage she had set—little maimed children behind bars!—to emphasize her point, laying responsibility for human suffering squarely with those most politically and commercially powerful. She also demanded that consumers be aware of and scrupulous about the connection between their purchases and the workers who created them.

The editorial page of the *New York Times* responded with disdain:

Pretty nearly anything will go down with the average audience, and that is the reason why Mother Jones and others like her are able to obtain so ready a hearing. . . . We are probably justified in assuming that the voice of the Coney Island lions in response to Mother Jones' harangue signified that they found it very cheap and sawdusty in the detail of the stuffing, and that from most and probably all points of observation she was a tedious and oppressive incubus, to be coughed down out of hand like a bad speaker in the House of Commons.

President Roosevelt, vacationing on Long Island, refused to meet with Mother Jones and her delegation of children. The marchers straggled home, the mill strikes in Kensington were broken, and most of the marchers returned to work.

However, if she'd lost this battle, Mother Jones and her colleagues would eventually win the war. Just as Ida B. Wells-Barnett reframed the debate on lynching, Mother Jones's fierce advocacy and high public profile helped change America's perception of child labor and labor generally. At the beginning of her career, unions were viewed as a violation of property rights and an enemy of free markets. (Of course, only a hundred years before, ownership of property had been a prerequisite of full citizenship.) Many methods were used to prevent employees from any attempt at collective bargaining, including the frequent use of the courts and the police. Upon request, judges routinely issued injunctions against striking or organizing. It was at one of Mother Jones's court appearances, for violating such an injunction, that a prosecutor was said to have called her "the most dangerous woman in America."

Many people still know Mother Jones's name, but very few know her full story. Within a decade of the children's march, thanks in part to her shrewd use of publicity, the concepts of collective bargaining and worker safety were no longer considered un-American. The United States Congress would investigate and take steps to improve working conditions across the country. There would be a growing campaign to abolish child labor. The *Times* would run a lengthy, respectful profile of the "tedious and oppressive incubus." And Mother Jones would even become a cordial correspondent with the man she had derided as a "hobo and bum"—John D. Rockefeller Jr.

Mary Harris Jones

Not much is known of Mother Jones's early life. Public records are scarce and Jones herself was not an entirely reliable source. What is known, however, helps explain her unflinching advocacy for the underdog, her class-consciousness, her adamant support for unionized labor, and the emotional intensity she brought to her cause.

In *Mother Jones: The Most Dangerous Woman in America*, Elliott J. Gorn concludes that Mary Harris was born in County Cork, Ireland, in the summer of 1837. (Later, she'd claim May 1, the international labor holiday, as her birthday. She'd also pad her age, celebrating her hundredth birthday in 1930 when she was actually a few months away from her ninety-third.) Along with thousands of other Irish, the family emigrated to Canada during the years of extreme poverty that followed the potato famine. In the six years from 1847 through 1853, approximately 1.2 million people fled Ireland. Hundreds of thousands of them emigrated to the United States, where they faced harsh prejudice.

Mary must have shown a talent for schoolwork since she continued through high school and qualified as a teacher. In 1859 she taught briefly in Michigan, then moved to Chicago, where she worked as a dressmaker. Soon she moved farther south to Memphis, Tennessee, where she resumed teaching. In late 1860 or early 1861 she married George Jones, a skilled foundry worker employed at a large machine shop. She probably left teaching then, since many schools refused to hire married women as teachers, and over the next several years, the couple had four children.

In her autobiography, Mother Jones described her husband as a "staunch member" of his union, and every month, the *Iron Molders' International Journal* arrived at the home. It's not unreasonable to assume that Mary, intelligent and well-educated, read the journal and discussed it with her husband. Certainly she agreed with the union's motto: "Equal and exact justice to all Men, of whatever state or persuasion."

In 1867 Memphis suffered an outbreak of yellow fever, one shorter and less widespread than the 1878 epidemic that would devastate Ida B. Wells's family. But in both, most of the victims were those who could not afford to flee the city and lived in close proximity to each other: blacks and poor whites. The fact that both Wells and Jones experienced their agonizing personal losses in that social context probably brought them to a heightened awareness of social inequalities and a hardened resolve to fight them.

Among the yellow fever victims in 1867 were George Jones and all four of Mary and George's children. Mother Jones rarely even mentioned this catastrophic loss, but she wrote this description in *The Autobiography of Mother Jones*.

All about my house I could hear weeping and cries of delirium. One by one, my four little children sickened and died. I washed their little bodies and got them ready for burial. My husband caught the fever and died. I sat alone through nights of grief. No one came to me. No one could. Other homes were as stricken as mine. All day long, all night long, I heard the grating of the wheels of the death cart.

After the union had buried my husband, I got a permit to nurse the sufferers. This I did until the plague was stamped out.

How completely shattering this loss must have been, especially for a young mother who had come of age amid the dreams of other Irish immigrants who wanted to raise their children in the land of opportunity. The sheer will it took to pick herself up from this blow is hard to imagine. Perhaps the totality of the disaster is what made her endlessly resilient and daring. Nothing that happened in the future could ever be worse.

Husband and children buried, Mother Jones returned to Chicago, but not to teaching. Instead, she and a partner opened a dressmaking business, which gave her another vantage point on socioeconomic inequality. "We worked for the aristocrats of Chicago," she recalled, "and I had ample opportunity to observe the luxury and extravagance of their lives. . . . I would look out of the plate glass windows and see the poor shivering wretches, jobless and hungry. . . . My employers seemed neither to notice or care."

Soon Mary Harris Jones was caught up in yet another disaster. In the windy October of 1871, Chicago was suffering from the effects of a long drought that had turned the city's wooden buildings to kindling. Small fires broke out around the city and were successfully put out before they spread, until the evening of October 8, when a fire started in the O'Leary family's barn, in a heavily Irish neighborhood.[1] As the fire raced through the city, Jones was one of thousands who fled to the lakeshore with whatever belongings they could salvage. Even there, the heat and blowing embers repeatedly forced them out into the freezing water. Another lakeshore refugee later wrote:

> The sparks and cinders were falling as fast and as thick as hailstones in a storm; and soon after daylight, to our discomfort and danger, the piles of household stuff which covered the ground everywhere began to burn. . . . An hour later, and the immense piles of lumber on the south of us were all afire, and then came the period of our greatest trial. Dense clouds of smoke and cinders rolled over and enveloped us, and it seemed almost impossible to breathe. Man and beast alike rushed to the water's edge, and into the water, to avoid suffocation. There was a mixed mass of human beings, horses, dogs, truck-wagons,

---

[1] Soon it became repeated as fact that Mrs. O'Leary or her cow started the fire by knocking over a kerosene lantern during milking. Given the widespread anti-Irish prejudice of the time, many accounts went on to accuse the woman of stupidity, incompetence, drunkenness, even willful malice. In his book *The Great Chicago Fire and the Myth of Mrs. O'Leary's Cow*, Richard F. Bales makes a case for exonerating both the woman and her cow; he argues that the blaze was started, probably accidentally, by the neighbor who first reported it.

and vehicles of all descriptions there . . . all with their backs to the storm of fire which raged behind them.

The fires swept through Chicago all night and into the following day, reducing the city to ashes. Three hundred people died, seventeen thousand buildings were destroyed, and over a hundred thousand were left homeless.

The Gilded Age

The last decades of the nineteenth century were distinguished by an unregulated business environment in which the most powerful companies moved quickly to establish monopoly control. The labor force, increasingly composed of poor immigrants, had no leverage over the terms and conditions offered by employers, which widened the income gap further. Several fledgling unions formed in an effort to provide workers with some bargaining power. The Knights of Labor, founded in 1869, was one such union. It was open to all workers, skilled or unskilled, in all trades and industries. In 1880 the Knights took the radical step of accepting women members. Although it is not clear whether Jones joined, Terence Powderly, head of the Knights during its years of fastest growth, became a lifelong friend of hers.

Economic downturns added to the ranks of the unemployed, who began to organize and campaign for public assistance, but mostly encountered violence and cruel disdain. For example, the *Chicago Tribune* warned that too much charity would dull the ambitions of the poor. Surely Mary Harris Jones, observing the excesses from her vantage point of profound loss, concurred with Mark Twain's parody of a well-known Protestant catechism: "What is the chief end of man?—to get rich. In what way?—dishonestly if we can; honestly if we must. Who is God, the one only and true? Money is God. God and Greenbacks and Stock—father, son, and the ghost of same—three persons in one; these are the true and only God, mighty and supreme . . ." In 1873, Twain published his first work of extended fiction (written in collaboration with Charles Dudley Warner), a novel that put a name to the times: *The Gilded Age*.

A financial panic in 1873 set off a terrible economic crisis, with unemployment rates in some cities reaching 25 percent within a year; the young unions abandoned the idea of strikes as pointless. Then, in 1877, four railroads, acting in concert, cut workers' pay for the second time in a year, this time by 10 percent, even while they paid stockholders' premi-ums in full. It was a breaking point, and workers walked off the job. Even after President Rutherford Hayes sent troops to break it, the strike held. On July 19 workers in Pittsburgh immobilized the railyards, and twenty died in the violence that followed. In retaliation, the men destroyed rail-road property, torching buildings and mangling the rails themselves. In her autobiography, Mother Jones claims to have been in Pittsburgh for this event. Her biographer, Elliott Gorn, doubts that she was actually there, but what is really interesting is that she wanted to have been there. I think she was always yearning to find scenes as dramatic in their human suffering as the one in which her husband and children died and then, cathartically, find a way to right the wrongs and relieve the pain.

The name "Mother Jones" first appeared in print after she joined a demonstration of unemployed people known as Coxey's Army. In 1894, in the midst of yet another crippling economic depression, a small-business owner named Jacob Coxey had organized this group to march on Washington and deliver an unprecedented message: the govern-ment should create jobs. Mary "Mother" Jones was described as a vol-unteer traveling with this radical group, making speeches, raising money, and looking after the marchers. The *Kansas City Star* referred to her as the "mother of the commonwealers." Soon she found a more specific constituency—the coal miners.

Organizing Coal Miners

At the turn of the last century, for both unionists and industrial-ists, coal mining was a central battleground. As the fuel that drove so many new industries, coal was an immensely profitable business. It was controlled by a small group of powerful men, none more power-ful than John D. Rockefeller, the founder of Standard Oil.[2]

---

[2] By 1890, Standard Oil controlled more than 90 percent of the refined oil distributed in the United States. The same year, the Sherman Anti-Trust Act was passed to regulate this and similar monopolies. Standard Oil's ongoing market domination, despite the act, attracted the attention of muckraking journalist Ida Tarbell. Her detailed exposé of the company's business practices ran for nineteen installments in *McClure's Magazine* and in 1904 was published as a book, *The History of Standard Oil*. The resulting public outcry led to closer scrutiny of the company and in 1911, the monopoly was broken. Rockefeller re-mained one of the wealthiest men in America and one of its most important philanthro-pists. His son, John D. Rockefeller Jr., continued and significantly expanded his father's philanthropy, leaving a particularly impressive legacy in environmental conservation.

The miners themselves had no power. Most were immigrants, at first from the United Kingdom and later from southern European and Slavic countries. The rest were former field workers, sharecroppers and, in growing numbers, bankrupt farmers. The luckier men found work with one of the more enlightened and responsible mine operators. The others toiled in extremely dangerous conditions with little hope of change.[3]

Each year thousands of miners died in cave-ins, explosions, and other workplace accidents. Many more suffered from respiratory diseases, such as black lung, and from the crippling effects of constant hard labor underground. John Brophy, who worked with Mother Jones and the United Mine Workers, had followed his father into the anthracite mines of Pennsylvania at the age of twelve. In his memoir, *A Miner's Life*, he wrote that the typical mine had a main tunnel about five feet high, and individual workplaces turned off it as it descended deeper and deeper to follow the coal seams. In larger mines, miners known as "company men" dug the main tunnel, laid down track for the coal cars, and advanced workplaces about 350 to 500 feet, carving them about thirty feet wide but only a few feet high. However, smaller mines often required the miners to do this work themselves. The miners' workplaces were separated by pillars about twenty feet thick. Using blasting powder, picks, and shovels, often lying down or crouching in the cramped spaces, miners stripped the ore from the seams. "One of the most exhausting things about mine work," wrote Brophy, "was the necessity of spending a ten- or eleven-hour day without a single chance to stand erect and stretch." As he worked, the miner cut through one pillar to the next workplace, a practice called "retreating"

---

[3] My grandfather, Albert Gore Sr., a native of Possum Hollow, Tennessee, began his career as a teacher in rural Tennessee in 1926, while boarding with coal miner Arkley Gore ("We could never prove any kinship but probably were cousins") in a town "named High Land—but known as 'Booze' since it was an active manufacturing center for moonshine." He was struck by the long hours, meager comforts, and harsh physical toll of the mining life. When he entered politics, as the commissioner of labor for Tennessee governor Gordon Browning, "Remembering Arkley Gore's coal-mining experience, I took seriously my responsibility for administering the Mine Inspection Law," as he wrote in *Eye of the Storm*. "I was horrified to learn that the inspectors I had inherited from the previous administration made not even the least pretense of actually entering the mines to check on working conditions. It was necessary to dismiss them all, and, with the approval of the Governor, to purchase testing equipment and to hire qualified men who would report on the actual conditions. Here, too, one met with personal hostility, and the only shield one could erect against such animus was the conviction that social reforms must be carried out even if they offend the vested interest."

or "robbing." When several pillars were cut through in a row, the roof became unstable and timbers were brought in to support it. Miners learned to sense when the roof got "heavy" and the pillars "soft," and the coal became easier to unearth. At some point, the timbers would begin splintering and the miners could hear the roof "working," a sound like rolling thunder that could last for days. Seasoned miners spoke of developing a sixth sense that let them work the softened pillars as long as possible without getting crushed in the inevitable cave-in.

Each miner loaded his haul into the coal car that ran regularly on the track in the main tunnel and was hung with a metal tag that bore the miner's number. The accuracy of the "checkweighman's" measurements of the amount each miner extracted was a constant source of tension and dispute between the miners and operators. After the coal was weighed, it was dumped in a massive chute, or tipple, that carried it to a barnlike structure for loading. "Breaker boys" sat beside the black rivers that came rattling down and sorted out the rocks from the lumps of coal. In the dim light and dusty air, beneath the watchful eye and ready stick of a boss, they hunched over their work, developing rounded shoulders and narrow chests as well as damaged eyes and lungs. It wasn't rare for boys as young as eight to begin a lifetime of mining with a job as a breaker boy.

The miners' jobs were controlled by the company, which also frequently controlled the nearby housing, stores, schooling, medical care, and law enforcement. The result was a "company town" where workers were controlled and exploited.[4] (In West Virginia, 94 percent of the miners lived in company towns.) Often, miners were paid in scrip, which was worthless anywhere but company-owned businesses. Knowing they had a captive market, company stores charged high prices for their goods, including the tools and materials the miners needed for work. Brophy listed the costs at the company store at the Pennsylvania mine where he worked. A twenty-five-pound keg of black powder, enough to last two weeks, cost $1.50 to $1.75—almost a

---

[4] The song "Sixteen Tons," made famous by Ernie Ford, was written by Merle Travis, whose father worked in the Kentucky coal mines. Its chorus was inspired by the answer his father gave to neighbors who asked how he was doing: "I can't afford to die. I owe my soul to the company store."

day's wages. Lard oil for the miners' lamps was fifty cents a gallon. Picks and augers had to be sharpened every couple of weeks, which cost another fifty cents. The checkweighman was paid out of the miners' wages, costing each miner about fifty cents each payday. If a doctor was provided, each man paid a flat fee from each pay packet, about seventy-five cents for a single man and one dollar for a family. "A miner got his pay twice a month, twenty or thirty dollars, less the deductions and his rent and store bill," recalled Brophy. "The miner typically [ended] each period with a small debt carried from pay period to pay period, and sometimes inherited from father to son . . . it had its value in keeping a man from trying to better himself by leaving town or agitating against the company."

As the companies grew wealthier and more powerful, business and government in the mining regions became more and more intertwined, and this trend was most pronounced in West Virginia. Mining executives or their cronies filled the legislative, executive, and judicial branches of the government. For example, the attorney for the mining company was the son-in-law of the company's founder and a good friend of the judge who presided over the legal proceedings. Thus, nominal state laws restricting mine work to those over fourteen and forbidding payment in scrip were completely ignored. And there was hardly any semblance of free speech or democracy: dissident newspapers were confiscated, company critics were fired and kicked out, and union organizers were brutally harassed by the local police. During elections, mine guards, privately employed and armed, served as poll watchers and sometimes even filled out the miners' ballots.

Despite their heated rhetorical defense of a free marketplace, the owners organized before the workers did, making deals both to keep wages low and to prevent any uprising among their employees. Early legislative proposals for an eight-hour day, safer conditions, or a minimum wage were killed by these "citizens' alliances" of powerful businessmen who had strong ties to the government. Safety measures were considered an unnecessary expense. "Flesh and blood," explained one labor leader, is cheaper than "iron and steel."

Owners viewed collective bargaining—and the demands of workplace safety as well as the wage and hour regulations it engendered—as a violation of property rights, unethical as well as illegal. The reigning philosophy was that God had entrusted the factory owners with their property to administer as they saw fit, and their first duty was to maximize income to owners and shareholders. As Reading Railroad president George E. Baer put it, "The rights and interests of the laboring man will be protected and cared for—not by the labor agitators, but by the Christian men to whom God in his infinite wisdom has given the control of the property interests of the country, and upon the successful management of which so much depends."

In a serendipitous pairing of cause and activist, Mother Jones became an organizer for the United Mine Workers in 1900, ten years after the union was formed. The workers needed an impassioned champion, someone who would devote every waking hour to their cause and make them heard. Mother Jones needed an all-consuming mission, a focus for her visceral sense of justice, her abundant energy, and her powerful sorrow and rage.

On the Soapbox

Small in stature, Mother Jones often stood on a box, a table, or a wagon bed so that she could be seen and heard in a packed hall or crowded field. Extraordinarily self-assured, she never spoke from a text or even notes. She captivated and motivated crowds through sheer rhetorical skill. Observers described her voice as "audible in

Jones giving a speech in Seattle. (courtesy University of Washington Libraries, Special Collection, UW9948)

every part of the hall," carrying "to the outermost listener," "clear and commanding." Poet Carl Sandburg called it a "singing voice," saying, "Nobody else could give me a thrill just by saying in that slow solemn orotund way, 'The Kaisers of this country are next, I tell ye.'" According to Brophy, "She dressed conventionally, and was not at all unusual in appearance. But when she started to speak, she could carry an audience of miners with her every time. Her voice was low and pleasant, with great carrying power, she didn't become shrill when she got excited; instead her voice dropped in pitch and the intensity of it became something you could almost feel physically." She must have been a hard act to follow. After one rally, a reporter wrote, "Mother Jones made the other speakers sound like tin cans."

Jones controlled the room when she spoke, even when her listeners did not speak English. Another miner and UMW official who worked with Mother Jones, Fred Mooney, described her ability to transcend language barriers. In 1919, Mother Jones and Mooney were dispatched to organize miners in a particular region. Mooney wrote later,

> I was introduced as the first speaker and after speaking for about 40 minutes, outlining the policies and principles of the United Mine Workers of America, without getting an audible response from the meeting, I decided to quit. I did so by introducing Mother Jones. "What is the matter with this bunch, Mother?" I inquired. "I can't move them."
>
> "Yuh damn fool, don't you know that not one of them understands a word of English?" she said, and laughed heartily at my expense. Mother Jones talked shop to them by telling them that the bosses were through kicking them around, etc. We organized five local unions and installed the officers that evening.

Upton Sinclair, whose muckraking book *The Jungle* shocked readers, including President Theodore Roosevelt, and helped spur regulation in the meatpacking industry, wrote of his friend, "Hearing her speak, you discovered the secret of her influence over these polyglot hordes. She had force, she had wit, above all she had the fire of indignation—she was the walking wrath of God."

Her passion comes through in her writing, too. While in the field, she kept up with the UMW leadership through typewritten missives reporting on meetings, arguing strategy, and denouncing owners and traitorous "snakes" within the union. Most of the letters show that Mother Jones—a former schoolteacher—was perfectly capable of producing standard grammar and spelling. Others demonstrate that under pressure, in a hurry, or stirred by emotion, she was considerably less attentive to these details.

In both speeches and letters, Mother Jones soon developed a number of themes and techniques she'd turn to again and again. She often framed the miners' fight in sweeping terms, as a battle against powerful but corrupt enemies: mine owners, "society ladies with their poodle dogs," politicians, the White House itself: "We will have [President William McKinley's adviser] Mark Hanna digging coal!" she exclaimed. Hanna was considered the real source of power and a corrupting force in the McKinley administration, and, according to McKinley biographer Margaret Leech, he was widely depicted as "a brutal, obese plutocrat, the symbol of sly malice and bloated greed, covered with moneybags and dollar signs. Behind this monster, the little candidate cowered in his big Napoleonic hat. Hanna was the puppet-master who pulled McKinley's strings; the ventriloquist who spoke through the dummy, McKinley; the organ-grinder for whom the monkey, McKinley, danced." Mother Jones reveled in such imagery and instinctively knew its populist power.

Although she often cited Jesus Christ and God, Jones scoffed at organized religion, dismissing the clergy as "sky pilots" who had nothing to offer the working man.[5] Like Ida B. Wells-Barnett, she constantly admonished people to not let religion dull their drive to better their own circumstances. At least once, she quoted a priest who "told the men to go back and obey their masters and their reward would be in Heaven . . . The miners left the church in a body and came over to my meeting. 'Boys,' I said, 'this strike is called in order that you and your wives . . . may get a bit of Heaven before you die.'" At the same time, she claimed

---

[5] Gorn points out a family irony: Mary Jones's brother, William Richard Harris, became a Catholic priest in Ontario. His obituary in March 1923 praised his oratorical skill and prolific theological studies. As adults the two apparently never spoke or corresponded.

moral authority for the miners' cause: "We marched the mountains, every one who took up Christ's doctrine—not the hypocrites but the fighters." Mother Jones preferred to hold her meetings in schoolhouses rather than the churches that the miners often reserved, telling them, "Your organization is not a praying institution. It's a fighting institution. It's an educational institution along industrial lines. Pray for the dead and fight like hell for the living."

Mother stressed working-class solidarity as its own article of faith, reminding the men that their common interests crossed the boundaries of language and skin color. Ever ready for a hot spot, Jones traveled to Mexico during that country's revolution and spoke optimistically of an international brotherhood of workers. In speeches, she constantly stressed the need for unity. "I believe we will get together and stay together and bury all personalities," she said in an early speech. "We will join hands together for the emancipation of the human race. We do not live for ourselves alone." She never tackled segregation or racism directly, and she occasionally indulged in the anti-Chinese rhetoric commonly used in the West against immigrant labor.[6] Even so, Jones constantly articulated the need to overcome ethnic divisions, and she was pointedly inclusive toward African-Americans, perhaps having been bound to them by shared suffering during the yellow fever epidemic. At the 1902 UMW convention, she said, "One of the best fellows we have is the black man. He knows what liberty is; he knows that in days gone by the bloodhounds went after his father over the mountains and tore him to pieces, and he knows that his own Mammy wept and prayed for liberty. For these reasons he prizes his liberty and is ready to fight for it." Later, she urged the miners to ignore skin color and band together, warning them, "if you work long for the coal companies you won't have any skin about you." Only through unity could they succeed: "Stop your bickering and be men, and let capital know it."

Jones had no patience for the internal power struggles endemic to the labor movement. Perhaps it was in part because, as a woman, she

---

[6] In the late nineteenth century, Chinese immigrants were blamed for declining wages and growing unemployment. In 1882 Congress passed the Chinese Exclusion Act, which suspended Chinese immigration and declared Chinese in the United States ineligible for citizenship. The act was renewed in 1892 and, in 1902, Chinese immigration was banned completely. Not until 1943 were Chinese immigrants eligible for United States citizenship.

would never be in contention for a leadership role that she so consistently scolded the jockeying for control. Again and again she warned the men to beware the "snakes" among them that would use the union for their own selfish interests. Throughout her career, she would resist ideologies or theoretical frameworks and scoff at those who seemed to put their own egos above the cause.

Jones, herself an immigrant, was remarkably deft at framing the labor movement as the true expression of American liberty. For her, the fact that mining companies silenced their critics with force and refused to acknowledge the grievances of their own workers was an affront to freedom itself. Again, from her 1902 UMW speech: "I have wondered many times what Patrick Henry would say, Patrick Henry who said, 'Give me liberty or give me death,' and who also said, 'Eternal vigilance is the price of liberty.' . . . I say with him, 'Give me liberty or give me death, for liberty I shall die, even if they riddle my body with bullets after I am dead.'" When Mother Jones recalled her confrontations with powerful institutions, she almost always cited the Bill of Rights or gave the example of an American hero to bolster her connection to the grand American tradition.

In her autobiography, Jones remembered being questioned about why she did not find a higher calling than "agitating." "'There was a man once,' said I, 'who had great gifts and a knowledge of men and he agitated against a powerful government that sought to make men serfs, to grind them down. He founded this nation that men might be free. He was a gentleman agitator!'" She was describing George Washington. She cited Abraham Lincoln and Jesus Christ in similar terms. At a time when many people believed it was the unfettered marketplace that made America great, she reminded them of the quintessentially American Bill of Rights. When she was asked whether she had a permit to speak, she responded, "Yes, the one issued by Thomas Jefferson." And at times, she drew on all the themes at once, as in this impassioned closing to a speech: "Oh, God Almighty grant—Oh, God Almighty grant—God grant that the woman who suffers for you suffers not for a coward but for a man. God grant that. He will send us another Lincoln, another Patrick Henry. God grant, my brothers, that you will be men, and the woman who bore you will see her God and say, 'I raised a man.'"

On a more pragmatic level, Jones had a shrewd sense of how to capture public attention and sympathy. She sometimes paused mid-speech to address reporters: "Mr. Newspaperman, I want you to print what I have said!" "Put that down, Mr. Reporter!" "Let the boys who are here for the papers spread the news that you are the jolliest, most harmonious, and loving family there is in the nation." Even if there were no reporters present, this device signaled to the miners that they had an audience, that they weren't invisible. She also knew the power of showing as well as telling. In 1899 she came to speak to striking miners in the company town of Arnot, Pennsylvania, during a time when the strike was in danger of faltering. The company threw her out of her boardinghouse at eleven o'clock that night, and she was taken in by a mining family. In her autobiography Jones noted this about the miner: "He held the oil lamp with the thumb and his little finger and I could see the others were off. His face was young but his body was bent over." The next morning, the family that had taken her in was evicted.

> The family gathered up all their earthly belongings, which weren't much, took down all the holy pictures, and put them in a wagon, and they with all their neighbors went to the meeting. The sight of that wagon with the sticks of furniture and the holy pictures and the children, with the father and mother and myself walking along through the streets turned the tide. It made the men so angry that they decided not to go that morning to the mines. Instead they came to the meeting where they determined not to give up the strike until they had won the victory.

"No Nation Is Greater than Its Women"

Mother Jones's physical presence—her age, her gender, her austere, matronly style—were essential elements of her persona. She constantly referred to the miners as "my boys." Like any mother would, she nagged them to study more and drink less. For twenty years, in speech after speech, she warned them that she wouldn't live much longer and they would have to carry on after she was gone.

Jones distinguished between ladies—"created by the parasitical class"—and women, "made by God Almighty." Mother Jones expected the miners' mothers, wives, sisters, and daughters to be women. She organized them into "mop brigades" to fend off scabs and prevent defections among the strikers. "Women are fighters," she proclaimed in a speech before the UMW. "You will never solve the problem until you let in the women. No nation is greater than its women." She often spoke directly to the women, as in this description of a speech in Pennsylvania, addressing a gathering of miners' wives and daughters. One especially gushing news account described:

> Walking to the edge of the platform, "Mother" Jones stretched out her arms to them, and in her thrillingly sweet voice said "Sisters!" . . . The faces awoke, the souls back of them kindled. For an hour the speaker walked to and fro, telling the deeds of the mothers of the past and sisters and wives. The listeners drew nearer. They leaned their elbows on the platform, and lifted their faces to drink in the words. Their bosoms heaved, and the tears rolled unheeded down their cheeks.

Jones scoffed at the women's suffrage movement as a frivolity of "sentimental society ladies." She told a crowd at Cooper Union in 1912, "What do the suffragettes know about economic conditions anyway? Why, if the women had the vote, the first thing they would do would be to ally themselves with the capitalist class against the workingmen. That's what they would do. Woman suffrage is nothing but sentimental philosophy."

Jones's own class consciousness often blinded her to many potential alliances and limited her reach. In 1920 she shared a stage with the brilliant social reformer Jane Addams at a Chicago rally against civil rights abuses, but she never paid homage to Addams's efforts. When prominent women of New York City gave a dinner in her honor, Jones shocked and offended them by announcing her opposition to the vote. She scolded the "ladies" who were preoccupied with their own right to vote but had not done everything already within their power to help the poor families who were enslaved by industry. "I have no vote and I've raised hell all over the country." Jones also repeatedly stated her firm belief that women belonged in the domestic sphere and used that as a reason why they shouldn't be allowed the vote. She told the New York Times, "In no sense of the word am I in sympathy with women's suffrage. In a long life of study of these questions, I have learned that women are out of place in political work. There already is a great responsibility on women's shoulders—that of rearing rising generations." Surely the fact that this responsibility had been cruelly wrested from her fueled this attitude toward gender roles and her own exemption from them.

In a testament to the slow emergence of the early women's movement, Jones would change her mind about suffrage, even using women voters to her advantage.

"Medieval West Virginia"

In the early years of the twentieth century, despite the many obstacles they faced, the UMW succeeded in organizing the Central Competitive Field in western Pennsylvania, Ohio, Indiana, and Illinois. Wages increased (by one estimate, from $270 a year to $522 in the six years from 1897 to 1903), as did union membership, which rose to over a hundred thousand by 1900. But one key state proved too treacherous to penetrate.

West Virginia[7] provided one-third of the nation's bituminous coal, but the state's miners accounted for only two percent of the UMW membership. The conditions there were by far the worst in the country, and mine safety was virtually ignored. The mining death toll exceeded that of every other state combined.

The Fairmont Coal Company controlled the northern region. The coal that was produced there was the hard, anthracite variety; it was heavily used in industrial processes and thus demand for it was increasing exponentially. Unlike the miners of the bituminous soft coal found in the Central field, anthracite miners had not gained any leverage to negotiate with the companies. As conditions worsened and some miners protested, the company escalated the violence and intimidation with which it silenced dissent. Betting on the force of her personality, UMW head John Mitchell named Mother Jones an "international delegate" of the UMW and sent her to the Appalachian hills. "I dislike to ask you always to take the dangerous fields," Mitchell

---

[7] A mountainous state with relatively little lowland plantation agriculture, West Virginia seceded from Virginia in 1863 so as to remain in the Union. The new state's motto became *"Montani semper liberi,"* or "Mountaineers are always free."

wrote, "but I know that you are willing to go where you can perform the best service." It was in what she dubbed "Medieval West Virginia" that Mother Jones was first arrested.

Traveling with "the Mother Jones Band" and making what she called "raids" on mining towns, Jones stormed into the Mountain State and dared anyone to cross her. When the UMW called a local strike on June 7, 1902, violence in the area increased. Jones herself was nearly trapped on a covered bridge by strikebreakers in an incident in which a colleague of hers was beaten and badly injured. In her autobiography, Mother Jones described ripping up her petticoat to stop the bleeding from "great, open cuts" on the man's head.

Even after this brutality, Fairmont won an unprecedented legal victory. Federal Circuit Court Judge John J. Jackson, a Lincoln appointee, issued a sweeping injunction against any union activity, labeling it a conspiracy to injure the plaintiff, a coal company financier. On June 20, as Mother Jones was speaking to a crowd near Clarksburg, a federal marshal came forward and, citing Judge Jackson's injunction, announced that she was under arrest. By her own account, she insisted on finishing her talk, concluding with an admonition to "keep up this fight! Don't surrender! Pay no attention to the injunction machine at Parkersburg. The Federal Judge is a scab anyhow. While you starve he plays golf. While you serve humanity, he serves injunctions for the money powers." She and several others were arrested and promptly taken to Parkersburg, eighty miles away, and held for several days. Mother Jones insisted that she go to the same cell block as her "boys," rather than the more comfortable lodgings the jailer offered in his own apartment.

Never one to prioritize physical comfort, Jones seemed almost delighted to go to jail. A year earlier, she'd addressed the UMW convention, saying, "No battle was ever won for civilization that the jails and the scaffolds did not hold the salt of the earth." Released on bond from West Virginia, she addressed the same convention, vowing to fight on: "I have been served with injunctions in quantities sufficient to form a shroud around for me when I am cold in death."

Mother Jones's trial began July 24, 1902. After the United States district attorney supposedly condemned her as "the most dangerous woman in America," he added that she and her cohorts were "vampires that live and fatten on the honest labor of coal miners in this country," and accused Jones herself of being the hapless tool of sedi-tious forces. "It seems to me that it would have been better far for her to follow the lines and paths which the Allwise Being intended her sex to pursue." The defendants each received a sixty-day sentence, though Jones's was suspended.

Mother Jones's arrest and trial in what she called "this God Cursed Monopolistic State" only fueled her growing legend. Shortly after the trial, a poem appeared in the UMW journal:

> *For the Soul and the spirit of old Mother Jones*
> *Will March up and down*
> *Like the soul of John Brown,*
> *Till justice shall vanquish our burdens and groans*
> *And kill all injunctions on old Mother Jones*

Child Labor

In these years, child labor in industries was on the rise. Of course children have always worked on farms and in family workshops and stores, but the nature of the work in the industrial era was dramatically different. It was repetitive—one step on an assembly line over and over, day after day, week after week. The hours were longer—as much as ten hours a day, six days a week. The conditions were far more harmful—almost always indoors, operating noisy and dangerous machinery in air clogged with fumes, dust, or lint. Moreover, unlike work on a family farm or in a family store, the products and profits were separate from their families and communities. It was preposterous to equate child labor in these factories with the pre-industrial family tasks, yet the own-ers of industries did just that.

The United States Department of Labor estimated that in 1900, one in six children under the age of sixteen was employed. Because of widespread padding of workers' ages and the numbers of workers who simply weren't counted, this figure is undoubtedly low. Many states set minimum ages for workers, but few enforced the limits. For instance, Pennsylvania banned workers under age twelve but re-quired no documentation or proof of age beyond a parent's say-so. Children as young as six were routinely sent into the mills by parents desperate for additional income. Some states were more lax than others. In the canning factories of the deep South, very young children reportedly shelled shrimp from three in the morning until the next afternoon. The mother of one five-year-old complained he could "make fifteen cents any day he wants to work but he won't do it steady." Factory owners often preferred workers under sixteen because they got away with paying them less, sometimes half the rate for an adult worker. Children were more obedient and their smaller size made them useful for work with crowded and complicated machines.

Massachusetts passed the first child labor law in 1842, and a few states followed, though enforcement was lax. By 1879, only seven states had passed any age restrictions on the workforce, with an average minimum age of eleven. While reformers pushed for national standards to prevent factories from evading laws by moving to less restrictive states, such laws were fought fiercely by legislators from Southern states with significant textile interests. The Southern Cotton Manufacturers successfully challenged the constitutionality of federal child labor laws and also fought off state laws. Textile factory owners spoke glowingly of the benefits of child labor: "Children are brought to the mills by their parents because the work is lighter, the pay is better, and they have better opportunities for improvement and enjoyment than on the farms. I appeal to the legislature and to the state in behalf of these people not to interfere with their privilege to work when and where they will. Georgia is suffering more from idleness than she is from ignorance. Instead of requiring that anyone who wants to work should bring a certificate that he had been to school, I would rather see a law requiring that any one who wished to be educated at public expense should bring a certificate showing that he had been at work." They also issued dark warnings about the consequences of child-labor legislation: "The agitation for such laws always comes from representatives of labor unions, and the people of Georgia do not know what dangerous elements they are dealing with when they give any kind of support to these agitators. . . . Their efforts lead inevitably to paternalism and socialism."

Through talking with the miners and their wives, Jones became aware of the conditions in textile mills, where many of them sent their children to work. In her autobiography, she describes infiltrating several factories employing child labor and seeing the conditions there, including the horrible, deadening atmosphere and the frequent injuries (including dismemberment and mutilation) suffered by child laborers. I

Jones in a West Virginia mine camp helping a mother dress her children. (courtesy Kerr Archives, The Newberry Library, Chicago)

imagine she had a moment in one of these noisy, dingy, crowded factories when she looked at a few of the small bodies on some sort of assembly line and realized that this was her new cause.

In late May 1903, workers in hundreds of textile factories in Kensington, Pennsylvania, went out on strike. They were facing an open-shop push by their employers, members of the National Association of Manufacturers. The workers were paid meager wages, but the long hours in such harsh conditions were obviously even worse: the strikers announced that they were willing to take a pay cut if the factories would reduce the workweek from sixty hours to fifty-five. Of the one hundred thousand strikers, approximately sixteen thousand were children under the age of sixteen. Soon after the strike began, Mother Jones traveled to Kensington and met with the mothers of the striking child workers. These women explained that they were desperate for income and the mill operators encouraged child labor by looking the other way when the mothers lied about their children's ages. "In a single block in Kensington, fourteen women, mothers of twenty-two children all under twelve, explained it was a question of starvation or perjury. That the fathers had been killed or maimed in the mines," recounted Jones. When on occasion some official noticed underage children in the factory, the owners claimed that the child had simply "wandered in." It was almost impossible to prove otherwise.

Mother Jones knew that the only way to end the suffering of these families was publicity, her weapon of choice. She seized on the idea of a national law, claiming that would eliminate the threat of factories avoiding the law by moving from state to state, allow standardized inspections, and impose substantial penalties for violations. And she came up with a novel means of drawing attention to the cause: the Children's March.

Jones convinced the mothers of almost a hundred children, all of whom were obliged to stay off the job during the strike, to let them go with her from Kensington to New York. There is no evidence that she promised them any particulars about safety or finances, but these women, already accustomed to sending their children into dangerous factories, were undoubtedly beaten down by the despair of their lives and the uncertainty of the union's ability to improve them. On a hot and steamy July day, the march set off: Mother Jones, the children, and about twenty union operatives.

In Princeton, New Jersey, directly across from the famous university, Jones pointed to ten-year-old marcher James Ashworth. "Here's a textbook on economics," she told the crowd. "He gets three dollars a week and his sister who is fourteen gets six dollars. They work in a carpet factory ten hours a day while the children of the rich are getting their higher education." In Trenton, a crowd of five thousand people gathered to hear Mother Jones, who, one newspaper said, spoke at "a mile-a-minute gait" for two solid hours. The marchers' reception varied from city to city, with Newark, New Jersey, judged the most hospitable. "Most of the saloons in the district where working people live or work are holding open house and everything is free to members of the army," reported the *New York Tribune*. "When 'Mother' Jones learned this she gave her followers a talking to that has been obeyed and they are abstaining from strong drink."

Soon after they set out, the *New York Tribune* reported that marchers kept dropping out because of the crushing heat. After a few days, Mother Jones sent home six "very bright and very pretty" girls because "I found out that this roaming was not good for them—that they and I were misunderstood." After the rally in New Brunswick,

New Jersey, the *Times* reported that "Mrs. Jones spoke to about three hundred people who were not very much impressed with her talk. She denounced child labor, saying that children were pitched from the cradle to the factories to sweat out their lives for the capitalists." The next day, again according to the *Times*, Jones was "at her wits' end to keep her army together," that "she made another speech upon the street tonight, in which she denounced capital, child labor, and things in general," and that the army "looked tired and disgusted with the whole thing." By the time they reached Rahway on the fourteenth, the army had dwindled to only about thirty children, and public interest in the rallies was uneven, with several described in terms such as "poorly attended" and "end[ing] with a fizzle."

The initial *Philadelphia Inquirer* story on the march mentioned that Mother Jones intended to go to Oyster Bay "for the purpose of calling the attention of President Roosevelt to the strike." However, she soon became more coy about her intentions, telling one reporter, "Oh, that's only a joke! Sometimes it takes extraordinary means to attract ordinary interest. Morgan and Roosevelt are names that attract attention at once, and I guess that is why I used them in talking to some reporters. Don't you think they could be put to a worse use than to get people interested in opposing child labor?" Perhaps Mother Jones herself hadn't made a decision about confronting Roosevelt, or perhaps she felt the uncertainty would stir up more interest. Whatever the reason, it's fascinating to see how this elderly, poor immigrant woman captured national attention on the issue of child labor, and sustained a spontaneous, canny repartee with the press corps.

On July 15 she sent President Roosevelt an open letter asking for an audience and promoting a national law banning child labor. In contrast to her lively, earthy speeches, she wrote respectfully and formally, asking "that the children be taken from the industrial prisons of this nation, and given their right of attending schools, so that in years to come better citizens will be given to this republic." The theme of creating a virtuous citizenry, which echoed the Founding Fathers, was one she returned to often. "These little children, raked by cruel toil beneath the iron wheels of greed are starving in this country which you have declared is in the height of prosperity . . . We ask you, Mr. President, if our commercial greatness has not cost us too much by being built on the quivering hearts of helpless children?"

As the march neared New York City, the crowds grew. On July 17 the army reached Newark, and the *New York Times* reported that "'Mother' Jones tonight, with as much enthusiasm and confidence as she has displayed all along the route taken by her and her army, addressed a large gathering at an open-air meeting in front of the Court House. Surrounded by her trusty followers and several hundred natives, 'Mother' Jones laid bare the facts which she said she expects to show President Roosevelt should the Executive grant her an audience. She was enthusiastically cheered by her listeners." The next day, in Paterson, New Jersey, "Helvetia Hall was packed to the doors to-night by an enthusiastic throng of men and women who turned out to hear Mother Jones and her lieutenants" and who gave her a "great reception."

Mother Jones also got a powerful new talking point when New York City's acting police commissioner denied the marchers a parade permit and announced that "the police will be instructed to arrest her if she attempts to parade her army." The city had just played host to Prince Henry of Germany and Mother Jones tore into the extravagant welcome laid out for that "piece of rotton royalty [sic]" and lambasted the federal government for spending thousands on the prince's entertainment while her children were striking over pennies per hour.

Jones leading a march in Trinidad, Colorado in 1913. (courtesy Kerr Archives, The Newberry Library, Chicago)

The next day, New York City mayor Seth Low instructed the commissioner to grant a permit to Mother Jones. Soon the mill children were on a ferry crossing the Hudson, staring in awe at the Statue of Liberty and the city's towering skyline. At 7:30 P.M. on July 23, Mother Jones assembled the marchers in front of the Labor Lyceum on East Fourth Street and led them uptown to Madison Square Park, at Twenty-third Street and Madison Avenue. Some marchers beat drums, others waved signs, and several more held out an American flag. So many people tossed coins into the flag that one reporter said it came to resemble "a huge bag of money."

Pleading fatigue, Mother Jones didn't make an extended speech that night but she did speak briefly to the crowd, with her arms draped on two marchers—"bright eyed lads" she called them—who flanked her. Noting that she and her "little band of slaves" had just completed a ninety-two-mile trek, she said, "We are quietly marching toward the President's home. I believe he can do something for these children, although the press declares he cannot. Congress last year passed a bill giving $45,000 to fill the stomach of an old prince, and he endorsed that, and if he could do that he surely could tell Congress to pass a bill that would take the children out of the God-accursed mills and put them in the schools."

After a brief stay in the city, the group made its way to Coney Island, where Frank Bostock hosted them at his circus. Bostock apparently shared Mother Jones's flair for publicity. When the marchers left, the circus owner loaned them an elephant to lead the parade down the shore. "The children got stuck in the sand banks," Mother Jones later said, "and I had a time cleaning the sand off the littlest ones."

Jones decided that the best way to approach Roosevelt would be to first meet with his ally, New York senator Thomas Platt. Apparently he was known to eat breakfast at the Oriental Hotel and so they headed there. There are different accounts of what happened. According to one observer, they simply arrived after Platt had already left for Manhattan. In another version, Platt eluded Mother Jones by sneaking out the back of a restaurant and boarding a train. Yet another account (possibly apocryphal but very appealing) said that the children got the elephant to sit on the train tracks in order to block his train from leaving.

Though they didn't ever actually see Platt, the hotel steward treated them all to breakfast. Afterward, the local police arrived to move them along. According to one report, "'Mother' Jones was much pleased, saying it was the most gratifying defeat she had ever administered to 'an aristocratic capitalism.' 'We make them take water,' she said, 'and their actions showed that with all of their financial power the handful of penniless crusaders scared them.'"

And on that note, the March of the Mill Children fizzled out. The last of the marchers returned to Kensington the first week in August, and a week later, the unions gave in. The factory owners refused to make any concessions and the strikers could not hold out any longer. Not surprisingly, the whole effort was widely deemed a failure. However, the march was a vital part of the growing awareness that eventually enabled the passage of laws to protect children from exploitation. The wheels of progress were moving slowly, and Mother Jones reached down and cranked them. Jones also cited some immediate measures of success. For one thing, "The children were very happy, having plenty to eat, taking baths in the brooks and rivers every day. I thought when the strike is over and they go back to the mills, they will never have another holiday like this."

Jones also credited the march with spurring more permanent change. "Not long afterward," wrote Jones in her autobiography, "the Pennsylvania legislature passed a child labor law that sent thousands of children home from the mills, and kept thousands of others from entering the factory until they were fourteen years of age." One year after the march, a group called the National Child Labor Committee was formed to investigate conditions and advocate for reform. Lewis Hine went into the field, gathering stunning documentary photographs for this group, raising yet more awareness of the issue. In 1907 a federal bill banning child labor was defeated. In 1916 a similar bill was passed but ruled unconstitutional by the Supreme Court. It was not until 1938, under the leadership of Labor Secretary Frances Perkins, that the federal government finally regulated child labor.

Paint Creek

In the years after the children's march, Mother Jones continued organizing workers in coal and copper mines, in breweries and telegraph offices and streetcars. She left the UMW to work for the Socialist Party, headed by her friend Eugene Debs, and she was an early member of the radical Industrial Workers of the World, also called the IWW or the Wobblies, but apparently she never felt fully engaged with either group. Still infatuated with Mexico, Jones also became involved in protesting the kidnapping and assault of Mexican revolutionaries by American police and became so visible an advocate that President Taft agreed to meet with her. After the revolution overthrew Porfirio Díaz in 1910, she traveled to Mexico as the guest of the new president, Francisco Madero. Soon after, she left the Socialist Party and rejoined the UMW.

Then, a decade after the 1902 arrest that first brought her wide national attention, a replay of sorts brought her to the peak of her influence and public profile. Once again, Jones was organizing miners in West Virginia. Once again, she was jailed under dubious use of government power. Once again, she used her jail cell as a pulpit to bring even greater attention to the cause of miners and all workers.

After more than a decade of organizing efforts, the UMW still wasn't as strong in West Virginia as it was elsewhere, but the miners had become more open to the union's message. Travel to and within the mountainous Kanawha County, a major source of bituminous coal, was difficult, characterized by steep trails and railroads built in narrow creek-cut canyons. Landmarks such as canyons and creeks were used to identify nearby mines; the Paint Creek mines were some of the few solidly organized ones in the state. During contract negotiations in March 1912, the UMW chapter for Paint Creek asked for a raise along with automatic deductions for union dues. The owners, fearing that concessions would erode their profit margins, refused, and the manager of the largest mine, Quinn Morton, convinced the rest to break off talks and withdraw union recognition.

The miners, including many outside the union, went on strike. Morton evicted the strikers and their families, who then set up a tent city in Holly Grove, just outside the strike area. As the walkout spread to the mines at nearby Cabin Creek, the operators grew more and more determined not to offer any concessions. They began recruiting strikebreakers in Eastern cities and hired several hundred armed guards from the notoriously violent Baldwin-Felts Detective Agency. A squad of Baldwin-Felts men, whose arms included a machine gun, manned a fort just outside the miners' tent colony.

When the strike began, Mother Jones was in Montana speaking to a group of copper miners. She immediately returned to West Virginia, the region she'd first struggled to organize in 1904, and began a ferocious Mother Jones–style campaign. Barred by injunctions from setting foot on company land, she trudged through creek beds to reach groups of miners and deliver her impassioned speeches. There is a detailed record of her speeches from this time because the Coal Operators Association paid to have stenographers record[8] several she gave in August and September.

On July 26, sixteen men died after shooting broke out between guards and strikers. The state's moderate Republican governor William E. Glasscock sent in three state militia companies to prevent further bloodshed. Speaking days later, Mother Jones condemned him as a hypocrite. He had claimed to be "helpless" to assist the suffering mining families, yet, as she pointed out, "the governor wasn't helpless when the operators asked him for two Gatling guns to murder the miners. He wasn't helpless then."

In addition to the blistering attacks on the governor, the mine owners, and organized religion, these speeches included several standard themes: the importance of solidarity; words of support from outside the camp and the state; the essential justice, even holiness, of their cause, which assured them of eventual success; the direct link between the workers and the true spirit of Washington and Lincoln.

In these speeches, Mother Jones added a new motif, that of extending solidarity to the militia members, working men like them-

---

[8] The stenographers' records capture the on-the-fly exuberance of a Mother Jones rally. Emphasizing a point, she tells the stenographer, "Put that down!" The miners holler out responses and she picks up on them.

(Cries of: "Tell it Mother, I heard it.")
I will tell you. I want you all to be good.
(A voice: "Yes, I will. We are always good.")
They say you are not, but I know you better than the balance do.
Be good. Don't drink, only a glass of beer. The parasite blood-suckers will tell you not to drink beer, because they want to drink it all, you know. They are afraid to tell you to drink, for fear there will not be enough for their carcass.
(Cries of: "The Governor takes champagne.")
He needs it. He gets it from you fellows. He ought to drink it. You pay for it, and as long as he can get it for nothing any fellow would be a fool not to drink it.

selves: "Let me say to you, I don't want a single officer of the militia molested in any way. I am not going to say to you don't molest the operators. It is they who hire the dogs to shoot you." By emphasizing the distinction between the operators and the militia, she not only stressed one of her standard messages but also lessened the possibility for more bloodshed.

As she continued speaking and organizing, the strike held and then spread. The mine operators began to focus on her as the real cause of all the labor unrest.

On September 2, Glasscock announced the formation of a committee to investigate the strike and recommend terms of a settlement. The three-man committee included a preacher, a militia officer, and a state tax commissioner. (Perhaps the politically correct mix of the day?) At the same time, Glasscock officially imposed martial law, sending in 1,200 troops. Gorn describes the results: "Glasscock's declaration of martial law became an excuse for a massive abuse of power. The military took jurisdiction over cases that began before a state of insurrection was declared and that occurred outside the martial-law zone. Equally important, prisoners' rights to legal counsel, to not incriminate themselves, to habeas corpus, and to trial by jury were suspended."

Throughout the rest of 1912 and into 1913, Jones continued organizing in the region, then traveled to Washington and New York to draw media attention to the strike. At her best, she was the personification of the feisty, fearless underdog. At Cooper Union, Jones denounced the conditions in West Virginia and, as she had so often, skillfully employed her own image: "What is the power of a Gatling gun compared with the power of an old gray-haired woman?"

While Jones was in the Northeast, the Glasscock committee issued a nominally even-handed but inconsequential report, which criticized both sides without making any recommendations for a settlement. On February 7 further violence erupted. A strikebreaker at Paint Creek was injured on the job, and strikers shot at those carrying him to the doctor. Shooting broke out on both sides. That night, Quinn Morton organized a posse armed with rifles and machine guns and loaded them aboard an armored rail car. With the cooperation of officials from the Chesapeake and Ohio Railroad, a train car called the "Bull Moose Special" rolled into the Holly Grove strike camp.

West Virginia native and UMW official Fred Mooney was at Holly

Grove that night. In his account, the strikers had been warned but were still caught off guard when the Bull Moose Special arrived earlier than expected. The miners had been gathered in the communal mess tent, some playing music, when they heard the sound of the train whistle.

Instruments were thrown aside and rifles were secured from music, the most inspiring thing known to man, these men leaped to arms, ready to defend the only place they could call home. From music to death. Can one imagine more of a change from one extreme to the other?

The toot of the engine whistle was a signal to the occupants of the armored coach to open fire. Machine guns spouted streams of bullets from windows on both sides of the coach. . . .

The fight was not to be one-sided for long, however. All at once spurts of flame leaped out of the darkness on every side. From behind trees, creek banks, and knolls, rifles cracked and bullets shattered glass in the armored coach. A bullet found its way to the hand of the engineer; some of his fingers were shot off. The armored coach was riddled with bullets. It looked like a sieve.

Cesco Estep was one of the strikers. He and his wife lived in a tent near the dugout. Mrs. Estep was outside the dugout when the armored train opened fire. Cesco said to her, "Hurry, dear, get inside quick."

These were the last words Cesco Estep spoke on earth. His wife was no more inside the entrance when an explosive bullet from the armored coach struck him on the right side of his face. He fell at the entrance of the dugout, his entire face shot away.

Bullets flew! The strikers began anew, and Mrs. Estep was in the thickest of it. The Mauser she had picked up from beside the body of her dead mate cracked incessantly, and she was no mean shot.

One striker had his gun shot in two while he held onto it; his hands were numb for hours. The fight became too hot for the death special and soon after the engineer's fingers were shot off he steamed up and pulled out.

Over the next few days, violence in the area increased and Glass-cock again imposed martial law. Mother Jones demanded a meeting with the governor and traveled to Charleston with a small group to press the issue. Gorn describes the hysteria Mother Jones now inspired: "The *Charlotte Daily Gazette* warned that she came at the head of five hundred armed miners to assassinate the governor. City Hall's bell tower rang out a riot warning, while local police and National Guard troops massed to defend the capitol. Mother Jones never made it past the Charleston train station."

"I Am a Military Prisoner"

Mother Jones and forty-seven others were arrested and jailed in the martial-law zone of Pratt, West Virginia. As always, she immediately began sending out impassioned letters. "The civil officers picked me [up] on the streets of Charleston threw me into an auto," she wrote to a fellow UMW official, "brought me 22 miles [to] the marshall law prison. . . . O the Villains they shot a man dead while he was takin his wife to Shelter She gave birth to a babe while they were buring him Shot a woman through the leg Talk about brutality heavens this beats anything." Her many errors reveal her haste and fury.

The spectacle of her arrest, at her proclaimed age of eighty, and her determination to draw maximum publicity resulted in national outrage and, finally, the political will to confront the abuses of power in coal country. Idaho senator William E. Borah, a maverick Republican, introduced a resolution to investigate conditions in the mines of West Virginia, and from her cell, Jones wrote to thank him. "I am in confinement now for a week at the age of 80 years. I am a military prisoner. . . . Senator, do what you can to relieve these wretches and the coming years will call you blessed."

On March 11, 1913, the *New York Times* reported that Jones was "on trial for her life before a military court, charged with conspiracy to murder. If she is convicted she will be subject to the death penalty by shooting. . . . She made fiery speeches which, it is charged, kindled the courage of striking miners so that they fought with mine guards, a number of whom were killed. She has rejected offers of amnesty made conditional on her leaving West Virginia." Jones and the others arrested sought a civil trial, but the circuit court ruled that the state was within its authority to declare martial law and try the union leaders in a military tribunal. Jones reveled in defiance and said, in words similar to those spoken by Ida B. Wells-Barnett, "I am eighty years old and haven't long to live anyhow. Since I have to die, I would rather die for the cause to which I have given so much of my life. My death would call attention of the whole United States to the conditions in West Virginia."

Trial records are incomplete, and there's no official record of the verdicts. On March 20 and 21, twenty-five defendants were released unconditionally. Nineteen more were released, apparently on some form of probation, on March 22. The remaining defendants, including Mother Jones, remained in custody apparently having been found guilty.

By now West Virginia had a new Republican governor, physician Henry Hatfield. Unlike Glasscock, Hatfield made it a point to meet with union officials and miners, as well as operators and militia officers. Throughout the court martial, the UMW and the operators had been negotiating, and on March 21, a settlement was announced. It provided for, among other things, the right to organize, a formal grievance procedure involving miners as well as managers, and a ban on importing strikebreakers.

Mother Jones was thoroughly at home in prison and, in a way that reflects her acute sense of her own role in the struggle, seemed energized by the experience. She continued her correspondence with union members, elected officials, and journalists, and the UMW sent a secretary to her once a week to help her keep up. Working with Senator Borah across party lines, Senate Majority Leader John Worth Kern of Indiana was pushing hard to pass the resolution to investigate conditions in West Virginia. The spectacle of a prim-looking old lady behind bars was a public-relations goldmine. During a floor debate, West Virginia senator Nathan Goff dismissed Mother Jones as the "grandmother of all agitators," not imprisoned at all but merely "confined in a pleasant boarding house." In response, Kern read into the record a telegram that Mother Jones had smuggled out: "From out of the military prison walls, where I have been forced to pass my eighty-first milestone of life, I plead with you for the honor of this Nation. I send you the groans and tears of men, women and children as I have heard them in this State, and beg you to force that investigation. Children yet unborn will rise and bless you." Three days later, on May 7, 1913, Mother Jones was released.

Speaking in New York City soon after, Mother Jones described her court martial as "the first move ever made by the ruling class to have the working class tried by military and not civil courts." She scolded the crowd in Carnegie Hall for standing by and letting it happen. "Moral cowards! If you had only risen to your feet like men and said 'We don't allow military despotism in America! Stop it!' A lot of moral cowards you are. Not a word of protest did we get out of you, but instead you sat idly by and let these things be."

That same month, the United States Senate debated the imposition of martial law in West Virginia while Mother Jones and fellow labor officials listened from the gallery. Senator Borah championed their cause: "If in such cases," he said, "the Governor of the State can close the doors of the court and deny the right of trial by jury, when the courts are able to proceed with cases under their jurisdiction, and we, the United States, are forced to sit idly by and see it proceed, we become Mexicanized in forty-eight hours." In June 1913 the Senate Subcommittee on Education and Labor opened investigations into the conditions at Paint Creek.

In this moment of her triumph, the *New York Times* ran a lengthy interview with Mother Jones, an article that's remarkable in many ways. The approving tone contrasts with that of the previous decade's editorial condemning the "tedious and oppressive incubus" at the head of the children's march. In the June 1, 1913, article the reporter wrote, "I had gone [to her hotel] with eyes ready for the blood-red flag. Instead I got calm sociology, interspersed with humor." She was indeed calm, even conciliatory: "I have as little patience with the workingman who cries that all employers are hard-hearted wretches as I have with the employer who declares all workingmen to be mere brutes who must be managed or ground into the dust." But most extraordinary is Mother Jones's extended metaphor likening the epidemic that killed her family to an "economic disease" laying waste to America's workers. In an extremely rare reference to her personal tragedy, she says, "My husband died of yellow fever in the South, and the same disease made widows by the tens of thousands. It is making no more widows, because we have mastered it. The world is suffering, to-day, from an industrial yellow fever, no less fatal but, I am certain, as preventable." She wove the trope through a lengthy discussion of the labor movement: the progress of

Jones in Chicago, photographed for the *Chicago Daily News* (courtesy Chicago Historical Society)

the past decade, the need for continued progress, the good to be gained from co-operation and fairness between workers and owners. She closed the metaphor by saying, "The capitalist and the striker—both men are all right, only they are sick; they need a remedy; they have been mosquito-bitten. Let's kill the virulent mosquito and then find and drain the swamp in which he breeds."

Colorado

The next battleground was Colorado, and it soon became the scene of the worst violence yet. Mother Jones first arrived on the scene after a UMW organizer was shot and killed on the street in Trinidad, Colorado, on August 16, 1913. She arrived to find the miners agitated by the refusal of the Colorado Fuel and Iron Company (controlled by John D. Rockefeller Jr.) to negotiate with them about their demands: an eight-hour day, union recognition, and an end to private guards. With Jones behind them, the miners went on strike on September 23.

As in West Virginia, the families were immediately evicted and set up tent cities outside the strike zone. The largest camp, at Ludlow, housed over a thousand families, speaking two dozen languages among them. The coal companies brought in guards armed with machine guns and a Baldwin-Felts–designed armored car, the "Death Special." With the encouragement of Mother Jones, the miners also armed themselves. Several shooting battles broke out over the next few weeks, and as the violence increased, operators pushed Governor

Elias Ammons, a Democrat, to take action. Finally, on October 28, he sent the Colorado National Guard to take control of the Trinidad area. Still, the violence did not subside.

Ever since her arrival in Colorado, Mother Jones had been speaking and organizing, writing letters to politicians and publications. In late 1913 she traveled to the East Coast to make the case for federal intervention, and to El Paso, Texas, to block the importation of Mexican strikebreakers. While she was out of the state, General John Chase, commander of the Colorado National Guard troops, barred her from reentering the strike region. Though Governor Ammons hadn't declared martial law, he made no objection to Chase's illegal declaration. According to Chase, Jones was a threat because "she inflames the minds of the strikers." Jones declared that the governor could not keep her out of Colorado even with military force. Furthermore, in a striking embrace of the suffrage movement she once disparaged, Jones said, "He had better go back to his mother and get a nursing bottle. He'll be better there than making war on an 82-year-old woman in a state where women vote."

Mother Jones arrived in Trinidad on January 4, 1914, and was immediately "deported" to Denver. Chase issued a statement saying "Mrs. Jones was met at the train this morning by the military escort acting under instructions not to permit her to remain in this district. The detail took charge of Mrs. Jones and her baggage, and she was accompanied out of the district under guard after being given breakfast. The step was taken in accordance with my instructions in order to preserve peace in the district. The presence of Mother Jones here at this time cannot be tolerated. She had planned to go to the Ludlow tent colony of strikers to stop the desertion of union members."

As always, opposition from the state had an inverse effect on Jones: it spurred her on. She returned to Trinidad on January 12 and immediately was seized by the local militia and taken to jail. In what came to be known as "the Mother Jones riot," a thousand mine women and children marched in her support and were met by one hundred armed, mounted troops, including General Chase himself. Chase ordered the group to halt and when they continued moving forward, lost control of his horse and tumbled to the ground. Amid laughter from the women and children, Chase ordered a charge, in which six women were seriously injured. This incident is a dramatic illustration of the thin skin of some powerful men, of the personal insecurities that led them to be oppressors. Mother Jones, like Ida B. Wells-Barnett, sought to expose the cowardice behind the brute force.

Soon after, the UMW filed a habeas corpus complaint seeking Jones's release. On March 6, the Colorado Supreme Court scheduled a hearing for March 16. Eager to avoid a precedent that would force the release of all the prisoners, Chase ordered the release of Mother Jones on March 15.

As soon as militia troops had escorted her out of the martial zone, Jones boarded a train for Trinidad but was arrested before it got there. A week later she wrote an open letter to the public from "an underground cell surrounded with sewer rats, tinhorn soldiers, and other vermin. . . . Not even my incarceration in a damp, underground dungeon will make me give up the fight in which I am engaged for liberty and for the rights of the working people . . . John Bunyan, John Brown and others were kept in jail quite awhile, and I shall stand firm." Clearly Jones saw herself as a modern John Brown, a woman of action, standing firm for principle, freeing the enslaved.

Prison, of course, has an illustrious tradition as a bully pulpit, the pinnacle being Martin Luther King Jr.'s *Letter from Birmingham Jail*, and Jones's flair for the dramatic increasingly thrived in her letters from this period. The eyes of the nation again were on this elderly woman being held, as she wrote in one open letter, "incommunicado in an underground cell . . . I have only to close my eyes to see the hot tears of the orphans and widows of the working men and hear the mourning of the broken hearts and the wailing of the funeral dirge, while the cringing politicians whose sworn duty it is to protect the lives and liberty of the people crawl subserviently before the national burglars of Wall Street who are today plundering and devastating the State of Colorado economically, financially, politically and morally."

This time Jones was released after twenty-three days. In the meantime, the commission began to focus on Colorado and other states as well as West Virginia. As the undisputed labor heroine of the Colorado coal conflict, Mother Jones was a sought-after witness. Jones testified before the United States House Commission on Mines and Mining, where she described conditions and recommended federal intervention.

Another featured witness was John D. Rockefeller Jr., representing the operators. The Rockefeller-controlled Colorado Fuel and Iron Company dominated the state's coal production, and Rockefeller Jr., the acting head of CFI, had become the de facto leader of the operators' coalition. Through the charitable Rockefeller Foundation and other good works, Junior (as he was known) consciously sought to redeem the family name from what many saw as the stain of Senior's aggressive business practices. Yet Junior also admired his father ("the most completely fearless man I ever met") and believed that unions were anti-American. On the stand he stood firm for the principle of "open camps," claiming he would never tolerate organized labor.

He was asked, "And you would defend this even if it costs all your property and kills all your employees?"

"It is a great principle," he responded.

The Ludlow Massacre

April 20, 1914, was Greek Orthodox Easter, the holiest of days for believers. The Greek families among the strikers celebrated early that morning, joined by Italians, Mexicans, and Eastern Europeans. Later, members of the Colorado state militia and Baldwin-Felts guards—with their Death Special—surrounded the strike camp at Ludlow, Colorado, and, at about ten A.M., opened fire. The strikers and their families had dug shelters underneath the tent platforms, and while the men returned fire, the women and children took shelter in these shallow pits. The battle lasted for over 14 hours. Near dusk, when the strikers ran out of ammunition, the troops moved in as desperate strikers and their families fled. Strike leader Louis Tikas was clubbed and then shot to death at point-blank range. Then the worst: militiamen began setting fire to the miners' tents, and at least a dozen women and children died in their refuges.

The next day, Rockefeller received the following wire from his representative in Colorado: "Unprovoked attack upon small force of militia yesterday forced fight resulting in probable loss of ten or fifteen strikers, only one militiaman killed. . . . Suggest your giving this information to friendly papers." The Colorado National Guard set up a committee to investigate, which interviewed no miners and declared that the strikers planned the whole incident. The spokesman added that most union members were "ignorant, lawless, and savage

South-European peasants." Despite these strategic interpretations, the facts of the massacre were indisputable, and a great public outcry against the Rockefellers soon arose. Demonstrators gathered outside Rockefellers' offices at 26 Broadway in New York, with one speaker calling for Junior to be shot down "like a dog." At the family estate, local fire departments were called out to blast demonstrators off the fences with fire hoses. Even Helen Keller, the international icon and inspiration for her triumph over disability, who had received financial assistance from the Rockefeller family, denounced Junior, telling reporters that he was "the monster of capitalism. He gives charity and in the same breath he permits the helpless workmen, their wives and children to be shot down." The only deaths related to these protests occurred when a bomb went off as several Wobblies were assembling it in their apartment. It was widely assumed that the bomb was intended for Junior.

Jones must have heard news of the massacre with a mixture of profound grief and eagerness to seize the moment for publicity. She began a new campaign, making Ludlow the centerpiece of her appeal for funds to support the Colorado strikers. In a speech to a labor convention in Pittsburg, Kansas, she described the massacre: "The horrors of it cannot be depicted by human pen, or penned into the history to come. When these children were piled up, sixteen that we know of, don't know how many more were roasted whose bodies were never found, and those bodies were piled up one after another and carried to their last resting place, how many people in the United States grasped the horror of that thing?"

In the strike area, the violence escalated. President Wilson, under increasing pressure to send in federal troops, asked Rockefeller to meet with the head of the House Subcommittee on Mines and Mining, to discuss potential solutions. At the meeting Rockefeller remained inflexible. According to Chernow: "Wilson was stunned by this brazen indifference to a presidential request, telling Junior, 'it seemed to me a great opportunity for some large action which would show the way not only in this case but in many others.'" The president sent federal troops into Colorado soon after.

In the aftermath of Ludlow, John D. Rockefeller Jr.—and his public image—underwent a remarkable transformation. Drawing on his own sense of fairness and his religious faith, he revised his views of the ac-

ceptable social costs of maintaining an "open shop." Canadian economist Mackenzie King, hired as the head of the Rockefeller Foundation's
newly formed Department of Industrial Relations, played a key role in
the evolution of his boss's rigidly anti-union views into a more moderate stance. In 1914 Rockefeller turned to former journalist Ivy Lee, who
was pioneering a new field: public relations. In January 1915 Rockefeller testified before the United States Commission on Industrial Relations in a hearing held at City Hall in New York. Lee insisted that rather
than be escorted in through a side entrance as before, Rockefeller enter
the hearing by the front door, in full view of the public. He did so, shaking hands with Mother Jones and other organizers along the way. His
testimony was remarkably more conciliatory. He even recognized labor's right to organize, adding that the owners also had a right to resist.

The next day, during a recess in the hearing, Rockefeller stopped
Mother Jones in a hallway, taking her hand in his. The *Washington
Post* recorded their exchange:

> "Our interests are mutual," he said to her. "We both want
> peace. We'll bury the hatchet. I wish you would come with me
> to Colorado as soon as my presence before this commission is
> no longer required."
>
> "If you'll come with me to Colorado you'll prove yourself
> the greatest man history ever produced!" exclaimed Mother
> Jones. Mr. Rockefeller blushed and gazed at her keenly and
> with the suggestion of a smile.
>
> "I think you're flattering me," he protested.
>
> "No," Mother Jones replied earnestly. "I never flatter. I
> throw more bricks than bouquets."

On the stand, Rockefeller admitted that he'd previously taken a far
too narrow view of his responsibilities as a director: "I should hope
that I could never reach the point where I would not be constantly
progressing to something higher, better—both with reference to my
own acts and . . . to the general situation in the company. My hope is
that I am progressing. It is my desire to."

For the rest of her life, Mother Jones would alternately praise and
curse Rockefeller. Not long after their hallway meeting, she condemned
his proposals as "a sham and a fraud," yet when his mother died, sent

Jones with (l-r) President Calvin Coolidge, First Lady Grace Coolidge and Theodore Roosevelt Jr. in 1924 outside the White House. (courtesy Library of Congress, Prints and Photographs Division)

him a gracious note of condolence and later declared that their antagonism had been "squared."

The Telegram Lie

Mother Jones continued organizing and agitating into the 1920s, but as she grew older, her judgment seemed to waver and her propensity to exaggerate and inflame grew worse. For instance, at a rally in 1919, she said, "I'll be 90 years old the first of May but by God if I have to, I'll take ninety guns and shoot the hell out of 'em. For every scab on the mills there is a woman that reared him. Women, the destiny of the workingman is in your hands. Clear hell of every damned scab you can lay hands on. We'll hang the bloodhounds to the telegraph poles. Go out and picket."

The most embarrassing episode, one which marks the end of her effectiveness as a UMW organizer, occurred in August 1921 during a strike among coal miners in Mingo County, West Virginia. One of the strikers was ambushed by the mine owners' private guards and shot to death. A week later Mother Jones and a thousand miners marched on Charleston and unsuccessfully petitioned the governor for a settlement. Frustrated, the miners began gathering in Marmet, a small town just south of Charleston, and declared that they would go en masse to Mingo County and end martial law by force.

Even though she had fanned the flames of their resolve, Jones became convinced that the miners' march would result in their slaughter and so sought to stop it. I think it was her pride—and her temperamental aversion to calming people down—that pushed her to make the biggest mistake of her career: on August 24 she told the men that President Harding had sent her a telegram promising that, if the miners dispersed, he'd work to end the "gunman system" in the state.

Astonished, the local UMW officials asked to see the telegram. When she refused to give it to them, they drove to Charleston, phoned the White House, and learned that she had fabricated the message. Within days, as many as eight thousand miners were on the march, all of them deeply disappointed in Mother Jones, calling her a "sellout" and "traitor."

The march was a disaster. The miners were stopped in Logan County and waged a three-day running battle until United States Army troops were called in. Hundreds of miners were charged with offenses including insurrection and murder. Most of the charges eventually were dropped, but as the legal proceedings dragged on for years, the union coffers were drained. By the end of the decade, the UMW had virtually disappeared from West Virginia.

Her Last Years

During the 1920s, Jones's health began failing. She lived for a few years at the home of her old friend Terence Powderly, former leader of the Knights of Labor, and his wife, Emma. She disappointed colleagues in organized labor by appearing on the White House lawn with President Coolidge, who was running for a second term (he had assumed office from the vice presidency when Warren Harding died, and he would go on to be elected in 1924) and Theodore Roosevelt Jr., the son of the former president, who was running against Al Smith for governor of New York (he would lose to Smith). Although some in the labor movement had reached out to these Republican candidates, neither had been very receptive to their concerns. Jones, who was most likely being used as a pawn, seemed to enjoy the attention at a time when her influence was vastly diminished.

After Terence Powderly's death in 1924, Emma's health began failing, and in 1929, Jones moved to a Maryland farm owned by Walter and Lillie Mae Burgess, two other old friends. On May 1, 1930, she celebrated her one-hundredth birthday (actually her ninety-third), an event she'd planned for more than two years. John D. Rockefeller Jr. sent a congratulatory telegram.

Mother Jones died six months later. Labor leaders from around the country came to pay tribute, and a requiem mass was sung in Saint Gabriel's Church in Washington, D.C. The president of the Chicago Federation of Labor accompanied the body to be buried in Mount Olive, Illinois. Jones was an effective but divisive figure to the end. In the eulogy that was broadcast on the radio, Reverend J. W. R. McGuire said, "Wealthy coal operators and capitalists throughout the United States are breathing sighs of relief while toil-worn men and women are weeping tears of bitter grief. The reason for this contrast of relief and sorrow is apparent. Mother Jones is dead."

Alice Hamilton

Is it sensible to assume that what is American is necessarily wisest and best, or even that it is unchangeable? Surely we should have enough humility to re-examine our national ways and decide quite objectively if they are the best possible for us. Personally, I am very loath to accept the verdict that a dependence on the benevolence of the uppermost class toward the lowest class is the only possible American way of solving the problem of the poor, or even that it makes for a healthy state and contentment at the bottom of society.

—ALICE HAMILTON

ALICE HAMILTON WAS A VERY UNLIKELY-LOOKING MUNITIONS inspector—a small, slight woman in her early forties, with an air of calm and gentility. Writing in 1926, one journalist described her as a "tweed-clad figure walking intrepidly on narrow planks hundreds of feet above the ground alongside of vats of seething sulphuric acid; dropping down vertical ladders into the dense darkness of copper mines; crawling on hands and knees into remote stopes;[1] listening in

---

[1] Stopes are terracelike excavations made when mining ore in very steep veins.

back rooms of saloons or union headquarters to strange tales in halting foreign tones; listening with equal attention in polished offices to the fluent statistics of captains of industry."

By 1915, when American plants began producing weapons and chemicals for the Allies, Hamilton had already spent more than five years exploring the dirtiest and most dangerous corners of industry. She was among the few Americans qualified—and curious—enough to investigate the effects that these new chemicals and processes had on the workers and recommend safeguards for them.

Her job was complicated by the fact that her employer, the Department of Labor, had no legal authority over these new factories. Hamilton later wrote, "could only tell me to follow my old procedure, visit the plants I knew and pick up gossip about the others." She had to secure permission to inspect factories from various military officials, and rely on tips to locate them. When she set about to determine if there was TNT poisoning among the enlisted men in the navy, Hamilton kept running into obstacles until the young assistant secretary of the navy, Franklin D. Roosevelt, agreed to meet with her. "He received me very graciously and, what was far more important, he listened carefully to my plea. Then he sent for an Admiral, who came in, resplendent in white and gold and blue, a gorgeous creature who made me feel like a drab peahen. I cannot remember how Mr. Roosevelt did it but I know that in some way he secured from the Admiral the permission I needed and in such a way that the gorgeous gentleman never lost face."

In her memoirs she describes her effort to investigate the making of picric, a component of explosives produced using nitric acid.

On one of my first trips in New Jersey, while I was waiting in a small railway station, I noticed a Negro and a white man standing near, and the eyes of all who were waiting for the train were turned on them curiously. "Look at the canaries," somebody whispered. The white man was of a leaden hue, thin and weary-looking, but touched into incongruous comedy by smears of orange stain on his cheekbones and deeply dyed yellow eyebrows and hair. The Negro was frankly comic, nails of bright orange standing out from his black hands, hair and eyebrows orange-dyed, a golden burnish over the high spots on his face, the palms of his hands a deep yellow. I edged over and, being greeted with a friendly grin by the Negro, ventured a question: "Dyeing cotton goods?" "No, Miss, we're working over to the Canary islands, making picric for the French." . . .

I found the Canary Islands that same day off in the meadows with wide stretches of farmland about. It was not possible to visit the plant then, I needed a permit from the central office, but from the road I could see strange forms hurrying about—black men in motley garb with great stiff aprons, colored orange, woolen shirts eaten away to rags, high boots streaked with yellow, flaps of leather hanging down against their hands. As I was looking, orange smoke began to rise, rolling out in thick clouds that sank and spread over the ground and then sluggishly rose and rolled away, paling as they went, while a crowd of grotesque men came running out from a long shed and stood waiting for the fumes to scatter. A dog with his gray coat stained in absurd yellow spots came out from the guarded gate. Near the barrier to the east the land rose a little and the trees there were blackened and withered, for the west wind swept the gases in that direction and they blight whatever they touch.

This was only one of countless investigations Hamilton made, not only of munitions plants but also of textile mills, copper mines, enameling factories, and Pullman-car painting sheds. She saw men and women poisoned and crippled by their work, and she tried to convince their bosses to improve working conditions. Through a combination of intelligence, honesty, humor, courtesy, and persistence, she succeeded surprisingly often. But she also helped develop standards and legislation to protect all workers, and the safeguards she secured still save lives. Like Mother Jones, she respected the workers and advocated for them, but Hamilton was also able to communicate and negotiate with the foremen, factory owners, and financiers. Her work led to a more intimate understanding of the experience of the poorest workers, and it was invaluable in achieving such major policies as workers' compensation and antipollution regulations. She was a pioneer in the field of occupational medicine and, at the height of the Industrial Revolution, one of the only physicians who made workplace safety her mission, a distinction that earned her an appointment to the Harvard faculty—the first woman chosen. Finally, she was a clear voice for responsible internationalism, whose experience studying in Germany led her to revisit the country in its darkest hours and to prophetically warn America about the rise of fascism. Her influence, which began in the 1910s, culminated in the New Deal.

The Homestead

One of the things I find endearing about Alice Hamilton is her strong bond with her family, an extraordinarily close-knit, intellectual clan in Fort Wayne, Indiana. The Hamilton estate, which the family called "the Homestead," encompassed lawns, woods, gardens, and three elegant old houses occupied by the extended Hamilton family. "There were eleven cousins living in the same big place. We needed no 'outsiders,' having our own games, our own traditions and rules of conduct," Alice wrote in her memoir *Exploring the Dangerous Trades.* Throughout her life, Alice would remain especially close to the cousins nearest her own age, Agnes Hamilton and Allen Hamilton Williams, and they were known among the family as the Three A's.

The Three A's: Alice (seated) with her two cousins Agnes Hamilton and Allen Hamilton Williams in 1893. (courtesy The Schlesinger Library, Radcliffe Institute, Harvard University)

The family's wealth had been amassed by Alice's grandfather, Irish immigrant Allen Hamilton, who arrived in Fort Wayne as a fur trader in 1823. As the frontier became settled and Fort Wayne grew, he invested in businesses and real estate. By the time Alice was born in 1869, the family was financially comfortable, with most of its

The Hamilton sisters in 1894: (l-r) Norah, Margaret, Alice and Edith. (courtesy The Schlesinger Library, Radcliffe Institute, Harvard University)

assets in real estate. However, the Hamiltons prided themselves not on money but on culture.

In Alice's immediate family, there were four girls—Edith, Alice, Margaret, and Norah—and one boy, Arthur, known as Quint. The Hamilton sisters, none of whom ever married, disdained the society girls of their milieu, who favored fashion and courtship, and chose instead to focus on education, charity, and work. Alice's sister Edith, eighteen months older, studied classics at Bryn Mawr College and became headmistress of Bryn Mawr School in Baltimore. After her retirement, she began translating and publishing classic texts. Lively and engaging, Edith Hamilton's writing interpreted the ideas of ancient civilizations for modern readers, and her books became widely read and quoted.[2] Margaret studied biology and taught in at Bryn Mawr School in Baltimore, where she also worked in administration. Norah, who struggled with her health, was an accomplished artist. She illustrated Alice's memoir as well as several of Jane Addams's

---

[2] Following John F. Kennedy's assassination, both his widow and his brother Robert found consolation in *The Greek Way*, which, in the words of Arthur Schlesinger Jr., "opened up . . . a world of suffering and exaltation—a world in which man's destiny was to set himself against the gods and, even while knowing the futility of the quest, to press on to meet his tragic fate." Robert Kennedy became a dedicated reader of Edith Hamilton's work, and *The Ever-Present Past* provided him with an often-used quotation: "to tame the savageness of man and make gentle the life of the world."

books and held art classes at Hull House. Quint, born in 1886, was seventeen years younger than Alice. He became a professor of French and Spanish at the University of Illinois at Urbana. The only one of the children to marry, he and his wife had no children themselves.

Their father, Montgomery Hamilton, one of five children and the younger of two boys, was a reserved, intellectual man who stressed the importance of education for all his children, boy and girls. He thought that the schools put too much stress on American history and arithmetic, so the Hamilton children learned at home, largely through reading what appealed to them. All five received a strong grounding in languages: Latin from their father, French from their mother and tutors, and German from a local teacher and the family's servants. Despite his obvious influence on their intellectual development and interests, the children weren't especially close to their father, who had a prickly personality and a drinking problem.

Alice's mother, Gertrude Pond Hamilton, was the heart of the family. An intelligent woman, fluent in French and Spanish and well-versed in contemporary literature, she shared her interests, including a passionate political sensibility, with her children. Alice later wrote:

> She could blaze out, even in her old age, over tales of police brutality, of the lynching of Negroes, over child labor and cruelty to prisoners. She made us feel that whatever went wrong in our society was a personal concern for her and for us. But her indignation was not so much against the individual policeman or prison warden; it was against the whole class and especially the system which made such cruelty possible.

Alice remembered her mother telling her, "There are two kinds of people, the ones who say 'Somebody ought to do something about it, but why should it be I?' and those who say 'Somebody must do something about it, then why not I?'" Hamilton would base her career and her life on that simple yet daunting question—"why not I?"

"A Larger Life"

Alice Hamilton decided early on that she wanted "a larger life." She settled on medicine "because as a doctor I could go anywhere I pleased—to far-off lands or to city slums—and be quite sure that I could be of use anywhere." Her training—first at "one of those little third-rate medical schools which flourished in the days before the American Medical Association reformed medical teaching" and then at the University of Michigan—confirmed her choice, and she thrived on the scientific method, which "fostered a spirit of inquiry, a habit of following a problem to its solution if possible, of accepting only what could be proved."

Witnessing the sheer power of cause and effect also inspired her. "I shall never forget the revelation that came to me when I saw through the microscope the cells which make up the human body, and realized that later on, I should be looking at these cells changed by disease— that the actual process of disease could be viewed by the human eye." Hamilton was equally fascinated with chain reactions in social policies and equally driven to inquire, analyze, and adapt her thinking to new evidence.

In her second year of medical school, Alice was one of three students selected to assist on the wards at the university's hospital. In an early letter, she describes one patient, an expectant mother with "a disease that bad women often have . . . It seems so dreadful, for she is so young, so utterly alone and has probably been so wicked." (Barbara Sicherman, who edited Hamilton's collected letters, surmises that the patient suffered from gonorrhea.) Over the next few letters, Hamilton's empathy overcomes her initial edge of prudishness as she comes to know the woman and her situation. Hamilton holds the woman's hand during labor, listens to her fret over whether or not to keep the baby, and intercedes with hospital staff to allow the woman to remain a few extra days to fully recover. (In the end, the woman gave up her baby and returned to her family.)

In 1894 Hamilton interned at the New England Hospital for Women in Boston. Her experience there was both wrenching and inspiring. This was the era of the house call, so Hamilton visited many patients in their homes and saw their deprivation for herself. All her patients were desperately poor and many were unwed mothers, disgraced and abandoned. She was able to help some of them in limited ways—making extra visits to patients or finding them new lodging—but she was frustrated by her inability to make significant changes.

After completing her year-long internship, Hamilton struggled to figure out her next step. She knew she didn't want a clinical practice and that she was interested in bacteriology and pathology, but she wasn't sure how or where to begin research work. She briefly returned to Fort Wayne to help care for two of her sisters. (Margaret was injured in a carriage accident and Edith had abdominal surgery.) Then she and Edith spent a year studying in Germany, which Alice tremendously enjoyed. She cultivated a personal understanding of the complexities of German society and an enduring interest in learning from the experiences of other cultures, an interest she obviously shared with Edith. During this period Hamilton was reading the work of progressive social reformers: Richard Ely, Franklin Giddings, Jacob Riis, and Jane Addams, who would become a mentor and close friend.

Like Alice Hamilton, Jane Addams was the daughter of a large and well-off midwestern family. She grew up in Cedarville, Illinois, the eighth of nine children. Her father was a politician, a Civil War veteran, and a friend of Abraham Lincoln. (Lincoln addressed him in letters as "My Dear Double D'ed Addams.") She found the inspiration for Hull House during a visit to Toynbee Hall in London's East End where she observed students from Oxford and Cambridge universities living and working among the city's most underprivileged, providing legal aid, home visits, lectures, and debates. When she returned to the United States in 1889, she and her friend Agnes Starr leased a large house on the corner of Polk and Halsted streets in Chicago, and established Hull House.

Hull House was located in the heart of one of the city's poorest districts, where immigrants from dozens of countries struggled to get a foothold in the American culture and economy. Largely neglected and often reviled by city officials and better-off Americans, residents of the Nineteenth District faced overcrowding, inadequate sanitation, high unemployment and extremely low income (for the average family, five dollars a week—roughly one hundred dollars today). Because of Addams's strong pragmatic bent, her original idea of assisting the poor by having the well-off live among them soon evolved into a broad-ranging array of services and activities: employment agencies, continuing education, legal counseling, health care, political lobbying, union organizing. Hull House[3] became a beacon to those interested in aggressive measures to alleviate poverty, and Addams herself became world-famous for her innovative social work and advocacy.

On one of her many speaking tours, Addams visited Fort Wayne shortly after Hamilton finished medical school. In her memoir, Alice recalled the visit as personally pivotal:

> [Addams] was already famous, though Hull House was not more than six years old. Norah brought the exciting news to Agnes and me, and we three went to hear her in the evening. I cannot remember my first impressions; they blend into the crowd of impressions that came in later years. I only know that it was then that Agnes and I definitely chose settlement life.

When she went to Chicago, however, Alice worried that settlement life would not choose her. "[Hull House] is so tremendously cultured," she wrote to Agnes, "and all the people seem to be specialists in sociology or kindergartening, or manual training or art or music or anything else that is taught there. I know I never would be accepted by them. You see they have a dreadful custom. They accept you for a six weeks' probation and then vote whether or not you are valuable enough to remain. Wouldn't it be pleasant to be voted out?"

Hull House

Hamilton applied to Hull House in 1897, only to be told that there were no openings. She got a job teaching at the Women's Medical School of Northwestern University in Chicago and soon after, Hull House notified her that there was a place available after all. Hamilton kept up with her teaching but lived and worked at the settlement. She passed the dreaded vote at the end of her probationary period and would remain connected to Hull House for the rest of her career. "I

---

[3] The original building is now a museum on the University of Illinois campus, but Hull House continues its work in Chicago with a variety of programs, including senior services, child development support, and assistance to small businesses.

should never have taken up the cause of the working class had I not lived at Hull House and learned much from Jane Addams, Florence Kelley,[4] Julia Lathrop[5] and others," she reflected.

Although Addams was the pillar of American empathy with the immigrant poor, it was actually Addams's lack of sentimentality that Hamilton found most inspiring, her "mixture of sweetness and aloofness, of sympathetic understanding and impersonality, and the total absence of that would-be-charm and false intimacy which school and college had made me dislike heartily in older women." Addams refused to romanticize or condescend to the people served by Hull House. Hamilton, who also disdained paternalism, wrote in her memoir:

> As one reads [Addams's] earlier writings one sees that she was moved not only by the greater inequalities and injustices of society but perhaps even more by less evident, more intangible and rarely voiced evils from which men and women suffer but which sociologists often miss. She knew, because she understood people, that political equality meant little in comparison to social equality. . . . Contempt, she said, is the greatest crime against one's fellow man. So she looked upon Hull-House as a bridge between the classes, and she always held that this bridge was as much of a help to the well-to-do as to the poor.

---

[4] Florence Kelley inspired and influenced countless reformers with her intensity and passion. Kelley founded the National Consumers' League and served as its head from 1898 until her death in 1932. The League sought to educate consumers on the underlying consequences of their purchases and convince them to use their pocketbooks to push for reform.

[5] Julia Lathrop joined Hull House in 1890, and three years later she was appointed to the Illinois Board of Charities. Over the next year, she personally inspected all 102 county poorhouses, farms, and charity institutions and published her findings, which eventually led to a restructuring of the system. Lathrop then focused on treatment for the mentally ill, arguing for separate treatment facilities for the mentally and physically ill as well as other reforms. She also pushed for the creation of Chicago's juvenile court system, the first in the world. In 1912, President Taft selected her to head the new Children's Bureau in the Labor Department, a position she held until 1921. During her tenure the bureau undertook research and recommended policies in a number of areas: infant mortality, child labor, financial assistance for mothers, child nutrition, juvenile delinquency, out-of-wedlock birth rates, and care for the mentally disabled.

Addams also shared and encouraged Hamilton's preference for measurable, visible change. "She was a pragmatist in the best sense," Alice wrote, "holding that anything one had learned in college and from travel must be tried out in actual life. 'Truth must be put to the ultimate test, the test of the conduct it dictates and inspires.'" Addams led a network of women reformers who advocated for changes in labor laws, old age insurance, public health programs, and compulsory public education for many years before the New Deal made these advances viable on a national scale. Starting with her work at Hull House, Alice Hamilton took her place among this group.

At Hull House, Hamilton found sustaining friendships and the "larger life" she craved. Her life there was earnest and purposeful but never humorless. For example, she began a summer tradition of nightly bicycle rides, which even the matronly Addams occasionally joined.

> We leave the nineteenth ward steaming and choking and melting and in fifteen minutes we are on the lakeshore drive spinning along with the air fresh on our faces and the lake before us and the moon just coming up. We usually go to one of the most distant beer gardens . . . and stay for an hour or so drinking delicious cold Bavarian beer from stone mugs, then we mount again and reach home between eleven and twelve. And after a cold bath one goes to bed feeling deliciously instead of all melted and miserable as I usually do in such weather.

Besides the long-term residents of Hull House, there were many others who volunteered for briefer periods of time, plus an endless stream of visitors—progressive and radical activists, artists, and reformers from all over the United States and the world. The most colorful radicals didn't influence Hamilton much. In her memoirs, she describes some she liked personally but considered ineffective, and others who put her off, including IWW leader Big Bill Haywood: "a great towering hulk of a man with a truculent, defiant way of speaking, not at all impressive or convincing." Hamilton had no patience for theoretical reform, and a keen eye for hypocrisy. She recalled escorting one visitor on a tour of the neighborhood. As he talked passionately about the desperate need for vacation schools for poor children in the London slums, he shoved aside the slum children right in front of him. Hamilton thought to herself, "You may love humanity but you certainly do not love your fellow man."

Hamilton developed a profound respect for the immigrant families she worked with at Hull House. "Life in a settlement does several things to you. Among others, it teaches you that education and culture have little to do with real wisdom, the wisdom that comes from life experience. You can never, thereafter, hear people speak of the 'masses,' the 'ignorant voters,' without feeling that if it were put up to you whether you would trust the fate of the country to 'the classes' or 'the masses,' you would decide for the latter."

Hamilton's first project at Hull House was a "well-baby clinic" in which she cared for infants from the surrounding slums and taught their mothers about nutrition and hygiene. Jane Addams let her use the basement, provided her with a dozen little bathtubs, and sent mothers and babies down to her for care. Hamilton, sensitive to cultural differences among the immigrants, learned to adapt her textbook doctrines to the mothers' hands-on knowledge, but one incident in particular shows that she was not infallible. "I found I could get past the Italian mothers' dread of water if I followed the bath with an alcohol rub and anointing with olive oil," she recalled in her memoir. Here, it was the Italian mothers who were right. As Hamilton would soon discover, Chicago's public water system was vulnerable to the same contamination as these mothers had rightfully grown to fear in their native country.

Much as Hamilton loved Hull House, her multiple roles there, combined with her teaching, left her exhausted and tortured about her professional options. In June of 1899, when she had been there a little over a year, Alice wrote to her cousin Agnes Hamilton:

> People in the house got into the habit of referring to me everything which had the remotest connection with medicine so that in a way I had a good many demands on my time, though it was all so scrappy that I had the feeling of being pulled about and tired and yet never doing anything definite. About January I began to get very tired and I think my work at the school would have been just about all I could manage. . . . You see if I could make up my mind just to be a professor of pathology in the

Women's Medical School and do what work I could do at Hull House I think I could manage it all right. But I don't think that would be right, even if it were possible. I think I can do good work in science, the men I have worked for have all told me so, and if one can do good work, one must, don't you think so?

Typhoid

In 1902 a typhoid epidemic struck Chicago. The Nineteenth Ward contained less than 3 percent of the population but suffered more than 14 percent of the casualties. Alice threw herself into finding out why. After investigation and analysis, she presented her findings to the Chicago Medical Society in January 1903 and published them in the *Journal of the American Medical Association* the next month. Her conclusion: the typhoid outbreak was spread throughout Chicago's poor neighborhoods by flies. "In Chicago the effect was most gratifying," she recalled. "A public inquiry resulted in a complete reorganization of the Health Department under a chief loaned by the Public Health Service, and an expert was put in charge of tenement-house inspection." Pamphlets on reducing insect populations were distributed throughout the area.

Eventually, the real cause of the typhoid epidemic was discovered: a pumping station in the Nineteenth Ward had malfunctioned, which caused whole neighborhoods to drink and bathe in sewage-tainted water. The city had delayed repairs, allowing the virus to spread. Hamilton's conclusion that flies were at fault inadvertently helped the city cover up the entire incident. Alice must have had a stark moment of self-doubt and embarrassment, but what I find impressive is how she pulled out of it: with reinvigorated respect for the population she served, with pointed ire at lackadaisical public officials, with a determination both to improve public services for the poor and to set the record straight, even though she would have to contradict other people's public praise of her work. "For years, although I did my best to lay the ghosts of those flies, they haunted me and mortified me, compelling me again and again to explain to deeply impressed audiences that the dramatic story their chairman had just rehearsed had little foundation in fact."

Cocaine Trials

Around this time Hamilton also confronted an early version of an enduring urban scourge: the sale of addictive, illegal drugs to children. In her memoir she describes the moment that a Hull House colleague "discovered that cocaine, 'happy dust,' was being sold to our schoolboys by agents of drugstores, who would stop the boys on their way home from school, give them a pinch of the powder to snuff up, and ask them how they liked it." Alice observed that the boys, once addicted, would "commit a crime to get it, hold up and rob, smash drugstore windows, intimidate drug clerks."

Though cocaine wasn't declared illegal under federal law until 1914, the druggists could be prosecuted under state law. Hamilton was drawn into the Hull House campaign because of a legal loophole: the law did not bar sales of very similar drugs, synthetic alpha- and beta-eucaines. One of the few ways to distinguish them from cocaine is that cocaine dilates the pupils, while eucaines do not. Hamilton went to the court to test the seized drug and testify as to the results. At first she tested the drug on rabbits, but the defendants' lawyers stirred up so much sympathy for the lab animals that she began to use herself as a test subject.

> I tested the powders on myself for I knew it would not injure my eyes and other people were quite understandably reluctant to take the risk. I used to go around the laboratory with one wide and one narrow pupil till everyone was so used to it that they took no notice. But one day [her supervisor] came in much amused to tell me that a doctor who had been talking with me went to him in great agitation to say that I evidently had a tumor of the brain.

This badly crafted law was frustrating, but what really enraged Hamilton was the corruption of the entire system. The new law that was passed to close the eucaine loophole (due in part to Hamilton's efforts) resulted in several convictions upon appeal, but all were eventually overturned due to a technicality in the revision of the law. "That seems to me," Hamilton later wrote, "as absurd as if the Health Department should refuse to test the water of a proposed reservoir, saying, 'No, we cannot tell you if this water is contaminated or not. You must put in the system and let the people drink the water, then if they get sick we will tell you whether it is typhoid fever and whether you must look for another water supply.'"

Perhaps it was then that Hamilton realized that her own judgment about public policy could be superior to those in charge of it. "As an American, nothing mortified me as much as the system of criminal law in Chicago," she wrote, "for it was impossible to explain it or to defend it to the immigrants whom one wanted so much to inspire with confidence in our American form of government."

Finding Her Calling

Hamilton's work in the early 1900s reflected a deepening interest in discovering how and why poor people were disproportionately affected by disease. In 1903, the year after the ill-fated typhoid investigation, she helped organize the Committee on the Prevention of Tuberculosis of the Visiting Nurse Association[6] and over the next few years she undertook several related studies. She cited extreme fatigue, poor sanitary conditions, and long working hours as contributing factors. Sicherman points out that although Hamilton herself doesn't mention them, these studies are "her earliest exploration into the relation between occupation and disease." Hamilton also joined a committee on midwives cosponsored by Hull House and the Chicago Medical Society.

In 1907 Hamilton read Sir Thomas Oliver's *Dangerous Trades*, which documented the many, often disfiguring and even fatal illnesses and injuries that afflicted workers in new industries in England. Though her colleagues assured her that these hazards didn't apply to American factories—"for our workmen were so much better paid, their standard of living was so much higher, and the factories that they worked in so much finer in every way than the European, that they did

---

[6] Chicago's VNA was similar to the Visiting Nurse Service (VNS) in New York, founded by Lillian Wald, another pioneer of the settlement house movement. The VNS was founded in 1893 and quickly became a model for civic organizations seeking to provide health care to indigent or homebound populations. It was linked with Wald's Henry Street Settlement, and both organizations received financial backing from philanthropist Jacob Schiff. New York's VNS and Henry Street are still in operation.

not suffer from the evils to which the poor foreigner was subject. This sort of talk always left me skeptical"—Hamilton knew from her own experience that American factories were hardly models of safety and hygiene. Oliver's book came at the right moment: it intrigued her and focused her desire to challenge the social order that so routinely sacrificed powerless people in the name of profits. As she wrote many years later,

> The worker was as truly under the power of his employer as was the peasant under the power of his overlord in the Middle Ages, with one exception: he could quit his job, but often that meant starvation. . . . When our Industrial Revolution had reached its peak, the leaders of big business or manufacturing, of mining and smelting, of oil production and refining, had behind them all the forces of law and order, which meant not only the state police but their private police forces, and also the law courts, the injunction judges, even the Supreme Court.

One of the success stories Oliver documented was the eradication of phossy jaw in Great Britain. White phosphorus, used in making matches since the 1830s, produced fumes that could enter a worker's body through an unfilled dental cavity. Painful abscesses developed, and the bone and flesh of the jaw became inflamed and often died, necessitating amputation. In severe cases, a victim's entire jawbone had to be removed. In the 1880s, Salvation Army founder General William Booth began a campaign against phossy jaw. Among the most compelling elements of his campaign were his visits to the homes of phossy jaw sufferers, accompanied by reporters and lawmakers, visits in which Booth would dim the gas lamp so the assembled observers could see the greenish-white glow of the affected areas. In 1891 Booth established a matchmaking factory using the safe red phosphorous, and by the turn of the century, white phosphorous use, and new cases of phossy jaw, had been eliminated in Great Britain and Europe. American factories eventually followed this lead.[7]

---

[7] Diamond Match Company held the United States patent for sesquisulfide, a safe substitute for white phosphorous. On January 28, 1911, the company voluntarily gave up the patent to "allay suspicion of monopoly" and help eradicate phossy jaw. In 1912 the Match Act taxed matches made with dangerous white phosphorous. Phossy jaw soon became virtually unknown.

Even after the eradication of phossy jaw in America, many industrialists still refused to acknowledge that the United States could learn from the experiences of other countries. Hamilton later reflected that phossy jaw had been "the simplest problem of industrial poisoning so far encountered." Soon Hamilton would encounter more difficult cases, and entrenched resistance from factory owners. She also would run up against the philosophy of unfettered competition in business, and a widespread belief in American exceptionalism—the certainty, contrary to evidence, that American working conditions were inevitably superior to those in Great Britain and Europe.

Hamilton's first action for workplace safety took place in 1908 when she published an article entitled "Industrial Diseases: With Special References to the Trades in Which Women are Employed," the first article about industrial disease to be published in the United States. In it Hamilton argued that it "was very improbable that all American employers would voluntarily take the precautions which stringent legislation has had to force upon the foreign employers." Hamilton preemptively challenged the idea that her openness to "foreign" ideas was somehow un-American.

This article, as well as the word of mouth about her work in and around Hull House, made Alice Hamilton a recognized expert in public health. She was asked to consult with the American Association for Labor Legislation on how to curtail industrial diseases and was one of the few scientists to participate in labor conferences. When the governor of Illinois assembled a commission to study the "poisonous trades" in 1910, he appointed Hamilton to be its special investigator.

The Illinois Investigation

Hamilton and the other researchers had no previous investigations to use as a model. They didn't even have a definitive roster of factories or industries to examine. Starting from scratch, they drew up a list of dangerous substances used in manufacturing and divided it up. In addition to her responsibility for supervising the entire project, Hamilton took on an investigation of lead. She spent the next year engaged in "shoe-leather epidemiology," visiting all but three of the twenty-five known American white lead factories. "So interesting did I find it," she wrote in 1929, "that I never went back to the laboratory, and ever since then I have been following the trail of lead, mercury, nitric acid, carbon disulphide, carbon monoxide, explosives, aniline dyes, benzol, and a long list of chemicals with complicated names which would suggest little to most readers but which are interestingly varied in their uses and in their effects on that more or less unconscious victim, the worker."

Hamilton identified lead-using industries, from paint to electric cables, and began looking for cases of lead poisoning (also called plumbism or lead colic) among the workers. Plumbism, resulting from breathing lead dust or lead fumes, had severe effects, ranging from hardening of the arteries to wasting, tremors, anemia, early senility, even death. Many factories kept sloppy and incomplete employee records. At one typical plant, Hamilton had to track down cases among, as she put it, "men who came from the Serbian, Bulgarian, and Polish sections of West and Northwest Chicago, and were known to the employing office only as Joe, Jim, or Charlie, with no record of their street and number!"

The workers themselves were often reluctant to talk to her at work, in front of their bosses, so Hamilton interviewed them at home, in taverns—wherever she could find them.

> As I remember it, the most nearly complete figures I secured in [the Illinois investigation] were obtained by examining about one hundred and fifty sanitary-ware enamellers who, luckily for me, were on strike at the time. Most met me in the rear room of a Polish saloon, the rest in a shack which they had turned into temporary headquarters. There, without any fear of losing their jobs, they were quite ready to let me find out whether or not they were "leaded." But usually the cases were picked up here and there from doctors, hospitals, priests, apothecaries, and by following clues through city tenements and workers' cottages.

She also discovered many previously unknown sources of danger and achieved results from preemptive efforts. For instance, no one outside the industry realized that one step in the enameling of bathtubs and sinks involved grinding down lead-filled glaze, which filled the workplace with toxic dust, but Hamilton discovered it when she found severe and widespread plumbism among the grinders and enamelers. In another instance, she successfully appealed to a large stockholder in Pullman Railroad to use his influence to change painting methods in order to prevent the dust that was giving the workers lead poisoning. "Changes took place with breathtaking speed, and by the end of 1912 there was a modern surgical department with surgeons in charge, an eye specialist, and a medical department to supervise the 500-odd painters."

Once Hamilton had identified unsafe conditions at a plant, she wrote a report documenting the problems and their effects on the workers and suggesting specific steps to improve conditions. Hamilton had a centrist, pragmatic temperament, with none of the fiery combativeness of Wells-Barnett or Jones. Both gentle and authoritative, she helped many leaders of industry to see what was happening on their watch and to respond to, in Lincoln's phrase, "the better angels of their natures." For example, Edward Cornish of the National Lead Company, initially "indignant and incredulous" when Hamilton informed him that men were being regularly poisoned in his plants, proved to be receptive to Hamilton's pitch, which included twenty-two documented cases of severe lead poisoning among his workers and specific recommendations for safeguards. Cornish promised to follow all of her directions, including hiring doctors to regularly examine the men. "He was better than his word," she rejoiced.

The results of the Illinois investigation were dramatic and far reaching. Through careful research and documentation, Hamilton proved that every year thousands of workers in the state were subjected to accidents, disease, and death without any recourse or accountability. Several months later, Illinois passed an occupational disease law that mandated compensation for industrial diseases, and other states followed suit. Once the employers realized they would have to insure against possible claims, the insurance companies got involved to make sure the causes for the claims were removed. Hamilton had made such a name for herself—and for industrial medicine—that she was asked by United States Commissioner of Labor Charles O'Neill to conduct national surveys.

National Surveys

Perhaps in part because other people's expectations of her would never be all that she knew she was capable of, Hamilton defined a broad role for herself. "The Illinois Commission expected me to report back to it and in such a way that no factory described in the report could be identified," she recalled. "That I did, of course, but I could not feel the whole of my responsibility was thereby discharged. . . . How could I hope that a cold, printed report which would satisfy the Commission would serve to do away with the pressing dangers?" Hamilton resolved to take her own knowledge and persuasive powers directly to the men in charge of the system. She often recalled a conversation she had in 1911 with a manager of a big plant, a man "of breeding and something of a philanthropist," who responded to her incredulously: "Why, that sounds as if you thought that when a man gets lead poisoning in my plant, I should be held responsible." This was exactly what she thought—and exactly the change she achieved.

One of her insights, echoing the work of Ida B. Wells-Barnett and Mother Jones, was that owners justified their abuse of the workers by dehumanizing them. "Many times in those early days I met men who employed foreign-born labor because it was cheap and submissive, and then washed their hands of all responsibility for accidents and sickness in the plant, because, as they would say: 'What can you do with a lot of ignorant Dagoes, Wops, Hunkies, Greasers? You can't make them wash if you took a shotgun to them.' They deliberately chose such men because it meant no protest against low wages and wretched housing and dangerous work, no trouble with union agents; but rather a surplus of eager, undemanding labor."

Employers also justified their practices through the "assumption of risk" argument. If the employees didn't like their working conditions, they could leave. If they chose to stay, they were accepting those conditions as terms of the job. This argument ignored several facts. First, the risks were largely hidden from the workers. Also, most workers had families to support. "It sometimes seemed to me that industry was exploiting the finest and best in these men—their love of their children, their sense of family responsibility," Alice lamented. Finally, the workers' options were extremely limited. "For an employer to say to his work-people, 'If you don't like the job, get out,' may in many instances be like a captain saying to his sailors, 'If you don't like the ship, get overboard,'" she explained.

Employers and their representatives often made bogus excuses to evade responsibility for workers' health. For instance, many firms provided a company doctor for the employees, but most of the physicians were very well aware of who paid their salaries and acted accordingly. As Alice wrote, "The physician attached to a large lead smelter (he had, however, never been inside it) told me that he had always advised the men to scrub their fingernails so as to avoid lead poisoning. I had just been over the plant and had seen the lifting and dumping of a huge roasting pot, the red-hot ore falling with a crash to a grating, and the men running up into the cloud and dust and fumes to break with hoes the larger pieces and push them through the grating. These were the men who were to escape poisoning by brushing their nails."

At least once, after inspecting a particularly dangerous factory that was poisoning its workers at a fast clip, Hamilton considered abandoning her courtesy and patience. As she recalled it, white lead was scattered everywhere and the men worked ten-hour days breathing lead dust. They even ate their lunches with unwashed, lead-coated hands and went home with lead in their hair and all over their skin and clothing. The foreman who gave her a tour sensed her dissatisfaction and "had a sudden inspiration—'I'll show you something you will like,' he said—and led me into a big stable where great dappled gray horses were standing on a clean brick floor, eating from clean mangers, and rubbed down till their coats shone. 'Mr. B. is awful proud of his dray horses,' he said. 'He thinks nothing is too good for them.'"

That night she considered writing a muckraking article to expose and embarrass the factory owner. The fact that she chose not to write the exposé reflects her commitment to long-term effectiveness over instant gratification. "The one plant might be reformed by such an attack, but the result would be to shut me out of most of the others," she reasoned. The next day she met with "Mr. B" and realized there was no point in confronting the doddering old man. Instead she spoke to the plant manager. He asked for her analysis and recommendations in writing and "carried out far-reaching changes in equipment and method so that the place was unrecognizable."

As Hamilton's work put her firmly on the side of those most exploited and marginalized, her progressive political philosophy deepened. "It was they who did the heavy, hot, dirty, and dangerous work of the country. In return for it, they met little but contempt from more fortunate Americans." Hamilton was determined to address systematic injustices she saw, so at odds with the "city on a hill" image of America that she had absorbed in her childhood. Hamilton believed that the fruits of capitalism should be shared by labor as well as owners, and that wealthy Americans should bear some responsibility for how their wealth is produced.

Alice Hamilton's genteel manner and hands-on practicality belied the extent to which she was challenging the prevailing political philosophy. She sought to change what she described as "industrial feudalism," by which sovereign states could "maintain their right to neglect the health and safety of their wage workers if they wish to." No matter how thrilling the individual victories, she felt that "so long as the health, safety and contentment of the working class are left largely to the good will and intelligence of the employing class, there will always be dark spots of neglect and ignorance and callousness." Hamilton became increasingly willing to work to change the system of accountability through government policies, the only way to go over the heads of recalcitrant factory owners. She credited Julia Lathrop with teaching her "a much-needed lesson, that harmony and peaceful relations with one's adversary were not in themselves of value, only if they went with a steady pushing of what one was trying to achieve."

"Joyous Ruthlessness"

World War I was a watershed for the developing field of industrial medicine. As Alice described, the war "not only increased the dangers in American industry; it aroused the interest of physicians in industrial poisons." The increased interest inspired some newspapers (notably the *New York World*) to run investigative reports on industrial poisoning, such as radium poisoning among workers making luminous timepieces and tetraethyl lead poisoning from gasoline additives. In both cases, the public attention led to quick resolution of the problems. Hamilton was thrilled at these victories but also recognized that, as with phossy jaw, these were relatively simple problems to solve and did not necessarily pave the way for the harder ones. In both cases, inexpensive substitutes for the dangerous substances were readily available and the manufacturing processes themselves weren't hazardous. That wasn't the case in many of the new weapons industries.

Through her extraordinary resourcefulness, Hamilton was able to investigate many factories and workers involved in production for the war, including the "canaries" at the picric plant. Although she immersed herself into her investigations of the munitions industry with her treasured impartiality, she found her discoveries profoundly depressing. "It was not only the sight of men sickening

Hamilton (at age fifty) in Chicago in 1919, the year she became the first woman to join the Harvard faculty. (courtesy The Schlesinger Library, Radcliffe Institute, Harvard University)

and dying on the effort to produce something that would wound or kill other men like themselves . . . but it was also my helplessness to protect them against quite unnecessary dangers." This was an especially bleak period for Hamilton, a committed pacifist.

From various platforms, Hamilton argued for protections for these workers, such as England and France had adopted, but she found few who were willing to listen. With the war, American exceptionalism had only increased, and Hamilton found herself fighting against something new, a "joyous ruthlessness" that swept the ranks of those making money off the war preparations. When the committee of physicians appointed by the War Labor Board, of which Hamilton was a key member, recommended cost-effective protection against TNT, picric acid, nitrous fumes, and other poisons, they "could not prevail against the arrogance of the manufacturers, the indifference of those higher up, and the contempt of the trade unions for non-union labor."

Her position as chair of the Committee on Industrial Poisons of the National Consumers' League—and later its general chairman—

gave her another platform from which to explore these topics. She learned to use the public conferences to garner support for change. As she wrote her Hull House colleague Florence Kelley, "It is, after all, the weapon of publicity which we hold up our sleeves that impresses them and makes them ready to do what we tell them to." When she did get publicity, Hamilton was often frustrated that more people—especially women—didn't rally to the cause, and she became resentful of what she saw as the single-mindedness of the suffrage movement.

Conflict within the Women's Movement

Alice Hamilton felt a special responsibility as a woman because so many qualified male scientists had ignored industrial medicine, thinking it, as Alice said, "tainted with Socialism or with feminine sentimentality for the poor." She was proud to be among the progressive women reformers addressing problems ignored by others, but Hamilton often disagreed with the leading suffragists and feminists of her day. For one thing, many suffragists had allied their cause with the temperance movement, while Hamilton saw the issue as a way to unfairly blame people for their hardships.

Hamilton came around to the view that equal rights for women were critically important, but initially she felt that those leading the charge were too obsessed with the vote, to the exclusion of important social issues all around them. Hamilton wrote to Addams about her conflict with Carrie Chapman Catt, "She isn't a big woman, none of the absolute suffragists are, they never had a chance to get broad."

Hamilton did support suffrage but prioritized other "social justice" proposals, including protective legislation for women workers, who were especially exploited in factories and often had children, either at home or in tow. When Alice Paul immediately followed the success of the Nineteenth Amendment with a proposal for the Equal Rights Amendment in 1921, women reformers were deeply divided. In her biography of Eleanor Roosevelt, Blanche Wiesen Cook describes the divide as one between two factions: "social feminists," including Kelley, Hamilton, Addams, and Eleanor Roosevelt; and "militant feminists," including Alice Paul and Crystal Eastman, who felt that they should seize the moment to eradicate all laws that discriminated on the basis of gender.

Hamilton initially opposed the Equal Rights Amendment proposed in 1921 by Alice Paul and the National Women's Party because she feared it would jeopardize new legislation limiting working hours for women. While Hamilton would have preferred all workers to enjoy the protection of an eight-hour day, she felt it was "better not to give up the ferry boat before the bridge is built." In a 1922 letter to Edith Houghton Hooker, editor of the National Women's Party journal, *Equal Rights*, Hamilton articulated her sense of women supportive of the ERA.

I could not help comparing you as you sat there [over a "friendly cup of tea"], sheltered, safe, beautifully guarded against even the uglinesses of life, with the women for whom you demand "freedom of contract." The Lithuanian women in the laundries whom the Illinois law . . . permits to work seventy hours a week on the night shift; the Portuguese women in the Rhode Island textile mills, on long night shifts . . . the great army of waitresses and hotel chambermaids, unorganized, utterly ignorant of ways of making their grievances known, working long hours and living wretchedly. To tell them to get what they should have by using their right of contract is to go back to the days of the Manchester School in England, when men maintained that there must be no interference with the right of women and children to make their own bargains with their employers in the cotton mills or at the pitheads. It is only a great ignorance of the poor as they actually are, only a great ignorance as to what is possible and what is impossible under our supposed democracy and actual plutocracy, that could make you argue as you do. . . . [If] you succeed in rescinding all the laws of the country discriminating against women and do it at the expense of present and future protective laws you will have harmed a far larger number of women than you will have benefited and the harm done to them will be more disastrous. . . . Remember, when you think me over-strenuous, that I have lived for twenty-two years among the poor and that for twelve years I have studied trades employing all sorts of labor. . . . The working woman is a very real person to me.

According to Cook, Hamilton's analysis had a profound effect on Eleanor Roosevelt, who rejected the "self-serving aristocrats who cared little and understood less about the needs of the poor" in favor of "the vision of reform created by that earlier generation of community activists, unionists, and radicals led by Florence Kelley, Jane Addams, Lillian Wald, Rose Schneiderman, and Dr. Alice Hamilton." (Hamilton eventually converted to the pro-ERA position and publicly supported the amendment in 1961, when President Kennedy appointed her chair of the Commission on the Status of Women.)

Alice Hamilton believed there were innate differences in the thinking and behavior of men and women. In fact, she saw her work as a sort of feminine righting of the Industrial Revolution. She recalled a conversation with a foreman who believed true workplace improvement depended on the presence of women in the workforce. Men, he said, see all the workers as part of the industrial system, whereas women immediately think of them as fathers, brothers, husbands, and so are naturally more humane in their treatment. Hamilton agreed. She also believed that male foremen and workers would listen to her, whereas they might hear the same criticism from a man as a challenge.

Hamilton also agreed with Mother Jones that a woman's primary responsibility was to home, husband, and children. Neither of them had faced the challenge of balancing their activism with child rearing, which undoubtedly made the conviction tidier and easier to maintain. In a letter to her cousin Agnes Hamilton, Alice criticized their cousin Allen's fiancée, a medical student, for continuing to train for a career while she planned for a family. Hamilton wholly accepted that her devotion to her work was its own kind of marriage, an all-or-nothing proposition. Unlike the diary of Ida B. Wells-Barnett, Hamilton's collected letters never reveal a strong need to have a home and children of her own. Perhaps she thought of the thousands of children she worked with as hers. A young woman who'd been one of the infants in Hamilton's early well-baby clinic at Hull House recalled that "ever since I was a baby she has wanted to know everything; when she comes back [to Hull House] now, the first thing, she takes you up to her room and makes you tell her everything—how your job is, and about the boys, and all about your sinus and your family."

Harvard

When Harvard University invited Hamilton to be its first woman faculty member in 1919, it did so grudgingly. The school wanted to establish a presence in the now-accepted field of industrial medicine, and Hamilton was the only obvious choice. Still, she was a woman, and so the invitation caused a stir. Headlines included "Very Feminine Is Dr. Alice Hamilton, the First Woman to Break Down Sex Barrier and Join Harvard Faculty" and "The Last Citadel Has Fallen."

Harvard made two stipulations to its offer: Hamilton would never be allowed to participate in commencement ceremonies, and she would not receive the treasured faculty football tickets. Hamilton found the restrictions silly and responded to the honor with characteristic self-deprecation, attributing her appointment to luck and the newness of her field. As she wrote one of her cousins, "I am not the first woman who ought to have been called to Harvard."

Hamilton made a stipulation of her own: she would teach at Harvard only half the year so that she could spend the other half at Hull House. She usually left in February and stopped along the way to give lectures at Bryn Mawr College and tour various factories and plants. At Harvard she contributed to the *Journal of Industrial Hygiene* and recruited so many other authors to write articles that one editor claimed she had "literally kept it going." She convinced the presidents of several lead companies to fund a three-year, no-strings-attached study of lead poisoning, and she gave regular cogent lectures on the health consequences of working in "dangerous trades" and how to improve them.

When the war ended in 1918 and the munitions factories closed, Hamilton had felt a new sense of possibility for industrial medicine. She became a sort of national resource for the new waves of scientists and reformers who had become interested in it. She also turned her attention to the devastation of the war. Hamilton and Jane Addams went on a Quaker relief mission to Germany, where Alice, using her language and medical skills, was gripped by the urgency to help the starving, impoverished people. The defeated nation was suffering under a blockade designed to force them to accept the harsh terms of the Versailles treaty. During the war, Britain had maintained a sea blockade against Germany, monitoring shipping through the English Channel and the North Sea. Although the armistice of November 11, 1918, ended the armed conflict, the blockade continued, devastating the civilian population. Many Germans, including children, died of starvation. Germany finally signed the treaty on June 28, 1919.

Alice's view, and her clear articulation of it, was truly prophetic.

A relief mission to Germany in 1919: (l-r) Jane Addams, unknown woman in background, Aletta H. Jacobs, Marion C. Fox, Joan M. Fry, Alice Hamilton (courtesy The Schlesinger Library, Radcliffe Institute, Harvard University)

She lambasted her own country's refusal to recognize that, in addition to being cruel, the blockade was strategically wrongheaded because it made Germany more unstable. Years later, Hitler would cite the terms of the Versailles treaty and the effects of the blockade as a justification for Germany's military buildup and territorial aggressions.

In December 1919 Frederick Shattuck, a prominent Harvard professor, asked Hamilton to stop making public pitches for the Quaker relief centers in Europe. Shattuck, a major fund-raiser for the industrial hygiene program, explained that other funders were disturbed by having a "pro-German" professor on the faculty. Her response was classic Hamilton: "I am afraid I cannot write you what I know you wish to hear from me, that your statement of my relation to Harvard University and its bearing on my espousal of an unpopular cause has made me decide to drop all efforts to help the children of Germany. What I have said in public about Germany and the Germans is based on what I saw there last July. It was a pitiful, heartbreaking sight and all that made it endurable was the thought that by seeing the misery with my own eyes I should be able to tell people over here about it with more convincing force and perhaps induce some of them to help."

After the War

Hamilton witnessed the backlash of intolerance and suspicion of foreigners after the war. Some of the reactions were rather silly, such as the campaign to rename sauerkraut "freedom cabbage." Others did real damage, including the infamous Palmer raids, in which thousands of accused or suspected radicals and subversives were arrested, often on flimsy evidence or mere accusation. Many of the foreign-born were immediately deported. The raids infuriated Hamilton, who had come to know both the political motivations behind the use of such force and the innocence of those it was so often used against. Immigrants were especially targeted, although, as she knew, the vast majority of them were innocent, hardworking, and believed deeply in the ideals of their adopted country. The idea that they assisted the "spread of Bolshevism" was ridiculous to her. She supported efforts to provide legal assistance

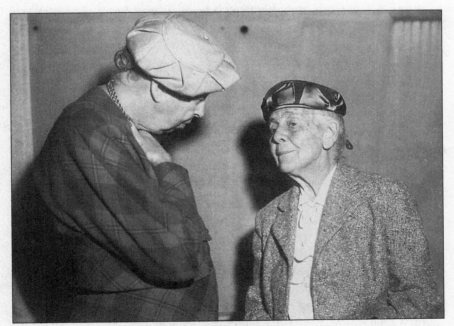

Alice Hamilton with Eleanor Roosevelt in 1958. (courtesy The Schlesinger Library, Radcliffe Institute, Harvard University)

for those imprisoned or threatened with deportation, and became an outspoken advocate on behalf of radical immigrants Nicola Sacco and Bartolomeo Vanzetti, convicted of murder in a dubious trial. Alice reacted to these assaults on civil liberties with passion, writing a friend, "It stirs me up more than anything in the world and makes me angrier, this imprisoning people for their opinions."

Hamilton loathed the "resolute isolationism and xenophobia which descended on us after the war." Later she would write, "As I followed our national policy after the last war I could find little to accept, much to deplore. We were so unbearably smug in those days." It is at these moments that I most love Alice Hamilton: her wit and conviction are crystal clear. She was troubled that the United States "severely ignored" the League of Nations, and she was eager to help rectify this situation when asked to join the League of Nations Health Committee, the only woman and one of only two Americans. "When, after 1924, I took every chance to speak in public about the Health Committee, I always felt my hearers' minds close with a snap, so skillfully had they been conditioned against it."

As a member of the League Health Committee, Hamilton traveled to other countries to analyze their health care systems and pick out the features that might be usefully replicated in America. In 1924, she accepted an invitation from the U.S.S.R.'s Department of Health to survey their national program for industrial hygiene. She spent a month there, returning full of mixed feelings about the experience. She disapproved of the stifling effects of Communism and the lack of individual liberties. "Russia is a terrible, terrible country. No matter what the theory of government is it is carried out by means of privilege to a small group in which all power is concentrated and by terrorism over the rest of the population," she wrote her family. Yet she admired the sense of equality—especially between the sexes—and the commitment to public health. All in all, she was relieved to be back in America, where she was on the frontier of the Industrial Revolution and its challenges to humanity. "There was more industrial hygiene in Russia than industry," she wryly observed.

As Hitler was gathering his forces and consolidating power, Alice continued her advocacy on both domestic and foreign policy: "The test of the fascist regime is not the prompt dispatch and arrival of trains, nor is the test of the American industrial regime the apparent efficiency with which it functions. The real test lies in the way it works under ignorant and indifferent and narrow-minded employers, and perhaps we must ask—though here I am venturing outside my own field—whether or not it encourages independence, resourcefulness, initiative, and the capacity for co-operation in the working class; for on those qualities in that class depends the future of democracy in the United States."

The Big Lie

In August of 1933 Hamilton and Addams joined Eleanor Roosevelt at Lillian Wald's home in Connecticut to discuss their recent relief mission in Germany. Hamilton, whose perspective was especially valuable since she had studied and lived in Germany, related her impressions of the mistakes of the Versailles Treaty, the rise of Nazism, and the complete brutality of the Hitler regime. Eleanor was so shaken that she invited Hamilton to come relate her impressions directly to the president, which she did on August 25. According to Blanche Wiesen Cook's analysis, Hamilton made a big impression on F.D.R. "Alice Hamilton was detailed and ardent in conversation with the President and First Lady. Then "within five days of Hamilton's visit, FDR sent his first letter to Ramsay McDonald since the London Economic Conference: 'I am concerned by events in Germany.'"

Hamilton was especially interested in understanding Hitler's method of propaganda. The October 1933 issue of the *Atlantic Monthly* included her review of *Mein Kampf,* which she read in the original German. This is a very early review of the book, extraordinarily insightful long before most people recognized the horror of Nazi Germany. With the same clarity of vision that led her to study and fight lead poisoning, she saw the danger Hitler posed. It is one of many cases where those in power should have listened to her earlier.

> Good propaganda limits itself to few points, and these it embodies in slogans and uses over and over till the last individual has felt the effect. . . . If you give the masses the least hint that there is a glimmer of light on the other side, you start doubts, uncertainty. . . . Remember that the bigger a lie is, the more readily it is believed by the masses. For the simple man is not really corrupt. He does tell small lies and therefore sees

through them; but he cannot imagine anyone deliberately telling a thundering lie, so when he reads or hears it, he believes it. . . . To the foreigner the success of the method is shown by the stereotyped answers that are given again and again by different people when they are confronted with any particular question, and by their bewilderment when the answer is challenged.

Although Hamilton did not advocate any specific changes in United States refugee policy toward Germany, she did call attention to what was happening under Hitler. Based on her personal connections to German citizens, she observed, "Speak about the Jewish situation and at once you are told of the hordes of Eastern Jews who flooded the country, of the excess of Jewish lawyers in Berlin. You are asked why the outside world always attacks Germany when it was quite indifferent to Mussolini's strong-arm methods and to the Bolshevist massacres. . . . The doctrine Hitler teaches his followers is simple, easily grasped by the most ignorant. Germany was betrayed in the war by Jews, Communists and Liberals."

Now in her sixties, Hamilton was still an ardent internationalist, determined that the United States should learn from both the triumphs and mistakes of the rest of the world. She was also essentially a humanist, always leery of political theories that discounted the preciousness of individual lives. And she was ever ready to adapt her ways of thinking. Once a pacifist, Hamilton was in favor of the United States's entry into World War II.

"With Her Own Eyes"

Hamilton's clear-eyed ability to connect internationalism and social justice, to see things that others couldn't, is inspirational. She was ahead of her time in almost every aspect of her work, even in minor ways. For example, in a pioneering version of ergonomics, Hamilton discovered that the paralysis of the fingers endemic among stonecutters was due to the use of air hammers—"the drearily familiar story that has followed the introduction of every labor-saving device." She did this by testing the device herself, noting what muscles it strained, and then examining the men who used it constantly. Hamilton also made several proposals to develop a sort of impartial consulting firm that could give expert advice to business and labor about workplace health and safety. Although this idea was a little too farsighted, in 1923 she was named medical consultant to General Electric. "For the first time I found myself obliged to go into the less obvious and less direct hazards in industry, such as the underlying causes of fatigue, improper seating, dazzling lights, noise and vibration, lack of nourishing midday meal and such, factors I had never paid much attention to when my mind was riveted on lead and mercury and benzol."

She was pleased by the attitude at General Electric, noting with satisfaction that CEO Gerald Swope remarked at a conference that he wasn't worried about malingerers among his workers because "most men are pretty honest." Hamilton agreed, saying that in her experience, "workers are more often likely to conceal illness, out of fear of losing their job, than to exaggerate it, to say nothing of deliberately cheating about it."

As Americans became accustomed to health regulations in industry, even Hamilton's adversaries came to recognize the value of her work. In 1933 Bradley Dewey, the president of a chemical company, wrote to S. P. Miller, who sold solvents. "I don't know what your company is feeling as of today about the work of Dr. Alice Hamilton on benzol poisoning," he wrote. "I know that back in the old days some of your boys used to think that she was a plain nuisance and just picking on you for luck. But I have a hunch that as you have learned more about the subject, men like your good self have grown to realize the debt that society owes her for her crusade. I am pretty sure that she saved the lives of a great many girls in the can-making plants and I would hate to think that you didn't agree with me."

Hamilton also noticed the progress made in management's attitude toward workers. "Twenty years ago," one plant supervisor told her, "if anyone had told the old president that I was popular with the men, he would have fired me because he would have been sure that I was not getting enough work out of them." This gave her great satisfaction because it indicated the paradigm shift she had fought for: instead of valuing subjugation, many owners valued worker morale and welfare.

In 1936 Eleanor Roosevelt attended an event honoring Alice Hamilton, and afterward, she wrote to her close friend Lorena Hickok: "[Dr. Hamilton] is such a dear. So gentle and unassuming and yet look at what she's done! A lesson to most of us who think we have to assert ourselves to be useful. . ." Later in the letter, she went on to say, "I was feeling rather annoyed until I realized tonight how small it all was, sitting by the sweet faced woman who has probably given the impetus to workman's compensation and research into industrial disease and saved countless lives and heartbreaks!"

Hamilton's influence was pervasive in the Roosevelt administration. She was named a medical consultant to the Department of Labor in 1935; fittingly, she made her last industrial study in 1937, under Secretary of Labor Frances Perkins. Initially Hamilton had set out to investigate the new rayon, or "artificial silk," industry on her own, driven by the knowledge that it used carbon disulfide, a neurotoxin that she had encountered decades before in the rubber industry. "What the silkworm achieves by digesting mulberry leaves, the viscose manufacturer achieves by treating wood pulp or cotton fibers with chemicals, of which carbon disulphide is the most important," she explained.

Hamilton immediately found cases of paralysis, loss of vision, and mental incapacitation among the rayon workers, but when she spoke to factory owners and state officials, she found complete lack of interest. "This prolonged neglect, both by the medical profession and by state government officials," she wrote, "can be explained only by the fact that the most important plants were situated in states where labor laws and labor inspection were practically nonexistent or very imperfectly administered, and where, no matter what sickness the worker contracted, he could claim no compensation from the company employing him."

After failed attempts to rectify the situation on her own, she appealed to Secretary Perkins and found a sympathetic ear. With official backing from the Department of Labor, Hamilton conducted an extensive investigation, finding huge percentages of rayon workers whose health and lives had been ruined. She then published her findings, as well as her prescriptions for change, and, with Perkins's help, secured passage of compensation laws and a radical reform of the rayon process. "The control of this dangerous trade," she recalled, "was slow in coming but when it came, it was astonishingly rapid and complete."

At the end of her career, Hamilton received recognition for the role she had played in humanizing the Industrial Revolution. In 1935, when Harvard named her professor emeritus, she remarked that it was "a great honor and pleasantly ignores my sex." She also received several honorary degrees and was honored by the American Medical Association for her lifetime of achievement. In 1943 she published her memoir, *Exploring the Dangerous Trades.*

Although she stopped her regular work on industrial medicine, she remained a presence in the field and a beacon to others who sought to put science to work for the common good. Named New England Medical Woman of the Year in 1956, she pointed out, with typical self-deprecation, "I have done absolutely nothing for more than ten years." Actually Hamilton continued to travel, write, and engage in politics in her old age. In 1961 she published a long article in the *Atlantic Monthly*, in which she took the opportunity to debunk the myth of the so-called "good old days" of laissez-faire economics that conservatives were already longing to bring back.

> A woman of ninety years has lived through that period, has seen it with her own eyes, has seen not only the front door and the parlor and master bedroom but the cellar and the back yard with the garbage pails. To her the country as it is now seems much better, has shed many injustices, much blindness, ignorance, arrogance, even ruthlessness. Perhaps it is worthwhile for an old woman, much of whose life was spent among the submerged working class, to tell what life was really like underneath the pleasant, comfortable Victorian surface.

Which Alice proceeded to do, with a wealth of detail, passion, and wit. Alice Hamilton was a woman of vision and consequence, whose application of scientific knowledge and steady moral compass made the United States stronger and more humane in tumultuous times.

On September 22, 1970, Alice Hamilton died at her home in Hadlyme, Connecticut, at age 101.

Frances Perkins

I didn't come here to work for the press anyway. I came to work for God, F.D.R. and the millions of forgotten, plain, common working men.
—Frances Perkins

ON FEBRUARY 22, 1933, NEW YORK CITY WAS PICKING ITSELF UP after a freakish storm with sixty-mile-an-hour winds that toppled chimneys, upended pushcarts, and turned signs into dangerous projectiles. (Fortunately, there was only one fatality, a woman struck by an oncoming train when she chased her windblown hat across the tracks.) The *New York Times* documented other events of the day that revealed, in ways large and small, the effects of the economic storm battering the country. That same morning, in the Bronx, a jobless man—one of the desperate faces behind the state's 32.6 percent unemployment rate—tried to "earn breakfast money by putting up a [clothes]line" and fell twenty feet to his death. Winthrop W. Aldrich, head of Chase National Bank, appeared before the Senate Finance Committee to "express faith" in the nation's banks, despite the fact that some nine thousand of them had failed since 1929 and as much as $2 billion in deposits had simply evaporated.

In the midst of this misery and uncertainty, the state industrial commissioner was summoned to the president-elect's home on East Sixty-fifth Street.[1] She knew she was about to be offered the post of labor secretary and, despite lingering uncertainties of her own, she would accept. Frances Perkins later described the scene when she arrived at Franklin and Eleanor Roosevelt's townhouse.

> The place was a shambles. . . . The constant flow of visitors left the small staff of servants powerless to retain any semblance of order. Furniture was broken. Rugs were rolled up and piled in a corner. Overshoes and muddy rubbers were in a heap near the door. The floor was littered with newspapers. Trunks were jammed into one corner, and in another stood boxes containing Roosevelt's papers which . . . had to be sorted and filed for reshipment to Washington.

Frances went up to Roosevelt's second-floor study and waited while a "stocky blond man whom I did not know" had his interview with the president-elect. When F.D.R. emerged from his study and greeted her, he introduced the man as Harold Ickes, the incoming secretary of the interior, who would be the only member of F.D.R.'s cabinet—besides Perkins—to serve from the beginning to the end of the administration.

Perkins came in with the practical, grounded attitude that had carried her through decades of public service. "If Roosevelt was going to be President, or if [former New York governor Al] Smith was going to be President—they were the only two people whose Presidential aspirations I had ever been interested in—my concern was to see that they were Presidents who promoted the line of social justice I thought important." She brought a list of objectives that she was deeply committed to, objectives that formed the backbone of the New Deal: public works projects to reduce unemployment, standards for minimum wages and maximum hours, abolition of child labor, unem-

---

[1] Roosevelt's first inauguration would also be the last to take place on March 4. The Twentieth Amendment to the United States Constitution set the inauguration for January 20 at noon, thus shortening the "lame duck" period between the November election and the inauguration. Passed by Congress on March 2, 1932, the amendment was ratified on January 23, 1933. F.D.R. took his second oath of office on January 20, 1937.

ployment insurance, and old-age insurance. She had a vision for vigorous federalism, with the Department of Labor holding conferences, launching programs, and persuading states to copy each other's successes. As she recalled it, Roosevelt heartily endorsed her plans "and so I agreed to become Secretary of Labor after a conversation that lasted but an hour."

But before formally accepting, there was one more thing she had to do. Perkins traveled upstate to visit her husband, Paul Wilson, in the sanitarium at White Plains where he had lived on and off since his mental breakdown fifteen years earlier. She knew that, brilliant as he was, in his condition he wouldn't be able to comprehend or analyze the situation. But she was still committed to their marriage and said later that she "would never dream of doing a thing that he hadn't been informed of and consulted about in advance." She later recalled, in her matter-of-fact tone, that he was "in a good controlled mood" and, after being assured that she would visit him regularly, gave his blessing.

Frances Perkins's legacy extends far beyond being the first woman cabinet secretary. Many of the safeguards of contemporary working life—Social Security, a minimum wage, workers' compensation, unemployment insurance—were set under her guidance. These were issues she had devoted years of study and hard work to, from her days investigating factories to her work for New York governor Al Smith and then his successor, F.D.R. Many contemporaries dismissed her as a stiff and unimpressive figure whose rise to the president's cabinet was due largely to the efforts of prominent supporters, such as Eleanor Roosevelt. I find this assessment unfair. Throughout F.D.R.'s term, she displayed tenacity and foresight, persevering in the face of a politically motivated smear campaign that culminated in impeachment proceedings. Through her efforts, the work of Mother Jones, Alice Hamilton, and other labor activists was protected and advanced and became part of the civic structure we take for granted today.

Ancestry

Fannie Coralie Perkins was born in Boston in 1880 to a well-to-do family descended, on both sides, from the Puritan settlers of New England. Early on, the family moved to Worcester, in central Massachusetts, where Fannie's father ran a successful stationery business. She had one sister, Ethel, four years younger.

Fred and Susan Perkins were traditional, conservative New Englanders who taught their daughters that the poor were generally lazy and sinful, that unions were evil, that preoccupation with such superficial things as physical beauty or pleasure was wrong, and that respectable women should work only when absolutely necessary and then only in certain professions such as teaching. They were personally generous people, active in their Congregational church and helpful to neighbors in need, but they opposed the kind of civic activism that would inspire their daughter.

Perkins often told the story of one early lesson in Yankee pragmatism. When she was twelve years old, her mother took her to a Boston millinery shop and picked out a tricorn hat—the style with the brim turned up on three sides, reminiscent of the American Revolutionaries she descended from. "My dear, this is your hat," her mother told her. "You should always wear a hat something like this. You have a very broad face. . . . Never let yourself get a hat that is narrower than your cheekbones, because it makes you look ridiculous." Young Fannie listened to her mother's blunt assessment and the tricorn hat became her trademark.

Another influential figure in Perkins's family was her grandmother, Cynthia Otis Perkins, whom the family visited every summer in Newcastle, Maine. Grandmother Perkins, who imparted lessons about hard work and the resistance of vanity, was a descendant of James Otis, an early American statesman who famously denounced the "arbitrary power" of the English government and was credited with coining the phrase, "Taxation without representation is tyranny."

Perkins had another extraordinary, if less well-known, ancestor: Mercy Otis Warren, James Otis's sister and one of the leading intellectuals of the early Republic. Warren was an accomplished poet and playwright who wrote an early (possibly the first) history of the American Revolution. As Joseph Ellis writes in *Founding Brothers*, "Mercy Otis Warren's *History of the American Revolution* (1805) defined the 'pure republicanism' interpretation, which was also the version embraced by the Republican party and therefore later called the Jeffersonian interpretation." She was also an influential advisor to President John

Adams, but had a falling out with him over her treatment of him in her groundbreaking book.

Throughout her life, Frances (as she would later call herself) was anchored by the sense of identity and purpose provided by her heritage. She often explained her actions by citing her "New England blood" or "Yankee" sensibility. The fact that her family tradition was itself "revolutionary" seemed to allow her to reconcile the essential irony of her personality: even while advocating sweeping changes in government policy and challenging the conventional notion of women's work, she described herself as a conformist. She had a burning desire to create the social justice that she regarded as America's destiny, yet also felt a strong sense of propriety and tradition. She was a prim radical.

Formative Years

The first of several turning points in the life of Frances Perkins occurred at Mount Holyoke, a distinguished small college, which had been founded in 1831 by Mary Lyons in order to train women to do socially valuable work. It was home to several intensely intellectual and demanding women professors who had a huge impact on Perkins, who attended Mount Holyoke from 1898 to 1902. Nellie Esther Goldthwaite taught sophomore chemistry and emphasized intellectual honesty and rigor in all aspects of life; Perkins recalled that it was under Goldthwaite's guidance that "for the first time I became conscious of character." History professor Annah May Soule required her students to visit nearby factories and record their observations of the grim working conditions there. Professor Soule's approach was a very early example of what would become known as social or economic history, and her interest in personally observing working conditions prefigures Alice Hamilton's later studies as well as Frances's own lobbying tactics. For Perkins, this experience "opened the door to the idea that the lack of comfort and security in some people was not solely due to the fact that they drank, which had been the prevailing view in my parental society."

While at Mount Holyoke, Perkins first encountered the fiery woman who would become her friend and mentor: Florence Kelley, Alice Hamilton's colleague and the executive secretary of the National Consumers' League, or NCL, which aimed to abolish child labor and sweatshops through public awareness, consumer pressure, and the improvement of state laws. Professor Soule's students had organized a Mount Holyoke chapter of the NCL, and on February 20, 1902, Kelley came to address them. She spelled out the economic consequences of their individual buying decisions: when they purchased items made by "sweaters," their money enriched the company owners while the desperately poor women and children who actually made the dresses or hats were paid little and driven hard, often in horrible working conditions.

In *Madame Secretary*, his biography of Perkins, George Martin explains that "Kelley's dynamic personality, her practical experience, her demand for dramatic improvement, and the 'sense of crusade' surrounding her all appealed to Fannie." Thirty years later, in her eulogy of Kelley, Perkins said, "She took a whole group of young people, formless in their aspirations, and molded their aspirations for social justice into some definite purpose, into a program that had meaning and that had experience and that had practicality back of it."

By the time she graduated from Mount Holyoke, Perkins, deeply influenced by her professors and Florence Kelley, longed to participate in the reform movement. She also wanted to have her own career and struggled to find one that was both socially acceptable and interesting to her. She was offered a job as a chemist in a canning factory, but her parents forbade her to accept it, deeming the job unsuitable. They also frowned upon her interest in professional social work. Fannie Perkins, not instinctively rebellious, would have liked to conform to her family's expectations, but she wasn't happy as a genteel do-gooder. The fact that she deliberately chose a harder, less-traveled path so early in life reveals her strong character and—despite all the stoicism—her essentially passionate nature. Rather than stay in the comfort of her family's home and expectations, she explored her options.

In search of some direction, she visited the renowned New York Charity Organization Society, which sought to help the impoverished and combat the causes of poverty. The director, Edward T. Devine, told Perkins that before she could be effective, she needed real life experience and knowledge. He encouraged her to continue teaching and volunteering and gave her a reading list. Perkins already had been influenced by her reading of *How the Other Half Lives* by the Danish-born American journalist Jacob Riis. Using the new technology of flash photography, Riis documented urban tenement life, bringing the suffering and squalor vividly to life and revealing it to affluent America for the first time. *How the Other Half Lives* influenced countless reformers and politicians, including Alice Hamilton and Theodore Roosevelt. After reading Riis's book, Perkins later wrote, she "straightaway felt that the pursuit of social justice would be my vocation."

Perkins found a job as a substitute teacher at an academy in Connecticut, then took a full-time job at a school in Worcester, Massachusetts. While there, she began volunteering at a settlement house in one of the city's poorer districts. She wrote to the Mount Holyoke alumnae update that she ran a "most interesting Girls' Club. Girls from 14 to 16 and most of them working in factories and stores already. We meet twice a week now and on one night we have gymnasium work and gym games—they are all hollow-chested and never get any exercise after being cramped up all day."

Through the club, Perkins found herself integrated into the struggles and injustices experienced by the destitute working girls. One member, Mary Hogan, had her hand cut off by a candy-dipping machine at the factory where she worked. The management bandaged her and sent her home without any further treatment or support. Outraged, Perkins took up Mary's cause, seeking medical help and financial compensation. She enlisted the support of others in the community and worked passionately, eventually securing compensation for the girl: one hundred dollars. This experience, which was so shocking and immediate, seemed to confirm Perkins's belief that the entire system that workers existed in had to be reformed. Private charity couldn't prevent accidents and circumstances like Mary Hogan's.

Perkins then accepted a job at Ferry Hall, a girls' boarding school in Lake Forest, Illinois, with connections to Mount Holyoke. She taught physics and biology and also served as the dormitory head. Two changes underscored the watershed nature of her time at Ferry Hall: she dropped the name Fannie in favor of Frances, and she left the Congregational church of her upbringing for the Episcopal church. While she never explained the reasons for these changes, they seem to have been motivated by her increasing independence and personal sense of propriety.

"I Had To Do Something"

Not surprisingly, Perkins was soon drawn further into the settlement house movement. She volunteered at Chicago Commons, located in the Seventeenth Ward, then spent school holidays both there and, increasingly, at Hull House. Her sense of mission, which had begun to take shape at Mount Holyoke and at the girls' club, solidified during these years. "I had to do something about unnecessary hazards to life, unnecessary poverty," explained Frances. "This feeling . . . sprang out of a period of great philosophical confusion which overtakes all young people."

At Hull House, Jane Addams was a source of guidance and inspiration for Perkins, as she had been for Alice Hamilton over a decade earlier. Later Frances wrote, "Miss Addams taught us to take all elements of the community into conference for the solution to any human problem—the grasping politician, the corner saloon-keeper, the policeman on the beat, the president of the University, the head of the railroad, the labor leader, all co-operating though the latent desire for association which is characteristic of the American genius."

One of Frances Perkins's responsibilities at Hull House echoed her experience with Mary Hogan. Addams asked Perkins to secure wages that were being unjustly withheld from poor immigrant workers, an experience that led to a full-scale revision of her view of the labor movement. She had been raised to believe that "unions were an evil to be avoided, if possible. You did good to the poor with charitable relief, friendly visiting . . . mother's clubs and that sort of thing." Perkins now "began to see that unions were the only powerful force to stand up for these individuals and make sure they were paid the wages they had earned." Just as her experience with Mary Hogan had changed her attitude toward the suffering poor, this role changed her attitude toward unions.

In the fall of 1907 Frances Perkins left her teaching job to become executive secretary of the Philadelphia Research and Protective Association, which advocated for the young women who were streaming into the city from rural America and overseas. Away from home and unprotected, these girls were at great risk of being exploited by employers and would-be pimps. Theodore Dreiser's *Sister Carrie* described the young women as Perkins probably saw them—"bright, timid, and full of the illusions and ignorance of youth," vulnerable to the "cunning wiles" of the city. Frances's parents did not approve, but Perkins loved her job and its occasional "strange and thrilling experiences." While walking home one night, she realized she was being followed by two men, associates of Sam Smith, operator of corrupt employment agencies and "lodging houses" that preyed on her clients. Alone and frightened, Perkins turned, thrust her umbrella at the men and shouted out, "Sam Smith!" Startled, the men turned and ran, and Frances reached home safely.

After this, she pushed harder for help from the police and the courts. Their rapid success in putting Sam Smith and his ilk out of business taught her a lesson she never forgot: it's possible to work within the system. Flawed, even corrupt public officials could be instruments of social justice. It seemed she also learned something else: her persona as an educated female social worker afforded her a considerable amount of power. For the rest of her career, Perkins relished the opportunity to lean on the consciences of politicians, who, more often than not, wanted some reassurance that they were acting virtuously.

Displaying her lifelong drive for self-improvement, Perkins enrolled in graduate school at the University of Pennsylvania, where she studied sociology and economics. Clearly an exceptional scholar, after a year she was awarded a fellowship to the New York School of Philanthropy at Columbia University. She moved to the city in 1909, excited to be "in the very heart of both the theoretical and practical efforts to socialize the life of the modern city."

Hell's Kitchen

To complete her Columbia research project on urban malnutrition, Perkins moved into Hartley House, a settlement house serving a section of Manhattan called Hell's Kitchen. This was the heyday of Tammany Hall, the powerful and corrupt organization that served as the executive committee of the New York State Democratic Party. Hell's Kitchen was controlled by Thomas ("The") McManus, whom a columnist had dubbed "the Devil's Deputy from Hell's Kitchen." Perkins later recalled how her appeals to McManus and his associates brought immediate relief to the distraught women and children she represented. Unlike the charity organizations, which studied the merits of each situation, the Tammany bosses, focused on vote-getting for the next election, simply greased wheels and delivered. Perkins, though never under any illusions that they were angels, recognized the benefits of partnering with them.

Perkins received a master's degree in political science from Columbia University in 1910. Her thesis, *Some Facts Concerning Certain Undernourished Children,* concluded that "temporary relief is necessary, and its method may well deserve discussion, but it is after all only an expedient to head off malnutrition until society adjusts itself and provides adequate incomes and adequate education to all its workers." Through study and hands-on experience, Perkins had come to believe that engaging in the political process was the only way to achieve real, lasting social justice.

Her next job allowed her to put this philosophy into action. In 1910 Perkins became executive chairman of the New York Consumers' League, which had been organized by reformer Lillian Wald. Her first assignment was to produce a study of sanitary conditions in New York City bakeries (where, among other unsanitary conditions, she sometimes found cats sleeping on worktables) and file the report and recommendations with the city Board of Health. She was also the league's representative in Albany, lobbying for legal protection for workers. Frances worked closely with Florence Kelley, who still headed the National Consumers' League, and became her protégée. Kelley was "a firebrand and a driver," recalled Perkins, "but there was something sweeping and cleansing in her anger. She was never little, never mean. 'Frances,' she would say, 'You have got to do it.' Then she would give me that steely look."

The Triangle Shirtwaist Factory Fire

On November 26, 1910, a factory fire in Newark, New Jersey, killed twenty-five people and injured forty, even though a firehouse was right across the street. Nineteen of the dead had tried to escape the only way available: jumping out of fourth-floor windows. In Manhattan, the fire chief announced that the city's current codes offered no protection from a similar disaster. "A fire in the daytime," the chief warned, "would be accompanied by a terrible loss of life." The Consumers'

League resolved to generate public pressure to change the fire codes and, before she was finished with her bakery report, Perkins began investigating factories to document the problems and devise solutions.

It was a huge project; the 1910 census counted 26,000 factories with 650,000 employees in greater New York. By late March, Perkins was still in the midst of it. On the afternoon of Saturday, March 25, 1911, she was having tea with her neighbor in Washington Square when they heard fire engines nearby and ran across the small park to see what was happening. On the northwest corner of Washington Place and Greene Street, flames were bursting from the top floors of a ten-story building.

Inside, approximately six hundred employees of the Triangle Shirtwaist Company—mostly girls and young women—had been finishing the day's work and preparing to go home when the fire broke out. The blaze immediately spread, feeding on the finished clothing and piles of fabric cuttings. A few people on the tenth floor escaped by climbing to the roof and across to the adjoining building, but most of the panicked workers were trapped. There was one fire escape, which led nowhere and soon collapsed. The elevators, which hadn't been properly inspected, had broken down earlier that day. Desperate girls crowded at the windows, the fire roaring behind them.

Perkins recalled, "Without saying much of anything, we all went down the steps and just went towards the fire. It was just about that time that they began to jump. It was the most horrible sight." Firemen struggled to reach the women, who were too high up for the truck ladders, and onlookers tried to help. One witness reported, "I saw four men who tried to catch the girls. They seized a horse blanket from a truck horse in Waverley Place and held it out. It gave way like paper as the girls struck it."

It was all over within half an hour. One hundred forty-six young women burned to death or died on the sidewalk. Seven bodies were never identified. There was never an accurate count made of the injured.

Over the next few days, an investigation revealed that the factory owners regularly kept most of the doors locked or barred to prevent theft and limit union organizers' access. No fire drills had ever been held. The oily sewing machines were crammed very close together, and the flammable scraps were allowed to pile up into drifts on each floor before they were hauled away. These appalling details kept public attention focused on the tragedy and led to a growing consensus that such conditions should be illegal.

On April 2, 1911, a memorial meeting was convened at the Metropolitan Opera House. Thousands of New Yorkers packed the hall and heard civic leaders, social workers, philanthropists, and clergy preach sermons, recommend reforms, and push for donations. (As president of the Consumers' League, Perkins had a place on the stage but did not speak.) Then labor leader Rose Schneiderman, of the Shirtwaist Makers Union, approached the podium. She was a young woman, so tiny that she looked even younger. Even decades later, Perkins remembered Schneiderman's "fiery red hair" and the fact that "she couldn't have come up to my shoulder." That day Perkins had noticed the younger woman shaking, from either nerves or rage. Eighteen months before, Schneiderman had led a strike demanding union recognition, shorter hours, and better safety measures. Triangle was one of the companies that broke the strike by firing union members. The public had reacted with indifference. Schneiderman began softly but soon her voice filled the theater.

> I would be a traitor to these poor burned bodies if I came here to talk good fellowship. We have tried you good people of the public and found you wanting. The old Inquisition had its rack and its thumbscrews and its instruments of torture with iron teeth. We know what these things are today: the iron teeth are our necessities, the thumbscrews the high-powered and swift machinery close to which we must work; and the rack is here in the firetrap structures that will destroy us the minute they catch fire.
>
> This is not the first time girls have been burned alive in the city. Every week I must learn of the untimely death of one of my sister workers. Every year thousands of us are maimed. The life of men and women is so cheap and property is so sacred. There are so many of us for one job it matters little if 143 are burned to death . . .
>
> You have a couple of dollars for the sorrowing mothers and brothers and sisters by way of a charity gift. But every time the workers come out in the only way they know to protest against

conditions which are unbearable the strong hand of the law is allowed to press down heavily upon us.

Public officials have only words of warning—that we must be intensely peaceable and intensely orderly, and they have the workhouse back of their warnings. . . . The strong hand of the law beats us back when we rise—back into the conditions that make life unbearable. . . . I can't talk fellowship to you who are gathered here. Too much blood has been spilled. I know from my experience it is up to the working people to save themselves. They can only save themselves by a strong working-class movement.

Schneiderman took her seat to echoing silence from the audience. Yet Perkins remembered this as the most moving speech she'd ever heard.

While the Triangle Shirtwaist factory fire was widely publicized and horrified all Americans, it specifically galvanized New Yorkers, causing many to question the lack of safeguards for these mostly immigrant workers. "These were the days when nobody expected the government to do anything," Perkins recalled. After the fire, "they certainly embraced the idea that there might be a law which could be properly enforced which would prevent this type of disaster."

The courts found that the building's owner, Joseph Asch, had followed the existing regulations. Asch eventually settled individual suits, paying survivors approximately $75 for each life lost. Triangle Company owners Isaac Harris and Max Blanck were acquitted of manslaughter and collected almost $65,000 from their insurance company—about $445 for each dead employee. The public was outraged.

Following the Harris and Blanck acquittals, an editorial in the *New York Tribune* expressed the frustration and pessimism many felt:

Of all the various individuals who should have known that the hundreds of shirtwaist workers in Harris & Blanck's place worked in peril of their lives—proprietors of the factory, city and state inspectors, superintendents, and those who passed on plans and licenses, all the personnel engaged in the empty farce of protecting lives in workshops—out of the whole list of those whose responsibility seemed more or less obvious, the public prosecutor chose the proprietors, the ones whose responsibility might not surely be demonstrated. The charges against them have not been established to the satisfaction of a jury. There is little hope that the bringing home of personal guilt to any one of the many who took desperate chances with the lives of those workers in Washington Place may teach a salutary lesson of official or private responsibility.

New York State Factory Investigating Commission

Under increasing pressure for meaningful reform, the state legislature named the New York State Factory Investigating Commission, chaired by State Senator Robert Wagner with Assemblyman Al Smith as vice-chair. Perkins was called to testify, and after demonstrating her intellect and knowledge of factory conditions, she was appointed director of investigations. This pivotal moment perfectly illustrates Perkins's extraordinary intelligence, passion, and ability to seize an important moment, and it led directly to her work with Smith and then F.D.R.

Excited that her skills were now in the specific service of the social justice movement that so inspired her, Perkins threw herself into the task. Under her leadership, the commission went beyond the issue of fire safety to,

Perkins in 1911 when she was executive secretary of the Factory Investigation Commission, showing the reporters the only fire escape available to workers in one factory.

in her words, "report [on] all kinds of human conditions that were unfavorable to the employees, including long hours, including low wages, including the labor of children, including the overwork of women, including homework put out by the factories to be taken home by the women. It included almost everything you could think of that had been in agitation for years. We were authorized to investigate and report and recommend action on all these subjects. I may say we did."

Characteristically, Perkins found inspiration in the belief that she was fulfilling a lofty duty. While a lesser, more vain person might have scoffed at factory inspections as gritty and mundane, she defined the work as heroic and seemed to have a gift for the self-fulfilling prophecy. "Factory inspection is of vast importance, not only to the people who work in the factories, but to the entire community, and such work well done may be looked upon as service to one's country," she said.

Instead of describing bleak working conditions in a report, Perkins showed the commissioners the realities of factory employment.

> . . . we used to make it our business to take Al Smith, the East Side boy who later became New York's governor and a presidential candidate, to see the women, thousands of them, coming off the ten-hour night shift on the rope walks in Auburn. We made sure that [State Senator] Robert Wagner personally crawled through the tiny hole in the wall that gave egress to a steep iron ladder covered with ice and ending twelve feet from the ground, which was euphemistically labeled "Fire Escape" in many factories. We saw to it that the austere legislative members of the Commission got up at dawn and drove with us for an unannounced visit to a Cattaraugus County cannery and that they saw with their own eyes the little children, not adolescents, but five-, six-, and seven-year-olds, snipping beans and shelling peas. We made sure that they saw the machinery that would scalp a girl or cut off a man's arm. Hours so long that both men and women were depleted and exhausted became realities to them through seeing for themselves the dirty little factories. These men realized something could be done about it from discussions with New York State employers

who had succeeded in remedying adverse working conditions and standards of pay.

Al Smith called it "the greatest education he'd ever had." As governor, he would support reshaping the state's labor laws, providing for workers' compensation, health and safety standards, and strict limits on weekly hours for child labor. New York's statewide reforms led the way for the national reform.

Decades later, in a lecture at Cornell's School of Industrial and Labor Relations, Perkins recalled the results of her commission's final report, issued in 1915:

> It was laid on the table before the legislature, and by this time, Al Smith was the speaker of the House and well on the way to be governor. We had a very favorable audience and much of the legislation was enacted into law . . . within a couple of years. . . . As I have thought of it afterwards, [this legislation] seems in some way to have paid the debt society owed to those children, those young people who lost their lives in the Triangle Fire.

The Fifty-four-Hour Bill

During the early months of her work on the factory investigation commission, Perkins continued lobbying for the NCL's major legislative goal: a state bill barring women and boys under eighteen from working more than fifty-four hours per week. In addition to progressives such as Al Smith and Robert Wagner, Perkins also worked closely with a legislator known as "Big Tim" Sullivan, a colleague of The McManus and a Tammany Hall boss representing the Lower East Side of Manhattan. He favored Perkins's bill, which would benefit his constituents, so he took her under his wing when she was lobbying in Albany. She remembered him as one who crystallized her view that even imperfect politicians could be instrumental for social justice. In a way that echoed her own visceral sensibility about fairness, she described his virtue: "He was real," she said later. "You didn't have to show him statistics on the incidence of fatigue poisoning to make him understand that a girl's back aches if she works too much."

Because the fifty-four-hour bill would never have passed in its original form, Perkins agreed to several changes to win crucial votes. On March 27, 1912, the day the bill came up for a floor vote, the canning industry demanded an exemption. There was no time for consideration or consultation. To get the bill passed, Perkins agreed to the exemption, but she was sure Kelley would be furious. "At that moment, I became an adult. I pictured Mrs. Kelley's face when I brought the word in. I thought of all she would say. I was terrified, but I said, 'Yes, let us take what we can get.'"

Even this last-minute compromise almost broke down when Perkins realized she was still short by one vote. Big Tim Sullivan, her champion on the floor, voted early and then, assured that the bill would pass, headed for the ferry down to New York City. After he left, two wavering legislators were convinced to switch sides and vote against the bill. In the midst of procedural scrambles leading to a re-vote, Perkins sent a message to Big Tim. In traditional heroic fashion, Sullivan arrived in the nick of time. He strode into the chamber, bellowing "Record me in the affirmative!" just before the chamber doors were locked for the closed vote. Perkins remembered Sullivan telling her, "It's all right, me gal; we is wid ya. De bosses thought they was going to kill your bill, but they forgot about Tim Sullivan. I'm a poor man meself. Me father and me mother were poor and struggling. I seen my sister go out to work when she was only fourteen and I know we ought to help these gals by giving 'em a law which will prevent 'em from being broken down while they're still young." The fifty-four-hour bill passed, and New York had its first child labor law—more than eleven years after the children in Mother Jones's march carried signs demanding "55 Hours—Or Nothing."

Perkins was awake all night, dreading Florence Kelley's reaction to the cannery compromise. The next morning, Kelley threw her arms around Perkins's neck, saying, "Frances, Frances, we have won; you have done it!" Not a word of rebuke. The experience was a crucial lesson for Perkins. She became, in a friend's words, "a half-loaf girl: take what you can get now and try for more later."

"A Primitive and Primary Attitude"

During this time Frances cultivated the persona she would maintain for the rest of her career, a matronly presence that, like Mother Jones, she felt had an effect of control over many men. She first realized this in 1913, during an extraordinary exchange with Democratic state senator James J. Frawley.

As part of an intraparty battle for control, the Democratic-controlled legislature had just impeached the Democratic governor, William Sulzer, and Frawley was chair of the committee investigating Sulzer. When Frances saw Frawley in a capitol hallway, she greeted him. He looked at her, startled, and said, "Oh, Miss Perkins, we've done a terrible thing!" Then he grabbed her hand, pulled out his handkerchief, and began to sob. He was extremely upset about betraying a colleague. "Oohh, it's a dreadful thing! . . . No one wants to ruin him. . . . We had to do it. He wouldn't give us any way out. Oohh, it's a dreadful thing." All the while he clung to Frances's hand while she made comforting noises. Finally, with one last enormous sob, he said, "Every man's got a mother, you know." He dropped her hand and wandered off.

At first, Perkins thought of this as a funny story. But later she realized its significance. "The way men take women in political life is to associate them with motherhood. They know and respect their mothers—ninety-nine percent of them do. It's a primitive and primary attitude. I said to myself, 'That's the way to get things done. So behave, so dress, and so comport yourself that you remind them subconsciously of their mothers.'"

Marriage and Family

While she had a broad range of friends and an active social life in New York, Frances Perkins was in no hurry to marry. Though her friend Sinclair Lewis, still a struggling writer, half-seriously proposed to her, she remained single until age thirty-three. On September 26, 1913, she married Paul C. Wilson, an economist interested in good government and a man the *New Yorker* later described as "one of the most civilized and intelligent men on Manhattan island." Perkins broke with tradition by keeping her maiden name. "My whole generation was, I suppose, the first generation that openly and actively asserted—at least some of us did—the separateness of women and their personal independence in the family relationship," she later explained.

The decision was also influenced by her husband's career. Wilson was assistant secretary to the reform mayor John Purroy Mitchel, who had campaigned on a promise to clean up Tammany Hall corruption. As mayor, Mitchel was responsible for many of the social conditions and policies that Perkins criticized. Frances felt that "using [Wilson's] name every time I made a wild speech in Buffalo about fire hazards in New York City . . . might be an embarrassment to the Mitchel administration."

Perkins did join forces with her husband when the Mitchel administration sought to deal with the 1914 economic downturn and the resulting mass layoffs. She worked with his friend, Henry Bruère, chamberlain of the city, to develop policies to help those affected. Having focused mainly on working conditions, Perkins received an education on a different social ill. It was "the first contact I ever had with mass unemployment," she recalled.

Frances experienced great personal turmoil during this period, all of which she handled with characteristic stoicism. In the spring of 1915 her first baby died shortly after birth, a tragedy she rarely spoke of at all and never in any detail. In 1916 her father died. At the end of that year, her daughter, Susanna Winslow Wilson, was born. Perkins finished up her work at the Committee on Safety and took a volunteer position as the executive secretary of the Maternity Center Association, which, in what hardly seems a coincidence, sought to improve the health of newborns and their mothers. She was preparing to withdraw from public life to concentrate on her family.

After 1918 that was no longer possible. That year Paul Wilson suffered a mental breakdown from which he never fully recovered. "He was sometimes depressed, sometimes excited. . . . From 1918 on there were never anything but very short periods of reasonably comfortable accommodations to life." Wilson likely would be diagnosed with bipolar disorder today but at the time, there was no useful diagnosis and no effective treatment. The social stigma of mental illness made the situation even more isolating and difficult. For the rest of his life, Wilson was unable to work and most often required constant attendance. "Sometimes he was hospitalized, sometimes not. Sometimes he would go off on a little trip. Sometimes he would have an attendant that was called a secretary," Frances dryly explained later. "There was great variety in the whole process." Perkins became the sole breadwinner of the family. Giving up her hopes of having another baby, she left her volunteer job and joined Al Smith's campaign for governor.

Al Smith

The name Frances Perkins is inextricably linked to that of Franklin Delano Roosevelt, but Al Smith, not F.D.R., is the man most responsible for launching her career. A brilliant politician with a remarkable record of progressive reform, Smith has largely been overshadowed by his successor as New York governor. But as Frances Perkins always maintained, much of F.D.R.'s program was built on Smith's innovations. Looking back, it is striking how closely the New Deal's rhetoric and substance were prefigured in the Smith administration in New York State. When Roosevelt was president, Perkins recalled him saying, "Practically all the things we've done in the Federal Government are like things Al Smith did as Governor of New York. They're things he would have done if he had been President of the United States."

Smith, a Catholic with Irish roots, was a cart driver's son born and raised in the shadow of the Manhattan anchorage of the Brooklyn Bridge. (The bridge itself was completed when Smith was nine years old. While it was still under construction, his father took him across to Brooklyn and back on the teetering catwalk used by the workers.) After his father's death, Smith left school at age fourteen and began working to help support his mother and sister. His first job was as a carting company runner, delivering messages to the firm's drivers. He also worked at the Fulton Fish Market, bickering and bargaining with fishermen, other brokers, and hotel and restaurant representatives. He later quipped that FFM was where he received his higher education. After Smith married Catherine Dunn, always known as Katie, he needed a more stable job. Instinctively drawn to politics, he joined up with the Tammany Hall political machine. Despite Tammany's well-deserved reputation for corruption, he never engaged in graft himself and, throughout his career, pushed for an end to patronage and payola.

First elected to the state assembly in 1903, Al Smith soon grew frustrated. As an obscure Democratic backbencher in the Republican-dominated legislature, he had no access to important committee posts, and the system's byzantine procedures and dense legalese baffled him. He began reading and cross-referencing each and every bill that hit his desk, educating himself in the law and legislative procedure.

That was exactly what he was doing when a colleague introduced him to Perkins. Learning that she was the chief lobbyist for the fifty-four-hour bill, he warned her, "It's still in committee and not moving very fast. Better ask for a hearing." Relying on the bill's sponsor to push it through, Perkins hadn't realized that there would be no hearing unless she asked for one. This was the first of many valuable political lessons she received from Smith.

Long before he became governor, Smith encouraged her to go out on the speaking circuit in support of suffrage, so she could learn to deal with hecklers and develop her public voice. Perkins was at her best around down-to-earth, gregarious personalities such as his because they brought her out of her shell, a shell created by shyness and, increasingly, her desire to protect her family.

Smith also persuaded her to become a Democrat. Although her family had been entirely Republican, Perkins's early work for reform had led her to join the Socialist Party. She kept this affiliation secret because her father was "explosive" about Eugene Debs. As she began to lobby for progressive legislation (and became more practical in her approach), she allied with Democrats but considered herself an independent. Of course, Perkins did not even have the right to vote[2] until 1918, the year she turned thirty-eight, and by that time, she was firmly involved with Al Smith's campaign for governor. After he won, he called her into his suite at the Hotel Biltmore and, puffing on his cigar, explained, "Good people need to be in the party, not outside looking in. If they're inside, doing their full duty by the party, voting, getting out the vote, helping with the campaigns and making what they know

---

[2] New York State passed a full-franchise law for women in 1917, which took effect the following year. The Nineteenth Amendment, establishing federal suffrage for women, was passed by Congress on June 4, 1919. By the summer of 1920, thirty-five states had ratified the amendment—one short of the required two-thirds majority. Of the remaining undecided states, only Tennessee agreed to call a special session. The tale of that historic session is often told throughout the state, and I've heard versions of it all my life. In August 1920, the national press converged on Nashville to cover the battle, and Carrie Chapman Catt arrived early to team up with local leaders to spearhead the final push. Partisans on both sides of the issue indicated their position by wearing or carrying roses—yellow for pro-suffrage, red for anti. On August 18, legislators and observers crowded into the sweltering statehouse for the vote. Two roll-call votes resulted in a 48-to-48 deadlock, and the third roll-call began. Harry Burns—at twenty-four, the youngest member of the legislature—stood up to vote, the red rose in his lapel drooping in the heat. He voted "yea" and opened the vote for women. In the pandemonium that followed, angry opponents of the bill demanded to know why Burns had changed his vote. (In some versions of the story, Burns had to hide in the attic until tempers cooled.) He explained, "I know that a mother's advice is always safest for her boy to follow, and my mother wanted me to vote for ratification."

available to everybody, then they have some influence. Then the party takes up a good and wise program."

The newly elected governor appointed Perkins to the State Industrial Commission, a position unprecedented for a woman. When Perkins told Florence Kelley the news, Kelley "burst into tears and she said exactly what Al Smith said she would say. 'Glory be to God. You don't mean it. I never thought I would live to see the day when someone we had trained and whom we knew knew industrial conditions, cared about women, cared to have things right would have the chance to be an administrative officer.'" Representatives of unions and manufacturers objected, claiming that one of their own should have been chosen in place of Perkins. Smith responded by saying, "I appointed Miss Perkins because of her ability and her knowledge of the department of labor and statutes affecting labor. She was very active in the legislative investigation that led to the labor code." As for those who said the commission was unsuitable for a woman, Smith pointed out that millions of women were employed in industry in New York and so it was entirely appropriate to have a woman on the commission.

The Rome Copper Workers' Strike of 1919

The highlight of this period of Perkins's career was her deft handling of the copper workers' strike of 1919 in Rome, New York. The copper workers, mainly Italian immigrants, earned less than any other industrial workers. In 1919 the Rome factory owners extended their hours without a corresponding increase in pay. Moreover, the workers could clearly see that the copper executives were making fortunes at their expense. "They could see the evidences of fortunes in the fine new houses and snappy automobiles which they were driving around," Perkins explained. In the beginning of June, the copper workers went on strike. They demanded an eight-hour day and a raise so that their wages would be equal to those made by workers in the Connecticut copper mines.

The executives refused to meet with labor representatives, insisting that they would address grievances individually but would never accept collective bargaining. This attitude was common among manufacturers in all industries and it infuriated the workers. One Rome mill owner, James Spargo, went far beyond this standoffishness and disrespect. Spargo reacted violently to protests from his workers, throwing them down stairs, verbally berating them, and, at least once, shooting a gun into a crowd. When a group of workers in the Spargo Wire Company sent him a proposal for compromise, he ripped it to shreds and sent it back with a note that read, "Kiss my ass and go to hell." On July 14, 1919, after yet another physical assault on one of their number, the copper workers attacked the obviously unstable Spargo, a riot ensued, and the mayor called on Governor Smith to send state police. He obliged but, in addition, sent Frances Perkins.

After arriving on an overnight train, Perkins established a rapport with both sides. She had asked a well-liked labor mediator based in Albany, "Packy" Downy, to meet her there, and he introduced her to the crowd of workers. She spoke directly to the crowd, explaining that Governor Smith had sent her and that she intended to hear all their grievances. She personally spoke to the union organizers who had appeared on the scene, as well as to various workers. On the employers' side, she mainly dealt with their counsel, T. Harvey Ferris, a state senator who had supported her appointment to the commission. While they often disagreed during the bargaining, neither doubted the other's good faith. Fortunately, Ferris was an honest man who respected her authority and was willing to compromise. Also fortunate was the fact that the employers seemed eager to settle the strike. The fact that Perkins refrained from using all of her power, which included the ability to convene hearings and subpoena both witnesses and records, reflects how brave and secure she was, especially as the only woman among so many clearly testosterone-fueled men. One of Perkins's great strengths was her strategic use of restraint. In this case she was able to open channels of communication in part because she had impressed the interested parties with her own coolheadedness and command of the facts.

She also averted further violence. All along she had implored Smith to remove the police, who, she felt, were making matters worse. One night she learned that some workers had hidden a cache of dynamite and intended to set it off to provoke a clash with the authorities. She literally defused the situation by brokering a deal with a union leader that if the police left, the workers must dump the dynamite into a nearby canal. Despite Senator Ferris's arguments that the police should stay, Perkins prevailed in convincing Smith to call them off. That night she and two workers' representatives watched as masked strikers hauled the explosives down to the canal—one man wheeled the dynamite in a baby carriage—and tossed them into the water.

Perkins was gaining ground in her negotiations, but Spargo had stymied her efforts by leaving town and refusing to return. When approached by written communication, he responded with a detailed, graphic, and obscene letter condemning the workers and their concerns.

Keeping the letter in reserve, Perkins called for a public hearing with her fellow commissioners in attendance. On August 4, the Rome courthouse was packed with workers and townspeople, and representatives of the workers and the factory owners made their case before the commissioners. Finally, the argument came down to one issue: the owners' refusal to deal directly with the workers. On this, they would not budge.

The commission chair was John Mitchell, former head of the United Mine Workers and colleague of Mother Jones. Perkins advised him to make one last appeal on behalf of the workers and their right to have their grievances heard. Then, in a brilliant move that reflected her shrewd understanding of the nature of the men in the room, she handed him Spargo's letter and told him to finish by reading it aloud, forcing the employers to face up to the insults heaped on the workers. Reluctantly, Mitchell agreed.

First, he made an impassioned plea on behalf of the strikers.

> These are workmen. These are human beings. God made them. They live here. They work here. They must be treated like human beings and when they are not, the resentments that gather are terrible indeed. Because they have been so insulted, they are so insistent upon having what they believe to be right and just and having it guaranteed by the State Industrial Commission.

Then he began reading the Spargo letter. The reaction was exactly what Perkins had predicted. Mitchell hadn't finished more than a sentence or two before the panicked employers stopped him. Mortified by their colleague's crudeness, they gave in and pledged to meet with the workers and reach an agreement.

In Al Smith's autobiography, he recalled the impression Perkins made. After Frances Perkins had managed to arrange a conference between the adversaries, one of the officers of the Rome Brass and Copper Company said to the state attorney, "Do us a favor and ask the Governor where he found that woman."

In 1920, national issues swept Smith, along with most Democrats, out of office. The postwar hangover and impatience with the League of Nations was one problem. Another was widespread suspicion of Democrats as the party of immigrants. But while the national ticket lost New York by 1.2 million votes, Smith was defeated by a slim margin of 75,000 votes. It was clear that he would run in the next election and likely win. In the interim, Perkins served as executive secretary of the Council on Immigrant Education, a project set up by businessmen to help immigrants assimilate, and Smith went to work for a friend's trucking company. As expected, Al Smith prevailed in the 1922 race for governor and immediately named Perkins to the Industrial Commission. He had already set his sights on higher office.

The 1924 Democratic Convention

During the 1924 Democratic convention in New York City, the party split into two incompatible factions, divided along many lines: East versus South and West, urban versus rural, immigrant versus native-born, Catholic versus Protestant, wet versus dry. These divisions had long existed but by 1924 they had erupted into open conflict. The 1920 census revealed that, for the first time, a majority of Americans lived in cities. These urbanites began to demand a voice in the party while the more traditional members resisted giving up power. Each faction had a favorite at the convention: the urbanites backed New York governor Al Smith (Catholic, anti-Prohibition, machine politician) and the rural members supported William McAdoo (Protestant, pro-Prohibition, Wilson's treasury secretary and son-in-law).

The convention site only exacerbated the factional division. The Smith-supporting hosts were generally opinionated, competitive, and confrontational, and the visitors were not charmed. Many "dry" Southerners regarded cities as sinks of sin and iniquity, and New York as America's own Sodom and Gomorrah. The city's outreach efforts to the delegates included a renamed Fifth Avenue a-flap with flags as "the Avenue of States"; state-themed window displays at Macy's, Gimbel's, and Altman's; and regional exotica such as butterscotch pie and chili con carne served in the cafés near the old Madison Square Garden. Still, hostilities flared in the sweltering Garden.

One issue dominated: whether or not to include a platform plank condemning the Ku Klux Klan by name. Along with blacks and Jews, Catholics were targeted by the nativist Klan, so the urban coalition demanded the group be singled out. The rural Democrats resisted and finally won by a tiny margin, but only after an ugly battle, with late-night debates, angry speeches, and brawls on the convention floor. At one point it seemed that only the presence of a thousand armed New York police officers averted a full-scale riot. And that was before the delegates had even started choosing a candidate.

Perkins, as chairman of the platform committee of the Women's De-mocratic Union and a member of the Smith administration, had an aisle seat near the speaker's platform. As the nominating speeches for president began, her attention soon focused on someone other than her boss.

Franklin Roosevelt had been designated the titular head of the Smith campaign and picked to deliver one of Smith's nominating speeches, due more to his social stature than to any affinity between the two men. When Smith asked why Roosevelt should make the speech, one of his advisers responded, "Because you're a Bowery Mick and he's a Protes-tant patrician and so he'll take some of the curse off of you." Roosevelt had been a rising star in the Democratic Party until 1921, when he was stricken with polio; this speech would mark his return to the public eye. His withered legs encased in steel braces, F.D.R. was assisted down the aisle to his seat by his son James. (Later, James said his fa-ther had gripped his arm so tightly that he had "bruised it up.") When it came time for the speech, James helped him to the speaker's platform and up the steps. Roosevelt took up his crutches and began his slow journey to the podium alone. The crowd hushed as Roosevelt made his way forward, legs dragging. When he reached the stand, the crowd cheered. Unable to release his grip on the podium and wave, Roosevelt threw his head back in that trademark dazzling smile. As he spoke, Perkins noticed Roosevelt's hands shaking with strain as he clutched the podium to keep himself upright. Yet his voice never wavered.

The speech, written by Smith's staff, ended with an allusion to Wordsworth's poem "Character of the Happy Warrior," a reference

Roosevelt had objected to as obscure. He was overruled, and so the speech closed with the line that gave Smith the nickname he would carry for the rest of his life: "He is the happy warrior of the political battlefield."

The audience went wild. In *Empire Statesman*, his biography of Smith, Robert Slayton describes complete chaos in the Garden, as delegates marched through the aisles waving banners and shouting slogans and singing along with a half-dozen bands playing a half-dozen rousing tunes. Banks of giant fire sirens brought in for the occasion were cranked up, creating, in Slayton's words, "an electronic wail of apocalyptic proportions that drowned out frail human speech and unnerved most mortals."

The bedlam gave Perkins time to act. Watching and listening to Roosevelt, she had grown worried about how he would manage his departure from the podium. "I saw around him all those fat slob politicians—men—and I knew they wouldn't think of it." As he spoke, she organized the women near her. When the crowd let loose and Roosevelt began to turn away from the podium, the women rushed up and gathered around as if to congratulate him, shielding his awkward movements from the audience. This tactic, which soon became routine, seems emblematic of Frances Perkins's political service to Roosevelt in the years to come.

The balloting began on Monday, June 30, and dragged on through day after day, with no nominee gathering the necessary two-thirds of the votes. The *New York Times* described the scene as delegates "lumbered about, weary but nervously on edge, hollow-eyed, jumpy, but exhausted, painfully stumbling along on the same old treadmill." The platform fight had been so poisonous that both factions' favorites, McAdoo and Smith, had to withdraw. Finally, on the 103rd ballot, dark horse candidate and stockbroker John W. Davis became the Democratic candidate. The convention adjourned in the early morning hours of July 10, and the frazzled delegates finally headed home, ten days later than they'd planned.

"The Perfect Job"

That November, Calvin Coolidge easily beat Davis. In the race for New York governor, Smith scored a resounding victory over Teddy Roosevelt Jr., winning by over a million votes. He immediately named Perkins head of the Industrial Commission.

Perkins later described it as "the perfect job" for her because through it, she could make "constant progress toward practical achievement of social justice." Perkins began studies of factory hazards and worked to improve communications between different governmental divisions.

Like Alice Hamilton, Perkins deeply believed that the power of the government should be used to protect individuals from the abuse of corporate or industrial power. She also concurred with Hamilton's belief that what could be done, should be done. "If you had knowledge there was a hazard and did nothing about it, then if something happened, you were to blame. . . . So during that period I really pushed very hard for the adoption of many codes." Perkins's efforts dovetailed with Hamilton's, as when she pushed for the law that made the manufacturers of chemicals responsible for toxic side effects. She knew that the companies would respond when they found out that "it costs money to poison people."

Frances Perkins was making a reputation for herself, even outside the United States. On March 12, 1927, a reporter for the British newspaper the *Manchester Guardian* wrote, "I have met a considerable number and wide range of interesting women in the United States but none who has impressed me more than this squarely built woman. . . . Under her guidance a comprehensive and enlightened factory code is being worked out and applied, which is transforming factory and workshop conditions as they affect the safety, health and comfort of the worker; and worked out largely in friendly cooperation with the use of the most up-to-date scientific counsel and advice from engineering and other experts."

In 1928 Smith headed the Democratic ticket as the party's presidential candidate, with Franklin Roosevelt tapped as the party's candidate for New York governor. Traveling the country campaigning for Smith, Perkins was shocked at the extent of the anti-Catholic bias he faced. In the South, she encountered what she described as "some of the most terrible fantastic prejudices and dreadful yarns that I have ever heard." In Maryland someone took her to see the estate said to be already purchased for the Pope, from which he'd dictate policy to the Smith White House. "It was pointed out to us. They knew it for a fact," Frances marveled.

On the trail the Smith campaign faced ugly demonstrations of bigotry. When Smith went to Oklahoma City, he was greeted by burning crosses. The next night, an evangelist preacher delivered an address to an audience of thousands—in the same hall in which Smith had spoken—entitled "Al Smith and the Forces of Hell." My grandfather, then an ambitious high-school principal campaigned for Smith throughout Middle Tennessee and found the same raw prejudice against Catholics that Perkins described. In *Let the Glory Out*, he recalled hearing a Baptist preacher speak to a packed house, denouncing Smith's candidacy: "'Normalcy' was still the magic word: in my community this meant 'no war, no rum' (legal, that is), and 'no Catholic in the White House,'" he recalled. Slayton describes how, in the South and the West, bigoted slander "[turned] a man's bid for the White House into one of the most revolting spectacles in the nation's history."

Herbert Hoover won the presidency in a landslide—58.2 percent of the popular vote versus Smith's 40.9 percent. Though the South was then a Democratic stronghold, Smith took only six of the thirteen former Confederate states, often by tiny margins. (He won Alabama by only seven thousand votes.) Smith overwhelmingly lost in his home state of New York, taking only four counties. Franklin D. Roosevelt was elected governor of New York, and Frances Perkins had a new boss.

Governor Roosevelt

Perkins had first met Franklin Roosevelt soon after she moved to New York. Years later she recalled a party in 1910 where she chatted briefly with a tall, thin young man who was interested in politics and distantly related to the current president, Theodore Roosevelt. Shortly after that, when Perkins was lobbying for the fifty-four-hour bill, Franklin Roosevelt was a state senator—an unimpressive one, in her opinion. While he didn't oppose the bill, he also did nothing to support it. Perkins later recalled, "I took it hard that a young man with so much spirit did not do so well in this, which I thought a test, as did Tim Sullivan and The MacManus, undoubtedly corrupt politicians."

Perkins admired the F.D.R. she'd come to know in the years since. He was far less frivolous than before, more sympathetic, more attentive to the struggles of his fellow citizens. She was certain that his own terrible battle with polio had deepened and strengthened his character. In *The Roosevelt I Knew*, she wrote,

I noticed when he came back that the years of pain and suffering had purged the slightly arrogant attitude he had displayed on occasion before he was stricken. The man emerged completely warmhearted, with humility of spirit and with a deeper philosophy. Having been to the depths of trouble, he understood the problems of people in trouble. Although he rarely, almost never, spoke of his illness in later years, he showed that he had developed faith in the capacity of troubled people to respond to help and encouragement. He learned in that period and began to express firm belief that the "only thing to fear is fear itself."

While some considered F.D.R.'s patrician charm and Harvard pedigree his main selling points, Perkins never displayed such snobbery. She seemed genuinely, and strongly, drawn to his ideals and the possibility that he would implement them on a national scale. Perhaps her own lineage also kept her from being overawed by F.D.R.'s family credentials and allowed her to build an alliance based on mutual respect and common cause.

Perkins's relationship with Eleanor Roosevelt was more complicated. They were both intelligent, accomplished, hardworking women with similar goals and beliefs, but their personalities clashed. Frances admired Eleanor's warmth and exuberance but was astonished by her openness. Martin recounts an evening during F.D.R.'s years as governor when Eleanor told Perkins about her difficult childhood. Frances was touched, and then later surprised to read similar stories in print. She recalled, "It embarrassed me that she should put all that in a book to be read by everybody and anybody. I had kept it absolutely secret. Frankly, any candid picture embarrasses me."

Despite the fact that they never bonded personally, the two women were always political allies and Eleanor was an early advocate for Perkins. After F.D.R. won his first gubernatorial race, Eleanor and other women active in the Democratic Party began promoting the appointment of women to key positions in the new administration. Roosevelt wrote her husband on November 22, 1928, "I hope you will consider making Frances Perkins labor commissioner. She would do well and you could fill her place as chair of the Industrial Commission by one of the men. . . . These are suggestions which I am passing on not my opinions for I don't want to butt in." Eleanor's biographer Blanche Wiesen Cook surmises, "The fact is that in 1928 Perkins was appointed because ER and her associates thought it would be a good idea; and women were appointed to several other key positions because of the activities of the women's committee which ER did so much to develop."

Perkins later testily downplayed Eleanor Roosevelt's role in advancing her career, saying, "I always knew him better than I knew her." This and other chilly remarks may have played a role in creating the increasingly cool relationship she had with Eleanor. They probably also reflect Perkins's desire to be taken seriously rather than be seen as a token woman or the first lady's representative in the cabinet.

In any event, Eleanor's role shouldn't overshadow the fact that Perkins was undeniably a great asset to the incoming governor and obviously qualified to fill the post. As she had demonstrated in the hearings after the Triangle Shirtwaist factory fire, as head of the investigation commission, and in her handling of the Rome strike, she was knowledgeable, intelligent, articulate, poised, and persuasive. She was also instinctively loyal and thoroughly committed to a progressive agenda. Moreover, she was the vehicle through which Roosevelt continued and expanded the progressive policies developed under Al Smith. In fact, Roosevelt eventually took credit for the thirty-two labor reform acts achieved by Wagner, Smith, and Perkins on the New York State Factory Commission, for which he had actually provided virtually no support.

When the newly elected Governor Roosevelt asked Perkins to serve as the state industrial commissioner, she asked if he'd consulted Smith. Roosevelt had and, by his own account, Smith felt that while Perkins was extremely competent, it might not be wise to make her the head of the commission, in charge of an all-male group. As she wrote in *The Roosevelt I Knew*, Roosevelt

> told me this with a chuckle, adding, "You see, Al's a good progressive fellow but I am willing to take more chances. I've got more nerve about women and their status in the world than Al has."
>
> I laughed too, but I could not resist the temptation to say, "But it was more of a victory for Al to bring himself to appoint a woman, never appointed before, when I was unknown, than it is for you when I have a record as a responsible public officer for almost ten years."

Frances and her twelve-year-old daughter Susanna Wilson after she was sworn in as New York commissioner of labor on January 14, 1929. (courtesy Bettman/Corbis)

In a preview of her meeting with President-elect Roosevelt four years later, Perkins asked whether Roosevelt would support her agenda as industrial commissioner: rooting out corruption, controlling child labor, and regulating working conditions. He agreed, beginning a new phase of a professional relationship that would change history.

"The Human Race Just Doesn't Lie Down under These Things"

Previous industrial commissioners had lived in Albany, but Perkins was reluctant to uproot her family. Susanna, now twelve, had her friends and school (the Brearley School) in New York City. Wilson was at home struggling to keep his mood swings in control. Though he tried to support his wife's career, he seemed to be becoming more morose and unresponsive—in George Martin's somewhat cruel words, "a kind of nonperson," whose charm and wit were fading away. Frances soon realized that it made sense to stay in the city, which had the added benefit that most of the state's industry was located there. She usually spent only one or two days a week in Albany, often staying in the Governor's Mansion. Shortly after her appointment, the family moved to a new apartment at the corner of Madison Avenue and Eighty-ninth

Street, where they remained for the next thirty-five years, through numerous long-term sublets.

Though Frances tried to maintain something of a normal family life, strains were showing. While she undoubtedly had even more demands on her time than before, she also seemed to feel more emotionally distant from her daughter. She wrote to a friend:

> I have to give you the advice I always give everybody. Enjoy your children while they are *little,* and never postpone the practice of companionship until they are, in your view, old enough to be companionable. At just the age when they are old enough to be companionable they begin to be tremendous individualists and interested only in themselves and their own generation.

While Roosevelt agreed to support his commissioner's agenda of reform and regulation, the stock market crash on October 24, 1929, shifted Perkins's priorities. New York State, with its extensive manufacturing base, was especially hard hit. The state unemployment rate in 1929 was 6.2 percent. It jumped to 17.2 in 1930, then 24.3 in 1931, and 32.6 in 1932. "The specter of unemployment—of starvation, of hunger, of the wandering boys, of the broken homes, of the families separated while somebody went out to look for work—stalked everywhere."

Perkins focused on enforcing workers' compensation regulations and revamped the New York State Public Employment Service to make it more responsive to and respectful of the unemployed. The improved service placed many thousands in jobs but couldn't keep up with the increase in joblessness. Frances refused to be intimidated by the scale of the problem. "The human race just doesn't lie down under these things," she later said.

On January 22, 1930, in the middle of this despair, President Hoover announced that the economy was on the upswing. Perkins was suspicious because she'd heard about "swindlers" in the Department of Labor willing to cook the books for political gain. She gathered her own experts and used the New York State unemployment figures to project a national analysis, which showed that unemployment and the economy in general were getting worse. In the heat of her indignation, without checking with Roosevelt, she held a widely publicized press conference. Afterward the governor called and, to her relief, cheered her on. She remembered him telling her, "Bully for you. That was a fine statement and I'm glad you made it. . . . If you had asked me, I probably would have told you not to do it, and I think it is much more wholesome to have it right out in the open." After this act of political courage, Perkins was looked to as a national authority on the true unemployment toll.

She built on this platform by advising Roosevelt to appoint a committee to study the unemployment problem. In this and other endeavors, she often joined forces with Eleanor Roosevelt, who was close to the network of women, including Lillian Wald, Jane Addams, and Alice Hamilton, who had been pushing a social justice agenda for some time. On October 2, 1930, Eleanor wrote to Franklin, "Miss Perkins came to see me today and she has a secret offer which will be made if you agree. The commission she got together to look into the public employment department will recommend if you are agreeable that a commission similar to the old age pension one be appointed. . . . It looks good to me for it would take into account middle aged and physically handicapped, etc. and let you get the jump on Hoover, but they won't move till you let me know what you think."

Many of the commission's recommendations foreshadowed the New Deal approach to come. At that time the workweek included Saturday, and the workday often lasted ten hours or more. The commission recommended reducing hours to allow a greater number of workers to fill the jobs, and also advised development of government-sponsored work projects. The commission concluded its report by noting that "the public conscience is not comfortable when good men anxious to work are unable to find employment to support themselves and their families." In January 1931 Roosevelt called a multistate conference on unemployment, a move that put him on the national stage.

The First Woman in the Cabinet

After two terms as New York State governor, F.D.R. was named the 1932 Democratic candidate for president. Perkins provided his election staff with information and policy suggestions for combating the economic collapse, and Roosevelt made the promise of help to those affected by the Depression the centerpiece of his campaign. While she supported Roosevelt's candidacy, Perkins did not campaign for him. After a brief period of relatively good health, Paul Wilson suffered another serious setback in 1932 and Perkins had to see to his care. By the time Roosevelt defeated Hoover that November, Wilson was settled again in the sanitarium.

The president-elect now had to select his new cabinet, and because of the dire employment situation, one especially crucial appointment was the secretary of labor. The women activists in the party pressed F.D.R. to nominate Perkins. Mary Dewson, chair of the Women's Activities Committee for the Democratic Party and friend of Eleanor, explained that it wasn't personal friendship that motivated their promotion of Perkins: "She is like Kipling's cat that walks alone. It was just that I admired her work for trade unionism and for better working conditions."

Again, I believe that F.D.R. might well have appointed Perkins without this push from his network of women supporters: she was outstandingly qualified. But Frances herself was reluctant to take the

appointment. In addition to well-founded anxiety about how the male labor leaders would respond, "the idea of moving to Washington horrified me. . . . My husband was ill in a hospital. . . . I didn't want to give up living with my child." Upon hearing the rumors that F.D.R. had settled on her for labor secretary, Perkins wrote him to suggest other candidates, reasoning that "for your own sake and that of the U.S.A. I think that someone straight from the ranks of some group of organized workers should

Perkins in 1931, as industrial commissioner for the state of New York, with two New York businessmen who worked with her on the Industrial Commission of labor, Max Meyer of New York City and Maxwell Wheeles of Buffalo. (courtesy Mount Holyoke College Archives and Special Collections)

be appointed." Roosevelt responded with a note that simply read, "Have considered your advice and don't agree."

In February 1933, after their brief meeting in his townhouse, President-elect Roosevelt announced the appointment of Frances Perkins as secretary of labor. There was an immediate uproar from the ranks of both labor and industry. As the *New Yorker* noted, "William E. Green, president of the American Federation of Labor, told the press that Miss Perkins was a lovely woman personally but that as Secretary of Labor she would be entirely unacceptable to organized labor, and that the Federation would have no dealings with her." Perkins called a press conference the following day and commended Green as "a man of great integrity, vision and patriotism." If he and other labor leaders could not come by her office, she would go to them at theirs, she cordially offered.

Perkins and her daughter, Susanna, boarded the train from New York to D.C., carrying a black dress for the incoming secretary to wear at the inaugural festivities. A friend had helped find it, since Perkins herself didn't have time to go shopping. When asked to describe the gown, she said it was "precisely as ordered: Rock of Gibraltar, rather, with a dash of style, and a discreet touch of feminine appeal." She also brought a selection of work clothes and a good-luck token given to her by Mary Brannigan, a woman who worked scrubbing the floors of the Industrial Board offices in New York. It was a transparent paperweight that, when shaken, sent a pink snowstorm swirling around the Virgin Mary.

On March 4, 1933, Frances Perkins was sworn in as the first woman to serve in the United States cabinet. Two factors made the transition especially difficult for her. The first was the extraordinary amount of attention and speculation she generated. Perkins was not merely a new cabinet member in a new administration but a historic and controversial choice. Everything she did was news. A *New Yorker* profile published in September 1933 gives an example of the tone:

The help gyrated around, exchanging impressions—pale and anxious little clerical people; plumper, ruddier assistants and guards. In hallways, and around water-coolers, they gathered, whispering to one another what they knew. Item: She has a crisp way about her, but real nice eyes. Item: She wears dark, tailored clothes and eyeglasses when she works. Item: Who's Who says she is a sociologist. Item: She dictates fast, too fast for most stenographers, and with a Boston accent. *Labor* is *laboh*; *masses* is *mawses*; *Frances* is *Frawnces*; *clear* is *cleah*. Item: She is a married woman and a mother, and she still calls herself Miss. And yet, when her personal staff asked how they should address her (the usual designation is "Mister Secretary"), "Oh, call me Madame Secretary," Miss Perkins said.

By 1935 Perkins was well-known enough to be lampooned by *Vanity Fair*. That fall the magazine ran an "Impossible Interview" between Perkins and another famous female, child star Shirley Temple:

PERKINS: Little girl, don't you know that child labor is a blot on America's escutcheon?

SHIRLEY: What is child labor, Aunt Fannie?

PERKINS: Child labor is when little girls like you have to work.

SHIRLEY: Poohie, I don't work. I dance and sing and make faces. I'm cute. . . . I got a gold statuette from the Motion Picture Academy and a kiss from Irvin S. Cobb.[3]

PERKINS: Now I *know* you're being exploited!

SHIRLEY (*tossing a curl or two*): Yah, you're jealous cuz you aren't an actress.

PERKINS: Well, the coal miners voted me their favorite comedienne.

SHIRLEY: Besides, I get $1,250 a week.

PERKINS (*startled*): What's that? Good land, child, why didn't you say so in the first place? Let the workers of the world unite! California—here I come!

This type of lighthearted spoof is something all politicians and other public figures face. But throughout her tenure, a disturbing

---

[3] Cobb was a portly, cigar-chomping humorist, actor, and raconteur. At the Academy Awards ceremony in February 1935, he declared Miss Temple "the world's greatest gift of joy and happiness." He then presented her with a widely photographed kiss on her dimpled cheek and a special award for her work in 1934, a year in which she appeared in ten movies. Temple received her Oscar two months before her seventh birthday.

"Impossible Interview" by Covarrubias for *Vanity Fair*'s September 1935 issue. (courtesy Miguel Covarrubias/Vanity Fair/The Conde Nast Publications, Inc.)

number of the attacks on Perkins slighted her looks, her femininity, or the role her emotions played in her decisions. For example, during the United Auto Workers sit-down strikes of 1937, one reporter described her as "on the verge of tears" after "the strain of her constant endeavors" to reach a resolution. There is no evidence that Perkins ever cried in public and her stoic nature makes it very unlikely, but the image of the labor secretary as a weepy weakling persisted and grew. Her biographer George Martin describes one apocryphal anecdote that made the rounds: Perkins begging Roosevelt to punish the head of General Motors for exploiting his workers and Roosevelt responding, "Frances, this is a democracy, not a tyranny of tears."

Later the *Saturday Evening Post* practiced a bit more amateur psychoanalysis, describing Perkins as "earnest, rather humorless, briskly official, and full of that eager little executive air which is the earmark of the old-fashioned feminist and social worker—she conceals her trepidation behind an official standoffishness and an air of importance which are completely alien to her real self." One particularly delirious profile summed up Perkins as follows: "Take three parts of Joan of Arc and three parts of New England Puritan, being careful not to discard the witch-burning core; add one part of Sphinx; season with sugar, red pepper, and vinegar, and pour the mixture into a plain black dress. Chill, garnish with plenty of authority and a small string of pearls. That's Frances Perkins, a dish usually served with hot tongue or cold turkey."

As intelligent as she was, Perkins undoubtedly lacked the skill to deal with the press, and each new publicity assault caused her to clam up even more. She was so wary of the trivial, frivolous angles that the reporters dwelled on, so eager to stick to policy, that she would talk in a dry, contained way to reporters, "as if she had swallowed a press release," according to one observer.

"On affairs of state she deals with reporters admiringly, putting before them with warmth and candor not only the surface structure but the inner sweep and meaning of her news," wrote the *New Yorker*. "But when they come around for a little human-interest story . . . she writhes and parries questions with a remote, patrician contempt [which] irritate[s] the press corps not a little now and then." During Roosevelt's second term, in one of the first lady's many public communications (this one was a *Good Housekeeping* article about women in the administration), Eleanor Roosevelt wrote that while Perkins had done a good job as labor secretary, "She has never really learned to handle the press, so her newspaper contacts are bad. This is partly because she is suspicious of reporters, and those around her, trying to protect her, accentuate this suspicion. . . . This inability to deal with the press is, I think, [her] greatest weakness." I think Perkins's mistrust of the press was entirely reasonable and largely due to a desire to protect the privacy of her daughter and husband, but she clearly did lack the public relations skills that could have made her even more effective.

Perkins also often annoyed powerful politicians by keeping them waiting or bluntly contradicting them. While she surely knew how to soften disagreement, she didn't always bother to do so and was just as likely to say, "No, you're wrong about that. Quite wrong." She tended to draw a tight inner circle and shut others out, creating outspoken and embittered critics.

And she made gaffes, often out of carelessness, such as when she said, "the whole South of this country is an untapped market for shoes," a remark which, not surprisingly, infuriated Southerners. Perkins claimed that she was simply making an economic point. "I could have talked about the market for bed sheets in Oregon—it's unimportant." But obviously, the damage was done.

The second unusual difficulty the new labor secretary faced was setting up domestic arrangements for herself and her family, a task most other cabinet members relied on their wives to handle. Once again, Perkins didn't want to uproot either her husband or her daughter. Susanna, now sixteen, lived with the family of a classmate in Manhattan, and Perkins's husband remained in his sanitarium in upstate New York. On the weekends, Perkins took the train back to the city to be with her daughter and visit Paul during his better spells.

During her first year as labor secretary, Frances shared a house in Georgetown with a friend from the Maternity Center Association, Mary Harriman Rumsey. "Rumsey," the daughter of railroad magnate E. H. Harriman and the widow of a prominent sculptor, came to Washington to help the Roosevelt administration. Her brother Averell, who became head of the National Recovery Administration and later a distinguished diplomat and philanthropist, remarked that Mary had convinced him to join the New Deal because it "marched with humor and humanity to create a secure future" and "put industry in its proper place." Rumsey was the perfect balance for Frances, bringing her into a warmer, more intimate circle of the New Dealers, adding wit, social connections, and the ability to play hostess.

For a year the two women shared a lively home, entertaining many artists and politicians, including the first lady. Rumsey was at the center of Eleanor Roosevelt's social circle and a catalyst for the first lady's biweekly "air our minds" luncheons, which Frances Perkins regularly attended along with a handful of other women. But on December 18, 1934, at age fifty-two, Rumsey died from complications after a riding accident, and the social scene ground to a halt. "The color seems to be wiped from the face of life with the going of Mary," wrote Isabel Greenway, another luncheon participant.

For the rest of her time in D.C., Frances lived alone in an apartment and had a much less active social life. Rumsey's death seems to have marked the end of a comfortable relationship with Eleanor Roosevelt, who sat with Perkins during the funeral services. Without the social grace of Rumsey to ease their conversations, the exchanges between the two women soon became entirely policy based. They continued to work together, but Perkins often harshly rejected some of the first lady's suggestions and seemed quietly resentful of her. Perhaps the fact that Eleanor wielded power because of her marriage sparked Perkins's grief about her own husband. But I think there was another reason. Perkins, a loner, derived much of her power from her own close relationship with F.D.R.—not romantic, but somewhat familial—and seemed annoyed that his unusually professional partnership with his wife always trumped his alliance with her. The discontent was by no means one-sided; some observers felt that Eleanor envied Frances's education, her independence, and her autonomous identity.

It is a shame that Perkins and Eleanor Roosevelt came to such odds, because early on, the first lady had impressed Perkins with her willingness to engage in intellectual and political conversations with other women. In an observation that says much about Frances's experiences with most other Washington women, she noted that "Eleanor Roosevelt talked to women in the frankest, pleasantest terms. There wasn't any of this waiting for the men to come in. . . . Some women don't open up or show off at all until the gentlemen come in from dinner. Some quite brilliant women have nothing to say while the ladies wait in the drawing room. They won't say a word. They're brilliant, witty, entertaining the minute the gentlemen come in. . . . It's all right but you notice that that particular kind of woman doesn't care a hoot what you say or what you think. You are just another woman. There are very few men who won't open up except before women." Frances seemed much more comfortable with the men she worked with during the White House years. She simply didn't have the talent for friendship to enable her to seek out and connect with like-minded women, and as the press attention took its toll, she became almost single-mindedly focused on her work.

Cleaning Up the Department of Labor

While her personal relationships were often strained, even Perkins's harshest critics acknowledged her effectiveness at cleaning up the Department of Labor. When she took over in March 1933, the offices needed a literal clean-up to remove clutter, dust, grime, and an infestation of enormous cockroaches. The infestation of corruption was, of course, more serious. The Department of Labor's original mandate included immigration regulation and enforcement. Under Perkins's predecessor, these powers were abused by the "Garsson Squad," described by the *New Yorker* as "an undercover organization of seventy-one detectives and stool-pigeons employed to investigate violations of the alien labor laws, Bolshevism, moral turpitude, grand duchesses, foreign movie actors who overstay their leaves, and similar menaces." The squad was infamous for staging spectacular raids without warrants and throwing accused illegal immigrants in jail without evidence or cause.

In her first press conference as labor secretary, Perkins announced she was disbanding the squad, effective immediately. She also revealed the large salaries they'd been paid and the considerable expenses they'd charged to the department—information that had been labeled "classified." Contemporary press accounts compared Perkins's action to that of her ancestor James Otis, who in 1761 denounced British officials for searching without a warrant. "It's in our family tradition," acknowledged Perkins.

Fighting corruption was one of Frances Perkins's great achievements in government. In an otherwise unflattering profile, one journalist noted, "Her severest critic will accord her the compliment that the whole Department has been made more efficient, free from corruption."

Perkins also refocused the Department of Labor, concentrating its efforts on workers' needs. She met with three senators—Robert F. Wagner of New York, Robert La Follette Jr. of Wisconsin, and Edward P. Costigan of Colorado—to assist in drafting a bill for unemployment relief by federal grants to the states. This bill became the basis for many of the work-relief programs of the New Deal, including the Civilian Conservation Corps (CCC). In the process Perkins had to soothe the concerns of organized labor, who felt that this new approach was, in the words of AFL president William Green, "a form of Sovietism." She and others eventually softened this opposition and Roosevelt signed the bill into law on March 31.

In an effort to send a signal of respect to organized labor, Perkins organized a conference of labor leaders at the department, held the same day that the CCC bill was signed. Almost all of the heavyweights attended—John L. Lewis of the UMW, Dan Tobin of the Teamsters, Sidney Hillman of the Amalgamated Clothing Workers, and "Big Bill" Hutcheson of the carpenters' union, to name a few. Perkins also made an extra effort to include women, such as Rose Schneiderman of the Women's Trade Union League. Frances skillfully handled the mix of egos and concluded the conference with a ten-point summary of recommendations to the president: unemployment relief through federal aid to the states; protection against employers using the relief to supplement sweatshop pay; public works projects to invigorate basic industries; a total ban on child labor; use of public buildings to offer services, such as education, to the unemployed; limitation on weekly hours; increased hourly wages; minimum wages in certain industries; Department of Labor oversight of minimum wages and conditions of work; and a guaranteed right of workers to organize and to select representatives.

Most of these recommendations were broad and already established on the New Deal agenda, but Perkins achieved a major political victory by making the labor leaders feel some ownership of them, and she ended the conference with vastly more respect than she began it. There is a striking disparity in Perkins's social skill in pursuing policy goals and her difficulty coping with relationships in other situations. She was happiest and most secure when she was clearly subsumed in her cause.

Frances Perkins also reorganized the department from within to avoid the jurisdictional disputes and inefficiency that she found so frustrating. One key was recruiting skilled consultants in policymaking and, separately, skilled administrators to make sure an approved policy would be put into action. In 1935 she appointed Alice Hamilton as a medical consultant. Later Hamilton would write, "I have no hesitation in saying that this Department should be given a large share of credit for the improvement now seen in the dangerous trades. The public does not realize how greatly the Labor Department has expanded and developed under Secretary Perkins, but I, who have known it since its foundation in 1912, have seen it pass through a promising childhood and a troublesome adolescence, to its present capable adult self."

The New Deal

The years 1932 and 1933 were the bleakest of the Great Depression. The nation's annual unemployment rate approached 25 percent, with estimates of the number of unemployed ranging from 13.3 million to almost 18 million. Roosevelt had to declare a "bank holiday" in March 1933 to keep the entire industry from imploding under the pressure of failures. In the 1932–33 academic year, eighty thousand college students dropped out and twenty thousand rural schools shut down because of lack of money. "We were improvising under a terrible pressure of poverty, distress, despair," Perkins recalled. "Therefore, whatever was done was done too quickly to think about all the implications."

Immediate relief came through the Federal Emergency Relief Act, based on the earlier work of Perkins and another influential New Dealer named Harry Hopkins. Hopkins, a former settlement-house worker and Red Cross official, had first met F.D.R. while working on the Al Smith presidential campaign. The men had a good rapport from the start and, when Roosevelt became governor, Hopkins joined his administration and began working with Frances Perkins. After the 1929 crash, Hopkins ran the state's Temporary Emergency Relief Administration, putting people to work in parks and other public facilities—clearly a forerunner of New Deal programs. Like Perkins, Hopkins followed Roosevelt to the White House and became one of the president's most effective deputies and closest confidantes.

In Washington Frances and Harry crafted a national equivalent of their successful state program. Their strong working relationship with progressive senators such as New York's Robert Wagner, who knew both Hopkins and Perkins well from their prior positions in the governor's office, led to the swift passage of the Federal Emergency Relief Act. In fall 1933 Hopkins became the head of the Federal Emergency Relief Administration (FERA), and within a month, had put more than 4 million men to work. While Hopkins distributed aid to state and local governments, Perkins put her mind to drafting legislation that would give the president authority to revive the economy and create a social safety net.

Here Perkins faced a new complication, one that hadn't applied to her work in New York State: the argument that the legislation was an unconstitutional overreaching of federal power. At the time, there was no precedent for the kind of sweeping programs that Perkins and the other New Dealers envisioned. She had to find, as she described it, "a method by which federal labor legislation could be written so as to be constitutional."

The first major attempt to revive the economy was the National Industrial Recovery Act (NIRA), which created the National Recovery Administration (NRA) and gave the president authority to regulate industry across the country, as well as to institute a public works program. The NIRA, signed into law on June 16, 1933, would eliminate unfair trade practices, reduce child labor, establish a minimum wage and maximum hours, and guarantee the right to collective bargaining: essentially, it was Perkins's dream agenda. However, six months after Roosevelt signed it into law, the Supreme Court ruled most of the NIRA unconstitutional, on the grounds that the federal government did not have the power to regulate commerce within the states. (The public works program did pass constitutional muster and continued to thrive, helping millions of Americans weather the worst of the Depression.)

Perkins was disappointed but determined. "I always think that something can be salvaged out of a wreck," she later observed. She and other New Dealers began drawing up more legislation to achieve their goals, in smaller increments and within the bounds of the court's interpretation of the Constitution. The new laws and policies setting federal standards in the workplace came in rapid succession: the National Labor Relations Act, the Public Contracts Act, and the Fair Labor Standards Act, among others.

"To Build the Future with Sanity and Wisdom"

While Perkins played a role in much of this legislation, she was particularly involved in crafting another pillar of the New Deal: the Social Security Act. As the chair of Roosevelt's Committee on Economic Security, she was authorized to explore methods to create a form of insurance for the elderly. Perkins recalled Roosevelt's words as he assigned her the task: "You care about this thing. You believe in it. Therefore I know you will put your back to it more than anyone else, and you will drive it through."

Her first stumbling block was her ideological clash with fellow committee member Harry Hopkins. Hopkins believed that all unemployment relief and social insurance should be merged so that any citizen, upon proof of old age, unemployment, or ill health, could receive government payments from the general tax revenues. Perkins argued that the plan was too extreme to gain public approval, and was too much like "the dole," which Roosevelt had always outspokenly opposed. By now, Perkins and the president shared a vision of properly structured social insurance: a three-tiered plan, with private annuities available to anyone who could afford them; a broad-based, mandatory insurance system collected through taxes and available to all retirees; and a needs-based program of old-age relief for the very poor. Eventually, Perkins prevailed in the debate with Hopkins.

On January 4, 1935, in his State of the Union address, Roosevelt announced his intention to provide a security net including "unemployment insurance, old-age insurance, benefits for children, for mothers, for the handicapped, for maternity care, and for other aspects of dependency" but also pledged to put people to work because "to dole out relief . . . is to administer a narcotic, a subtle destroyer of the human spirit."

The premise of Social Security as Perkins understood it then came under attack from the right and, unexpectedly, from within the president's own cabinet. Treasury Secretary Henry Morgenthau, alone among the committee members, voiced his opposition to the government's contribution to Social Security out of its general revenues, countering with two proposals: that it be funded entirely from a 1 percent tax on employers and employees, and that domestic and agricultural workers be considered exempt, effectively excluding the majority of black workers. Morgenthau's suggestions provoked opposition from liberal groups, especially the NAACP, who referred to it as a "Lily White Social Security System." Though shocked, Perkins calmly resolved to continue pressing for universal coverage. Again she found herself on the same side as Eleanor Roosevelt, and they were both relieved when F.D.R., in a fireside chat on April 28, 1935, signaled his intention to insure everyone through government contributions to the system: "Our responsibility is to all the people of this country."

The commissioners also studied various ways to organize and implement a national health insurance program, but to no avail. The problem was so complicated, and opposition from the medical community so extreme and adamant, that health insurance was cut from the plans of the New Deal. (Later, during the labor shortages of World War II, employees' wages were capped to prevent inflation. Unable to offer higher wages, employers instead competed for workers by offering benefits such as paid health insurance, which is one reason the United States is the only industrialized country with health insurance tied to employment.)

While struggling to find a way to draw up the legislation so it would pass constitutional muster, Perkins found the solution in a supposedly unofficial setting: a tea party. As Perkins once wisely pointed out, "In Washington you don't go to parties because you want to go, you know; you go because you have to go." Thus she dutifully attended a party hosted by Mrs. Harlan Fisk Stone, wife of the Supreme Court justice. When the two of them found themselves in conversation, Justice Stone asked Perkins how the old-age insurance project was coming along and she described her efforts to ensure it would pass constitutional muster. Stone glanced around the room and then whispered to her, "The taxing power . . . my dear; the taxing power is sufficient for everything you want and need."

By her own account, Perkins instructed her staff to draft the legislation accordingly. The final wording of the Social Security Act was drawn up during late-night meetings at her home in the days before Christmas 1934. It provided for old age benefits and unemployment insurance to be financed by specifically earmarked payroll taxes. In 1937 the Supreme Court issued a series of rulings that held the Social Security Act was constitutional because it was based on the federal taxing power. (One of the three relevant majority opinions was written by Justice Stone.)

While the bill was before Congress, Perkins delivered a national radio address to explain the new Social Security program.

We now stand ready to build the future with sanity and wisdom. . . . It has taken the rapid industrialization of the last few decades, with its mass production methods, to teach us that a man might be a victim of circumstances far beyond his control, and finally it took depression to dramatize for us the appalling insecurity of the great mass of the population, and to stimulate interest in social insurance in the United States. We have come to learn that the large majority of our citizens must have protection against the loss of income due to unemployment, old age, death of breadwinners and disabling accidents and illness, not only on humanitarian grounds, but in the interest of our national welfare.

She pointed out that it was important to have a national program to avoid competition between states, but she acknowledged the need for each state to have wide latitude in developing its program. She explained, "For those now young or even middle aged, a system of compulsory old-age insurance will enable them to build up, with matching contributions from their employers, an annuity from which they can draw as a right upon reaching old age. These workers will be able to care for themselves—with modest comfort and security."

This and other addresses led one observer to declare, "Miss Perkins's strongest point is still her great ability in clarifying to the public complicated problems of legislation." I think this clarity grew out of her own clear-mindedness about their purpose and her refusal to be distracted by the horse-trading aspects of legislation.

The day that Roosevelt signed the act into law, Perkins received a phone call alerting her that her husband had escaped from the sanitarium in White Plains. As the major public face of the act, she at-

F.D.R. signing the Social Security Bill in August 1935. Behind him are (l-r) Representative Robert Doughton, Senator Robert Wagner, Secretary of Labor Frances Perkins, Senator Pat Harrison, and Representative David J. Lewis. Perkins had just learned that her husband escaped from a sanitarium in upstate New York and boarded a train to look for him immediately after the ceremony. (courtesy Library of Congress, Prints and Photographs Division)

tended the signing ceremony at the White House before hurriedly boarding a train to New York. She traveled north, apparently bearing this emotional burden alone, located Wilson, and saw to it that he was safely settled back into his institution. As always, she stoically fulfilled her duties. Perhaps her experience coping with the pain of this marriage inoculated her against some of the poisonous barbs she received in her professional life. Those barbs which began early in her career, would grow sharper and more numerous in the years to come.

The Longshoremen's Strike

Most Americans, having suffered the worst of the Depression and found that the government's programs resulted in concrete benefits, celebrated the New Deal. However, there was a powerful minority that bitterly opposed the agenda and chose Frances Perkins as their primary target. Her enemies, searching for ways to discredit her, seized upon her handling of the longshoremen's strike of 1934 to launch a sustained attack on her patriotism.

That spring the longshoremen and maritime unions on the West Coast began negotiating with the shipping companies for, among other things, better pay and union-run hiring halls. The negotiations stalled, and on May 9, twelve thousand workers in ports from San Diego to the Canadian border walked off the job. A joint strike committee was formed, and eventually Harry Bridges, a labor activist and former longshoreman, became its informal head. Bridges was a charismatic Australian who'd lived and worked in the United States since age sixteen.

The companies quickly hired strikebreakers, temporary workers who were well paid and well treated by the companies, which angered the strikers all the more. One strikebreaker described the generous treatment and said that while he couldn't even begin to guess how much the companies were spending on the scabs' room and board, it was clear that the owners had "decided to work their ships at any cost save that of giving in to the strikers." Although the replacement workers managed to unload ships, they lacked the skill needed to load the holds. The boilermakers' and machinists' unions—in a show of sympathy—refused to work. Because the Teamsters also refused to cross the picket lines, unloaded goods couldn't be trucked away and tons of cargo remained on the docks, the perishables rotting. Within days, in the San Francisco port alone, ninety-four ships were stacked up.

As the strike continued, its effects spread. Sawmills, logging camps, industrial plants of all kinds began shutting down, unable to send out finished goods or restock raw materials. Edward McGrady, the Department of Labor negotiator, became more and more frustrated. At one point, he accused the unions of working in tandem with Communists, but he soon backed off. For her part, Perkins was certain that intransigence on both sides was far more of an issue than Communist influence, but she was unable to intervene without the president's authority.

As the situation grew more tense, San Francisco mayor Angelo Rossi made increasingly panicky and inflammatory public announcements. On June 22 he called Perkins to say that the shipowners had put together a small fleet of trucks to begin moving the backlogged cargo, and the ports would reopen June 25. The first load actually left the docks Tuesday, July 3, driving past throngs of police and strikers lining the Embarcadero. Violence soon erupted and by the end of the day, there were reports of nine policemen injured, with two civilians shot and eleven more hurt badly enough to be hospitalized.

The Fourth of July holiday brought a brief respite, and then, on Thursday, July 5, just after eight A.M., the trucks again rolled away from the piers. In *A Terrible Anger*, David Selvin describes what happened next.

> Lines of police—"Mounties, motorcycle, and just plain flatfoots with extra long nightsticks dangling from their belts," one eyewitness said—held the swelling crowd, tense and silent, to the far side of the Embarcadero. A police patrol car came screaming down the Embarcadero, the witness said. A police captain jumped out, ordered, "OK, boys, let 'em have it." Tear gas bombs were fired directly into the crowd; Mounties charged. An elderly man went down, blood streaming from his head. The crowd retreated up Rincon Hill, police following.

Violence continued through the day; more than seventy people were wounded. When two strikers, Howard Sperry and Nick Bordoise, were killed by police gunfire, the bloody sidewalk where they died became a memorial, marked with chalked messages and piles of flowers, guarded by longshoremen. The California governor called out the National Guard, while negotiations continued to stall.

Then, on July 16, the city shut down as Teamsters, butchers, laundry workers, and thousands more marched in solidarity with the long-shoremen. President Roosevelt, on his way to Hawaii for a vacation, left Secretary of State Cordell Hull[4] in charge of the government. (The Twenty-fifth Amendment, which provides that the vice president take over when the president is absent or incapacitated, wasn't enacted until 1967.) The strike panicked Hull, who was certain it was a subversive plot, one that threatened the national government itself, and he announced his intention to send federal troops to break it.

Perkins's response recalls her approach to resolving the Rome copper strike twenty-five years before. She believed the widespread strike was motivated by sympathy with the longshoremen and would be over soon if conciliatory measures were taken. The presence of troops would only exacerbate bad feelings and prolong the strike. Her experience with labor negotiations, her style, and her fundamental belief in both labor rights and nonviolence combined to make her adamant in standing up to Hull. She later recalled telling him, "I call it serious for us to use troops against American citizens who as yet haven't done anything but inconvenience the community. . . . I cannot tell you how serious it would be, politically, morally, and for the basic labor-industry, labor-government relationships of the country, if we were to do this." As Hull and his allies continued to push for federal military intervention, Perkins announced, "I will have to make it a matter of record that I demand, I insist, that you send a message to the president by naval communications telling him what you propose to do and get an answer from him authorizing it."[5]

Perkins then immediately contacted the president herself, explain-

---

[4] While Hull was quite conservative in his domestic political views, he was also bold and progressive on foreign affairs. My grandfather greatly admired Hull, who shared his hometown of Carthage, Tennessee. In *Eye of the Storm*, he wrote, "In a hall on the Senate side of the Capitol there is a bust of Cordell Hull. . . . The legend on the bust reads, 'Father of the United Nations'—a great epitaph for a great man who spent his life promoting [our] democratic ideal among the nations of the world. . . . With a typically American pragmatic idealism, Cordell Hull affirmed that it was in the self-interest of each nation to cooperate in promoting the welfare of the international community of nations."

[5] Perkins also clashed with Joseph Kennedy, then chairman of the Maritime Commission and soon to be appointed ambassador to Great Britain. Kennedy wanted the National Mediation Board to step in, and he demanded that Perkins change course. She explained that the time was not ripe for the government to impose its own will. "The government cannot dictate any settlement. This country would not be a democracy if it could." "The time," Kennedy steamed, is "overripe for ruin."

ing the situation and warning him of Hull's intentions. Roosevelt, perhaps also swayed by his acute political instincts about the importance of labor in his base constituency, agreed with her reading of the situation. In the end there was no federal intervention and the adversaries submitted to arbitration.

As Perkins predicted, the general strike was called off within the week and on July 31 the longshoremen's strike ended. Untold millions of dollars had been lost, a total of seven strikers had died, and countless more had been injured. In October 1934 the results of the arbitration were announced. The longshoremen got a wage increase and their maximum straight time (the hours worked before overtime pay was required) was set at thirty hours per week. They also agreed that hiring halls would be jointly run by management and the unions but the dispatcher would be selected by the union. It was essentially a compromise.

"A Terrible Winter"

Although the strike was over, Perkins's troubles were just beginning. Several politicians began demanding Harry Bridges's deportation, accusing him of being a Communist infiltrator intent on using strikes to overthrow the government. The Department of Labor, then in charge of immigration questions, researched his background and found that Bridges was in the country legally and, though he had associated with Communists, he himself had never joined the party or advocated a Communist revolution.

Frances Perkins, resisting calls to deport Bridges, soon came under attack herself. She was rumored to be Bridges's lover, possibly his secret wife, maybe his mother-in-law, and definitely his comrade in Communism. Ugliest of all were the anti-Semitic attacks. A widely circulated pamphlet, published by the American Vigilante Intelligence Federation of Chicago, elaborated that Perkins was born with the name Watzki and came to the country in 1910 as a dedicated Communist. Further proof was offered: her department had "decreased alien deportation 60 percent." Eventually Perkins issued a formal press statement: "If I were a Jew, I would make no secret of it. On the contrary, I would be proud to acknowledge it." She was frustrated and disgusted by what she called "the utter un-Americanism of such a whispering campaign."

In light of the rise of Hitler, the anti-Semitic attacks must have seemed particularly alarming. Perkins had already become concerned by what she felt was an increasing spread of Nazi propaganda in the U.S. As early as 1933, she presented evidence to F.D.R. of the active promotion in the U.S. of "anti-Jewish, pro-Nordic and extremely nationalistic views."

The rumors, the whispering, and the pressure continued, and Perkins succumbed slightly, allowing the Department of Labor to begin deportation proceedings in March of 1938. The next month, a federal court ruling gave her reason to delay. The Fifth Circuit Court of Appeals in New Orleans ruled on an immigration case, *Kessler v. Strecker*, that raised similar issues. The court found that Strecker, a Polish immigrant, could not be deported on the sole grounds that he had once been a member of the Communist Party as long as he was no longer a member when he applied for United States citizenship. Perkins announced that she would wait for the Supreme Court to review this case before acting against Bridges.

The attacks on Perkins intensified through the summer and fall. The House Un-American Activities Committee, chaired by Texas Democrat Martin Dies Jr., warned Perkins that she would face impeachment if she did not deport Bridges immediately. Members of the California American Legion testified before the committee, accusing her of "gross malfeasance of office" and blaming her "red-coddling" policies for Communist infiltration at California's Stanford University. The Labor Department was accused of deliberately refusing to deport thirteen Communist aliens in Detroit. Hate mail poured in and editorials demanded her resignation. At her public appearances, someone always asked about her association with Bridges, the Communist Party, or both. "It was a terrible winter," she recalled. "There was hardly a day when I didn't pick up the paper and read that someone else had denounced me, or some organization had passed a resolution—it was extremely painful." As the Dies committee hearings wrapped up in December 1938, it can't have lifted her spirits to read in the *Washington Post* that "after several months of stormy hearings, a survey by the American Institute of Public Opinion indicates the rank and file of American voters believe the hearings have justified themselves and should be continued."

It would have been so much easier for Frances Perkins to simply go along with the demands for deportation, but she stuck with her conscience and was one of the few who stood up for Bridges. In January 1939, Secretary of the Interior Harold Ickes, often a critic of Perkins, described a cabinet meeting in which the Bridges case was discussed. "There was not a single one in this lot that would justify the arbitrary expulsion of Bridges from this country—Bridges himself denies that he has ever belonged to any communist organization. There is no record that he has ever advocated the overthrow of the Government by force and violence—So far a United States Circuit Court of Appeals has held that he is not deportable and this case is on appeal to the Supreme Court. Yet notwithstanding all this there is great clamor throughout the land for his deportation and this has reflected adversely upon Miss Perkins and the Administration."

Ickes added that the chairman of the Democratic National Committee, also the postmaster general, "burst in with the remark that, whether Bridges was a communist or not, the people of the country believed that he was and believed that he ought to be deported—In effect, he said that whether he was deportable or not, Bridges ought to be sent out of the country for the sake of the Democratic party." Roosevelt responded that, unless there was unassailable legal proof, Bridges should not be deported.

On January 24, 1939, J. Parnell Thomas of New Jersey, a Republican member of the Dies committee, called for the impeachment of Perkins and two of her colleagues, Gerard D. Reilly and James Houghteling. In February Perkins and Reilly appeared before the House Judiciary Committee. As they walked to the hearing room, she asked Reilly, "Do you remember the priest that walked beside Joan of Arc when she went to the stake?" It was the first time he realized how much the entire ordeal had unnerved her.

On March 24 the committee announced that there wasn't enough evidence to warrant impeachment. The ten Republican members concurred in that unanimous opinion, yet they published an addendum stating that Perkins and her subordinates had been "lenient and indulgent of Harry Bridges."

The Bridges case was finally resolved when the Supreme Court upheld the Fifth Circuit ruling in the *Strecker* case. Now an alien could not be deported because of Communist Party membership as long as he or she was not a member at the time of arrest or application for cit-

izenship. Perkins appointed the dean of Harvard Law School to conduct a hearing as to whether or not Bridges could be deported under
this standard. The finding was that he could not. Bridges remained in
the United States and became a citizen in 1945.

All the hearings and all the investigations didn't stop the smears
and innuendoes. The press never fully repudiated the most unfounded
charges that had been made against Perkins, and seemed content to
write her off rather than recognize her heroic defense of civil liberties.[6]
Typical was an article in the *Saturday Evening Post*, which opined that
"Miss Perkins is not a Communist, not even remotely a Communist
sympathizer. She is as true a Democrat in her convictions as any I have
ever known. But she represents the classic type of soft-minded liberal
whom the Stalinists behind the scenes know how to exploit for their
own purposes."

I don't believe Perkins was exploited by anyone. She viewed unions
as essential to protect workers against powerful corporate interests and
she stood by her principles, angering powerful interests who were facing a cut in profits. This approach was consistent with the one she took
in the controversial 1937 United Auto Workers sit-down strike, cen-
tered in Flint, Michigan. For weeks, the situation teetered on the brink
of bloodshed until, in part because of Perkins's careful handling of the
situation, the strike ended with GM's historic recognition of the UAW.

This was a huge victory for labor and put wind in the sails of the
movement, making Frances Perkins all the more reviled by some of the
businessmen affected by subsequent strikes. After spending an afternoon with Perkins, Eleanor Roosevelt wrote a friend about the extraordinary attacks the labor secretary had endured: "How men hate a
woman in a position of real power!" Actually, I believe it was her inflexible principles and her refusal to be intimidated by their power that
caused those men to hate her.

---

[6] After the press frenzy prompted by the impeachment announcement, the dis-
missal of the charges received so little attention that one congressman, John Martin
of Colorado, took it on himself to issue a statement: "After months of nation-wide
publicizing of unjust and unfounded charges against an official, the final result is her-
alded by no blare of trumpets and is scarcely brought to the notice of the public,
which for months and months has been fed with promises that the public official
would be found guilty of high crimes and misdemeanors and of betrayal of public
trust—All fair-minded people should reprobate and condemn the campaign carried
on against them, more pregnant with possibilities of danger to our institutions than
even the subversive forces they were charged with being in league with."

Showing enormous bravery in standing up to the xenophobia and intolerance of the times, Frances Perkins also tried to use her influence to protect refugees, especially the large numbers of Jews feeling persecution in the 1930s. Frustrated by the entrenched opposition to her proposal to remove restrictions on immigration in order to "relieve the strain on a terrorized people," Perkins sought the help of the first lady, and together they worked to prevent the deportation of Jews who were in the United States illegally.[7] As Blanche Wiesen Cook recounts, "Perkins was embattled over each case, and confronted a mostly hostile Congress and State Department. Although ER responded to each letter sent to her by needful refugees and forwarded most of them to Perkins, unless FDR issued an executive order there was no hope for a policy change."

World War II

World War II finally changed the tone in Washington and put the red-baiting to rest, for a while. Calling herself "anything but a pacifist," Perkins felt that "all of Europe was overrun by a tyrannical mob" and the United States would have to act. On July 18, 1940, as the war became inevitable, the Democratic Party took the unprecedented step of nominating F.D.R. for a third term. That November he defeated Wendell Willkie.

Perkins already had tried to bow out of the cabinet many times, but F.D.R. always convinced her to stay. After the 1940 election, she asked Eleanor Roosevelt to help her convince him to agree to a turnover at Labor. The first lady spoke to her husband and responded to Perkins in a note. "The answer is no, absolutely no. He's got to think about the war, the appropriate diplomacy, the foreign policy problems and all that. He just can't put his mind on a new person operating in this field. You do understand each other. That's that. It can't be done." At the next cabinet meeting Roosevelt elaborated. Perkins recalled him saying, "You know me. You see lots of things that most people don't see. You keep me guarded against a lot of things that no new man walking in here would protect me from."

---

[7] In January 1944 F.D.R. did sign an executive order to create the War Refugees Board, which is credited with helping as many as 200,000 European Jews reach safety. Roosevelt's delay in taking action and his earlier executive order establishing the Japanese internment camps are now widely criticized.

Perkins and F.D.R. on December 17, 1943, just after his return from the Tehran Conference. (courtesy F.D.R. Library)

After the United States entered the war, Perkins had her department develop evacuation plans for city children in case of bomb attacks. She assigned the Civilian Conservation Corps to wartime preparations. However, she did not have oversight of wartime production and found her influence limited.

During the war years, unemployment dropped and the economy improved. In 1944, in his fourth presidential campaign, Roosevelt defeated Governor Thomas Dewey of New York.[8] Perkins again tried to resign but soon realized that F.D.R.'s health was so poor that the time

---

[8] Thomas E. Dewey first came to public notice before he was thirty-five years old when, as a New York special prosecutor, he broke up the racketeering and loan sharking rings run by Dutch Schultz, Lucky Luciano, and a host of lesser-known gangsters. He was elected governor of New York in 1942 and his term was marked by several accomplishments, including a state law barring racial or religious discrimination in hiring, a revamped labor mediation board, and a large-scale highway building program. After losing to Harry Truman in 1948 (his second presidential run) Dewey continued to serve as governor until 1954, and thereafter focused on building up his law practice, which proved very successful. An influential figure in the Republican Party, he also was open to bipartisan efforts. He later built a very cordial relationship with President Johnson, who wanted him to chair a new national commission on crime. Dewey was an early and longtime supporter of Nixon, and in 1968, at the age of sixty-six, he turned down President Nixon's offer to put him on the Supreme Court. He died three years later.

wasn't right to press the issue. Their last real contact took place just before Inauguration Day, after a cabinet meeting. Later, she wrote of the moment when, with tears in his eyes, F.D.R. took her hand and thanked her for her service. "It was all the reward I could ever have asked, to know that he had recognized the storms and trials I had faced in developing our program, to know that he appreciated the program and thought well of it, and that he was grateful."

F.D.R. died of a cerebral hemorrhage on April 12, 1945. Perkins was the first to arrive at the hastily called cabinet meeting, and she stood with Harry Truman's wife and daughter when he took the oath of office. Soon after, Eleanor Roosevelt advised Bess Truman to hold a press conference. Mrs. Truman asked Perkins whether she ought to do it, confiding, "It terrifies me. I don't even think of public affairs." Perkins told her, "No, Mrs. Truman, I don't think you ought to feel the slightest obligation to do it. Mrs. Roosevelt is an unusual person. She enjoys it. There certainly isn't anything the press has a right to ask you."

Perkins's successor immediately issued a statement announcing, "The duty of an officer in this Department is to accept the laws as Congress has written them and as the Courts have interpreted them." This was a clear rebuke to Perkins's proactive approach, but she had no second thoughts. Just after her resignation, in a letter she wrote to her old friend Felix Frankfurter, she explained that all the personal attacks and media scrutiny had been worth it because of what she had been able to achieve for "the millions of forgotten, plain, common working men."

Her Last Years

Perkins spent the next decades writing and teaching. Needing income, she accepted a publisher's contract for a memoir of F.D.R. *The Roosevelt I Knew*, published in 1946, was generally well received. In a review, Arthur M. Schlesinger concluded that "Frances Perkins has discharged her obligation to historians with grace, fidelity, and insight," and the *New York Times Book Review* described it as a "penetrating yet generous evaluation" of the man and his career, "a portrait, admittedly incomplete though it is, [that] will last because it is essentially true." However, the book brought out old frictions between Perkins and Eleanor Roosevelt, who clearly did not like it. While Eleanor apparently never explained what offended her, friends suspected that she felt Perkins had played down the first lady's role in her husband's career.

In 1947 President Truman appointed Perkins to the U.S. Civil Service Commission, reviewing complaints and accusations against federal employees. Influenced by her experiences as labor secretary, Perkins was very careful to protect the privacy of those who appeared before the commission. She made three crucial rulings intended to limit potential abuses: failure to report a brief membership in the Communist party should not be grounds for discharge, a person's loyalty should not be gauged by his willingness to inform on others, and the government had no role in searching out and punishing moral flaws in its employees. When an acquaintance asked if she might be overstating the potential for abuse, she gave him a withering glance and replied, "Don't forget: I was the secretary of labor during the Harry Bridges case."

In 1951 Paul Wilson came to live with his wife for the last year of his life. One can only imagine how emotionally challenging this last chapter of their marriage was, but Perkins remained loyal and stoic, and mourned him when he succumbed to "a long illness" on December 31, 1952. A week later, Perkins resigned from the Civil Service Commission.

In 1955 Perkins took a job teaching at Cornell University's Department of Labor Relations, where she was a popular and admired presence. One of her colleagues recalled, "Apart from the important public life that she had, she was inestimably outstanding as a person and personality. If she came into a room where she was unknown, people would at once know that someone special had entered. She was recognizably an important person—her demeanor, her carriage, her style of dress, her eyes, everything about her marked her as someone very special. One was tempted to address her as 'Your Ladyship.'"

While at Cornell, Perkins began making notes and conducting research for another biography, *The Al Smith I Knew*. (Among the surprises she unearthed: Tammany Hall's most famous son was only one-quarter Irish, on his mother's side. His father was a mixture of Italian and German and his mother was half English.) She felt that Smith's groundbreaking work in progressive politics had been forgotten and she wanted to give her old friend his due. Although she died before completing her research, the 1969 biography *Al Smith: Hero of the Cities* drew on her work.

Perkins at age 83 at a dinner commemorating the 50th anniversary of the Department of Labor on March 4, 1963. She is entertaining President John F. Kennedy by describing the size of a cockroach in her desk when she first arrived at the Department. (courtesy Mount Holyoke College Archives and Special Collections)

During these years, she also grew closer to her daughter. Because of circumstances and temperaments, the family had, in a friend's words, "all lived separate lives." Susanna, strong-willed and artistic, tended to clash with her mother, while Frances tended to overwhelm her daughter. In 1954 Susanna and her husband, artist Calvert Cogge-shall, had a son they named Tomlin. Frances adored the boy and enjoyed being a grandmother.

On March 4, 1963, Perkins joined President John F. Kennedy to commemorate the fiftieth anniversary of the Department of Labor. She entertained the audience by describing the enormous cockroaches she found upon entering the department's offices. The following year, the *Washington Post* noted that the "spry octogenarian with a dry wit" participated in an all-day meeting organized by the Department of Labor. In 1980 the newly completed building housing the department would be named in her honor.

Frances Perkins died on May 14, 1965, after several strokes. The secretary of labor at the time, Willard Wirtz, paid her tribute: "Every man and woman who works at a living wage, under safe conditions, for reasonable hours, or who is protected by unemployment insurance or Social Security, is her debtor."

Virginia Durr

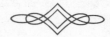

The struggle is not just a struggle by or for the Negroes but a struggle to make this country the kind of country we promised it would be, and if we fail, we simply fail as citizens and the country fails and we are in danger of slipping down the slippery slope into violence, police terror and a form of the corporate state. The main thing I stress is positive action and positive values and positive thought too.

—Virginia Durr

In February 1954, as the country awaited the Supreme Court ruling in *Brown v. Board of Education*, Senator Jim Eastland of Mississippi was on a continuing crusade against what he regarded as the twin evils of integration and Communism. He'd already declared that a ruling against segregation would prove that the Supreme Court was under Communist control. As chairman of the Civil Rights Subcommittee, he ensured that no civil rights bills would pass by simply refusing to convene the committee. He also stuffed the Congressional Record with volumes of dubious "evidence" of connections between civil rights groups and Communism.

Eastland, also head of the Senate Internal Security Subcommittee, had decided to target the Southern Conference Educational Fund, a group dedicated to ending segregation. He'd subpoenaed one of SCEF's leaders, Aubrey Williams, the former head of F.D.R.'s National Youth Administration and an early civil rights activist. Ostensibly, Eastland wanted to question Williams about his participation in a recent radio debate on school desegregation, in which he'd argued against Herman Talmadge, governor of Georgia. Even though Williams and Talmadge were the only debaters, Eastland also subpoenaed several other people, including a woman named Virginia Foster Durr.

At first glance, Virginia seemed to be an odd target for the subcommittee. She was the mother of three daughters at home and one who was grown and married. She was the daughter of an old Alabama family, a former Junior Leaguer, a gregarious and exuberant socializer. She was married to Clifford Durr, lawyer, Rhodes scholar, and son of another old Alabama family. Virginia's only recent affiliation was with an organization called United Church Women.

But Durr was anything but a stereotypical Southern socialite. The United Church Women was an interracial group that included Coretta Scott King, and it was broken up when the members' names were published, prompting vandalism and death threats against them. Years earlier, while her husband worked on the New Deal, she had put together a wide-ranging coalition in support of abolishing the poll tax, and then turned the group's efforts to the fight against segregation. She was a founding member of the interracial Southern Conference for Human Welfare, a groundbreaking effort to bring together disparate liberal groups in the South in order to abolish the poll tax, end violence against labor organizers, and work towards integration.

She and her husband were also supporters of the Highlander Folk School, a controversial integrated retreat in Middle Tennessee that held workshops on voting rights and civil rights activism. (Later that year, Virginia would personally arrange for her friend Rosa Parks to visit Highlander, an experience that would lead to the Montgomery bus boycott.) Virginia was one of many women who built the civil rights movement from the ground up, challenging the social mores of their time and convincing others to do the same. She worked for political change with and through a web of friends inspired by her boundless charm, energy, and persistence.

Virginia's story is particularly compelling because she went through her own personal transformation, from an unquestioning racist to a firebrand for racial equality. In his foreword to Virginia's memoir, *Outside the Magic Circle*, her friend Studs Terkel explained the origin of the title. Virginia had told him that a well-brought-up Southern woman had three options: play the Southern belle, acting all the time; go insane; or "step outside the magic circle"—become a rebel, abandon privilege, and challenge convention. "Ostracism, bruises of all sorts, and defamation would be her lot, " he summarized. "Her reward would be a truly examined life. And a world she would otherwise never have known." Virginia, always clever with words, always embracing life experience and human potential, stepped out of the magic circle. Her story is uplifting not only in its personal triumphs but in its telescoped view of what our culture goes through in those paradigm-shifting, tumultuous times. Virginia understood that there are certain intangible, illogical, "magical" forces that compel people to stay inside a safe zone, unquestioning of the social order around them. It is her rich inner understanding of this that makes her so prescient, so likeable, and so funny.

Roots

Born near Birmingham, Alabama, on August 6, 1903, Virginia was the youngest child of Sterling Foster and Anne Patterson Foster. Her brother, Sterling, was the eldest, and Josephine was the middle child. Virginia described her family as "genteel but poor," clinging to the notion that they were Old South aristocrats and "keeping up with the Joneses at great effort, trying to make a fifteen dollar dress look like a hundred dollar one."

Virginia's contemporary William Faulkner said of the South they knew, "The past is never dead. It's not even past." Though it had ended more than forty years before she was born, the Civil War was a real presence in Virginia's childhood. At social gatherings, old Confederate veterans bent down to kiss her cheek, the unpleasantness of the whiskey and tobacco on their breath tempered by her sense that they were heroes of a tragic war with an unjust end. She was raised on tales of her family's past glories: gallant Confederate officers, grand plantations, hundreds of loyal slaves. Her father had grown up "in this atmosphere of wealth and abundance and servants" on the family's plantation in Union Springs, Alabama. Her mother's family, the Pattersons, were said to have had a majestic plantation in Tennessee tended by hundreds of slaves. As an adult, she learned that the "plantation" was a small brick house surrounded by a farm and the "hundreds" of slaves shrank to perhaps a dozen. The Civil War legacy was real, though. Her grandfather had served with Nathan Bedford Forrest, widely considered the most effective cavalry leader of the Confederacy. After the war, Forrest became one of the founders of the Ku Klux Klan (which took its name from the Greek *kuklos*, or circle). Both he and Virginia's uncle, Malcolm "Ham" Patterson, were elected to the United States Congress from Tennessee. Ham Patterson went on to become governor of the state.

Virginia grew up with two black women she deeply loved and admired, and it was those relationships that planted the first seeds of doubt about the doctrine of "Negro inferiority." A woman Virginia called "Nursie" was like a second mother who bathed her, fed her, watched over her, and put her to sleep every night. Nursie's daughter Sarah was Virginia's closest playmate. Through the summer months, Virginia, Nursie, and Sarah stayed at the Foster plantation. Grandmother Foster "never had to do anything in her life but be charming," and the real power in the household was a former slave named Easter. Wearing an immaculate white dress and white apron, with a starched white bandana tied around her head, Easter ran the whole enterprise. Virginia remembered her as tremendously dignified and "probably one of the smartest women I ever knew."

Virginia's vivid recollection of one incident in her childhood underscores its symbolic importance to her later views of Southern race relations. Just before her seventh birthday, Virginia was told that, instead of the traditional backyard barbecue with her mostly black playmates, she'd have her party in the front yard with only white children invited. She threw a tantrum until her parents agreed to have the usual barbecue in the morning and a second celebration in the afternoon.

At the time, Virginia's Aunt May, a woman Virginia remembered as "so fashionable and so unpleasant," and May's daughter Elizabeth were staying with the Fosters. During the barbecue, Elizabeth said to Sarah, "I'm not going to eat any chicken that your black hand has touched, you little nigger," prompting Virginia to tell her cousin to go to hell. At the afternoon party, when Virginia realized all the guests were white children whom she did not know, she had another fit and smashed in her cake.

That evening at dinner, Aunt May turned to Virginia's mother and said, "I really think you have to do something about her because she's so high-tempered, such a bad child." After a third temper tantrum, Virginia was banished from the table and ran to find refuge with Nursie. As they sat on the back porch, Virginia curled in Nursie's lap, they both overheard Aunt May tell Virginia's mother, "I think it's terrible that you let her sit in her lap and sleep with her and kiss her and hug her. You know all these black women are diseased."

Despite the fact that Nursie had been a central figure in the Foster home, providing constant nurturing care as well as cooking and cleaning, neither Virginia's mother nor her grandmother said a word to defend her. Deeply offended, Nursie and Sarah left the house the next morning and never returned. Virginia was devastated. She tracked down Nursie at her next job and repeatedly begged her to come back to the Fosters', to no avail.[1]

As an adult, Virginia viewed this incident and thousands like it as both symptom and cause of the South's pathology. "If you have . . . slept in the bed with your Negro nurse, if you have kissed and hugged and sat in [Negroes'] laps and have loved them so much and been so close to them, and then all of a sudden you are told by your mother and your father and your aunts and your uncles and the whole of white society that they are inferior people and they should not be treated like other people, it makes you feel that there is something wrong with you. It sets up a terrible conflict in people and I think they get to be schizophrenic. . . . That's why so much of the literature of the South is full of conflict and madness, because you can't do that to people."

---

[1] Decades later, while living near Washington, D.C., and working on the repeal of the poll tax, Virginia got to know a writer for the *Chicago Defender*, a woman named Mrs. Spraggs who was also from Birmingham. Twice Mrs. Spraggs mentioned that her mother-in-law was visiting her, had known Virginia in Birmingham, and would like to see her. Virginia agreed but made no special effort, since she didn't remember ever meeting anyone named Spraggs. Finally Mrs. Spraggs said that her sister-in-law, Sarah Spraggs, was visiting and wanted to see Virginia. "All of a sudden, I realized who she was—Nursie's daughter. I had never known the last name of Nursie, the love of my life, who had raised me from a baby for all those seven years. It just shows how completely backward I was. . . . Nursie by that time had died. I had missed seeing her because I didn't know her name." Virginia did meet Sarah for lunch, at a Chinese restaurant that agreed to serve them in a private room. Sarah remembered that last birthday party at the Fosters', especially Virginia's telling her cousin to go to hell. "She had remembered that all her life, and I remembered it too."

But as a child, Virginia couldn't understand the conflict and the madness so clearly. After that moment of indignant understanding at age seven, the magic circle, the force of socialization, closed around her again. She loved the film *Birth of a Nation* and enjoyed the parades staged by the respected gentlemen of the Ku Klux Klan. Virginia grew up thinking of the Klan as "something noble and grand and patriotic that had saved the white women of the South" from sexually predatory black men. "Politicians would make speeches about pure white Southern womanhood—and I believed it. I was pure white Southern womanhood and Southern men had died for me and the Confederate flag was flying just to save me. I got to thinking I was pretty hot stuff, to have the war fought for me." As for the many light-skinned black people, Virginia's father informed her that was "all due to the Union Army." She recalled, "Well, I just accepted it. I didn't know what it meant, but I took it for granted that the Union Army caused them to be different colors. There were answers to everything even if the answers didn't always make sense."

Virginia also, quite naturally, wanted to feel as if she belonged to the social groups she entered as a teenager. However, she was a bit awkward and extremely nearsighted. Although she got glasses at sixteen, she was told to avoid wearing them. "When I dated," she recalled, "my mother would hide the glasses, and she would never let me wear them at dances or parties. In the days before talking movies they would flash signs up and I could never read them. I could hardly see Marguerite Clark or Mary Pickford or Wallace Reid, who was my hero. I couldn't see the leaves on the trees. Everything was a blur."

Josephine, "beautiful, sweet and charming," had all the attributes of a great Southern belle and was one of the local celebrities. "A man was proud to be seen with them. It gave him status. Their cities were proud of them. . . . They were not on the stage but they were playing a part all the time. They were the epitome of success, and oh, I wanted to be like them so badly. But I knew I wasn't. . . . I never had the feeling that the belles had of being irresistible." Despite the fact that her feelings of insecurity were exacerbated by being compared to her sister, Virginia always felt close to Josephine, whom the family called "Sister," and seemed to feel protective of her.

Looking back on their lives as girls and young women, Virginia felt that Sister had been overshadowed her entire life by two powerful men: first their father, and then her husband, Hugo Black, who became a legendary New Deal senator and liberal Supreme Court justice. When Black began courting Josephine in 1919, he was a labor lawyer, which was not a profession considered appropriate in the Fosters' circles, so he had to work to charm the entire family. He was a "wonderful influence" on sixteen-year-old Virginia, bringing her books to read and talking to her about unions. Black was also very generous to the Fosters, even helping them financially on occasion, and they all remained devoted to him. However, as his career took off, Virginia felt the marriage stifled her sister.

> Hugo absolutely worshipped Josephine. I never saw a man love a woman more than he did or work harder to get her. He did everything in his power to make her happy, except give her her freedom. He gave her everything he could think of. There was not a wish of her heart that he didn't satisfy, but she never had one hour's freedom from that time on. She was Mrs. Hugo Black. He expected her to subordinate herself to his life and his ambitions. It never occurred to him otherwise.

Josephine also suffered from depression, which likely contributed to her early death on December 7, 1951, at age 52. Virginia later said, "I think if Sister had ever been able to hate evil as I do she might have been saved, but she never could. And perhaps that is not the way to salvation—but at least it gives you an outward target for your angers and they are not turned inward." Clearly, the relationship between the sisters was a complicated one, but it was also loving and mutually supportive. As Mrs. Hugo Black, Josephine introduced Virginia to many colorful political leaders, and Virginia's support of Hugo's liberal stances must have been a source of comfort to the Blacks.

Another element of the magic circle was the way Virginia's peers and elders reacted to the growing poverty around them. Birmingham's economy depended on textile mills and steel plants. Many of the plants were owned by out-of-state corporations indifferent to the community, and the managers at all the plants went to great lengths to keep the workforce unorganized. Factory jobs were low-paying and dangerous but still better than sharecropping or anything else available. Poverty was widespread, among both blacks and whites, and Virginia couldn't help but notice it. Her parents gave her the same reassurance Frances Perkins's family had given her.

The poor white children were very pale and thin with stringy hair. The textile mill children always looked thin and pale and had white hair and white eyebrows and eyelashes [from pellagra]. The poor black children always looked ashen. They wore flour sacks as clothes, with nothing under them. And they often had two great streams of snot hanging down from their nose. They were very unattractive looking. I would feel sorry for them and ask my family about them and they would say, "This is just the way they are. They are born this way. They don't have any pride or ambition. If you gave them anything they would just get drunk or spend it on something foolish. They are immoral and spend their money unwisely . . ." We were brought up, or at least I was brought up, to believe that the distribution of wealth was ordained by God . . . it was a very comforting thought, you see, because when you saw people starving and poor and miserable, you thought, "Well, it isn't my fault. I didn't do anything to cause it. God just ordained it this way."

The Foster children were sent to good schools, as much to keep up appearances as out of respect for education. Virginia went to a boarding school in Washington, D.C., the National Cathedral School for Girls, and then to Massachusetts to attend Wellesley, which she called "the greatest adventure of my life until then." She joined the Southern Club and met several men who would become lifelong friends.

Virginia loved the intellectual challenge and lively social environment, and she couldn't wait to return for her sophomore year. Her first night back, she remembered, "I went to the dining room and a Negro girl was sitting at my table. My God, I nearly fell over dead." Virginia immediately went to the head of the house and explained that she couldn't possibly eat at the same table as a black person and the other student would have to be moved. The woman informed Virginia that there'd be no change in the seating arrangements and she had two choices: sit at her assigned table or withdraw from school.

Virginia talked it over with her roommate, who told her, "I just think you're crazy. Last summer when I was visiting you down in Alabama, you kissed and hugged that old black woman who was cooking for you. I wouldn't have kissed and hugged an old black woman, but you did. Why would you kiss and hug them but not eat with them?"

Virginia explained that it was just the way things were, just the Southern way of life. She loved the cook but would never, ever dine with her.

Lying awake all night, Virginia finally realized that she actually didn't care about sitting with the girl. The real problem was that she was terrified of what her father, a rabid segregationist who worked at the polls administering "literacy tests," would think of her if he found out about it. She decided to go ahead and eat meals with the black girl but make sure her father never knew. She later admitted that the decision had nothing to do with principle. She was having the "time of her life" at Wellesley and didn't want to leave. But the incident did make her realize that it was other people's view of her, rather than her view of black people, that drove her segregationist thinking. She explained that it "may not have been crucial at the time but it was the origin of a doubt." It must also have been a rekindling of the feisty sense of justice Virginia had shown at her seventh birthday party, a spirit that had been dampened by the years in between.

Soon after, Virginia had to leave Wellesley anyway. The boll weevil infestation of the 1920s caused cotton prices to soar and land values to plummet, wiping out the Fosters' income. "The boll weevil ate up my education," she joked.

Virginia and Clifford

Virginia met Clifford Durr at church in Montgomery, not long after she returned from Wellesley. Later she said he caught her eye because "he was tall, blond, and blue-eyed and wore English suits, not the seersucker suits that looked like pajamas that most Southern boys wore." He also knew Virginia's family, having been a fraternity brother of her brother, Sterling.

The Fosters, worried that Virginia might not marry well, were delighted by this Rhodes scholar from a well-off family whose great-uncle had fought in the Civil War with Virginia's great-uncle. They invited him for lunch immediately and the young couple was soon engaged.

Virginia and Cliff married on April 7, 1926. They honeymooned in Pass Christian, Mississippi, on the Gulf Coast, where they—and their marriage—survived a hurricane and food poisoning. "I came back from my honeymoon pregnant," Virginia recalled. "I had not known the first thing about marriage, to say nothing about birth control. . . . We thought that a perfectly innocent and ignorant girl had a better

Virginia with two of her children, Clifford Judkins Durr Jr. and Lucy in Seminary Hill. (courtesy Ann Durr Lyon)

chance of getting a good husband. It was pretty hard on the man, I must say, to marry a woman who didn't know what it was all about."

Their first daughter, Ann, was born the following year. The Durrs would have four more children. Clifford Jr. was born in 1935, followed by Lucy in 1937, and Virginia, whom everyone called Tilla, in 1939. Their youngest, Lulah, was born in 1948, when Virginia was in her forties.

Throughout their marriage, Virginia bolstered and sustained Clifford and also influenced and participated in his career. (This reminds me very much of the role played by my grandmother Pauline Gore and surely applies to many other smart women whose options for an independent career were limited.) Clifford, too, was always supportive of Virginia, even when he disagreed with her. They were very different in temperament, Clifford as measured and restrained as Virginia was impulsive and ebullient. As their daughter Lucy recalls, "they filled each other's gaps" and encouraged each other "to think about things in a different way."

The Depression in Alabama

With the excitement of Wellesley becoming a distant memory, Virginia began living the life she'd been trained for, that of a respectable and socially prominent young wife and mother. She was an officer of the Montgomery Junior League and active in her church. She joined a sewing circle and played bridge.

As the Depression set in, the South sank further into poverty. The Fosters lost almost everything, including the mortgaged plantation, and moved in with Virginia and Cliff. Through the Junior League, Virginia began volunteering for the Red Cross, which, with no government relief of any kind, was one of the few sources of help available to the desperately poor. Virginia and other volunteers visited families to certify those who were totally destitute and thus eligible for the stipend of $2.50 per week. "I began little by little to wake up to the world," Virginia later said of this time. With her maturing sense of practical idealism, she convinced the farmers who were dumping milk they could not sell to instead let the Red Cross distribute it. She also organized free concerts with music provided by local policemen's and firemen's bands.

When confronted with the suffering, Virginia found it harder to comfort herself with her parents' myth that all these people were poor because they deserved to be. People laid off from the plants and mills were pleading for any kind of work. Families evicted from company housing sought any shelter they could find, even in abandoned coke ovens. Hugo Black's tutorials on the labor movement must have also made her more open to understanding the larger forces at work. "I saw more accumulated misery than you can imagine. What bothered me the most was that these poor people blamed themselves for their situation. They never said, 'We are destitute because U.S. Steel doesn't treat us as well as they treat the mules.' The mules got whatever they needed to stay alive, but the people got nothing." Like Mother Jones and Ida B. Wells-Barnett, Durr developed a strong dislike of those who professed to have strict morals yet did nothing to help the poor, and first on this list were ministers who preached hellfire and brimstone to suffering families. "I got so I wanted to kill these preachers. I thought it was dreadful to tell those people they were poverty-stricken because they had sinned!"

Hugo Black was elected to the United States Senate from Alabama in 1932 and through him, Clifford was offered a job heading the bank insurance program for the Reconstruction Finance Corporation (RFC). Virginia had heard a lot of criticism of the new president and first lady, most of it focused on their hypocrisy as wealthy Americans who took up the cause of the improvident. "That was a great word people used—improvident. You hadn't provided for the future, you see. You were poor and it was your own fault." Virginia struggled with this theory, wondering if part of the problem could lie in the irresponsibility of others with more power.

The prospect of joining the New Deal was thrilling to Virginia, who, despite all the negative things she had heard, felt that at least this administration was trying to do something to help those in need. Ever adventurous, she was also eager to get to know a new city, though she still sought out people and places that reminded her of home. When an acquaintance familiar with Washington asked where she wanted to live, she replied that she would like to be somewhere where people were "poor and genteel." The friend directed her to Seminary Hill, a suburban neighborhood in Virginia, and that's where the Durrs settled.

The New Deal

Virginia thought the socially ambitious wives of the other RFC men were a "horrible bore," but the Durrs did develop a lively circle of friends. Clark Foreman, a friend from her Wellesley days, was now working for Harold Ickes in the Department of the Interior, and he and his wife became close friends of the Durrs. They also got to know a young congressman from Texas "with a great big Adam's apple, as thin as a string bean," Lyndon Johnson, and his wife Lady Bird. "He was always on the job and always remembering birthdays and Christmas presents and everything else. He was a constant politician," Virginia remembered. Economist John Kenneth Galbraith and his wife, Kitty, lived near the Durrs in Seminary Hill. "If I went in the car pool in the morning, I would sit on somebody's knees, usually Kenneth Galbraith's, which were very bony, I must say. He was very nice about it. He was the biggest, and I was rather large and heavy. And we were always crowded. It was a very interdependent life."

Through the social gatherings of this group, Virginia bonded with Stella Landis, a Mississippian whose husband clerked for Justice Louis Brandeis on the Supreme Court. With Stella, Virginia visited with the wives of justices and grew close to the "marvelous, interesting" Mrs. Brandeis. Virginia soon began to follow the great New Deal legal cases as well as the political discourse.

The Durrs and the Blacks only socialized on occasion. Virginia remembered that after Black joined the Supreme Court in 1937, he avoided social discussion of any issues that might pertain to a case. "Hugo and Sister's dinner parties were pretty dull because nobody could talk about anything very much. They were always so afraid it would come before the Supreme Court. We usually talked about roses and tennis. And sometimes Bill Douglas would sing hymns."

Through Josephine, Virginia met Eleanor Roosevelt, who greatly inspired her. "I thought she was absolutely lovely. She was a tall, slender woman and had brown hair and beautiful eyes. The lower part of her face was not very attractive but she was such a lovely person to be with that she gave the impression of beauty and graciousness and charm and cordiality. So I decided I would volunteer for the Women's Division [of the Democratic National Committee] mostly because I knew Mrs. Roosevelt worked with them." Virginia focused on the party's goal of getting rid of the poll tax "so white Southern women could vote." At that point, the DNC avoided the race issue by focusing on the economic barriers it created for women and poor whites generally.

Campaigning Against the Poll Tax

As Virginia would soon come to realize, the poll tax issue was inextricably linked to race. Poll taxes were instituted after Reconstruction with the main goal of disenfranchising blacks. State standards differed, but most poll taxes were cumulative, meaning that anyone registering for the first time had to pay not only that year's tax but the tax for every year since the voter became eligible. This alone eliminated many voters, including poor whites. Since the advent of poll taxes, voting rates in Southern states had steadily declined. In 1940 Southern writer George C. Stoney published an article on the poll tax, "Suffrage in the South," which contrasted the overall voting rate in the United States—64 percent—with those in poll tax states.[2] Texas had the highest turnout, at 33.5 percent, and South Carolina the lowest, 14.1 percent. As a result, the South was ruled by a virtual oligarchy of planters and corporate interests—hardly a true democracy. In Stoney's words: "one-third democracy for one-sixth of the nation."

Most Southern states also administered various tests which were, in effect, forms of intimidation. Literacy tests were common and rarely enforced against white voters. Stoney wrote, "Electors are required to 'read, write and explain' any passage of the state constitution chosen by the registrar, who is the sole and final judge. Many Negro college

---

[2] An excerpt from "Suffrage in the South" spells out the practical effects of the poll tax in Alabama:

Eight people sitting on the porch down in Green Pond, Ala., were talking about the triple-A farm program and the chance [U.S. congressman from Alabama William] Bankhead has of replacing [Vice President John Nance] Garner on the 1940 ticket. Four wrinkled-faced farmers and their faded wives they were. Yes, they went to the Holiness Church, and they had the usual Alabama back-country hatred of the Negro, but they also read the newspapers and they knew what issues were in Congress. In other words, these ordinary Alabama poor whites were politically conscious. As for the chances of their getting into the political game:

"We might just as well be outside the fence a-lookin' through a knothole," the oldest one of the eight laughed. Only two of the eight voted—or could vote under Alabama's cumulative poll tax law. These two men had paid their $1.50 every year. A third had voted until the drought of 1933. With no election that year he saw no reason for putting out $1.50 he didn't have. Next year $3 was the price he had to pay to vote, and cotton was selling for 5 cents a pound. He couldn't spare that much. Now a vote for Bankhead in the Democratic primaries next spring will cost him $11.50. He won't vote. (For men the tax is cumulative from the age of twenty-one. Women pay from the time they first vote. In both cases the first vote is free.)

"Lord, that's jus' like me," his wife spoke up. "They drug me out and hauled me down when Bryan was arunnin' in '24. I hadn't voted since. Wonder what they'd charge me now?" We figured it out. It came to $22.50. "That's as much as I give fer that cook-stove yonder," she answered, "and hit'll last me a heap longer!"

In this community of 300 people, only twelve citizens could be named who "had the vote."

professors have been denied the ballot under such procedure. There are other hurdles for the Negro would-be voter. He may find himself in a line of people waiting to register—a line that never moves. Often this registrar tells him to go out and find some white man who will 'vouch' for him. . . . If all this fails to discourage, then intimidation often begins. As a result, the average Negro concludes: 'What is the use of starting trouble just to cast a vote in a meaningless election?'" Virginia recalled her own father coming home from work as a registrar, saying, "I swear to God, there was a damn nigger there today who had been to Harvard. Harvard, mind you! And, you know, you just couldn't hardly think of enough questions to ask him that he couldn't answer. But I did." It is no wonder that Virginia kept feeling drawn back into the fold of accepting racism and segregation: her family was intimately involved in upholding it.

Virginia's pivotal moments all hinge on personal relationships, and her friendship with Clark Foreman was an especially emotional one. While a student at the University of Georgia, Foreman had witnessed a horrible lynching and the experience had made him a passionate advocate of racial equality. Upon his arrival in D.C., he hired a black secretary, which Virginia said caused "an absolute storm throughout the whole government." When Clark visited the Durrs soon after, Virginia, still clinging to the notions of her upbringing, accused him of betraying his heritage.

> We got in the most awful fight you have ever known in your life. . . . He said, "You are just a white, Southern, bigoted, prejudiced, provincial girl." Oh, he just laid me out. I got furious and I said, "You are going back on all the traditions of the South. . . . What do you think of the Civil War? What did we stand for?" White supremacy, of course. When they left, Cliff said "Well, I don't think you'll ever see him again."

Actually, the Foremans invited them to dinner the following week and the two couples became close friends. Virginia's friendship with Clark played an important role in her ongoing political development. Clark and Virginia eventually realized that they were kindred spirits, both from traditional old Southern families, both gregarious, charming, and curious people and both willing to change their minds about the political notions they had grown up with. Clark was, she once wrote, "blood of my blood, bone of my bone." Foreman's Georgia boyhood had intimately acquainted him with racists and racism, so he understood Virginia's struggle and slow transformation.

At one of the Foremans' dinners, Durr met Mary McLeod Bethune,[3] the unofficial liaison between the New Deal and the black community. In Virginia's words, Bethune "looked like an African queen. A large woman, and homely, but with an air of grandeur. She always carried a stick engraved with her name that President Roosevelt had given her." Clearly the stick had social meaning for both Bethune and Durr and underscores, yet again, the pervasive influence of Eleanor Roosevelt, who had insisted that Bethune be given a prominent position. That night Virginia and Mary McLeod Bethune talked about the poll tax.

Virginia recalled that Bethune played a big role in convincing her to merge her poll tax activism with the fledgling civil rights movement. "You sweet Southern ladies are never going to get the laws changed. Your husbands have power, but *you* don't have any power," said Bethune, "and the only way you're going to get the right to vote is to line up with the blacks. . . ." Through Bethune, Virginia got to know other politically active black women, notably Mary Church Terrell.[4] As they talked, they discovered that Virginia Durr's grandfather had been a good friend of Mary Church Terrell's grandfather, who was white and who had taken the unusual step of providing for his illegitimate black children. Terrell, poised, intelligent, and honest, made a big impression on Virginia. Although Virginia's mother had taught her that black women must never be called ladies, she saw that Bethune and Terrell "were ladies in every sense of the word."

Inadvertently, the legislators she lobbied also encouraged Virginia to make the connection between civil rights and ending the poll tax.

---

[3] Bethune was a teacher who founded the Daytona Normal and Industrial Institute for Negro Girls (now Bethune-Cookman College) and became instrumental in the black women's club movement. During the Roosevelt administration, she was director of Negro affairs in the National Youth Administration from 1936 to 1944 and also advised the president on African-American issues.

[4] Terrell, born in Memphis the same year as Ida B. Wells, was herself a remarkable public servant. She, along with Wells-Barnett, was present at the 1909 convention that founded the NAACP (unlike Wells-Barnett, she was invited to be on the Committee of Forty). Later she spoke out for suffrage and for an end to segregation.

One particularly striking moment occurred when she escorted a group from the Mississippi Women's Society for Christian Service to visit Senator Eastland as part of their efforts to lobby against the poll tax:

> It was hot summer and they were all dressed like the ladies in Mississippi and Alabama dress, which I think is very pretty— light voile dresses, white shoes, white gloves, white beads, and white hats with flowers on them. They looked very lovely, I thought—very Women's Society. . . . Everything started off very pleasantly until they came to the poll tax. . . . [Senator Jim] Eastland jumped up. His face turned red. He's got these heavy jowls like a turkey and they began to turn purple. And he screamed out, "I know what you women want—black men lay- ing on you!" That's exactly what he said. . . . It was so embar- rassing to these ladies that their Senator had said such a thing.

The La Follette Hearings

In the summer of 1938, Virginia became fascinated by the hearings held by Wisconsin's senator Robert La Follette to expose and address the oppressive, often violent, tactics used against workers who tried to bargain collectively. Many of the tactics were the same as those used in Mother Jones's day: firing union members, attacking organizers, secur- ing injunctions against organizing or meeting, evicting workers and their families. According to a study commissioned by La Follette's com- mittee, during the years 1934 through 1936, big industries spent over $80 million to crush union efforts. In addition to practicing espionage, the owners often amassed weapons and established a campaign of sys- tematic intimidation.

Virginia was amazed at the power the plant owners and operators exercised over their workers. These "nice looking men with white hair . . . would say 'But we started the town,' and La Follette would say, 'But you bought all these guns and machine guns and killed all these people at the strike.'" And they would respond with, in her words, "a bunch of pious lies." She was horrified and fascinated by the testimony: the violent clashes between union men and operators, the hired thugs willing to kill strikers. "You could just feel murder and death in that hearing room." In these hearings, Virginia saw the dynamics of economic power laid bare and finally understood the poverty she had seen around her as a child. "This is where I got my education," she said.

Virginia also had another reason to immerse herself in these hearings. That spring, the Durrs' three-year-old son had died of a burst appendix. The doctors had not diagnosed the appendicitis correctly and, with penicillin not yet available, it was hopeless. "I was terribly depressed and the La Follette hearings diverted me," she recalled. "It was an exciting summer and it did take my mind off my little boy's death, at least during the day."

When the hearings turned to the Tennessee Coal, Iron and Railroad Company (TCI), the most powerful employer in the industrial center of Birmingham, Virginia was horrified to learn that some of her family's friends were on the company committee formed to keep out labor organizers. She immediately sent telegrams to "these high-class gentlemen" informing them of what she had learned in the hearing and asking whether they had anything to do with it. In return, she received sheepish letters that, as she recalled it, read, "I can assure you that our only objective has been to maintain law and order and we had nothing in the wide world to do with all this shooting and killing and holding incommunicado."

The hearings' star witness was Joseph Gelders, a fellow Alabamian. Gelders had been a physics teacher at the University of Alabama, initially apolitical but increasingly distressed by the horrific poverty around Tuscaloosa. Early in the Depression, under a controversial policy promulgated by the Agricultural Adjustment Act and designed to create scarcity and drive up prices paid to farmers, the government ordered the slaughter of livestock and the destruction of crops. Gelders thought the policy was wrongheaded, and Virginia agreed: "Killing pigs when people were hungry and plowing up cotton when they didn't have anything to wear seemed irrational." Gelders began reading up on economics and political philosophy and holding meetings in his home. During a trip to New York, he met with some more radical groups, contacted the Communist Party, and resolved to do something to help alleviate the suffering he saw back home.

Upon his return to Alabama, Gelders began organizing sharecroppers, who had nothing to eat and barely anything to wear, and whose children suffered from rickets, pellagra, and hookworm.[5] The local antiunionists swiftly and viciously targeted him. One night, on his way home, he was picked up and taken over the mountain by a group of men. They stripped him, beat and kicked him relentlessly, and left him for dead. He managed to crawl to the roadside, where someone picked him up and took him to the hospital. Gelders's testimony was central to the hearings and he impressed everyone not only with his resilience but also with his thoughtfulness and courtesy.

Virginia was riveted and inspired by this tale of a man enduring such abuse for his efforts to help the very people whose suffering she had consciously ignored as a girl. "A child who's shaking all over with rickets because he doesn't get any calcium is a pretty horrible sight . . . I was in my twenties before I woke up to it, and it had been right around me all the time," she recalled. Through the hearings and her growing friendship with Gelders, Virginia came to see the links between the civil rights movement and the labor movement, both opposed by a power structure intent on keeping the poor divided, dependent, and fearful. The man who was said to be the ringleader of the Gelders beating, Walter "Crack" Hanna, went from being the head of the U.S. Steel private police force to leading the Alabama National Guard. Hanna had taken over as chief of the U.S. Steel force after his predecessor, Eugene "Bull" Connor, was elected police commissioner of Birmingham. (Twenty years later, Connor would shock the world with his brutal reaction to nonviolent protesters.)

The political climate was so charged that it became risky to express any liberal views on race. Even the idealist Hugo Black, then a United States senator, was intimidated. "Hugo encouraged me all he could to do what I was doing, trying to get rid of the poll tax and work

---

[5] All three conditions are linked to poverty and deprivation. Rickets, caused by a lack of vitamin D, softens and weakens the bones, often resulting in permanently bowed legs. One of the most common sources of vitamin D is cow's milk, but poorer families could not afford to keep a cow or buy milk. Pellagra, a B-vitamin deficiency, causes sores and rashes on the face, trunk, and arms; pale, bleached-looking skin and hair; and severe depression. Sufferers can develop pica, a compulsion to eat dirt. Poor Southerners' diet of salt pork, cornmeal mush, and crude molasses lacked sufficient B vitamins. Varying the diet or simply adding brewer's yeast readily cures pellagra, but this wasn't widely accepted by physicians until 1937. Hookworm is spread through fecal contact. In places with inadequate privies, or none, the parasites can burrow in through bare feet. A severe infestation causes anemia and exhaustion. These diseases, their causes and symptoms, helped contribute to outsiders' stereotype of the South as unhealthy and alien, its inhabitants lazy and dull-witted.

with the Democratic Women's Committee, but publicly he never took a stand," Durr recalled. The political leaders in the Democratic National Committee ordered the Women's Division of the DNC to hold off on the campaign against the poll tax because it was upsetting many Southerners in the New Deal coalition.

Virginia, with newfound resolve, began to employ her unusual talent for friendship to find and connect allies who did want to fight the poll tax. The first lady was part of the social network she cultivated. Eleanor Roosevelt biographer Blanche Wiesen Cook writes that "in the spring and summer of 1938, some of ER's happiest days were spent with Aubrey Williams' extended circle of Southern liberals and race radicals who met regularly in the home of Alabama's Clifford and Virginia Durr."

The Southern Conference on Human Welfare

Eleanor Roosevelt, who had also been moved by the story of Joseph Gelders, became a major supporter of the organization that became the most significant platform for Virginia Durr to take her fight back home: the Southern Conference on Human Welfare (SCHW). The SCHW was the brainchild of Lucy Randolph Mason, a native Virginian from an aristocratic family who was a passionate New Dealer.

A close confidante of the first lady, Mason was especially focused on eradicating the oppression of labor in the South and had been working with the Congress of Industrial Organizations (CIO). Mason and Gelders made an especially shrewd pitch to the Roosevelts: that it was in their political interest to promote the cause of labor in the South, specifically with regard to the poll tax. Mason wrote to Eleanor: "The only hope for progressive democracy in the South lies in the lower economic groups—particularly the wage earner. The power holding group, meaning the capitalists and manufacturers and business men, are distinctly reactionary and as a rule opposed to the present Administration [but] among the rank and file . . . both in cities and on the land, the president is adored. Yet this is a group so largely disenfranchised by the poll tax requirements of eight Southern states." Having convinced the Roosevelts, Gelders and Mason brought the idea to Virginia Durr, who enthusiastically joined and began planning the SCHW's first meeting in Birmingham.

FDR had specifically endorsed the idea of putting the poll tax on the

SCHW's agenda, but neither he nor the organizers of the conference were prepared to directly address the issue of segregation. As Diane McWhorter describes in *Carry Me Home*, the conference organizers went South hopefully, intent on building a coalition of various New Dealers, such as union members, liberal political clubs, church groups, and public-works employees, to work together on race and labor issues under the organizational sponsorship of John Lewis's CIO. "But Gelders and the other southerners should have recognized the folly of thinking they could win their region's hearts and minds without confronting its soul of racism," McWhorter writes, "especially in the place that was the country's laboratory of segregation, Birmingham."[6]

I think Durr, a hometown girl, must have realized that they were bound to confront racism; that understanding makes her energetic work in organizing the conference all the more impressive. In preparation, Durr helped organize the conference agenda, putting together reports on the poll tax and on Southern coverage of the La Follette hearings. In 1938 the Southern Conference for Human Welfare held its first meeting in Birmingham, Alabama. The first night, November 20, left Virginia "full of love and hope." Bankers mingled with sharecroppers, blacks with whites. The keynote speaker was Frank Graham, president of the University of North Carolina, who declared "The black man is the primary test of American Christianity and democracy. . . . Repression, whether it be of the Negro, Catholic, Jew or laborer, is the way of frightened power."

The next morning "frightened power" arrived with a vengeance. Bull Connor, then the public safety commissioner and the main enforcer of segregation, had announced that anyone who defied Birmingham's segregation statutes would be arrested. After several integrated workshops, the conference attendees convened at the Municipal Auditorium and found it surrounded by black Marias, the large vehicles used to transport arrestees. Connor had driven a peg into the front lawn, tied a string to it, and threaded the string through the doors of the auditorium and down the central aisle, commanding that the blacks sit on one side and the whites on the other.

In one of the most striking moments in United States history, First

---

[6] McWhorter recounts a joke from that time, about a black man in Chicago who woke up and told his wife that Jesus had come to him in a dream and told him to go to Birmingham. His wife asked, "Did Jesus say he'd go with you?" The man replied, "He said he'd go as far as Memphis."

Lady Eleanor Roosevelt sat in the black section and was told to move by the Alabama police. Then, as Virginia recalled, "she got a little folding chair and put it in the middle of the aisle." Although many joined the first lady in resisting the order, Connor succeeded in bullying the conference into segregating itself. One attendee, Communist labor leader Hosea Hudson, remarked years later that if a few powerful whites had stood up to Connor, "All that stuff that Reverend King and them went through trying to break down segregation, what they had to suffer, and some people's murder, could have been stopped that day." We'll never know.

Amazingly, the mainstream press did not even cover this moment. The *New York Times* account focused on the economic reforms called for at the conference, the inclusion of grassroots organizations rather than outside experts, the first lady's busy schedule that day, and the president's supportive letter. In the lead paragraph, the reporter described the conference as a "determined attack on the difficulties and misfortunes which recently have led to the designation of this region as the nation's No. 1 problem."

A very brief *Washington Post* article headlined "'Jim Crow' Issue in Welfare Group" stated blandly, "A controversy over segregation of colored and white delegates enlivened sessions of the Southern Conference for Human Welfare today after the group's race relations section adopted a resolution demanding suspension of 'Jim Crow' laws." The next day's *New York Times* ran a similar article, noting a resolution passed opposing Jim Crow laws and expressing "disapproval of the action of Birmingham city officials in rigidly enforcing separation ordinances." Only the black press saw the incident for what it was. The weekly *Afro-American* ran an editorial about the first lady's actions: "If the people of the South do not grasp this gesture, we must. Sometimes actions speak louder than words."

The SCHW adopted thirty-six resolutions, including one demanding that the four falsely accused "Scottsboro boys"[7] who remained in

---

[7] In March 1931 nine young black men riding a freight train from Chattanooga to Memphis were accused of raping two white women in the same boxcar. While the train was in north Alabama, a mounted posse blocked the tracks and captured the accused, loaded them on a flatbed truck, and drove to Scottsboro, Alabama. The men narrowly escaped lynching when Alabama governor B. M. Miller ordered out the National Guard. The Scottsboro case became an ongoing legal circus. Although the evidence against them was dubious and one of the alleged victims recanted and became a defense witness, all nine defendants were convicted. They served significant time in prison before being vindicated.

The Durrs in 1941 after Clifford was sworn in as an FCC Commissioner: (l-r) Virginia, Tilla, Clifford, Lucy, Ann (courtesy Ann Durr Lyon)

prison be freed; several calling for more public funding of housing, educational institutions, and public facilities used by blacks; and even one prescribing integrated SCHW meetings. Virginia herself made a speech that didn't directly mention segregation but reflected her path to the cause of civil rights: she decried the South's poor educational system and demanded more honest reporting, instead of the collusion between "the huge propaganda machine" of business and the "controlled press."

The significance of all the challenges to Jim Crow that occurred at the meeting thrilled Virginia, and I surmise it was then and there that she experienced her final conversion to the fledgling civil rights movement. She was pleased when her new friend Mary McLeod Bethune caused a stir by insisting on being called "Mrs. Bethune" from the platform rather than "Mary," which is how she had been addressed by one white speaker. "That sounds like a small thing now but that was a big dividing line. A Negro woman in Birmingham, Alabama, was called Mrs. at a public meeting," Virginia later observed.

The conference ended with Hugo Black accepting the Thomas Jefferson Award. He described it as "a symbol confided to me for the many southerners who stand with Jefferson in the belief that good government must give first importance to promoting the welfare and happiness of all human beings by assuring equal justice to all and special consideration to none." Like Virginia, he avoided specifically mentioning the elephant in the room, but it was clear to all that he was referring to race.

"I can see that meeting now," Durr recalled many years later. "White on one side and black on the other and Mrs. Roosevelt and Hugo standing on the platform." Bull Connor had clearly won this battle, but the real war against segregation was about to begin. As McWhorter described it, the conference's "chief achievement would be its gift to posterity: It had initiated the key white players of the future civil rights movement—their names were Virginia and Clifford Durr, Aubrey Williams, Myles Horton, and James Dombrowski."

After the conference closed, the Alabama Democratic Women's Club called for an investigation of the event's financial sponsors, and Congressman Martin Dies of HUAC announced that a "committee agent" was investigating whether SCHW was "inspired by Communists." Despite the threatened opposition, the SCHW continued to organize events, focusing more and more on race issues. The group succeeded in integrating a hotel in Washington, D.C., by hosting a dinner for none other than Justice Hugo Black, with an integrated guest list. Virginia helped to organize the dinner, cultivating support from both Republicans and Democrats. "Of course, a lot of Republicans backed us in order to create friction within the Democratic party, because the poll tax issue always split the Southern Democrats from the rest of the party," she explained. Virginia's social savvy was crucial to navigating these crosscurrents: "I have always been more personal than ideological. I like people for themselves more than I do for their ideas. Sometimes they change their opinions and take on what I regard as crazy ideas, but I don't throw them off and say they're heretics. I like to agree with people, but I don't mind disagreeing with them."

Although she was now comfortable supporting integration, Virginia's interest in voting rights was still at the center of her activism. As Southern conservatives continued to resist giving up control of the polls, Virginia became more determined to defeat them, and more certain that her values coincided with those of the integrationists.

After the Birmingham meeting, the SCHW began serious work on the poll tax issue. Virginia did the networking in Washington while Gelders organized out in the field. In 1939 they succeeded in convincing Congressman Lee Geyer of California—who was, according to Virginia, "a lovely man and a great student of American history"—to introduce a bill ending the poll tax. The head of the Judiciary Committee was Hatton Sumners of Texas, "the epitome of the Southern conservative," who did everything possible to block it. Another Texas congressman, Maury Maverick, a member of the SCHW and chair of the poll tax committee, succeeded in getting a hearing for the bill. The evidence in support of repeal was overwhelming. Even though Sumners prevented the hearings from being printed (and Maury Maverick was defeated in the next election), the bill finally passed the House.

In 1941 SCHW's poll tax committee was spun off as a separate entity, the National Committee to Abolish the Poll Tax, or NCAPT. Virginia had assembled a broad coalition—labor unions, the NAACP, the Negro Elks, many Christian organizations and churches, several women's organizations, Bethune's Council of Negro Women, and, for a while, the White House. Virginia was a natural at coalition building because of her ability to charm and connect with virtually anyone. "I had no money and no power but I got along with the disparate groups who were backing the anti-poll tax bill." Soon the poll tax coalition had more members than the SCHW.

Both SCHW and the poll tax committee soon drew the attention of the growing horde of red-baiters. At first this was just an "irritating diversion" from what was generally a time of hope and progress. Even when Martin Dies, another congressman from Texas, became chairman of the newly organized Special Committee to Investigate Un-American Activities, Virginia and her friends didn't take it seriously. "He even called Shirley Temple a Communist . . . it was just so stupid," she recalled.

Several people approached Virginia with lists of alleged Communists in her organizations, demanding that they be expelled. There were some Communists in the SCHW, but they were by no means advocating an overthrow of the government. In fact, their main issue was voting rights—the basis of a functional democracy. But the Dies committee and other conservative institutions, such as the Constitutional Education League, an industry-funded source of propaganda, discredited the whole conference by equating it with Communism and singled out Virginia herself for attack. When Tennessee senator Kenneth McKellar[8] filibustered the poll tax bill in the Senate, he condemned her by name. Durr recalled, "Well, McKellar got up on the Senate floor and you never heard such carrying on about me. Here I was a flower of the Old South and my grandfather had been the congressman from Memphis and my uncle had been Ham Patterson, the governor of Tennessee, and why in the world would a woman like that turn into a—I think he called me a Communist, a nigger-loving Communist."

The campaign took its toll and key supporters started to distance themselves from both SCHW and NCAPT. I imagine there were some who were committed to the New Deal agenda and to racial justice, yet backed away because they did not want to threaten a winning coalition by association with the people who had been successfully smeared. Those on the right exploited this dynamic and the Durrs were among those who were increasingly ostracized. "When these red-baiters get out to mow you down and destroy you, a lot of them may be dumb, but they really make a concerted effort. There is no doubt about that," Virginia said.

What resources remained of the SCHW were funneled into the Southern Conference Educational Fund (SCEF), which focused on ending segregation. Virginia worked with Louis Burnham (a black activist who once wore a turban to pass as a "foreigner" and thus be allowed to enter a segregated hotel) and Aubrey Williams to focus the efforts of the SCEF on voter registration. Virginia believed that it was crucial to get people to the polls, not only to achieve democracy,

---

[8] My family's favorite political story involves Senator McKellar, whom my grandfather successfully challenged in the 1952 Democratic primary. McKellar was an entrenched incumbent who served as chairman of the appropriations committee, and Gore was a young congressman. McKellar's campaign covered telephone poles, roadside trees, barns, and storefront windows with signs reading, "Thinking Feller/Vote McKellar." It was my grandmother, Pauline, who came up with the Gore campaign's response, posted underneath each one: "Think some more/And vote for Gore."

but to build a "countervailing force against the reactionary power in the South."

By now Virginia had begun to supplement her own personal understanding of the pathologies of the South by reading the works of W. J. Cash and C. Vann Woodward, both of whom published rich, insightful accounts that combined sociology and history. She met Woodward in the late 1930s, shortly after he published *Tom Watson: Agrarian Rebel*, which detailed the biracial Populist coalition of the 1890s. The two became lifelong friends and correspondents. Woodward's interpretation of the Populist heritage of the South gave Virginia and many Southern New Dealers hope that their region would put prejudices aside in favor of common interest in social progress. She wrote to him, "I have an invincible belief that if the right people ever get together something is bound to happen."

Instead, there was increasing pressure to drop the race issue in order to keep the Southerners in the New Deal coalition. When DNC chair James Farley (the same man who'd urged Roosevelt to deport Harry Bridges) ordered the Women's Division to cease all work on the poll tax issue, Virginia resigned in protest and continued working on the issue in Congressman Geyer's office.

Eleanor Roosevelt helped Durr find a Senate sponsor for the bill, Claude Pepper of Florida. But then, the Southern conservatives filibustered the bill and killed it. This was a major defeat and it was doubtful the bill would get another chance. Roosevelt himself had become reluctant to offend the Southern politicians he needed to support his push to enter World War II. Virginia, clearly moved by the news of the atrocities in Europe, was totally in favor of fighting against Hitler. While she understood the new political dynamics, she was still disappointed when F.D.R. transformed himself, as she put it, "from Dr. New Deal to Dr. Win-the-War."

She recalled one meeting at the White House with Eleanor Roosevelt. "She had us out for tea on the south portico overlooking the Washington Monument and she couldn't have been more gracious and sweet and kind." Mrs. Roosevelt asked what she could do to help with the anti–poll tax effort. After a brief conversation, she excused herself, saying, "Before we go any further, I think I had better speak to Franklin and see what his ideas are." Upon her return, she looked very upset. "She said that as far as Franklin was concerned he wasn't going to touch the poll tax with a ten foot pole and she couldn't have any open part in it either."

"A Strange Household"

Through her lively social circle in Washington, Virginia became friends with Jessica "Decca" Mitford[9] and her husband, Esmond Romilly, in 1939. The couple had just arrived in the United States from Spain, where he'd fought with the Republicans against Franco. The next year, when Esmond left to join the Canadian Air Force, he asked Virginia to look after Decca. Virginia was scheduled to go to Chicago for the 1940 Democratic convention, where she'd appear before the platform committee and lobby for the poll tax issue. Reluctantly, she took Decca along. On the drive to Chicago, they kept having to pull over for Mitford, who was stricken with terrible morning sickness. The situation didn't improve when they arrived in Chicago. Virginia later said, "They didn't have air-conditioning then, and the coliseum must have been 110 degrees in the shade. It was horribly hot, and the ladies' room was just miles away. So I said to [Texas congressman] Maury Maverick, 'You know, I've got a young English girl with me who throws up all the time. What in the name of God are we going to do?' Maury had on a great big hat, a sombrero, made out of really fine felt. So he went over and swept off his hat like Sir Walter Raleigh and said to Decca, 'Madame, use my hat if you need it.' Well, Decca said she felt like Queen Elizabeth. . . . Fortunately, she didn't throw up in his hat, but she kept it in her lap all the time."

---

[9] There were six daughters in the aristocratic, eccentric Mitford family. Jessica ran off with Esmond Romilly, Winston Churchill's notoriously "red" nephew; she later became a journalist and wrote several books of nonfiction, the best-known of which is *The American Way of Death*, a scathing examination of the funeral industry. Diana married a Guinness heir, then left him for the leader of the British Union of Fascists; the two were imprisoned during World War II and Pamela, the "quiet sister," took in Diana's two children. Unity became friendly with Hitler, Goebbels, and other prominent Nazis; when England joined the war against the Axis, she attempted suicide by shooting herself in the head and remained a semi-invalid for the remainder of her life. The oldest Mitford sibling, Nancy, wrote several witty and sharp novels that drew on her family, notably *Pursuit of Love* and *Love in a Cold Climate*, as well as several other books. The youngest daughter, Deborah, married a duke and wrote two books that mixed memoir with tales of restoring her husband's family estate. The only son, Tom, was killed in World War II.

Despite the rocky start, the two had "the greatest time you can imagine." They began referring to the baby-to-be as Dinky Donk, in honor of the Democratic mascot, and the nickname stuck. (Though the girl was officially named Constancia at birth, she was always called Dinky Donk, or Dink.) Virginia and Decca got along so well that Decca moved in with the Durrs while awaiting her husband's return. Soon after the baby's birth and just before the United States entered the war, Esmond was killed in combat. Needing comfort and support, Mitford and her daughter remained with the Durrs.

The Durrs had a full house throughout the war. They had three girls, and Virginia's mother moved in with the family during what Virginia called a "bout of melancholia" and "wept and wept all the time." Virginia, hearing about a Japanese butler named Mr. Yamasaki who'd been fired because of his nationality, immediately offered to take him in, not realizing he had a wife and son. She made room for the entire family, and Decca hired the Japanese woman to be Dinky Donk's nanny. "We had a strange household. My little girl Tilla and Decca's little girl Dinky Donk and the little Japanese boy Hiroshi, all called Cliff 'Daddy.'"

The Durrs' Japanese guests combined with Decca's complicated and contradictory family background must have aroused suspicion. Add the Durrs' involvement in the civil rights movement, and it's no wonder the FBI visited the house on a regular basis. "They were always two big old dumb goofs who wanted to look around and see if there were any aerials and if we were transmitting messages to the Japanese." They even raided Mr. Yamasaki's personal belongings (revealing a stash of girlie photos—"I thought [he] would die in his tracks") and seized his camera for the duration of the war. "It got to the point where the children would cry out, 'Mama, milkman's here. Mama, laundryman's here. Mama, FBI's here.'"

Durr seemed to relish all of these colorful characters in her home, and these were apparently happy, if hectic, years. A favorite family story describes Vice President Henry Wallace's visit to the Seminary Hill house to see Clifford Durr, at home during one of his frequent bouts of severe back pain. Virginia, never a fastidious housekeeper, prepared by getting the vacuum out of the closet and clearing a path from the front door up the stairs to the bedroom. Lucy wistfully recalls her "involved but distracted" mother, and it's clear that all Virginia's daughters sometimes longed for her to pay more attention to them. Lucy remembers her mother's response to a question about why she didn't behave like the other mothers they knew, keeping house and baking cookies: "I suppose I could be like those mothers in Germany who were baking cookies while children were being burned in ovens!" Lucy says, "We probably just thought, 'oh, there she goes again.'"

Virginia's daughters can trace the connection between their mother's political activism and the increasing chaos in their home. Listening to the oldest sister, Ann, describe how Virginia made smocked dresses for her in Birmingham, the younger three looked at each other in shock, thinking, "We were lucky to have clean underwear!"

Jessica Mitford's description of her first encounters with Virginia captures not only her domestic eccentricities but also her intense charisma. A friend took Mitford to a breakfast attended by several New Dealers, where

> I sat next to a tall southern woman in a huge white hat. She introduced herself to me as Virginia Durr. She spoke in a sort of soft scream [and] her approach to conversation was that of the frontal attack. As soon as she learned I was English, she fired question after question at me:
>
> "Well, what in the world do you think of Mr. Chamberlain? I think he's just poifectly awful . . . Whereabouts did you live in England? I've always been so fascinated by English country life! What in the world did you do all day long? How much do youall pay your servants in England? What does steak and kidney pie taste like? I just adore Jane Austen, and Cranford, and I would so love to go to England some day . . ."
>
> I was a little ruffled by the insistent barrage. . . . Mrs. Durr made me feel outnumbered, as though I were being cornered by a roomful of reporters.

The Durrs invited Decca and Esmond to dinner the following night and Virginia greeted them exuberantly:

> "Why, I'm so absolutely delighted that youall could come! Cliff, honey, go get them a drink. Come on in, and meet Lucy and Baby Sister." She led us into the drawing-room, one end of which was filled with a tangled mass of small children. Mrs.

Durr strode among them, sorting them out, and produced Lucy, a beautiful little blond child of two. Baby Sister, a new-born infant, was kicking placidly in a pram in another corner of the room. . . .

Mrs. Durr settled down for some more inexorable questioning, completely oblivious of the bedlam which filled the room. Occasionally an extra loud wail would produce some reaction: "My Lord! Children, won't youall please keep quiet and play nicely . . ." Eventually, without any particular prompting, the children gradually dispersed and Lucy stumped off to bed. In the unnatural quiet that followed it was noticed that Baby Sister had been crying for some time ("My lands! We forgot to feed Baby Sister!"). She was quickly pacified with a bottle, and the grown-up conversation proceeded without further interruption. . . .

Listening to [Virginia and Esmond] talk, I already began to form a different view of Mrs. Durr. She was a real spellbinder, I decided, whose peculiar charm lay in her enormous curiosity about people, her driving passion to find out things, to know about details and motives, to trace big events to their small human beginnings. No wonder she loved Jane Austen!

The Truman Years

After 1945, in the wake of F.D.R.'s death and during the increasingly conservative postwar years, the progressive movement began to collapse, and the SCHW and NCAPT with it. "The poll tax committee died the same way the Roosevelt coalition died, the way the whole liberal movement of the United States died," explained Virginia. "It became exclusively anti-communistic. The red-baiting had been happening from the beginning of the conference in 1938, but it got worse and worse." The FBI infiltrated both organizations, which Durr took with her usual good humor. "We were always having strange young men come in saying they wanted to be volunteers. . . . The first thing they would always want to do when they came in was to get hold of the mailing list. We would not only give it to them, but we'd say we'd appreciate their making several hundred copies of it because we needed more copies to send out all over the country. This was in the days before photocopying machines, of course, so these young men would work for hours on end cranking out mimeograph copies."

With impressive clarity of vision, Virginia consistently stood up to the red-baiters. "My position on the Communists is as it has always been," she later explained, "that they represent the extreme left of the political circuit, and I often disagree with their programs and methods. But I see so clearly that when one group of people is made untouchable the liberties of all suffer, and our Democracy is on the way to ruin. I see and feel so clearly how it has crippled the lives and hopes of both the Negro and white people of the South." Virginia not only felt that tolerance of dissent was essential in a civilized society, she acted on those feelings, raising her own voice and defending those outside the mainstream.

While Virginia refused to be drawn into the purging mania, the tide was against her. Eleanor Roosevelt left the SCHW in 1946. The CIO banned all unions that did not bar Communists, and when the SCHW and the NCAPT refused to conduct a purge, it too ended its participation. Soon, the organizations' membership dwindled to "left-wing unions, the civil rights organizations, and some of the religious organizations. . . . We stood by our principles but people didn't stand by us," Virginia lamented.

In 1941 Clifford Durr started a new job as an attorney for the Federal Communications Commission. He remained there until 1947, when President Truman succumbed to the political pressure and issued an executive order establishing a loyalty oath for all government employees and setting up a loyalty review board with broad powers to question employees accused of suspicious activities or associations. Truman was well aware of the possibilities for abuse but went forward, hoping to stave off the worst (perhaps by appointing ethical commissioners such as Frances Perkins). He wrote his wife, "If I can prevent [it], there'll be no NKVD [Soviet Secret Police] or Gestapo in this country. Edgar Hoover's organization would make a good start toward a citizen spy system. Not for me."

In *The White South and the Red Menace*, George Lewis examines the activities of segregationists during the civil rights era, especially their red-baiting and their policy of "massive resistance." According to Lewis, Truman's loyalty program legitimized suspicions that the fight for civil rights was inextricably linked with Communism, giving

the idea the federal government's stamp of authority. Defendants before the Loyalty Review Board might be asked what they thought
about the Red Cross policy of segregating blood donations by race,
whether they'd ever invited blacks into their home, or even about the
books and records they owned.

Virginia recalled, "If the investigators found anything in your past
or your present that made you suspect at all, you came up before the
committee, which was composed of leading citizens. But you were accused by nameless people. The committee wouldn't say John Jones
who lives at 1727 Oak Street saw you at a meeting of the Spanish War
Relief back in 1936 and what do you say to that. If you'd ever been *for*
Republican Spain, you were tainted. They would say T-17, a confidential informant of the FBI in whom we have the utmost trust, says that
you were at this meeting."

Clifford Durr refused to take the oath or administer it to his employees and I imagine this was one of the instances where Virginia's
fiery resolve and good sense of humor sustained him. "Cliff went to
see Truman and told him that he could not accept reappointment for
the FCC and that he was against the loyalty oath," Virginia recalled.
"Truman told him that he was just trying to get ahead of [New Jersey
congressman] Parnell Thomas, who was then head of the Un-American
Activities Committee." The committee had become a vehicle for enemies of the New Deal to discredit its leaders. In retrospect, Truman
acknowledged that the entire loyalty oath enterprise was a mistake, a
"terrible" idea.

Virginia herself was so disappointed with Truman that she actively
supported Progressive Party presidential candidate Henry Wallace, an
aggressive critic of Truman's Cold War policies. She also threw her
own hat in the ring as the Progressive Party candidate for the Senate,
challenging the firmly entrenched Harry Byrd. This was one of many
times Virginia's activism caused tension with her brother-in-law, then
a Supreme Court justice. "Uncle Hugo was sometimes anxious about
Mother's involvement, worried that it would taint him," explains Lucy.
Though Hugo Black and the Durrs remained close after Josephine's
death, this tension continued, flaring up when Virginia made her most
daring public stands.

It was clear that her campaign never stood a serious chance, but it
gave her a platform to speak out about racial equality and strong pub-

lic education. She had come to such a clear, personally informed view of these issues that it must have been frustrating to have lost the footing that the SCHW and NCAPT had given her in the national debate.

After leaving the FCC, Cliff set up a private practice in Washington, D.C. His first client was Roy Patterson, a World War II veteran who'd been wounded and decorated for valor and bravery. Having taken a government job, Patterson was forced to go through the loyalty oath process. He was fired because he frequented the Washington Book Shop, which sold Marxist books and ran an integrated coffee shop. Patterson explained to the committee that the shop sold cheap, interesting records and he liked the fact that blacks and whites drank coffee together. As Virginia later put it: "A member of the committee asked, 'Why in the world would you, a Texas boy, want to drink coffee with Negroes?' . . . He responded that in the war he fought beside Negroes and came to realize that they're just like everybody else, human beings." Clifford got his client's job back, but Patterson was again brought before the board and fired. "It just stirred Cliff up terribly." The large corporate clients Clifford was expecting avoided him after the publicity surrounding the Patterson case, recalled Virginia. "So our income began to go down, down, down."

Yet Clifford continued to take the loyalty board cases. "Cliff would come home and throw up and have sick headaches. It made him not only furious but sick." The Supreme Court affirmed the board's practices, even though use of anonymous informants made a fair hearing impossible. "Hugo and Bill Douglas dissented in the cases that went to the Supreme Court but all the cases were confirmed anyway. . . . The Court upheld faceless informers; it upheld loyalty orders; it upheld people being fired because some FBI agent, whose name wasn't revealed, said they had been at a meeting of the Spanish War Relief. It just got worse and worse," Virginia lamented.

In 1949 Clifford Durr became president of the National Lawyers Guild, an organization started by New Dealers as an alternative to the then-conservative American Bar Association. The guild was committed to challenging Cold War abuses of civil liberties, and Durr was happy to have it as a base. When California congressman Richard Nixon launched an attack on the guild, using information provided by the FBI, Clifford was put under surveillance, which would continue for twenty years. He also had been teaching a class at Princeton but was fired when some alumni found out about his connections and, according to Virginia, "had fits." At this point the Durrs were struggling to make ends meet, so while Clifford looked for work, Virginia taught English to bring in some cash. Her pupils included the Romanian ambassador and several Czech and Polish diplomats.

By this time, Ann had graduated from college and was working at Hull House. The Durrs' three younger daughters were still at home: Lucy was in high school, Tilla in junior high, and the youngest, Lulah, was a toddler. Worried about what the future might hold, Virginia wrote to Ann, "I am frankly terrified of going to Alabama. I think I could manage all right, but only by suppressing myself constantly and conforming to a pattern which I think is utterly evil." More understated than his wife, as always, Clifford wrote, "Independence of mind can be an expensive luxury."

Denver

In 1950 Clifford got a new job as general counsel of the Farmer's Union Insurance Corporation and the Durrs moved to Denver, Colorado, where the union was headquartered. Virginia was always more at home in the world of people than "in the world of nature," but she was happy to have a decent home and steady income.

They were still settling in and adjusting when, in spring 1951, Virginia received a mailing from renowned chemist and peace activist Linus Pauling, circulating a petition opposing American bombing in North Korea. Virginia didn't think the petition was radical, or her signing of it brave or even noteworthy. She wrote later, "It seemed to me that no one who had any sense would want to bomb above the Yalu and get in a war with China. I wrote on the answering card that I did not believe in bombing above the Yalu and signed my name and sent the card off. I never thought anything more about it. I never even told Cliff about it."

Days later the *Denver Post* ran a story headlined, "Wife of General Counsel of Farmer's Union Insurance Corporation Signs Red Petition." Clifford's boss immediately called Virginia and demanded that she withdraw her support of the American Peace Crusade and publicly repudiate it and its leaders. He'd already had a retraction letter written up for her to sign and read it to her over the phone. Virginia's recollection of the letter illustrates how mad it made her:

> Dear Sir,
> In reply to the article which was published this morning in the paper I want to say that I have been duped by the Reds. And I am sorry, and I beg your pardon. I did not know it was a Red petition. Please forgive me. I'm just a poor weak woman and my husband's been sick. If you'll just realize that I'm an idiot and a fool, and I'm just crawling on my hands and knees, everything will be all right—I hope.

While Virginia was trying to decide what to do, her husband came "hobbling up the walk" on his crutches. (He'd just returned to work after recovering from back surgery.) His boss had shown him the letter and explained that if Clifford didn't convince his wife to sign it, he'd be fired. With characteristic loyalty and conviction, Clifford simply said he'd never allow his wife to sign such a letter, and walked out.

Back to Alabama

In May 1951 the Durrs traveled to Washington, D.C., for Ann's wedding to Walter Lyon. (The couple soon moved to Thailand, where Walter worked with the U.S. Public Health Service. In 1953, he was called back because of an unspecified problem with his security file; Virginia was certain it was because of his link to the Durrs.) After the wedding, Clifford and Virginia returned to Alabama, settling in Clifford's hometown of Montgomery. Clifford dryly welcomed the return: "I was so glad to get back to Alabama because here in Alabama I know who the sons-of-bitches are, but in Washington I so often got fooled." Virginia was glad to be back in familiar surroundings, where "I will hear the sound of rain again . . . my hair will curl again," but she also knew her life in the segregated South would be like "living in a closed room, simply struggling for air."

The Durrs would remain in Alabama for the rest of Clifford's life, though Virginia did travel as much as possible. During those decades, she kept in touch with friends through witty, impassioned, observant letters. Besides helping to open up the closed room and relieve the suffocating isolation she felt, those connections also allowed her to carry on in her effort to motivate and organize the front against segregation.

In Montgomery, Clifford opened a law practice and Virginia became his secretary. She resigned her organizational affiliations and political posts, not only because of time and money constraints, but also because they were living with Clifford's mother, who was very traditional and had always slightly disapproved of Virginia's activism. And, as Virginia admitted, they were simply tired and needed time to refuel. "Even in a battle, the wounded are entitled to some rest. . . . Our ammunition has plumb run out."

Despite his intention to settle into a noncontroversial practice, Clifford began representing poor blacks who'd been cheated and exploited by loan sharks and deceptive insurance policies, cases that obviously didn't pay well at all. "He took one of those cases all the way to the Supreme Court of the United States and got twenty-five dollars for it," Virginia recalled. Still, he persisted. These cases enraged and offended Clifford because the perpetrators were upstanding white businessmen. "Every time Cliff got one of those cases where a Negro had been cheated by an insurance company or secondhand automobile dealer, he felt a sense of shame, as a Southern white man, that anybody would treat helpless people that way." As he put it, echoing his wife's words, "I'm not basically an ideological person. But you move instinctively when you see somebody being kicked around."

Virginia's endless curiosity and sociability drew her into new friendships with an enormous array of people and she kept in touch with old friends, such as Aubrey and Anita Williams, and Jessica Mitford. During this time the Durrs also became close to E. D. Nixon, head of the Progressive Voters League and leader of the Alabama NAACP. Virginia appreciated Nixon's blunt, no-nonsense style: "When I called Mr. Nixon 'Ed' once, he told me in his usual flat-out manner, 'Don't ever call me "Ed" because I would be lynched if I called you "Virginia" and until I can call you by your first name, don't call me by mine.' Good advice." Through Nixon they met Rosa Parks, a seamstress and an officer of the local NAACP chapter. Virginia hired Parks to do some sewing for her, and the two became friends.

At this point Virginia's only active public effort for integration was her membership in the United Church Women, open to black and white members of any church in Montgomery; Coretta Scott King was among the members. "We used to meet and pray and sing and hold hands and have a cup of tea afterwards," Virginia recalled. During one meeting a local segregationist made note of the license plate numbers of the attendees. A few days later the women's names, telephone numbers, and addresses were published in his newsletter, *Sheet Lightning*.

The retribution was swift—harassing phone calls, threats, vandalism. Fearing loss of business, some men even took out ads in the paper disassociating themselves from their own wives or daughters. "That broke the group up. We never met after that."

Virginia felt increasingly isolated. "For so many years—so long that I had begun to take it for granted—I have been in communion with people that believed and worked for a solution to the ills of the world." Now she felt that she was "utterly cut off . . . I listen to the conversations here and it is sometimes like a long dirge." Then came the Eastland hearings.

The Eastland Hearings

"Nobody thought I was a Communist," explained Virginia. "Even Jim Eastland didn't think I was a Communist. He thought I was a 'fellow-traveler,' which was even more dangerous. The sin that Cliff and I committed in those days was that we weren't such *anti*-communists."

Virginia powdering her nose defiantly at the Eastland hearings in 1954. (courtesy Ann Durr Lyon)

And, of course, racial equality was associated with Communism in the minds of Southern conservatives. The Durrs' involvement in the Highlander Folk School must have played a role in feeding Eastland's ire, as he had publicly condemned the retreat as a Communist outpost. The *Nation* speculated that there may have been another motive for this attack on Virginia: "It would not be far-fetched to assume that the attack on Mrs. Durr, who had not been associated with the S.C.E.F. since 1950, was a crude attempt to get Justice Black to excuse himself in the impending Supreme Court decisions on segregation in the public schools." Whether or not that's true, Virginia's work for integration had made her many powerful enemies.

Shortly before the hearings opened, she made two phone calls, both intended to deflate the relevance of the hearing and embarrass Senator Eastland, and both reflective of the strong friendships that made her such an effective advocate. The first was to Lyndon Johnson, then the majority leader of the Senate. As she recalled it, "Lyndon got on the phone and I said, 'Lyndon, what are you doing sending those bloodhounds down here after Aubrey and me?'" and Johnson responded, "Why, honey, I don't know a thing about it." Virginia asked that if he couldn't stop the hearings, could he at least make sure that no Democrats attended. Johnson promised to do what he could.

She then called George Bender, a Republican congressman from Ohio and an ally in the fight against the poll tax, and asked him to keep the Republicans away. The hearings opened the next morning with only Eastland and the subcommittee lawyer in attendance. Virginia arrived with Clifford, who'd been suffering from heart and back problems but insisted on attending both as legal counsel to Aubrey Williams and Myles Horton and to support his wife. Clifford had originally planned to represent Virginia, too, but an old friend, a "very conservative" lawyer from Montgomery named John Kohn, insisted that he handle her defense.

Virginia was scheduled to testify on the second day of the hearing. After watching the first day's testimony, she was so furious that she stayed up late that night, preparing a statement to read from the stand. It began, "I have the highest respect for the investigatory powers of Congress. I think that's an important function. But from what I saw going on yesterday, this is not a proper exercise of Congressional powers—This is nothing but a kangaroo court. . . . I stand in utter and complete contempt of this committee."

As she took the stand, Virginia was told that she would not be allowed to read her statement into the record. Furious, she decided to remain silent, refusing even to exercise her Fifth Amendment rights. At first she planned to ignore all questions but, in deference to her brother-in-law Hugo Black, she answered an emphatic "no" when she was asked if she was a Communist or under Communist control. To all other questions, her answer was, "I stand mute." Eastland grew more and more frustrated, barking, "Answer that question!" Virginia played the untouchable Southern lady, occasionally taking out her compact and powdering her nose. Finally she was allowed to leave the stand.

Later that day an FBI informant named Paul Crouch swore he was a former Communist and knew Aubrey Williams and other witnesses from party meetings and planning sessions. Suddenly the questioning shifted to Clifford. Was he a Communist? Yes, Crouch said, Clifford was definitely a Communist, one of the leaders. Clifford insisted on being sworn in. He denied that he'd ever been a Communist, despite what Crouch said. Later he recalled the close of his testimony: "'Now, both of us are under oath, and it's your responsibility as chairman of this committee to see that one or the other of us is indicted for perjury.' Well, of course, nothing was ever done about it."

Another of the witnesses called before the committee was the Durrs' friend Myles Horton. Horton was a Tennessee native who first became interested in social change the summer before his senior year at Cumberland University, when he was sent to Ozone, Tennessee, to set up vacation Bible schools. It was 1927 and while the rest of the country seemed to be booming economically, Ozone was not. The area's resources—timber and coal—had been stripped and the people who remained seemed sunk in misery. Myles invited the parents of the children attending Bible school to talk about their concerns, which turned out to be eminently practical—getting a job, testing a well for typhoid, trying to replant clear-cut hillsides. Horton helped search out answers, often finding them within the community. This was the beginning of what would become the Highlander Folk School's philosophy: encourage people to express their concerns, help them focus their questions, and trust them to develop useful answers.

Two years later, at the Union Theological Seminary, theologian Reinhold Niebuhr had a profound influence on Horton just as he would on Martin Luther King Jr. John M. Glen, author of a history of Highlander, wrote, "[Horton] was drawn to Niebuhr's attacks on corporate capitalism and the flaccid idealism of the social gospel, his clear commitment to the interests of the working classes, his call for new forms of education, and his concern with the relationship between spiritual values and material welfare." When Horton decided to open a teaching center based on these ideas, Niebuhr encouraged him, providing crucial support and guidance. Highlander Folk School opened in 1932, in Monteagle, Tennessee.

For the first years of its existence, Highlander focused on labor issues, such as organizing and worker education. From the beginning, Horton was determined that Highlander be integrated, but it wasn't until 1944 that significant numbers of African-Americans attended the school. Gradually, desegregation and civil rights issues came to dominate the school's curriculum. By the time Horton was called before Eastland's committee, Highlander's fight against segregation had earned the school a nationwide reputation as a radical hotbed of agitators, subversives, and fellow-travelers.

Horton did not remain long on the witness stand. Immediately he and the attorney tangled over the relevance of the questions and Horton's insistence on explaining his answers. Finally Horton burst out, "Mr. Chairman, you listened to Communists and ex-Communists talk here—won't you listen to an American citizen talk?" As Eastland banged his gavel for order, Horton read aloud from a statement on civil rights by President Eisenhower until Eastland ordered him removed from the courtroom. As two U.S. marshals dragged him to the door, Horton shouted, "They're treating me like a criminal!" Then, to Eastland, "You are just putting on a show here, that's all!"

Toward the end of the week Crouch once again took the stand. This time he testified that he knew Virginia Durr as a "fellow traveler" who had helped pass state secrets to Communist spies, secrets Virginia had extracted from then–first lady Eleanor Roosevelt. As he left the stand he passed near Clifford, who suddenly snapped, jumping over the jury rail and lunging for Crouch, shouting, "You goddamn son of a bitch, I'll kill you for lying about my wife like that!" Clifford was removed by marshals and collapsed in the hallway, suffering a mild heart attack. In his history of the civil rights movement, Taylor Branch describes this as a breaking point for Durr's career: "The normally judicious Durr exploded in a rage . . . and photographs of guards restraining him landed on the front page of the *New York Times*. After that, Durr lost most of his remaining clients in Montgomery. He became a threadbare patrician, explaining patiently why he thought a confluence of events had reduced him to such a state."

After Clifford recovered he and Virginia returned home to Montgomery, Alabama, a place Virginia had come to think of as "enemy territory." The Durrs experienced a greater degree of social shunning, and their income suffered even more. "We had never had a big practice, but what we had began to slide away. I don't believe very many people thought Cliff and I were trying to overthrow the government by force and violence or that we were revolutionaries or Communists. They just didn't want to be touched by all the bad publicity." The Durrs' opposition to segregation had already made them suspect among their peers, and the Eastland hearing made them unfit for polite society. "It was like being peed on by a polecat," Virginia memorably declared.

Still, there was one benefit: "I was grateful that my cover as a nice, proper Southern lady was blown. . . . I could begin to say what I really thought." Virginia began attending political meetings again and got involved in the local NAACP.

Later, remembering the celebrations of Civil War veterans in her youth, she remarked, "I used to think it was funny that my husband Cliff and I were accused of trying to overthrow the government by force and violence just because we were trying to get voting rights for people. . . . Those who actually did try to overthrow the government by force and violence became great, honored figures in the South, whereas we, their grandchildren, were reviled."

After the *Brown v. Board of Education* ruling, the Durrs were ostracized not only for their own activities and beliefs, but increasingly because of their relationship with Hugo Black, who was considered a

traitor in his home state of Alabama because of his liberal opinions[10]
and official endorsement of desegregation. (Ironically, when F.D.R.
nominated him for the U.S. Supreme Court in 1937, Black was widely
condemned in the North because of his past membership in the Ku Klux
Klan.) At school the Durrs' three daughters were taunted about their
uncle. In front of the entire class, one of Tilla's teachers looked at her
and said, "You just tell your uncle I'm not going to teach any nigger children. I don't care how many laws they pass." And in what Virginia regarded as the most painful episode, six-year-old Lulah, who was all
ready "in a little white ruffled dress with a big sash" for a birthday
party, was abruptly disinvited when the host found out who her family
was. Virginia had called to confirm the time and, after a pause, the other
parent said, "Mrs. Durr, there will be no party this afternoon as far as
your daughter is concerned because I wouldn't have a child of yours in
my house."

Durr could tolerate being insulted herself, but she hated to see her
children treated as pariahs. She did everything she could to get them
out of the local environment of hatred and scorn. She wrote in the

---

[10] In more than thirty years on the bench, Black established a judicial record as a
strong supporter of the Bill of Rights and an advocate for extending its protections to
the state level. In an interview three years before his death, he cited his dissent in
1947's *Adamson v. California* case as one of the important opinons of his career. The
basic issue was whether the Fifth Amendment protection against self-incrimination
applied to state legal systems, and the court ruled it did not. Dissenting, Black wrote
that in his judgment, "the language of the first section of the Fourteenth Amendment,
taken as a whole, was thought by those responsible for its submission to the people,
and by those who opposed its submission, sufficiently explicit to guarantee that thereafter no state could deprive its citizens of the privileges and protections of the Bill of
Rights." At the very end of his career, Black wrote the majority opinion in the 1971
Pentagon Papers case, in which the Nixon administration tried to bar the *Washington
Post* and the *New York Times* from printing secret and damaging documents about its
Vietnam War policy. Black wrote that the press has a duty "to prevent any part of the
government from deceiving the people and sending them off to distant lands to die of
foreign fevers and foreign shot and shell." In his conclusion, he responded to the government's declaration that publication would threaten the nation's security: "The word
'security' is a broad, vague generality whose contours should not be invoked to abro-
gate the fundamental law embodied in the First Amendment. The guarding of military
and diplomatic secrets at the expense of informed representative government provides no real security for our republic. The framers of the First Amendment, fully
aware of both the need to defend a new nation and the abuses of the English and colonial governments, sought to give this new society strength and security by providing
that freedom of speech, press, religion, and assembly should not be abridged."

This was the last case Black heard. Three months later, he suffered a debilitating
stroke and retired from the court; he died eight days later, on September 24, 1971.

summer of 1954, "I have gotten a job for July and August as Assistant Cook at a Camp in Vermont and in payment they are giving Tilla her tuition and Lulah too. I am so thrilled over the chance to get them in a good inter-racial camp where they will have healthy surroundings." When Lucy was accepted at Radcliffe, Virginia arranged for a work-study program to cover expenses. In 1956 Virginia borrowed money from Jessica Mitford to enroll Tilla in the Cambridge School in Weston, Massachusetts. Later, Lulah recalled, "It was amazing to have your parents considered such demons and [then] go to a place where they're considered such heroes. It was so liberating to be able to embrace all that after having a childhood where so much of it had to be quiet."

Rosa Parks and the Montgomery Bus Boycott

In the spring of 1955 Virginia got a call from Myles Horton at Highlander Folk School, asking if she knew anyone who would be a good candidate for a scholarship to Highlander. She immediately thought of Rosa Parks. The two women often discussed politics, including the injustice of the segregated transportation system, and Virginia thought Rosa would love the civic workshops on fighting Jim Crow. "She had complained about the bus to me," recalled Virginia, "and discussed it many times. She told me how she'd pay her money and then have to run around to the back door to get in, and the driver would slam the door and ride off leaving her standing on the curb after she'd paid her money. She resented having to get up and give her seat to white people." Parks was interested in going to Highlander but could not afford the trip, so Virginia raised the necessary funds.

That summer, Rosa participated in workshops led by the great Septima Poinsette Clark, who by then was training hundreds of blacks every month to vote and to participate in the civil rights movement. Rosa remembered that when she arrived at Highlander, she was perennially tense and upset, feeling that she "had been destroyed too long" by the cruelties of Jim Crow. The *Brown v. Board* decision had given her some hope of racial equality, but reactionaries in Alabama had nearly crushed it. At Highlander she learned that "I could not help others free their hearts and minds of racial prejudice unless I would do all that I could within myself to straighten out my own thinking and

Myles Horton, E.D. Nixon, and Virginia (l-r) around 1978 (courtesy Ann Durr Lyon)

respond to kindness, to goodwill from wherever it came." The complete intermingling of the races at the school astonished and delighted her. "I was forty-two, and it was one of the few times in my life when I did not feel any hostility from white people."

When she returned, Parks found it even harder to tolerate the routine humiliations of everyday life under Jim Crow. Virginia later wrote Myles and Zilphia Horton: "When [Rosa] came back she was so happy and felt so liberated and then as time went on she said the discrimination got worse and worse to bear after having, for the first time in her life, been free of it at Highlander."

At this point, Parks was a sophisticated political activist, very well aware that for months efforts had been underway to find a good test case to take on Montgomery's segregated transportation system. In fact, she and the Durrs had been involved in one such effort earlier that year. In March 1955, Clifford Durr had assisted NAACP lawyer Fred Gray in Claudette Colvin's case. Colvin, a fifteen-year-old black student, was arrested for refusing to give up her seat on a city bus in Montgomery. While Colvin shouted that it was her constitutional right to be treated the same as a white person, the police called her a "black bitch" and a "black whore" and dragged her off the bus.

After Colvin's arrest, Parks headed an NAACP committee to raise money for the legal battle. Virginia helped with fund-raising, soliciting friends across the country, specifically writing Parks's contact information as the place to send funds. Then state NAACP president E. D. Nixon discovered that Colvin was pregnant. Reluctantly, he decided that hers couldn't be the rallying case, since opponents would focus not only on her fierce resistance but also on her "immorality." Fred Gray, with Durr's assistance, continued representing Colvin, who was found guilty of assault and battery. There was a boycott following the decision but it was limited and lasted only a few days.

Then came the famous evening of December 5, 1955, when Rosa Parks boarded a bus crowded with black people and found a seat for the ride home near the front of the bus. A few stops later, when several white men got on, the driver announced, "Niggers, move back." Parks refused to move. The driver walked back and confronted her, and when she still refused, he called the police. Parks was hauled off the bus and arrested.

She used her call from jail to contact E. D. Nixon, who immediately phoned Clifford Durr. "About six o'clock that night the telephone rang," recalled Virginia, "and Mr. Nixon said he understood that Mrs. Parks had been arrested, and he [had] called the jail, but they wouldn't tell him why she was arrested. So they thought if Cliff called, a white lawyer, they might tell him." As Taylor Branch describes it, "Durr promised to find out what he could from the jail, and soon called back with a report: Rosa Parks was charged with violating the Alabama bus segregation laws. That was all. When he volunteered to accompany Nixon to make bond for Mrs. Parks, Nixon accepted the offer readily. In fact, he told Durr to wait for him to come by. They would convoy to the city jail. When Nixon pulled up at the Durr home, Virginia Durr was waiting outside with her husband, ready to go too."

When they arrived at the jail, Virginia was distressed to see her dignified friend treated like a criminal. "That was a terrible sight for me," she recalled, "to see this gentle, lovely, sweet woman, whom I knew and was so fond of, being brought down by the matron." Nixon and the Durrs drove Parks home, where they sat down with her husband and her mother to discuss the options. Virginia recalled that Parks's husband, Raymond, was very reluctant to let her make a test case out of it. "It was like a background chorus, to hear the poor man, who was as white as he could be, for a black man, saying 'Rosa, the white folks will kill you.'" Cliff explained the various possibilities for getting the charges dismissed, if she chose not to pursue the case. Nixon, knowing that she was the perfect plaintiff, pleaded with her to stick with the case. Parks, well aware of what she was doing, agreed. They knew that the case, with all the necessary appeals, would require the resources of the NAACP. As Virginia said later: "So that night it was decided that Mrs. Parks would challenge the bus ordinance on constitutional grounds, and Fred Gray would represent her. It would be an NAACP case and Cliff would do all he could to help Fred, but Cliff would not be the lawyer of record."

Nixon organized the bus boycott, and he and other black leaders asked the young preacher Martin Luther King Jr. to lead the boycott's sponsoring organization, the Montgomery Improvement Association (MIA). As a national organization, the NAACP was often condemned as a group of "outside agitators," so the purely local MIA was set up specifically for the boycott.

At the first MIA meeting, King gave an electrifying speech in which he framed the fight ahead of them in epic, moral terms that echoed Ida B. Wells-Barnett. "If you will protest courageously and yet with dignity and Christian love, when the history books are written in future generations the historians will pause and say, 'There lived a great people—a black people—who injected new meaning and dignity into the veins of civilization.' That is our challenge and our overwhelming responsibility." Virginia felt King at that moment claimed his place as the movement's "undoubted leader."

Virginia had met Dr. King several times and attended many of his speeches, and she felt Coretta Scott King was a great Southern lady. Initially, she was a little wary of the overtly religious component of his message and felt more comfortable with old-time civil rights organizers like E. D. Nixon. But in retrospect, she acknowledged that King broke the easy, automatic linkage of integration and Communism. "He started the movement in the churches, so when the people started trying to red-bait the Negro movement, they had to go into the churches and red-bait Jesus Christ—pretty difficult to do."

Virginia drove boycotting black workers to and from their jobs and helped raise money for Parks, who lost her job, was unable to find another, and had her rent raised. But Durr recognized that she and all sympathetic whites had a supporting role in the blacks' fight for equality, and she admired their resolve. Most blacks did not acknowledge to whites that they were participating in the boycott, even to known supporters like the Durrs. Instead they explained they were walking because their bus had broken down or for medical reasons. Nevertheless, they kept walking. Virginia said, "the unity of the black people was the most amazing thing I have ever seen in my life."

The Durrs were accustomed to being ostracized, but their public support for the boycott took their shunning to a new level. Virginia recalled that "the first thing that happened to whites like us who were sympathetic to the boycott was that we lost our businesses. People didn't come to us. We got a reputation. My husband got mighty little law business after he took a very decided stand. People like my husband and Aubrey Williams [publisher of the *Southern Farmer*] realized that they were cutting their own throats. Aubrey lost all of his advertising, every bit of it."

Many white women who weren't at all sympathetic with the issues behind the boycott but couldn't manage without help drove their maids, cooks, and nurses themselves, prompting the Montgomery mayor to call for them to stop aiding the boycotters. The response, as Virginia recalled it, was an outraged refusal:

Well, you have never heard such a roar of indignation in your life as came from the white women of Montgomery. They were just furious at [Mayor] Tacky Gayle. They said, okay, if Tacky Gale wants to come out here and do my washing and ironing and cleaning and cooking and look after my children, he can do it, but unless he does, I'm going to get Mary or Sally or Suzy. And they said, "Sally has never had a thing to do with that boycott in the first place. She told me she only stays off the buses because she's scared of those hoodlums that might hurt her."

A vast deceit went on. Everybody knew everybody else was lying, but to save face, they had to lie. . . . The black women needed those jobs. They weren't paid very much, but that's all the income many of them had. They couldn't afford to say, "I'm supporting the boycott." So the white women lied and the black women lied. And the maids kept coming and the white women kept driving them back and forth to work.

Viewing Southern culture with the intimacy of an insider and the perspective of an outsider, Durr sought to understand the human motivations behind such evil, and wrote her impressions in letters to friends. Writing to Decca, she described the reaction of Cliff's family to the boycott.

They stay silent for the most part when we are around [but] are heart and soul with the other side and his Aunt who is completely outspoken about the "niggers" thinks they should all be sent back to Africa. She told Mary who bathes her, rubs her back, cleans up after her, feeds her, nurses her when she's sick . . . that "you niggers are not citizens of this country, you ought to go back to Africa if you don't like it here." And Mary with her eyes simply snapping said "Well when the Lord wants to send me back just let him send a chariot to take me, but when he takes us all back to Africa I don't know who is goin' to look after the white folks." That is what makes the whole thing so completely and obviously and wholeheartedly ridiculous, that the White South rests on the Black South. . . . Reason has flown out the window and nothing is left but hysteria—pure hysteria.

"To Sweep the Sea Back with a Broom"

Virginia was especially interested in the mentality of white Southerners who went along with racism even though they sensed it was immoral. "There was another kind of terror," she explained in an interview years later. "Some whites were scared that they wouldn't be invited to the ball, to the parties. It's a terror of being a social failure, of not making your way in the world. Now that's not nearly as bad as being lynched or killed or beaten up. But it's a terrible fear; that's the fear that possesses most men today." She was sympathetic to this fear—the power of the "magic circle"—because she had felt it, but that sympathy strengthened rather than diminished her opposition to it.

The harm segregation did to blacks was obvious, but Durr also saw the less visible damage racism inflicted on whites. When her brother, Sterling, died, she wrote to Clark Foreman, "He knew something was wrong but not what was wrong and he never really believed in himself. How many of these sweet, charming Southern men have you and I known, lovable, kind, wanting everyone to love them and really wanting to love everyone else, who simply were thwarted and distorted by this savage and cruel society." Later she observed of the typical white Southerner, "I still think it is economic competition that he fears, and he sees in the Negro and has seen for a long time, the shadow of his own helplessness and poverty and fear and degradation, and it is like a man trying to cut off his own shadow."

Virginia also was certain that the segregationists' rage was partly a product of the toxic obsession with interracial sex. During the Freedom March, she wrote, "They accuse all the Marchers of immorality, public fornication, Negro mixing. . . . It reveals the real cesspool that lies below the surface here and is the cause of the horrible brutality, fierce resistance and irrational behavior. It would take a trained Freudian to discover the roots of the behavior of some of these men who have slept with Negro women all their lives, had children by them, still do, and then get up and scream white supremacy and deny their own children. It certainly produces brutes." The obsession with protecting "pure white Southern womanhood" from black brutes infuriated her. Discussing several of Cliff's rape cases, she wrote, "I sometimes feel we southern white women are some kind of obscene goddesses that they make these burnt offerings to. 'Burn the Nigger, burn the Nigger' is what you hear . . . and there is something so awful and horrible about it, especially when no white man gets the death penalty for rape in any case and of course when it occurs with a Negro woman they never even believe it is rape."

Virginia was a prolific letter writer to foes as well, and she, like Ida B. Wells-Barnett, was not afraid to challenge newspapers to report the truth. Upon his inauguration in January 1959 as Alabama's governor, the openly racist John Patterson (a cousin of Virginia's) vowed that if any effort was made to desegregate the public schools, they would be shut down. In response to a desegregation suit filed by the MIA, the city commission had already closed the zoo and all thirteen city parks, which remained closed until 1965.[11] Virginia immediately wrote a letter to the editor protesting the closing of public facilities and soon found her front lawn littered with obscene pamphlets. (Under intense pressure, MIA withdrew its suit, and soon after, Martin Luther King Jr. left Montgomery for Atlanta.)

Virginia also raised money and recommended friends such as Ella Baker for teaching and speaking engagements. She urged influential friends, including Eleanor Roosevelt and Senator Lyndon Johnson, to strike at segregation by targeting Southern military bases. "If the Army and the Air Force would make some protests about their personnel being segregated that would help more than anything as the South certainly does not want to lose all those federal installations." The emphasis on economics again echoes the strategies used by Wells-Barnett and Perkins. President Kennedy's assistant attorney general for civil rights, Burke Marshall, became a regular correspondent. She sent him information about local civil rights issues and violations and also gave him suggestions about how to get Southerners to comply with desegregation orders.

---

[11] This and similar tactics were part of the segregationist policy of massive resistance, the philosophy of which was declared in the "Southern Manifesto" of 1956. Early that year, a group led by Strom Thurmond of South Carolina and several other Southern politicians wrote up and circulated the document, which declared the *Brown v. Board* decision unconstitutional and announced the signatories' refusal to abide by it or any law intended to enact it. By March 1956, all the Southern senators had signed the manifesto, with three exceptions: Lyndon Johnson of Texas, Estes Kefauver of Tennessee, and my grandfather, Albert Gore Sr. of Tennessee.

From then on, despite the enactment of desegregation, the fury behind massive resistance only strengthened and it greatly contributed to Gore Sr.'s defeat in 1970. Just months before that election, the U.S. Senate approved the nomination of Minnesota judge Harry A. Blackmun to the Supreme Court after President Nixon's first two nominees, G. Harrold Carswell and Clement F. Haynsworth Jr., were rejected after heated debates about their "strict constructionism" which would have affected decisions about the federal government's enforcement of civil rights legislation within the states. (Blackmun would go on to author the opinion in *Roe v. Wade* three years later.) My grandfather's votes against both Carswell and Haynsworth were used against him in the 1970 Senate campaign. One ad that was run at saturation levels and was emblematic of the Republican Party's "Southern strategy": "On Gun Registration, Tennesseans said No, but Albert Gore said Yes. On Busing of School Children Tennesseans said No, but Albert Gore said Yes. On School Prayer, Tennesseans voted Yes, but Albert Gore voted No. On Carswell and Haynsworth Tennesseans said Yes, but Albert Gore voted No. Isn't it about time Tennesseans said No to Albert Gore?"

In her letters to friends, Virginia expressed alarm at the increasing sense of anarchy and sadness at her continuing isolation. "The terrorization still goes on to anyone that sticks their neck out, telephone calls, anonymous letters but above all, lack of any work, no jobs. Brutal economic pressure and brutal social pressure," she wrote to Decca in 1959. During these times, she felt lonely and isolated and took great solace in her correspondence. "It is hard from down here to know how much of the country really is behind the effort to desegregate."

Yet she never lost her sense of humor. Writing about the increasing violence, she referred to segregationists as "'Strom' troopers." After Montgomery city officials agreed to desegregate the public libraries and then removed all the chairs, she observed, "The idea was that if libraries had to be integrated, everybody had to stand up. Vertical integration apparently was more tolerable." Describing a Civil War commemoration, she wrote, "The funniest thing is that while strict segregation is observed, in all the doings they have a troupe of dancers in black face to represent the happy slaves! Actually! No Negroes allowed but a whole troupe of white people with their faces blackened to represent them. How crazy can people get?"

While Virginia carried on her correspondences, attended meetings, made speeches, and worked on legal cases with Cliff, she was also concerned for her husband's health. Clifford, one of the few white lawyers in the area who would take on civil rights cases, was tremendously overworked, and the burden was aggravating his back and heart problems. His law practice continued to consist mostly of black clients who had been exploited or abused. He regularly took cases of police brutality and worked closely with NAACP lawyer Fred Gray defending black men arrested for rape—a death-penalty charge—based on dubious or clearly fabricated evidence. It was important work, but exhausting and endless: like "trying to sweep the sea back with a broom," or "chipping pieces off an iceberg," as Virginia put it. Without very many clients who could pay, money was tight, but harder still was the fact that the Durrs were shunned by mainstream white society. "We live on a narrow edge of tolerance."

The Durrs also spent a lot of time at their country home in Wetumpka, Alabama, called the "Pea Level." Clifford inherited the land and built a rustic cabin there, taking on the construction himself despite his chronic back problems. The Pea Level became a refreshing retreat. The Durrs invited friends, both black and white, to spend time with them there—a brave act for all involved. Lucy recalls that amid the talk and laughter, there were moments of real fear: "The black people would leave before dark. Whenever a dog would bark, you could just feel the tension. . . . But Mother and Daddy used to just sort of dismiss it."

While the Durrs would never be fully accepted in Montgomery, their isolation eventually did ease a bit. "Montgomery goes on its merry way to hell," she wrote. "But it is lucky for us that we do have such interesting visitors for we are far from being favorites here in Montgomery, although we do have now a few staunch friends we can count on." As the civil rights movement grew, the Durrs' home became a way station for traveling activists and organizers, a development Virginia loved. Occasionally, she became frustrated with "Northern hit-and-run liberals" who came south as saviors and left a few weeks later, leaving the problems behind. But overall she enjoyed getting to know the new generation of activists.

Virginia occasionally bristled over the stereotyping of Southerners by these activists. In June of 1960 she attended the wedding of Shelagh Foreman, Clark's daughter, in New York. Joan Baez sang at the wedding and afterward, according to Virginia's account, lay down on the floor and went to sleep. The next day, as Virginia was visiting with the Foremans, who had a houseful of guests, she asked one of the young men to go buy her a pack of cigarettes.

> Joan Baez spoke up and said, "I suppose you're used to ordering black people around all your life, so you think you can order us around."
>
> "My Lord," I said, "I don't know why it's such a terrible request to ask a young boy to go out and get a package of cigarettes."
>
> "Well, you just bring that Southern arrogance with you and think you can order people around because you've been ordering black people around all your life."
>
> I was absolutely astonished at such rudeness and I said, "Well, evidently you don't approve of anybody from the South." Then she got on a long diatribe about the South and the way we were treating the blacks and all.
>
> "You don't approve of me either, do you?" she said finally.

"Well, no, actually I don't." By this time I was furious.

"Why don't you approve of me?"

"Well, in the first place," I said, "I thought your behavior yesterday at the wedding was extremely odd and very rude. I think if you want to take a nap you don't have to lie down in the middle of the floor and go to sleep and make everybody step around you. You just made yourself conspicuous and you certainly caused other people a great deal of inconvenience. I think it was pure exhibitionism." Oh, she practically bared her teeth at that.

Three years later Virginia wrote to the Foremans that she forgave the singer after Baez and Bob Dylan refused to appear on the popular ABC folk-music program *Hootenanny* because the show had blacklisted Pete Seeger. Seeger was one of the central figures in the folk music movement and he remains a dedicated supporter of progressive causes. (In 2006, Bruce Springsteen brought Seeger's work to a new audience when he released *We Shall Overcome: The Seeger Sessions*.) Virginia had known Seeger since the Seminary Hill days—he played at a campaign event during her 1948 Senate candidacy—and it infuriated her that the national media had censored him.

Virginia Durr urged people to stand up for what they believed in, but she was also astute in her judgment of when to compromise with imperfect politicians. She wrote to Decca in 1960, "I disagree completely on 'sitting this one out' but can't take time to go into it thoroughly. Actually a non-vote is a vote for Nixon, and I do not think as bad as Kennedy is that he is as big a scoundrel as Nixon." After watching Nixon woo the civil rights groups and still lose the black vote, she accurately predicted that his coalition would reach out to the segregationists. (Later, when he was in the White House, Virginia wrote a friend, "O! that nasty Nixon. Just to see him on TV makes me break out with the itch.")

Freedom Rides

In December 1960 the Supreme Court issued a decision—written by Hugo Black—that affirmed an earlier ban on segregation on interstate transportation and extended the policy to the associated terminals, waiting areas, and restaurants. In practice, buses on Southern routes remained segregated, as they had since the original 1946 ruling. The following year, the Congress of Racial Equality[12] (CORE) assembled an interracial group for a "Freedom Ride" through the South. On May 4 a dozen people boarded a bus in Washington, D.C. They planned to arrive in New Orleans on May 17, the seventh anniversary of the *Brown v. Board of Education* decision.

At first the ride was largely uneventful, with only minor scuffles and confrontations. On May 14, Mother's Day, the group reached Atlanta and split up for the trip to Birmingham—one group boarded a Trailways bus, the other a Greyhound. The Greyhound was the first to reach the only stop, Anniston, Alabama. Immediately, an angry mob attacked, bashing the sides of the bus and slashing its back tires. The driver pulled out of the parking lot, followed by attackers in about twenty cars and trucks. A few miles down the road, tires shredded, the bus stopped, and the driver leaped out and ran. Then someone threw a firebomb into the bus, and the passengers scrambled out the exit door in back. Just after the last passenger left, the fuel tank exploded. Miraculously, no one was seriously injured.

When the Trailways bus arrived in Anniston, it too was attacked, and several men forced their way onto the bus and beat the passengers indiscriminately. Eight members of the mob stayed aboard when the bus left Anniston.

In Birmingham, Police Chief Eugene "Bull" Connor and the local Klan chapter had made plans to greet the Freedom Riders, agreeing that the Klansmen would have fifteen minutes to beat their victims before the police arrived from the station across the street. Connor also vowed to avoid arresting any of the attackers. (He later said few police officers were available because it was Mother's Day.) The Trailways bus arrived in Birmingham at 4:15 and the Klansmen attacked with pipes

---

[12] The Congress of Racial Equality was founded in 1942 as the Committee of Racial Equality by an interracial group of students at the University of Chicago. Its first leaders were white student George Houser and black student James Farmer. CORE began protests against segregation in public accommodations by organizing sit-ins and other nonviolent direct actions. Although CORE was founded as a nonhierarchical, decentralized organization, there was growing tension between the local and national leadership, and by the early '50s, the organization had lost influence. The 1954 *Brown v. Board of Education* decision revitalized CORE and the organization was at the forefront of many of the most visible civil rights projects: the 1960 lunch counter sit-in protest in Greensboro, North Carolina; the original Freedom Rides in 1961, 1963's March on Washington; Freedom Summer in 1964. Three activists killed that summer, James Chaney, Andrew Goodman, and Michael Schwerner, were members of CORE.

and clubs, beating on heads and kicking and stamping on those who fell. Onlookers cheered on the Klan and soon joined in the attacks. A reporter described how "toughs grabbed the passengers into alleys and corridors, pounding them with pipes, with keyrings, with fists. One passenger was knocked down at my feet by twelve of the hoodlums, and his face was beaten and kicked until it was a bloody pulp." The police arrived shortly after 4:30 and the crowd dispersed. There were no arrests.

The Freedom Ride almost ended there. The driver refused to continue and both companies feared losing another bus. Negotiations between the companies and the riders went on for two days, with the atmosphere growing more and more tense. The riders, in fear for their lives, flew to New Orleans.

Reinforcements arrived from Nashville, Tennessee after several activists there decided the Freedom Ride had to go on. Diane Nash,[13] one of the organizers, said later, "If the Freedom Riders had been stopped as a result of violence, I strongly felt that the future of the movement was going to be cut short. The impression would have been that whenever a movement starts, all [you have to do] is attack it with massive violence and the blacks [will] stop." A group of ten, including John Lewis, now a U.S. congressman from Georgia, arrived in Birmingham and began discussions with the bus company. On May 17, the Birmingham police put them under "protective custody" in the jail. John Lewis later wrote, "We went on singing, both to keep our spirits up and—to be honest—because we knew that neither Bull Connor nor his guards could stand it. Later on Connor would tell reporters that was one of the worst things about this experience for him—listening to the sound of our singing." On May 19, at two A.M., Connor announced that the group would be driven to the Tennessee border and dropped off. When the riders refused to move, the police carried them out to the cars. From the state border, the riders made their way back to Nashville, changed clothes, and returned to Birmingham.

Also on May 19, Governor John Patterson, who had been refusing to return calls from President Kennedy, spoke to the attorney general,

---

[13] Diane Nash, the daughter of a middle-class family in Chicago, was a charismatic civil rights activist best known for her role in the 1960 Nashville lunch counter sit-ins. During the rally at City Hall, Nash—beautiful, intelligent, self-confident—confronted the governor. The next day's *Tennessean* ran a banner headline: "Integrate Counters—Mayor." Working with SNCC, she went on to help plan and implement events such as the march from Selma. Recently she reflected on her role in the early days of civil rights: "I [am] very satisfied. . . . My living has made a difference on the planet. And I love that. I really do."

Robert Kennedy. It was by all accounts a brief conversation and not at all cordial. Kennedy had already sent a Justice Department aide named John Seigenthaler to Birmingham to monitor the situation, and Patterson refused to negotiate with anyone but Seigenthaler, apparently because he was another southerner, a native of Tennessee.

After a heated conversation, during which Patterson declared that blood would flow in the streets if Alabama schools were integrated, Seigenthaler secured the governor's assurance that state police would escort the Freedom Riders' bus to Montgomery, where the city police would take over.

On May 20, twenty-one riders accompanied by two Greyhound officials left Birmingham. The bus was preceded and followed by highway patrol cars, with carloads of reporters at the end of the motorcade. A state highway patrol airplane droned overhead. Traveling at ninety miles an hour, it didn't take long to reach Montgomery. Immediately, the escort vanished and there were no city police to take their place.

As the bus pulled into the station, everything was quiet. "And then, all of a sudden, just like magic, white people everywhere," said Freedom Rider Frederick Leonard. The mob shouted and pounded on the bus while the riders tried to figure out how to escape safely. Finally Jim Zwerg, a white rider, walked off the bus. While the crowd was busy attacking him, the other riders exited. Some escaped but others were badly beaten, as were several people who tried to stop the beatings. John Seigenthaler was assaulted, knocked unconscious, and left bleeding in the street for half an hour. Lewis remembers that his briefcase "was ripped from my fingers. At that instant, I felt a thud against my head. I could feel my knees collapse and then nothing. Everything turned white for an instant, then black. . . . I learned later that someone had swung a Coca-Cola crate against my head." Finally the Montgomery police arrived and the violence died down. Again, there were no arrests. Lewis remembers coming to as the Alabama attorney general "stood over me and read aloud an injunction forbidding 'entry into and travel within the state of Alabama and engaging in the so-called "Freedom Ride" and other acts or conduct calculated to promote breaches of the peace.'"

Jessica Mitford was staying in Montgomery with the Durrs that weekend, and she and Virgina went downtown, where a massive crowd had assembled. Before Virginia had parked the car, Decca had hopped out to head for the bus station. Virginia pushed through the crowd and made her way to Cliff's office, which overlooked the station. As she remembered it:

> I felt absolute stark terror. I'd lived in Montgomery for ten years. We'd gone through the bus boycott and the *Brown* decision and all the things that had happened after the *Brown* decision. We'd gone through the Eastland hearing. What terrified me so was that the people who were shouting and holding up their babies to "see the niggers run" were just ordinary Montgomery people who had come downtown on a Saturday, as they usually do, to shop. And they had turned into a raving mob. It destroyed the confidence I'd been building up for ten years. . . . These were the people I was living among and they were really crazy. They were full of hatred and they were full of bigotry and meanness.

Martin Luther King Jr. flew into Montgomery, and a gathering to honor the Freedom Riders was held at Reverend Ralph Abernathy's First Baptist Church. Mitford borrowed the Durrs' Buick to drive over, arriving to find that hundreds of whites had already surrounded the church. She went inside, and during the gathering more than a thousand people joined the mob. They threw bricks at passing drivers, torched a parked car, and loudly threatened to "clean the niggers out." A few dozen federal marshals struggled to control the crowd and finally sprayed them with tear gas. Local police and state troopers joined the marshals and they eventually dispersed the crowd. The rioters weren't finished; they stayed in the neighborhood and regrouped. Finally, the National Guard was called in and martial law declared. At dawn, when Decca and the others could safely leave the church, she discovered that the destroyed car was the Durrs' Buick. A National Guardsman drove her home in a jeep.

Robert Kennedy asked the Riders to take a "cooling-off period" but they insisted on continuing. CORE cofounder Jim Farmer said later, "We'd been cooling off for 350 years. . . . If we cooled off any more, we'd be in a deep freeze." The Freedom Ride continued into Mississippi, where several riders were arrested and sentenced to sixty days in the state penitentiary. It never reached New Orleans.

Lady Bird Johnson and Virginia (courtesy Ann Durr Lyon)

Her Legacy

In the case of the Freedom Rides—as well as some other landmark events of the civil rights movement—Virginia Durr was more of an insightful observer than a heroine on the front lines. Yet she remained a major force for good. Not only did Virginia bravely dissent from the mainstream around her, she rallied the troops and lobbied those in power.

After years of vociferously urging her old friend Lyndon Johnson to take up the cause of civil rights, Virginia was thrilled when, as president, he signed the Civil Rights Act of 1964.[14] (After signing the bill, he reportedly remarked, "We've just delivered the South to the Republicans for a generation.") Virginia and Clifford were welcomed as family when they traveled to Washington for Johnson's inauguration

---

[14] Though my grandfather never considered himself one of the heroes of the civil rights movement, over his career he compiled an impressively progressive voting record on civil rights. However, he did vote against the landmark Civil Rights Act of 1964. He felt that as written, the bill was "an extreme grant of power to unelected, often faceless executive officials" but later admitted the vote was a terrible mistake. My father remembers arguing with him across the dinner table, trying to get him to change his mind, and said later, "It was the first time I can remember, one of the only times, feeling I was right and he was wrong on a matter of public importance."

Virginia at the 50th anniversary of Highlander Folk School in 1982 with Ralph Tefferteller and Bernice Robinson. (courtesy Highlander Research and Education Center)

in January 1965. Later that year, Virginia savored victory over the poll tax at last, when LBJ signed the Voting Rights Act. Later Virginia grew more and more frustrated by Lyndon's escalation of the Vietnam War; but her affection for Lady Bird never wavered.

When the racist George Wallace took control of the Alabama Democratic party, Virginia became a founding member of the National Democratic Party of Alabama (NDPA), which was headed by a black dentist named John Cashin. The party sought to realign the choices of Alabamans with the national spectrum as well as mobilize the black electorate. She attended the 1968 Democratic Convention as a delegate of the NDPA, pledged to antiwar candidate Eugene Mc-Carthy. Clifford and Lulah went to the train station to pick her up when she returned. Clifford caught sight of Virginia stepping onto the platform and said, "She still takes my breath away." They'd been married for forty-two years.

As the civil rights movement progressed, the Durrs' contribution began to be recognized. On December 13, 1972, Lyndon Johnson wrote Virginia to report on the civil rights symposium he'd organized: "I only wish that you could have been with us because a long, long time ago you taught me so much, by precept and example, about the dignity and opportunity to which each is entitled regardless of color, birthplace, ancestry, and all other ways in which many have been ignored and disdained."

In May 1975 Clifford died of a heart attack. Virginia was devastated. Though she was a social, gregarious, and flirtatious woman, Clifford had been her one sustaining companion. Soon after his death she told their daughters, "Now that your father has died, I don't know who is going to put the brakes on me." Almost two decades later, at her ninetieth birthday party, someone asked what one wish she'd like to be granted. She said, "I wish I could spend one more day with my husband."

Virginia also continued to host friends and family at the Pea Level and never ceased her political preoccupations. She considered most young adults of the '80s and '90s superficial and selfish, especially compared to their '60s and '70s equivalents: "Really, what they want to do is get prepared for good jobs, live a pleasant life, eat health food, and have healthy children. They've shrunk!" In a hilarious speech at Virginia's ninetieth birthday celebration, her grandson Fain Hackney recalled his earliest memories of his grandmother holding court.

> We children were left to our own devices as the grownups gathered on the porch and in the living room to discuss politics and world affairs endlessly. In the cacophony of voices that wafted into the other parts of the house where we were playing, my grandmother's voice was the loudest and most constant. . . . The children did not speak at the dinner table, except to nod when we were asked whether we were aware that the world was going to hell in a handbasket unless we, the future leaders of America, took a stand against racial injustice, economic inequality, and all Republicans.

In her later years, Virginia divided her time between the Pea Level, Montgomery, and Martha's Vineyard, where she made many friends. One of them, writer William Styron, described sitting with Virginia in a summer garden:

> She speaks in her murmurous soft voice of bygone times, of political friends and enemies, of old defeats and triumphs. She

Virginia and her old friend Rosa Parks ca. 1982. When Virginia died, Rosa said, "I celebrate the life of Mrs. Virginia Durr, whose upbringing and privilege didn't prohibit her from wanting equality for all people." (courtesy Ann Durr Lyon)

sits erect and commandingly, welcoming talk as others welcome dinner. . . . For a moment the warrior vanishes and in her place sits the nice southern lady conversing as nice southern ladies do, chatting of kinfolk—both the quick and the departed—of home and land, of people's amorous entanglements, lesser and greater scandals, dogs, mortal ailments, the weather. . . . [Then] she returns to matters that most seriously inflame her heart—the misconduct of human beings, their propensity for wreaking cruel havoc on each other, the mean handiwork of scoundrels in high places. Her eyes glint with a new brightness, her voice swells with indignation, and I realize that for most of a lifetime her being has been wholly animated by the need to make sense of an only partly understandable dream.

The dream is justice. How curious, yet how fitting, that this grand ardor should dwell in the breast of a slave owner's granddaughter born in Birmingham, Alabama.

Virginia Durr died on February 24, 1999, at the age of ninety-five.

Septima Poinsette Clark

In teaching them and thereby helping them raise to a better status in life, I felt then that I would not only be serving them but serving my state and nation too, all the people, affluent and poor, white and black. For in my later years I am more convinced than ever that in lifting the lowly we lift likewise the entire citizenship.

—SEPTIMA CLARK

I am always very respectful and very much in awe of the presence of Septima Clark because her life story makes the effort that I have made very minute. I only hope that there is a possible chance that some of her great courage and dignity and wisdom has rubbed off on me.

—ROSA PARKS

Her name might be generally unknown today, but she was a powerful influence on many of us at that formative time.

—REPRESENTATIVE JOHN LEWIS

JULY 31, 1959, MARKED THE FINAL DAY OF A WEEKLONG SERIES of workshops at the Highlander Folk School. Both controversial and influential, Highlander brought together people from all over the country and the world to participate in integrated workshops on voter registration, community organizing, and desegregation activism. At that time such a mission would have been remarkable anywhere in the United States. In that region—rural Tennessee—it was downright heretical.

Earlier that year, a state legislative committee had explored the possibility of shutting down the school by revoking its nonprofit charter. The committee heard testimony that people at Highlander indulged in "very questionable activity" and "immoral, lewd and unchaste practices." Arkansas's segregationist attorney general Bruce Bartlett was called as an expert witness and literally outlined the charges against the school. On the hearing room chalkboard, he drew a web of liberal, integrationist organizations and people, with Highlander Folk School at its center—"the center of Communism in the South." Later the *Chattanooga Sunday Times* would report that several committee members "felt that the ultra-liberal positions of Highlander officials place them in the class of 'left-wingers'" and that the school should not have a tax-exempt charter. However, after they "found no evidence of subversion" at Highlander, this committee decided to allow the school to keep its charter and continue in its mission.

Septima Poinsette Clark was crucial to that mission. Sixty-one years old, with more than forty years of teaching experience, Septima was Highlander's education director. She'd crafted the school's citizenship classes, which prepared African Americans not only to meet voting requirements but to become leaders in their communities, spreading civic activism throughout the South. The gentle force of her personality—loving, open-minded, determined to see the best in everyone, unshakable in her political convictions—fueled Highlander's ongoing success.

That Friday night, the Highlander attendees held a celebratory banquet in the dining hall and then began watching a documentary entitled *The Face of the South*. About ten minutes before nine P.M., just after the narrator said, "They went to the schools that we gave them, which weren't very good," the door flew open. Septima's eleven-year-old granddaughter Yvonne, who lived with her, remembers opening the front door outside the auditorium and finding a white man in plainclothes, who blew past her to where the workshop was meeting. Eighteen armed law enforcement officers, both uniformed and plainclothes, burst into the hall. Leading the officers was District Attorney General Ab Sloan, accompanied by Grundy County Sheriff Elson Clay and Tennessee Bureau of Criminal Identification Agent

Kenneth Shelton. A reporter and photographer for the *Chattanooga Free Press* were also on hand.[1]

Sloan, apparently aware that Highlander founder and executive director Myles Horton was out of the country, approached Septima and told her that he had a warrant to search the premises for liquor. (Highlander was in a dry county.) Septima remembered later, "I said to them, when they came to me: 'Just go in that kitchen and look all over. You won't even find cooking sherry in there.' It was so funny." Shortly after the search began, Clark was officially put in custody. Two workshop attendees objected and they too were held by the police.

Then a young folk musician named Guy Carawan, who was spending his first summer at Highlander, began to strum "We Shall Overcome" on his guitar[2] and the other Highlanders took up the song. Septima remembered hearing a young woman improvising a new

---

[1] For many years, the *Chattanooga Free Press* was the afternoon paper and the *Chattanooga Times* was the morning paper. The *Free Press* was a conservative, tabloid-esque paper while the *Times* was much more restrained in tone and generally progressive. The *Times* was first published by Adolph S. Ochs on July 2, 1878, and became successful enough that, in 1896, he was able to buy a struggling newspaper called the *New York Times* and begin overhauling it. Ochs's only child, his daughter Iphigene, married a journalist named Arthur Hays Sulzberger in 1917 and the next year, Sulzberger joined the *New York Times* staff, eventually taking control of the paper and increasing the company's holdings.

[2] The old spiritual, "I'll Overcome Someday" ("Deep in my heart, I do believe, it will be all right some day . . . I will see his face some day . . .") was first politicized in the 1940s, when a group of black, female tobacco workers in Charleston, South Carolina, took it up as their strike anthem. Carawan made the song part of his repertoire that first summer at Highlander and afterward, playing and teaching it at demonstrations, rallies, and pickets throughout the country. As David Halberstam has written, on April 19, 1960, the song became forever linked with the struggle for civil rights. In the early hours of that morning, the home of Nashville attorney Z. A. Looby (counsel to the Nashville sit-in activists) was bombed; fortunately, neither he nor his wife was injured. When word spread of the bombing, thousands marched silently through the streets and gathered at City Hall. Carawan picked up his guitar and began "We Shall Overcome." According to Halberstam, "Some of the leaders like [James] Bevel, [Bernard] Lafayette and [John] Lewis, who had already heard the song at Highlander, took it up immediately. . . . The others who had heard it before but had not sung it during a demonstration took it up. Suddenly the sound seemed to sweep across the courthouse square. Verse followed verse, the sound becoming ever more powerful. . . . It was religious and gentle, just right for a Gandhian protest, but its force and power were not to be underestimated; it not only emboldened those who were setting out on this dangerous path, but it helped affect and bring in those on the sidelines, those watching television at home who had seen young blacks, immaculately behaved and dressed, beaten up by white thugs or cops, thereupon sing this haunting song. It was an important moment: The students now had their anthem."

verse—"We are not afraid, we are not afraid tonight." As the officers kept searching, the Highlanders kept singing, verse after verse, which "made the police feel nervous," she recalled. Guy Carawan was soon arrested, too.

After they found no liquor in the main hall, the officers began searching the rest of the buildings, as well as the cars parked on campus. Septima reported later that they destroyed Highlander documents, ripped pages from a book by Martin Luther King Jr., and seized personal items, including cash. Finally the searchers gained access to the locked basement of Horton's home and, at last, discovered some booze. Many people on the Highlander staff, including Septima, were teetotalers and, as Yvonne recalls, Myles and Septima were both keenly aware that the police might raid the premises at any time and were accordingly careful and discreet. The story she always heard was that the liquor had been planted. The *Nashville Tennessean* reported Sloan's rundown of the haul: "a quart bottle containing some gin, flask with a little rum, a quart bottle full of rum, and a 10-gallon keg containing, 'in my [Sloan's] opinion, two or three gallons of what looks and smells like wildcat or white whiskey.'"

When the police told Septima she would be taken into custody, she arranged for a woman attending the workshop to look after Yvonne. Clark and the three men were taken to the county jail in Altamont, arriving at about one A.M. While she was being processed, Sloan teased Septima, asking if she'd had "a good taste of that liquor." Clark, a woman known for her patience and good humor, snapped back that she'd be happy to take a blood-alcohol test so he could see for himself. Her offer was ignored.

While Septima waited to be bailed out, she sat in her cell (with "all the stuff" from the men's room upstairs pouring down the wall each time the toilet was flushed) and passed the time by singing "Michael, Row the Boat Ashore," a song activist and singer Harry Belafonte had recently taught at Highlander. At about two-thirty A.M., a Highlander teacher paid Clark's $500 bail. (Yvonne remembers her grandmother's return to Highlander: "It was the only time I ever saw her smoke a cigarette.") The three young men who'd been arrested with Clark weren't allowed to post bail because Sloan wanted to keep them in jail overnight "to sober up."

It was a ridiculous statement. None of the four had been drinking at all and Sloan knew very well that there'd been no alcohol anywhere near the Highlander dining hall. It was an elaborate charade; everyone involved knew the raid was part of the ongoing campaign to shut down Highlander because it preached and practiced integration. In newspaper coverage the next day, Ab Sloan admitted as much. He noted that the committee's unsuccessful attempt to revoke Highlander's charter indicted it "mostly on integration and communism, and I wasn't satisfied I could be successful at that. I thought maybe this [raid for liquor] was the best shot and I think now I'll be successful."

Eventually, he was successful, though it took almost two years of contentious hearings before Highlander was shut down for good, at least in its Monteagle, Tennessee, location. In the meantime, Myles and Septima had made arrangements for Martin Luther King Jr.'s Southern Christian Leadership Conference to take over Highlander's classes under the auspices of its Citizenship Education Program. By 1963 almost 26,000 blacks in twelve Southern states had attended Septima Clark's citizenship classes and become voters. That year, 400 local citizenship schools educated and trained over 6,500 adults. Later Septima would estimate that the program directly reached 100,000 people in all, and it is impossible to measure the impact that each of them, in turn, had on their communities.

I first heard of Septima Clark from a friend whose grandmother, Maggie Sanders, knew and loved "Miss Seppie," as most people called her. She spoke of Septima's warmth and kindness, her courage and her quiet yet forceful influence on those around her. Septima's example inspired Maggie not only to pursue an education but to insist that her own children do so as well: "Being with her encouraged me to go do things myself."

As I learned more about Clark, I was astonished that she is not well known. She had a pervasive and catalytic effect on the civil rights movement—not just through the classes she taught, but also through her constant efforts to keep the movement grounded in principles of compassion and respect. She concentrated on the less-visible but still essential work of the movement, "the underground things," as one relative put it. In his groundbreaking book *Parting the Waters* (dedicated to Clark's memory), Taylor Branch described Septima's character as "a miraculous balance between leathery zeal and infinite patience." Her way with people, her determination to inspire and empower, created a groundswell.

The summer before the raid, a divinity student and sharecropper's son named John Lewis attended a Highlander workshop, eager to become part of the growing civil rights movement. Observing him, a visiting teacher scoffed at the idea that he might have leadership potential: he stuttered, his grammar wasn't perfect, he didn't read particularly well. Septima responded, "What difference does that make?" All of those things could be learned, and more important, the people he needed to lead already understood him.

Septima was right. Two years later Lewis helped orchestrate the historic sit-ins that desegregated Nashville's lunch counters. He was among the Freedom Riders badly beaten in Virginia Durr's Montgomery, and he was knocked unconscious on "Bloody Sunday," when a peaceful march from Selma to Montgomery was attacked by mounted police with bullwhips, clubs, and tear gas. These and other brave protests meant that Lewis was arrested forty times, arrests often accompanied by severe physical abuse. He became a founding member and chairman of the Student Nonviolent Coordinating Committee[3] (SNCC), a longtime worker for voting rights, and in 2006 he was reelected to his eleventh term as the United States congressman from Georgia's Fifth District.

Lewis wrote about that first weekend at Highlander in his memoir, *Walking with the Wind*:

> What I loved about Clark was her down-to-earth, no-nonsense approach and the fact that the people she aimed at were the same ones Gandhi went after, the same ones I identified with, having grown up poor and barefoot and black. I sensed then, and this belief would grow as the years went on, that the

---

[3] The Student Nonviolent Coordinating Committee (SNCC) was formed in 1960 by black college students determined to participate in and help shape the growing civil rights movement. In addition to direct action such as sit-ins and the Freedom Rides, SNCC focused on voter registration. At its peak, the Freedom Summer of 1964, SNCC sent as many as six hundred activists into the poorest, most isolated parts of the South to encourage and facilitate voter registration. The 1965 "Bloody Sunday" march is credited with boosting popular support for the Voting Rights Act of 1965, which President Lyndon Johnson signed into law in August. The act suspended (and later banned) the use of literacy or other voter qualification tests that had been used to keep blacks off voter rolls.

lifeblood of the movement was not going to be the spokes-men—the schooled, sophisticated, savvy upper crust who might be the best at speechmaking and press conferences. They would be the leaders, naturally, but it was going to be the tens of thousands of faceless, nameless, anonymous men, women and children—men like my father, women like my mother, children like the boy I had been—who were going to rise like an irresistible army as this movement for civil rights took shape. Septima Clark was one of those people.

Septima was a transformative teacher to thousands of blacks—some young, educated, and affluent but many older, illiterate, and poor—who, touched by her influence, became the voters, the marchers, and the organizers of the civil rights movement. I am especially moved by the fact that Septima rejected bitterness and hatred in favor of compassion and selfless pragmatism, even when insulted, ignored, and fiercely challenged by the political powers of the day.

Childhood

Septima always credited her parents with instilling in her self-respect, a strong work ethic, integrity, and a love of learning. Her father, Peter Porcher (pronounced "por-SHAY") Poinsette, was born a slave on the plantation Casa Bianca, located on the banks of the Wando River near Charleston, South Carolina. The plantation belonged to Joel Poinsette, the botanist and former ambassador to Mexico who brought the famous flaming red plant—dubbed the "poinsettia"—to the United States.

At the end of the Civil War, the newly free Peter Poinsette went to work on a Clyde Line steamship traveling a route between Charleston and New York. On one of his stops, he met the striking, self-assured Victoria Warren Anderson. Victoria's father was a member of the Muskhogean tribes on the Georgia Sea Islands. Her mother, who was Haitian, died when her children were very young, and Victoria and her two sisters were sent to Haiti, where an uncle worked as a cigar maker. Vicky thrived in the Haitian schools, her sharp mind stimulated by the rigorous European-style curricula.

When they reached marriageable age, she and her sisters were sent back to the United States.

Victoria and Peter married and settled in Charleston, South Carolina. Septima was born May 3, 1898, the second of the Poinsettes' eight children. *Septima*, Latin for seven, also means "sufficient" in Haitian Creole, and the baby was named for an aunt in Haiti, Septima Peace. Septima joked later, "I was supposed to be sufficient peace, but I certainly wasn't sufficient, and I don't know about peace, because I did so many things that wasn't peaceful."

Remembering her parents, Septima said Peter was a "gentle, tolerant man," while Victoria was "fiercely proud," eager to point out that she'd never been a slave. Perhaps because of her Haitian upbringing, she was remarkably unintimidated by the pervasive prejudice against blacks and taught her children fearlessness: "She wanted you to be able to stand your ground, regardless of where you were or whatever happened." Decades later Septima recalled one incident from her childhood, when a police officer ran onto their property.

> My mother said, "What are you doing in my yard? Who told you you could come in here? You're not supposed to come into my yard."
>
> The policeman replied that he was pursuing a criminal.
>
> She said, "I'm a little piece of leather, but I'm well put together, so don't you come in here."
>
> My mother did many things like this. I appreciate them because I really feel that it helped me to be able to stand in front of the Klansmen and the White Citizen's Councils, of large groups that were hostile. I never felt afraid, and I think it was due to the fact that my mother showed so much courage back in those early days. I felt that if she could do it way back then, then I could.

The Poinsettes insisted that their children get a good education. Septima attended a private school for African-American children, taught in the home of a local matron. In the fourth grade she began attending the public school, where she first encountered a white teacher. At first the transition was unsettling, but then, as she later

This 1924 snapshot shows Septima Poinsette (right) with her brother Peter and his wife Lucille. (courtesy Avery Research Center at the College of Charleston)

described it, "a small thing happened that was to have a powerful effect on my whole life, I do believe. A man came to the school and gave a show in which several canaries did some sort of act. I remember little about the act but it must have impressed me considerably at the time. The teacher assigned us to write a story about the canaries. I must have written . . . a very good paper, because she praised me for it before the class. This sudden recognition did something for me. From then on I felt better about going to public school."

At the end of the ninth grade, Septima was ready to seek work to help her parents put food on the table, but her mother insisted that she continue her education at the Avery Normal Institute. Avery, founded in 1865 by the American Missionary Association, was the only school in Charleston that offered a college-preparatory curriculum for African Americans. Coming up with the necessary tuition was a struggle for the Poinsettes and so Septima herself took a job babysitting for a black couple in her neighborhood to help pay the bills. Despite the financial worries, she found the world of knowledge at Avery to be "paradise."

Recognizing Septima's unusual intelligence, her teachers pressed her to go on to college. Avery's principal collected information about Fisk University and discussed the prospect with the Poinsettes. Septima knew that, despite their enthusiasm, her parents could never afford to pay for it, so she resolved to find work as a teacher. However, she never gave up on getting a college degree. (After decades of summer school, she would receive her B.A. from Benedict College in 1942 and her M.A. from Hampton Institute in 1955, just before she went to Highlander.)

Teaching on Johns Island

Because the Charleston public schools did not hire blacks, it was a challenge for Septima to find work. With the help of a local minister, she secured a teaching position on Johns Island, a tiny piece of lush land just off the coast of South Carolina. The population of Johns Island, as well as the other nearby Sea Islands, was overwhelmingly African-American, descended from slaves brought over from Africa and the Caribbean in the early nineteenth century.

Until the 1930s, the Sea Islands were reachable only by ferry. Because of this isolation, the residents developed a distinct language and culture, called Gullah. (According to one theory, the word "Gullah" originated from Angola, pronounced "n'gulla," the coast from which many slaves left Africa.) Like many of the African languages, Gullah relies primarily on singular nouns and the present tense. Linguists have traced Gullah words to many African languages, including Wolof, Igbo, Temme, Twi, Mende, and Kongo. Some of these words, such as the Temme *nanse,* or spider, remained within Gullah, while others, such as *yam* and *okra,* spread into English. Many of Gullah's adaptations of standard English are vivid and descriptive, such as *dayclean* for dawn, or *shut mout* for secretive. Because slaves were rarely taught to read or write, Gullah remained an oral language.

When Septima arrived on Johns Island in 1916, there were fourteen schools for blacks and three for whites. The black schools generally had more than double the number of pupils the white schools had, and Septima described her student body as "a mass of children from tiny little things to mature persons," all with varying degrees of education. There was also a huge variance in teacher salaries. At one point Septima taught 132 pupils for thirty-five dollars per month while the white teacher in the school nearby taught three pupils for eighty-five dollars per month.

Septima never knew how many students would attend on any given day. "On rainy days when no work could be done in the fields we would have a large attendance. But if by noon the sun came out, the plantation overseer would ride up to school and call for the tenants' children." Entire families were contractually obligated to provide labor on demand in exchange for rations of staple food such as flour, rice, fatback, and molasses.

Another challenge was coping with the primitive conditions. Her school had two rooms for all 132 students, with a chimney in the middle for heat. The only light came from the windows on two sides, rough openings with no glass or screens, covered only by shutters. There was no chalkboard, so she wrote out lessons on old paper bags. The only furniture was a row of backless benches, so the students sat on the floor and propped their papers on the benches to write. But Septima found—and cultivated—a love of learning in her students. Most of them had to walk several miles over muddy roads or paddle across creeks with no bridges to get to school, but they told her that they were happy to be there instead of working in the fields.

Septima herself lived in an attic room, with so many gaps between the boards that the wind whistled through. During her first winter on Johns Island, she got chilblains, a kind of frostbite, from walking in the almost-freezing mud. The natives advised her to put her feet in hot baked potatoes, an old folk remedy that must have brought them relief but didn't solve the problem for Septima. Instead she learned to protect her feet by wrapping them in towels before slogging through the mud.

Even in this harsh setting, Septima loved teaching, right from the beginning. Unlike Ida B. Wells, who became a teacher because it was one of the few respectable professions open to her and never found much satisfaction in the work, Septima was a natural educator—patient, kind, and eager to help people gain confidence as well as knowledge. It was on Johns Island that she first experimented with the techniques she came to rely upon in her work in the citizenship schools: translating the rich oral tradition into writing, using tracing to practice words, and respecting whatever experience and skills each student brought to the classroom.

With no textbooks to work from, she began by talking to the students and encouraging them to tell stories about the island, its trees, animals, people, and events. Septima wrote the stories down and taught from them, word by word, incorporating the Gullah language at the same time she was guiding the students toward standard English.

> When I taught reading, I put down "de" for "the," because that's the way they said "the." Then I told them, "Now when you look in a book, you're going to see 'the.' You say 'de,' but in the book it's printed 'the.'"

When fraternal organizations like the Masons (to which Wells's father had belonged) spread to the island, the parents of Septima's pupils began to approach her for help in filling out applications or writing speeches. Septima worked with them as she had their children, querying each student, writing down his answer, and using it as a guide to help develop the speech. The islanders easily memorized their speeches and soon wanted to read and write themselves. Septima began teaching night classes, which the adults attended after they came in from the fields.

She thrived on the teaching, the busy schedule, and the rich culture, saying later that Johns Island was "never boresome." She was instrumental in improving conditions and methods in the Johns Island schools, creating textbooks and organizing the classrooms to better facilitate learning. She organized a parent-teacher group, participated in the local sewing circle, attended wakes, enjoyed the fiddling and dancing at the celebration that followed the cotton harvest, ate coconut and peanut candy hot from an iron pot when it was time to boil the sugarcane for molasses. The islanders welcomed Miss Seppie, and she loved and respected them.

Decades later she recalled the progress of several students from her early years on Johns Island: the first black engineer at the navy yard, a successful lawyer in New York, a teacher in Charleston, and one of the leaders of the local citizenship school. She later wrote, "It was the Johns Island folk who, if they did not set me on my course, surely did confirm me in a course I had dreamed of taking even as a child, that of teaching and particularly teaching the poor and underprivileged of my own underprivileged race."

Campaign for Black Teachers

In 1919 Septima returned to Charleston to teach at Avery Normal. She also joined the NAACP and became active in its campaign to force the state to hire black teachers in the Charleston public school system. White citizens opposed the change, even though the school system itself would remain segregated and the black teachers would work only in the black schools.

This was another formative experience for her, one that introduced her to the work and rewards of political organizing. "I volunteered . . . and started visiting the grassroots people [to gather petition signatures]," she recalled. "Soon we brought a tow sack—we called it a croaker sack, I remember, back in those days—with more than 10,000 signatures. . . . I remember the number because of the fact that a white legislator known then as One-Eyed Tillman had declared [that we] would never be able to get 10,000 signatures. The law [allowing black teachers in the public schools] was passed. . . . We had been victorious in this, my first effort to establish for Negro citizens what I sincerely believed was no more than their God-given rights." Soon, she herself was teaching in the public schools, as well as pursuing her own B.A. during the summers.

Nerie Clark

In January 1919, Septima Poinsette met a handsome navy cook named Nerie Clark and invited him to church. The date must have gone well, because in May Nerie got a three-day pass to pay Septima a surprise visit. The trip from Norfolk, Virginia, to Charleston and back took two days, and on his one day in town, Septima was busy with school duties. That evening she waited with Nerie at the railroad station, and when he boarded his train, she gave him a passionate send-off: "I . . . kissed him so hard that the blue dye rubbed off his uniform onto my white shirtwaist."

A year later the couple married, over the objections of her family. Her "caste-conscious" mother didn't like the fact that Nerie was several shades darker than Septima, and both her parents pointed out "that Nerie Clark was virtually a stranger—I'd seen him on only two occasions—and that my family knew nothing about his family, since his being from way up in North Carolina made him almost a foreigner to them." But as Septima recalled, "I had never fallen in love before, I had a feeling that this was my chance. This was my life, so I went ahead with it."

Because of his work, Nerie Clark was often away from home, so Septima suffered the death of their firstborn alone. The baby girl, Victoria, was born with an intestinal deformity and died when she was twenty-three days old. Septima was devastated, and the fact that she had named the girl after her own disapproving mother made her grief even deeper. Not long after, Nerie was discharged from the navy and the Clarks moved to Dayton, Ohio, where their second child, a son they named Nerie, was born. While in the hospital recovering, Septima learned that work wasn't the only thing keeping her husband away from home: he was practically living with a mistress. Nerie asked her to leave Dayton and, stunned, she and her infant son moved in with her sympathetic in-laws in Hickory, North Carolina. Ten months later they got word that Nerie Sr. was dying of kidney disease. She arrived back in Dayton "in time to say good-bye to my deeply ashamed husband." Increasingly prizing her independence, Septima decided there and then to never marry again. Her granddaughter recalls her explaining, "No man is going to tell me how to raise my son."

During this painful time Septima never succumbed to self-pity or resentment. In her memoir, *Echo in My Soul*, she described Nerie Clark as "an industrious and courageous man with a deal of pride and a great liking for comfortable surroundings (which, for him, included fashionable clothes) and . . . he was, indeed, a generous, good man." She's more candid in *Ready from Within*, published more than two decades later. She acknowledges her husband's infidelity yet displays no anger. By then, the betrayal was more than fifty years in the past, but her actions at the time speak of her remarkable capacity for forgiveness. She recalls that to prepare for his funeral, she "pieced together all the sweet notes he had written me, so the minister could help the family feel good." Her husband's mistress sent flowers and, understandably, Nerie's brother threw them away. Septima reflected, "I would not have done that. I would not allow hate to enter my heart. I felt sorrow for my husband rather than anger. I pitied any person who could not keep his vows."

Columbia, South Carolina

In 1926 Septima took another teaching job on Johns Island. She found some improvements: "the school's grounds had been mowed, the outside of the building had been painted with creosote, and outdoor privies had been built. . . . And soon I would learn that a health supervisor and a teaching supervisor had been employed to visit the schools on the island." But illiteracy was rampant still, and the economic life of the island was so sluggish that most young people left. During this time, her son, Nerie, then about three, came down with whooping cough and measles. As he was recovering, he slipped away from his caregiver and walked to Septima's school. "Coughing, exhausted, he greeted me, grinning, 'Here I is, Seppie.' . . . I decided at once that as much as I loved him and wanted him to grow up under my own care and guidance, it would be best for him to live with his father's parents. So I sent him back to Hickory." Soon she also made up her mind to try someplace new: Columbia, South Carolina.

She found Columbia refreshingly open. Unlike Charleston with its rigid social distinctions, no one in Columbia cared that her father had been a slave or that her mother took in laundry. Describing the difference between the two cities, she wrote, "When the Negro doctors in Columbia had their meetings, they would invite not only their wives and their more elite friends to the social functions but also their patients. They left no one out. And I like that, though I still love Charleston!"

It was in Columbia that Septima first attended integrated meetings, joined the Federated Women's Club, and did charity work for underprivileged girls. Nerie left his grandparents and lived with her for a year when he was in the seventh grade. Septima planned on having him stay with her permanently, but the situation just wasn't workable. Nerie was used to living on a farm with "room for him to range about," plenty of food from the garden, and milk and butter from the cow. Boarding-house life, with its constricted spaces and "dainty salads and cereals," didn't suit him. He returned to his grandparents' farm, and mother and son maintained their relationship through regular visits.

These separations hurt Septima—in *Freedom's Daughters*, Lynne Olson recounts that Clark "burst into uncontrollable tears" after each reunion—but she always remained on good terms with her in-laws and appreciated their support. Nerie Clark finished high school at sixteen and left college to fight in World War II. Eventually he married and had six children, all of whom were close to "Mama Seppie." The youngest of the six, David, was mentally challenged and lived with Septima from the time he was a baby. (One of his siblings remembers that while doctors had predicted David wouldn't live past age twelve, he lived to be twenty-eight.) The relationship between Septima and her son was loving but "formal," Septima's granddaughter Yvonne, who also lived with her, remembers. "Not hugging and kissing and close, like it always was with us."

Septima doesn't mention it specifically, but her inability to earn enough to have her son live with her may have been an extra motivation for her involvement with an early campaign for racial equality: the fight for equal pay among teachers. Black teachers in Columbia public schools were paid about half as much as white teachers with equivalent education and experience, even though—as on Johns Island—they often worked under much harsher conditions. Another teacher, J. Andrew Simmons, was spearheading the effort to equalize the pay scale, with assistance from the NAACP and one of their young lawyers, who would go on to be a legendary force for civil rights and the first African-American Supreme Court justice, Thurgood Marshall. Septima, who helped gather evidence and record affidavits, was thrilled when the courts decided in the teachers' favor. (Later she described this effort as "my first radical job.") In response, the Columbia school district required all teachers to take the national teachers' examinations. While some teachers resigned rather than take the test, Septima passed with an A and her salary immediately tripled. I imagine that the successful outcome reaffirmed her self-confidence and refined instinct for taking important risks.

Meeting at the Y

When her mother fell ill in 1947, Septima returned to Charleston to care for her in her last year. As she had during her eighteen years in Columbia, she immersed herself in the civic life of her hometown. She helped with fund-raising for the Tuberculosis Association—which, through her extraordinary contributions and personality, she succeeded in integrating. She said, "We Negroes felt that if we weren't able to integrate our efforts to get rid of a dread scourge like tuberculosis, then we just shouldn't work at it." In addition, Clark served as chairman of the YWCA's board, which was also integrated at this time. While at the Y she had an experience that highlights her ability to rise above the baser elements in others in order to find some common ground for progress. The Y had hired an executive secretary, a shy young woman, who soon was targeted by the "rougher boys of the neighborhood [who] would walk into the building and do childish pranks to annoy her." The board decided to approach the mayor to request a two-pronged solution: an increased police presence near the building to deal with the immediate problem, and a city recreation program to help keep the boys out of trouble in the future. Septima arrived at City Hall with two colleagues, both white women. What followed struck me as something like a mirror image of Virginia Durr's experience in the meeting with Jim Eastland.

> The mayor had not known when we made the appointment that one of the three women coming to see him was a Negro. As we walked into the office, he was standing up. He seated the two white women and then sat down himself, with his back to me. Then I sat down behind him.
>
> The white women were indignant at his treatment of me and they flushed to their ears. But I remained calm, outside and inside. We had come down there for a purpose and I resolved to let nothing keep me from doing my part to see the purpose accomplished.

Septima laid out their case calmly, and the mayor agreed to both proposals. After the women left, Septima's colleagues told her how distressed they were at the mayor's behavior, and she assured them she appreciated their kindness. Remembering the event later, she wrote, "But I refused to be disturbed by what happened. 'Well, I do know one thing,' I said to them, 'we got something done this morning and regardless of the way he treated me, I think he must feel now that hereafter he can sit with his face toward a Negro woman.'" For her part, Septima felt that she'd learned several things, "including the virtue and efficacy of having patience and seeing things from the long view, and not permitting myself the costly luxury of losing my temper."

At the next YWCA committee meeting, Septima simply reported

what the mayor had agreed to, not mentioning the man's affront. In *Echo*, she wrote, "I am mentioning it now only to give emphasis to my contention that hating people, bearing hate in your heart, even though you may feel you have been ill-treated, never accomplishes anything good." Although I am sympathetic to the leadership style of other women in this book who stood on principle no matter what the cost to their cause (Ida B. Wells-Barnett is the strongest example, and I'm sure she would have stormed out of the meeting, confronted the mayor and certainly publicized what happened), I find this aspect of Septima's character refreshing. It clearly enabled her to influence people on the large scale that she did, as well as maintain her own peace of mind.

The Warings of Charleston

Through her involvement in the YWCA, Septima became friends with the most reviled white couple in Charleston—Federal Judge Waties Waring and his wife, Elizabeth. Waring, a member of a prominent local family, was appointed to the bench in 1942 with the expectation that he would protect and defend the old guard. But after his racial views were transformed during his time on the bench, he shattered that notion. When he and his first wife (from another prominent local family) divorced and he married Detroit native Elizabeth Avery, he began to make his break from the old guard. Septima remembered him saying, "You know, a judge has to live with his conscience. I would sit in a courtroom, and I would see black men coming in that I knew were decent men, and they were considered bums and trash because they were black. And I would see white men that I knew were bums and they were considered gentlemen. I just couldn't take it any longer."

In his biography of Waring, *A Passion for Justice*, Tinsley Yarbrough cites a specific case as the spur for Waring's transformation. On February 12, 1946, a newly discharged black army veteran and Bronx native named Isaac Woodward Jr. boarded a bus near Camp Gordon, Georgia, headed for his wife's home in Winnsboro, South Carolina. That night he was taken off the bus in a small town near Columbia called Batesburg, arrested for public drunkenness and disorderly conduct, and held overnight. The next morning he pleaded guilty and paid a fine. It was noted during his court appearance that Woodward's eyes appeared unusually "red and swollen." That day

Woodward checked in to the Columbia veterans' hospital, where he remained for three months. During his arrest, he'd been beaten and rendered totally blind.

Civil rights groups began demanding justice for Woodward. In September federal charges were filed against Batesburg police chief Lynwood Shull, accusing him of blinding Woodward with a blackjack. Waring presided over the trial, which revealed that during the stop in Batesburg, Woodward asked the bus driver to wait while he found a restroom. The white driver cursed him and ordered him to sit back down. Woodward responded, "Talk to me like I'm talking to you. I'm a man just like you," and left the bus. When he returned, he was arrested and beaten. At the end of the testimony, Waring asked the all-white jury to "put aside prejudice and give due justice," while one of Shull's attorneys warned the jury, "If Lynwood Shull is convicted today, you will be saying to the public officers of South Carolina that you no longer want your home, your wife, your children protected." The jury took only twenty-five minutes to acquit Shull.

Elizabeth Waring attended the trial. Enormously disturbed by what she saw, she began a thorough examination of the social dynamics of the South. As Virginia Durr had, she turned to books: W. J. Cash's *Mind of the South* and Gunnar Myrdal's *An American Dilemma*, along with other examinations of the segregated South. She shared her readings with her husband, who later said, "I couldn't take it, at first. I used to say it wasn't true, it couldn't be. I'd put the books down, so troubled I couldn't look at them. We'd get in our car and drive through the night, miles and miles, just thinking and talking."

As a result, Waring banned segregated seating in his courtroom, hired a black bailiff, ordered that the lists of prospective jurors not indicate their race, and ruled in favor of equal pay for black teachers. In 1947 he declared "white primaries" unconstitutional, ordering the local Democratic Party to either allow blacks to vote in the primaries or be held legally accountable. Within three days of his announcement, 4,360 blacks registered in Charleston County, and 30,000 blacks voted in the next Democratic primary.

Waring's actions greatly impressed Septima:

Several days before the election [in August 1948], some of the whites made a statement that if blacks attempted to vote in the primary, then blood would be running down the streets like water. Judge Waring said to them, and had the press print it, that, "If that happens, I'll put you in jail, and you'll stay there for the rest of your life. These people have a right to vote, and so they will vote."

You know, that was a quiet election. Election day used to be a terrible thing around Charleston. Guns were always out. During the election just before this one, a young white reporter was killed. There would always be some death. But Judge Waring stopped that.

There would always be some death. This was the context of Septima's political activism, which included seeking out allies like the Warings. Their friendship must have been one of the first times she saw white people willing to be partners in the fight for racial equality, which was clearly very important to her. Yvonne remembers that her grandmother "adored the Warings. She talked about them all the time" and kept a portrait of them in her home.

After learning about Waring's stance in support of voting rights for blacks, Clark decided that Elizabeth would be a good choice to address the next meeting of the black chapter of the Charleston YWCA. (While the YWCA board was integrated, it maintained segregated chapters.) Elizabeth Waring was glad to oblige, but once word got out anticipating her speech, in Septima's words, "all hell broke forth."

Despite pressure from blacks and whites, Septima refused to withdraw the invitation and Elizabeth refused to withdraw her acceptance. In fact, she called the national YWCA office to report the pressure—which only increased. Whites objected to the flouting of Jim Crow convention, and blacks feared the funding stream from white foundations would dry up. Septima and Elizabeth both were subjected to attacks, and Septima remembered receiving hostile and obscene phone calls, to which she'd respond, "Thank you," and hang up. She also recalled Judge Waring's advice to post someone at each of the light switches the night of the speech, "because if the Klan comes in, the first thing they're going to do is turn your lights out, and then you'll have a terrible time."

That night, Septima wrote, Elizabeth Waring "talked plainly and laid it on."

Speaking of Charlestonians generally, she told them they were decadent and low-down and she promised they would be getting their just deserts; she told them that one day as she was riding a city bus she saw on it a picture of the Pilgrims praying. Why, she asked sarcastically, would they put such a picture on a bus that had the Negro riders herded at the back; it was a terrible thing to do, she declared, a terrible way to treat people. She really laid the whip to the backs of the people of Charleston and the South.

Afterwards, Judge Waring handed out typed copies of his wife's speech, instructing the reporter present to print it exactly as written. Not surprisingly, it created an uproar.

Clark's friendship with the Warings caused problems for her within the black community as well. At one faculty meeting, her fellow teachers berated her for her association with them. "They said it just proved what white people were saying, that the real reason that blacks wanted integration was to socialize with whites." Pointing out that her accusers valued their own freedom in making decisions about their lives such as selecting their own cars and clothes and spouses, Septima responded calmly, "I have a right to select my own friends." Her refusal to go along with these conventions led to more obscene and threatening phone calls, as well as the loss of her more conformist friends.

Septima was frustrated by the more affluent blacks who did not want to ruffle feathers by standing up to the powers behind segregation. "Material things were more important to them than the human value things," Clark lamented. In some cases this cowardice was a version of the force of socialization that kept whites from questioning the social structure, what Virginia Durr described as the magic circle.

As Durr did, Clark faced opposition to her involvement in the civil rights movement within her own family, who were concerned for both her and themselves. They didn't want her to jeopardize her stable job or her physical well-being, and they also feared for their own financial and physical safety. She sought to change their minds but never admonished them, saying that "everyone is entitled to their feelings."

Highlander

Septima Clark first went to Highlander in the summer of 1953, at the suggestion of another black teacher who had discovered that it was the only place in the South where blacks and whites could meet together and talk about early childhood education. Immediately the threads of Septima's interests and experiences began coming together, and she found her calling.

She was instinctively drawn to Highlander's cultural director, Zilphia Horton, a warm woman and a talented musician who wove singing throughout the school's programs. John Lewis remembered, "It didn't matter whether you could carry a tune or not, everyone sang. Even me, and I *cannot* sing." Like his wife, Myles Horton was warm and sociable, but he also had an intense, challenging Socratic style, pushing students and teachers alike to move beyond comfortable actions and responses.

Well aware that the school was being monitored, Horton wryly put the Knoxville FBI office on the Highlander mailing list. The FBI agents, with their J. Edgar Hoover-instilled mania for documentation, dutifully included all the material in their file on Highlander, along with letters from paranoid neighbors and reports from undercover agents. Hundreds of people from all over the country mailed in accusations and supposed documentation of Communist infiltration at the school. Hundreds more asked the FBI whether the charges of subversion and anti-Americanism they'd heard were true. So many people wrote in with similar questions that the FBI developed a boilerplate response:

> The Highlander Folk School has been the subject of numerous allegations that it is a communist school and the headquarters of communism in eastern Tennessee, due primarily to its interracial character. These allegations have not been substantiated. The Bureau has not investigated this organization.

Often the response also included a selection of Hoover-authored pamphlets, such as *What You Can Do to Fight Communism and Preserve America*.

Septima found the school's optimistic, daring spirit exhilarating. As she put it, "Highlander workshops weren't set up merely to theorize and ponder problems; they expected and demanded that theory and discussion and decision be galvanized into action and achievement." Every session ended with each person answering the question, "What do you plan on doing when you get home?"

Horton recognized the value of Clark's teaching style and encouraged her to visit often, which she did, spending school holidays teaching there. The summer of 1954, she helped to prepare two pamphlets, *A Guide to Action for Public School Desegregation* and *What is a Workshop?* She also brought promising recruits to Highlander, such as Esau Jenkins from Johns Island. Jenkins was a confident man, a natural leader who'd established a successful bus company carrying Johns Islanders to Charleston. Highlander provided the training, support, and structure that enabled him to make real changes on the island. When he was asked what he planned to do when he got home, he said he would enter the race for school trustee, just to prove that a black man could run for office and not be killed.

In the summer of 1955, at Virginia Durr's behest, Rosa Parks enrolled in Highlander Folk School. Clark had implemented her teaching methods throughout the school. Parks recalled how Septima "just moved through the different workshops and groups as though it was just what she was made to do, in spite of the fact that she had to face so much opposition in her home state and lost her job and all that. She seemed to be just a beautiful person and it didn't seem to shake her." Clark's strength and steadiness combined with Horton's wit drew Rosa Parks out. "Myles Horton just washed away and melted a lot of my feelings of hostility and prejudice and feeling of bitterness toward white people because he had such a wonderful sense of humor," Parks recalled. "I often thought about many of the things he had said and how he could strip the white segregationists of their hardcore attitudes and how he could confuse them, and I found myself laughing when I hadn't been able to laugh in a long time."

That same summer, Alice Poinsette, the youngest daughter of Septima's brother Peter, stayed at Highlander. She had just graduated from high school and worked as a gofer, fetching coffee and pencils and helping her aunt look after Yvonne. She recalled that Septima used the workshops to "give courage to people" and specifically drew in a reluctant Parks:

> The one thing that struck me about her workshops—and I remember this with the Montgomery people so well—is that she said you can't solve a problem if you are still emotionally involved in it. So the first session was getting all those feelings and anger and stuff out of you so we can start talking about, "Well, what can we do from here?" And in fact, she got on me

Septima with Rosa Parks at Highlander (courtesy Highlander Research and Education Center)

because [during that session] Rosa was doing Yvonne's hair and Rosa just said, "Oh, I don't want to be in there with all that screaming and hollering"—and people did, you know. They were just that angry. Septima said to me, "Who's supposed to be doing Yvonne's hair?" and I said, "I am." "Well, why is Rosa doing it?" . . . I finally convinced Rosa to go. I said, "Seppie told me *I* have to do the hair and *you* have to go to the workshop."

Alice recalls being at Hampton Institute months later and picking up the newspaper to see Rosa Parks on the cover. "I just screamed and cried because I knew that took a lot of courage for her to do that." (As for the bus boycott, Alice says, "They had planned that whole thing out" at Highlander.)

Parks has said that her experience at Highlander was critical to her decision to put herself on the line for the cause. "People always say that I didn't give up my seat because I was tired, but that isn't true," she explained later. "I was not tired physically, or no more tired than I usually was at the end of a working day. I was not old, although some people have an image of me as being old then. I was forty-two. No, the only tired I was, was tired of giving in. . . . I had decided that I would have to know once and for all what rights I had as a human being and a citizen, even in Montgomery, Alabama."

"When I heard the news," recalled Septima, "I said, 'Rosa? Rosa?' She was so shy when she came to Highlander, but she got enough courage to do that."

Brown *and NAACP membership*

After the landmark *Brown v. Board of Education* decision, the Charleston public school system required all teachers to list their organizational affiliations on questionnaires. The South Carolina legislature concurrently passed a law that said no city or state employee could belong to the NAACP. Despite the obvious consequences, Septima listed her membership and was summarily dismissed, with no official explanation. Almost sixty years old, after forty years of teaching, Clark had no job and no pension.

Disappointed by the lack of solidarity among her fellow teachers, most of whom either resigned from the NAACP or hid their affiliation with it, Septima longed to change their minds. She later called her inability to convince the other black teachers to fight against the unjust law "the big failure of my life." Septima signed and mailed 726 letters asking them to protest. Only eleven teachers responded and only four agreed to accompany her to a meeting with her supervisor, who just shrugged and said that Septima was ahead of her time. According to Alice Poinsette Frazier, her father, Septima's brother Peter, was frustrated and upset that his sister, whom he'd helped put through school, would sacrifice her job. "I could just feel the tension in the house. . . . He said, 'She had a good job. Why did she have to do this? Why couldn't she just be like everybody else?'"

This moment tellingly reflects Clark's courage of conviction. She wrote 726 letters and considered it her own "failure" that they weren't successful—an astounding testament to her belief in civil liberties and the strength of her convictions. "I felt then—and I feel now—that a kind Providence directs us when we strive to do what we think is right," she explained.

Soon after her firing, Myles Horton offered her a full-time job as

Septima reading with her granddaughter Yvonne with their integrated doll collection in the background (courtesy Yvonne Clark)

education director at Highlander and she moved there with her granddaughter. (Yvonne remembers lying in Myles Horton's garden that first summer, drinking lemonade and gazing up at "these enormous sunflowers that would turn and face the sun.") Septima continued to put into use everything she'd learned in her decades of teaching and activism. She developed workbooks that were respectful of the adult students and imparted practical civic knowledge. "There's not a mention of dogs, cats, bunnies, chickens, not one exhortation to 'Come, Muff, see Puff.' Instead, at the top of the page is a roughly outlined map of the United States . . . Underneath this map is a half page of text under the simple title *Our America*." Other chapters included "Political Parties in South Carolina," "Taxes You Must Pay in South Carolina," "Social Security," "Your Health Services and How to Address Officials." Despite the many charges of anti-Americanism hurled at Highlander, this was hardly subversive material, except, of course, in that it enabled and encouraged blacks to be full citizens.

Spreading Citizenship Schools

The first citizenship school on Johns Island developed over a period of years out of a collaboration among students and teachers. The first person to raise the idea was one of Esau Jenkins's bus passengers, Alice Wine. One morning she told Jenkins, "I don't have much schooling, Esau. I wasn't even able to get through third grade. But I would like to hold up my head with other people; I'd like to be able to vote. Esau, if you'll help me a little when you have the time, I'll be glad to try to learn the South Carolina laws about voting, and if I can learn the laws and get qualified to vote, I promise you I'll register and I'll vote." Jenkins began teaching all the bus riders the relevant material and some, including Alice Wine, did register, but he knew they needed a much larger program, and so he turned to Highlander.

During 1955 Myles Horton made several visits to the island and that summer, Septima and Esau Jenkins brought twelve Johns Islanders to Highlander for residential workshops. In his article "The Birth of Citizenship Schools," David P. Levine describes one workshop:

> During an evening session, a Johns Island group presented "How Buddy Votes," a reenactment of how one man became convinced of the power of the ballot and also persuaded his father to register. During the play, Buddy Freeman and Esau Jenkins played themselves, and Clark played Buddy's wife. A sense of Jenkins' political gospel is captured in the dialogue. He exhorts Buddy to vote, arguing, "If you do not go to the extreme in doing something then the Lord cannot help you. You have a houseful of children, you need his help. But He cannot help you if you don't go down and register to vote, that you can get the things that are necessary for you and your children's health sake." Jenkins's mention of health care for children would have resonated with blacks back on Johns Island. In 1953 sixty-eight children on the island had died during a diphtheria epidemic.

By 1956, Horton, Clark, and Jenkins were looking for a place to hold classes. School administrators and preachers were afraid to host them, so Highlander loaned the Progressive Club, the voter education group Esau Jenkins had founded, $1,500 to buy a building. Classes were held in the back of the building and, partly for camouflage and partly because it was needed, a co-op store occupied the front.

The first teacher they recruited was Septima's cousin, Bernice Robinson, who'd just returned to Charleston after a number of years in New York. Robinson protested, saying she'd be happy to *help* the teacher but not to *be* the teacher. Eventually they convinced her that if she didn't agree, the school couldn't open, so she gave in. On January 7, 1957, Bernice stood before her first group of fourteen students.

She followed the pattern set by Septima years before: "Bernice and her students would tell stories about the things they had to deal with every day—about growing vegetables, plowing the land, digging up potatoes. Then they would write down these stories and read them back. Any words they stumbled over, Bernice would use in the spelling lesson." She also had her own innovations. Some of the students had young daughters they didn't want to leave home alone, so Bernice began sewing and crocheting lessons for the girls.

From the very beginning, the literacy lessons were always directed at civic participation and empowerment, and the Johns Island school was very successful at getting people to register and vote. The most immediate incentive was Esau Jenkins's promised run for a seat on the school board. "People wanted to vote so that they might vote for Esau," Septima explained. His campaign encouraged many black islanders to register for the first time, and that increase in eligible voters changed the political calculus. The next year, a white judge in a tight race approached Jenkins to ask for support. Jenkins recalled, "I told him that if he would promise to treat them [blacks] better, make them realize they are human beings when they come into the court, not charging them with everything or just assuming they are wrong, but just give them what belongs to them—if they are right, let them know they are right—I said, we will vote for you. We got a few Negroes voting, and if you got fifty percent of your people, the rest of the Negroes would certainly turn the tide." In a stirring example of Clark's growing influence, the judge won his race and his treatment of blacks measurably improved.

Each citizenship school led to others. "You see, one thing spreading out starts others. It's like the pebble thrown into the mill pond," said Septima. With their increased success, political attacks against Highlander began to spread too, with the favored technique still being the right-wing standard: red-baiting.

The rumors about Communist activity at the school were so fantastical that they included the idea that the roof of Myles Horton's house was flat so that Soviet helicopters could land on it. Virginia Durr's nemesis, Mississippi senator James Eastland, got in on the act with his subcommittee on Internal Security, and Georgia Governor Marvin Griffin appointed a special commission specifically to investigate Highlander "so the people of Georgia will know where some of the South's racial trouble originates." The commission concluded that the school was a "communist training school" to promote "methods and tactics for precipitating racial disturbances."

In 1957, the year after he rose to fame in the Montgomery bus boycott, Martin Luther King Jr. came to the school's twenty-fifth anniversary celebration as the keynote speaker. The event, open to the press, drew reporters from many different papers, including, unbeknownst to the Highlander leadership, a Communist publication called the *Daily Worker*. During the proceedings, an undercover agent for Governor Griffin's commission snapped a picture of Dr. King sitting near this reporter. The photograph was reproduced on billboards around the South as "proof" that King had attended a "Communist training center." Myles Horton responded with a statement denouncing the "irresponsible demagoguery" and calling for "equal opportunity." Supporters of Highlander, including Eleanor Roosevelt and Reinhold Niebuhr, signed the document. As the forces of reaction gathered strength throughout the South, the attacks on Highlander increased, finally culminating in the raid of July 31, 1959.

Hearings After the Highlander Raid

On August 6, 1959, a preliminary hearing on the liquor possession charge against Septima was held before two Grundy County justices of the peace. Her attorney, Cecil Branstetter, demanded the right to question the informant whose sworn testimony had been used to justify the search warrant. The motion was denied, and the testimony against Highlander began. One state witness testified that she had seen a black man and a white woman having sexual intercourse in the school library, on a date before the library had been built. Another witness, Dr. Wilford Owen, head of the theology department at the University of the South in Sewanee, Tennessee, testified that he had once been offered a choice of beer or orange juice at a social gathering. He added that he'd never seen drunkenness, immorality, or the sale of liquor during his visits to the workshops there. In Owen's opinion, the school's bad reputation resulted from the fact that "some people in Sewanee disagree with integration of any sort, or improving race relations."

Branstetter's only defense witness was Septima Clark. She said that the only liquor found the night of the raid had never been in her possession and in fact was found in Horton's home and not on Highlander property. District Attorney General Ab Sloan shook his finger in Clark's face and threatened her with a perjury charge if she "falsifie[d] the records" of the school, and in his summary roared that Highlander was "an integrated whorehouse." The court upheld the possession charge.

Next Sloan petitioned Circuit Court Judge Chester Chattin for a "padlock order" shutting down the entire Highlander campus as a "public nuisance." On September 16, Judge Chattin ordered the administration building temporarily padlocked, while the other eleven buildings remained open. Shortly after Chattin's order was applied, on September 26, Myles Horton told the members of a workshop, "You can padlock a building. But you can't padlock an idea . . . you can't kill it and you can't close it in. This workshop is part of the idea. It will grow wherever people take it."

Ordinarily the authorities' next step would be to file for a permanent injunction against the school, but Sloan dropped that request and asked instead that Highlander's charter be revoked on grounds that it was operating a racially integrated private school in violation of Tennessee law. Finally, in February 1960, the Grundy County circuit court judge revoked the school's charter on the grounds that it had "permitted integration in its school work" and that Myles Horton had improperly enriched himself through the school. In April 1961, Highlander lost on appeal.

Throughout the entire ordeal, Septima kept organizing workshops and planning for the continuation of the citizenship schools. No matter how much antagonism was directed her way, she refused to respond in kind. Her description of her encounter with Ab Sloan at that preliminary hearing reflected her confidence and good humor: "I knew he was all stirred up inside. I could see the veins sticking out in his neck, and I thought to myself, that man won't even be able to digest his dinner tonight. Me, I went home and ate hearty as you please."

The Southern Christian Leadership Conference and Dorchester

Septima Clark and Myles Horton, anticipating the loss on appeal, had already taken Highlander into a new phase by joining forces with

Martin Luther King Jr.'s Southern Christian Leadership Conference (SCLC).[4] As early as the fall of 1958, SCLC organizer Ella Baker[5] had visited Highlander with this partnership in mind. Baker knew that Clark's workshops were aimed at registering illiterate blacks, and she was especially impressed by the fact that Clark recruited so many women to be citizenship teachers. John Lewis later recalled in his memoir, *Walking with the Wind*, that "one of the hallmarks of Highlander's reputation [was] that women were as involved as men in all the seminars and workshops and were treated with as much respect."

Other SCLC leaders, including King himself, were attracted to the partnership because it enabled them to conduct a coordinated, multipronged campaign, with the students of SNCC continuing to lead sit-ins, King acting as a national spokesperson, and Septima Clark registering voters. Also appealing was the fact that many influential foundation officials were already impressed by Clark and her programs: the SCLC desperately needed more funds.

Initially, it wasn't an easy transition. Some in the national movement had opposed King's joining with Highlander because of concerns that the school's reputation would taint the SCLC. Some of the Highlander loyalists—including Septima—bristled at what they saw as the inner circle's top-down approach and its exclusion of women.

---

[4] After the success of the Montgomery bus boycott, several community leaders expressed interest in continuing and expanding similar protests. As head of the Montgomery Improvement Association, which had led the boycott, Martin Luther King Jr. organized the Negro Leaders Conference on Nonviolent Integration, held in Atlanta on January 10–11, 1957. Sixty ministers from ten Southern states attended. (During the conference segregationists in Montgomery bombed the black First Baptist Church and several homes, including that of Rev. Ralph Abernathy, who was attending the conference. Fortunately no one was killed or badly injured.) The conferees voted to form a new organization that would, after a few name changes, become the Southern Christian Leadership Conference.

[5] Like Septima Clark, Ella Baker was a quiet but powerful presence in the civil rights movement. Born in Norfolk, Virginia, in 1903, she listened to her grandmother's stories of slave revolts and the whippings her grandmother received for refusing to pair up with the slave the owner had chosen for her. Baker went to Shaw University in Raleigh, North Carolina, and graduated as valedictorian. She moved to New York City and became involved in promoting women's rights and economic power through collective bargaining. In 1940, she became a field secretary, then director of branches, for the NAACP and was associated with the organization until 1957, when she moved to Atlanta to set up the SCLC. Baker shared Clark's impatience with hierarchical, centralized structure and the "great leader" approach to organizing. As she said, "strong people don't need strong leaders." She left the SCLC after two years and organized the conference of young activists that led to SNCC.

But the alliance went forward, and Septima's methods—as well as her talent for turning people into leaders—became an engine for the next phase of the civil rights movement. As the SCLC records state, "The CEP [Citizen Education Program] was established in 1960 when Septima P. Clark, a literacy teacher at the Highlander Folk School, convinced Martin Luther King Jr. that literacy training and political education would spur voter registration among African-Americans in the South. Highlander Folk School's CEP was disintegrating under pressure from the hostile Tennessee State government, and the SCLC essentially took over the Highlander program, bringing Clark on the smooth transition."

In an appeal for funding for this new project, Martin Luther King Jr. wrote a letter describing the techniques Septima had developed. "Through Myles Horton and Septima Clark, professional educators, a method to train individuals for these purposes was developed and tested for a period exceeding five years," he wrote. "This program was designed to equip persons for citizenship starting with the teaching of reading and writing in order to become registered to vote. . . . SCLC has accepted the invitation to use this educational plan and consider its unique advantages in filling the need for developing new leadership as teachers and supervisors and providing the broad educational base for the population at large through the establishment of citizenship schools conducted by these new leaders throughout the South."

In 1961 Clark became the director of education and teaching for the SCLC, reporting directly to Andrew Young, the minister from New Orleans whom King had recruited to coordinate his efforts. The SCLC soon headquartered its citizenship school program at Dorchester, a former Congregationalist retreat near the Georgia coast.

Like Highlander, Dorchester was an oasis from the surrounding tensions, its sturdy brick buildings surrounded by lush oak trees draped in Spanish moss. From there, Septima presided over a mass movement to train local leaders to disperse throughout the South and teach others to read, write, register, vote, and peacefully protest. "The people who left Dorchester went home to teach and to work in voter registration drives," Clark recalled. "They went home, and they didn't take it anymore. They started their own citizenship classes, discussing the problems in their towns. 'How come the pavement stops where the black section begins?' Asking questions like that, and then know-

Clark with guests at Highlander in front of the library (courtesy Highlander Research and Education Center)

ing who to go to to talk about it, or where to protest it." One student told how the intensive five days at Dorchester transformed her view of what was possible. "The cobwebs are moving from my brain," she explained.

Beatings in a Mississippi Jail

By now the segregationist campaign of massive resistance had gone beyond threats and property destruction. The civil rights workers themselves came under attack, as did their sympathizers or those perceived to be sympathizers. Septima recalled one horrible incident in Marion, Alabama, where a policeman was threatening to beat the mother of a black man. "He ran up to put his arms around his mother, and they shot him in the groin. He died the next day. We lost thirty people, from northern Virginia to eastern Texas, during the time we were working in the civil rights movement to get people registered."

There's no way to calculate the number of Septima's colleagues who were beaten and injured. One was Annell Ponder.

Ponder was Septima's teaching assistant at Dorchester when, in early 1963, she was recruited to set up a citizenship school in Greenwood, Mississippi. Ponder arrived at the beginning of March. The week before, on the last day of February, a SNCC volunteer had been shot in the neck and nearly killed. Under intense pressure from the public and the Kennedy Justice Department, county authorities arrested three men for the shooting but deferred the trial indefinitely. Greenwood was only one of the danger spots in the South. That spring bombings, beatings, and shootings spread throughout the region. SNCC and other student groups responded with increased intensity. By May the protests had coalesced around Birmingham, Alabama, where Bull Connor's police force set attack dogs on protesters and had them blasted with fire hoses.

The first week of June, Ponder was back in Dorchester with several recent graduates of the Greenwood literacy program, attending a teacher-training workshop. The group included forty-five-year-old sharecropper Fannie Lou Hamer,[6] already a community leader in Sunflower County, and sixteen-year-old June Johnson, who'd first been drawn to the movement by a crush on the local SNCC coordinator and was now a dedicated activist.

On June 9 the group boarded a Trailways bus back to Greenwood, full of enthusiasm after an intensive week of training. Even the meals at Dorchester—featuring offerings such as "Freedom Fighting Hot Rolls," "Full Citizenship Barbecued Chicken," "Literacy Potato Salad," and "Brotherhood Punch"—reminded the brand-new teachers of their goals and the means to achieve them.

That afternoon, when their bus stopped in Winona, Mississippi, the

---

[6] Hamer would become the most visible face of the Mississippi Freedom Democratic Party, which was created by SNCC as an alternative to the state's white-controlled Democratic Party. After she and other MFDP activists were barred from the 1964 party convention in Atlantic City, they challenged their exclusion from the convention floor, an act that helped open the party leadership to minorities. Later, Hamer's summary of her motivations would become famous. Jerry DeMuth, writing for the *Nation*, interviewed Hamer, who explained that she'd become involved with political and civic activism because "I was sick and tired of being sick and tired." The sentence became so deeply linked with Hamer that her family had it engraved on her headstone.

group walked into the white section of the waiting area. Spotting them, the waitress yelled, "I can't take it no more!" and flung her order pad at the wall. Several police officers and a highway patrolman approached them and ordered them to leave, Ponder's indignant reminders that segregation was now banned in interstate transportation falling on deaf ears.

Standing outside the station, Ponder decided she couldn't take it anymore, either. She began writing down the license plate numbers of the cruisers so she could file a complaint. Soon the entire group was under arrest.

At the jailhouse, June Johnson was the first to be questioned. She was taken to the booking room and asked, Are you a member of the NAACP? Who pays you? What kind of trouble are you planning? The officers began by slapping the teenager, then one clouted her on the back of the head with his nightstick. They locked the sobbing girl in a cell and brought in Annell Ponder. She acknowledged that she'd taken down the plate numbers so she could file a complaint, and she refused to address the men as "sir" as long as they called her "nigger" and "bitch." She also told the policemen that she and her friends did not hate them, which I suspect made the men as angry as anything else she said.

When the police started beating Ponder, they went much further than they had with Johnson. (Taylor Branch reports that they cursed Bobby Kennedy as they repeatedly knocked the woman to the floor, dragged her upright, and flattened her again.) She emerged bloody and bruised, with a chipped tooth and one eye knocked askew. She made it back to the cell only by holding onto the wall as she walked.

Then it was Fannie Lou Hamer's turn.

Three white men came into my room. One was a state highway policeman (he had the marking on his sleeve) . . . They said they were going to make me wish I was dead. They made me lay down on my face and they ordered two Negro prisoners to beat me with a blackjack. That was unbearable. The first prisoner beat me until he was exhausted, then the second Negro began to beat me. I had polio when I was about six years old. I was limp. I was holding my hands behind me to protect my weak side. I began to work my feet. My dress pulled up and I tried to smooth it down. One of the policemen walked over and raised my dress as high as he could. They beat me until my body was hard, 'til I couldn't bend my fingers or get up when they told me to. That's how I got this blood clot in my eye—the sight's nearly gone now. My kidney was injured from the blows they gave me on the back.

Civil rights workers in the South always left detailed itineraries when they traveled, so when Ponder and her students didn't arrive back in Greenwood on schedule, her colleagues started making phone calls. The answers they got from Winona seemed suspiciously vague. When SNCC member Lawrence Guyot drove to the jail and asked about Ponder and her students, he was arrested and beaten himself.

Eventually Robert Kennedy's Justice Department charged five Mississippi police officers with civil rights violations. The trial was held in December 1964, in the federal building in Oxford, Mississippi. Septima Clark and Ella Baker were there every day, supporting the young activists. The defense attorney dismissed Ponder's testimony as the sort of lies taught at the "Communist training school, Highlander." Clark wrote her old boss Myles Horton, "Your name has not been called but the school as the sponsor was mentioned many times. The man in front of me said, 'I know Russia had something to do with it.'"

Despite the extensive evidence—including the testimony of the two black prisoners who claimed they beat the women under duress—all five defendants were acquitted. The jury deliberated an hour. Lawrence Guyot was furious at the obvious injustice, but Clark simply told him, "You can be bigger than this." Baker added, "Look beyond this foolishness. Don't let it stop you."

Pebble in a Mill Pond

Clark went back to Dorchester determined to redouble her efforts in training teachers, but she also checked up on the field workers with increasing frequency. She often traveled alone, putting herself at great personal risk. Local KKK chapters or White Citizens' Council groups sometimes surrounded the building where she held meetings. Once, in Grenada, Mississippi, they set fire to a church five minutes after she and her citizenship school trainees had left. Clark herself tested the desegregation rules, insisting on sitting in the front section of the bus. "They asked me to move," she remembered, "but I didn't. I reminded them that we had a law now that said we could sit anywhere on the bus."

Clark sometimes took her granddaughter with her on these trips. According to Yvonne, "She never let me see the danger. She didn't take me along when it was really dangerous but there were times when we would sneak in and out of places, or we would pull down the shades, and it wasn't until later in life that I realized we were hiding from the police cars or from the white man out front." Even when they got home, there was a sense of being stalked. "The phones were tapped all my life," says Yvonne, "and there were always cars parked outside that shouldn't have been there."

Septima was one of many activists who stayed with Virginia and Clifford Durr when she passed though Montgomery, and she and Virginia became friends. During one of Clark's visits, Virginia noticed suspicious vehicles driving up and down the block past her house. Then a man identifying himself as a police officer called the house and asked Virginia to come to Cliff's office because of an apparent break-in. Suspecting the call was part of a plan to get Septima alone in the house, Virginia rushed her friend into the car. Eager to lose possible pursuers, Durr frequently stopped at green lights, dramatically powdered her nose, and then, just as the light turned red, shot through the intersection. Clark recalled telling Virginia, "I said, 'I'm really more afraid of riding with you than I am of those Klansmen' because I was so afraid that a policeman was going to stop her. . . . [Then] they would have gotten me."

Despite the danger, Septima loved her time in the field because she saw the results of the sessions at Dorchester or Highlander flourishing throughout the South. She kept in touch with her former students and before she went to visit them, she sent letters full of support, adding a gentle push when needed. "Politicians listen to voters," she wrote to Mildred Patterson of Farmville, Virginia. "You know how to help them get registered. It is important to get your Citizenship School started at once . . . Remember each morning I'm searching the mail for a letter from you. I'm expecting it to say what you have done and that you want me to see your group in action." It was signed, "Your concerned teacher, (Mrs.) Septima Clark."

She made it a point to collect information about the various local

Clark teaching at the Citizenship School on Johns Island with her cousin Bernice Robinson (standing) and their students in 1959. (copyright Ida Berman)

hurdles to voting in order to preemptively train people to clear them. Thus, in addition to her unique lesson books, which included quizzes on such topics as "What does the 14th amendment say?" and "Who is a citizen?" Septima also developed questionnaires to guide the structure of new classes. Those for students asked questions such as "What are the requirements for voting in your area?"

Each state had different requirements, most aimed exclusively at keeping blacks away from the polls. Congressman John Lewis recalls being asked, "How many bubbles are in a bar of soap?" In Georgia, a person had to answer twenty-four of thirty questions correctly in order to register. Some reported questions were "How may a new state be admitted to the union?" and "How many members are in the Georgia House of Representatives and how does the Georgia constitution provide for the seats to be apportioned?" Alabama had about twenty-four questions, one of which was "What is the definition of a thief?" Septima recalled that one teacher said she never could give the right answer, "because the registrar wanted her to say 'a thief is a nigger who steals.'" Accordingly, Septima had dictionary definitions reprinted for those going to Alabama polls.

The questionnaire Clark gave to her trained teachers asked them to assess their students' progress through questions such as "Has the student become a registered voter?" "Did he have difficulty reading or writing in connection with the registration?" "Did he vote?" "What chief reasons does he give for his choice of candidate?" "In what ways has he become more effective in community action?" These questions, with their concern for each individual's civic voice, reflect Clark's commitment to shaping thoughtful citizens, rather than those who would be susceptible to cynical politicians. "People should vote for candidates on the basis of the platforms they offer and the abilities they have, not because of what the candidates give them in the way of fish fries and cold drinks or even cold cash," she said.

Septima was also involved in fund-raising and wrote up progress reports to send to supporters. In one she described the various challenges to voting faced by blacks in the South: "These problems may include illiteracy; prevention and intimidation by local laws and mores; lethargy on the part of the people themselves; lack of information about registration and voting procedure; ignorance of the rights and responsibilities of first class citizenship; and many others." She went on to detail areas where these obstacles had been overcome, including Johns Island, where she proudly reported a huge leap in registered voters and "almost 100% voting of registered persons." And she recruited dynamic speakers and seminar leaders from around the country. She wrote to Reverend C. T. Vivian, SCLC's director of affiliates, requesting his participation: "You can stir them up and send them back home to attempt to change the faces of their community."

The "Mother Conscience"

While Septima's egalitarian approach had meshed easily with Highlander's principles, SCLC's more hierarchical philosophy did indeed create conflicts in her working relationships. She believed that it was the strength and goodwill of a popular movement, not "some government edict or Messiah," that would eradicate racism. Accordingly, she resisted the notion that one national star—even as bright a star as King became—should eclipse local leadership. This was an ongoing source of tension between Septima and Andrew Young, who was King's close confidant and the major liaison between the SCLC and Dorchester. At least once, Septima sent a letter directly to King, arguing that rather than leading all the marches himself, he should "develop leaders who could lead their own marches." As she painfully recalled, King read it aloud to the SCLC members and "they just laughed. . . . Whenever I had anything to say, I would put up my hand and say it. But I did know that they weren't paying attention."

Septima and Andrew Young had a productive, if sometimes tense, relationship. She was close to him and admired him (and he would become "like a second father" to Yvonne) but Clark didn't hesitate to call Young to task for straying from the mission of the movement. In December 1963 she complained to King about Young's lack of support for the Citizenship Education Program. "Many states are losing their Citizenship Schools because there is no one to do follow-up work. . . . It seems as if Citizenship Education is all mine, except when it comes time to pick up the checks." (Young pleaded exhaustion, both physical and emotional, but conceded he hadn't given the CEP the support it needed.)

More often, her objections had to do specifically with the hierarchical mindset. Young was ostensibly her boss but it was Septima who oversaw all the workshops, trained the new teachers, and spent time with the workshop participants. She insisted that these people receive courtesy and respect from everyone in the organization. One morning, shortly after she had arrived at Dorchester, Young stepped off a chartered airplane just as a group of students disembarked from an all-night bus ride. As he began to get himself breakfast, Septima stopped him, insisting that he not eat in front of the students unless he could feed them too. She warned him that people would stop trusting the movement if it was not focused on them and responsive to them.

"If you can pay all that money that the Marshall Field Foundation has sent us to rent a plane, why can't you give them two or three dollars to buy breakfast?" she asked. Failing that, he could share their discomfort.

"Septima, you are a saint," [he responded.]

"No I'm not a saint," she said. "I don't consider myself a saint but I do know that what you are doing is not wise."

As Clark's own selflessness shamed others into listening to her, she became, as Taylor Branch put it, "the SCLC's mother conscience." Yvonne recalls, "The young men—the foot soldiers, as we called them— all talked about my grandmother. J. T. Johnson, Tyrone Brooks, Leon Hall—they all told me stories about how she called them on the carpet [and] about how much they learned from her." On another occasion Septima scolded Reverend Ralph Abernathy for being so intent on flaunting his own importance that he deliberately kept his congregation waiting. She herself had refused a pay raise offered to her at the seventh annual convention of the SCLC, writing to King that she "couldn't accept it and feel perfectly free inside."

Septima's maternal touch is reminiscent of Mother Jones's admonitions to the miners and Frances Perkins's beliefs about powerful mens' reaction to women colleagues. Clark was generally a very calming, soft presence, but she knew when to use a sharp tongue and a steely look. Although the men held superior positions in the organization, she led by influencing them as well as carrying out her own work.

Clark was also constantly asking the SCLC leadership to pay more attention to the leadership potential and needs of women. "She had a real issue with how the SCLC had all males at the top and no females," according to Alice Poinsette Frazier. "She felt all these young ministers thinking, 'She's a lady, she don't know' before they realized she had been protesting since before they were born." Even at Highlander, an organization with a conscious commitment to bringing women into leadership positions, Clark had noticed the differences created by gender and class.

> It was funny to me, but most of the educated men seemed to have that trouble relating. They didn't have the patience at first to work in small towns or listen to the poor people who came in. Myles Horton had trouble sitting and listening to the people from places like Thomasville, Georgia, tell about the happenings there. It was hard for him to sit and listen to them say, "Now this happened the night that that cow had its calf on such-and-such a moon." He wanted them to come right to the point, and they wouldn't do it. [laughing] I found that true with most of the men.

At the SCLC, where there was no similar commitment, Septima grew more frustrated. After a breezy note from Young, in which he mentioned the heavy workload borne by the civil rights workers, Septima responded with detailed objections to "the kind of administration I greatly detest," adding that "I agree with you about the men with families but women have great responsibilities also. They need consideration too." Perhaps her own experience growing up with such a strong mother happily married to a quiet, gentle father gave her extra certainty about the leadership potential of women.

In any event, Clark regretted that King himself did not elevate more women in the civil rights movement, perhaps even herself. In response to a request for a preface to her 1962 memoir, *Echo in My Soul*, King obliged but chose to focus on her struggle to combine motherhood and a career rather than on her considerable accomplishments for civil rights. "*Echo in My Soul*," he wrote, "epitomizes the continuous struggle of the Southern Negro woman to realize her role as a mother while fulfilling her forced position as community teacher, intuitive fighter for human rights and leader of her unlettered and disillusioned people." How annoying this must have been; in the end Clark used a foreword by her colleague Harry Golden.

Despite the clash of styles and disparity of power, Clark and King did have a strong working relationship as well as a cordial friendship. Yvonne remembers his visits to Septima's home in Charleston, "eating okra soup and fried chicken." (She also remembers that, "One time he stayed over and the whole house smelled like Magic Shave.") Septima grew increasingly impressed with King's practice of nonviolence and the resonating power of his speeches. She was also, unlike some in the movement, fully supportive of his brand of civil disobedience. "We felt that in disobeying such unjust laws, the person resisting should do so openly but also in a nonviolent, peaceful manner. And he must willingly accept the penalty for breaking the law," she explained. King clearly valued Septima's work. When he traveled to Norway to receive the 1964 Nobel Peace Prize, Septima was one of a small group asked to accompany him.

As the reactionary forces became more defensive, younger and more militant civil rights activists began rejecting King's doctrine of nonviolence. Septima worried about leaders such as Stokely Carmichael, who was advocating the use of force as well as advancing a notion of separatism. With as keen an eye for irony as her friend Virginia Durr had, she recalled the time that King invited Carmichael to dinner and tried to impress upon him the principle of nonviolence. "Well, Stokely went right out that next Monday on Auburn

Avenue and had a lot of black boys with sticks smashing the windows of black merchants who failed to support Dr. King in his non-violent message."

In her inimitable style, Clark reached out to Carmichael and reinforced nonviolence as a tactic, even after King's murder. She described a dinner with him and six of his male friends at which she gave her nonviolence pitch. Although they resisted the message and some even mocked it, apparently Carmichael himself recognized her impact on him. As Septima recalled, years later, at a meeting, he said, "There's Mrs. Clark. Stand up, Mrs. Clark. She was the one who got me to realize that being violent was the one thing that I shouldn't do."

Septima lived her own life in accordance with the philosophy that communication and education were the strongest weapons against prejudice. Like Durr, who remained a close friend, she was upset by the black separatist movement and discouraged by signs of violent unrest. After the assassination of Dr. King, the first thing Septima did was to arrange for a traveling white minister and his family to stay with her. They were afraid that angry, grief-stricken blacks might seek vengeance and she wanted to give them comfort and protection.

"None of It Hurt My Heart"

Septima continued her work for the SCLC until 1972, when she retired to her native Charleston and settled in as a matriarch to both her extended family and to the network of activists who came from around the country and the world, having heard of her and her work. "I put a sign on her door once that said, 'Septima's U.N.,'" laughs Yvonne. As Septima grew older, she became more interested in exploring the gender divide in both white and black America. In 1968, Septima joined Virginia Durr as a member of the National Organization for Women, or NOW,[7] and campaigned for the Equal Rights Amendment. "I am all for women's liberation," Clark declared. She looked back on her life

---

[7] NOW was formed in October 1966 by several frustrated activists who had unsuccessfully fought to convince the Equal Employment Opportunity Commission to take seriously job discrimination against women. Betty Friedan, credited as NOW's founder, said later, "these very reluctant women" felt they had no choice but "to take the actions needed to bring women into the mainstream of American society, now, full equality for women, in fully equal partnership with men."

Septima with her grandchildren Eli Clark and Yvonne Clark at the dedication of an expressway named for her in South Carolina in 1978. (courtesy Yvonne Clark)

and its accomplishments with satisfaction and quiet pride but felt that the lack of leadership opportunities for women had been a detriment to the civil rights movement.

Until her death, Clark was on the cutting edge of the fight for civil and equal rights, always with an extraordinarily forgiving and open heart. She helped organize workshops for the American Field Service, raised scholarship money for black students, organized day care centers, and in 1975 became a member of the same school board that many years before had fired her for refusing to give up her NAACP membership. (After much legal wrangling, the school system also gave Septima her pension.)

In 1979 Septima received the Living Legacy award from President Jimmy Carter in a White House ceremony. Soon after, the landslide victory of Ronald Reagan shook the confidence of the large population of Southern blacks who had supported Carter. But, as Septima—"peering through thick, old-fashioned spectacles"—told the *New York Times*, "I've been through the civil rights, I went to jail in Tennessee, and none of it hurt my heart, none of it. I'm not going to let them make me angry. We'll just have to work with whoever is in there. That's what it takes for attitudes to change."

As time passed, she continued to see the fruits of her work in the citizenship schools. "From one end of the South to the other," Clark remarked in 1985, "if you look at the black elected officials and the political leaders, you find people who had their first involvement in the training program of the citizenship school." Septima deserves credit for lighting the way for those leaders and all of us who have access to a more inclusive political process. She always felt there was more work to be done, and education was key, often explaining, "If we can erase ignorance, we can have good citizens."

Septima always believed that the best could be brought out in everyone, and that the best leaders are found within their own communities. She was never afraid to challenge the powers that be or endure the results. Her genius was in laying the groundwork for social change, sensing opportunity where others felt despair and confusion. "I have great belief in the fact that whenever there is chaos, it creates wonderful thinking. I consider chaos a gift."

Septima Poinsette Clark died in 1987, at age 89, in a nursing home on Johns Island.

Dolores Huerta

Anger is important, but you have to use it in a positive way. My anger doesn't make me cynical because we have a solution, a way to change things, a formula—organization.

—Dolores Huerta

"Dolores is absolutely fearless, physically and emotionally," said César Chávez of his co-founder of the United Farm Workers (UFW). In January 1968, Dolores Huerta, forty farmworkers, and ten student volunteers headed east, from the strike fields in central California to New York City. Having seen the plight of migrant farmworkers—literally backbreaking work for ten or twelve hours a day, substandard housing, exposure to toxic pesticides, lack of basic facilities like toilets—and having spent the past six years helping them organize, lobby, and negotiate for safer, more humane working conditions, she was now prepared to launch an unprecedented new tactic: a national boycott. Huerta, dynamic and intense as always, arrived in New York determined to persuade eleven million shoppers to stop buying grapes. "When we got to New York," she recalled later, "it was something like four or five degrees above zero. The first day we went out on the picket line, one of the Filipino women fell down and hit her head on some ice and had amnesia for about an hour. Everybody was slipping on the ice and falling. But they had a heck of a lot of spirit."

Most of the fresh produce sold in the New York area was distributed through the Hunts Point Terminal Market, then the largest produce market in the nation. Dolores and the workers, picketing at Hunts Point, managed to convince people she described as "those hardened produce buyers" to begin considering the conditions faced by the workers who picked the grapes. The UFW then sent groups to Chicago, Boston, Los Angeles, and Detroit. In each city, the striking workers and volunteers met with church groups, labor unions, neighborhood associations, and other organizations, explaining the strike and signing up boycott supporters. Dolores also organized pickets at neighborhood groceries and major chains and, within weeks, awareness of the exploitation of migrant farmworkers spread across the country.

"I think we brought to the world, the United States anyhow, the whole idea of boycotting as a nonviolent tactic. I think we showed the world that nonviolence can work to make social change," Huerta recalled proudly. "I think we have laid a pattern of how farmworkers are eventually going to get out of their bondage. It may not happen right now in our foreseeable future but the pattern is there and the farmworkers are going to make it."

Dolores Huerta, the mother of eleven children, endured death threats, physical assault, twenty-two arrests (for nonviolent protests), and a hand-to-mouth, transient lifestyle in order to improve the lives of poor immigrant laborers. Uncommonly beautiful, favoring clothes of red and black (the official colors of the United Farm Workers) and pink lipstick, Dolores radiated feminine strength. As one profile described her:

> She is an effective speaker, whether at union meetings or on campuses, because she seems to relive the history of her cause each time she begins talking of it. She speaks rapidly, in a constantly hoarse voice, using her hands and her eyes to create images of men and women bent double in burning fields in California. Finely built and thin, with an intense yet serene

round face that is framed by straight black hair falling from a widow's peak to her shoulders, she makes you think of all the people she speaks for, the physically powerless but mystically driven, the strike-hardened and sun-tired men and women in the fields.

Huerta was on the forefront of the critical fight for immigrants' rights and fair labor practices of the second half of the twentieth century. Among her achievements for farmworkers are the first medical and pension plan, the first credit union, higher wages, more affordable housing, safer conditions, and their legal right to bargain collectively. A consummate grassroots organizer, she registered voters, lobbied elected officials, led strikes, and organized national boycotts, all in the face of powerful opposition, all in the name of a group that was so disenfranchised that many neither spoke English nor had a penny to their names.

In championing farmworkers, Huerta also coined the phrase that first gave some hope of political power to the group that Secretary of Labor Frances Perkins called "the most submerged class in the entire United States." It's a simple yet powerful statement: *"Si, se puede."* Yes, it can be done.

Her Roots

Dolores Fernandez was born in 1930 in Dawson, a mining town in northern New Mexico. Her father, Juan Fernandez, was a Mexican-American miner who occasionally worked on local farms to make ends meet after he was blacklisted for union activity. It was her mother, Alicia Chávez, how-

Dolores speaking during the grape boycott in the late sixties. (courtesy Walter P. Reuther Library, Wayne State University)

ever, who was the dominant force in the family and the biggest influence on her daughter.

When Dolores was a child, her parents divorced and she, along with her two brothers and two sisters, moved with their mother to Stockton, California, a farmworker community in the central San Joaquin valley. "My first exposure to union action," Dolores recalls, "was my mother's participation in the cannery workers' strike in Stockton, California, in 1938, which was run by George Meany, the future president of the AFL-CIO."

Alicia was determined to make a good life for her family even as a single mother amidst the desperation of the Great Depression. Alicia was, in Dolores's words, "a Mexican-American Horatio Alger type" who worked hard in the fields and then took shifts at a canning factory and as a waitress before she saved enough money to buy a restaurant. Then during the "relocation" of the Japanese during World War II, a Japanese family asked her to take over the operation of their seventy-room hotel. She did so gladly. As Dolores remembers, she "knew the restaurant business would be more difficult because during World War II, food rationing went into effect." Alicia also "welcomed the idea" of the whole family living together at the hotel.

Dolores, obviously infused with her mother's work ethic, also was deeply influenced by her generosity to the more vulnerable members of their community. Theirs was an integrated neighborhood that included families of many different origins: Japanese, Chinese, Filipino, Jewish, Mexican, African-American, and more. Alicia treated even those most different from her with respect and went out of her way to help the poor families of agricultural laborers, often allowing them to stay in her hotel for free. This maternal example of helping others had a profound effect on Dolores, as it did on Alice Hamilton and Septima Clark.

Dolores's mother clearly instilled a strong sense of self in her daughter, treating her with respect and expecting a lot in return. Although there was much that was conventional about Alicia's household, there was an unusual freedom from chauvinism. Dolores recalled, "At home, we all shared equally in the household tasks. I never had to cook for my brothers or do their clothes like many traditional Mexican families."

Alicia also encouraged her children to participate in cultural activities. "My mother was always pushing me to get involved in all these youth activities," Huerta recalled. "We took violin lessons. I took piano lessons. I took dancing lessons. I belonged to the church choir. . . . I belonged to the church youth organization. And I was a very active Girl Scout from the time I was eight to the time I was eighteen." In a recent interview she described the Girl Scouts as a strong influence in her early life, giving her confidence and providing her first leadership role. Wanting to provide a similar experience for others, she organized a storefront "youth club" that drew participants from the ethnically diverse neighborhood. "There were all these guys in zoot suits[1] playing musical chairs," Dolores remembers. But local police, responding to complaints about racial mixing, closed down the club. Dolores briefly reopened the club in the church of a sympathetic local minister but police pressure soon shut it down for good. "They actually ran [the minister] out of town," she laments. "There were lots of police recruited from the South to come to California. That was a problem."

As she grew older, Dolores increasingly confronted the disparity between her own family's values and the inequities around her. "When I got into high school, it was really segregated," she wrote. "There were the real rich and the real poor. I later realized we were poor too and I got hit with a lot of racial discrimination." She was a good student and was "crushed" when one of her teachers questioned whether she had actually written the essay she turned in. "That really discouraged me because I used to stay up all night and think and try to make every paper different, and try to put words in there that I thought were nice." After giving her As throughout the year, the teacher gave her a C for the class, explaining that she believed someone else had done the work for Dolores. "This is a common situation for Latino students," Dolores says now.

Alicia's parenting grounded her daughter so that, rather than

---

[1] The zoot suit was a brief flamboyant fad with origins in jazz culture. In the late 1930s and early 40s the look—long, broad-shouldered jackets worn with baggy pants nipped in at the cuffs—was adopted by Mexican-Americans who called themselves *pachucos*, and the zoot suit became linked with growing racial identity and pride. Like most extreme fashions, it puzzled and offended the mainstream, a response exacerbated by the racial association. Further, the extravagant use of fabric during wartime rationing was seen as deliberately provocative and unpatriotic.

doubting herself, Dolores was incensed when the world did not live up to her expectations. "I felt I had all of these frustrations inside me. I had a fantastic inferiority complex because I seemed to be out of step with everybody and everything. You're trying to go to school and yet you see all of these injustices." When she was seventeen, her mother took her to visit Mexico City and encouraged her to take pride in her ethnic heritage. "This trip opened my eyes to the fact that there was nothing wrong with Chicanos," she recalled. "Be yourself," was Alicia's gentle, guiding refrain.

Dolores stayed in touch with her father, whose own accomplishments later inspired her. After joining the migrant labor force, Juan Fernandez traveled through the fields of Colorado, Wyoming, Nebraska, and New Mexico. He became a volunteer organizer for the United Mine Workers in northern New Mexico and, in 1938, won election to the New Mexico state legislature, where he worked for progressive labor legislation. During World War II he served in the Civilian Air Patrol and during the Korean War he joined the navy. At age 51, Juan Fernandez fulfilled his lifelong dream of graduating from college.

Dolores married her high school sweetheart, Ralph Head, in 1948 and immediately had two children, Lori and Celeste. The marriage soon deteriorated: "He was probably not ready for marriage," Dolores says now. When the marriage broke up, she increasingly relied on her mother to care for her young children. Resolved to make some career for herself, the newly single mother went to the College of the Pacific for a teaching degree. At that point Dolores knew that she wanted to serve others but wasn't sure exactly what path she would take. "I knew there was something I was meant to do," she recalled. "I had a sense of mission."

In another parallel to Clark's experience, Dolores felt a call to political activism through her experience as a teacher. Faced with students largely from the families of local farmworkers, she found herself struggling to focus on lesson plans amidst her increasing awareness of the children's more basic needs. "I had students who didn't have proper clothing or shoes because of the poor wages their parents made. They were sick because their family had no health insurance," she explained. "I couldn't stand seeing kids come to class hungry and needing shoes. I thought I could do more by organizing farmworkers than by trying to teach their hungry children."

Farmworkers

I find Dolores's story particularly interesting because, in some ways, she picked up where both Alice Hamilton and Frances Perkins left off. Throughout the twentieth century, while workers in America's industries fought for safe working conditions and fair wages, agricultural workers were left behind. This disparity was partly due to the seasonal nature of farm work and the fact that the labor pool is often transient. However, as Huerta points out, there are other seasonal, transient laborers who manage to survive year-round—construction workers, for example. The farmworkers also were excluded because almost all were Latino immigrants, and racism played a powerful role in determining their treatment. Also relevant is the symbolic and emotional image of the family farm in American culture. Ironically, as farming became more mechanized and centrally owned, this image served to minimize the real plight of agricultural laborers.

When the New Deal established new safeguards—a minimum wage, unemployment insurance, the right to organize—for most American workers, it specifically excluded agricultural laborers. The 1932 National Labor Relations Act, which changed the practice of nullifying union activities through court injunctions, carved out an exception for agribusiness. Agriculture also was excluded from both the unprecedented Wagner Act of 1935, which paved the way for the big industrial labor unions, and the Fair Labor Standards Act, which set up policies for overtime pay. Secretary Perkins had actually pushed for some inclusion for farmworkers, such as applicable unemployment insurance and the right to collective bargaining, but to no avail. At the time she was criticized for exacerbating the administration's headaches about the farm income problem.

The result of these exclusions was second-class status for farmworkers. They were paid poor wages, which growers often reduced as a penalty for poor performance, compensation for the cost of the water they drank, or other punitive and arbitrary measures. In an echo of the company towns Mother Jones fought to end, workers sometimes were even driven to supermarkets or restaurants and forced to cash their checks for a fee or buy food they did not want. They were denied basic necessities such as toilets and adequate drinking water and, after enduring arduous physical labor for long hours, they often had only makeshift shelters to go home to. The language barrier and power gap between employer and employee left little possibility of bargaining.

Mexican Immigration

As always, the farm labor situation was tangled up in the issues surrounding immigration. Around the turn of the twentieth century, the expanding railroad system began to foster immigration throughout the Southwest. At the same time, large-scale commercial farms began operating in the newly irrigated regions of Texas and the Central Valley of California. While industrial mining also drew Mexican workers north, these new corporate farms soon became the primary employers of immigrant labor. The growers even were given the power to issue visas to the thousands of Mexicans crossing the border to work for them.

In 1910 the Mexican dictator Porfirio Díaz was voted out of office in favor of Francisco Madero, the populist reformer who hosted Mother Jones at the presidential palace. But within a year optimism in Mexico gave way to violence. Madero was assassinated by a Díaz loyalist and for almost a decade to follow, the nation was rocked by assassinations, bloody battles, coups, and counter-coups. The upheaval only spurred more immigration to the United States. As the United States geared up for World War I, new job opportunities opened up and Mexicans began moving to Chicago and other industrial cities. The population of Mexican nationals living in the United States—210,000 in 1910—increased to approximately one million by 1930.

This new demographic reality elicited nativist attacks, especially by those looking for scapegoats in times of economic downturn. Throughout the Southwest there was brutal discrimination against Mexicans and Mexican Americans. In addition to restrictions in businesses ("White Trade Only" signs appeared in some store windows), there was an effort to drive immigrants back to Mexico. The attacks only worsened as the economy faltered. During the Great Depression, over 500,000 Mexicans were deported, including many children who were United States citizens by virtue of their birth here. Even many of those who were in the United States legally were intimidated, tricked, or forced into returning to Mexico. Most of those who remained were once again employed as field workers.

Farming was hard enough on native-born workers. American farmers began struggling financially in the 1920s, and in the mid-1930s, their situation got even worse. In the driest regions of the Great Plains—southeastern Kansas and Colorado, and the panhandles of Oklahoma and Texas—drought and a relentless stretch of unusually fierce windstorms combined to strip the soil from thousands of farms. By 1934 the brutal winds had carried away as much as 100 million acres of fertile topsoil. The worst storm hit on April 14, 1935. One observer wrote, "The impact is like a shovelful of fine sand flung against the face. People caught in their own yards grope for the doorstep. Cars come to a standstill, for no light in the world can penetrate that swirling murk . . . We live with the dust, eat it, sleep with it, watch it strip us of possessions and the hope of possessions." Farm families loaded up jalopies with whatever they could save. Those without a car hitchhiked or rode the rails. Most headed west to California and the new start it offered. Regardless of where they came from, these "Dust Bowl" refugees became known as "Okies," their plight famously fictionalized in *The Grapes of Wrath* by Salinas, California native John Steinbeck. Steinbeck also wrote about the discriminatory treatment of "imported" workers. In a 1936 essay published in the *Nation*, he compared the situation of the Okies and that of immigrant laborers, who met not only oppressive tactics but also white landowners and bosses "inflamed to race hatred."

The growing prejudice against Mexican Americans extended from the farms to the cities, flaring up dramatically in the Zoot Suit Riots of 1943. On May 30 of that year, a Caucasian sailor was badly beaten by a group of Mexican Americans, and on June 3 a group of about fifty sailors set out to get revenge. They roamed the neighborhood near the Naval Reserve Armory, stripping and beating zoot suiters and burning their clothes. By the next day, more sailors had joined in. Running out of the preferred target, the armed bands organized "search and destroy" forays into Mexican-American neighborhoods, attacking indiscriminately. By June 6 civilians had joined the raids, and the worst violence occurred the next day, with soldiers, sailors, and marines arriving from as far away as San Diego and Las Vegas to participate in the beatings. Taxi drivers offered free transportation to white men headed to the riot areas, and the mob swelled to five thousand or more. The police took no action. According to one member of the force, "You can say that the cops had a 'hands-off' policy during the riots. Well, we represented public opinion. Many of us were in the First World War, and we're not going to pick on kids in the service." Finally, on June 8, senior military officials declared Los Angeles off-limits to soldiers and the shore patrol was ordered to arrest disorderly personnel. The official report, issued by a citizens' committee appointed by the governor, cited racism as the chief cause of the riot. L.A. mayor Fletcher Bowron dismissed the report, blaming juvenile delinquents and white Southerners for the unrest.

At the same time, as World War II once again tightened the labor supply, the United States negotiated the Mexican Farm Labor Program Agreement, known as the Bracero program, which went into effect in August 1942. Mexican workers hired as braceros received legal status for a specific period, with a minimum wage and certain standards for housing and safety ostensibly guaranteed. In practice, the worker protections and benefits mandated by the law were widely ignored. Though originally intended as a temporary wartime measure, the program continued for the next twenty-two years. There were several revisions and amendments to the agreement as the labor supply expanded or contracted and one side or the other claimed the stronger negotiating position. During the Cold War, ongoing immigration triggered a response from the Immigration and Naturalization Service: the bluntly named "Operation Wetback," which deported almost four million Mexicans by 1954.

As in the Colorado coal mines and Birmingham steel mills, employers resorted to extreme measures to prevent strikes or slowdowns, and because the production and harvest of food is so time-sensitive, the managers of commercial farms were especially intolerant of any labor unrest. Growers used many of the tactics Mother Jones and other early union organizers faced: intimidating and punishing workers who protested conditions, firing union leaders, hiring aggressive strikebreakers, obtaining injunctions against organizing or protesting. Using political influence, the growers sought to ban legal protection for farmworker organizations and shape immigration policy to keep a steady supply of cheap immigrant labor.

As Alice Hamilton had noted decades before, one underlying and pervasive tactic used by abusive employers is to think of and treat their workers as less than human beings. Huerta said later, "Growers dehumanize their workers. Why would you refuse to give workers a toilet?

Because if you don't give them a toilet then they're not human beings. Why would you allow workers to be sprayed with pesticides? Growers view farmworkers as tools."

The Community Service Organization

Looking for a way to provide meaningful help to her students, Dolores began volunteering for community organizations supporting migrant workers. She became an organizer for one of the failed strikes, impressing its leaders with her toughness and charisma. Then, through a former college professor, she met Fred Ross Sr., the head of the Community Service Organization (CSO), who was looking for Mexican Americans interested in grassroots organization.

Ross himself had come to the cause through his Depression-era work for the state of California. In 1939 he was assigned to oversee more than four thousand Dust Bowl refugees in the Arvin Migratory Labor Camp, Steinbeck's model for the labor camp the Joad family stopped at in *The Grapes of Wrath*. Ross followed an abusive and brutal director and it took time to earn the refugees' trust. He persisted in reorganizing the camp as a self-governing institution and watched as the suspicious, seemingly apathetic refugees rose to these new demands, taking on more autonomy and responsibility. Through this experience, Ross became convinced that community organization could transform the lifestyles of poverty-stricken populations.

Although Dolores was interested in going to work on behalf of the farmworkers, she was initially reluctant to join with Ross and the CSO. The red-baiters, so infuriatingly obstructionist to the work of Frances Perkins, Virginia Durr, and Septima Clark, had been effective enough to cause the young Dolores to have a moment of doubt before going to work with Ross. "I thought Fred Ross was a communist so I went to the FBI and had him checked out," Huerta recalled. "See how middle class I was. In fact, I was a registered Republican at the time." Dolores remembers that the FBI agents in the Stockton office "gave Fred a glowing report, as the CSO was also supported by the Daughters of the American Revolution and the Council of Churches." She decided to meet with Ross, and his articulate and heartfelt argument for empowering the poor and expanding the civil rights movement to include

Mexican Americans convinced her to join the CSO and, eventually, to switch political parties. "Fred showed me the proof of CSO accomplishments," Dolores remembers. "Street lights, clinics in the barrios, the first Mexican American elected to the L.A. city council, Ed Roybal."

Under Ross, the CSO also opposed segregation, led voter registration drives, pushed for more Latinos on the police force,[2] advocated for more Spanish speakers on staff at hospitals and government offices, and campaigned for better infrastructure and facilities in the barrios. Tall, charismatic, and completely bilingual, Ross was an effective leader. He immediately put Dolores to work on voter registration drives.

It was during her years with the CSO that Dolores married Ventura Huerta and had five more children: Fidel, Emilio, Vincent, Alicia, and Angela. Their family life was swallowed by the CSO agenda. "All the Huerta kids were born during the big CSO fights. I was always pregnant. I don't remember anything about Alicia's childhood except nursing her in the ladies' room during breaks in city council meetings or dropping her off at a friend's house," Dolores recalled. This reminds me of how Ida B. Wells-Barnett brought her nursing child to an antilynching lecture, and it's interesting to compare and contrast the way those two women approached the challenge of their dual roles. Whereas Ida had a period of time when she pulled back from her public activities and then went back to them when her children were older, Dolores went full steam ahead, with children either in tow or entrusted to friends or relatives.

The CSO was a formative period in Dolores's career, not only be-

---

[2] In the early postwar years, the Los Angeles Police Department (LAPD) responded to pressure from the CSO by setting up programs to reach out to community leaders, but police discrimination and brutality continued. One of the worst incidents came to be known as "Bloody Christmas." On December 25, 1951, seven young men, accused of underage drinking, were taken to the city center jail. About one hundred officers at the jail were celebrating the holiday with liquor donated by local merchants, and the prisoners were badly beaten: a broken cheekbone, a punctured bladder, a punctured liver, massive blood loss. The incident wasn't revealed until February 1952, in the wake of a separate brutality case involving the CSO chairman, Anthony Ríos. Eight officers eventually were indicted for their involvement in Bloody Christmas. Five were convicted, with only one receiving a sentence longer than one year. According to some historians, the protests and outrage over Bloody Christmas among the Mexican-American and black communities helped solidify the LAPD's image, within its ranks and among many residents, as a "thin blue line" protecting the peaceful, law-abiding, white middle-class.

cause she gained the skills and experience that fortified her later work but also because she met her professional soul mate, César Chávez.

César Chávez

Dark, slender, and preternaturally cool, César had already become a rising star of the Chicano movement. Born to poor farmworkers near Yuma, Arizona, he had labored in the fields as a child, thinning lettuce and sugar beets in the summer, planting onions in the winter, and traveling wherever there was a harvest to reap. In the off-season, the Chávez family lived in the San Jose barrio of Sal Si Puedes, a name that literally means "Get out if you can."

Taking that advice, César had joined the navy in 1944 and served a two-year stint. When he returned to Delano, California, he joined his father in a strike organized by the National Farm Labor Union, an AFL affiliate that had recently begun an organizing campaign in the area. César began to volunteer time in the union office, sweeping floors, among other tasks. But economic hardships also meant that he worked in the fields, along with his parents and three siblings, for long, tortuous hours.

In 1952, Chávez met a Roman Catholic priest, Father Donald McDonnell, who had been sent by the San Francisco diocese to build a parish in Sal Si Puedes. McDonnell followed the migrant workers from camp to camp, setting up portable altars and hearing confession outdoors. Confronted with such dire poverty and despair, he soon began to promote doctrines of social justice, encouraging the workers to band together to better their living conditions and thus their ability to raise healthy, strong children. Chávez, immediately drawn to this mission, became an assistant to Father McDonnell, who introduced him to the teachings of Gandhi and Saint Francis of Assisi. Chávez recalled, "As Father McDonnell followed legislation very closely, he introduced me to the transcripts of the La Follette committee hearings held in 1940 in Los Angeles. . . . These things began to form a picture for me." It was Father McDonnell who, when approached by Fred Ross in his search for local men who might help organize Sal Si Puede, gave him César Chávez's name.

Aware of sanctimonious social scientists who visited Chicano neighborhoods for research, Chávez was suspicious of Ross at first. However, at the urging of his wife, Helen, Chávez decided to meet with him. "I invited some of the rougher guys I knew and bought some beer," he recalled. "I thought we could show this gringo a little bit of how we felt. We'd let him speak for a while, and when I gave them the signal, shifting my cigarette from my right hand to the left, we'd tell him off and run him out of the house. Then we'd be even." But Fred Ross impressed him with his sincerity, knowledge of local concerns, and history of advocating for the rights of Mexicans in police brutality cases. Chávez immediately joined the CSO and, as he remembered it, "Fred Ross became sort of my hero."

Although Chávez was gratified by the work of the CSO, he was increasingly drawn to the task of organizing farmworkers. As Helen recalled, "César had always talked about organizing farmworkers, even before CSO. After all, we were both farmworkers, and my parents and his parents and our whole families." The CSO often supported strikes, but it did not want to start a new union.

In the meantime Dolores had become a star within the organization's ranks, known for her perseverance and passion. She was also becoming frustrated with the fact that the CSO did not take on the task of unionizing the farmworkers. "Farmworkers work very hard. They pick tons of fruits and vegetables—not pounds, *tons*—every day to feed the nation," she explained. "The people who feed us should earn enough so that they can nourish their own bodies. Growers live all year from a seasonal harvest. Farmworkers should be able to as well." She felt that in order to have a realistic ability to negotiate better wages and working conditions, they had to have their own union. "Workers who have a union contract aren't abused, yelled at, or treated like animals. . . . Workers without a union feel helpless. They think it's their fate in life to be victims."

In 1958, with the help of Father Thomas McCullough, Dolores established the Agricultural Workers Association. She was gripped by this new mission: it thrust her into the kind of hands-on, uphill struggle that she thrived on. But she realized, like so many women before her (Ida B. Wells-Barnett in her antilynching work, Alice Hamilton at Harvard, Septima Clark in the Southern Christian Leadership Conference), that many people were resistant to the idea of a woman taking a lead role. At first Dolores compensated by persuading men around her to take up the effort. "I made my husband, Ventura, quit his job to work for [AWA]," recalled Dolores. "Then my brother quit his job, and both worked full time without pay to organize the union. But Father McCullough didn't want me to be involved. He said that farm labor organizing was no place for a woman. So I kind of worked under cover, doing the work through my husband and my brother." Huerta recruited Larry Itliong, a leader of the Filipino workers, as well as leaders from other farmworker groups, including "Okies" and African-Americans. Father McCullough, Father McDonnell, and a third priest, Father Doogan, traveled to Washington, D.C., to make the case for a farmworkers' union within the AFL-CIO. When they were turned down, they established the Agricultural Workers Association (AWA) within the CSO.

A year later, the AFL-CIO changed its mind and established the Agricultural Workers Organizing Committee, and the AWA voted to join it. Labor organizer Norman Smith, who had made his reputation organizing autoworkers in the Midwest, was put in charge of the AWOC and tasked with a lettuce strike. It barely got off the ground. The situation of the farmworkers was so dire, so difficult, and so dif-

Dolores recruiting members for the National Farmworkers Association in September 1962. (courtesy Walter P. Reuther Library, Wayne State University)

ferent from that of the autoworkers, that Smith was unable to maintain solidarity.

At this point, Huerta and Chávez had not yet begun working together. "I had heard a lot about him from Fred Ross," she recalled. "César this and César that—but I didn't really get a chance to talk to him the first time I met him, and he didn't make much of an impression on me. I forgot his face. I know he was a great organizer, but he never showed it; it came out in the reports. He was very unassuming." As Smith and AWOC struggled with the lettuce strike, Dolores remembers, "I kept pushing to bring César to Stockton, as he had pulled a few successful strikes with local farmworkers and braceros, but others were adamantly opposed." Even though Dolores had initially organized the AWA, Father McCullough suggested that she stop organizing and "take care of her family." Huerta recalls, "My mother was present at the time and said to me, 'Do not listen to him. You are the one who has organized this, and you know what you're doing.'" Soon the AFL-CIO grew frustrated and reduced funding for the AWOC. Both Dolores and César were convinced of the need to continue, so they kept the AWA going until 1962, when they left to start the precursor to the United Farm Workers.

Dolores became especially effective when she moved beyond persuading men to front her efforts and innovated other ways to achieve her political goals. The sense of being excluded gave her, as it had Wells, Jones, Hamilton, and Perkins before her, a keen eye for opportunities to use bottom-up, grassroots tactics: recruiting people through publicity, harnessing consumer power, teaching people how to stand up for themselves. This sense of exclusion also planted the seeds of feminism in her consciousness, although they were slow to grow.

Dolores struggled with the fact that her passion for her work could not coexist with the expectations within her marriage. "I knew I wasn't comfortable in a wife's role," she explained, "but I wasn't clearly facing the issue. I hedged, I made excuses, I didn't come out and tell my husband that I cared more about helping other people than cleaning our house and doing my hair." Her ceaseless work, internal struggle, and continual childbearing took its toll on Dolores's family life. "It was difficult for us, too, to work for nothing, because I was having a baby every year," recalled Huerta. "They were hard times! In fact, it ended up in divorce."

This second divorce was acrimonious and resulted in a bitter custody battle. After temporarily abducting the children, Dolores's estranged husband took her to court. "He said I was a negligent mother," she recalled. However, the children themselves expressed a desire to stay with their mother and Dolores retained custody. In response to this emotional upheaval, Huerta threw herself into the cause. She traveled and worked constantly, often through the night. Huerta later recalled that her frenetic pace kept her from "going under," overcome by fears about the security of her seven children and guilt about her failed marriages.

Particularly intent on making a personal appeal to lawmakers, Dolores beat a path between the fields, her home in Stockton, and the state capitol. In 1961 she commuted daily to Sacramento to "lobby the legislators into passing laws for poor people. I knew nothing about lobbying before the day I began it. CSO just sent me, paying us through contributors' nickels and dimes, and said, 'You can do it.' I had to do it but at the same time I was too distracted to work. My husband was trying to take the kids away from me in court. I couldn't lose my children, but I couldn't quit working for people who counted on me." Adding to her stress, Dolores's mother was dying of cancer. Overwhelmed and emotionally distraught, Dolores sought solace in her faith. "I went into church and prayed. I took confession for the first time in years. When I left the church, I felt my way was clear to work to pass those bills. God would take care of the rest."

This palpable sense of sacrifice and heightened awareness of what was truly valuable led Dolores to bring an indignant intensity to every meeting with a politician. Her drive paid off for the CSO and the poor immigrants it represented. In 1961 alone, fifteen bills for which she had lobbied passed, including the removal of citizenship requirements for public assistance programs, making resident aliens eligible for old age pensions, disability assistance, aid for the blind, and disability insurance for farmworkers. She also ensured that Spanish versions of many government documents, including ballots, were made available. "All these bills were passed when my mother was dying and I was separating from my husband," Dolores recalled.

Chávez and Huerta pushed the CSO to start a union for farmworkers, but at the organization's 1961 convention, the majority voted against it. Several CSO leaders already affiliated with other unions argued that it would be "dual unionism." Others argued that it would be better to maintain CSO's focus on building the electoral strength of the Mexican Americans through citizenship classes, voter registration, and the promotion of Chicano leaders, all of which would be subsumed by the daunting task of starting a new union of these most vulnerable, unskilled, immigrant workers. "They said CSO was not a labor organization, it was a civic organization," recalled Huerta.

With the blessing of Fred Ross, César and Dolores left CSO to focus on labor organizing. As she remembered it, "One day, César called me over to his house and said, 'You know, farmworkers are never going to have a union unless you and I start it.'" He held no illusions about their chances for success. Dolores remembers that he told her they would not see a national union in their lifetime, "because the growers are too rich and too powerful."

As they planned the new union, César and Dolores also specifically discussed which one of them would take the lead role. "There was no disagreement that he would be the leader," she recalled, adding that she has never minded being less publicly prominent than her co-founder. "The fact that I did not get publicity, recognition, etc., is [because] even women reporters did not report on what women did. Remember, our organization was going on at the same time as the activity of the women's movement in the U.S." Dolores would soon become active in the women's movement, but when the UFW was founded, she did not yet see those issues as part of her mission.

The United Farm Workers

In 1962 Chávez and Huerta went to Delano and started the National Farm Workers Association (NFWA), the precursor to the United Farm Workers. They were still on good terms with Fred Ross, who provided frequent counsel to both of his protégés. Dolores brought six of her own children (the oldest stayed with his father) to live with Chávez's wife and their eight children and they began by joining the workers in the fields, picking grapes to finance the organization effort. "We wanted only people with a real commitment," recalled César, who always made it clear that he and Dolores were "the architects" of the NFWA.

They knew the tremendous obstacles to a union: the pool of farm-workers was seemingly endless and often seasonal, and as César described it, "The power of the growers was backed by the power of the police, the courts, state and federal laws, and the financial power of the big corporations, the banks, and the utilities." As Huerta explains, the growers hired workers through labor contractors and "the workers often had to pay bribes and did not have their Social Security, disability insurance, or unemployment insurance reported. Women were subjected to sexual harassment and the families had to keep quiet just to be able to work. These were the evil labor practices that we had to eliminate with the hiring hall." In addition, the growers had been known to resort to violence and threats to quell unrest. For Huerta and Chávez, these circumstances underscored why the civic goals of the CSO were impossible to achieve without giving the laborers their own power base.

They began by conducting a census of farmworkers, splitting the Central Valley in half. César with his wife and eight children went south, Dolores and her children went north. Thus began an austere and difficult lifestyle that Huerta kept up for most of her life. She often slept on the ground or in a car. She had barely enough money for food, much less clothing. "All of us have very exotic wardrobes," she lightheartedly pointed out. "We get our clothes out of donations." When necessary, she left her children in the care of other families, sometimes waking them in the middle of the night to move to a new camp. For this she was criticized from all corners, by fellow organizers, by farmworkers, and even by her own father. Huerta recalls, "my relatives thought I was crazy. Being a divorced woman, there is always a bit of disapproval. And I was leaving a good job." But she felt compelled to make what she called a "total leap of faith" because of a deep sense that this was her calling. She acknowledges that her children "suffered a lot of neglect" but she also felt that they all participated in an important cause at a pivotal time. "We were in crisis mode all the time . . . but there was a community and we looked after each other."

As the Huerta and Chávez families took the census, they also handed out leaflets describing their plan and began to sign people up as union members. Finally they organized a convention with delegates and elected officers, and the union organization was in place. "Our first office was César and Helen's house," Dolores recalled. "Then we moved into a small building with three rooms." Later the UFW would be run out of a building known as the Gray House, with meeting rooms for organizers and offices for a legal department and a boycott staff. Nearby in the Pink House was a health clinic staffed by volunteer physicians. Much of the UFW's work, however, was done out in the field.

Much like Mother Jones, Dolores seemed to bring religious fervor to the cause of labor. She spoke in terms of salvation, human dignity, and good versus evil. She once told a reporter that she had a dream about millions of farmworkers marching with silver crosses and marking their ballots with the crosses. Because of her vision, rhetoric, and ceaseless intensity, Dolores Huerta earned the nickname *"la Pasionara,"* the passionate one. Artist Luis Valdez, who worked with the UFW, later wrote, "People tend to forget that the 1960s were the sexist dark ages, even in the Chicano movement, as we called it, but Dolores was already way out in front. She was a woman, a Mexican American, a Chicana, cutting a swath of revolutionary action across the torpidity of the San Joaquin Valley."

Dolores and César

Chávez, struck by Huerta's loyalty and devotion, wanted her in a leadership role. "At first I wasn't going to be an officer," Dolores recalled, "but César said, 'You have to be an officer. The people who actually do the work are going to run this union.'" Huerta took it upon herself to make certain that the union stuck to that philosophy, and she proudly cites this focus on the workers as a major reason for the union's successes and longevity. "César's dream of having farmworkers run the union is an important part of what we do. All our field offices are run by farmworkers, all of our radio stations are run by people who've come out of the field, and we have several negotiators who used to be farmworkers."

Huerta frequently referred to César's vision and gave him full credit for the success of the union, while at the same time clashing with him behind the scenes. In her words, "Our success is due to the New Deal tradition among older Americans and the younger generation which responds to César's charismatic leadership."

These references to following his lead reflect her shrewd political instinct. Dolores was always slightly controversial because aspects of her personal life were at odds with the conservative social culture of many Catholic Mexican Americans, while César Chávez became immensely popular—indeed, iconic. In September 1974 César Chávez, along with several family members and colleagues, visited the Vatican[3], which issued an official statement of welcome which read, in part: "We are all, indeed, grateful to Mr. Chavez for the lesson which he brings to our attention. It is a very important lesson: To know how to be conscious of a terrible responsibility that is incumbent on us who bear the name 'Christian.' His entire life is an illustration of that principle; it shows a laudable endeavor to apply this principle, which means expending the effort that is required to put the Gospel into practice. What attracts our attention in a particular way is the commitment that is manifested: the commitment to work for the good of one's brothers and sisters, to be of service to them in the name of Christ, and to render this service with a full measure of all the energy one possesses." No doubt Dolores matched César in commitment and energy, but she would never be publicly embraced by the Vatican. Chávez undoubtedly was the public face of the movement, and Dolores understood and accepted that. She also recognized the practical utility of Chávez's ability to use and project Christian doctrine. Virginia Durr's comment that Martin Luther King's theological approach made his message resound all the more because it was "pretty hard" to "red-bait Jesus Christ" also applied to Chávez.

Dolores also felt that it was virtuous to forgo credit for one's humanitarian work, even if she did not always achieve such a standard. She once recalled a piece of wisdom from her mother that had guided her: "She always, from the time we were very little, always said, 'When you see that something needs to be done, especially someone needs help, you have to help them. And don't expect any compensation or reward for what you've done because what you're doing is a reward in itself. And if you expect a reward or you expect compensation, then you take away the grace.'" This notion of grace, akin to Septima Clark's "kind providence," lies at the heart of what gave the women in this book the courage to light the way where others would not. It is not selflessness so much as it is faith in their own sense of right and wrong.

---

[3] The Roman Catholic Church was very supportive of Chávez's efforts on behalf of workers. Pope Paul VI granted him a private audience—a rare honor—where the Holy Father released his own statement. An excerpt: "Our welcome goes this morning to César Chávez whom we are happy to receive as a loyal son of the Catholic Church and as a distinguished leader and representative of the Mexican-American community in the United States. ... In the spirit of our own predecessors in this See of Peter we renew the full measure of our solicitude for the human and Christian condition of labor and for the genuine good will of all those who lend support to this lofty vocation."

Dolores's public demurrals should not cloud the leadership role she did play. The fact that her role has faded in the retelling of the account of the movement she cofounded is unfortunate because it misses a more interesting story. Huerta was not only compelling and brave but also an innovator of grassroots organizing skills that are still critical to real social change. Huerta's role was essential: without her, Chávez and the UFW might never have gotten off the ground. As one Chávez biography describes it, the relationship between César and Dolores was "symbiotic . . . he functioned as the catalyst, she was the engine."

Dolores explained that their relationship was also tumultuous—in a good way. "César and I have a lot of personal fights," Dolores admitted, "usually over strategy or personalities. I don't think César himself understands why he fights with me. We have these heart-to-heart talks every six months or so on how we're not going to fight anymore and how demoralizing it is to everybody else that we do. But then, like the next day, we'll have another fight." Dolores took this dynamic as a sign of their closeness and of his respect for her. She knew she was needed, not only by the farmworkers but also by Chávez himself. "He knows I'll never quit so he uses me to let off steam; he knows I'll fight back anyway," she said.

Chávez and Huerta were different in temperament and background. Her education and "middle-class" upbringing complemented César's authority and experience as a farm worker. And, unlike the calmer, more reserved Chávez, Huerta was more than willing to go head to head with anyone. "I think we really built on each other's strengths a lot," said Huerta. "I think I had more experience in dealing with Anglos than he did because César was always very uncomfortable, because he always felt that politicians would sell you out."

But as impressed as he was by her tenacity, César was also troubled by her lifestyle. This was exacerbated by her romance with his brother, Richard, who also worked with the UFW. Dolores and Richard had four children: Juanita, Maria Elena, Ricardo, and Camila. As one contemporary profile put it, "Chávez, a traditionalist in his own home life, is said to privately disapprove of Dolores' divorces, her living now with his brother, and her chaotic way of raising her kids." His disapproval softened over time, especially after their marriage. "Initially he felt our relationship was just a whim," Dolores explains. But later "he not only accepted it but supported it and our four children."

However, César and Dolores continued to argue throughout their

Dolores with fellow UFW organizers and three of her children (copyright 1978 George Ballis/Take Stock)

years working together, the fights often fueled by the differences in their backgrounds and family lives. When Chávez really wanted to get to her, he would tell her that she was not Mexican.

Huerta is disarmingly honest about her feelings. She has often spoken of her anger and overwhelming feelings of guilt—about her divorces, her time away from her kids, her lack of interest in being a homemaker—and it seems that she also felt some guilt about not being the kind of "Mexican" that César Chávez was. When she and César were building the union, she said, "I know I have a terrible temper. It might be that I am still suffering from guilt about my divorce, and from the feeling that I shouldn't really be the leader people see in me. . . . If you haven't forgiven yourself something, how can you forgive others?" Having carried with her, from childhood, the consciousness that she came from a more privileged background than most of the others around her, she sought to understand the world from the farmworkers' point of view. "I am a logical person," she explained. "I went to school and you learn that you have to weigh both sides and look at things objectively. But the farmworkers, I believe, know that wrong is wrong. They know that there's evil in the world and that you have to fight evil."

At times she seemed to reshape some of her interests and behavior in order to fit an image that the farmworkers would admire. Once, with an interviewer, she enjoyed herself in a mariachi bar, reapplying her pink lipstick and dancing in her seat. "I could never go to a bar in Delano without a man and carry on like this," she said. "The farmworkers wouldn't like it." When a reporter asked about her many children, Huerta responded, "Poor people think big families are strong families and I love my kids."

"Motherhood Kinds of Things"

Dolores took on personal responsibility for bringing women into the union. Her own pushing of boundaries definitely inspired more women to move into leadership positions, and, like Septima Clark in the citizenship program, she herself promoted them. Historian Margaret Rose observed that "Huerta's union activism is atypical. She rebelled against the traditional constraints upon women's full participation in trade union activism, competing directly with male colleagues in the UFW." In fact, under her guidance, soon nearly half of the UFW's organizers were women, and women ran the credit union and some of the clinical programs. However, at least in the early days, Huerta was far from a feminist.

Huerta, like both Jones and Hamilton, initially subscribed to a view of gender roles that put a premium on women as the center of family life. Huerta felt that recruiting women was the key to recruiting whole families and that women had innate skills that were useful in the union. "Women have one advantage over men—their egos aren't so involved. They can compromise to get what they want instead of forcing a showdown all the time." And, like Perkins before her, Huerta used the power of the maternal image when dealing with her political adversaries, almost all of whom were men. In negotiations, she first "focused on motherhood kinds of things, like clean water and toilets." Over and over, she sensed her opponents softening in the face of this approach and cultivated her role as a sort of feminine conscience.

Like both Jones and Perkins, Huerta often described the spectacle of degraded womanhood—young mothers unable to properly care for their children—as among the worst consequences of unbridled greed. Child labor was then, and continues to be, a major problem among migrant workers, a problem Huerta remains determined to solve. "A couple of weeks ago," she began one anecdote, "I saw a woman in a tomato field during a school day. She had three of her kids out there with her and when she saw me she started apologizing. She said, 'I had to take them out of school because we didn't have enough money to buy groceries.' They're out there every single day, little kids picking tomatoes with their hands too small to even cover the damn tomato. The big question for workers is, How can we survive? You go to their homes and see that they're barely making enough to feed and clothe their children." Dolores excelled at using such anecdotes to make the plight of the poor instantly comprehensible.

She also understood that growers were more embarrassed to use force against women, at least if reporters were present. Like Mother Jones, she communicated well with the media and staged emotional protests, such as when she included women on the front lines of the strikes, coaching them to kneel and pray as the other side sought to forcibly remove them. She also felt that women made the protests more peaceful by their example. "The participation of women has helped keep the movement nonviolent," she once surmised.

The First UFW Strike

Before the grape boycott that made them famous, the UFW focused on flowers. The first major UFW strike was in the rose industry. Rose grafters crawl on their knees for miles, slitting and inserting buds into rose bushes at top speed. They had come to the UFW and complained of numerous abuses, including the fact that they were being paid about $6.50 per thousand rose plants instead of the promised $9. The UFW met with the workers and resolved to strike for the promised wages. This strike, though unsuccessful, was an early show of Dolores's mettle. César Chávez recalled its beginning: "We had a pledge ceremony on Sunday, the day before the strike started. Dolores held the crucifix, and the guys put their hands on it, pledging not to break the strike."

The first day of the strike, the UFW had to send someone in to the company foreman to explain the workers' demands. "Thinking that maybe a woman would have a better chance," César recounted, "we had Dolores knock on the door about 10:30." Having held the crucifix, she then led the way, confronting the management and articulating the union's demands. The foreman screamed at her and called her a Communist, but she stood her ground and attempted negotiation until the police came and told her to leave. Then she went around personally to the homes of the striking workers and pressured them not to give in to the companies.

Mount Arbor Rose Company brought up replacement workers from Tangansiguiero, Mexico, to break the strike. This was a pivotal moment for the UFW, which offered all its benefits to the undocumented workers. "Everybody was angry," recalled César, "and we sent a letter to the mayor of Tangansiguiero denouncing them. In those little Mexican towns, they have an old building where people go to read the news. On one side they list things like stray animals and on the other they have a list of criminals. The mayor was so upset, he put our letter on the side with the criminals, in effect classifying them as such. . . . There was a lot of criticism of the Tangan. Today I think everyone from there is a Union member, and they are all good Union members." Chávez and Huerta both were talented at spreading the élan of union solidarity and used it to address the constant supply of illegal migrant workers, building alliances rather than shutting people out.

The Grape Strike

The great grape boycott began with a strike among Filipino workers in Delano. Led by Larry Itliong, who was now in charge of the Agricultural Workers' Organizing Committee (AWOC), the Filipino grape workers complained of arbitrarily lowered wages and horrible conditions. The owners of the farms were receiving higher and higher prices for their grapes but still paid their employees less than a living wage. They responded to the strike by threatening violence and locking the workers out of the camps they had been living in.

Dolores, who got to know Itliong when she recruited him to help organize the AWA, again took the lead. She immediately went to the picket lines to assess the situation and determine whether the UFW should get involved. "Dolores and Larry were in constant touch, and Dolores reported to me every day," recalled Chávez.

Soon, with Dolores strongly advocating for the strike, César Chávez called a UFW meeting at Our Lady of Guadalupe Church in Delano. They selected September 16—Mexican Independence Day—for the meeting. "The strike was begun by the Filipinos, but it is not exclusively for them," César said to the crowd. "Tonight we must decide if we are going to join our fellow workers in this great labor struggle."

The UFW voted to strike and adopt the same demands as the Filipinos: $1.40 an hour, 25 cents a box.

With the show of solidarity, the situation quickly escalated. The growers fought back fiercely. Delano city officials repeatedly sent inspectors to union headquarters. Visitors to the headquarters were tailed by police. It wasn't always clear who the agents of intimidation were, but the growers' private security and local law enforcement seemed to work together. Picketers were beaten, driven off the road by cars and tractors, and sprayed with pesticides and agricultural chemicals (chemical weapons really, and insult was added to injury because the UFW was fighting to limit the workers' exposure to them). While few attackers were arrested, dozens of strikers and their sympathizers were jailed. David Havens, a migrant ministry worker, was arrested and charged with "disturbing the peace" for reading aloud "The Definition of a Strikebreaker," often attributed to Jack London.[4]

The arrest, which resulted in charges that were eventually dismissed on First Amendment grounds, was one of many that crippled the strike. "[Sergeant Gerald] Dodd was picking us off one at a time—harassment arrests—and we couldn't fight back effectively," recalled Chávez. He, Dolores, and several members of the union and the migrant ministry developed a plan to get the strikers' message out to the public beyond Delano. The plan was put into effect two days after

---

[4] This is the complete text, which Chávez called "strong medicine."

> After God had finished the rattlesnake, the toad, the vampire, He had some awful substance left with which He made a Strikebreaker. A Strikebreaker is a two-legged animal with a corkscrew soul, a water-logged brain, a combination backbone made of jelly and glue. Where others have hearts he carries a tumor of rotten principles.
>
> When a Strikebreaker comes down the street men turn their backs and angels weep in Heaven, and the devil shuts the gates of Hell to keep him out. No man has a right to scab so long as there is a pool of water to drown his body in, or a rope long enough to hang his carcass with.
>
> Judas Iscariot was a gentleman compared with a scab. For betraying his Master he had character enough to hang himself—a Strikebreaker has not. Esau sold his birthright for a mess of pottage. Judas Iscariot sold his Savior for 30 pieces of silver. Benedict Arnold sold his country for the promise of a commission in the British Army.
>
> The modern Strikebreaker sells his birthright, his country, his wife, his children, and his fellow man for an unfilled promise from his employer, trust or corporation. Esau was a traitor to himself. Judas Iscariot was a traitor to his God. Benedict Arnold was a traitor to his country; a Strikebreaker to his God, his country, his family, his class.
>
> A real man will never scab.

Havens's arrest and, as Chávez remembered, it was "perfectly set up and executed."

The UFW lined up several speaking engagements for Chávez at Bay Area colleges and, the night before he went to San Francisco, the union asked for members willing to risk arrest for picketing. Everyone at the meeting volunteered. The next morning the volunteers found a field being worked by strikebreakers and began picketing, shouting *"Huelga! Huelga! Huelga!"*—"Strike! Strike! Strike!" As expected, Dodd ordered them to stop. When they refused, he began arresting strikers and organizers, and a total of forty-four were hauled off to jail. Hours later, at Berkeley, Mills College, Stanford, and other stops, Chávez announced the arrests and asked students to pitch in their "lunch money" for the strikers and protest the arrests. That day Chávez raised almost seven thousand dollars and, more important, forged a tangible link between the farmworkers' struggle and the growing civil rights movement. In a sense, he and Dolores had closed the circle, beginning with the CSO's civic organizing, then building on those principles to create a new labor organization in the UFW, and now creating alliances with other organizations committed to the principles and power of nonviolent protest.

Huerta and Chávez were successful in taking the farmworkers' cause to a higher level because they recognized and seized their place in the sweeping social change of the sixties. In 1960 the lunch counter desegregation in Nashville was led by Diane Nash, John Lewis, and others who would go on to found the Student Nonviolent Coordinating Committee, or SNCC. In 1961 and 1962 the Freedom Rides tore through the South. In 1963 the march on Washington and Martin Luther King Jr.'s "I have a dream" speech electrified the civil rights movement. In 1964, during Freedom Summer, three civil rights workers—James Chaney, Andrew Goodman, and Michael Schwerner—were murdered in Mississippi. That same year President Lyndon Johnson signed the Civil Rights Act. During the summer of 1965, weeks before the UFW strike began, the march from Selma to Montgomery had riveted the nation. By the time of the strike, the connections between the farmworkers' struggle—*La Causa*—and the civil rights movement were clear. The next summer, Martin Luther King Jr. sent the UFW a congratulatory telegram: "As brothers in the fight for equality, I extend the hand of fellowship and good will and wish continuing success to you and your members. The fight for equality must be fought on many fronts—in the urban slums, in the sweat shops of the factories and fields. Our separate struggles are really one—a struggle for freedom, for dignity, and for humanity. . . . We are together with you in spirit and in determination that our dreams for a better tomorrow will be realized."

After La Causa first came to public attention, César and Dolores continued their efforts, organizing, publicizing the unjustified arrests of the strikers, and articulating the roots of the exploitation. In April 1966 the UFW organized a march from Delano to Sacramento, modeled on the Selma-to-Montgomery march, which generated enough attention to prompt the Congressional Subcommittee on Migrant Labor to hold hearings in California in the fall of 1966.

Senator Robert F. Kennedy attended the hearing in Delano and spoke to a UFW gathering. Shortly before the midday recess, Kennedy asked Sheriff Leroy Gaylen about a recent round of picket arrests. Gaylen explained that he'd arrested the pickets to prevent a riot, since the strikebreakers had threatened to "cut their hearts out" if the picketers refused to leave. Impressed, Representative George Murphy told Gaylen, "I think it's a shame you weren't there before the Watts riots."[5] Appalled, Kennedy said, "Can I suggest that in the interim period of time, the luncheon period of time, that the sheriff and the district attorney read the Constitution of the United States?"

The UFW also took advantage of another cultural phenomenon, the growing concern over pesticides. Rachel Carson's *Silent Spring*, published in 1962, awakened Americans to the dangers of increasing pesticide use: "For the first time in the history of the world, every human being is now subjected to contact with dangerous chemicals, from the moment of conception until death," she wrote. (My father remembers that his first awareness of and interest in the environment was when his mother, Pauline Gore, began talking at the dinner table about how

---

[5] On August 11, 1965, in the largely black area of Watts, a Los Angeles Police Department patrol car pulled over a man on suspicion of drunk driving. While the police questioned the driver and his brother, residents of the neighborhood gathered and more officers arrived. When the driver was arrested, a struggle broke out and several of the officers struck the driver and his brother with their batons. The crowd continued to grow, as did their anger, and after the police left, the rioting began. Over the course of six days, 34 people died, more than a thousand were wounded, and property damage totaled as much as $100 million.

Huerta with Senator Robert F. Kennedy in Delano in 1968 shortly before Cesar Chavez broke one of his fasts. Andy Imutan and Larry Itliong are in the background. (courtesy Walter P. Reuther Library, Wayne State University)

important Carson's book was.) Dolores and the UFW drew on the new public awareness that Carson created and made protection of farm-workers from pesticide exposure a standard part of any contract.

The Grape Boycott

Encouraged by the public response to the strike, Chávez and Huerta, in conjunction with their friend and mentor Fred Ross, orga-nized a consumer boycott against table grapes from offending farms. Soon the powerful growers found a way to derail the boycott by chang-ing the labels on their grapes. Chávez remembered:

We had great difficulty in boycotting labels because the labels many times were not attached to the grapes. When the grapes go to the serving trays in the market, the boxes aren't with them.

Our own troops were confused. They didn't know which la-bels to boycott, which not to boycott. People who wanted to help were also confused. And out of all this confusion came the idea.

Fred [Ross] and Dolores found how to attack the riddle. They said, "Look, all the growers are now involved, right? Let's boycott all of them!"

I immediately rejected the idea.

They explained to me that it was the only way you could do it, because then the grapes became the label itself. That made it clear to me.

Then it was just a question of the principles and the morals involved.

César insisted they had to give the growers one last chance, but as the negotiations stalled, he agreed to the general boycott. (The UFW succeeded in getting a union contract with DiGiorgio farms, so the slogan became, "Boycott California grapes—except DiGiorgio.") In January 1968 Dolores went east and began her spirited leadership of the pickets, rallies, and press conferences that made the grape boycott such an unprecedented success.

During the course of the boycott Dolores noticed a difference between her approach and that of male leaders. She recalls, "I decided to start with the small, independent stores and move up to the bigger chains," whereas "the macho attitude was to take on the biggest store first." In 1969, after one of his fasts, César fell ill and by then, Dolores had "cleaned up the eastern states" and returned to California, where she invigorated the boycott. "They were still fighting the big chains," she remembers, but with the new approach, "we won the boycott." Huerta was a steely and inspiring field commander. Throughout the country volunteers flocked to the cause and she often led pickets herself, keeping morale high with impassioned speeches.

The boycott was especially gratifying to Huerta because it reassured her sense that society at large would not long tolerate such inequities. "We took the fight from Delano to New York, Canada and Europe," Huerta remembered. "The vast majority of people don't like to see injustice. Farmworkers' poverty is so extreme and the growers are so wealthy. People look at the way farmworkers live, they see the things farmworkers don't have, and they ask, Why? Why aren't these workers paid fairly? It's not the consumers' fault. Consumers shouldn't feel bad, but they should be concerned. They should help ensure that the people who are feeding them are not exploited or abused."

The growers had prepared for worker unrest by forming an organization—the South Central Farmers Committee—complete with attorneys and consultants, but they had no way of dealing with the theatrical

PR campaign and the newfound spirit among the workers. Picketing, bullhorns, flag-waving, and finally the boycott all amounted to a strategy that was "agonizing" to them. The media swarmed to the scene and the growers were depicted as greedy and cruel. "Growing grapes was never our problem," confessed one grower, Harry Steinovic. "Our problem was handling the media." He and other growers were deeply hurt by what they saw as an unfair depiction of them as lacking in compassion and fairness. "We paid prevailing wages. We were just competing with other growers for unskilled labor."

As the chief negotiator for the UFW, Dolores brought the same emotional intensity to the negotiating table that she had brought to field organizing, soon earning a reputation as a formidable adversary. She was not afraid of confrontation and was determined to hold growers accountable for their treatment of their workers: "The growers I was negotiating with were the same ones who had pulled rifles on us, beat us with boards, put me in jail." She sometimes brought workers with her to negotiating sessions and spoke to them in Spanish throughout, which upset the growers. Dolores explains, "My speaking to workers in Spanish was to keep them apprised at all times of what was going on in the negotiations and to ask their opinion. As a negotiator, you are on the go between the employers and the workers." But some found her style uncomfortably intense. "Huerta is a brave woman," said Nicholas Petris, then chairman of housing and urban affairs in the California legislature, adding, "She's a believer, not a broker for her cause." César Chávez himself sometimes joked about "unleashing Dolores" on the growers.

Effective as she was, the growers began attacking Huerta personally. One PR man representing the growers used both racial and gender stereotypes to discredit her: "Dolores Huerta is crazy. She's a violent woman, where women, especially Mexican women, are usually peaceful and pleasant. You can't live wrought up like she does and not be crazy." According to Dolores, "What the growers hated was my persistence at getting the articles approved and my tenacity in trying to get good, strong contracts. You have to remember that conditions for the workers were primitive, toilets non-existent. One county supervisor called one of the Filipino workers a monkey at the negotiating table. Another one made a proposition to an attractive woman on our team in front of her husband. When things like this would happen, I would naturally object. One attorney said, 'What do you have against love?' when we brought up the foreman's sexual harassment at the table."

In 1970 about thirty growers came to the UFW offices and signed historic new contracts in front of the national press. They were three-year contracts that paid for unemployment insurance, health care, and a deduction for union dues, and they ceded some managerial decisions to the union. "We lost the PR battle and we paid for it," recalled Steinovic. "We learned that we weren't in control of everything, and we acknowledged our loss by signing a union contract with the United Farm Workers."

The results of these and subsequent contracts were significant. As the lead negotiator, Huerta proudly ticked off the progress: "Our workers earn higher wages than non-union workers. Our workers are covered by a pension plan. Our workers and every member of their families are covered by our major medical plan . . . [We have] a grievance procedure so we can get people back to work if they've been fired unjustly. Workers on contract have seniority rights so they'll be re-hired when the season's over." Having used the newly expanded mass media to achieve some momentum on the issue, she immediately took the fight back to the California legislature. Working overtime in Sacramento, Huerta secured unemployment insurance for farmworkers.

In the late 1960s and early 70s, the UFW tangled repeatedly with California governor Ronald Reagan. Unfazed by the national wave of nostalgia that followed Reagan's death in 2004, Huerta minced no words when remembering him. She told an interviewer, "Reagan was very much opposed to collective bargaining." She pointed out that he had never met with the farmworkers face to face, and he had once told an interviewer that the union's five-year boycott on grapes was immoral. Still outraged, she recalled, "He actually was eating grapes during the grape boycott." Citing his repeated vetoes of legislation that would have extended unemployment insurance to farmworkers, she summarized, "Reagan did very harsh things for poor people."

The Battle with the Teamsters

In 1973, when those hard-won contracts began to expire, the largest and wealthiest union in the world, the International Brotherhood of Teamsters, challenged the UFW. The Teamsters had been expelled from the AFL-CIO in 1957 because of corruption and ties to organized crime. (Robert F. Kennedy served as counsel to the Senate committee investigating union corruption.) According to some contemporary observers, Teamster leaders seemed intent on putting a wedge into the union movement for their own gain (like the self-serving "snakes" that Mother Jones warned of). They wanted to reap the union dues and build their national political influence, while at the same time enjoying a cozy relationship with the powerful growers. William Grami, a smooth and ambitious executive, was the chief strategist for the Teamsters when they decided to go after the UFW's contracts.

The Teamsters offered the growers a very minimal version of what the UFW had fought for—slightly increased wages with no major protections or benefits. The growers, resentful from the acrimonious negotiations that preceded the 1970 contract, leapt at the chance to work with another, much less demanding union. "The Teamsters became an alternative and we signed contracts with them that were quite favorable," explained one grape grower. According to Huerta, "The Teamster contracts were not enforced and gave the workers no protection. The whole thing was a ruse to get rid of the UFW, cooked up by the head of the Teamsters, Frank Fitzsimmons, the head of the farm bureau, Allen Grant, and President Nixon. Workers were fired if they did not sign Teamster cards."

The Teamsters' collaboration with the growers was devastating. At its peak, the UFW had 55,000 members. After the Teamsters moved in, the membership dropped to 10,000, which resulted in a scarcity of funds, major cuts in the programs the UFW offered, and an understandable dive in morale. One grape grower asserted that the UFW over-reached and lost support when it established a centralized hiring hall. Having won so many victories only a few years earlier, the union "antagonized their own members because they wanted to control them," he said. But Huerta saw the "control" as essential to empowerment, especially since it was the farmworkers themselves running the union. "We know the work can be organized so people settle down in one place with their families and control their lives through political power and their own union—which they run themselves . . . The union helps farmworkers stabilize their lives, settle down in a community, and send their kids to school."

Huerta and Chávez turned to the AFL-CIO for support and fought fiercely to maintain the allegiance of the farmworkers. As Huerta explained, the minor increases in wages that the Teamsters offered were merely a Band-Aid for the workers. "Farmworkers kill themselves working, living nowhere, traveling all the time, putting up with the pesticides because the growers want it that way," she said. "It's a feudal system which higher wages won't change."

Dolores Huerta worked harder than ever to help the UFW regain the lost ground. She made speeches, passed out literature, and made countless personal appeals to the workers and their families, passionately persuading them that they were the lifeblood of the UFW, that the union was by, for, and of the farmworkers themselves. When it was time for the election, Dolores was so worried about foul play that she persuaded the UFW election monitor to take Dexedrine to stay alert while the ballots were counted. When the returns were in, the UFW had won back all the contracts, defeating the mighty Teamsters.

Despite the victory, the Teamster challenge had shaken the UFW. They had to keep up their efforts, even in farms where they'd won contracts, because the Teamsters continued their organizing push and challenged contracts as they expired. Throughout the strike areas, growers' alliances with law enforcement and civic officials remained

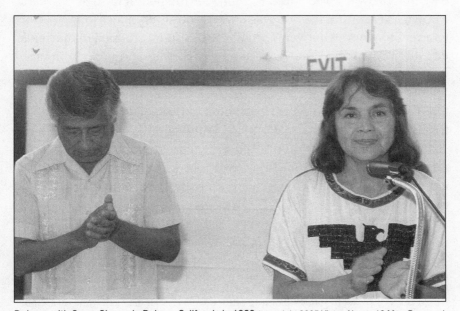

Dolores with Cesar Chavez in Delano, California in 1989 (copyright 2005 Victor Aleman/ 2 Mun-Dos.com)

strong and by the end of 1973, over 3,500 UFW strikers and organizers had been arrested, most for violating injunctions or unlawful assembly. When the attacks on the strikers became more violent,
Chávez and Huerta maintained their original philosophy of nonviolence, but this lack of response did not defuse the situation. On August 13, 1973, picket captain Nagi Daifullah was beaten to death by a
Kern County deputy sheriff. Two days later, Juan de la Cruz, one of
the original di Giorgio strikers, was shot and killed.[6] Both deaths
were later ruled accidental. The violence ebbed a bit but the Teamsters continued to pour money and staff into their campaign to replace the UFW. They finally backed off in the late seventies, in the
face of changing labor legislation, ongoing corruption scandals, and
the leadership vacuum that followed the mysterious disappearance of
influential former Teamster head Jimmy Hoffa.

Throughout the seventies, the UFW continued to achieve reforms
in the agricultural industry. In 1975, the Agricultural Labor Relations
Act was passed, the first law to recognize the collective bargaining
rights of farmworkers in California. They approached the California
Rural Legal Assistance to bring the case that resulted in the abolition
of the short-handled hoe, a device which was emblematic of the cruel
way that growers prioritized profits over the health of their workers.
Known as *el cortito*, the hoe was only twenty-four inches long, forcing
workers to work bent over. The long hours spent stooped in the fields,
day after day, meant that debilitating back pain and lifelong injuries
were common among farmworkers. At one hearing on the issue,
female farmworker and organizer Jessie de la Cruz told a grower,
"Just stand up and hold the tips of your shoes and walk up and down
this room and see how many times you can do it." But growers resisted all efforts to get rid of *el cortito*, claiming that its short length
afforded more control and that, without it, thinning and weeding
would not be done as effectively and the crop would not be big
enough.

César Chávez's own back specialist said that work with *el cortito*

---

[6] This wasn't the first UFW fatality. Eighteen-year-old Nan Freeman, a student
from Massachusetts, was struck and killed by a truck while walking a picket line at Tal-
isman Sugar Company in Florida. Nor would it be the last—in 1979 Rufino Contreras
would be shot to death while talking to lettuce workers. Huerta still mourns all four,
calling them "our martyrs."

was to blame for his chronic pain, and other doctors concurred that it was crippling farmworkers across the state. It was, in the words of one labor activist, "a flat-out symbol of oppression—a way to keep control of workers and make them live humbled, stooped-over lives." Other states had already shifted to a long-handled hoe, but the growers in California did not budge. Finally, in 1975, the UFW personally lobbied Governor Jerry Brown, who saw to it that *el cortito* was banned.

Born-Again Feminism

As Huerta got older, she experienced what she refers to as a "born-again commitment to feminism." Like Wells-Barnett, Jones, Hamilton, Perkins, Durr, and Clark—all of whom had moments of doubt that the movement for women's rights of their day was concomitant with their specific concerns about social justice—Huerta eventually would become fully committed to the women's movement, part of its lifeblood.

Dolores was influenced in particular by her friendship with one of the most influential American feminists, who had come to the UFW in 1967 as a freelance journalist volunteering to help with public relations: Gloria Steinem.[7] Steinem recalls that Huerta was "intense, focused, a great speechifier at rallies" and "totally authentic" in her leadership of picket lines and demonstrations at a time when there were really no other women in union leadership positions. Yet Huerta was initially closed to the growing movement for reproductive freedom for women and accepted the chauvinistic attitudes toward women activists as inevitable.

As Steinem put it, Dolores went through the same kind of awakening that so many other women did in the sixties and seventies—including Gloria herself, who used to whisper her ideas to men in meetings and responded gratefully when told "You write like a man"—just on a

---

[7] Steinem helped to organize press for the march from Delano to Sacramento and to strategize about how to manage the fact that local law enforcement had made it clear that they would not protect the farmworkers from violence. She also helped to organize a UFW benefit at Carnegie Hall. One of the reasons Steinem left the UFW (although she stayed in touch with them) was that they refused to provide family planning help to the women farmworkers (and wives of farmworkers) who would "come to the clinic literally on their hands and knees pleading" for it. At that time, Dolores, as well as César, viewed the dissemination of birth control and availability of abortion as immoral.

more circuitous route. In the end it was the link between the exploitation of the farmworkers and the condescension to women in general that converted Dolores to feminism and made her question the way that others had viewed her gender. "She saw that adversaries of the farmworkers were the same as those against the women's movement," according to Steinem.

Feminism came quite naturally, albeit late, to Huerta, who had always bucked convention and was tired of feeling ashamed of it. "The women's movement has done a lot towards helping me not feel guilty about my divorces," she explained. Through it, Huerta found a way to apply her political philosophy to herself. "We want to go on and cut a path for our life," she says of women, "and we shouldn't let anyone stand in our way." Huerta was a founding member of the Feminist Majority Foundation board, on which she still serves, as well as an early and active member of NOW. She's spoken at many rallies and marches on behalf of the women's movement, including the March for Women's Lives in 2004.

Although she had always sought to make the environment in the union hierarchy more welcoming to women by promoting them to leadership positions and encouraging their participation in the strikes and boycotts, Dolores began to communicate with the men about it.

Huerta with Gloria Steinem in 1996 (courtesy Jenny Warburg)

"We were in our board meeting," she recalled, "and the fellas all joking, talking, this and this. I just started making a little check mark every time that they made a sexist statement. . . . And then they would catch themselves. I mean, because they—it was sort of an educational process for them also because they didn't realize. And I remember one of César's security guards saying to me, 'Dolores, when you walk in the room, the whole climate changes.'" She also helped found the Coalition for Labor Union Women, always seeking new ways to bring women to leadership roles. "I always made it a point to encourage and promote women and to mentor and support them," she said recently. "It's hard for women to fight for decision-making roles, but that's where they need to be. My message is that women are not servants and are not sex objects. We are needed in public life because we think differently. We have a different perspective."

Dolores has become an outspoken advocate for opening up women's choices in balancing work and family obligations. In one interview she remarked, "I have friends who were single parents and had to accept welfare but continued with their schooling. Now they have M.A. and Ph.D. degrees; the fact that a woman gives birth to a baby doesn't mean that she can't go out and seek her career path." She articulated a solid point in the debate about motherhood and career paths: it's not true that women can't have it all—they can. They just can't have it all at one time. Or, as she put it, "There's a song called 'El Rey' with a phrase that says 'You don't have to be the first one to get there, but you have to know how to arrive.'"

Huerta has also argued that part of being a good parent is connecting to the community. In an editorial published in May 2005, she asserted that children benefit from their mothers' civic activism. "Mothers today often say that they are concerned about what is happening to America. But most feel that they just can't afford to 'get involved' . . . getting kids involved with us develops their conscience and confidence in their own power to do good."

Pesticides

Since the awareness generated by Rachel Carson's *Silent Spring*, the UFW had been successful in including contract terms regulating the use of chemicals, but most growers were not inclined to limit their use without more outside pressure to do so. "Getting a union contract is one of the biggest tools in working to ban pesticides," Huerta observed. But soon it was time to take the campaign beyond the contracts and into the national political arena.

The most toxic pesticides resulted from the unprecedented Industrial Revolution chemical processes that Alice Hamilton studied and sought to regulate. As my father, Al Gore, wrote in *Earth in the Balance,* there was a "whole new generation of powerful compounds created in the chemical revolution, which picked up speed after World War II; over the past fifty years, herbicides, pesticides, fungicides, chlorofluorocarbons (CFCs), and thousands of other compounds have come streaming out of laboratories and chemical plants faster than we can possibly keep track of them." Huerta and Chávez became alarmed about the impact of pesticides when they saw the crippling effects on farmworkers, including birth defects, sickness, and death.

A continued push to raise public awareness was a key part of the effort, and Huerta became an effective spokesperson. "The pesticide manufacturers push pesticides like they're candy through their marketing," she explained in one interview. "Many of the growers I've negotiated with across the bargaining table don't even know the dangers of these pesticides. . . . A lot of manufacturers push pesticides on the growers so they don't know what they're using and they overdose, using more pesticides than they have to."

In 1984 the UFW drew up a list of "the dirty dozen" pesticides that caused health problems among farmworkers. Among them were methyl bromide, DDT, and aldrin. "God knows how many workers have died from methyl bromide," said Huerta. "I personally know one family where the woman's husband got sick working in the strawberries in San Diego. He got on a bus and went home and died in Tijuana." Having raised awareness about the issue, Dolores was invited to testify before Congress. When she did so, lawmakers close to the growers and the chemical manufacturers threatened perjury charges, specifically insisting that she was lying about the effects of DDT. But eventually, as the scientific proof mounted about the effects of indiscriminate use of the chemical, DDT was nationally banned. Huerta followed the same course of action with parathion and other pesticides, first banning it within UFW contracts, then fighting for legislation.

Protection from pesticides became, and remains, one of the UFW's major issues. In 1984 the UFW called for another grape boycott (this one less successful than the first) to protest excessive and dangerous pesticide use. In 1988 Chávez fasted for thirty-six days to call attention to the dangers of pesticides, his third major fast and the longest one. Although it did result in increased consumer awareness, pesticides remain a terrible worker hazard, one Huerta continues to combat.

Politics and Dissent

While some advocates let the perfect be the enemy of the good, turning up their noses at flawed candidates and sitting out election cycles, Dolores Huerta embraced the political process. Like Virginia Durr, Dolores has always gotten behind the candidates she feels will champion her issues, from helping Robert Kennedy win the California Democratic primary, to campaigning hard as a chair of Women for Kerry in 2004. Her steadfast presence on the campaign front lines has come at a personal cost, and once led to a terrible beating.

In San Francisco in 1988, Huerta participated in a peaceful demonstration outside a $1,000-a-plate fundraiser for presidential candidate, and then vice president, George H. W. Bush. She was handing out literature on the danger pesticides created for farmworkers (promoting the second grape boycott, which Bush had dismissed) when the crowd was pressed against a police barricade and ordered by law enforcement officers to move back. In an incident caught on videotape, Huerta, then fifty-eight years old, was clubbed by police officers. She sustained serious internal injuries, including six broken ribs and a spleen so damaged that it had to be removed in emergency surgery. UFW field representative Henry Wallace charged, "It was a totally unwarranted, brutal attack. This 110-pound woman did not take on the tac [tactical] squad."

San Francisco's mayor Art Agnos, a friend and ally of Dolores's, was so appalled that after visiting her in the hospital, talking by phone to Chávez, and reviewing the videotape, he held a press conference. As the *Los Angeles Times* reported, Agnos said he was able to identify Huerta in the police tape and clearly saw that she was moving in compliance with police instructions. "If you read her lips, she is saying, 'I am moving,'" Agnos said.

As Susan Ferris and Ricardo Sandoval wrote in *The Fight in the Fields*, "Controversy gripped the city for days afterward, as César and civil rights activists demanded a thorough investigation. Initially there were doubts that the officer had acted improperly; but the case broke wide open when a subsequent review of television news footage clearly showed the officer striking Huerta. In 1991, the city settled with Huerta out of court for $825,000, a sum that inspired her to joke that she would have to open a bank account. In all her years of volunteerism with the UFW, she had never so much as applied for a credit card. Huerta said she intended to use the money to help groups organizing women."

Huerta used the settlement money to set up the Dolores Huerta Foundation. Several years later, the *Los Angeles Times* reported that police conduct in the case had shaken public confidence in the department.

In 1993, César Chávez died while traveling on union business, staying with a farm family near his Arizona birthplace. Though the death was unexpected, it was also unsurprising. Chávez's physical health had been damaged by years of work in the fields and by his repeated, extreme fasts.

On April 29, more than 35,000 mourners gathered for an outdoor mass in Delano—the largest funeral for an American labor leader. His twenty-seven grandchildren approached the altar to lay down a wooden carving of the UFW eagle, and a short-handled hoe. After delivering a eulogy for her friend and colleague of more than forty years, Dolores returned to her work for the organization they'd built together. "I've always been comfortable in a leadership role," she said in 2005. "I had a tremendous advantage as the founder of the union, the negotiator, setting up the ranch committees. I had a great deal of respect from the workers and the public. This still applies to this day." At the same time, she did not take Chávez's place at the head of the union, endorsing Arturo Rodriguez instead.

In 2000, Dolores Huerta suffered a brain aneurysm so severe that she wasn't expected to survive. She remained hospitalized for months and then, with characteristic spirit, fought her way back to health. After slowly regaining the ability to walk, talk, and eat, she led a 165-mile UFW march from Bakersfield to Sacramento in 2001. The purpose of the eleven-day march was to pressure Governor Gray Davis to sign a bill forcing growers to submit to arbitration when negotiations with farmworkers stalled. "When she's there, people know it's serious," said one politician at the rally in Sacramento. Dolores Huerta addressed the crowd, telling them, "When Gray signed [the bill declaring] César Chávez Day, he gave me a copy of the bill with a note calling me his 'conscience.' Now we'll learn if he hears his conscience." Although powerful growers argued that higher wages and more benefits for the farmworkers could put them out of business, Governor Davis signed the new law into effect on September 30, 2002. "Dolores has an incredibly strong symbolic and charismatic presence, but more than that she [understands] the strength of the grassroots," said New York politician Fernando Ferrer.

In 2003 Huerta officially resigned from the UFW and devoted herself to her foundation. At its first fundraiser, which honored her mentor Fred Ross Sr., she announced that the foundation's goal was to send organizers into communities to "show people how to work together and take on the issues that are affecting them." She proudly laid out her vision for political activism on behalf of the Americans she now sees as most vulnerable. "Immigrants are the new civil rights movement," she

Dolores with two of her daughters, Maria Elena Chavez and Juanita Chavez in La Paz, California in 1986 at the UFW headquarters. (copyright 2005 Victor Aleman/ 2 Mun-Dos.com)

declared. "There is a backlash against them and they need to know how they can participate in the political process."

Huerta, still traveling and speaking out, is now married to her long-time partner, César's brother Richard Chávez, and keeps in close touch with her children. She proudly lists their diverse professions: attorney, paralegal, medical doctor, performing artist, therapist, chef, administrators, teacher, filmmaker, emergency room nurse. When asked what kind of people she wanted her children to be, she replied, "tough, political, responsible, and loving," a combination of attributes that Huerta herself exemplifies.

In countless situations, Dolores Huerta displayed extraordinary courage, defending others and lighting the way ahead. At the core of her actions is the lesson her mother taught her: to respect and help fellow human beings in need. "We need to respect people who do things with their hands: farmworkers, carpenters, mechanics," she told one reporter. "Just because you don't have a college degree it doesn't make you a lesser person." Dolores has clearly helped many young women find their political voices; she was recently surprised to see her own face on T-shirts commemorating *La Causa*, right alongside César's. "It's because of the Latinas," she told me. "They want to see a woman's face."

I am inspired by the longevity of Huerta's work and the way in which, even as she has become more recognized for her achievements, she continues to reach out, spreading hope and self-respect. In 2003 Huerta visited the Stockton elementary school named in her honor and told the students, mostly children and grandchildren of farmworkers: "Your parents and grandparents do the most sacred work in the world. They feed everybody."

Helen Rodriguez-Trias

Individuals and leadership are crucial, but we should never deny the need for organizations and movements because they shape individuals.
—HELEN RODRIGUEZ-TRIAS

IN 1970 THE COUNTRY SEEMED TO BE FRACTURING ALONG THE fault lines that had become increasingly apparent during the previous decade. In May, in the wake of the Cambodia invasion and the killings of student protesters at Kent State University and Jackson State University, massive antiwar rallies were held all over the country. In New York, construction workers in hard hats, some armed with lead pipes and crowbars, left their World Trade Center workplace and violently broke up an antiwar protest on Wall Street as brokers and office workers cheered.

Of course, the war was only one source of division. Another was the growing women's movement. On August 26 tens of thousands of women in cities from coast to coast marked an all-day "Women's Strike for Equality." After identifying a woman with an unfamiliar courtesy title, the *New York Times* helpfully explained that "'Ms.' is used by women who object to the distinction between 'Miss' and 'Mrs.' to denote marital status."

Soon it was a woman addressed as "Dr.," Helen Rodriguez-Trias, who would figure in another New York social drama. At Lincoln Hospital in the South Bronx, the Pediatrics Collective, made up of young, radical residents sporting bell-bottoms, long hair, and love beads, joined forces with the Black Panthers[1] and the Puerto Rican Young Lords[2] to take control of the hospital administration. They had personally escorted some staff members out of the building, explaining that they were no longer needed because they were not sensitive to the needs of the community that Lincoln served—well over 300,000 people, 80 percent Puerto Rican, 20 percent black, overwhelmingly poor. As the revolutionary atmosphere thickened, a hand-painted banner sprawled from one window: *"Bienvenido Al Hospital Del Pueblo"*—Welcome to the People's Hospital.

Established in 1839 as a nursing home for runaway slaves, Lincoln had fallen into such disrepair by 1970 that most people casually referred to it as "a dump" and the *New York Times* described it as "universally deplored as inadequate and obsolete." Clinics were run in overcrowded hallways, and there were long waiting lists for vital services. In 1969 (a month after Woodstock), the hospital administration had decided to address the perennial staff shortages by tapping the stream of "socially conscious and politically aware" young medical students. They wound up with the Collective.

Tensions mounted when the group forced the resignation of Lincoln's head of pediatrics, a distinguished Jewish physician who was born in Belgium and had fought the Nazis. Dr. Arnold H. Einhorn, understandably agitated by all of this, pleaded his case in public, prompting charges of racism and the arrival of the press corps, the

---

[1] The Black Panther Party for Self-Defense was founded in 1966 by black nationalists Huey P. Newton and Bobby G. Seale, who were motivated by frustration with the limited gains of the civil rights movement. Advocating creation of separate judicial, educational, and self-defense systems, the Panthers set up social service organizations within the black communities that were underserved by public works, ran youth breakfast programs, and worked to purge inner-city neighborhoods of drug dealers. In later years, the Panthers were weakened by FBI infiltration, internal power struggles, and increasing corruption and violence among some members.

[2] The Young Lords, a Puerto Rican nationalist group founded in 1968, advocated empowerment of poor Puerto Ricans in both Chicago and New York and highlighted inequalities in public services. They protested the discriminatory routes of the Sanitation Department, demanded Puerto Rican independence, and established social service programs modeled on those of the Black Panthers.

Jewish Defense League, and various other advocacy groups. The Pediatrics Collective members, pointing out that many of them were Jewish as well, forged ahead, while the Black Panthers and Young Lords manned "grievance desks" in the hospital lobby.

Officials in charge of the municipal health care system began to look for a solution; they settled on finding a replacement for Dr. Einhorn, who had by then requested a transfer. Their choice was forty-one-year-old Helen Rodriguez-Trias, a woman who had grown up and been educated in Puerto Rico and was, according to the *New York Times*, "a pediatrician with impeccable professional credentials and a personality that indicated she could get along with the collective." Helen, who had been recruited by Einhorn a year earlier, began her new job in the middle of this ferocious political atmosphere. "I don't think they [the collective] know the kind of dynamite they are playing with in the communities" said Dr. Joseph English, the head of the city's Health and Hospitals Corporation, which administered Lincoln and other public hospitals. Furthermore, she received no welcome bouquets. When asked whether the appointment was a response to the Young Lords' demands, Dean Labe Scheinberg said, "So far as I'm concerned it's merely a coincidence. She was the only person available."

Helen, a beautiful brunette with clear, smooth skin and lovely almond-shaped eyes, combined an overachieving academic brilliance with a knack for relating to people of very different backgrounds. She constantly switched from English to Spanish throughout her day, speaking to patients, colleagues, and political leaders with equal forbearance and respect. A friend and colleague says Helen epitomized the line from the Rudyard Kipling poem "If": "If you can talk with crowds and keep your virtue / Or walk with kings nor lose the common touch."

Like Alice Hamilton, Rodriguez-Trias brought zeal, pragmatism, and supreme analytical skills to the field of public health. She loved to organize political movements from the ground up, was open-minded and versatile, and never lost sight of her goal. Helen's enduring legacies—from the first neonatal care unit on the island of Puerto Rico, to the effective campaign to stop coerced sterilization, to bridges she built within the women's movement (which had struggled with racial and class tensions ever since the days of Ida B. Wells-Barnett's friendship with Susan B. Anthony and Mother Jones's disparagement of the suffragists), to her work to protect victims of domestic violence and curtail the transmission of HIV/AIDS—all reflect her foresight and passion.

Childhood

The youngest of three children, Helen was born in 1929 in New York City to Puerto Rican parents. The family returned to Puerto Rico when she was very young, and Helen ended up moving back and forth between the island and the city throughout her life. Her father, Damian Rodriguez, was a reasonably successful businessman but also an alcoholic, which led to financial instability, family separations, and emotional turbulence: "When he drank, his urbanity disappeared and he threatened us with violence in a booming, rough voice." Throughout it all, Helen's Aunt Estela was the children's "most constant nurturer," while her mother, Josefa Trias, "struggled to keep our family together."

Helen deeply admired Josefa, who imparted a strong work ethic and a sense of civic responsibility. "My mother was a very avid fighter for what she thought was right," said Helen. As a schoolteacher, she fought for education reforms, such as a school lunch program, arguing that "children could not learn with just a few swallows of sugarless coffee in their stomachs." Josefa also fought for the right to teach classes in Spanish, which had been banned since 1898, when the United States took control of the island from Spain.[3]

Clearly influenced by her mother, Helen developed an early and strong political sensibility:

> During my sixth summer, spent as were many childhood summers, with my mother's cousins in the small highland town of Cayey, Puerto Rico, I went to a circus for the first time. The

---

[3] The Spanish-American War marked a major turning point in the international role of the United States. As Edmund Morris wrote in his biography of Theodore Roosevelt, the acquisition of Guam, Puerto Rico, and the Philippines was very controversial. "The ideological gulf yawned even wider when [McKinley was persuaded] that occupation of Spain's former colonies should continue well beyond the armistice. . . . Powerful commercial, strategic, and moral arguments to this effect had been advanced by young soldiers—Theodore Roosevelt among them—campaigning for McKinley's reelection. They had trumpeted the islands as new markets for America's superabundant production, cited naval research in favor of a global defense system, and looked to Congress to ensure that America would hold on to what the Supreme Court euphemistically called its 'unincorporated territories.'"

huge tent held many wonders including a woman who hung suspended by her teeth as she twirled in the air, spangled costume glittering, body gracefully arched. Walking through the circus later, my eyes caught the half-open flap of a worn low tent. Behind it was that same woman, thin and tired, nursing a tiny baby. She sat on a bare mattress on the ground, enveloped in semi-darkness and mixed human smells. Much later in life, I recognized these as the smells of poverty in my country. The nation of which my children, grandchildren, and I form part—in whose soil my parents, grandparents, and great-grandparents lie—is much like that circus. Where the tourists tread is the glitter of hotels, casinos, expensive restaurants, and the other props of the trade. Where people really live, work, love, and nurse their children, the rank smells of poverty prevail. My history is intertwined with my nation's.

Even when she was very young, Helen knew she wanted to be a doctor because "it combined the things I loved the most, science and people." In what seems to have been the early instinct that leads so many future doctors to medicine, Helen felt a calling to, in her words, "be part of the healing community." It was a familiar calling, as she later said: "My mother's people were spiritualists, one of my aunts a medium and healer well-known in those parts. Perhaps the scientific interests also sprouted then in the fertile black soil of the garden."

Helen also credited one early science teacher with kindling her interest: "In second grade she had us doing experiments, for example, on why things burn and what happens if you take oxygen away from something that's burning. That really was a tremendous eye-opener for me."

In 1939, when Helen was ten, her parents divorced. Poverty and unemployment were rampant and Josefa, unable to find work in the depressed economy of Puerto Rico, decided to go back to New York City. According to Helen, she was "seeking a better life, like many Puerto Ricans before her." Helen's twenty-year-old brother Damian, known as Pepito, continued with engineering school, and her fourteen-year-old sister Gladys, settled with friends and school, remained with Aunt Estela. Already adventurous and optimistic, young Helen was a bit apprehensive about the move but nonetheless excited: "I knew I would see marvelous things like snow, be up in high buildings looking down at tiny cars and people, travel by train for the first time and live in an apartment building with what seemed hundreds of people."

Helen and Josefa settled in Washington Heights, a working-class community whose residents came from a variety of backgrounds: Irish, Italians, Greeks, Puerto Ricans, blacks, and Jews. Josefa wanted to avoid living in El Barrio, the Puerto Rican enclave, because she deplored the conditions there, but she insisted that Helen speak Spanish at home.

Helen recalls those first few years in the city as a time of isolation. They lived in a series of furnished rooms or shared apartments and Josefa, whose bilingualism was considered undesirable, was unable to get a teaching license. Instead, she took piecework—sewing beads on collars, stitching feathers to hats, assembling gloves—until finding steadier work as a cook and housekeeper.

When Helen entered the American elementary school system, she immediately sensed that she was perceived as different—and less worthy—than the white students. She became aware of her ethnicity in a way she never had been before. The way she was treated, the comments, the assignments, all reflected the notion that Hispanics were a sort of lower caste. Helen learned English quickly but it was a struggle to adapt and be accepted. She said later, "In Puerto Rico racism was subtle. There wasn't the kind of separatist racism like in the United States. I wasn't used to this." Despite good grades, she was placed in remedial classes. "When I graduated from the sixth grade, I ended up in a class considered to be of the poor students . . . all this must have been because of my name. It wasn't the grades."

One teacher realized Helen's potential and probably changed her life. "One day I was called upon to recite a poem, and I knew the poem by heart. The teacher said, 'Why are you in this class?' She moved me to the class with the bright kids. . . . I might have just as well gone down the tubes academically if that teacher hadn't moved me out of that class. This is an example of how pivotal teachers are. So many children are misplaced, tracked, or put in environments that don't foster learning." Helen internalized this realization in two ways—first by trusting her own abilities and second by realizing the effect that a caring individual in a position of power can have on others. Throughout her life she mentored other women and encouraged them to believe in their own potential.

While she recognized the advantages this new status offered, at first it cut her off from her heritage. She said later, "I learned quickly to 'pass' by not being too different from the others. The pressure toward becoming 'American' was too great to resist. I would soon say I was proud of being a 'gringo' although I wasn't sure what that meant."

Despite these efforts and her obvious intelligence, Helen was constantly reminded that she was considered both different and inferior. She was one of two Puerto Rican girls in a high school chemistry class, and whenever one or the other approached the blackboard, the teacher sang the chorus of a song made popular by Dean Martin: "Mañana, mañana is good enough for me." Another teacher told her she was "too dark" to wear the colonial costume donned by the honor guard to take down the flag during school ceremonies.

By her senior year, Helen was no longer hurt by these insults, her thinking stimulated by an economics teacher who engaged the class in debates about segregation, rent control, and other social policy legislation. She embraced

Helen's high school portrait signed "To my dear papa" (courtesy Laura and JoEllen Brainin-Rodriguez)

political studies and joined the school's Pan American Club, which included students from Colombian, Dominican, and Puerto Rican backgrounds. However, after the club organized in support of Puerto Rican independence, the school disbanded it. (Ironically, the school had first organized the club in honor of Teddy Roosevelt's "Good Neighbor" policy.)

University, Marriage, and Children

Clearly, Helen was destined for higher education. Because tuition in the United States was so expensive, Josefa suggested she enroll at the University of Puerto Rico, where she was awarded a full scholarship. In 1947, when Helen was eighteen, she returned to her childhood home. It was a bittersweet experience:

> Every ocean wave, flower, palm tree, every inland road covered by arches of flaming poincianas filled me with tremendous joy of rediscovery. I sang with joy perched in the back of my brother's jeep as we rode to the beach, laughed with the people on the bus to a mountain town as a countryman struggled to get a pig on board. The beauty of the land, sea, and people moved me. It was the poverty that overwhelmed me. The nearly forgotten smells were there, the sight of San Juan's huge slums . . . was unforgettable.

Within months, political controversy cut short her first year in college. A supporter of Puerto Rican independence, Helen joined a strike that began in the spring of 1948, when the university president refused to allow the student council to invite a controversial nationalist leader to speak. In response, the student body voted to strike and for weeks, the campus was roiled with protests: picketing students were jailed, beaten, and tear-gassed, and many leaders were suspended or expelled. While she wasn't at the center of the movement, Helen's involvement invigorated and engaged her. She recalled later, "I was peripheral to the student movement, but began to identify with the political struggles of the island. I think it was part of my formation, too, to have been part of a movement to change society."

Helen's brother Pepito, now working as an engineer, was helping her with living expenses. Learning about her participation in the strike, he demanded that she stop. "He said, 'You just go to school. If you're going to be involved with anything political, forget it. I'm not supporting you.' So [after finishing her freshman year when the campus reopened] I packed up and went back to New York."

Her involvement in the strike led her to other young activists in the city, including the man who would become her first husband. Helen was asked to write an account of the Puerto Rican student movement for a publication called *New Foundations,* where she met a young man named David Brainin. He recalls her charisma and charm: "She always had leadership skills. She was not only articulate, she wrote well too." Within six months, the two married; Helen was nineteen, David twenty-three. "Youthful exuberance," he remembers.

David shared Helen's experience as an outsider—as a Jew, he had faced the anti-Semitism that was more open and prevalent before World War II—and so the two of them were, in David's words, "both sensitive to the discrimination against blacks." Together they became involved in the movement to end job discrimination, joining pickets and canvassing efforts to that effect. In the summer of 1949, one incident led to their involvement in the campaign of U.S. Congressman Vito Marcantonio,[4] the legendary liberal representative of East Harlem. Brainin recalls:

> Helen was pregnant with Jo Ellen and we were living on 108th Street in a first-floor apartment and we had some friends over with different skin colors. We had met them when we were picketing the A&P because they weren't hiring blacks or Puerto Ricans there. Some of our neighbors started yelling through our windows and I went outside to persuade them to stop, and all of a sudden I was in a fight. Other people started fighting

---

[4] A friend and protégé of Mayor Fiorello LaGuardia, Marcantonio—known to everyone as "Marc"—represented East Harlem in Congress for fourteen years, from 1935 to 1937 and 1939 to 1951. His constituents were a mixture of African Americans and immigrants, mainly Italians and Puerto Ricans, and he was a relentless fighter for both their immediate needs and the larger issues that concerned them. As early as the 1940s he took up civil rights issues, including an investigation into racial discrimination in Major League Baseball. During World War II, he fought discrimination against Italian Americans, and was an early and strong supporter of Puerto Rican self-determination. He became an ally of Virginia Durr in the fight against poll taxes and she described him as "one of the most trustworthy men I have ever worked with," a skilled politician with "a marvelous sense of humor." Though never a Communist himself, Marcantonio fiercely supported the free-speech rights of Communists. In 1951 he successfully defended W. E. B. Du Bois, by then a member of the Communist Party of the USA, after Du Bois was indicted on charges of failing to register as a foreign agent. Marc's unapologetic liberalism stirred up intense opposition. Between the 1950 primary and the general election—a matter of weeks—the New York *Daily Mirror* ran fifty-eight inaccurate, near-libelous articles with headlines such as "Marc in Photo with Harlem Vice Queen" and "Marc's Underworld Machine." He was defeated in that race and died in 1954, at age 52.

and the police came and everyone took off. The next day I went to Marc's office to let him know what was going on in his district and whether he would do anything about it—and he did. He called in his district captain and he made him come to our place and make peace.

David explains that this sort of political engagement was just what he and Helen "expected of each other. It didn't seem extraordinary at the time." Their first child, Jo Ellen, was born not long after, an experience Helen later described as her "first conscious contact with the health care system in the United States," one that left an indelible mark.

"I was conveyed in a wheelchair (women in labor weren't supposed to walk) to the dingy, bare labor room of the ward service," Helen recalled. After telling the physician that she did not feel prepared for natural childbirth, "the young doctor expressed disappointment at my decision, and then spent the remaining hours of the night shift discussing with a colleague, within my hearing, the clinical details of the tearing of tissues in childbirth. All the while I writhed in pain, fear, and loneliness, with an unsympathetic nurse admonishing me to keep quiet." Later Helen discovered that she was an "unwitting control subject in an experiment involving 'primiparas [women giving birth for the first time] with and without emotional support.'" This experience shaped Helen's career, making her empathetic to patients and passionate about improving health care for women.

After their daughter was born, David and Helen began looking for an area with a lower cost of living and a union presence. When David got a job in a steel mill, they moved to Lorain, Ohio, which had a small but growing Puerto Rican community. After landlords objected to their black visitors, the couple bought an old house on the GI Bill and began renovations.

Soon Helen found it impossible to manage all the demands on her time and energy and turned to her mother for help. Josefa took care of Jo Ellen in New York while Helen and David renovated the house. By the time Josefa brought Jo Ellen back to Ohio a few months later, Helen was already pregnant with her second child. Laura was born in January of 1951, and their son David was born eighteen months after that. The couple discussed the idea of Helen finishing college and continuing on to medical school, but it was financially impossible.

Life was chaotic and draining. "Having three children in two and a half years was horrendous," Helen later said. The intense demands and unequal burdens of parenthood began to drive the couple apart. As she recalled, "The loneliness and isolation finally led to our separation. My husband was away a great deal. Between his job and the organizational work, he got a great deal of satisfaction. But I was home alone with small children who were very demanding, and the strain became unendurable. I remember going for days without talking to adults. I longed for company." I imagine that this trying scene helped fuel Helen's political engagement in the seventies, but it also temporarily dampened her strong sense of mission in life, which she had felt so keenly during her school days.

Her mother came to stay and help with the children from time to time, and Helen came to feel completely dependent on her. When Josefa discovered a malignant lump in her breast and returned to Puerto Rico for a radical mastectomy and recovery, Helen decided to take the three children and go with her. By this time Jo Ellen was three, Laura was almost two, and David was five months old. "My decision arose out of sheer desperation and pain. At twenty-five I was embarrassed to need my mother so desperately." Remembering her first marriage decades later, Helen felt "compassion now toward the naïve neophytes we once were," but it was clear the situation could not continue. Helen said later that, as she left for Puerto Rico, "I did not want to admit it to Dave or myself, but I think I knew then that I would not be back."

Medical Training in Puerto Rico

This time, no doubt tempered by the failing marriage and sheer hard labor of child care, Helen was also determined to follow her childhood dream of being a doctor. When she met the man who would become her second husband, she was looking for someone to support her in this, and he did. "Dave came to Puerto Rico in an attempt at reconciliation but I already had a lover, whom I later married. My lover was divorced with two sons," she later explained. Helen's mother strongly objected to the new relationship and urged her to reconcile with Dave. As Helen recalled, her mother said, "'He may not be the ideal person. He has a bad temper, but he's sober and decent and the father of these children. That counts for a great deal.'" But

Helen's lover "was seductive and passion got in the way of reason. When I told him I wanted to study medicine, he suggested I stop working right after we got married and start school right away." She divorced Dave and enrolled again at the University of Puerto Rico. Shortly afterward, her mother died of cancer.

Now twenty-seven years old, Helen threw herself into her studies, achieving the same recognition of her natural intelligence that she had when she was in elementary school. Although she felt "on top of the world" at the time, she later regretted that "I was not a great mom when I was in training. During the premedical years, I had more time with the kids, but with the pressures of med school I had no time or energy to spare." Although Helen periodically had hired help, her second husband was the primary parental presence at home.

While it was intellectually stimulating, medical school was also, in her words, "a period of conformism . . . a period of fear, actual fear of change." The rigorous curriculum was demanding, of course, but it was also repressive and demoralizing. She recalled "the simple dehumanization of us as students, the way we were treated, carried over into the dehumanized way we might see patients—as cases, totally depersonalized. A whole defensive armor was built up to ward us from any emotional rapport—with patients, with each other, with ourselves." One of seven women in a class of fifty-two, Helen felt they were singled out for particular hostility, as when it was only the women who were assigned to conduct the class dissection and presentation of male genitalia. Helen felt constant pressure to shrug off provocations and harassment, to "pass" as she had when she was a young girl new to America, to "absorb much more material than was possible" just to keep up.

Rodriguez-Trias's intense work schedule affected her children, of course. Her son David recalled that he sometimes "felt shortchanged. Why was my mom not home to cook a meal every day?" When Laura was a first-grader, she answered a question about what her parents did by saying that her father was an economist and her mother "studies and sleeps." Helen's absence was all the more painful because of the intensity of her presence. David recalled, "One of the most troubling sensations growing up was seeing how she could click onto one of us, establish that connection, that unique experience that is talking with my mom. And just as fast she'd break the connection and give someone else a turn. That instant when she clicked off always left a void because her energy is so beautiful and so strong."

Helen graduated from medical school first in her class, pregnant with her fourth child, Daniel. As her daughter Jo Ellen recalled, "My mother didn't graduate first by a slim margin; she graduated first with eight medals. It was in all the papers. She had three kids and was six months pregnant at the time, and she was one of only four women in her med school class. What she told me was that she was so terrified she would come out last that she had to blast through."

She began her residency at the university hospital in San Juan, at a time when the hospital was in the midst of a transition from the municipal health system to the national one—a period of "absolute chaos." She started having labor pains as she was cutting a cast off a patient's leg and, once Daniel was born, the on-duty schedule meant she saw him only every other day. Yet amid the stress, she maintained her characteristic poise and presence. Jo Ellen described her mother at this time:

> I remember her coming home from her internship, dressed in her (stylish) version of the white uniform: a tailored white skirt (she had a seamstress make that for her), a crisp white shirt and the official-issue jacket. I remember her white Penaljo sandals were spattered with blood. I went to hug her, with my nose ready for someone sweaty with normal end-of-the-day body odor, only to be greeted by a very fresh and soft scent of lavender.

After finishing the year-long residency, Helen decided to go into pediatrics because of "a sense of potential—I can do a lot of early prevention work. I love children, and I identify with mothers a great deal." She began working for the Department of Pediatrics, an experience she describes as "crucial in changing my perspective" from individual to public health care. Asked to take on a new job directing the department's newborn service, Helen found a chaotic and disorganized program: understaffed, neglected, with inadequate hygiene and a resultant high death rate from preventable diseases. In the fight to build a proper program, she noticed that her best allies were the public-health personnel. Once the reforms were in place, the death rate among newborns at the hospital dropped by half within three years.

After a fellowship in perinatal physiology, Helen joined the Clinical Research Center. There, she pioneered a system of training teams across the island that worked together to gather statistics on newborns to track diseases and outcomes that would then be used to develop a focused perinatal care program. Working on this proposal—"getting statistics together, talking to people, and finding out who was doing what all over the island"—was so fulfilling that she decided to move into public health.

Helen's insights, determination, and sheer organizational ability in achieving these professional goals, while also managing her four children, is impressive enough. Yet she was also formulating a more mature political sensibility. "I could not stop my emerging consciousness from developing," she said later. "I was aware of the unfairness of the contradictory decisions often forced upon women."

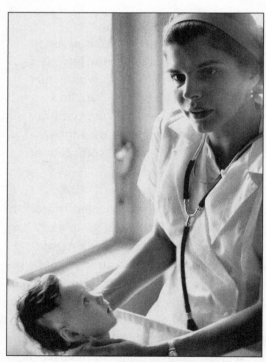

Helen working in the neo-natal clinic she directed in Puerto Rico (photo by Jim Hansen, *Look* magazine collection, Library of Congress)

During these early years of medical training and practice, Helen saw several cases that vividly illustrated the exploitation of poor women in particular: a mother of eleven children denied her request for sterilization; a mother of five who died during a tubal ligation performed by inexperienced and overwhelmed medical staff; women denied pain medication during difficult deliveries; countless tragic deaths from botched abortions. "As an intern on the obstetrical service, just after I had my own fourth baby, I saw woman after woman come in with bleeding or infection from incomplete abortions. Some met their death among the soiled bed curtains under the ministrations of the trainees of our wards." Helen felt a "deep communality" with the patients around her and she began to see the connections between their experiences and the political system.

Crisis at Home

As her professional life was flourishing, Helen's second marriage was unraveling. Her husband became verbally abusive and controlling, expressing resentment about her career and blaming her for any issues that came up with the children. He said things like "You can't get a raise. I don't want a wife who earns more than I do," and "You doctors are such bores at parties. I have never met people like you, always talking about your work." When their young son began to dress in girls' clothes, the boy's father wanted to punish him. When Helen disagreed, he insisted that she and Daniel go into psychotherapy. "When Daniel was five," she remembered, "a child psychiatrist shattered me with his conclusion: 'In my experience, when a boy wants to dress like a girl, he is being encouraged, and I rather suspect that you, Helen, are the one who is encouraging him.'" At the same time, her teenage daughters were becoming increasingly rebellious.

Helen was overwhelmed with guilt and confusion about what exactly was wrong in her home. Her husband interspersed his verbal attacks on her with "romantic interludes of intense wooing" and kept trying to convince her that she was the one harming the family. "I suspected I had poisoned my children. I had three rebellious teenagers and a severely disturbed child, or so I thought. The next day we took the children to a favorite, secluded beach. I swam out, crying, and considered going under—the only time I have considered suicide." Remembering her obligation to her children, she swam back to shore and resolved to make changes and "heal the harm."

In 1970, Helen and her second husband divorced. By now, her three oldest children were grown: Jo Ellen, twenty-one, lived in Boston, while Laura, twenty, and David, eighteen, lived in Puerto Rico. Knowing that the island "was not a happy place for divorced women" and wanting a break from places and people connected to her former husband, she applied to and was accepted into the Master's in Public

Health program at the University of California at Berkeley. With a year to wait before she began her studies, she decided that she might as well gain some ambulatory-care experience at a community hospital in the U.S. On a trip to New York, a friend at Lincoln Hospital in the South Bronx suggested that she apply for a job in the hospital's community pediatrics program. She interviewed, was accepted, and within three weeks she and Daniel had moved to New York. During those first weeks, as Helen was helping the ten year old adjust to what was an "alien environment," she experienced the most devastating realization of her life.

That Thanksgiving, Jo Ellen visited Helen and they talked about the transition to New York. Helen was uncertain about how to handle Daniel's father's request that the boy spend summers in Puerto Rico with him. When Helen said she thought it was good for children to be with a father figure, Jo Ellen finally snapped, "Bullshit. Let me tell you what kind of father he was." She then told her mother the crushing truth: Helen's second husband had sexually abused both her and Laura for several years until, at age fourteen, Jo Ellen stood up to him and demanded that it stop.[5]

It came as a total shock. As Jo Ellen recalled, "Her jaw dropped and she burst out crying. She felt angry and betrayed." While Helen was in medical school, she'd been grateful to have her husband handle most of the day-to-day child care and housekeeping. He seemed to be the stable presence they needed. "He came from a large and apparently close family, with a mother considered by everyone a saint. Ashamed of the broken family I grew up in, I trusted his ways with the children more than my own."

Most painful was the fact that she had not seen the signs, had not been there to protect her daughters, and—how awful this must have been—they had felt unable to tell her about it. Laura explained, "When

---

[5] Helen and her daughters were interviewed in the early 1990s for a book called *The Conversation Begins*, written by a mother and daughter to, as the subtitle puts it, "talk about living feminism." Helen begins her account bluntly: "Shortly after I joined the women's movement in 1970, my daughter Jo Ellen told me that she and her younger sister had been sexually abused by their stepfather, whom I had divorced four months earlier." She never mentions her second husband by name, referring to him only as "X."

I was twelve I nearly told my mother what was happening but my sister talked me out of it. We needed to protect mom. On some level I think we felt responsible for the demise of her first marriage, as kids are wont to do, so it was years before the truth came out."

Of course, Helen was racked with guilt. She recalled seeing only one sign of the abuse and she wished she had pursued it. "During my third year of med school, I arrived home one evening to find seven-year-old Laura in our bed. Irritated with her, which I deeply regret, I said sharply, 'To your bed. You know I don't like children in adult beds.' At the time, X feigned deep sleep. The next day he said, 'Last night you pulled a fast one on me, accusing me of something improper with Laura. She was just sleeping here and so was I.' He attacked me as disturbed and evil-minded, and I cried and apologized, convinced that my view of men was distorted. I never suspected again. I wish I had been able to say to Laura, 'Come here, baby. I won't be angry with you, and I will always love you, no matter what you tell me is happening.' She might have told me then and spared the girls years of abuse and me years of being deceived."

In the course of dealing with this revelation, Helen questioned her decision to spend so much time outside of the home. "I regret not being more attentive, not taking more time with the kids. Above all, I regret not having learned more from my mother, a wise woman, before I lost her."

In the immediate aftermath, Helen and her daughters talked about what they should do next. Jo Ellen recalled: "My mother has a wonderful sense of drama, and she imagined that we might confront him like the chorus in a Greek play, singing, 'I accuse you, I accuse you.' Then, one by one, we'd dump buckets of paint on his head: 'Brown is for the lives you've covered in shit, yellow is for your coward's eyes, green is for envy, red is for the blood on your hands.' I said, 'Mom, I don't think that is really practical. But it's a great image.'"

Under the pretense of discussing the visitation arrangements, Helen made an appointment to see X in Puerto Rico and brought the girls and their brother David along. They all went into his office and recounted the abuse to his face. He was so unsettled that he actually jumped out of his second-story office window. "I last saw him cowed and shaken," Helen said, "sitting on a grassy knoll ten feet below the window, a small crowd gathering. The man who had terrorized my children had become a nothing. After he got up off the lawn—amazingly—X called the police and had Helen and her daughters arrested at the airport and charged with assault, battery, and attempted murder. The charges were eventually dropped.

The way Helen handled this—the most wrenching crisis of her life—shows how unflinching a person she was. As Jo Ellen said, "My mother is an incredible person who has left her mark on many agencies and people over the years. To me, that is all well and good, but it was her reaction to my stepfather's abuse that gave me the sense that the advocacy work she had done for children everywhere, she was willing to do for us. Going to bat for us was the most healing thing she could have done. The experience of the confrontation was very liberating for us."

Jo Ellen and Laura admired their mother and her accomplishments but did express resentment about her absence from their lives. Laura said, "I am constantly approached by people, especially in public settings, who say, 'Your mother is so wonderful. You're so lucky she's your mother.' And she was a good mother in terms of the values she passed on, the intelligence and the passion. But I didn't feel particularly mothered. She was never present in the traditional sense that moms are supposed to be present. . . . I felt resentful that she was gone so much. I always felt she wanted to be mother of the world but not my mother."

While coping with this trauma, Helen came to feel that "the women's movement was a matter of personal survival to me." What had first brought her into the fold was what she described as "the great contributions of feminists to the demystification of the health care needs of women," but facing abuse in her home made feminism sink in on a deeper level. She sought to make it a matter of personal survival for others too, and as a pediatrician, began to address the issue of abuse,[6] teaching doctors and parents to recognize warning signs. She also took on a cause that she stayed with for the rest of

---

[6] In fact, sexual abuse of children is distressingly common. Every year, in the United States, approximately 150,000 cases are reported and confirmed and it is likely that at least that many more never come to light. There is some evidence that children who are not living with both biological parents are at higher risk of being sexually abused, possibly because they might also have other risk factors, such as less integration with extended family members and lack of a long-term bond between caregiver and child.

Dr. Rodriguez-Trias attending to a line of mothers and babies in Cidra, Puerto Rico in 1964. (photo by Jim Hansen, *Look* magazine collection, Library of Congress)

her life: protecting women and children from all kinds of domestic violence.

The Lincoln Hospital Years (1970–1978)

Helen's professional life proved to be no refuge from the tumult of her personal life. Entering the hospital for the first time during the Young Lords takeover, "I found myself in the middle of a struggle that had begun before I left Puerto Rico, in which now I was a major factor." Helen was struck by both how familiar and how alien it was.

My first impression on walking along the crowded, dirty emergency room all too reminiscent of the San Juan Municipal Hospital of the fifties where I had trained, were the faces of parents and children wearily waiting; and of the doctors, bearded, long-haired, and oddly oblivious to an occasional comment on hairiness in Spanish. They seemed to be working seriously, and their manner was kind. The take-over and the doctors appeared as unrelated phenomena, but I later learned they were not. I was to gain a better understanding of social change in the late sixties as I learned the history of community unrest and the response of the professionals.

The bearded doctors, the Pediatrics Collective, had earlier allied themselves with the Young Lords to develop better community care. This, as well as their general philosophical approach, put them at odds with the more traditional leadership at the hospital. Factions developed, with some demanding the reinstatement of Dr. Einhorn as the director of the pediatrics service and others arguing that Dr. Rodriguez-Trias should assume control.

She was sympathetic to the Collective's goals. Soon after arriving, she attended a meeting "with a group of house staff and people from the community, who spoke of their commitment to better health care and to change in society," which corresponded with her own beliefs and goals. As she later put it, "I think my sense of what was happening to people's health . . . was that it was really determined by what was happening in society—by the degree of poverty and inequality that you had."

When Helen finally became the uncontested director of the pediatrics service in 1971, she faced the task of rebuilding the service and found that while she agreed with the goals of the Collective, their means were less impressive. The more she met with them, the more she found them "irritating, fascinating, challenging, and frequently frustrating." They insisted on endless discussions with little attempt at compromise and resisted structure and hierarchy, refusing to have a chief resident and resenting Helen's insistence on "precision and discipline."

At one meeting, some of the residents expressed frustration with Helen's decision-making, saying that she didn't understand that the Collective was there to give power to the community.

> I said, "You can't give away what you ain't got, and you haven't got any power. And furthermore, if you're talking about being here because there is a community that is interested in being able to control its destiny in health care, then you are not going to give anything to anybody. You are agents of that community. . . . I think you have to sit with yourselves and find out why you're having these feelings at a time when we should be acting jointly to strengthen the program. . . . You had Einhorn who was autocratic, who was politically alien to you, and who couldn't stand you. Now you've got me, and I'm Puerto Rican, and I understand you politically. We're close politically but not

identical by any means, and you are very unhappy. So I think you just have to find out what the hell is going on, and I'm tired and I'm going home." This was almost a breaking point in the midst of all these crises.

But the next day when I stepped in to make rounds in the nursery, for once everybody was standing there washed, gowned, looking attentive. A couple of people apologized and said that after I had left, they had the best meeting that they had ever had because they got into the whole question of racism and attitudes, working in the community, and their basic ideology.

Politically aware and engaged as she was, Helen had no patience with rigid ideology, with unproductive anarchy justified as fairness or open-mindedness. She later said, "My own orientation is very much in terms of groups that can function in a disciplined way, that can agree on a line, on an ideological principle that they may translate into programs. I found it very hard to work with a group that sometimes had fifty opinions, and then generally ended in not doing anything, because the differences couldn't be resolved. I fought a kind of magical belief that process was an end in itself."

Yet she also was extremely skilled at using process to include people in productive decision-making. She reached out to doctors, patients, administrators, and politicians, guiding the institution through this harrowing period. As one activist who knew her at that time recalled, "people who [normally] wouldn't sit at the same table together would sit with Helen." Slowly, meeting by meeting, decision by decision, Helen came to command respect throughout Lincoln and its neighborhood. She later described the evolution of her leadership style during this time: "There were times when you could actually find better points of unity when you were less confrontational and more reasonable and actually listened to other people more and not just see them as being off the deep end, or evil."

Her time at Lincoln was a pivotal experience in many ways. She later recalled it as the time when she shook off the last vestiges of conformity and isolation: "I felt I had literally crossed a bridge. I could never lead the quiet, respectable life of an academician again. Nor did I want to."

At Lincoln, Helen again witnessed the tragic consequences of substandard care, especially poor reproductive health care for women. She observed that the process of pregnancy and birth was often made intimidating to women, especially those who did not speak English and felt powerless. She felt that mothers had been cruelly sidelined in the medicalization of childbirth,[7] which left poor and immigrant women especially disoriented and disempowered. As she put it, by the sixties "any delivery of an infant in a hospital was an elaborate, frequently traumatic procedure, fraught with the discomfort of monitors, extensive laboratory tests, intravenous medications, analgesia, episiotomies. . . . The risk of a cesarean section was increasing, with rates from 20 to 30 percent becoming common. Nurse-midwifery programs were virtually nonexistent. It was practically impossible to obtain any but the most interventionist forms of childbirth."

Rodriguez-Trias also saw that affluent women always had access to medically safe abortion if they felt they needed it, but if "a poor woman needed an abortion, she came to the university hospital in the middle of the night and said she had fallen and was having a miscarriage. Some were already infected from incompetent or even self-attempted abortions." All too often, in the days before legal abortion, doctors would make a deal with poor women to perform an abortion if they agreed to be sterilized.

Helen enjoyed being part of the palpable growth and progress of the women's movement. All over the country, women were gathering to support one another and come up with solutions to common problems. For instance, in Boston a group of women began to meet weekly to talk about their experiences with the medical system. They took turns researching and teaching each other and eventually formed the Boston Women's Health Book Collective to publish *Our*

---

[7] Beginning in the late nineteenth century, scientific advances resulted in the shift of medical care from the home to the clinic or hospital. While there were obviously many benefits from this, there have also been some negative effects. With childbirth specifically, physicians (overwhelmingly male) supplanted midwives (overwhelmingly female) and tended to see birth as a process to be managed and controlled. Many mothers have complained about medicalized births that were humiliating, scary, and isolating, such as Helen's experience with Jo Ellen. Many writers—including Virginia Durr's friend Jessica Mitford—have argued for a more balanced approach to childbirth, but the medical model has not changed much. As Naomi Wolf wrote in *Misconceptions*: "A decade after Jessica Mitford's exposé of troubling birth practices, *The American Way of Birth*, and almost a quarter century after Suzanne Arms's exposé of high-tech birth, *Immaculate Deception*, alerted women to problems in the birth industry, the reforms these books sought are far from realized."

Bodies, Ourselves, which encouraged women to learn about their bodies and become active in maintaining their own physical health. That first, cheaply produced newsprint volume sold over a quarter of a million copies. In a foreword to a later edition, Rodriguez-Trias wrote that she'd read the book with a "surge of joy," feeling that "the authors spoke to me as if I had been part of their discussion group." *Our Bodies, Ourselves* soon became part of the reference library for Lincoln Hospital, "used for classes, discussions, and teaching materials for community groups." The first mass-market edition was issued in 1973, and it became an immediate best-seller. With its message of women's empowerment and autonomy, it also came under fire from the growing religious right. *Our Bodies, Ourselves* continues to sell briskly and has been translated into nineteen languages.

Energized by these changes and conversations, Rodriguez-Trias attended many women's rights conferences, organized a consciousness-raising group for Latinas, and shared with many audiences her views and insights on public health, and specifically women's health. On one occasion Helen's audience included Gloria Steinem, who recalled that she was not only charismatic but very clear and intelligent, never resorting to overly medical or politicized language. Steinem said later, "I remember thinking this woman is very smart because I understand every word she says."

Many of Rodriguez-Trias's most powerful presentations highlighted individual women's experiences with inequities in the health care system as a way of illustrating women's need to stand up for their rights as "by far the most frequent users of health services for themselves, their children, or other dependent family members." At the 1974 American Public Health Association (APHA) meeting, she described women's health issues "in the context of my experience as a pediatrician in a Black and Puerto Rican ghetto. The availability of services to poor women, and particularly to third world women, makes for sharp class distinctions." She then recounted the story of a twenty-three-year-old Puerto Rican woman, Mrs. Castro, who had an IUD implanted at the Bronx Municipal Hospital. She soon developed severe abdominal pain and went back to the hospital. She was turned away, but returned later, in worse pain. Again she was denied treatment and died at home of a massive internal hemorrhage. On the second visit, Mrs. Castro's husband had demanded care for his wife but the doctor implied that she was faking it. Helen pointed out, "The same medical school that is responsible for care at that municipal hospital has on its staff two prominent pediatricians who edited a text of *Pediatrics* that indexes 'Puerto Rican Syndrome' as a term for hysteria." With a vigilance and attention to language reminiscent of Ida B. Wells-Barnett, Helen was instrumental in changing the stereotypes of Latinos, which she saw as integral to achieving equitable health care. In response to her letter of protest, this derogatory phrase was removed from later editions of the textbook. "A small victory, perhaps," she reflected, "but one which strengthens our own consciousness of the need to struggle and grow."

Coerced Sterilization

As she smoothed tensions at Lincoln, Helen worked with the Young Lords to promote a pragmatic agenda for change, which included taking aim at the discriminatory care received by Latinas and other women of color. Negative stereotypes fed this discrimination on several levels. As sociologist Leo Chávez has documented, Latina fertility is consistently portrayed as far too high, resulting in an out-of-control birth rate that drains social services and threatens the American cultural identity. One example he cited was an article in the June 22, 1992, *National Review,* whose cover featured a depiction of the Statue of Liberty with her arm raised in a "stop!" gesture, saying, "Tired? Poor? Huddled? Tempest-Tossed? Try Australia. Rethinking Immigration." These notions, like the association of hysteria with Puerto Ricans, laid the groundwork for abuse and exploitation. Helen recognized this dynamic, calling it the "intellectualization of sexism and racism."

---

[8] Some male Young Lords had early on taken a liking to the chauvinistic ways of the Black Panthers, so the women Lords organized an insurrection to prevent their group from becoming equally male-dominated. It began when Denise Oliver attended a Black Panthers meeting in Newark, New Jersey. When she entered the room, she realized that she was the only woman there to participate in the meeting. The other women were there to serve the men refreshments in a particularly bizarre way. "Women crawled into the room on their hands and knees wearing elaborate headdresses decorated with fruit," she recalled. Taken aback, Oliver fired questions at the Black Panther leader, who ignored her. Furious, she stormed out, returned to New York City, and called a meeting of the women Young Lords, where she argued for an aggressive feminist agenda (including reproductive rights), warning that unless the male Lords took their agenda seriously, "we would end up on our hands and knees with fruit on our head." They launched a campaign inspired by Aristophanes's *Lysistrata*: the Young Lords women refused to have sex with their partners in the group unless their demands were met. Apparently the protest was successful, since the Young Lords became and remained a group where women were fully included.

The Young Lords, guided by powerful and charismatic women, had already adopted a feminist agenda, but needed focus.[8] "She was giving us political direction," recalls Esperanza Martell, who worked with Helen in the Latin Women's Collective (which grew out of the feminist wing of the Young Lords) and now heads the House of Women's Power in the South Bronx. "She was able to synthesize people's pain and confusion and help them move into action, to transform anger into collective power."

One element of the agenda was eradicating a politically motivated abuse that would become one of the central issues of Helen's career: coerced sterilization. Although it had been happening all around her in Puerto Rico as well as New York, Helen did not actually realize the full extent of it until later. One evening, at the invitation of the Committee for Puerto Rican De-Colonization, Helen attended a screening of a Bolivian movie called *Blood of the Condor* at New York University. The movie depicted the plight of Quechua Indian families who were forced to move from the mountains to the city in search of work. *Blood of the Condor,* wildly popular in Latin America, also made the rounds of colleges and counterculture gatherings in the United States. The cultural genocide theme was dramatized in a scene in which Peace Corps workers sterilize Quechua women against their will. (The Peace Corps always denied they'd sterilized any Bolivians, and there's no evidence to suggest they did. However, the program's advocacy of birth control was seen by the Bolivian left as coercive. Because of the political climate, Bolivia expelled the Peace Corps in 1971.)

The organizers of the event had invited Helen to give a presentation after the film, a brief talk about how this theme applied to Puerto Rico. Helen began reading books and conducting interviews to prepare. "That was when I first personally began to understand what had been happening in Puerto Rico during the time I was there as a medical student, as a young mother, and as a practicing pediatrician. During those years of 1956 to 1970 I had been totally oblivious to the campaign to sterilize women that was a social policy. I began to understand that social policy could creep up on you without it being explicit public policy."

La Operación

What she found was shocking. During the 1960s, sterilization became so widespread in Puerto Rico that it was called simply *La Op-*

eración. Puerto Rico had the world's highest sterilization rate, a rate concentrated overwhelmingly in poor communities. By 1965, fully one-third of Puerto Rican women of childbearing age had undergone the irreversible procedure. Although Helen never personally saw coerced sterilization while practicing in Puerto Rico, it was during these years that she first became aware that her native island was a testing ground for medical drugs and procedures. Early versions of the birth control pill were tested on Puerto Rican women, with the first sizeable study conducted in 1956 in San Juan, Puerto Rico. (Birth control became an option in 1937, as a result of Margaret Sanger's groundbreaking work in the United States.) Many women experienced severe side effects from the high experimental dosages. Some died of heart attacks that were probably a result of pulmonary embolism. As Helen put it later, "I was working in Puerto Rico in the medical school in those years, the decade of 1960 to 1970. And one of the things that seemed pretty obvious to us then was that Puerto Rico was being used as a laboratory."

Although the Puerto Rican medical establishment characterized sterilization as a healthy "option" for women who chose it, in reality it was performed on many women without their realizing that it would disable them from childbearing forever. "Women were usually asked to sign a consent right after delivery, in a strange place, while weak, and without fully understanding that '*La Operación*' was irreversible, Helen wrote." Some young women were even sterilized before they had a first child, and many were convinced to consent by the threat of withdrawal of social services and other heavy-handed tactics. Sometimes the women did realize the consequences and specifically declined the procedure, but it was done anyway.

American social scientists were able to promote sterilization in Puerto Rico because of the island's unique relationship to the United States. After the United States took control of Puerto Rico from the Spanish, sugar barons were allowed to establish large plantations, evicting small farmers and causing poverty and unemployment to surge. From then on, the United States had a sort of imperial presence, and there are ongoing political debates on the island about which is the best course: statehood, independence, or continued status as a United States territory. (Helen favored independence.) The first wave of Puerto Rican migration to the United States began in the 1930s and swelled as jobs opened in the factories involved in war production. Racism towards the newcomers immediately flared up, while the Puerto Ricans who stayed on the island faced increasingly hard times with rising unemployment. In the 1940s many large United States industries relocated to Puerto Rico, attracted by favorable tax structures and a large supply of cheap labor, but large numbers of Puerto Ricans continued to immigrate to the United States looking for economic opportunity. Strong ties remained between immigrants to the United States and their relatives in Puerto Rico, and many families, like Helen's, actually moved back and forth a few times.

As the economy in Puerto Rico continued to struggle through the 1950s and 60s, the population grew restless in the face of the obvious disparity of wealth and lack of opportunity. Those in power increasingly answered demands for better social services by suggesting population reduction. This notion handily deflected the demand for better social services and implicitly blamed the people in need. It also disrespected the right of women to choose how many children to have and made the island more vulnerable to birth control testing. One contemporary commentator described Puerto Rico as "crowded, impoverished and ripe for an intensive birth control program—a prototype underdeveloped country on America's own doorstep."

The Puerto Rican government began a campaign to encourage sterilization. The surgery was widely offered at little or no cost, while most other forms of contraception were scarce and expensive. Physicians often recommended sterilization, counseling that other forms of birth control required a lot more work and could fail. During this time, in a survey of 850 single Puerto Rican women, 22 percent said they knew about sterilization—a far higher percentage than those familiar with condoms or diaphragms. Helen's experience practicing medicine in this environment (in addition to her firsthand experience with childbirth and child care) led to her lifelong interest in making birth control widely available. It also helped her immediately and viscerally grasp how thoroughly sterilization abuse had become entrenched on her native island.

Eugenics

This coercive practice had its roots in the American eugenics movement, which maintained that the human race would benefit from prudent breeding, and social policies should therefore discourage reproduction of the "unfit." In 1907 President Theodore Roosevelt, a longtime eugenics enthusiast, lamented "race suicide" in America, explaining that "the greatest problem of civilization is to be found in the fact that the well-to-do families tend to die out; there results, in consequence, a tendency to the elimination instead of the survival of the fittest."

Many eugenics advocates readily admitted that they defined some people as inferior regardless of their actual behavior or abilities. In a speech to the State Medical Association of Texas in 1911, Dr. Malone Duggan of the state's Society of Social Hygiene put it this way: "No doubt many with criminal and perverted strains have been prevented from becoming themselves criminals and perverts in fact, but they are criminals and perverts still, in that they transmit the same strains to their children, who, under less favorable environments, will develop the same morbid characters."

Resentment about taxes was just as prevalent then as today, and the idea that eliminating bad people would reduce the amount each household had to pay to the state was seductive. "It is a reproach to our intelligence," wrote C. B. Davenport in *Heredity in Relation to Eugenics* in 1911, "that we as a people, proud in other respects of our control of nature, should have to support about half a million insane, feeble-minded, epileptic, blind and deaf, 80,000 prisoners and 100,000 paupers at a cost of over 100 million dollars a year." From 1900 to 1920, roughly thirty-two hundred institutionalized people in the United States were sterilized under eugenics-related programs. During the first half of the century, about two-thirds of all states enacted legislation permitting sterilization programs, most with a focus on institutionalized persons, some with a potentially broader reach. Between 1907 and 1960, over sixty thousand people deemed mentally ill, retarded, or criminal were sterilized without their consent.

The definition of "unfit" kept expanding, with race also playing an increasing role and non-European descent judged decidedly inferior. A prominent eugenics researcher, psychologist Henry H. Goddard, was invited to Ellis Island in 1913 to screen out "morons" among the immigrants. In *Intelligence Classification of Immigrants of Different Nationalities* (1917), he analyzed the mental capabilities of the immigrant population and concluded that of those he tested, 83 percent of Jews were "feeble-minded," along with 80 percent of Hungarians, 79 percent of Italians and 87 percent of Russians. In the late 1920s, Goddard recanted some of his theories and expressed regret that his methods had been flawed, but the damage was done, and his initial ideas were picked up by others. As late as 1932, eugenics activist Harry H. Laughlin, a schoolteacher who had recruited many prominent physicians to the cause, said, "Our studies show also that the compulsory feature is now soundly established in long practice. They show also that the subject for sterilization does not necessarily have to be an inmate of an institution, but may be selected with equal legality from the population at large. It remains to be seen whether the states can extend sterilization to apparently normal individuals who have come from exceedingly inferior stocks, judged by the constitutional qualities of their close kin." As Puerto Ricans migrated to the United States, they also became targets. In 1935, the prominent eugenicist Mariann S. Olden, who believed that "biological checks" were needed to prevent crime, wrote that "a study has just been completed of Puerto Rican children in the schools of New York City; it states: 'Puerto Ricans are adding greatly to the tremendous problem of sub-normal school retardates of alien parentage.'"

After World War II, as the horrors of Nazism came to light, forced sterilization programs ended in most institutions. But while pushing sterilization was no longer part of a coordinated eugenics movement, the practice retained a lingering following and was always an arrow in the quiver of those seeking to dehumanize groups on the lower end of the socioeconomic spectrum.

The Committee to End Sterilization Abuse (CESA)

After Helen learned the history in Puerto Rico of coerced sterilization—which had reached its height while she was a practicing physician there—she realized she had found her cause. Her skill at synthesizing people's pain and emotions was critical to not only raise awareness of the issue but also to encourage people to share their experiences and come together to change policies and perceptions. She also had a keen sense of how to effectively communicate these needs and emotions to people in positions of authority.

Her efforts began with a powerful presentation that night at NYU, and afterward she talked with audience members about similar abuses in the United States. The evening was a second turning point for Helen, and one that built on the dramatic awakening she experienced after learning of her daughters' abuse. After that profound illustration of how clandestine violations of women can be, she now confronted the reality of an abusive and unacknowledged social policy being implemented all around her. She spoke to several people about the issue, including a young psychiatrist in Brooklyn who recounted many coerced sterilizations he knew about personally. Helen became the driving force in the formation of a small group that began to meet regularly and eventually became the Committee to End Sterilization Abuse (CESA). In those early days, Helen hosted meetings at her apartment, where she quietly made sure everyone had a chance to lead a meeting and no one's concerns went unheard.

The more Helen researched sterilization abuse, the more she realized how rampant it was among poor communities of color in the United States. It was clearly an unwritten policy in urban hospitals across the country to recommend sterilization for poor women who gave birth to multiple children. From 1970 to 1974, female sterilizations in the United States increased from 192,000 to 548,000. Among women with less than a high school education who were sterilized, 14.5 percent were Caucasian, 31.6 percent were black, and 35 percent were Hispanic.

Sterilization also was horrifically imposed on Native Americans by the federal government's Indian Health Service (IHS), with coercion ranging from the threat to withhold government aid or take away a woman's existing children, to the performance of the procedure during an unrelated surgical operation, without the patient's knowledge. Bertha Medicine Bull, a leader on the Montana Lame Deer Reservation, claims that two fifteen-year-old girls were sterilized without their knowledge when they had appendectomies. Barbara Moore recounted the story of her own child's birth. The child died after a C-section delivery (she demanded an autopsy that concluded that the cause was "inconclusive") and Moore was sterilized. Moore and other Native American activists characterize the sterilization abuse on Indian reservations as an extension of the genocide of their people. A 1976 federal investigation uncovered the fact that in the four-year period from 1973 through 1976, 3,406 Native American women were sterilized without their consent. Of that group, 3,001 were between the ages of fifteen and forty-four. (Because only four out of twelve IHS facilities were studied, a total estimate of Native American women coerced into sterilization is 12,000.) In 1979 another report revealed that most IHS hospitals routinely sterilized women under age twenty-one.

The frequency with which African-American women in the South underwent forced sterilization caused it to be referred to as a "Mississippi appendectomy." In fact, civil rights activist Fannie Lou Hamer was a victim of exactly that abuse. She went to the hospital for the removal of a uterine tumor and later found out that she had been sterilized during the procedure. Hamer shared her personal experience in order to highlight the abuse and, in one speech, claimed that a full 60 percent of black women who came through her hometown hospital in Mississippi had been sterilized, many without their knowledge. By the end of the 1970s, many states had considered bills proposing mandatory sterilization of women on welfare. Even though none of these passed, the administration of sterilization programs reflected the goal of reducing certain populations.

Two high-profile cases were particularly important to Helen's understanding and presentation of the issue. The first was the Relf case. Minnie Lee and Mary Alice Relf, African-American girls aged twelve and fourteen, were sterilized in a federally funded program in Montgomery, Alabama, in June of 1973. As Helen recalled, "The Southern Poverty Law Center found out about the girls and interviewed the mother, who said she thought she was consenting to the girls getting a contraceptive." Representatives of the program had called her to offer birth control shots, so she brought the girls into their clinic. The mother signed the consent form with an X because she couldn't read or write, and both girls were permanently sterilized. The Relf case went to federal court, where the judge enjoined the federal Department of Health, Education, and Welfare to come up with guidelines to prevent sterilization abuse. "Although Congress has been insistent that all family planning programs function purely on a voluntary basis," he wrote, "there is uncontroverted evidence in the record that minors and other incompetents have been sterilized with federal funds and that an indefinite number of poor people have been improperly coerced into accepting a sterilization operation under the threat that various federally supported welfare benefits would be withdrawn unless they submitted to irreversible sterilization."

The second important case was *Madrigal v. Quilligan*, a class action suit brought against the Los Angeles County Medical Center by a group of Hispanic women who were sterilized in the early seventies, right after giving birth, in public hospitals, without giving informed consent. None of the women in the class were native English-speakers, and the consent forms were only available in English. Some were never even asked permission. Some were told erroneously that the operation was reversible.

Shockingly, the nurses and doctors often pressured these women during their labor and even after they had been drugged. Some medical staff remarked that more children would be a "burden on the government." In several of these cases, the sterilization resulted in marital tensions, not to mention depression. The hearings in the *Madrigal* case were widely publicized and resulted in significant reforms in California, such as the adoption of bilingual consent forms and the enforcement of a waiting period.

The new HEW guidelines, drawn up in 1974, banned sterilization of minors and others who were incapable of giving consent; stipulated a 72-hour waiting period; required a written statement demonstrating consent; and mandated the right to refuse sterilization, even if consent previously had been given. However, they applied only to federally funded programs, exempting local, state, and nonprofit programs. Further, without any monitoring or enforcement mechanisms, these guidelines were routinely violated, especially in hospitals and clinics that served Native Americans, immigrants, and the poor.

Helen's group rose to the challenge and worked to remedy the situation. In 1975 CESA joined with members of various citizens' groups and the Health and Hospitals Corporation of New York City to form an advisory committee on sterilization guidelines. As Helen described the committee, "Most of the members were women involved in patient advocacy and who at the same time represented New York's various clinic communities."

I was struck by Helen's reluctance to claim credit for herself in her accounts of the fight against sterilization abuse, a reluctance that seems to reflect her personality rather than the reality of her role. According to Barbara Seaman, "Helen modestly described her struggle against sterilization abuse without specifically situating herself as the principal founder, which of course she was." Public health activist Elsa Rios looked on Helen as a mentor; she remembers Helen as someone who "embodied a very traditional cultural trait, that you don't call attention to yourself all the time and it's not always all about you. A kind of humbleness without being self-effacing."

Like Septima Clark, Helen strongly believed that it was essential to make people feel included in the leadership of an important political movement. As one person close to her recently described it, Helen disliked the "celebrity status of political leaders" because it distanced them from the needs of the people they were supposed to represent. She felt "it was a trap when leaders fell in love with the microphone," and she believed that positive leadership came about when people joined together to help others. Her approach and rhetoric seem to echo the famous words of anthropologist Margaret Mead: "Never doubt that a small group of thoughtful, committed people can change the world. Indeed, it's the only thing that ever has."

CESA set up several goals: to educate, to demand free access to birth control, to establish guidelines for informed consent before sterilization, and to initiate legal actions against those who abuse patients' rights. A 1975 CESA publication pointedly quoted a recent report from HEW: "It is possible that we may see sterilization become as important in family planning in the fifty states as it already is in Puerto Rico." Helen made it her mission to expose the ugly underbelly of this policy: "More efficient means of sterilization can be used against poor and non-white women, both here in the United States and abroad (as in India) to make it easier to induce or coerce them, against their will, to give up their right to determine for themselves whether or not they will have children."

Helen recalls that CESA's publicity efforts—"speaking to colleagues, in churches, organizing workshops in youth clubs, reaching out to social groups . . . radio shows"—resulted in a huge influx of people into the movement, many of them wanting direct personal help. It was an illuminating and wrenching experience.

> It wasn't about political analysis. Someone would call in and say, "Three years ago, I was told I had something wrong with my uterus and they took it out and I don't have any children and I'm only twenty years old and I don't know what's hap-

pening." . . . What I learned is that when you are organizing around an issue, you should be prepared to have some concrete services available for people. You need to know where people can get help. Do not assume that all others will be interested in your issue as you may be, as a political issue, or as an issue of public policy, or as human rights or whatever it is that is your driving ideal. I remember one radio show when we had at least twenty calls and at least half of them were people calling for help, and we weren't ready for it. It was a painful experience for me.

Led by Helen, CESA proposed new guidelines to protect women from coerced sterilization: a thirty-day waiting period between a request for sterilization and the surgery; the proposal for sterilization had to come from the woman herself; consent could not be solicited during childbirth or abortion; information on sterilization's permanence and other fertility control options must be given in writing, in the woman's native language.

Rodriguez-Trias continued to adapt her style of advocacy as she saw what worked and what didn't. She recalled that as she was helping to draft guidelines for the Health and Hospitals Corporation, she and her colleagues went to "every single hospital in the system, there were fifteen of them, each with an ob-gyn department director. I recall that there was not one of the directors who was willing to listen about the guidelines. In part their antagonism was because the document we prepared trying to justify why guidelines were needed actually started out with a list of all the abuses. If you tell people that under their service, their command, their watch, these terrible things are going on, they stop listening right there. You just are not going to make your point, and so we ended up with this infuriated bunch of doctors. After reflection, we realized that we could have said things differently and gotten a more attentive audience."

Helen applied her gentle, persuasive style to local efforts as well as to her growing role as a national advocate for women's health. Judy Norsigian, executive director of the organization Our Bodies Ourselves, recalls hearing Helen speak at the first grassroots conference on women's health, held in 1975 at Harvard University. (Although the university was a reluctant host, the conference brought 2,500 people to the university where, fifty-six years before, public health pioneer Alice Hamilton had become the first woman faculty member.) Norsigian recalls that Helen was magnetic and convincing, an obvious role model for women who wanted to tackle the complicated political issues of the day. "She was soft-spoken but commanding," remembers Norsigian. "Here was this beautiful, articulate, sensitive woman who never ram-rodded anything yet was tenacious."

Rodriguez-Trias viewed the regulations she proposed for New York City as a model for the nation, which they did indeed become—but only after overcoming strong opposition from unexpected sources.

Friendly Fire

"We were unprepared for the ferocity of the opposition to our guidelines," Helen recalled. "Our files, replete with angry letters from obstetricians, organizations involved in family planning and population control, and other groups, attest to the length and difficulty of our struggle."

Some of the strongest opposition came from elements within the women's movement, such as Planned Parenthood and NOW, who saw easy access to sterilization as part of their agenda. The experience of many women—largely white and relatively affluent—had been difficulty getting sterilized when they requested it. At that time a formula called the rule of 120 was often used. A doctor would approve a woman's sterilization request only if her age multiplied by the number of children she had equaled 120. Thus, for example, a woman of thirty would have to have four children to be considered a valid candidate, regardless of the woman's own assessment of her situation and desires. "Perversely," according to Helen, "[sterilization] was being promoted, if not downright pushed or coerced, for others—women of low income, women of color, women who, for whatever reason, the provider decided should not have more children." (In addition, it was being pushed internationally on vulnerable women in places like India and Bangladesh, who were often not informed of other methods of birth control.) As Helen later said, "The [women's movement] was very diverse, but the more public positions articulated by the movement didn't concern the experiences or concerns of women of color or of poor women." Despite this powerful opposition, the coalition Helen had assembled prevailed: in April 1977, Public Law 37 passed the New York City Council by unanimous vote.

Throughout these debates, Helen was amazed by the disparity in experience and opinion but hopeful that communication could galvanize the whole movement. "I began to understand that we were coming to different conclusions because we were living different realities," she explained. "While young white middle-class women were denied their requests for sterilization, low-income women of certain ethnicity were misled or coerced into them. . . . We had to listen to each other. We had to find out each other's reality."

Helen worked by conversing with different groups of women and encouraging them to share their experiences. Rather than promote acrimony, she brought people together. "She had an ability to transcend class lines," says activist Esperanza Martell. "She could do it at a parents meeting in any barrio or with the President of the United States." At first, it was paramount that the less powerful women be heard. Helen recalled that at various conferences, "The Third World Women, as we called ourselves then, would get together and craft a social and economic agenda. . . . When we did our presentation, it turned the whole conference around, made it more concrete, and focused it on important issues. I saw this happen in many forums. The women of color would state their positions and it would become another meeting. You really had to deal with the inequities."

Again, Helen put the women she worked with front and center, not only by referencing their experiences but by inviting them to be speakers, guests at her own parties, and leaders of demonstrations and lobbying efforts. "Helen believed you could get a lot done if you don't demand credit for it," says Seaman. "She loved to let the real folks working on the issue get credit. Most advocates thank them at the end of a speech but Helen wanted them to be the ones making the speech."

In the late seventies, CESA merged with a new organization, the Committee for Abortion Rights and Against Sterilization Abuse, or CARASA. As with CESA, Helen was a pivotal presence in CARASA, which became a sort of watchdog group over the enforcement of the regulations, as well as an attempt to bridge factions of the women's movement. As Steinem recalled, many women came to realize that opponents of all kinds of women's rights were eager to promote divisions based on race and class in order to impede progress. Looking back, Helen described the many concerns that had continued to be addressed within the same tent.

> For many years the struggle for reproductive rights was hampered by disunity and lack of a common agenda. Working through years of painful debates and frequent misunderstandings, white women and women of color were finally able to engage in more productive dialogue. . . . We are still learning to provide safe spaces for our discussions and to listen to each other with creativity. We are still learning that to work on commonalities, we first have to be clear on the differences.

Women's Health

The same year she helped establish CESA, Helen also became a founding member of the Women's Caucus of the American Public Health Association.[9] She attended the association's 1971 meeting to give a presentation on sterilization in Puerto Rico. She later described the experience:

> That was the year that public professionals provided jobs for people in the community who came into health work. I joined because I felt it was the leading public health organization. I became a member in 1972 and have been active ever since. APHA has always provided a home for people in public health with a broad view of what public health is. Public health is really about people's life conditions and how these conditions do or do not promote health. APHA is committed to equity and ending all barriers, and has always been committed to civil, human, and health rights. It's a wonderful place for women to be.

---

[9] The American Public Health Association was founded in 1872, primarily to stop the spread of communicable diseases by advocating for better sanitary conditions. Over the years their focus has broadened and currently the APHA encompasses twenty-four sections, each based on a specific discipline, such as gerontological health, epidemiology, public health education, and nutrition.

Rodriguez-Trias used the caucus to analyze the relationship between the status and circumstances of American women and the pervasive inequities in health care. Women make twice as many visits to doctors as men because of their childbearing and child-rearing roles, she often explained, and they are also more likely to be taken advantage of, ignored, or given substandard care. She felt that until any broader changes could be made, poor women needed to be supported on a sustained basis by those who would stand up to the system. "There is no doubt in my mind," she wrote, "that on the spot, knowledgeable and aggressive health advocates who represent a community point of view are deterrents to gross neglect of patients' rights." Cynthia Pearson, a colleague of Helen's who is currently at the National Women's Health Network, says, "One of her greatest gifts to women's health was her insistence that we not only listen to women's descriptions of their experience with health care, but that we build policies and programs that acknowledged those experiences and responded to them."

Every time the gaps opened, Helen wanted to be there to close them, yet she never compromised on her deeply held principles. In January 1978, she attended a weekend "teach-in" to commemorate the fifth anniversary of *Roe v. Wade*. Another goal was organizing a public awareness campaign to protest the passage of the Hyde amendment, which withdrew federal funding for abortions (but continued funding sterilizations). The talk was all about economic disparity, coat hangers, "back alley butchers," and the inability of so many lawmakers to see the discriminatory effects of the new law. Helen agreed with this consensus but found that there was still a major disconnect about the dangers of *La Operación*. One woman stood up and angrily attacked the idea that women did not support sterilization on demand, saying, "It's my body and no one else's." Helen rose to answer, relaying the reality of what had gone on in Puerto Rico and in New York, the treatment of Fannie Lou Hamer, the women in the *Madrigal* case, and the Relf girls. "It's the slight inconvenience of a thirty-day waiting period versus the danger of many instances of abuse. Frankly, I would choose to inconvenience the few."

Helen also advocated for international safeguards against sterilization abuse, which put her squarely in the debate over population control efforts. For some early feminists, the willingness of population control advocates to embrace birth control made them natural allies. That changed after the Supreme Court's 1965 decision in

Griswold v. Connecticut, which guaranteed married couples the right to use contraceptives; once birth control was seen as a right, the tenuous alliance began to loosen. The evolution of the concept of "reproductive rights," which Helen contributed to, crystallized the feminist position that the goal was to empower individual women with birth control choices, not to try to make the choice for them.

Her Vision

Helen continued to bring her vision of inclusiveness and respect to each new professional and educational position she held. In 1978 she left Lincoln and became the associate director of pediatrics for primary care at St. Luke's-Roosevelt Hospital Center and director of Roosevelt's Children and Youth Program, with a $2 million annual budget and 38,000 patients per year. In 1981, an interviewer described a confident, welcoming presence:

> Dr. Helen Rodriguez-Trias sits at the round table in her office . . . her rust-colored dress showing beneath the white jacket. The curtains gently float and ebb with the breeze as occa-

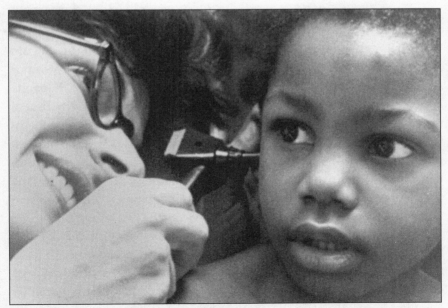

Helen examines a young patient in New York City (courtesy The Helen Rodríguez Papers at the Center for Puerto Rican Studies, City University of New York)

Helen and Eddie shortly after their marriage in 1987 in Puerto Rico (courtesy Edward Gonzalez)

sional buses rumble by on the street below. On every available surface there are tidy clusters of reports, letters and pamphlets.

During that interview, she described her experience at Lincoln and the surprising degree of racism she'd encountered at her new position. Despite the fact that 60 percent of the patients were Hispanic, she met resistance when she tried to increase the number of bilingual social workers. Certain white colleagues didn't meet her gaze in meetings, preferring to address her white assistant. "Racism is the hardest nut to crack in this country. It will get cracked by people becoming conscious of their own need to change society. . . . If I can persuade that physician to work along with a few of my plans, eventually some degree of professional respect will evolve."

She went on to outline other aspects of her developing philosophy. She pointed out that women—herself included—weren't taught one of the most basic realities of taking charge of a group: "Leadership means encountering hostility. Even if you are a beloved leader, there will be enemies. A lot of us, especially women . . . are unprepared not to be loved or even to be hated." Despite negative reactions and heated emotions, a successful leader keeps the situation from escalating: "It is important to acknowledge people's anger without fanning it."

In November of that year, Helen's personal life took a turn for the better. The day after Thanksgiving, she met a blind date friends had set her up with: Eddie Gonzalez, a former labor organizer from a family of Puerto Rican immigrants who taught labor relations and conflict resolution at Cornell. As Gonzalez recently recalled, "She had just gotten back from Cuba, where she wasn't supposed to be, and she walked into the room with this big smile. I fell in love with her that day."

Fighting Domestic Violence

In addition to her focus on reproductive rights, Helen also continued to raise awareness of domestic violence and sexual abuse throughout her career. Discussing health empowerment for women, Rodriguez-Trias said, "I try to emphasize the need to improve health conditions: where we work, where we live, what our environment is like, what are the chances of you or someone in your family being victimized by violence, traumatized by violence? What are your chances of tranquility unless your kids are safe in school and at home? All of these elements in life are determinants and definers of our health."

The recognition of domestic violence as a crime and a major cause of death and injury to women began to spread in the early seventies. Before then, it was common for severe, repetitive violence to go unaddressed, with police officers routinely telling both people to simply "take a walk around the block" to cool off. Helen was among the early advocates for change in perceptions and laws regarding domestic violence victims. She also lobbied for more forceful prosecution of all rape crimes at a time when date rape, or acquaintance rape, was not acknowledged as a crime. Dorchen Lietholdt, an attorney who represents domestic violence victims, worked with Helen in an organization called New York Women Against Rape. She remembers Helen as someone with a "deep understanding" of the issues involved and a "gentleness, sincerity, and integrity" that allowed her to navigate complicated political turf wars and actually get things done. In the 1980s she was a critical force behind the establishment of a policy that

trained emergency room workers to recognize signs of domestic violence and assist victims in getting help. She also helped assemble the
evidence and arguments that encouraged the New York State health
department to create the groundbreaking Joint Commission on Accreditation of Healthcare Organizations (JCAHO) to set standards and
policies for treatment of domestic violence victims. In January of 1992,
the JCAHO revised its manual for hospitals to require that "standards
previously addressed only to management of child abuse and rape victims be expanded to include victims of spousal and elderly abuse," with
noncompliance possibly resulting in the hospital's being shut down.

In order to accomplish this, Rodriguez-Trias drew on the political
relationships she had established during the campaign against sterilization abuse. Seaman says of Helen, "I might even say (as a compliment) that she had a bit of the 'ward heeler' in her soul. That is, she
might do a political favor for this one, and then ask the recipient of the
favor if they would return the kindness by doing such and such for so
and so."

I imagine that Helen always kept her daughters' abuse in mind
when fighting this battle, a personal connection which helped fuel her
extraordinary passion and insight. In 1999 Helen coauthored, with
Janet Nudelman, a paper entitled "Building Bridges between Domestic Violence Advocates and Health Care Providers," which pointed out
that "concern for women's health is growing, and the need to respond
to domestic violence as a major women's health issue is being raised
by mainstream policymakers and health organizations alike." For
Rodriguez-Trias, the women's movement and public health movement were one, both about combating the inequities of power that
caused people pain. She later explained that "the women's movement
is about survival, about finding our strength and using it to help other
women. We reach out to each other to build a different kind of society,
one where women are equal to men in power and where children are
truly prized."

AIDS

In 1985, Rodriguez-Trias became director of the pediatric primary
care program at Newark Beth Israel Medical Center, a position that
led her to a new fight. Dismayed by the number of children with AIDS

she encountered in the walk-in and primary-care clinics, she became convinced that prevention and management of HIV infection had to become an integral part of all aspects of the health care system.

With her typical thoroughness and analytical skill, she tackled the problem on multiple levels. She began to campaign for clinical trials for low-income HIV-infected women, contacting other health advocates and political leaders. In 1988 she established the New York State Department of Health AIDS Institute, and between 1987 and 1989, she headed the New York State AIDS Institute. As her colleague Carole Marte explains, "She was very influential in establishing HIV standards of care, particularly for the poor, marginalized, and women. Soon, New York became a model for quality assurance in HIV care nationally." Rodriguez-Trias also worked on AIDS as an active member of the board of the National Women's Health Network, which has honored her legacy by creating the Helen Rodriguez-Trias Women's Health Leadership Program, which helps train new generations of public health advocates.

Rodriguez-Trias also spoke out forcefully against the prejudice and marginalization that contributed to the spread of AIDS. In a presentation at the 1989 meeting of the APHA, she wisely said: "The identification of HIV in male homosexuals in the United States brought forth virulent forms of longheld prejudices and fears. . . . The fact that the HIV epidemic has spread widely has not yet sufficed to consider that it affects the 'general population.' . . . I think the very exclusion of whole categories of people from the 'general population' has retarded an acknowlegement of our own ultimate personal individual and collective vulnerability." The only way to combat this false containment of the disease was to "recognize our common humanity," regardless of HIV status.

On a policy level, she argued for a greater alliance between the philosophy of public health and the concrete reality of health delivery. Community hospitals and clinics were overwhelmed by the same factors that led to the spread of HIV: the drug epidemic, homelessness, poverty. She envisioned a renewed integration of public health professionals with frontline health care professionals and, with characteristic optimism, described the problem as an opportunity to spur a "broad social reform movement toward health of the world's people."

Full-Time Activism

Throughout the eighties, Helen experienced increasingly overwhelming demands on her time. "She always carried two aspects of her life, the clinical and the political," Gonzalez explains. After the two married in May 1987, Helen resolved to focus more on the political aspect of her work. This was facilitated by the couple's move to California and her leadersip role in advocacy groups there. Soon she found an ideal platform from which she could pursue all her public health concerns.

In 1993, with Eddie as her campaign manager, Helen announced her candidacy for the presidency of the organization. Through two decades with the APHA, Rodriguez-Trias had developed a following and earned the respect of her peers and she quickly built support for her campaign. He remembers, "It was close and I was standing in the back of the room with other supporters of hers, and when her name was called as the winner, I just started to cry."

As the first Latina president of the APHA, Rodriguez-Trias used her one-year term to forward an agenda of inclusivity and equity in health care. This new position gave her the opportunity to travel the country and speak with large groups of health care providers, spreading her messages about reproductive rights, domestic violence, AIDS, and equity in health care. A colleague, Dr. Adriana Linares of the University of Texas School of Public Health, assessed her influence: "Her keen insight into what it takes to get Latino health issues surfaced and addressed in a mainstream world has been very effective, especially around women's issues, reproductive concerns and protecting children's health." Another colleague recalled that Helen never forgot her ethnicity and used it to be inclusive in every aspect of her work: "At a time when Puerto Rican women were sorely missing from the professional health fields, she stood as a beacon of hope to those she served."

When Rodriguez-Trias stepped down as APHA president, she didn't slow down. She joined with Marie Harvey of the Pacific Institute for Women's Health, where the two were co-directors from 1996 to 1999. Harvey recalls Rodriguez-Trias's energy as contagious and motivating: "She was passionate about taking research findings and changing things with them" and was in those years especially focused on "bringing efforts for pregnancy prevention and HIV prevention under the same umbrella." At the Pacific Institute, Helen directed the Partners' Study, which examined the male role in reproductive decision-making and condom use, and resulted in recommended guidelines for public health clinics. "I'm at a point that I don't talk about contraception without talking STD or HIV," Helen said. "We've done everybody a great disservice by separating these things." She was a passionate advocate for the widespread availability of condoms: "What's important is that information be accompanied by access."

During Helen's tenure, the Institute also launched projects around the world designed to empower women and lobby for their access to health care, including contraception and abortion. She developed a public health mentoring program in Eastern Europe and Latin America and continued networking among these activists for the rest of her life. She also maintained her influence in Puerto Rico, where several public health initiatives she founded are still in operation. Particularly moved by the stories of rape victims who were unable to have their pregnancies terminated, she worked to spread the availability of the full range of reproductive health services to countries as diverse as Brazil and Uganda.

Helen attended the 1994 International Conference on Population and Development in Cairo, where she lobbied for the inclusion of reproductive rights, and assurances that population control efforts would not be forced on women. Helen's efforts, along with those of other advocates, resulted in the adoption of Principle 4: "Advancing gender equality and equity and the empowerment of women, and the elimination of all kinds of violence against women, and ensuring women's ability to control their own fertility, are cornerstones of population and development-related programs."

She also wrote prolifically—introductions or forewords for books on topics that engaged her, editorials for newspapers, professional essays. She always expressed herself clearly yet not dismissively. One of the few times she sounds upset is in an insightful 1997 essay: "During the recent election, I found most upsetting the blame heaped on the current administration for complex and painful problems, such as the rise in substance abuse by young people or the persistent issue of teen childbearing. Much of the talk comes from those who have long opposed health education and services in schools—the same people who begrudge kids getting honest information or skills development in regard to sex and drugs. It's time to stop the hypocrisy and to talk straight—to ourselves, each other, and, above all, to young people."

In 1998 Rodriguez-Trias embarked on a new project when she was named to California's Managed Health Care Task Force. She was excited to be named a "consumer representative" because, as she put it, "women are not only the majority of consumers, caretakers and employees of managed care, but increasingly, principal decision-makers in health care matters for themselves and their families. As such, they stand to gain most from an improved system of health care." But she was disappointed when the task force chose not to require health plans to provide services in two areas that she felt were crucial: reproductive health services and infant care.

After the task force chair, Dr. Alain Enthoven, complained that these recommendations contained "coded language for abortion services," Helen responded with an open letter. "I expressed the conviction that use of words like 'coded language for abortion services' (which are necessary and legal) biased the discussion of women's need for a full range of reproductive health services." She also attacked the industry's resistance to mandated services in reproductive health and the lack of attention to the large numbers of uninsured Californians. Helen was also a vocal critic of Governor Pete Wilson's Proposition 187, which sought to deny undocumented immigrants and their children access to social services, including health care. She worked to bring this population into the system, publicizing the availability of public health programs and encouraging those eligible to use them.

Rodriguez-Trias had an uncanny sense of when to stand up to people and when restraint was more expedient. Cindy Pearson vividly recalls her standing on the steps of a Trailways bus, about to depart for a public health conference, answering Cindy's desperate question about whether or not to directly antagonize someone in a meeting. "No," Helen said. "There are only three reasons to confront someone: one is when you really have to make people who have no other voice be heard, one is when you have to rally your own troops, and the other is when there are simply no other options." Eddie Gonzales remembers one of her favorite mottos: "Don't confuse the mission with the vision."

Rodriguez-Trias receives the Presidential Citizen's medal from President Bill Clinton just before he left office in 2001. Age 72 and suffering from lung cancer, she died later that year. (courtesy Edward Gonzalez)

Her Legacy

Helen lived her life in a graceful balance of uncompromising idealism and down-to-earth practicality, always conscious of the need to lay a groundwork for positive change. In her words, "Nothing has the seeds of improvement and betterment unless there is really broad, conscious, education and community participation on an ongoing level." Helen herself shaped many organizations and her influence clearly rippled out, influencing movements throughout the country and around the world.

All her work flowed from personal conviction. Observing changes in managed care, she addressed the "gaps between rich and poor, well and poorly educated, medically indigent and consumers of elective high-tech surgery, owners of mansions and the homeless. . . . We still have a system that excludes, underserves, and even misserves all too many people. Above all, we need to create a grounding for a healthy public policy that redresses and salvages the growing inequities."

Helen's personal style—the effect she had on those around her—was a key part of her success. She was a fun-loving and gracious friend whose beauty radiated to others, even strangers. Marie Harvey recalls one evening when she, Helen, and Eddie were eating dinner at a restaurant, Helen with her preferred drink of beer with ice and lemon. They overheard some women at a nearby table pointing out Helen: "Look at what nice skin she has! It's because she drinks lemonade instead of beer." Helen was delighted.

She was also a profoundly empathetic person who had an exceptional ability to spread her spirit of humanitarianism. In her contributions to a National Institutes of Health Conference on Women's Health in 1997, she described the need for health care providers to communicate well with their patients and gave a few examples of shared cultural values of Latinos. Her description reflects so much that was wonderful about her, not least her belief that everyone deserves to be treated with kindness and respect. "Salient among [Latino cultural values] are *personalismo*, personal relationships that are warm and trusting. This shapes expectations and interactions with health care providers. *Respeto* and *dignidad* refer to observance of traditional expectations in form of address, dress, and professional and personal space. . . . When in doubt, more rather than less formality is advisable. Latinos expect social conversation to precede human transactions and as a prerequisite to establishing *confianza* or trust."

Helen at the White House with her granddaughter Zashari Brainin. (courtesy Edward Gonzalez)

Helen had a keen sense of the winds of social change and how to influence them. She once remarked that to be a good advocate, you have to both care deeply about the issue you are fighting for and also be able to "look around to see who else feels like you do and thinks like you do, or if there is already something going on that you can become a part of." She recognized what Septima Clark and others had discovered before her—that concerted effort by a dedicated few must precede widespread change. "There has to be a climate or event that wakes people up to an issue and gives them a vision of change. . . . It takes a lot of hard work and organization and some force driving people to move toward a vision to get us to a better place." In 2001 Helen received the Presidential Citizen's Medal in recognition of her work as "an outstanding educator and dynamic leader in public health." She clearly had inspired at least one young activist to make her case politely, passionately, with dignity, and without fear of the trappings of power. At the ceremony, her granddaughter Zashari Brainin took the opportunity to hand President Clinton a letter requesting an end to the bombing of Vieques, the Puerto Rican island used for decades as a training ground by the U.S. military.

Helen Rodriguez-Trias died later that year at the age of 72. In a letter included in her funeral program, she and Eddie wrote about their life together, lamenting "the long arm of smoking" that killed her and celebrating the legacy she left as a healer. "As we rush to complete this letter, during these few precious and emotional moments left to us, Helen reminds me again that life is for living: to be lived with the same love of life and passion for good and social justice for all people that was so much a part of her life, and our life together."

Gretchen Buchenholz

In this work, there are no glorious hills you top with flags. It doesn't look heroic to sit alone in a room with a scared child, being tender and gentle and pitting your caring against the weight of a terrible past. But that's what we do here. We love children back to life.

—Gretchen Buchenholz

A PIVOTAL MOMENT IN GRETCHEN BUCHENHOLZ'S LIFE OCCURRED because she went to the wrong address. A former college teacher and recently widowed mother, Gretchen was busy in April 1984 with two community projects—Merricat's Castle, an "inclusionary" preschool she had founded ten years earlier, and her then recent creation, the Yorkville Soup Kitchen. She was on her way to a city government office to get a day care permit for Merricat's when, by accident, she opened a door to an office where homeless families were waiting to be placed in one of the city's "welfare hotels." The scene Gretchen happened upon was that of a room crowded with children and people sleeping on the floor. "There were three bare crib mattresses with babies, not related to each other, with no diapers on, lying in each other's waste, having trouble breathing, their faces covered with filth."

And then, one detail she'll never forget, "there was a metal door that separated these families from the government office and that door had little knuckle dents on the bottom half of it from the children banging and asking for food."

Gretchen immediately went out and bought bread, peanut butter, apple juice, and diapers and took all that she could carry back to the children. She hurried to a phone booth to place three calls: to the Red Cross Disaster Office, City Hall, and the *New York Times*. She already knew that people were destitute in her own neighborhood—she had been out on the street helping them as a volunteer for the Coalition for the Homeless, as well as running the soup kitchen. Now, suddenly seeing the systemic roots of the problem, she resolved to find a solution. "I began to think this had to be changed," she said. "Something had to be done. I wanted to think of alternatives." In the process of conceiving of and creating these alternatives, through her organization the Association to Benefit Children (ABC), Gretchen Buchenholz has become one of the most effective child advocates in the country.

A dark-haired woman with rich brown eyes and angular features, Buchenholz has a no-nonsense style. Her staff jokes that her wardrobe is in "the catering uniform period," although sometimes she wears a colorful scarf around her neck and prefers Chinese slippers in the summertime. She's reluctant to talk about herself or her family, fiercely protective of the privacy of her six children, and equally reluctant to take credit for her accomplishments: creating innovative ways to feed the hungry, changing the system of housing homeless families from crime-ridden "welfare hotels" to transitional homes, ending the practice of warehousing "boarder babies" in hospitals, establishing a model for integrating disabled children into classrooms with other kids, successfully changing the policy regarding AIDS testing of newborns so that they can receive immediate medical care, securing medical treatment for poor children with debilitating asthma, and all the while supervising early childhood education centers full of young children born into extreme poverty. This is how she summarizes the programs she's built and why: "ABC is a response to the changing faces of poverty—hunger, homelessness, crack-addiction, AIDS—and was founded on behalf of poor children who have no voice. Its programs are designed to give children a foothold in the mainstream of life."

When I first met Gretchen to talk about part-time work at ABC, I was full of the guilt-ridden trepidation of someone who has walked right on by people in need. I was enchanted to find that Gretchen is not a harsh judge of character, but kind enough to be almost solicitous of human vulnerability. I was immediately charmed by the way she moves through life, her mittens attached with clips to her coat, drinking Coca-Cola, always aware of someone else who needs a hand, laughing, teasing. She is a delight to be around, to discuss movies (her favorites range from Eminem's *8 Mile* to *Angels in America*), try restaurants, and explore the New York of backyards with chickens, charm shops selling magic potions, entire makeshift shantytowns, and more. When she took me to see the programs she had started in East Harlem, we rode with Mr. Howard, a charismatic man with eyes and a voice like the actor Samuel L. Jackson, who, formerly homeless, raised four sons as a single father after his wife left them in 1989. He told me their names—Willie, Money, Cash, and Arthur—and explained that without Gretchen and the programs and personal touch she has provided, he could not have done it. In the two years that I worked part time at ABC, I heard countless such stories. The legacy she has already left has been personal, direct, and also "incalculably diffusive," thanks to the people she's inspired and the programs and policies she's developed that have been replicated across the country.

Growing Up

Gretchen Shadof was the youngest of three children raised by a single mother who worked in a factory at 37 West Thirty-seventh Street doing piecework, paid a certain amount for each item completed. "It was an actual sweatshop," Gretchen recalls. Despite the hardships, she had a happy childhood, filled with positive energy and a sense of belonging to a community. She played softball and basketball on Police Athletic League teams and credits that experience with teaching her two invaluable lessons: "keeping your eye on the ball, and working with a team." One day, reading a newspaper article about her team, she got a surprise. "I read that our precinct, the 42nd Precinct, was one of the poorest neighborhoods in the city and it was shocking to me, because that wasn't my mother's spin on things at all."

Gretchen's mother, Helen (when her colleagues at work, all male, called her "Miss Helen," she responded, "just plain Helen"), made the family feel as if they were fortunate and should share what they had. Gretchen remembers one of her sayings: "If someone has a loaf of bread under each arm, one of them is for another person." She saw her daughter's gifts and encouraged them. "She'd told me these stories about during the Depression when people were migrating, there were certain houses that gave food. And if a family was given food on the way, an X was put on the door so that the next family would know they were people who would give." Just before she died in 1982, Helen told Gretchen the story again and added, "You have an X on you."

Throughout her years attending public schools (in both Manhattan and the Bronx), Gretchen worked at jobs both before and after school, from Woolworth's to a publishing house to the Claremont stables. ("I worked with a redhead named Jimmy Flood, mucking out stables before school. I stank when I got to school," she laughs.) She

Gretchen practices balancing in the early sixties after one of her stable jobs. (courtesy Gretchen Buchenholz)

worked to bring home some money but also because various jobs "took me into neighborhoods that were different to meet people that were different."

One experience was particularly moving. When she was around sixteen, Gretchen took a job as a tutor with the State of New York, assigned to work with a blind girl in her home after school. She soon found that not only was the girl blind, both of her parents were blind too. The house was completely dark and roach infested, and the family made their way around by touch. Gretchen was profoundly moved by their existence, their love for one another, the way they cooked dinner and communicated. She also saw another need she could fill: this young girl had never learned how to care for her physical appearance. Gretchen helped her, brushing her hair and making stencils for her so she could put on lipstick. "It was so cool, so fun, with such concrete gains. I was so, so amazed. At first it seemed like the dark to me but it was really full of light."

When Gretchen finished high school, she went on to Hunter College in New York City, where she got a degree in sociology, and then to Columbia for her masters, also in sociology. She continued working a variety of jobs, at this point choosing ones that involved helping people one-on-one. It was through one of her jobs that she met the man who would become her husband, a child psychiatrist named Bruce Buchenholz. Along with some other mental health professionals, he was running a psychiatric hospital for adolescents which advertised for program therapists who could work with their patients in various therapeutic activities. Gretchen, whose love of horses had grown since the days mucking out the Claremont stables, took the job and designated horseback riding as her therapeutic activity.

"For My Own Children"

Bruce was significantly older than Gretchen, but, as evidenced by the fact that he was a professional recorder player, painter, sculptor, and photographer as well as a practicing psychiatrist, he shared her energetic approach to life. From the start, the relationship was supportive and loving, strengthened by the fact that they shared the same values and were both inclined to actively promote them. They married in 1963. The following year they joined Martin Luther King's March where Gretchen was inspired by the power of collective will and the sense of imminent positive change. Five years later Bruce and Gretchen took their two small children with them to the festival of "peace, love and music" known as Woodstock. Gretchen loved the performances—especially Crosby, Stills Nash and Young's "Wooden Ships," Jimi Hendrix's "Star Spangled Banner," and Joan Baez's rendition of "We Shall Overcome"—but mainly (and understandably) she remembers coping with cloth diapers in the rain.

When Gretchen decided that she wanted to start her own nursery school, one that included children with disabilities and reached out for those of all racial and economic backgrounds, Bruce was behind her. "I really wanted to do it for my own children," she recalled. "I wanted a good school that was also diverse. It came about from talking to friends on the playground." Gretchen asked her church, Holy Trinity on East Eighty-eighth Street, if they would lease her space to start the school. They agreed, and Merricat's Castle opened in 1974. Gretchen still attends Holy Trinity and continues to live on the same block where she and Bruce settled in 1963. (They moved across the street in 1969.)

Merricat's is also still going strong. The policy today is to reserve one-third of the spots for homeless (or very poor) children, one-third for special needs children, and one-third for the typically developing children from families who can afford to pay. "It's a tricky formula, but we keep the faith," Gretchen says with a smile.

Merricat's Castle and the other preschools Gretchen subsequently founded have become a model for "inclusionary" education, where children with special needs play and learn along with typically developing children. "What's important to children is whether or not another child is fun," Gretchen explains. "'Will you share? Will you play?' Children make magic like little gods. They can turn a chair into a spaceship, go to the moon, land the craft, and then turn it back into a chair. There is no problem playing with handicapped children when so much of play is magic."

The success of this model has paved the way for more widespread change. As documented in a 2004 *New York Times Magazine* cover story, "'Inclusion' is the latest in a series of evolving strategies for special-needs education," and is being tried for the first time in a New York City public elementary school. "Inclusion, as used by educators, generally means making a child with a disability a full part of the class. Instead of merely placing that child in a standard classroom for part or

Gretchen at Merricat's Castle preschool in 1978 with Norman the rabbit, who had previously been the "petting" rabbit at the Bronx Zoo. He was given to her by the chief veterinarian there, a good friend of hers. Norman became a beloved mascot for ABC in its early days. (courtesy Gretchen Buchenholz)

even most of the day and expecting him to keep up (a strategy often known as 'mainstreaming') inclusion involves rearranging the class—both in the physical space and the curriculum—to include him." The classroom profiled in this piece included a five-year-old, motor-impaired girl named Danielle, a graduate of one of ABC's preschools.

The 1980s

Though her good friend and colleague Marian Wright Edelman[1] calls Buchenholz "saintly and remarkable," Gretchen herself refers to her work in very simple, practical terms. "It's all about the children," she says, "and the incredible, devoted staff we have. They make it work. I'm like a plumber." Or, even more simply: "If you give children love and warmth and caring, they grow. Kindness does it all."

Saintly or not, Gretchen certainly doesn't humbly turn the other cheek when she is defending children in need. As she has demonstrated on national television, she doesn't hesitate to flatly declare, "You're wrong." She confronts opponents, including government officials, for falling short of their obligations. All this fight is used on behalf of children who have no political voice and no one else in their corner. When she is playing with, talking to, or holding those children, her love for them—and her impatience with those who refuse to help them—is clear. Abigail Disney, a philanthropist and Gretchen's friend, says she combines the spirit of Mother Teresa with the spine of Margaret Thatcher.

This combination was exactly what was needed in the 1980s, when massive budget cuts, increasing unemployment, and rising prices exacerbated the growing gap between rich and poor. Suddenly, in cities everywhere, Americans confronted an alarming rise in homelessness. There's no exact census but the lowest of the authoritative estimates concludes that in the 1980s and early 90s, 1.4 million Americans were homeless for all or part of the year, each year. Minorities made up the majority of the homeless—59 percent or more, as opposed to approximately 25 percent in the general population. The market for unskilled day labor had shrunk considerably, and the homeless were more likely to be unemployed and had an even lower income than their 1950s

---

[1] Perhaps best known for her work as the founder and chief executive officer of the Children's Defense Fund (CDF), Wright Edelman's entire career has focused on advocacy for the disadvantaged. As the first black woman admitted to the Mississippi Bar, she headed the NAACP Legal Defense Educational Fund office in Jackson, Mississippi, and went on to serve as counsel for Martin Luther King Jr.'s Poor People's Campaign. In 1973, she founded CDF, a respected and influential advocate for children and families. Wright Edelman has received numerous awards, including the Albert Schweitzer Humanitarian Award, a MacArthur Foundation fellowship, the Presidential Medal of Freedom, and the Robert F. Kennedy Lifetime Achievement Award.

counterparts. There were far fewer affordable housing options, so the homeless were not just more numerous but more visible. And for the first time, there were substantial, and growing, numbers of homeless women with children—21 percent of the total homeless in 1984, 40 percent by 1988.

Among the significant factors in the spread of homelessness were the increase in poverty and the reduction in programs to assist the poor. At the time, the federal government considered a working family of three "poor" if it had an annual income of $9,862 or less, hardly enough for shelter, food, and expenses. The national poverty rate climbed to 15 percent in 1982, amounting to 34.4 million Americans, with an additional 12 million living just barely above the poverty line. Food stamp programs that had been instituted in response to hunger in 1967, and had proved effective, had been slashed in the Reagan budget, along with a litany of other critical elements of the safety net: funds for public school lunches; food programs for senior citizens; child care assistance; the Women, Infants and Children (WIC) feeding program; and many similar programs. Suddenly, after having dropped steadily for over forty years, infant mortality was on the rise. And in its 1982 study of hunger in New York City, the Nutrition Watch Committee was "deeply shocked to discover that hunger, which had been largely eliminated through a variety of measures including food stamps and other feeding programs is again on the rise in New York."

Even as income dropped for the poorest Americans, it increased for the richest, widening the gap between the two. In 1979 the poorest fifth received 6 percent of the aggregate national income, the wealthiest fifth received 44.2 percent, and the wealthiest 5 percent of the country received 16.9 percent. In 1989 the poorest fifth received 3.8 percent, the top fifth 48.8, the top 5 percent 18.9 percent. A chief cause of this drop in income appears to have been the shifting composition of private sector jobs. While overall employment increased during the 1980s, the gains were in relatively low-paying service jobs while well-paid manufacturing jobs began to disappear. Far from being considered a problem, this growing disparity was celebrated. Gordon Gecko's mantra in the movie *Wall Street*—"Greed is good"—became a real-life motto for many, and Tom Wolfe's *Bonfire of the Vanities* described the new breed of Masters of the Universe, who felt it was a struggle to make ends meet on less than $2 million a year.

While income was falling, housing prices were rising, and the actual stock of housing the poor could afford was shrinking. (For statistical purposes, a house or apartment is considered affordable if the rent is no more than 30 percent of the household income.) One study measured availability of housing for Americans in the 25th percentile of income, meaning that they made less than 75 percent of the population. In 1970 there was an excess of 500,000 units affordable for this group; by 1989 there was a deficit of five million units.

Phasing out the system of state institutions for the mentally ill also added to the homeless population and made life even more challenging for the children mixed into it. This is not what the architects of de-institutionalization had envisioned. As originally planned by the National Institute of Mental Health (NIMH), the newly released patients would have access to a federally funded system of community mental health centers (CMHCs) offering housing subsidies, vocational training, and other assistance, and the states would use the money saved by closing the hospitals to assist with the transition. Instead the hospitals were closed before the support system was in place. According to the original plan, by 1980 there would be 2,000 CMHCs in operation. In fact, by 1978 there were 650. By 1984, 80 percent of the country's institutionalized mental patients—more than 400,000 people—were released into nursing homes, halfway houses, and single-room occupancy hotels. Follow-up care was minimal. By 1986 the NIMH had completely lost track of almost two-thirds of the schizophrenics who had been released.

Underpinning and accelerating all these changing structural factors was the Reagan Revolution. During his presidency, the upper income brackets benefited from tax cuts as well as a booming stock market. At the same time, the poor were widely dismissed as "welfare queens" who were taking advantage of public assistance. To many, the Reagan administration seemed oblivious to increasing poverty and eager to justify the cutting of government programs, including public school lunches. "This was the era of 'ketchup is a vegetable,'" recalled Gretchen.

The Reagan policy of "new federalism" meant that cuts in social programs trickled down to the state level. From 1980 to 1989, inflation-adjusted federal spending dropped in all social services: education, training, employment, and community and regional development. (Defense spending increased, as did Medicare and Social Security, but by far the largest gain—more than 140 percent—was in net interest on the ballooning national debt.) What federal funding went to states was more often awarded as block grants with few policy guidelines or spending directives, so the money could be and frequently was siphoned off for other purposes.

Of course, not every poor family went hungry or became homeless, but there's no doubt their numbers grew. Reagan's economic and policy changes stripped away much of what had been keeping some families afloat. In December 1988, on the brink of leaving office, Ronald Reagan sat down for an interview with David Brinkley of ABC News. Displaying his characteristic sunny outlook, Reagan assessed some of the hot-button issues that arose during his eight years in office.

On homelessness, he remarked, "They make it their own choice for staying out there. There are shelters in virtually every city, and shelters here, and those people still prefer out there on the grates or the lawn to going into one of those shelters." Even if his assertion about availability had been true, as Gretchen made it a point to find out, conditions in the shelters were often so horrific that the homeless—especially mothers—avoided them if at all possible.

Reagan also ignored the government's failure to follow through on the community mental health care network that was supposed to replace institutions. Instead he blamed the consequences on the mentally ill themselves, who "walked away from those institutions—they wanted freedom but they walked out to where there was nothing for them."

Hunger

In 1983 President Reagan appointed the thirteen-member Task Force on Food Assistance. One member caused a stir by declaring that African-Americans did not face a hunger problem. "Their problems are not food—they are probably the best nourished group in the United States," said Dr. George Graham, professor of international health and pediatrics at Johns Hopkins University, the only task force member with a medical background. "Don't tell me you're going to correct complex social problems by throwing food at them," he said, adding that the phenomenon of low birth-weight babies and premature births among blacks could be solved by cultural

Gretchen with students at Merricat's Castle preschool in 1985. (courtesy Gretchen Buchenholz)

changes such as "avoiding sex during pregnancy." Graham also informed a Senate committee that "the greatest threat to [low income groups'] health is over-nutrition." He'd also declared the Women, Infant and Children nutrition program "wasteful and unneeded." White House counsel Edwin Meese didn't help matters when he said he had seen no "authoritative evidence" of a hunger problem in America and that people went to soup kitchens "because the food is free and that's easier than paying for it."

After Graham's remarks were publicized, other nutritionists came forward to say that they were unaware of any medical evidence to support that argument, and Gretchen herself spoke out, bluntly dismissing his statement as "the cruel joke of a madman" and decrying his effort "to shift the focus away from human suffering and thereby away from government responsibility for that suffering." She also pointed out that the infant mortality rate in Harlem was 2.1 percent—much higher than the city rate of 1.5 percent. Since then repeated studies have shown that hunger causes real harm to children, affecting both their emotional and physical well-being. Moreover, if the family is short of food, the mother generally will feed her children before herself. Hunger has similar negative effects on adults, making an already stressful situation more difficult to deal with.

Nowhere was hunger in the midst of plenty more apparent than the small island of Manhattan, where limousines pulled away from midtown church services while the hungry stood waiting in line for food. Gretchen noticed such lines in her own neighborhood, where she ran Merricat's Castle out of Holy Trinity Church on East Eighty-eighth Street. She soon found herself handing out the preschool's leftover graham crackers and apple juice to the hungry and homeless outside its doors. "The knowledge that there were hungry people came to me right from the doors of the nursery school, which was at the church. So I asked the church, could we do a feeding program. That was how it started. And then it wasn't sufficient." One day Gretchen was particularly shocked to see a family eating a raw chicken because they had no home, no place to cook it. "That's when I realized how many homeless children there were. I was ignorant."

Buchenholz has always operated on two interlocking levels: immediate care and support for those in need, and long-term advocacy to improve public policies. "If you have hunger like this in one of the most affluent neighborhoods in New York, what must it be like in a poor neighborhood?" she asked herself, and resolved to find out. Soon she had become the head of the Committee on Hunger for the Coalition for the Homeless, handing out food to people in makeshift shelters all over the city and talking with them about their circumstances. Finding overwhelming need, she began lobbying city officials to expand existing programs providing sixty thousand meals a day to needy children and the elderly. "There are so many feeding centers and they are all overwhelmed," she told the *New York Times*. "We're not blaming Mayor Koch for the problem but it is his responsibility to do something about it."

As for immediate solutions: "I had seen signs in the country in the back of supermarkets that said buy an extra can of cat food or buy bird seed or buy something for a hungry animal, and I thought, Why don't we do that for children? And that's what I came to the church with. If we could get people to donate food—if we could get an alliance of churches and synagogues to come on board with that and put a box in the back of the church—and that's what we did."

Gretchen with her six children on Thanksgiving, 1992. (courtesy Gretchen Buchenholz)

Gretchen began talking up the program, promoting it whenever and wherever she could, and soon she became known as an articulate voice on the issue of hunger. Before her first television interview, she remembers feeling nervous and finding the steadiness and clarity that she needed in her husband, Bruce. She remembers how, over breakfast at the Mansion Diner that morning, he "kept my head straight on the subject," explaining that she didn't need to feel frightened, she didn't need to know every detail about the history of policies because she knew what she had seen, the hungry people she had met and tried to help.

After her appearance on a local PBS talk show, she got a call from a man named Harry Frelinghuysen, the first person to offer private funding to her food pantry project and eventually for ABC's programs. Gretchen recalled: "He called me up and he said—I remember his voice"—and she deepened her voice to imitate her late friend—"'Are there really hungry people in New York?' And he simply showed up with a check for five thousand dollars in his hand, wanting me to show him. So I did." It was at this moment that Gretchen felt herself become an advocate. "I felt that I could amplify the children's voices," she explains. "Here was this man in Far Hills, New Jersey, with sheep outside his window who called and wanted to do something—and we did something."

Sensing an opportunity, Gretchen recruited more supporters and began to experiment with ways to publicize the growing hunger problem. "There were people saying there were no hungry people or these people were in line for some other reason, they really would rather spend their money on vodka. There were attacks on the very people who were suffering, and I saw this opportunity to counterattack." This reminds me of Virginia Durr's analysis of the way people talked about poor children with rickets and pellagra during the Depression, the way Alice Hamilton noticed some factory owners make dehumanizing comments about immigrant workers, and even the racism encountered by Ida B. Wells-Barnett and others. The genius of all the women in this book is that they saw past these lines most people drew and challenged others to do the same.

The legal right to shelter for homeless families had been successfully established. Gretchen used this "opportunity to counterattack." Gretchen believed these families had the right to basic food as well, so she joined the coalition's hunger committee. She was working on this, running Merricat's, and taking care of her young children when, on July 17, 1983, Bruce Buchenholz died.

I can only imagine how difficult this must have been. Gretchen herself, always concerned foremost with protecting her children's privacy, doesn't really like to talk about her personal life. What is clear is that she resolved to find the same sense of balancing duties she had always had growing up. Now raising her children as a single mother, Buchenholz resolved to continue her mission to help those in need.

In 1985 the coalition helped produce a report entitled *The Summer Hunger Crisis*, which warned that the closing of public schools coupled with the ongoing drop in donations—of food, money, and volunteer time—meant that more children would go hungry. At a press conference marking the report's release, Gretchen said, "All of us have a vision of that day in June when school closes, of the doors opening up and kids pouring out into the summer sunshine in new sneakers, looking forward to a summer of joy and fun and growth and freedom. But last week public schools closed, and an unprecedented number of children in this state became captives of poverty, depriva-tion, hunger and suffering."

Gretchen is determined to find practical solutions for problems, and she has a gift for coming up with innovative ideas that are so workable that they seem obvious in retrospect. While continuing her lobbying work with the coalition, she came up with a plan to make ex-tra meals in the public school cafeterias and hand them out to home-less people after school hours. "It made sense. They already had the cooks and the kitchen. They just needed to make extra meals that we could give people after school. It was the least expensive way to feed people," she says.

Meeting Kevin Gill at the office of School Food Services—likely en-chanting him with her combination of humor, will, and compassion—she knew she'd found an ally. "He got it," she says. "It worked because he really helped us." He agreed to let her team of volunteers run a soup kitchen out of the cafeteria of P.S. 151. Each meal cost about ninety-five cents, and volunteers served the meals on-site and also handed them out to the homeless on the streets. Gretchen herself traveled around the city handing out plastic bags filled with sandwiches, a container of salad, fruit, and small cartons of milk to the growing number of people huddled in makeshift shelters or digging through garbage bins in search of food.

Eventually the Yorkville Soup Kitchen received some federal fund-ing through the Federal Emergency Management Agency (FEMA), the same group that dispenses relief for disasters such as hurricanes, but it was necessarily sporadic and limited. Congress authorized bills to use these funds to address what some saw as a hunger epidemic, but there was no comprehensive, permanent feeding program. A FEMA spokesperson explained that the assistance was "still considered a sup-plemental emergency program to supplement efforts at the local level."

The Yorkville Soup Kitchen—now called the Yorkville Common Pantry—also offered a support network to those in need, and it inspired similar operations in other parts of the city. "People should not walk by a homeless child, or a homeless adult for that matter, feeling that there is nothing they can do," she said. During this period one friend told the *New York Daily News* that Gretchen was a "one-woman social agency in helping homeless families find suitable shelters." Inspired by her ex-

ample, other churches and synagogues began to establish similar part-
nerships with school cafeterias, and some of her coworkers created innovative projects of their own. One Yorkville employee, Helen Palit,
founded City Harvest, a service that collects surplus food from restaurants and grocery stores and distributes it to food pantries and soup
kitchens. Helen credits Gretchen with giving her the inspiration, connections, and support to make City Harvest happen. In a letter to her
mentor, Palit wrote, "You were behind me, with me 100%. And now
City Harvest delivers free food to the Yorkville Common Pantry. The
circle is completed."

Amid these activities, Gretchen also founded the New York State
Committee Against Hunger, a joint project of the Coalition for the
Homeless and the New York Urban Coalition. This was the beginning
of the more concerted political approach that has become part of her
mission. "In 1985, in affluent America, poverty, yes, poverty, is the
greatest killer of children," she said in one of her presentations. "Yet
nothing serious has been done to protect our children from the devastation of hunger. Nothing serious has been done to prevent the stag-
gering number of low birthweight, premature infants born to ill-fed,
ill-cared-for, poor mothers. . . . Two weeks ago as I left my soup
kitchen, I found a small child sitting inside a soup kitchen garbage pail
eating the soup kitchen garbage. His mother was rifling through another pail looking for something to eat. It was the last week of the
month. This little boy, his mother, and his baby sister had walked
twenty blocks to get a meager meal. But we had too many people that
day and we'd turned them away." She went on to recount other heartbreaking examples of children who were literally starving in the middle of Manhattan. As a result of her speaking out, the reality of hunger
was revealed to many who had no idea it was going on in their midst.
"It was hidden," Gretchen explained. "We got some private funds and
made it clear that hunger was a problem in New York."

Once the problem was no longer hidden, New Yorkers demanded
action. Hundreds not only volunteered at and donated to projects such
as the Yorkville Common Pantry, they also began pressuring politicians
to do something about the problem. The Human Resources Administration issued a request for proposals, seeking new programs to feed
the hungry. Under Mayor David Dinkins (who became a close friend of
Gretchen's and is today a board member of ABC), beacon schools were

established to provide meals for hungry children after school and all year round. Slowly, the problem abated—though there are troubling signs that it is returning.

Gretchen, like all the other women in this book, believes in the preciousness of each individual and the moral imperative to give those in the most dire circumstances an opportunity to overcome them. Like Wells-Barnett, Jones, and Huerta, she wants to reveal the reality of suffering, having faith that most people will respond with goodwill. Like Perkins, Hamilton, and Rodriguez-Trias, she has a talent for challenging the status quo with her own practical solutions. Like Durr, she maintains her own sometimes mischievous sense of humor, recognizes the power of friendship, and gracefully accepts the complexities of human nature. But she reminds me most of kind and tough Septima Clark, drawn to the most neglected, most underestimated people—homeless families, disabled and sick children, recovering addicts—and driven by the joy in specific, individual moments when they light up with pride and confidence. What she does may be defined as charity by some, but up close it seems more like acting out of the way things ought to be. She seems, more than anyone I've met, to epitomize Gandhi's challenge to "be the change you wish to see in the world."

Homelessness

It was in this context that Gretchen chose not to shut the door to the Emergency Assistance Unit that she had mistakenly opened in April of 1984. She didn't tell herself that she was already doing enough. Instead, she shifted her efforts to focus on services for homeless families.

The *New York Times* article prompted by Gretchen's phone call outlined the basic perversity of the homeless program. One woman, a thirty-year-old mother of two who was seven months pregnant and on a methadone maintenance program, was considered "hard to place" because she had only two children; the welfare hotels preferred larger families because they could charge the city more. This woman and her children, along with forty other homeless people, including twenty-four other children, slept in metal chairs, cots, or on the floor, and did not get food until Gretchen arrived.

Gretchen was determined to conduct her own investigation into the extent of the problem. She was joined by Tom Styron, a Yale professor of psychiatry and Gretchen's friend from the Coalition for the Homeless, and the two of them set out on foot through the poorest neighborhoods of New York. "We were so dumb," she recalls. "We'd go in anywhere," including crack houses and abandoned buildings. What they found was heartbreaking and scary. Many families lived without water, electricity, or sufficient food. "They were living like cave people," she said. "They were scared we were coming to take something away from them and we had to explain, 'No, we want to help you.'"

As in all urban areas, homelessness in New York City began to rise, and become more visible, in the late 1970s. In 1979 Robert Hayes, who would later found the Coalition for the Homeless, filed a class action lawsuit on behalf of this growing population, arguing that the New York State constitution established a fundamental right to shelter. In 1981 the state and New York City settled the suit, establishing a right to shelter for homeless men and setting standards for adequate shelter. (Later, the Coalition for the Homeless filed suit to extend the right to women, and eventually to women with children.)

Early on, New York City's response was a patchwork of group shelters and welfare hotels. As the homeless population climbed, with more and more homeless families, the system proved horribly inadequate. The group shelter was essentially an enormous room filled with rows of cots. No privacy, little security. Families with children, even newborns, were mixed in with strange adults and exposed to all kinds of communicable diseases, among other hazards. One woman, Maria Vestres, and her four children were assigned to the shelter in the Bronx's Roberto Clemente Park. Vestres said, "I don't feel safe because there's too many people here, and I don't trust anyone when it comes to my kids." After a visit to the same shelter, Gretchen recalled, "The thing that really haunted me was a high-risk infant out of the hospital a few days, who weighed five pounds and who was having respiratory distress. The mother reported to me that the baby had several times stopped breathing and she had to breathe into the baby's mouth." She also noted that many children, some of whom obviously had colds, were playing around this baby due to the crowded conditions. "To place a high-risk infant in such a shelter is worse than stupid—it's criminal," she said.

Placement seemed to be almost random, with people sent from a group shelter, to a welfare hotel, to another welfare hotel, to another shelter, then a third welfare hotel, in a matter of a few weeks. "Some of this was unbelievable," Gretchen recalls. "Families were moved every night, with their lives stuffed in garbage bags, to the hotel, back again, four o'clock in the morning, from one hotel to another. It was pretty horrible."

The welfare hotels—dirty, vermin-infested places full of crime, prostitution, violence, and drugs—weren't much better than the shelters. Families shared filthy bathrooms with prisoners on work release, addicts, and drug dealers. The city government paid as much as $1,800 a month for a tiny, dreary room for an entire family; the hotel owners were actually making quite a profit. Many single mothers expressed frustration that they could not use some portion of that monthly rent to find their own apartment. But the funds used to pay for rooms in welfare hotels could not be put toward low-income housing because it was earmarked for temporary, emergency shelter. The federal government covered half this bill, and the city and state split the other half. Moreover, as Mayor Koch and others repeatedly stated, there was not very much low-income housing available.

The Martinique Hotel, once an elegant getaway, was perhaps the most notorious of the welfare hotels. In the 1980s it housed as many as 440 families with well over a thousand children. Half the children were under the age of five, including about two hundred infants and toddlers. The closest playground was a sliver of concrete near where Broadway and Sixth Avenue intersect, and getting there required crossing one of New York's busiest streets. Parents didn't dare let their children play in the hallways, territory staked out by drug dealers and prostitutes. Most of the families slept two to a bed in cramped and suffocating rooms with little floor space, certainly not enough for a crib or a desk. "I used to wake up in the night at the Martinique, hear the rats, and try to stuff things in the holes in the wall to keep them out," said one resident, a man who had lost his job at a hardware store, then lost the family's apartment and lived on the streets with his wife and children before moving into the hotel. "We'd put the baby between us in bed." Cooking wasn't allowed but most families used a hotplate anyway, risking eviction if they were caught. Only 15 rooms in the hotel had refrigerators and everyone else had to make do however they could (rigging up shelves outside the window in cool weather, keeping food and medicines in the toilet tank or sink). In the lobby, the clamor of

Gretchen with David Bright, whom she calls "one of my heroes," in 1986. (courtesy Gretchen Buchenholz)

despairing and frustrated people bounced off the lofty ceilings, and the reverberating echoes, in one visitor's words, "intensified the atmosphere of imminent violence." And the Martinique smelled—an "unfamiliar and pungent" odor powerful enough to cling to one's clothes hours after leaving.

In an old video shot inside the infamous hotel, Gretchen—slender, pretty, in an old-fashioned dress—enters the danger zone, rearranges it, challenges its very existence. She makes a record of the lives being lived out of sight of the affluent and powerful, and she forces people to understand the consequences of misguided public policies and too much private indifference.

During her work among the homeless, Gretchen was always most drawn to the children, and she began documenting their stories. "I was there every day and I often wrote their stories, I took their pictures. . . . It was important to me. The kids' words were important. What the kids thought was important. I wanted them to be heard." Because of her efforts, the kids were heard. Their words were picked up by the news media, published, and aired, contributing considerably to the growing awareness about homelessness.

The stories are terrible to read, much less live. "One time we heard of this murder and we looked and there was blood all over the walls," reported one girl living in a welfare hotel, "and it was really gross and no one even cleaned it up, it just wore off, but the blood just stayed there. Every time we walked down the hall it was still there." Another girl simply said, "There is a baby on the fourth floor that has scabies on her body. I don't think anyone is really trying to help." These transcripts also reflect Gretchen's gentle, respectful way with the kids. She asks them questions, listens for long stretches, and then affirms that what they are saying is important and invites them to share more.

One of the roughly 1,400 homeless kids in the Martinique Hotel became especially close to Gretchen, and was soon introduced to the entire country. The family of ten-year-old David Bright, who was one of four children of a thirty-five-year-old single mother, had been bounced between various shelters and hotels since his family lost their apartment in the Bronx in 1983. Articulate and clever, Bright became a face and voice for the plight of homeless children when he testified before Congress in March 1986:

> Hello. My name is David Bright. I am ten years old. I am homeless. I am often hungry. Right now, I live in the Martinique Hotel. The Martinique is a mad house. The hallways are dangerous. Many things could happen to you while you are in the hallways. The roaches and rats are a big problem too.
>
> I am often hungry because I do not get enough to eat. Homeless kids are taken to schools far away. When the bus comes late, I cannot even get breakfast at school. When I arrive, the bell rings, then the breakfast just stops. I just cannot think in school when I am hungry. My mind just stops thinking and this cannot go on forever.
>
> That is because I want to learn. I want to get a good education. Learning is fun for me. There are too many little kids in the hotel who never go to school. There just is not enough room in the school for them. Just like there are not enough homes for poor children and not enough food.
>
> When I grow up, I will be President of the United States. When I am President, every American will have a home. Every American will have a little money in his pocket. When I am president, no ten-year-old boy like me will have to put his head down on the desk at school because it hurts to be hungry.

After his testimony, David became, as the *New York Times* put it, "a kind of homeless everychild," bringing the plight of thousands to the attention of congressmen, senators, and citizens. He handled all the attention with remarkable aplomb. When New York City mayor Ed Koch publicly questioned his account, David simply said, "He's putting up a fight—right?" He also pointed out that the mayor's opposition might be personal rather than political: "I've got hair, and he doesn't." David and Gretchen keep in touch and, as of fall 2004, he was enrolled in college and doing well.

ABC

In 1986 Gretchen and Tom Styron incorporated under the name that her organization bears today—the Association to Benefit Children (ABC). Their first mission was to create a day care center inside the Martinique Hotel—"in what I liked to call the belly of the beast. And it was very difficult to open it," Gretchen remembers. "The city told us we couldn't open a day care center in a place, a building, that had so many violations and yet over a thousand families were housed there in that same building." But Buchenholz and Styron persevered, keeping political pressure on those in charge, as well as raising private money and looking for sympathetic partners. When the day care center did open, it was an oasis for the children and families that had felt so trapped and scared. "The stress of living in such a terrifying environment keeps hammering at the children," she said. "Our job is to rescue these kids before the damage becomes permanent. What you see is the quiet tenderness here, the time to wash a doll's hair, put jelly on toast."

Roy Grant, who helped set up ABC's child care center at the Martinique, later wrote about the experience. (The earlier descriptions of the hotel's noises and odors came from his essay.) Roy's account lays out in stark terms not only the terrible physical conditions but also the desperate emotional and financial struggles faced by the families and especially the children who lived there.

When Grant and the others began renovations in the room they'd use—1,100 square feet with high ceilings—it was completely empty, except for two small sheds that would be used for storage and office space. The door to the room was standing open and a toddler, a boy perhaps two-and-a-half years old, peeked in.

The boy took one look at this vast space and ran as fast as he could, crashing hard into the roll-down steel gate protecting one of the sheds. He fell backward, hitting the floor very hard. Much to our surprise, both he and his mother laughed delightedly at the incident. My first thought was how disturbed this behavior was, but then I realized how starved for physical movement a child this age might be at the Hotel Martinique. Behavior that seemed bizarre in another context may be perfectly normal in the abnormal environment of a homeless shelter.

When the center was completed—open, spacious, colorful—it seemed to affect other children in a similar way. Grant says that most children spent their first week at the center running aimlessly around the room before they settled into the routine and structure. Some had to be taught to play with each other, even how to play with toys. One little girl attended the center for six months before anyone heard her laugh. Over time, with lots of patience and guidance and love, the children blossomed. Even the most difficult kids responded to the attention, and the staff, trained to recognize potential problems, discussed possibilities and options with the parents and set up appointments for examinations and counseling as needed or requested.

Rewarding as it was, working with the children at the Martinique also could be frustrating and heartbreaking. Some parents—overwhelmed, suspicious, or exhausted—refused to cooperate with the staff on keeping up doctors' visits and treatments. Families were moved out with no notice and no way to arrange follow-up or transitional services. The head of another center told her staff, "Every month is September and every day is Monday. Do what you can in one day, without making great plans for the future, and hope that what is done will make a difference."

Lobbying for a more humane system of housing, Gretchen sought both public and private support to establish a model. She and Tom located empty apartments, raised funds to renovate them, hired homeless men to help renovate them, and moved families from the Martinique into them. Like others profiled in this book—Hamilton and Perkins in particular—Buchenholz felt a call to change the entire system that these people were suffering under. "We were kind of determined together, ultimately, to do something; we wanted to do service," Gretchen explained. "We wanted to do something about the issues. We wanted to actually get out and house people. The first families we housed were actually here on Ninety-third Street."

Tired of bureaucratic inertia, ABC filed a class-action lawsuit under the Child Welfare Reform Act of New York, demanding help in providing basic services to the children in the hotels. "At that point they were overwhelmed, they were warehousing families," Gretchen recalls. She felt that the litigation was necessary to break the logjam. Back then "there really weren't services for these families, and I'm talking about the kinds of things that day care could bring in. First of all, food—children didn't have enough to eat. Second of all, inoculations. Many of the children weren't inoculated. Just basic needs. Third, of course, services to families and education. And we were blocked at every turn. It wasn't easy to do."

Gretchen, like Alice Hamilton before her, has struggled with the issue of how much to use the media to call attention to the injustices and abuses she saw up close. On the one hand, the publicity can result in the public outcry that fuels social change. On the other, like the "muckraking article" Hamilton pondered, it can create resentment among more sympathetic public officials and a formidable backlash among more reactionary ones. The latter is what Gretchen believes happened after she boldly "snuck" an entire *60 Minutes* crew into the Martinique Hotel to document the squalid conditions there. After the piece aired, it created a bit of a backlash, as Gretchen recalls. "There were people in the Congress who wanted to stop the flow of money altogether. They focused on the fact that money was being squandered rather than on allowing the money to be used for permanent housing. And that's basically the kind of mind you were dealing with."

However, the setback was temporary. As a result of the increased public awareness of the reality of hunger and homelessness among children, there was more political support for funding low-income housing projects. The Koch administration developed the "Housing New York" initiative, a ten-year plan to create a total of 150,000 new housing units with a percentage set aside for the homeless. The program developed an average of 3,700 of these affordable apartments each year. The New York/New York Agreement pooled funds from the city and the state to create new housing with support services for the mentally ill. Welfare hotels and the barracks shelters began to be phased out, and the homeless population shrank, falling 29 percent between 1988 and 1990. "It's certainly true at the end of the Koch administration there was a great deal of housing and the hotels were in fact closed," says Gretchen. Unfortunately homelessness continues;

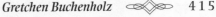

despite increasing economic instability and disparity, the social safety net is still remarkably flimsy and under increasing attack.

Transitional Housing and Day Care

After founding ABC, Buchenholz and Styron met a young, idealistic city official named David Saltzman who worked with them to establish ABC's first home for homeless families. Rosie and Harry's Place was named after two of its major benefactors: Harry Frelinghuysen, who had helped set up the Yorkville Soup Kitchen, and Tom's mother, Rose. It provided apartments for thirteen families and a day care and preschool on the ground floor. Gretchen's vision—that the children would be nurtured and schooled while their parents had a "home plate" from which to seek help and employment—quickly proved successful. The kids at Rosie and Harry's "look different so quickly," she marveled, "it's like a light has been turned on in their faces."

As the welfare hotels closed, ABC moved its early childhood programs to several locations on the east side of Manhattan. In each of these places, Gretchen has ensured that there is an inclusionary policy that incorporates children with special needs into the classroom. One center was All Children's House, whose name was inspired by one of her favorite quotes, by Carl Sandburg: "There is only one child in the world and the child's name is All Children." By 1989 All Children's House occupied a seven-story building off Fifth Avenue in Carnegie Hill, offering a home base to fifty-eight homeless children and thirty-eight children whose parents could afford the annual $7,200. In 1996, with underwriting and inspiration from Frank and Kathy Lee Gifford, Buchenholz opened Cassity's Place on East Eighty-sixth Street, which still provides day care to over one hundred children in need. Gerri Davis, the nineteen-year-old mother of two-year-old Ruben, explained, "Since Ruben went to day care, I feel he's more talkative. He runs his mouth all day—he's more open. He likes going. When I tell him the bus is going to leave, he puts his clothes on faster." As in all ABC programs, the children never have to say good-bye. When they move on to elementary and high school, they are invited to come back to ABC's after-school programs. "We hang with the child for the long haul," Gretchen says.

Gretchen often speaks of the richness of her life, and watching her with small children, it's easy to see what she means. Her face lights up; she treats each child completely as her equal, relishing their total honesty and vulnerability. Working from an office in one of ABC's early childhood centers, she takes a break to greet by name each of the tiny kids tumbling in off the bus, social workers clutching their hands and wiping their noses. Her office is welcoming too, with a big bowl of fruit on the mantel and a bigger stash of candy in the drawer. There is a rocking horse in case a child wants to ride, and she's perfectly happy to ride it herself, if that will make a child smile. The walls are covered with family photos—graduates of Merricat's nursery school, formerly homeless teenagers beaming from their high school snapshots, the Christmas cards of major benefactors, photos of foster kids reuniting with their birth parents.

Gretchen's work at ABC has been effective on a national scale because it has resulted in replicable models. Even though she is focused on the families in just one poor neighborhood—or perhaps because of that—Gretchen designs programs and services that have been used in cities all over the country. Says Marian Wright Edelman, "Gretchen and ABC have had an impact on thousands of lives through their direct services to children and families and also by designing their programs to serve as models for centers and services across the country that learn from them and develop similar or identical programs in their communities." As Gretchen herself put it, "Since [ABC] helps only a tiny fraction of the children in need" in the United States, "its projects ultimately are most useful as models of cost-effective programs."

David Saltzman also believes that the cost-effectiveness of model programs has been one of Gretchen's greatest—and least recognized—achievements. Rosie and Harry's Place "got people into independent housing cheaper, faster [than other programs] and it included supportive services," he explained. The program became a model for transitional housing for homeless families, now known as "tier two" housing. Supportive transitional housing, such as that provided at Rosie and Harry's, is now a standard and effective method of addressing homelessness. ABC's innovative use of Housing Opportunities for Persons With AIDS (HOPWA) funds, as demonstrated in ABC's Jamie Rose House, has also been replicated across the country. As a result, the reality for homeless families became safer and more hopeful at less cost to the taxpayers.

In this case, as in many others, Gretchen's ability to be both firm and gentle was critical to making progress. As David Dinkins puts it, "She is such a good person who believes so deeply that if one were to disagree

Gretchen at the 1996 ribbon-cutting ceremony for Cassidy's Place, which opened with generous support from the Gifford family. She is seated between Mayor Rudolph Giuliani and former mayor David Dinkins who are politically disparate but, as Gretchen teased after the ceremonial songs, both terrible singers. (courtesy Gretchen Buchenholz)

with her, they wouldn't doubt her sincerity and conviction. She conveys her point not by shouting or pounding on the table but by being persistent. And she never lets controversy or adverse opinions stop her."

Boarder Babies

Just as the homelessness crisis began to abate, American cities were hit with two epidemics that had devastating effects on children: crack and AIDS.

Crack first arrived in America's biggest cities in the early 1980s. As addiction rates among women grew, there were widespread reports of increased child neglect and abuse, abandoned babies, and the trading of (often unprotected) sex for crack. In New York, the number of babies born with cocaine in their system doubled within a year—from 407 in a six-month period in 1985, to 895 in the equivalent period in 1986. All too often their mothers abandoned them in the hospital and so, with a shortage of foster homes, the babies were left in bleak hospital cribs with no one to regularly hold, touch, and nurture them.

"It was horrible," Gretchen recalled. "When babies were big enough to stand up, they would put tops on the cribs, make them into cages. A healthy baby, treated like that, would never learn to trust or love anyone. They would lose the capacity. It was hard for the bureaucracy to change. They didn't understand the crack epidemic. They would leave babies in hospitals and think they had solved the problem. No one cared. There were babies with no names."

As with the welfare hotels, the city had a system that was both expensive and inhumane. On December 12, 1986, the *New York Times* reported that thousands of families had offered homes for the boarder babies but that no serious effort had been made to match the babies with prospective parents, in part because of red tape, in part because of a desire to match children with people of their own race. About 75 percent of boarder babies were black, and about 15 percent were Hispanic. Gretchen said, "We have gotten hundreds of calls from people who have been turned away on the telephones or have been told there are no babies or that because [the prospective adopters] are white [and the babies are black or Latino] they can't have them, regardless of the pain it has caused the babies." On February 8, 1987, the *New York Times* reported, "the number of boarder babies in the city may be far more than previous counts of 170."

Gretchen, not afraid to ruffle feathers and butt heads, was once again a critical force for change, speaking directly and starkly to those in power. "Unless the city makes children a priority, the problem is going to get worse," she said at a press conference. She went on to question whether the city's Special Services for Children, with a $410 million budget and 3,744 employees, had the "competence and willingness to care for the children." David Saltzman recalls, "It was costing a million dollars a year and it was cruel. Gretchen was the one who went in and got every one of those kids a home and changed the system and now there are no more boarder babies."

It was not an easy task. In December 1987, after publicity and persuasion failed, ABC brought a lawsuit to force the city to make immediate family placement a priority. "It's cruel and foolish to spend this money to cause harm to babies," Gretchen asserted. The money would be better spent on "an aggressive campaign to recruit foster parents and to increase the rates for foster families." Foster care stipends ranged from about $288 to $420 per month, depending on the age and needs of the child. By March 1988 the city had worked out a settlement

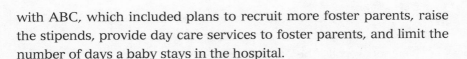

with ABC, which included plans to recruit more foster parents, raise the stipends, provide day care services to foster parents, and limit the number of days a baby stays in the hospital.

Marian Wright Edelman described the results:

> Now social workers begin immediately to work with troubled mothers to see if city or private support can help them take their babies home or allow relatives to care for them, or, if the babies cannot go to families, they are placed within seven days of medical readiness in a foster or pre-adoptive home. Though the law specifies no longer than a seven-day stay, Gretchen is proud of the collaborative efforts of social services across the state which have brought the average stay down to three days.

ABC not only eliminated boarder baby warehousing in New York but also provided technical assistance to advocate groups around the country, which meant that in forty-eight states, similar policies were eliminated without litigation.

The only exception was New Jersey. Ten years after ABC's lawsuit, New Jersey was the only state where the phenomenon of boarder babies persisted, with over seven hundred babies referred to child welfare offices every year, and an average of fifty-four healthy babies in hospitals awaiting placement every month. Gretchen filed suit again, asking the federal courts to force the state government to move babies immediately into foster care, if a return to their biological families was not appropriate. "Warehousing babies, keeping them from the love and nurturing of a primary care-giver, inflicts irreparable damage on them that costs the child and society for the whole lifetime of these babies," Gretchen argued once again. "The hospitals are not the villains here. The hospitals are trying to do something that is impossible, and that is to love babies and be a family. This is an unwillingness, on behalf of the state, to recognize the gravity and urgency of this problem." In speeches and interviews, in meetings with officials and politicians, she stressed the fact that no one benefited from this policy. "These babies are voiceless," Buchenholz said. "I hope that the state will implement a system and really will stop this cruel and expensive practice that really is an embarrassment to the citizens of New Jersey." On December 21, 1996, New Jersey agreed, under a consent decree, to implement a policy of quickly finding homes for the boarder babies, with ABC as a monitor of the process.

Gretchen recalls the "tremendous feeling of urgency" that propelled her to rescue the boarder babies and also to open another program, Variety House, where people were trained in how to care for children with special needs. She came and held and rocked many of the babies herself and took pleasure in showing others how to do the same. "We have a little boy in that crib," she explained in a 1991 documentary by the Robin Hood Foundation, "who is going to be a year old, who spent almost eleven months virtually encaged—the only mother he knew was a nipple wrapped in a rag—and here he has gained two pounds, he knows us, and we are going to find him a family because that is what every baby, every child, needs and ought to have."

It's worth noting that the media's most alarmist predictions about "crack babies" never came true. In 1985, days after a limited and preliminary study on the effects of prenatal cocaine exposure, CBS News ran a story featuring a social worker predicting that a crack-exposed baby in her care would be severely retarded and "barely be able to dress herself." Very quickly, "crack babies" became a staple of print punditry and TV tabloids. The *Columbia Journalism Review* reports that by 1987, the press had run more than a thousand articles on the subject. On one hand, these infants were innocent, "blighted by chemical exposure in the womb," or "the tiniest victims." On the other hand, they also were a looming catastrophe since, according to one columnist, crack exposure "interfer[ed] with the core of what it is to be human." Commentator Charles Krauthammer warned, "A cohort of babies is now being born whose future is closed to them from day one. Theirs will be a life of certain suffering, of probable deviance, of permanent inferiority. At best, a menial life of severe deprivation. And all this is biologically determined from birth."

In response, several states began filing charges against mothers after their infants tested positive for cocaine exposure at birth. A nonprofit organization called CRACK (Children Requiring a Caring Kommunity) paid mothers with a history of drug abuse so that they could be sterilized. Schools dreaded the coming onslaught of crack children who, with their inborn mental and emotional difficulties, were predicted to cost educational systems anywhere from $42 to $352 million. The fear and contempt trickled down to the students themselves.

The *CJR* article describes the experience of one boy whose parents were involved with crack:

> It started in fourth grade when his teacher asked him to read aloud. Antwuan stammered, then went silent. "He can't read because he's a crack baby," jeered a classmate. In the cafeteria that day no one would sit near him. The kids pointed and chanted, "crack baby, crack baby." Antwuan sat sipping his milk and staring down at his tray. After that, the taunting never stopped.[2]

It is this dehumanizing treatment that Gretchen and ABC sought to prevent. In fact, as documented in a 2001 report in the *Journal of the American Medical Association*, babies with prenatal cocaine exposure can grow up to be healthy, thriving children. The key factor for success is a support system to help overcome an environment of neglect, deprivation, and abuse, exactly what Gretchen provided.

HIV Testing of Newborns

It was through her work with sick and special needs babies that Gretchen took on the most controversial fight of her career—HIV testing of newborns. In the early nineties, New York tested every newborn for HIV infection, but the results weren't revealed to anyone. This "blind" test was simply an epidemiological tool, a way to track the spread of HIV. As a result, state officials knew how many babies were born HIV positive, but unless the mother chose to find out for herself, no one knew who they were.

Blind testing wasn't much of a controversy as long as there were no truly effective treatments for AIDS. But as research advanced and treatments improved, the knowledge of a newborn's HIV status could mean the difference between a short, painful life and a chance

---

[2] Antwuan left school in fourth grade and got involved in the drug trade. His parents soon lost custody of him. While in foster care, Antwuan returned to school and in the fall of 2004, was studying journalism at LaGuardia Community College and writing for *Respect*, a magazine produced by and for children in the foster care system. He helped produce a special issue of the magazine, "Crack Babies—All Grown Up," in which these adolescents and young adults described their experiences and successes.

at a happy childhood. The results of other mandatory tests, such as sickle cell anemia and syphilis, were automatically revealed to the doctor and patient, but the results of the HIV test stayed confidential. The rationale was that AIDS was so stigmatized that it was crucial to keep a diagnosis completely private.

At ABC Gretchen watched children sicken and die without their mothers or caregivers knowing that they were HIV positive. For example, a little girl named Marsha T. was born to an intravenous drug user and immediately placed in foster care. Although she had been tested for HIV at birth, no one was told that she was HIV positive. Her foster parents faced legal obstacles when they sought an HIV test because of the laws of confidentiality meant to protect Marsha's birth mother. Starting at two months old, Marsha developed several infections and was eventually hospitalized. Finally she was given an unblind test that revealed she was HIV positive, prompting her foster parents to start her on drug treatment immediately. Marsha survived but in the months she was untreated, the infection ravaged her system and caused serious developmental delays.

For Gretchen, who has based her life's work on doing whatever is possible to help these children, it was a singular hell to watch the tragedy of children's HIV infections compounded by the tragedy that they suffered and died without available medications that could have helped them. The emotional pain of seeing children like Marsha suffer fueled her particularly grueling fight against blind testing.

ABC's original complaint was prepared against Governor Mario Cuomo and his commissioners but never filed because its research and analysis convinced Cuomo to issue emergency regulations covering testing of children in foster care. Administration officials used their power of emergency revision to streamline procedures to allow the testing after good-faith efforts to locate a parent or legal guardian, and extended the testing period beyond age two to a "capacity to consent" on the part of the child. The new guidelines also included adoption of the same risk factors that indicated an HIV test for adults. However, when George Pataki took office, he suspended all previous emergency regulations, so on March 14, 1995, ABC filed suit on behalf of all New York children with HIV. The suit demanded routine, unblinded HIV testing of all newborns and appropriate treatment and counseling for HIV-positive children, their mothers, and their caregivers. "We are looking to identify children and get them preventative treatment to enable them to live whole child-hoods," Gretchen explained. The lawsuit called for a mandatory test within 30 days of birth, with the results revealed to the mother and the doctor, but no one else.

Gretchen's stance put her in opposition to many groups that might once have been allies, including the ACLU and the HIV Law Project, which both filed briefs on behalf of the state. Their rationale was that the mother's right to privacy precluded revealing her baby's HIV status unless the mother wanted to know her own status. In the early days, most newborns who tested positive did so only because of antibodies from the mother that crossed the placenta: about three-fourths of the babies themselves never developed HIV. There were also concerns that revealing the mother's status might cause her to lose custody or work or housing, and might drive her away from the social services that might otherwise help them. The real solution, according to this point of view, was to counsel these mothers and advise them to choose volun-tary testing.

This approach ignored two factors. The babies who were truly pos-itive—like Marsha—lost precious time before beginning treatment, and since 1991 a test had existed to determine the baby's HIV status sepa-rately from the mother's. Although a positive result would still indicate the mother's status, there was no longer the risk of a false positive.

Gretchen was frustrated by the infighting, the fact that the people whom she'd expected to be allies had become enemies instead. On tele-vision, she argued, "Everyone agrees that we should have good pre-natal care and counseling. But counseling has been a terrible failure in this state. We find that mothers find out anyway, and they usually find out when their child is stricken by an opportunistic illness (or a num-ber of them) and they are already too sick to treat. And that is when the mother finds out, and she is often furious, and they didn't even know they had a risk factor. She feels angry, guilty, helpless, and often furious. We need to look with immense respect at mothers with HIV. It's hard to hear this info and hard to hear it at birth, but I think it is worth it."

After Gretchen became the public spokesperson for unblinding the test, she was deluged with antagonism from AIDS activists. One flier at-tacked "Buchenholtz [sic], who presumptuously bills herself as the guardian ad litum for all the infant children in the care of New York State" and argued that "the Buchenholtz [sic] lawsuit seeks to force mandatory unblinded testing of all newborns in the state of New York. The intervenors seek to persuade the court that the issue is not as simply [sic] as it has been framed. The mandatory testing of newborns actually translates to the testing of pregnant women without their consent." On Tuesday, April 14, 1995, activists staged a rally to announce their opposition to the lawsuit. Many held signs saying "Stop Gretchen," and there was even one that said "Kill Gretchen." She received threatening phone calls and letters. It was the most harrowing time of her life, and all the while, "we were burying these children. They were dying in our arms. I was with the mothers at their funerals, and they didn't want this either."

While Gretchen and ABC paid for the funerals of the children they knew, there were hundreds more dying around the city. After discovering that poor children were buried on Hart Island by prisoners from Rikers Island, Gretchen obtained heartbreaking footage of hundreds of tiny wooden coffins labeled with numbers, awaiting burial. When ABC created a public service announcement, that footage was included. It's characteristic of Gretchen to confront and expose the very thing most people find too painful to face; because of her, more people began to care.

In September 1995 the state attorney general sought a settlement with ABC that protected confidentiality while also recognizing the necessity of prompt access to treatment and health care for HIV-positive infants and children. The settlement called for a revision of the state's consent form notifying mothers that their children would be tested and offering counseling on the question of whether they would like to know the child's results. Gretchen considered this a "beautiful" compromise, but it was not appreciated by organizations such as the HIV Law Project, Housing Works, and other advocacy groups who continued to demand that test results be kept secret. They assumed that Assemblywoman Nettie Mayersohn of Queens, who filed a bill calling for mandatory disclosure of all testing, had been coordinating with ABC and had been part of the settlement. However, because Mayersohn had not participated in the settlement, she wasn't bound by its terms and successfully reintroduced her bill which, unfortunately, in its final version did not include all the supportive services requested by ABC.

By now, the issue had become a hot one, and Governor Pataki was ready to sign the bill when it passed. Gretchen supported the Mayer-sohn bill, lamenting the loss of badly needed support services but reckoning it was better to get HIV-positive babies treated immediately and continue pushing for improvements. (Like Frances Perkins, Gretchen is a "half-loaf girl.") "Now, hardly anyone questions testing newborns," Gretchen says, "but what's so sad is that we didn't get the counseling and treatment."

At the same time, she also picked another battleground to protect children with HIV: the testing policies within the foster care system. In 1994 New York City alone had 47,000 children in foster care, and a 1993 study showed that 50 to 60 percent of this population was HIV-positive. Given that many of the diseases that killed or damaged children with HIV struck in the first three to six months of life, and the birth mothers were often unreachable, many of these babies still did not get an un-blind test until it was too late. Gretchen planned another lawsuit and began a targeted advocacy campaign. "In the case of foster children," she wrote in one editorial, "the state is breaching its constitutional and regulatory obligations to provide adequate medical care to the children in its care." This time, even the ACLU agreed. "The balancing comes out differently," said its legislative director, "because the state has acquired a right for children in foster care that it doesn't have for all children."

Largely as a result of Gretchen's advocacy efforts, New York State changed its policy and began routine HIV tests on children in foster care. The state agreed to a revised informed consent form for mothers of newborns that would inform them that their children would be tested and would lay out the potential consequences of their choosing not to know the results. In addition, if a mother declined to fill out the consent form at all, and the health care provider suspected that the child might be infected with HIV, he or she could declare a medical emergency and direct that an HIV test be done. As for foster care children, the state developed new regulations that required that all children entering the system be tested within five days. Thousands of HIV-positive children now receive effective treatment that keeps them healthy for years to come. Some of these children come to ABC programs every day, and their smiling faces tell the story better than I possibly can.

Even better news came in January 2005, with reports that AIDS in infants may be on the verge of being eliminated in the United States. Since 1990 the number of United States infants born HIV-positive dropped from approximately 2,000 to just over 200 in 2003. In New York City, the numbers dropped from 321 in 1990 to five in 2003. The actual transfer of the virus from mother to child was blocked by doses of the drug AZT—but the drug was only effective when taken during pregnancy. Until the unblinding Gretchen fought so hard for, too many women were discovering their HIV status only after they'd given birth, if at all. Once newborn testing was mandatory, it was easier to include HIV testing as part of the standard prenatal treatment. According to Dr. Guthrie S. Birkhead, director of the AIDS Institute at the New York State Department of Health, "The newborn testing became a safety net." Dr. Lucia Torian, in charge of HIV surveillance for the city, recalled that despite the suffering of the early nineties, New York's reporting lagged: "It is very hard for us to understand at this point. It felt from the public health point of view, and even from the personal view of the mother, not to be a rational stance."

"City Birds"

Of course there are still tragic, premature deaths among ABC children, caused by a variety of illnesses. Gretchen's philosophy is to honor the children in death and focus on making life joyous for the children still with us.

The playground outside Variety House includes a mural showing green grass, rivers, animals, and pigeons—"city birds," Gretchen explains with a smile. Many of the pigeons are marked with the names of ABC children who have died. Gretchen explained the tradition's start: "A boy named Wilfredo lived here while he was dying. His mother had already died of AIDS. He was a lovely boy. After he died, his father asked if we could bury him here in the playground. I said we couldn't but we would build a memorial to him. But I didn't know how. Then someone came up with the idea of putting his name and dates on one of the pigeons. After that, we did it for other children who died. It's a wonderful image of flying upward, above the earth, free of all pain. We think of this as holy ground."

One of the things I have found inspiring about Gretchen is her ability to endure heartbreaking losses. Having created a refuge for children in the most dire circumstances, some terminally ill, some facing seemingly limitless loss, pain, and need in their families, she must face tragedies. The way she does it seems guided by the "kind providence" that Septima Clark mentioned, that resolute inner calling to do the right thing despite the obvious personal costs. To watch Gretchen sit down every day with groups of children—knowing that among the adorable faces there are those suffering with AIDS, those with severe neurological damage from prenatal exposure to drugs or alcohol, those whose parents are in jail or have committed suicide or are simply, honestly struggling to make it—and to watch her sing songs, play with dolls, ask about their siblings, and really come to love them is astonishing. She claims that it is the generous spirit that emanates from the children themselves—as well as from the professional caregivers hired as teachers and therapists—that gives her strength. "Thee lift me and I'll lift thee and we'll ascend together," reads the Quaker proverb she keeps on the mantel in her office.

Another part of her secret seems to be assigning appropriately huge value to the small moments of progress and happiness. "The kids we start with are often challenged just to make it through, and the families we work with may have hard times for a lifetime," she says. "One thing to remember is that we're looking at success in terms of each child's progress on his or her own terms. Maybe it's standing up and taking a step, breathing more freely, maybe playing on his or her own, eating Cheerios with a spoon. We're not looking at Harvard for every kid. That's not our measure of success. They just deserve a happy childhood."

Asthma

Thirty years after she started Merricat's Castle, twenty-one years after she began her campaign to move homeless families out of welfare hotels, ten years after the HIV testing controversy, Gretchen continues to combine hands-on caregiving and large-scale policy work. She monitors individual ABC cases, manages the organization as a whole, and evaluates how public policies are working. When she feels a growing need and senses a systemic injustice, she resumes her fighting stance, lobbying, speaking out, and, if need be, turning to the justice system. Recently she took on the cause of homeless kids with asthma.

Asthma has become epidemic among poor, urban children, another example of the way social inequities impact health. City officials estimate that as many as 22 percent of children in the city's poorest neighborhoods suffer from asthma. Across the country, the asthma rate among children ages five to fourteen nearly doubled from 1980 to 1993. According to the Center for Children's Health and the Environment at Mount Sinai Medical Center: "Although there remains much to learn about the causes of asthma, it is clear that the increasing severity of the disease in the United States is concentrated in urban centers among children who live in poor conditions." These children are more likely to be exposed to both indoor and outdoor air pollution and less likely to have regular access to health care.

Of course homelessness makes asthma worse and harder to deal with. A 2004 study found that the rate of asthma among homeless children in New York City approached 40 percent—six times the national rate for all children. The homeless children were also more likely to suffer severe asthma attacks and inadequate, sporadic treatment. In turn, lack of ongoing treatment for asthma is linked to higher death rates from the disease. Homeless women show high rates of clinical depression, and depressed mothers are less likely to keep up with the preventive care needed to keep asthma under control.

As Gretchen went about her work with homeless families, bringing them out of shelters and into transitional housing, accepting the children in day care and preschool programs, she started hearing more stories about the debilitating effects of the disease: kids desperately gasping for air, unable to go out or run around. Asthma often put great strain on their bodies and, of course, added another element of fear and uncertainty to their lives.

The thing that made the situation especially hard to tolerate was that Gretchen knew that these kids were entitled to screening and treatment for asthma under federal law, but there seemed to be no way for them to get that care. In fact, the Medicaid Act provides that states receiving federal Medicaid funds must provide "periodic screening, diagnostic and treatment services" of diseases such as asthma for poor children. Gretchen knew one child, Dajour B., who had persistent, severe asthma and was often rushed to the emergency room, but he'd never received the regular, effective treatments that are readily available to more affluent children. When lobbying was not enough to break through the institutional inertia and inequity, ABC sued the city and won. The suit was settled within months and now, as Buchenholz happily notes, "thousands of children suffering from asthma will be properly treated."

Mental Health

Gretchen has shown her exceptional compassion and creativity in many ways, including by being willing to integrate mental health care into ABC's web of interlocking programs at a time when mental health care is still stigmatized and underfunded.[3] In a city where many wealthy people see psychiatrists to work out issues like how to get through the holidays, there is a stark lack of care available for indigent young people, who have a greater likelihood of being severely traumatized or seriously mentally ill. Gretchen, having seen many children with serious psychiatric conditions go without any treatment, felt another approach was needed.

This realization led to one of ABC's newest programs, a mobile mental health team called Fast Break, named after one of Gretchen's favorite basketball plays. She says, "We really believed that if you brought the [mental health] services to the people and didn't make it an added burden in their lives and you made it useful, people would use the services. And we were right. Plain and simple."

Fast Break's child psychiatrists and social workers are trained to go and respond to trauma and crisis, whether in a home, a school, or an arcade in the middle of the night. The team also responds immediately to children grappling with suicides, murders, and abuse of all kinds, in addition to the psychological stress of poverty and homelessness. The program has developed a relationship with local institutions and authorities, so that it receives referrals from both inside and outside ABC's other programs. As a Fast Break staff psychiatrist, Nina Freund, described, "Over the years, we've developed relationships with neighborhood schools. School guidance counselors, in particular, know all about us." In keeping with the philosophy of replicating pro-

---

[3] My mother, who watched her own mother struggle with mental illness, has been on the forefront of the effort to reduce the stigma of mental illness. One of the most exciting moments of the Clinton-Gore administration in our family was when she chaired the first White House conference on mental health, which included debate on measures to achieve parity, meaning equal attention to (and lack of stigma associated with) diseases of the brain and the body.

grams that work, the Fast Break team is collaborating with New York City's Gouverneur Hospital to help develop their own children's mobile mental health care program.

The team has been called on frequently after school shootings and suicides, but nothing else has been on the scale of what they, and the city, faced on September 11, 2001.

9/11/01

As soon as the planes hit the towers, the reality of the attacks began to sink in. Gretchen was one of millions of New Yorkers who watched in horror while frantically checking to make sure her own family was safe. After making sure everyone in the ABC programs also was safe and the situation there was under control, she rounded up medical supplies and bags of ice, gathered a volunteer team, and went downtown. Soon, it became clear that the families of the missing were those most in need of help, kids brought to crisis centers by family members looking for missing loved ones.

Starting Wednesday, September 12, ABC began to set up what became known as a "child space" in every one of the city's family disaster centers. Gretchen gathered toys and materials in English and Spanish to serve as tools for helping children deal with the trauma. She recruited all of ABC's disaster-trained staff and volunteers, past and present, to run the centers, first in the Armory on 27th Street and then at several more sites. "Everyone wanted to help," she recalled. "Every single hour these child care spaces were open from the day after the disaster all the way to the day the centers closed." At first, the child space workers collected DNA from the inside of the kids' cheeks, using a quick swabbing method the volunteers incorporated into a game. As the hope for their relatives' survival dwindled, the families' needs only intensified. For months after the attacks, ABC provided all of the child care at each of the city's assistance centers. During this time ABC developed a special backpack full of toys and tools to help children deal with trauma. Now these backpacks—filled with special dolls, crayons, paper, and "operating instructions" for adults—are ready in case of any disaster, whether on a small scale or a large one.

More than four years later, most still clearly recall everything we learned about the spirit of New Yorkers in the wake of September 11—the grit, the optimism, the can-do determination to overcome tragedy, the simple human compassion. Down at Ground Zero for as long as there was a need, Gretchen is one of so many New Yorkers who embodied that spirit. Once Safe Horizon, a nonprofit organization devoted to victim's services, took over running the assistance centers, ABC continued to provide child care and counseling for the families of the victims. "ABC's role has never been an upfront fancy one," says Gretchen. "We change the diapers. We watch the kids. Play with the kids. Provide what we call therapeutic day care, make a space for them, just like our classrooms. We have tried to make an environment where they could either forget for a while or talk about it or play about it or paint about it or not, in their own time and way. And we have hung in all the way." In September 2005, in the wake of Hurricane Katrina, New York City set up a Disaster Assistance Service Center (DASC) to meet the needs of the evacuees fleeing their devastated homes. Recognizing ABC's experience and expertise, the administration called upon them to set up a Child Space in the DASC. Gretchen led the effort, directing staff and volunteers who created a warm and safe environment for the children who had been through so much.

Gretchen playing with a child in one of ABC's programs. (courtesy Gretchen Buchenholz)

Her Work Continues

I am proud to end this book with stories from the life and work of Gretchen Buchenholz, not only because she is a friend, but because she is at the forefront of the struggle to overcome the effects of some of our worst contemporary scourges—homelessness, the day care crisis, AIDS, drugs, terrorism—and she is striving, as have many women before her, to stand up for those affected by the cruelest circumstances of their time and demand recognition of their human dignity. I have also found that within this daunting effort is a mentality that holds more keys to happiness than meet the eye—a gift for seeing and celebrating small moments of joy, marking tiny increments of progress, and feeling that there is always something we can do to help others.

Gretchen's love of innovation and her determination to fill gaps has made ABC a constantly adaptive, expanding force, one increasingly focused on helping whole families. While day care for young children is the cornerstone, this holistic approach has led to supplementary programs, also designed to be replicable. "No one funding stream covers the needs of families and kids for a whole day so we've blended them." ABC's latest and biggest family center, in Echo Park in East Harlem, is home to three Head Start classrooms, a technology lab for older children, after-school programs, a summer camp, and a baking school[4] for jobless parents of the children. "There is no finer public service than what Gretchen does," says Dinkins. "Her work is where the rubber meets the road, for real."

Gretchen says she draws her strength and vision from the individual children she sees every day. "They are heroic—often against all odds," Gretchen says. "These are children born into a life of terrible pain, suffering, and early death, yet they greet each day as one of potential and the possibility of hope and joy."

---

[4] Baked in the 'Hood enrolls thirty students in each cycle and there are three cycles each year. Roughly ten trainees from each cycle reach graduation, pass the Health Department test, and go on to work at some of New York's best-known restaurants: Bryant Park Grill, Ferrara's, America, City Bakery, BR Guest Restaurants, Greystone Bakery. The job bulletin board outside Baked in the 'Hood is a determinedly hopeful place, covered with typed notices on little white slips listing available jobs at various bakeries and restaurants: "line cook needed," "accepting applications for an assistant pastry chef," "counter cook position available."

Postscript

WHEN I BEGAN THIS PROJECT, I THOUGHT OF IT AS SOMEWHAT
therapeutic—an immersion in the past triumphs of progressive politics.
But as I completed the book I realized that what I had really learned was
less ideological than it was personal. The stories in this book, from Ida B.
Wells-Barnett's legal challenge to segregation to Gretchen Buchenholz's
service to the families of the victims of the attacks on September 11,
demonstrate that one individual can change the course of many people's
lives, that seemingly isolated acts of kindness and courage can ripple
out, as Septima Clark used to say, "like a pebble thrown in a mill pond."

The personal styles of all nine of these women, so critical to their
effectiveness, all lent themselves to grassroots methodology. It was
the constant contact with those they advocated for that grounded
their politics and, in the end, legitimized their work. When Mother
Jones strode into dangerous factories to remove young children from
the assembly line, when Frances Perkins brought legislators face to
face with sweatshop workers, when Septima Clark quietly sat down
and wrote hundreds of letters to her fellow teachers urging them not
to be bullied into resigning their NAACP membership, they were pioneering and consequential public servants. Although I initially focused on lesser known women in order to discover some new faces, I
found another benefit: their stories give insight into how political
movements are built from the ground up, often by people who never
receive credit for their eventual success.

There is an ideological underpinning to these nine stories as well. These heroines were, in essence, seeking to make the United States a more inclusive and just country, and they believed that the government should take a proactive role. As Ida B. Wells-Barnett wrote, "What material benefit is a 'leader' if he does not, to some extent, devote his time, talent and wealth to the alleviation of the poverty and misery, and elevation of his people?" This premise is always under attack from the right, with some drawing lines between people in order to justify civic inaction. The same spirit that animates racism inspires some to marginalize those in need (and their advocates), labeling them unworthy, defective, or treasonous. As strong voices on the political cutting edge, these nine women all felt the sting of ostracism and the truth of Eleanor Roosevelt's observation, "what is to give light must endure the burning."

I was fascinated to see how consistent the tactics of their enemies were: labeling them communists, implying that they were under the sway of others, questioning their sanity, charging that they were un-Amercan. The sentiment, which seems to have flared up in recent years, that patriotism is measured by how strongly one supports the decisions of those in power, has an established and shameful tradition. The stories of these prescient individuals remind us of the importance of honoring dissent. If past is prologue, then the mainstream will be wrong again, and a lonely voice like Alice Hamilton's or Virginia Durr's will be the one that, in the end, rings true.

One of the most inspirational aspects of learning about these women is the knowledge that there are so many others like them, in the present as well as the past. In an age of so much cynicism, there are still people who base their lives on the lesson public health pioneer Alice Hamilton learned from her mother: "There are two kinds of people in life. The ones who say 'Somebody ought to do something about it, but why should it be I?' and those who say 'Somebody must do something about it, then why not I?'" The nine women in *Lighting the Way* kept their eyes and minds open, asking themselves the latter question. My hope for my own children is that they recognize them, celebrate them, and join them.

Endnotes

Ida B. Wells-Barnett

The core biographical sources I relied on were Linda McMurry's biography *To Keep the Waters Troubled* and Wells-Barnett's own writings: her memoir, *Crusade for Justice*, edited by her daughter, Alfreda M. Duster, and *The Memphis Diary of Ida B. Wells*, edited by Miriam DeCosta-Willis. I also relied on two volumes of Wells-Barnett's work, *The Reason Why the Colored American Is Not in the World's Columbian Exposition*, edited by Robert R. Rydell, and *On Lynchings*, with an introduction by Patricia Hill Collins.

1 *We do not believe*: Ida B. Wells, *On Lynchings* (Amherst, NY: Humanity Books, 2002), 154.

1 *One evening in September 1883*: Linda O. McMurry, *To Keep the Waters Troubled: The Life of Ida B. Wells* (Oxford and New York: Oxford Univ. Press, 1998), 24. In *Crusade* only one incident of harassment on a rail car is described and the date is given as May 1884; I've followed McMurry's chronology here because Wells's account apparently was based chiefly on her memory, while McMurry cites court documents.

2 *"He tried to drag me"*: Ida B. Wells-Barnett, *Crusade for Justice: The Autobiography of Ida B. Wells* (Chicago and London: Univ. of Chicago Press, 1970), 18–19.

2 *In 1881, the legislature had passed a law*: McMurry, 27. Her account of the progress of Wells' suit and the legal context appears on 27–29.

3 *roughly equivalent to*: This and all present-day dollar equivalents were arrived at via the *Columbia Journalism Review*'s online Inflation Calculator, developed with the assistance of Professor Robert Sahr of the Oregon State University Political Science Department. The most recent year provided by the calculator is 2002. http://www.cjr.org/tools/inflation/index.asp

3 *The* Memphis Daily Appeal: quoted in *Crusade,* 19.

3 *"alike in every respect"*: McMurry, 29.

3 *In 1892 a cobbler named Homer Plessy*: The material on *Plessy v. Ferguson* is taken from *Landmark Cases*, a joint project of Street Law and the Supreme Court Historical Society, http://www.landmark-cases.org/plessy/home.html (accessed 28 February 2005). In the 1896 Supreme Court decision, the majority opinion maintained: "A statute which implies merely a legal distinction between the white and colored races—a distinction which is founded in the color of the two races, and which must always exist so long as white men are distinguished from the other race by color—has no tendency to destroy the legal equality of the two races. . . ." There was one dissenting vote, from Justice John Harlan, who said—with great foresight—"In my opinion, the judgment this day rendered will, in time, prove to be quite as pernicious as the decision made by this tribunal in the Dred Scott case. . . . The present decision, it may well be apprehended, will not only stimulate aggressions, more or less brutal and irritating, upon the admitted rights of colored citizens, but will encourage the belief that it is possible, by means of state enactments, to defeat the beneficent purposes which the people of the United States had in view when they adopted the recent amendments of the Constitution." The Southern states eagerly instituted separate accommodations of all kinds. [The quotations are from *History Matters*, a project of the American Social History Project/Center for Media and Learning (City University of New York, Graduate Center) and the Center for History and New Media (George Mason University), 2002. Harlan's opinion: http://historymatters.gmu.edu/d/5484. The majority opinion: http://historymatters.gmu.edu/d/5485/ (both accessed 28 February 2005).]

4 *"Went to see [Greer]"*: Ida B. Wells, *The Memphis Diary of Ida B. Wells: An Intimate Portrait of the Activist as a Young Woman* (Boston: Beacon Press, 1995), 140

4 Family Roots: The information on Wells' childhood comes from McMurry, 3–17, and *Crusade*, 8–16.

5 *"The only thing I remember"*: *Crusade*, 9–10

6 *"I do not remember when or where"*: *Crusade*, 9

6 *Shaw University*: Founded in 1866 by the Freedmen's Aid Society of the Methodist Episcopal Church and renamed Rust College in 1882, the school is still in operation as an accredited four-year liberal arts school, the oldest Historical Black College in the state. "About Rust," *The Official Rust College Web Site*, http://www.rustcollege.edu/about .html (accessed 1 March 2005)

6 Yellow Fever: Much of the information on the disease and the 1878 epidemic is drawn from *Yellow Fever and Public Health in the New South* by John Ellis (Lexington, KY: The Univ. Press of Kentucky, 1992), "Yellow Fever: Scourge of the South" by JoAnn Carrigan, in *Disease and Distinctiveness in the American South*, ed. Todd L. Savitt and James Harvey Young (Knoxville, TN: The Univ. of Tennessee Press, 1988), as well as several uncollected articles.

6 *The "fomite theory" held*: This and the account of the medical advances against yellow fever are taken from "Biography of Major Walter Reed," *Walter Reed Army Medical Center Online Visitors Center*, 21 December 2004. http://www.wramc.amedd.army.mil./welcome/history/ index1.htm (accessed 28 February 2005)

8 *about 20,000 people left*: Ellis, 46.

8 *"It was a freight train."*: *Crusade*, 12.

9 *"I took the examination"*: *Crusade*, 16.

9 *an astonishing 450 percent increase*: McMurray, 18.

9 *"thousands of lazy negro men and women"*: Leon F. Litwack, *Been in the Storm So Long: The Aftermath of Slavery* (New York: Vintage Books, 1980), 314.

9 *In August 1865 Tennessee governor William G. Brownlow proclaimed*: McMurry, 20.

10 *One of the worst riots*: McMurry, 20; Litwack, 281; Kenneth W. Goings and Gerald L. Smith, "Duty of the Hour," in *Trial and Triumph: Essays in Tennessee's African American History*, ed. Carroll Van West (Knoxville, TN: The Univ. of Tennessee Press, 2002), 230–231.

10 *"The late riots in our city"*: Alrutheus A. Taylor, *The Negro in Tennessee, 1865–1880*, quoted in Litwack, 281.

10 *"I will not begin"*: *Memphis Diary*, 37.

10 *"[he] came home with me"*: *Memphis Diary*, 74.

11 *"the confinement and monotony"*: *Crusade*, 31.

11 *This term originated in the late 1820s*: There is a great deal of information available online detailing not only the origins of the term "Jim Crow" but also the nature of this systematic humiliation and control. One of the most comprehensive sites is *The History of Jim Crow*, an educational resource linked to the documentary *The Rise and Fall of Jim Crow* offering a wealth of primary documents, interviews, photographs, historical essays and analysis. The home page is: http://www.jimcrowhistory.org/home.htm. Another excellent resource is the Web site of the Jim Crow Museum of Racist Memorabilia at Ferris State University, http://www.ferris.edu/news/jimcrow/menu .htm, which focuses on the ways African Americans were, and are, presented in advertising, cartoons, collectibles, and other cultural artifacts. The images on the site are given context through historical and analytical essays.

11 *"sluggish nature"*: *Memphis Diary*, 55.

11 *"It reads very well"*: *Memphis Diary*, 23.

11 *"A glance at all my 'brilliant?' productions"*: *Memphis Diary*, 100.

13 *"The* Sun *unhesitatingly accepts"*: *Memphis Diary*, 52.

13 *"the pleasant-faced, modest Miss Ida Wells"*: quoted in Mc-Murray, 99.

13 *"She has become famous"*: quoted in *Crusade*, 33.

13 *Fortune was a prominent black journalist*: "T. Thomas Fortune," *Notable Black American Men* (Gale Research, 1998), reproduced in *Biography Resource Center* (Farmington Hills, MI: Thomson Gale, 2005) http://galenet.galegroup.com/servlet/BioRC (accessed 6 March 2005).

13 *"My curiosity is satisfied"*: *Memphis Diary*, 52

14 *"What material benefit"*: originally published 12 September 1885 in *Living Way*, reprinted in *Memphis Diary*, 178.

14 *"I had an instinctive feeling"*: *Memphis Diary*, 23.

14 *"it is written in the faces"*: On Lynchings, 63.

15 *"The facts were brought out"*: *Memphis Diary*, 46.

15 *"The miscegenation laws"*: On Lynchings, 31.

15 *"double-consciousness"*: W. E. B. Du Bois, *The Souls of Black Folk* (New York: Vintage, 1990), 16.

15 *The rumors intensified*: *Memphis Diary*, 113.

15 *"I have been so long misrepresented"*: *Memphis Diary*, 114.

16 *"none [of the accusations] sting so deeply"*: originally published 1 January 1887 in *New York Freeman* (later renamed the *New York Age*), reprinted in *Memphis Diary*, 185.

16 *On a trip to Natchez, Mississippi*: *Crusade*, 43–44.

16 *"The correspondence I had built up"*: *Crusade,* 31.

16 *"I felt that some protest should be made"*: *Crusade,* 36.

17 The People's Grocery Lynchings: This incident is recounted in *Crusade,* 47–52, and McMurry, 130–149.

18 *"the mob took possession"*: *Crusade,* 51.

19 *"The only reason"*: *On Lynchings,* 14.

19 *No one was punished*: *On Lynchings,* 50; McMurry, 135.

19 *"This is what opened my eyes"*: *Crusade,* 64.

19 *While there's some dispute*: "Lynch Law." *The American Heritage Dictionary of the English Language,* 4th ed. (Boston: Houghton Mifflin, 2000), www.bartleby.com/61/, and the *Online Etymology Dictionary,* http://www.etymonline.com/index.php?term=lynch (both accessed 12 March 2005).

19 *Lynching became a routine business*: Much of the historical information on lynching in the post-Reconstruction South comes from Leon Litwack's introduction to *Without Sanctuary: Lynching Photography in America,* ed. James Allen (Santa Fe, NM: Twin Palms Publishers, 2000), 8–37. Litwack's earlier work, *Been in the Storm So Long,* also details on this dark period.

19 *Officially known as the Bureau of Refugees, Freedmen, and Abandoned Lands*: Elaine C. Everly, "Freedmen's Bureau Records: An Overview," *Federal Records and African American History* (Summer 1997, Vol. 29, No. 2), the National Archives and Records Administration, http://www.archives.gov/publications/prologue/summer_1997_freedmens_bureau_records.html (accessed 14 April 2005).

19 *In 1901, W. E. B. DuBois wrote an article*: W. E. B. Du Bois, "The Freedmen's Bureau," *Atlantic Monthly,* March 1901, vol. 87, issue 521.

19 *One Kentucky officer*: Litwack, 277.

20 *In Alabama, a young black minister*: Litwack, 279.

20 *"I went into that cellblock"*: *Without Sanctuary,* 21.

20 *"Our American Christians"*: *Crusade,* 154.

21 *the chilling and important book* Without Sanctuary: For four weeks in early 2000, the Roth Horowitz Gallery in New York hosted an exhibition called *Without Sanctuary*, containing dozens of these photographs. To meet the extraordinary interest in the show, *Without Sanctuary* then moved to the New-York Historical Society, where it drew over 50,000 visitors; it attracted similar crowds at other venues. The photographs are now at Emory University on a long-term loan. The dealer who assembled the images, James Allen, said, "It's important that people don't see these as a collectible. They really belong to the

nation, so that this enters into the vocabulary of the discussion about race." Photographs from the exhibition, as well as more from Allen's collection, were published in *Without Sanctuary*, along with essays by historian Leon Litwack, writer and critic Hilton Als, and Congressman John Lewis. The photographs themselves are presented without commentary. (Allen quote from Robin Pogrebin, "A Quest for Photographs He Could Barely Look At," *New York Times*, 13 January 2000.)

21 *"This is the way we do things here"*: *Without Sanctuary*, 11.

21 *"The lynching of three Negro scoundrels"*: quoted in *On Lynchings*, 42.

22 *"I felt that one had better"*: *Crusade*, 62.

22 *"The city of Memphis has demonstrated"*: *Crusade*, 52.

23 they had *"killed the goose"*: *Crusade*, 64.

23 *"Eight negroes lynched"*: *On Lynchings*, 29.

23 *"The fact that a black scoundrel"*: quoted in *On Lynchings*, 30.

23 *"to tie the wretch"*: *Ibid.*

24 *"We desire to put on record"*: Kenneth W. Goings and Gerald L. Smith, "Duty of the Hour: African American Communities in Memphis, 1862–1923." In *Trial and Triumph: Essays in Tennessee's African American History*, edited by Carroll Van West (Knoxville, TN: The Univ. of Tennessee Press, 2002), 235. I found several essays in this book invaluable in illuminating the Memphis of Ida B. Wells's time.

24 *"she has shaken this country"*: *On Lynching*, 94.

24 *"There is no word equal to it"*: *On Lynchings*, 55.

25 *conducted her own investigations*: One lynching Wells investigated in depth was that of Sam Hose, who worked for a Georgia planter named Alfred Cranford. Hose went to Cranford's home to ask for payment of back wages and permission to visit his sick mother. The two men quarreled, and when Cranford reached for a pistol, Hose flung an axe, killing Cranford instantly. Soon the story evolved into a tale that Hose had raped Mrs. Cranford in a pool of blood oozing from her husband's dying body and had then chopped him to bits. On Sunday afternoon, April 23, 1899, two thousand white Georgians traveled to a field near the town of Newman to witness or partake in his killing. The mob stripped him, chained him to a tree, put kerosene soaked wood around him and, before lighting the fire, chopped off his ears, fingers and genitals and skinned his face. One reporter noted that hundreds were looking on in "unfeigned satisfaction" as the flames consumed him. He was heard to cry out "Oh my God! Oh Jesus!" Even after the fire had died, people came to slice out body parts for keep-

sakes. One man reportedly took a piece of his heart to deliver to the Governor of Georgia who officially declared that Hose's crime had been "the most diabolical in the annals of crime." At the foot of the tree, the crowd placed a sign that said "We must protect our Southern women." The white press reportedly all these details, concluding the Hose was "a monster in human form." Wells conducted her own investigation, citing the accounts in white newspapers and doing interviews on her own. Her findings, which were later confirmed by an independent white detective, were that the two men had quarreled and Hose had killed Cranford in self-defense. According to Mrs. Cranford herself, Hose then fled the scene immediately. He never entered the house, much less assaulted her. [*Without Sanctuary*, 10]

25 *In February of 1818 Frederick Bailey*: Summary from Ted Widmer, *Martin Van Buren: The American Presidents Series*, Arthur M. Schlesinger Jr., general editor (New York: Times Books, 2005); "Frederick Douglass," *Notable Black American Men* (New York: Gale Research, 1998).

25 *"The big burly brute"*: *Crusade*, 65.

25 *"The above is a rough sketch"*: "Seay J. Miller," *Born in the Wake of Freedom*: *John H. Miller, Jr., and the* Richmond Planet, Library of Virginia exhibition, 6 October 2004, http://www.lva.lib.va.us/whoweare/exhibits/mitchell/miller.htm (accessed 28 February 2005).

26 *"awakening of the public conscience"*: *On Lynchings*, 57.

26 *"No other civilized nation"*: *On Lynchings*, 64.

27 *"in a plain, unvarnished, connected way"*: *On Lynchings*, 154.

27 *"Brave woman!"*: *On Lynchings*, 28.

27 *"Lee Walker, colored man"*: *On Lynchings*, 106.

28 *she spoke "for two hours"*: McMurry, 226.

28 *"she is spoken of"*: *Woman's Tribune*, 12 November 1892.

28 *"She spoke with singular refinement"*: *Crusade*, 146.

28 *"Miss Wells is a quiet, demure-looking"*: "She Pleads for Her Race," *New York Tribune*, 30 July 1894.

28 *A writer for the* Memphis Daily Commercial: quoted in McMurry, 214.

28 *"The moment the colored criminal"*: *New York Sun*, quoted in "As to Ida B. Wells," *Washington Post*, 2 August 1894, p. 4.

29 *"exaggerations which she has"*: "Not a Nation of Lynchers," *Washington Post*, 31 May 1893.

29 *Ida "had made her tour"*: "As to Ida B. Wells," *Washington Post*, 2 August 1894.

29 *"Miss Ida B. Wells, a mulatress"*: *New York Times*, 27 July 1894.

29 *"soft pedal on charges"*: *Crusade*, 220.

30 *"The colored race multiplies"*: quoted in *Crusade*, 151–152.

30 *Linda McMurry posits*: McMurry, 212.

31 the White City: Historian Robert Rydell, in his introduction to the reprint of the pamphlet Wells produced, *The Reason Why the Colored American Is Not In the World's Columbian Exposition: The Afro-American's Contribution to Columbian Literature* (Chicago: Univ. of Illinois Press, 1999), details the issues surrounding the pamphlet's original publication. "How Did African-American Women Define Their Citizenship at the Chicago World's Fair in 1893?" is one of many remarkable projects contained in *Women and Social Movements in the United States, 1600–2000*, developed by the Center for the Historical Study of Women and Gender at the State University of New York at Binghamton. The projects are available electronically at most libraries and by subscription. For more information, go the center's home page at http://chswg.binghamton.edu/index.htm. Ida herself discusses producing the pamphlet in *Crusade*, 115–120.

31 *a former slave named Nancy Green*: Rydell, xvi.

31 *One hundred seven years later*: "The Advertising Century: Top 10 Advertising Icons of the Century," edited by David Klein and Scott Donaton, *Advertising Age*/Crain Communications, http://www.adage.com/century/ad_icons.html, (28 February 2005).

32 *"Men talk of the Negro problem"*: Wolfgang Mieder, *No Struggle, No Protest: Frederick Douglass and His Proverbial Rhetoric for Civil Rights* (New York: Peter Lang Publishing Co., 2001), 347.

32 *"straight out to the fair"*: *Crusade*, 116.

33 *"echoes from that little volume"*: *Crusade*, 117.

33 *"gives Ferd her skirts"*: McMurry, 239.

34 *"I had not entered into the bonds"*: *Crusade*, 251.

34 *"realized what a wonderful place"*: Ibid.

34 *"I honestly believe"*: *Crusade*, 244.

34 *"all this public work was given up"*: *Crusade*, 250

34 *In 1895 Anthony attended a lecture*: *Crusade*, 227; "Color Line in the North," *Washington Post*, 9 April 1895; Lynn Scherr, *Failure Is Impossible: Susan B. Anthony in Her Own Words* (New York: Times Books, 1995), 42.

35 *Anthony promptly fired*: *Crusade*, 229.

35 *"I know of no one"*: *Crusade*, 255.

35 *The Fifteenth Amendment*: Steve Mount, *The U.S. Constitution*

Online, 13 September 2004, http://www.usconstitution.net/constam-notes.html#Am15 (accessed 28 February 2005).

35 *In 1898 these efforts*: Linda T. Wynn, "Toward a Perfect Democracy: The Struggle of African Americans in Fayette County to Fulfill the Unfulfilled Right of the Franchise." In *Trial and Triumph: Essays in Tennessee's African American History*, 395.

35 *"Neither [women or black men] have a claim"*: Scher, 41.

35 *"I had been with [Anthony] for several days"*: Crusade, 230.

36 *"Vicariously, she always wanted me to be a lawyer"*: Memphis Diary, 197.

36 *a "humorous record called"*: Memphis Diary, 198.

36 *"Even when there was no segregation"*: Memphis Diary, 196.

36 *"Mother was very displeased"*: Memphis Diary, 194.

37 *A prisoner under the charge of*: Crusade, 309.

37 *"It was not very convenient"*: Crusade, 311.

37 *"an increase of lynchings"*: Crusade, 317.

37 *"I was quite surprised"*: Crusade, 318.

38 *"endeavor[ing] to make me see"*: Crusade, 229.

38 *"besetting sin"*: Crusade, 286.

38 *"After looking us over"*: Crusade, 331.

39 *"We saw, as perhaps never before"*: Crusade, 280–281.

40 *"if you want to raise money in New York"*: McMurry, 279.

41 *the "powerful personalities"*: McMurry, 282.

41 *"Mother was with W. E. B. Du Bois"*: Memphis Diary, 197.

42 *"I did a foolish thing"*: Crusade, 281.

42 *In 1910 she joined*: McMurry, 287.

42 *"All through my childhood"*: McMurry, 300.

43 *The worst such incident*: Crusade, 383–395; McMurry, 314.

43 *"efforts to terrorize Negroes"*: Crusade, 389.

43 *A full-scale attack*: McMurry, 315.

43 *"had Bundy done what they charged him with"*: Crusade, 391.

44 *stating "that after repeated [requests] to officials"*: McMurry, 316.

44 *the material was "being used to stir up"*: McMurry, 317.

44 *In Chicago a riot was set off*: McMurry, 326. McMurry notes, "The Chicago riot was apparently painful for Wells-Barnett, who devoted a mere three and a half pages of her autobiography to the event," while entire chapters were devoted to her experiences in Cairo, East Saint Louis, and elsewhere.

44 *the massacre near Elaine, Arkansas*: There's little documentary record from the time, so there's confusion attached to every aspect of

the incident, including the name itself. The initial shooting took place at Hoop Spur and involved county law officers based in Helena, but most of the violence took place in and near the town of Elaine. *Crusade,* 397–404; McMurray, 327–329. Grif Stockley provides a detailed account of the riots and their aftermath in *Blood in Their Eyes: The Elaine Race Massacres of 1919* (Fayetteville, AK: Univ. of Arkansas Press, 2001).

45 *"Nightriding" refers to*: "nightriding, n.," the *Oxford English Dictionary*, 2nd ed., 1989. OED Online. Oxford University Press. http://dictionary.oed.com/cgi/entry/00184753 (accessed 14 April 2005).

46 *The NAACP hired Atlanta native Walter White*: Summarized from Gilbert Jonas, *Freedom's Sword: The NAACP and the Struggle against Racism in America, 1909–1969* (New York and London: Routledge, 2005).

46 *it was "already doing"*: Crusade, 401.

46 *"saw only a group"*: Crusade, 401.

47 *"You have talked and sung"*: Crusade, 402.

48 *credited her with "starting this whole movement"*: Ibid.

48 *"made a cool million"*: quoted in Stockley, 52.

48 *By all accounts*: summary from Stockley.

48 *"When my family came in"*: Crusade, 404.

49 *"A young woman recently asked me"*: Crusade, 3.

50 *"the awakening of the conscience"*: McMurry, 338.

Mother Jones

Elliot Gorn's biography, *Mother Jones: The Most Dangerous Woman in America,* was invaluable, as were Edward M. Steel's collections of Mother Jones's work, *The Correspondence of Mother Jones* and *The Speeches and Writings of Mother Jones,* and his account of her 1913 trial, *The Court-Martial of Mother Jones.* I also relied on the third Kerr edition of *The Autobiography of Mother Jones* and its detailed introduction by Fred Thompson. In writing about the Children's March, Stephen Currie's young-adult book *We Have Marched Together: The Working Children's Crusade* provided a good summary and interesting details.

51 *"I asked the newspaper men"*: Mary Harris Jones, *The Autobiography of Mother Jones* (Chicago: Charles H. Kerr Publishing Company, 1976), 71–72.

51 *"'Mother' Jones and her 'Army'"*: New York Times, 23 July 1903.

52 *"I am going to show Wall Street"*: quoted in Elliot Gorn, *Mother*

Jones: The Most Dangerous Woman in America (New York: Hill and Wang, 2001), 132.

52 *The strikers had been earning*: Gorn, 131.

52 *"There was a backdrop"*: *Autobiography,* 79–80.

53 *"Pretty nearly anything"*: "Oratory and Lions," *New York Times,* 2 August 1903.

54 *Mary Harris was born*: Gorn, 9.

54 *In the six years*: Gorn, 19.

55 *she married George Jones*: Gorn, 37.

55 *the* Iron Moulders' International Journal: *Autobiography,* 12; Gorn, 45.

55 *"All about my house"*: *Autobiography,* 12.

56 *"We worked for the aristocrats"*: *Autobiography,* 12–13.

56 *Soon it became repeated as fact*: summary from Richard F. Bales, *The Great Chicago Fire and the Myth of Mrs. O'Leary's Cow* (Jefferson, NC: McFarland & Co., 2002).

56 *The sparks and cinders were falling*: Lambert Tree, in *The Great Chicago Fire in Eyewitness Accounts and Seventy Contemporary Photographs and Illustrations* (New York: Dover Publications, 1979).

57 *Three hundred people died*: Gorn, 44.

57 *The Knights of Labor*: Gorn, 45.

57 *The* Chicago Tribune *warned*: Gorn, 47.

57 *"What is the chief aim of man?"*: Mark Twain, "Revised Catechism," originally published in the *New York Tribune,* 24 August 1871.

57 *A financial panic in 1873*: Gorn, 46–47.

58 *Her biographer, Elliot Gorn, doubts*: Gorn, 47.

58 *The name "Mother Jones" first appeared*: Gorn, 62.

58 *The Kansas City Star*: quoted in Gorn, 63.

58 *coal mining was a central battleground*: Gorn, 69.

58 *By 1890, Standard Oil controlled*: summary from Ron Chernow, *Titan: The Life of John D. Rockefeller Sr.* (New York: Random House, 1998).

59 *My grandfather, Albert Gore, Sr.*: Albert Gore Sr., *The Eye of the Storm: A People's Politics for the Seventies* (New York: Herder and Herder, 1970), 194.

59 *"I was horrified to learn"*: Albert Gore Sr., *Let the Glory Out: My South and Its Politics* (New York: The Viking Press, 1972), 201.

59 *Each year thousands of miners*: Gorn, 69.

59 *"One of the most exhausting things"*: John Brophy, *A Miner's Life* (Madison, WI: Univ. of Wisconsin Press, 1964), 45. His account of

life in the mines and mining towns appears on pp. 38–51. According to Brophy, "In a good seam of coal, a competent miner could get out four or five tons of coal in a ten-hour shift. Therefore, he earned about two dollars a day when he was working, barring complications, such as short time or time wasted on company work. If the miner could be sure of six days of work the year round, he could make a living, not a good one, but a living. But work was never that steady, nor could the average man have endured the strain if it had been. He had to get out his four or five tons a day by hand labor. Undercutting, drilling, blasting, loading, all were hand jobs, to say nothing of timbering, tracklaying, . . . and car-pushing, which made heavy demands on his strength and stamina without putting a penny in his pocket." Brophy, 46.

60 The song "Sixteen Tons": "'Sixteen Tons'—The Story Behind the Legend," *Tennessee Ernie Ford!*, http://www.ernieford.com/Sixteen%20Tons.htm (accessed 18 April 2005).

60 *In West Virginia, 94 percent*: Gorn, 90.

60 *A twenty-five-pound keg*: Brophy, 47.

61 *"A miner got his pay"*: Brophy, 63.

61 *business and government in the mining regions*: Gorn, 98.

61 *the owners organized*: Gorn, 102.

61 *"Flesh and blood"*: Stephen Currie, *We Have Marched Together: The Working Children's Crusade* (Minneapolis, MN: Lerner Publishing Group, 1996), 55.

62 *President George Baer*: Gorn, 84.

62 *Observers described her voice*: Mary Harris Jones, edited by Edward M. Steel, *The Speeches and Writings of Mother Jones* (Pittsburgh, PA: Univ. of Pittsburgh Press, 1988), xv.

63 *Poet Carl Sandburg called it*: Ibid.

63 *"She dressed conventionally"*: Brophy, 74.

63 *After one rally, a reporter wrote*: Speeches, xvi.

63 *"I was introduced"*: Fred Mooney, *Struggle in the Coal Fields: The Autobiography of Fred Mooney*, (Morgantown, WV: West Virginia Univ. Press, 1967), 278–279.

63 *"Hearing her speak"*: Gorn, 227.

64 *"Mark Hanna digging coal!"*: Speeches, 13.

64 *widely depicted as "a brutal, obese plutocrat"*: Margaret Leech, *In the Days of McKinley* (New York: Harpers, 1959), 77.

64 *Gorn points out*: Gorn 278–279.

64 *a priest who "told the men"*: Autobiography 89–90

65 *"We marched the mountains"*: Speeches, 74.

65 *"Your organization"*: Autobiography, 41.

65 *"I believe we will get together"*: Speeches, 8.

65 *In the late nineteenth century*: summary from Andrew Gyory, *Closing the Gate: Race Politics and the Chinese Exclusion Act* (Chapel Hill, NC: Univ. of North Carolina Press, 1998).

65 *"One of the best fellows"*: Speeches, 20–21.

65 *"if you work long"*: Speeches, 71.

65 *"Stop your bickering"*: Speeches, 143.

66 *"I have wondered"*: Speeches, 7.

66 *Jones remembered*: Autobiography, 47.

66 *she responded*: Autobiography, 24.

66 *"Oh, God Almighty grant"*: Speeches, 87.

67 *"Mr. Newspaperman"*: Speeches, 42.

67 *"Let the boys who are here"*: Speeches, 34.

67 *"Put that down, Mr. Reporter!"* Speeches, 45.

67 *"He held the oil lamp"*: Autobiography, 33.

67 *The family gathered up*: Ibid.

67 *"created by the parasitical class"*: Speeches, 59.

68 *"Women are fighters"*: Speeches, 304.

68 *"Walking to the edge"*: Boston Herald, 11 September 1904, quoted in Gorn, 120.

68 *"What do the suffragettes"*: "'Mother' Jones Not Afraid, *New York Times, 12 November* 1912.

68 *"I have no vote"*: Gorn, 232.

68 *"In no sense of the word"*: "'Mother' Jones, Mild-Mannered, Talks Sociology," New York Times, 1 June 1913.

69 *Wages increased*: Gorn, 76.

69 *A mountainous state*: summary from Otis K. Rice and Stephen W. Brown, *West Virginia: A History* (Lexington, KY: Univ. Press of Kentucky, 1993).

69 *"I dislike to ask you always"*: Mary Harris Jones, edited by Edward M. Steel, *The Correspondence of Mother Jones* (Pittsburgh, PA: Univ. of Pittsburgh Press, 1985), 32.

70 *Jones herself was nearly trapped*: Gorn, 95.

70 *"great, open cuts"*: Autobiography, 44.

70 *unprecedented legal victory*: Gorn, 95.

70 *"keep up this fight!"*: Autobiography, 49.

70 *"No battle was ever won"*: Speeches, 11.

70 *"the most dangerous woman"*: Gorn, 96.

71 *"It seems to me"*: Gorn, 97.

71 *"this God Cursed Monopolistic State"*: Correspondence, 21.

71 *"For the Soul and spirit"*: United Mine Workers Journal, 17 July 1902, quoted in Gorn, 100.

71 *U.S. Department of Labor estimated*: Gorn, 125.

72 *he could "make fifteen cents"*: Currie, 23.

72 *Massachusetts passed*: summary from Walter I. Trattner, *Crusade for the Children: A History of the National Child Labor Committee and Child Labor Reform in America* (Chicago: Quadrangle Books, 1970).

72 *"Children are brought to the mill"*: Mary Applewhite Bacon, "Unrest in the Southern Textile Mills," *Charities*, 18 July 1903. Trattner cites similar arguments in favor of child labor. For instance, one mill owner declared that the South's cotton mills were "the greatest and almost the only real friends that the poor whites of the South have. . . . [The children are] infinitely better off in the cotton mills than on the soil-polluted, disease-breeding, one-horse, privyless farms. . . . I view child labor as an actual blessing [in comparison]." (102)

72 *"The agitation for such laws"*: Ibid.

73 *In late May 1903*: Gorn, 131.

73 *"In a single block"*: Autobiography, 71.

74 *"Here's a textbook"*: Autobiography, 76–77.

74 *"a mile-a-minute gait"*: Currie, 28.

74 *"Most of the saloons"*: "Free Beer for Army," *New York Tribune*, 17 July 1903.

74 *"very bright and very pretty"*: "Army Crosses Delaware," *New York Tribune*, 11 July 1903.

75 *"Mrs. Jones spoke"*: "'Mother' Jones Keeps Moving," *New York Times*, 13 July 1903.

75 *"at her wits end"*: "'Mother' Jones Hard Pressed," *New York Times*, 14 July 1903.

75 *to Oyster Bay "for the purpose of"*: "Textile Strikers Start on Long March to New York," *Philadelphia Inquirer*, 8 July 1903.

75 *"Oh, that's only a joke!"*: "Army Crosses Delaware," *New York Tribune*, 11 July 1903.

75 *asking "that the children"*: Correspondence, 45.

75 *"These little children"*: Ibid.

76 *"'Mother' Jones tonight"*: "Mother Jones's Tired Army," *New York Times*, 18 July 1903.

76 *"Helvetia Hall was packed"*: "Mother Jones Determined," *New York Times*, 19 July 1903.

76 *"the police will be instructed"*: "Ready to Defy Ebstein," *New York Tribune*, 23 July 1903.

76 *a "piece of rotton royalty"*: Ibid.

77 *Mother Jones assembled the marchers*: "'Mother' Jones Arrives," *New York Times*, 24 July 1903.

77 *"a huge bag of money"*: Ibid.

77 *"We are quietly marching"*: "Mother Jones's Meeting," *New York Tribune*, 28 July 1903.

77 *"The children got stuck"*: Autobiography, 82.

77 *According to one observer*: "Fails to See Platt," *New York Tribune*, 28 July 1903.

77 *In another version*: Autobiography, 82.

77 *Yet another account*: Currie, 55.

78 *"'Mother' Jones was much pleased*: "Fails to See Platt."

78 *"The children were very happy"*: Autobiography, 74.

78 *"Not long afterward"*: Autobiography, 83.

78 *One year after the march*: Gorn, 141.

79 *the IWW or the Wobblies*: The Industrial Workers of the World, which seeks to organize all workers regardless of trade, was established January 1905 as a radical alternative to the moderate American Federation of Labor. The nickname's origins are uncertain. The IWW cites four theories: Chinese immigrant members pronounced the initials "Eye Wobbly Wobbly" and the others adopted it; the "wobbly saw" was a tool used by the early timberworker members; it started as a codeword for workplace sabotage; it was originally used as an insult but the members took it over in defiance. "What Is the Origin of the Term Wobbly?" Industrial Workers of the World, http://www.iww.org/culture/official/wobbly (accessed 7 March 2005).

79 *more open to the union's message*: Gorn proposes several reasons for this: growing class solidarity, a greater proportion of miners with families, development of a pro-unionizing "underground religious tradition" as opposed to the company-established churches. The operators, too, were drawing together as a coalition, perceiving themselves as under attack from their workers. "So when the time came to discuss new terms in 1912, the division between labor and management already ran deep." Gorn, 171.

80 *"the governor wasn't helpless"*: Speeches, 62.

80 *The stenographers' records capture*: Speeches, 100.

81 *"Let me say to you"*: Speeches, 60.

81 *Glasscock's declaration of martial law*: Gorn, 185.

81 *"what is the power"*: "'Mother' Jones Not Afraid," *New York Times* 12 November 1912.

81 *nominally even-handed but inconsequential report*: Gorn, 186.

82 *"Instruments were thrown aside"*: Mooney, 36.

83 *Gorn describes the hysteria*: Gorn, 187.

83 *"The civil officers picked me"*: Correspondence, 107.

83 *"I am in confinement"*: Correspondence, 107.

83 *"on trial for her life"*: "'Mother Jones' Defiant," *New York Times*, 11 March 1913.

84 *"I am eighty years old"*: Ibid.

84 *Trial records are incomplete*: Edward M. Steel, editor, *The Court-Martial of Mother Jones* (Lexington, KY: Univ. Press of Kentucky, 1995), 58.

84 *West Virginia had a new Republican governor*: Gorn, 191–192.

84 *the UMW sent a secretary*: Court-Martial, 59.

84 *"grandmother of all agitators"*: Court-Martial, 60.

84 *"From out of the military prison walls"*: Correspondence, 114.

85 *"the first move ever made"*: "Mother Jones Stirs Crowd," *New York Times*, 28 May 1913.

85 *"If in such cases"*: "'Mother Jones' at Debate," *New York Times*, 16 May 1913.

85 *The* New York Times *ran a lengthy interview*: "'Mother' Jones, Mild-Mannered, Talks Sociology," *New York Times*, 1 June 1913.

86 *Mother Jones first arrived*: Gorn, 204.

87 *Though governor Ammons hadn't declared*: Gorn, 206.

87 *Jones said, "He had better go back"*: Gorn, 208.

87 *"Mrs. Jones was met"*: New York Times, 5 January 1914.

87 *a thousand mine women and children marched*: Gorn, 209.

88 *Eager to avoid a precedent*: Ibid.

88 *"incommunicado in an underground cell"*: Correspondence, 125–126.

89 *The Rockefeller-controlled Colorado Fuel and Iron Company*: Gorn, 201.

89 *"the most completely fearless man"*: Ron Chernow, *Titan: The Life of John D. Rockefeller Sr.* (New York: Random House), 587.

89 *He was asked*: Chernow, 578. Chernow describes the family's response to Junior's testimony: "Almost tearful with joy at her boy's performance, Cettie wired him that his testimony 'was a bugle note . . . struck for principle.' A no-less-exultant Senior told a friend apro-

pos of Junior's testimony, 'He expressed the views which I entertain, and which have been drilled into him from his earliest childhood.' Until this point, Junior had not owned any shares in the Colorado company and acted only as his father's proxy. Now, Senior gave him ten thousand shares of CFI as a reward for his testimony." Chernow, 579.

89 *April 20, 1914, was Greek Orthodox Easter*: Gorn, 213.

89 *"Unprovoked attack upon small force of militia"*: Gorn, 213–214.

90 *Demonstrators gathered*: Chernow, 580.

90 *"the monster of capitalism"*: *Ibid.*

90 *"The horrors of it cannot be depicted"*: *Speeches*, 132.

90 *According to Chernow*: Chernow, 580.

90 *In the aftermath of Ludlow*: Chernow, 584–585.

91 *The* Washington Post *recorded*: "To End Labor War," *Washington Post*, 28 January 1915.

91 *"I should hope"*: Chernow, 586.

91 *"a sham and a fraud"*: Gorn, 222.

92 *sent him a gracious note*: *Correspondence* 134

92 *"I'll be 90 years old"*: "Mother Jones Urges Strikers to Violence," *New York Times*, 24 October 1919

93 *calling her a "sellout" and "traitor"*: Gorn 272

93 *her old friend Terence Powderly*: Powderly left the Knights of Labor in 1893, after fourteen years of leading the union through its most successful period. While he was Grand Master Workman of the Knights, he was elected to three terms as mayor of Scranton, Pennsylvania. He became a lawyer and joined the federal government as U.S. commissioner general of immigration, from 1887 to 1902 and then became chief of the Labor Department's Division of Information.

93 *She disappointed her colleagues*: Gorn, 287.

94 *"Wealthy coal operators"*: "Mother Jones Eulogized," *New York Times*, 8 December 1930.

Alice Hamilton

The two major sources for this chapter were Hamilton's autobiography, *Exploring the Dangerous Trades*, and *Alice Hamilton: A Life in Letters* edited by Barbara Sicherman. Blanche Wiesen Cook's two-volume biography, *Eleanor Roosevelt*, illuminated the role Hamilton and other progressives played in shaping Roosevelt's political philosophy.

95 *Is it sensible to assume*: Alice Hamilton, "State Pensions or Charity?" *The Atlantic*, May 1930, 686.

95 *"a tweed-clad figure"*: Elizabeth Shepley Sergeant, "Alice Hamilton, M .D.: Crusader for Health in Industry," *Harpers Monthly*, May 1926, 763.

95 *Stopes are terrace-like excavations*: "stope," the *American Heritage Dictionary of the English Language*, 4th ed. (Boston: Houghton Mifflin, 2000), www.bartleby.com/61/ (accessed 5 February 2005).

96 *"could only tell me"*: Alice Hamilton, *Exploring the Dangerous Trades: The Autobiography of Alice Hamilton, M.D.* (Boston: Little, Brown and Company, 1943), 184.

96 *"He received me very graciously"*: *Exploring*, 194.

96 *"On one of my first trips"*: *Exploring*, 184–186.

98 *"There were eleven cousins"*: *Exploring*, 25.

98 *The family's wealth had been amassed*: *Alice Hamilton: A Life in Letters*, edited by Barbara Sicherman (Cambridge, MA: Harvard Univ. Press, 1984), 14.

98 *In Alice's immediate family*: Sicherman, 11–14.

99 *in the words of Arthur Schlesinger Jr.,*: Arthur Schlesinger Jr., *Robert Kennedy and His Times* (Boston: Houghton Mifflin, 1978), 618.

100 *"She could blaze out"*: *Exploring*, 32.

100 *"There are two kinds of people"*: *Ibid.*

100 *she wanted "a larger life"*: *Exploring*, 39. All the quoted material in the paragraph comes from the same page.

101 *"I shall never forget"*: *Exploring*, 42.

101 *she describes one patient*: Sicherman, 47–52.

101 *In 1894 Hamilton interned*: Sicherman, 79–87.

102 *After completing her year-long internship*: Sicherman, 88–92.

102 *Jane Addams was the daughter*: The information on Addams and Hull House was taken from two sources: Addams's *Twenty Years at Hull House* (New York: MacMillan Co., 1910) and the Web site *Urban Experience in Chicago: Hull-House and Its Neighborhoods, 1889–1963*, a joint project of the College of Architecture and the Arts at the University of Illinois at Chicago, and the Jane Addams Hull-House Museum, http://www.uic.edu/jaddams/hull/urbanexp/. *Urban Experience* is a wonderful resource, offering a wealth of primary documents and photos as well as historical essays.

103 *Addams visited Fort Wayne*: Addams's speech was likely in connection with the publication of *Hull House Maps and Papers: A Presentation of Nationalities and Wages in a Congested District of Chicago*.

The book documented living conditions among several Nineteenth District communities (Italians, Bohemians, and Russian and Polish Jews) and argued against "sweating" and child labor.

103 *Hull House continues its work*: "About Hull House," Jane Addams Hull House Web site, http://www.hullhouse.org/about.asp (accessed 13 March 2005).

103 *"[Addams] was already famous"*: *Exploring*, 54. In January 1902 Agnes moved to the Lighthouse in Kensington, Pennsylvania the site of the Kensington mill strike that led to Mother Jones's children's march in 1903. The two settlement houses were very different philosophically. Hull House specifically avoided religious activities and programs, and Addams refused to equate settlement life with deprivation. The Lighthouse, however, was entirely religious. Its founder, Esther Kelly, disapproved of alcohol and secular forms of entertainment such as theater. Sicherman, 141.

103 *"[Hull House] is so tremendously cultured"*: Sicherman, 109.

104 *"I should never have taken"*: *Exploring*, 16.

104 *Florence Kelley inspired*: Kathryn Kish Sklar, "Florence Kelley," *The Reader's Companion to American History*, http://college.hmco.com/history/readerscomp/rcah/html/ah_049300_kelleyfloren.htm (accessed 13 February 2005). Kelley worked with attorney Louis Brandeis on the case *Muller v. Oregon*, which limited working hours for women. In preparing for the argument before the Supreme Court, Kelley and Brandeis included sociological data, a pioneering legal tactic. Now quite common, this form of argument is known as a "Brandeis brief." Kelley herself considered her most important accomplishment the Sheppard-Towner Maternity and Infancy Protection Act, passed in 1921, the first federal allocation for health care. Two childhood experiences shaped Florence's philosophy: one was a late-night expedition with her father, who had served in Congress as a staunch abolitionist, to Philadelphia's factories, where she saw other children working in terrible conditions; the other was the death of five of her siblings during infancy, which moved her to work towards improving infant health.

104 *Julia Lathrop joined Hull House*: "Julia Clifford Lathrop," *Women in American History by Encyclopedia Britannica*, http://search.eb.com/women/articles/Lathrop_Julia_Clifford.html, (13 February 2005).

104 *"As one reads [Addams's] earlier writings "*: *Exploring*, 59.

105 *"She was a pragmatist"*: *Exploring*, 65–66.

105 *We leave the nineteenth ward*: Sicherman, 124.

105 *"a great towering hulk"*: *Exploring*, 88.

106 *"You may love humanity"*: *Exploring*, 85.

106 *"Life in a settlement"*: *Exploring*, 72.

106 *"I found I could get past"*: *Exploring*, 69.

106 *"People in the house"*: Sicherman, 133.

107 *more than 14 percent*: Sicherman,135.

107 *"In Chicago the effect was most gratifying"*: *Exploring*, 99.

107 *"For years, although I did my best"*: *Exploring*, 105.

108 *"discovered that cocaine"*: *Exploring*, 100.

108 *"I tested the powders on myself"*: *Exploring*, 102.

108 *"That seems to me"*: *Exploring*, 103.

109 *"As an American"*: *Ibid*.

109 *the Visiting Nurse Service (VNS) in New York*: summary from Beatrice Siegel, *Lillian Wald of Henry Street* (New York: MacMillan, 1993).

109 *"her earliest exploration"*: Sicherman, 147.

109 *"for our workmen"*: *Exploring*, 115.

110 *"The worker was as truly"*: Alice Hamilton, "A Woman of Ninety," *Atlantic Monthly*, September 1961, 52.

110 *In the 1880s Salvation Army founder*: Melvin L. Myers and James D. McGlothlin, "Matchmakers' 'Phossy Jaw' Eradicated." *American Industrial Hygiene Association* 4 (1996), 330.

111 *Diamond Match Company*: *Exploring*, 117–118.

111 *phossy jaw had been "the simplest problem"*: Alice Hamilton, "Healthy, Wealthy—If Wise—Industry," *The American Scholar* (1:1938), 13.

111 *argued that it "was very improbable"*: quoted in Sicherman, 153.

111 *a recognized expert in public health*: Sicherman, 155.

112 *"So interesting did I find it"*: Alice Hamilton, "Nineteen Years in the Poisonous Trades," *Harper's Monthly*, October 1929, 580.

112 *"As I remember it"*: "Nineteen Years," 581.

112 *"men who came from"* "A Woman of Ninety," 54.

113 *"Changes took place"*: *Exploring*, 158–159.

113 *"He was better than his word"*: *Exploring*, 10.

114 *"The Illinois Commission expected me"*: *Exploring*, 7.

114 *"Many times in those early days"*: *Exploring*, 4.

114 *"It sometimes seemed to me"* *Exploring*, 125–126.

114 *"For an employer"*: Sicherman, 181.

115 *"The physician attached"*: "Nineteen Years," 583.

115 *As she recalled it*: *Exploring*, 135.

115 *"The one plant might be reformed"*: "Nineteen Years," 588–589.

116 *"It was they who did"*: *Exploring,* 6.

116 *"industrial feudalism"*: Sicherman, 239.

116 *"so long as the health"*: "Nineteen Years," 590.

116 teaching her *"a much-needed lesson"*: *Exploring,* 63.

117 *"not only increased the dangers"*: "Healthy, Wealthy," 17.

117 *"It was not only the sight"*: "Nineteen Years," 584.

117 *"joyous ruthlessness"*: Ibid.

117 they *"could not prevail"*: Ibid.

118 *"It is, after all, the weapon of publicity"*

118 *"tainted with socialism"*: Sicherman, 169.

118 *"She isn't a big woman"*: Sicherman, 279.

118 *When Alice Paul immediately followed*: Blanche Wiesen Cook, *Eleanor Roosevelt: Volume 1, 1881–1933* (New York: Penguin Books, 1993), 357.

119 *she felt it was "better not to give up"*: Sicherman, 254.

119 *"sheltered, safe, beautifully guarded"*: Cook v. 1, 358. The Manchester School, a political philosophy developed in nineteenth-century Britain, stressed the positive effects of an unhampered capitalist system. "Manchester School," the *Columbia Encyclopedia,* 6th ed., New York: Columbia University Press, 2001–04, www.bartleby.com/65/ (accessed 13 April 2005).

119 *According to Cook*: Cook v. 1, 358.

119 *She recalled*: *Exploring,* 291.

120 *"ever since I was a baby"*: Sergeant, 767.

121 *Headlines included*: Ibid.

121 *"I am not the first woman"*: Sicherman, 237.

121 *"literally kept it going"*: Sicherman, 238.

121 *She became a sort of national resource*: Sicherman, 281.

121 *the Versailles treaty*: The Treaty of Versailles, intended both to exact revenge and to prevent Germany from becoming a major power again, imposed war reparations on Germany, put its colonies under the control of the new League of Nations, reduced its European territory by 13 percent, limited its army to 100,000 troops, prohibited an air force altogether, and banned development or acquisition of certain kinds of weapons. Germany was reluctant to accept the terms of the treaty, which it had no part in negotiating, but the Allies were determined to impose them. In the words of Cambridge University historian Jay Winter: "The majority of the German nation shared the position that Hitler took on the Treaty of Versailles: that it was unfair, and that the imposi-

tion on Germany of sole responsibility for the war was wrong. . . . They were convinced that what happened to them was an injustice, so that the very way in which the Treaty of Versailles was forced on the German people stored up the material for the next round. . . . The problem was: what could be done that would enable the millions of people who had lost loved ones, to believe that somehow, those responsible for the deaths of their loved ones had paid the price for it—at the same time as reviving Europe with a strong Germany. There's no way to do that. Revenge and reconciliation are incompatible. They tried both and got neither." "The Versailles Treaty—A Grand Bazaar," *The Great War and the Shaping of the Twentieth Century* Web site, http://www.pbs.org/greatwar/historian/hist_winter_21_versailles.html (accessed 2 May 2005).

122 *"I am afraid I cannot write you"*: Sicherman, 248.

124 *"It stirs me up"*: Sicherman, 261.

124 *"resolute isolationism and xenophobia"*: Exploring, 299.

124 *"As I followed"*: Exploring, 423.

124 *"When, after 1924"*: Exploring, 299.

124 *"Russia is a terrible, terrible country"*: Sicherman, 276.

124 *"The test of the fascist regime"*: "Nineteen Years," 591.

125 *Hamilton and Addams joined Eleanor Roosevelt*: Blanche Wiesen Cook, *Eleanor Roosevelt: Volume 2, 1933–1938: The Defining Years* (New York: Penguin Books, 1999), 126–128.

125 *"Alice Hamilton was detailed"*: Cook v. 2, 126.

125 *Good propaganda limits itself*: Alice Hamilton, "Hitler Speaks: His Book Reveals the Man," *The Atlantic*, October 1933, 401.

126 *did not advocate any specific changes*: Cook v. 2, 127.

126 *"Speak about the Jewish situation"*: "Hitler Speaks," 402.

126 *"the drearily familiar story"*: Exploring, 201.

127 *"For the first time I found myself"*: Exploring, 290.

127 *She was pleased by the attitude*: Exploring, 291.

127 *"I don't know what your company is feeling"*: Sicherman, 311.

127 *"twenty years ago"*: "Nineteen Years," 585.

127 *"So gentle and unassuming"*: Cook v. 2, 366.

128 *"What the silkworm achieves"*: Exploring, 389.

128 *"This prolonged neglect"*: Exploring, 391.

128 *"The control of this dangerous trade"*: Exploring, 394.

128 *"a great honor"*: Exploring, 405.

129 *"I have done absolutely nothing"*: Sicherman, 398.

129 *"A woman of ninety years"*: "A Woman of Ninety," 51.

Frances Perkins

Madame Secretary, the biography of Perkins by George Martin, is both exhaustive and fascinating. Naomi Pasachoff's young-adult biography *Frances Perkins: Champion of the New Deal* is an excellent supplement, drawing on Perkins's oral history interviews at Columbia University. Blanche Weisen Cook's biography of Eleanor Roosevelt, so useful in the Alice Hamilton chapter, is indispensable here. Perkins's own book, *The Roosevelt I Knew*, highlights her relationship with the president. Two biographies of Al Smith also proved useful: *Al Smith: Hero of the Cities,* by Matthew Josephson and Hannah Josephson, includes much of Perkins' unfinished research for her own biography of Smith; Robert Slayton's *Empire Statesman: The Rise and Redemption of Al Smith* paints a vivid picture of politics in the 1920s.

130 *I didn't come here*: George Martin, *Madame Secretary: Frances Perkins. A Biography of America's First Woman Cabinet Member* (Boston: Houghton Mifflin Company, 1976), 374.

130 *a freakish storm*: "City Area Lashed by 60-Mile Gale," *New York Times*, 22 February 1933.

130 *a jobless man*: "Jobless Man Dies in 20-Foot Fall," *New York Times*, 23 February 1933.

130 *32.6 percent unemployment rate*: Martin, 219.

130 *Winthrop P. Aldrich, head of Chase National Bank*: "Aldrich has Faith in Nation's Banks," *New York Times*, 23 February 1933.

131 *The place was a shambles*: Frances Perkins, *The Roosevelt I Knew* (New York: The Viking Press, 1946), 150.

131 *Roosevelt's first inauguration*: "Notes on the Amendments," U.S Constitution Online, http://www.usconstitution.net/constamnotes .html#Am20 (accessed 28 January 2005).

131 *only member of FDR's cabinet*: Martin, 239.

131 *"If Roosevelt was going to be President"*: Naomi Pasachoff, *Frances Perkins: Champion of the New Deal* (Oxford and New York: Oxford Univ. Press, 1999), 69.

131 *"and so I agreed"*: Perkins, 152.

132 *she "would never dream of"*: Pasachoff, 74.

133 *"There, my dear, this is your hat"*: Martin, 5.

133 *"Mercy Otis Warren's History"*: Joseph J. Ellis, *Founding Brothers: The Revolutionary Generation* (New York: Random House, 2002), 213.

134 *"for the first time"*: Martin, 46.

134 *"opened the door"*: Martin, 50.

135 *on February 20, 1902*: Martin, 53.

135 *items made by "sweaters"*: Thirty-two years later, Labor Secretary Frances Perkins wrote "The Cost of a Five-Dollar Dress," published in the journal *Survey Graphic*. This anti-sweatshop essay took up the NCL's argument that consumers should be aware of the consequences, and the power, of their purchases. What strikes me is how contemporary her argument remains. It reads, in part:

> *The manufacturer who pays a living wage for a reasonable week's work under decent conditions cannot turn out attractive silk frocks to retail at $5 or less. The real cost is borne by the workers in the sweatshops that are springing up in hard-pressed communities. Under today's desperate need for work and wages, girls and women are found toiling overtime at power machines and worktables, some of them for paychecks that represent a wage of less than 10 cents a day. . . . Since [the sweatshop employer] cannot hope to meet union conditions or the requirements of the labor law, he goes to some outlying suburb where garment factories are not a feature of the local picture and where state inspectors are not on the lookout for him. Or perhaps he goes to a nearby state . . . where he believes labor laws are less stringent or that he will escape attention.*
>
> *His work force is made up of wives and daughters of local wage earners who have been out of work for months or even years and whose family situation is desperate. The boss sets the wage rates, figures the pay slips, determines the hours of work. His reply to any complaint is, "Quit if you don't like it." . . . The red silk bargain dress in the shop window is a danger signal. It is a warning of the return to the sweatshop, a challenge to us all to reinforce the gains we have made in our long and difficult progress toward a civilized industrial order.*

Originally published in *Survey Graphic*, 1933, quoted in Pasachoff, 76–77.

135 *"Kelley's dynamic personality"*: Martin, 53.

135 *"She took a whole group"*: Pasachoff, 15.

135 *she visited the renowned Charity Organization Society*: Martin, 53.

136 *she "straightaway felt"*: Perkins, 12.

136 *she ran a "most interesting Girls' Club"*: Martin, 55.

137 *I had to do something*: Martin, 64.

137 *"Miss Addams taught us"*: Benjamin Stolberg, "Madame Secretary: A Study in Bewilderment," *Saturday Evening Post*, 27 July 1940, 11.

137 *to believe that "unions were an evil"*: Pasachoff, 18.

138 *"strange and thrilling experiences"*: Pasachoff, 20.

138 *excited to be "in the very heart"*: Martin, 73.

138 *Perkins moved in to Hartley House*: Martin, 73.

138 *whom a columnist had dubbed*: Perkins, 12.

139 *"temporary relief is necessary"*: Martin, 74.

139 *"She was a firebrand and a driver"*: Russell Lord, "Profiles: Madame Secretary," *New Yorker*, 2 September 1933, 17.

139 *"A fire in the daytime"*: Martin, 78.

140 *The 1910 census*: Ibid.

140 *On the afternoon of Saturday, March 25, 1911*: Martin, 84.

140 *"Without saying much of anything"*: Pasachoff, 29.

140 *"I saw four men"*: "Stories of Survivors," *New York Times*, 26 March 1911.

140 *Over the next few days*: Martin, 85.

141 *On April 2, 1911*: Martin, 86–87.

141 *Schneiderman's "fiery red hair"*: "Lecture by Frances Perkins," *The Triangle Factory Fire* Web site, the Industrial Labor Relations School at Cornell University, http://www.ilr.cornell.edu/trianglefire/texts/lectures/perkins.html (accessed 28 January 2005).

141 *I would be a traitor*: Matthew Josephson and Hannah Josephson, *Al Smith: Hero of the Cities: A Political Portrait Drawing on the Papers of Frances Perkins* (Boston: Houghton Mifflin Company, 1969), 123. At the time of Scheiderman's speech, the estimate of deaths in the Triangle fire was 143. It would later be raised to 146.

142 *Yet Perkins remembered*: Ibid.

142 *"These were the days"*: "Lecture by Frances Perkins."

142 *The courts found*: Martin, 86.

142 *"Of all the various individuals"*: "147 Dead, Nobody Guilty," *Literary Digest*, 6 January 1912, accessed on *The Triangle Factory Fire* Web site, http://www.ilr.cornell.edu/trianglefire/texts/newspaper/ld_010612.html (accessed 28 January 2005).

144 *"report [on] all kinds"*: "Lecture by Frances Perkins."

144 *"Factory inspection is of vast importance"*: Pasachoff, 51.

144 *We used to make it our business*: Perkins, 22.

145 *"the greatest education he'd ever had"*: quoted in Pasachoff, 31.

145 *"It was laid on the table"*: "Lecture by Frances Perkins."

145 *"He was real"*: Lord, 18.

146 *On March 27, 1912*: Martin, 92–98.

146 *"At that moment"*: Lord, 18.

146 *"It's all right, me girl"*: Perkins, 14.

146 *"Frances, Frances, we have won"*: Lord, 19.

146 *"a half-loaf girl"*: Martin, 98.

147 *As part of an intraparty battle for control*: Martin, 145–146.

147 *"The way men take women"*: Martin, 146.

147 *On September 26, 1913*: Martin, 122.

147 *"one of the most civilized"*: Lord, 18.

147 *"my whole generation"*: Pasachoff, 36.

148 *"using [Wilson's] name"*: Ibid.

148 *It was "the first contact"*: Pasachoff, 37.

148 *she rarely spoke of at all*: Martin, 128.

148 *"He was sometimes depressed"*: Martin, 135.

148 *"Sometimes he was hospitalized"*: Ibid.

149 *"Practically all the things"*: Perkins, 157.

149 *Smith, a Catholic with Irish roots*: summary from Matthew Josephson and Hannah Josephson, *Al Smith: Hero of the Cities.*

150 *He warned her*: Josephson, 2.

150 *"explosive" about Eugene Debs*: Martin, 163.

150 Information on New York State suffrage: Ann-Marie Imbornoni, "Timeline of Key Events in the American Women's Rights Movement," InfoPlease, http://www.infoplease.com/spot/womenstimeline1.html. Information on the Nineteenth Amendment: "Notes on the Amendments," *U.S Constitution Online*, http://www.usconstitution.net/constamnotes.html#Am19. Information on the vote in the Tennessee legislature: A. Elizabeth Taylor, *The Woman Suffrage Movement in Tennessee* (New York: Bookman Associates, 1957); "The Nineteenth Amendment & the War of the Roses," Tennessee Federation of Republican Women Web site, http://www.tnfrw.org/amend.htm; and local lore told to the author.

150 *"Good people need to be in the party"*: Martin, 166.

151 *Kelley "burst into tears"*: Martin, 144.

151 *"I appointed Miss Perkins*: Pasachoff, 42.

151 *"They could see the evidences"*: Pasachoff, 45.

152 *Spargo reacted violently*: Martin, 155.

152 *She literally defused the situation*: Martin, 156.

153 *These are workmen*: Pasachoff, 47.

154 *"Do us a favor"*: Pasachoff, 49.

154 *In 1920 national issues swept Smith*: Robert A. Slayton, *Empire Statesman: The Rise and Redemption of Al Smith* (New York: The Free Press, 2001), 146.

154 *the national ticket lost New York*: Martin, 169.

154 *The 1920 census revealed*: Edward Ranson, "'A Snarling Roughhouse:' The Democratic Convention of 1924," *History Today* 7 (1994), 27.

155 *"the Avenue of the States"*: "City Salutes Delegates," *New York Times*, 23 June 1924.

155 *and regional exotica*: "Butterscotch Pie?" *The Nation*, 2 July 1934, 5–6.

155 *"Because you're a Bowery Mick"*: Slayton, 209.

155 *he had "bruised it up"*: Slayton, 210.

156 *In* Empire Statesman: Slayton, 211.

156 *"I saw around him"*: Martin, 184.

156 *delegates "lumbered about"*: Elmer Davis, "Delegates Take New Hope," *New York Times*, 6 July 1924.

157 *"the perfect job"*: Perkins, 57.

157 *"If you had knowledge"*: Pasachoff, 54.

157 *"I have met a considerable number"*: quoted in Pasachoff, 55.

157 *"some of the most terrible"*: Slayton, 317.

158 *"Al Smith and the Forces of Hell"*: Martin, 199.

158 *"'Normalcy' was still the magic word"*: Let the Glory Out, 39.

158 *Slayton describes*: Slayton, 317.

158 *Herbert Hoover won*: Slayton, 322.

158 *"I took it hard"*: Perkins, 14.

159 *"Franklin Roosevelt underwent"*: Perkins, 29.

159 *"It embarrassed me"*: Martin, 234.

159 *"I hope you will consider"*: Cook v. 1, 392.

159 *Cook surmises*: Ibid.

160 *Roosevelt eventually took credit*: Cook v. 1, 194.

160 *"told me this with a chuckle"*: Perkins, 55.

161 *Previous industrial commissioners*: Martin, 231.

161 *"a kind of non-person"*: Martin, 232.

162 *I have to give you the advice*: Martin, 209.

162 *The state unemployment rate*: Martin, 219.

162 *"The specter of unemployment"*: Pasachoff, 64.

162 *"The human race"*: Ibid.

162 *On January 22, 1930*: Martin, 215.

163 *"Bully for you"*: Perkins, 96.

163 *"Miss Perkins came to see me today"*: Cook v. 1, 426.

163 *"the public conscience"*: Pasachoff, 68.

163 *Perkins provided the campaign*: Martin, 232.

164 *"She is like Kipling's cat"*: Pasachoff, 68.

164 *"the idea of moving to Washington"*: Pasachoff, 71.

164 *Perkins wrote him*: Martin, 236.

165 *"William E. Green"*: Lord, 2 September 1933, 16.

165 *"a man of great integrity"*: Pasachoff, 75.

165 *"precisely as ordered"*: Lord, 9 September 1933, 22.

165 *"The help gyrated around"*: Lord, 9 September 1933, 20.

166 *Cobb was a portly*: Loriane Burdick, *The Shirley Temple Scrapbook* (New York: Jonathon David Publishers, 2001), 7.

166 *The magazine ran an "Impossible Interview"*: "Impossible Interview," *Vanity Fair*, September 1935, 33.

167 *"on the verge of tears"*: Martin, 403.

168 *Martin describes*: Ibid.

168 *"earnest, rather humorless"*: Stolberg, 9.

168 *"take three parts Joan of Arc"*: Walter Karig, "The Inscrutable Madame Secretary," *Liberty*, 15 October 1938, 42.

168 *"as if she had swallowed"*: Doris Kearns Goodwin, *No Ordinary Time: Franklin and Eleanor Roosevelt, The Home Front in World War II* (New York: Touchstone, 1995), 31.

168 *"On affairs of state"*: Lord, 9 September 1933, 22.

168 *"She has never really learned"*: Eleanor Roosevelt, "Women in Politics," originally published in *Good Housekeeping*, January 1940, accessed on line at the New Deal Network, http://newdeal.feri.org/er/er13.htm (28 January 2005).

168 *"was just as likely to say"*: Martin, 421.

169 *"the whole South"*: Karig, 22 October 1938, 50.

169 *Susanna, now sixteen*: Martin, 240–241.

169 *because it "marched with humor"*: Cook v. 2, 231.

169 *"The color seems to be wiped"*: Cook v. 2, 232.

170 *"[Eleanor Roosevelt] talked to women"*: Cook v. 1, 385.

171 *"a undercover organization"*: Lord , 9 September 1933, 20.

171 *"It's in our family tradition"*: Pasachoff, 82.

171 *"Her severest critic"*: Karig, 15 October 1938, 43.

171 *Perkins also refocused*: Martin, 249–251.

172 *Perkins organized a conference*: Martin, 252.

172 *Perkins achieved a major political victory*: Martin, 255.

172 *"I have no hesitation"*: Exploring, 417.

173 *The nation's annual unemployment rate*: Martin, 219.

173 *"We were improvising"*: Pasachoff, 83.

173 *Harry Hopkins*: In 1935 Hopkins was put in charge of the Works Progress Administration, where he presided over a successful program to put millions back to work. His single-minded drive earned him enemies and in 1938 he faced a grueling (but ultimately successful) confirmation hearing for secretary of commerce. A year later, exhausted and in poor health, he resigned that post. On January 1, 1941, he became the president's personal representative to London. His reporting on and analysis of the situation led to the Lend-Lease Bill, which was crucial to Britain's survival and Germany's eventual defeat. FDR called on Hopkins once more to serve as his aide at the Yalta Conference. Roosevelt died a few months after Yalta, and Hopkins resigned from government. In September 1945, President Truman awarded him the Distinguished Service Medal for his wartime efforts. Harry Hopkins died in January 1946. "Harry Lloyd Hopkins (1890–1946)," Eleanor Roosevelt National Historic Site Web site, http://www.nps.gov/elro/glossary/hopkins-harry.htm (accessed 4 February 2005).

173 *In fall 1933*: Martin, 220.

174 *"a method by which"*: Perkins, 214.

174 *"I always think that something"*: Pasachoff, 87.

174 *the new laws and policies*: Three of the most wide-reaching ones were: the *National Labor Relations Act*, which protected the right to collective bargaining. Championed by Senator Robert Wagner and signed into law on July 5, 1935, the NLRA also established the National Labor Relations board to prevent unfair labor practices; the *Public Contracts Act*, which mandated that workers producing goods worth at least ten thousand dollars under government contracts would not be required to work more than an eight-hour day or a forty-hour week and authorized the secretary of labor to set minimum wages and ensure safe working conditions. The act became law in June 1936 and was later upheld by the Supreme Court; the *Fair Labor Standards Act*, which drastically limited child labor and set maximum hours and minimum wages. Also called the Wages and Hours Act, the FLSA was signed into law in June 1938. Three years later, was ruled constitutional on the grounds that it covered only employees "engaged in interstate commerce." Martin, 387–395.

174 *"You care about this thing"*: Martin, 342–343.

175 *including "unemployment insurance"*: Cook v. 2, 233

175 *from within the president's own cabinet*: Cook v. 2, 248.

175 *"Lily White Social Security System"*: Ibid.

175 *"Our responsibility"*: Ibid.

175 *a national health insurance program*: Martin, 347.

176 *benefits such as paid health insurance*: Paul Starr, *The Social Transformation of American Medicine: The Rise of a Sovereign Profession and the Making of a Vast Industry* (New York: Basic Books, 1982), 311–312.

176 *"In Washington you don't go"*: Pasachoff, 90.

176 *"The taxing power, my dear"*: Perkins, 286.

176 *Perkins instructed her staff*: Martin, 348–349.

176 *"We now stand ready"*: Radio Address by Hon. Frances Perkins: 'Social Insurance for U.S.,'" *The History of Social Security: Social Security Online*, http://www.ssa.gov/history/perkinsradio.html (accessed 15 March 2005).

177 *"For those now young"*: Ibid.

177 *"Miss Perkins' strongest point"*: Stolberg, 65.

177 *Perkins received a phone call*: Martin, 356.

178: The Longshoremen's Strike of 1934: Much of the information on this strike was found in David Selvin's *A Terrible Anger: The 1934 Waterfront and General Strikes in San Francisco* (Detroit: Wayne State Univ. Press, 1996).

178 *they'd "decided to work their ships"*: quoted in Selvin, 91.

179 *he accused the unions*: Selvin, 106.

179 *"Lines of police"*: Selvin, 148. Joseph Roush, the Federal Laboratories salesman who supplied the tear gas, rode with the police and gave a field demonstration. Reporting to Federal Labs' vice president, he wrote, "During one of the riots, I shot a long-range projectile into a group, a shell hitting one man and causing a fracture of the skull, from which he has since died. As he was a communist, I have had no feeling in the matter and I am sorry that I did not get more." The vice president responded, "The report is splendid and we think enough of it to excerpt a large portion of it to send out to the men." Selvin notes that, in fact, the injured striker did not die. Selvin, 151.

180 *My grandfather greatly admired Hull*: Eye of the Storm, 47.

180 *"I call it serious"*: Martin, 320.

180 *"I will have to make it a matter of record"*: Ibid.

180 *Perkins also clashed*: Karig, 22 October 1938, 51.

181 *A widely circulated pamphlet*: Karig, 8 October 1938, 8.

181 *"decreased alien deportation"*: Pasachoff, 99

181 *"If I were a Jew"*: Karig, 22 October 1938, 55.

181 *"the utter un-Americanism"*: *Ibid.*

182 *As early as 1933*: Cook v. 2, 307.

182 *The attacks on Perkins intensified*: Martin, 409.

182 *Members of the California American Legion*: "Miss Perkins Held to 'Coddle' Reds," *New York Times*, 26 October 1938.

182 *The Labor Department was accused*: Ernest K. Lindley, "Deportation of Aliens," *Washington Post*, 10 February 1939.

182 *"It was a terrible winter"*: Pasachoff, 106–107.

182 *"after several months"*: George Gallup, "Public Feels U.S. Must Keep Eyes Open," *Washington Post*, 11 December 1938.

183 *"There was not a single one"*: Pasachoff, 105.

183 *"burst in with the remark"*: *Ibid.*

183 *"Do you remember"*: Martin, 414.

183 *"lenient and indulgent"*: Martin, 415.

184 *After the press frenzy*: Martin, 416.

184 *"Miss Perkins is not a Communist"*: Stolberg, 111.

184 *GM's historic recognition of the UAW*: In late 1936, frustrated by the company's refusal to negotiate with their union, workers in several General Motors plants refused to work but also refused to leave the plants. Soon the strike spread to include 112,000 of GM's 170,000 workers. Strike discipline was strong and damage to the factories minimal but there was enormous pressure, headed by GM's Alfred P. Sloan Jr., to send in state and national troops to oust the strikers. There was fierce public debate over the legality of the strike, whether the obvious trespass was enough to justify armed force and whether the strike might be a first step in Soviet-style collectivization of the industry. Even so, the strike remained a local issue and, according to Perkins's biographer George Martin, Michigan governor and strong FDR ally Frank Murphy played the crucial governmental role in the strike with Perkins offering support: conferring with him, coordinating strategy, and convening meetings among the parties. Perkins' chief role seemed to be counseling Roosevelt to stay out. In one conversation, they both agreed that the strike was "reprehensible." But, she asked the president, "after you've said it's reprehensible, then what? . . . My advice is not to call it intolerable or reprehensible or illegal unless we have a course of action to put immediately into effect." (Martin, 402.)

While FDR incurred the wrath of John Lewis by refusing to endorse the rights of the workers to hold their sit-down strikes, Perkins implicitly sided with the strikers by offering government mediation between the two sides and supporting Murphy's efforts to open communication between labor and management. On February 2 a Flint judge issued an injunction for the strikers to vacate the premises. Soon hundred of militiamen surrounded the plant in what became a prolonged blockade. With FDR refusing to back Lewis's point of view, the only thing that prevented a bloodbath was the steady, labor-friendly hand of Governor Murphy, with Frances Perkins as his ally. On February 11, 1937, General Motors recognized the United Auto Workers and began negotiations (Martin, 399–406.).

184 *"How men hate a woman"*: Cook v. 2, 456.

185 *in order to "relieve the strain"*: Cook v. 2, 344.

185 *"Perkins was embattled*: Ibid.

185 *Calling herself "anything but"*: Excerpts from *Frances Perkins: Champion of the New Deal* by Amy Pasachoff copyright © 2000 by Naomi Pasachoff. Reprinted by permission of Oxford University Press. Pasachoff, 114.

185 *"The answer is no"*: Martin, 437.

185 *"You know me"*: Ibid.

186 *Thomas E. Dewey*: summary from Richard Smith, *Thomas E. Dewey and His Times* (New York: Simon & Schuster, 1982).

187 *"It was all the reward"*: Martin, 394.

187 *Mrs. Truman asked Perkins*: Goodwin, 617.

187 *"The duty of an officer"*: Martin, 464.

187 *"for the millions"*: Martin, 375.

187 *"Frances Perkins has discharged"*: Pasachoff, 135.

187 *The* New York Times *Book Review*: Karl Schriftgiesser, "Madame Secretary," *New York Times Book Review*, 3 November 1946, 159.

187 *friends suspected*: Martin, 235.

188 *Truman appointed Perkins*: Martin, 476.

188 *"Don't forget"*: Martin, 477.

188 *succumbed to "a long illness"*: "Paul C. Wilson Dies at 77," *New York Times*, 1 January 1953.

188 *"Apart from the important public life"*: Pasachoff, 143.

189 *"all lived separate lives"*: Martin, 472.

189 *The* Washington Post *noted*: "Aides and Admirers Honor Miss Perkins," *Washington Post*, 18 November 1964.

189 *"Every man and woman"*: Pasachoff, 147.

Virginia Durr

Virginia's engaging personality comes through in her memoir, *Outside the Magic Circle*, which was drawn from many interviews, and in her letters collected in *Freedom Writer,* edited with care and affection by Patricia Sullivan. Another Birmingham native, Diane McWhorter, wrote a rich and compelling account of the city in the civil rights years, *Carry Me Home.* Taylor Branch's detailed histories of the civil rights movement, *Parting the Waters* and *Pillar of Fire,* were greatly helpful as well as fascinating. Finally, Lynne Olson's *Freedom's Daughters* provided a wealth of detail on Durr, as well as many other women who deserve wider notice. I'm also grateful to Rose Styron and Lucy Durr Hackney for interviews.

190 *The struggle is not*: Virginia Foster Durr, *Freedom Writer*: *Virginia Foster Durr, Letters from the Civil Rights Years,* edited by Patricia Sullivan (New York and London: Routledge, 2003), 292.

192 *Her friend Studs Terkel explained*: Virginia Foster Durr, *Outside the Magic Circle: The Autobiography of Virginia Foster Durr,* edited by Hollinger F. Barnard (Tuscaloosa, AL: The Univ. of Alabama Press, 1986), xi.

192 *"genteel but poor"*: *Outside the Magic Circle,* 42.

192 *had grown up "in this atmosphere"*: *Outside the Magic Circle,* 8.

193 *"Negro inferiority"*: *Outside the Magic Circle,* 5.

193 *"never had to do anything"*: *Ibid.*

193 *"probably one of the smartest women"*: *Ibid.*

193 *"I'm not going to eat any chicken"*: *Outside the Magic Circle,* 17.

194 *"I really think"*: *Ibid.*

194 *"I think it's terrible"*: *Ibid.*

194 *"All of a sudden"*: *Outside the Magic Circle,* 18.

194 *"If you have . . . slept"*: *Freedom Writer,* 213.

195 *"something noble and grand"*: *Outside the Magic Circle,* 45.

195 *it was "all due to the Union Army"*: *Outside the Magic Circle,* 24.

195 *"When I dated," she recalled*: *Outside the Magic Circle,* 49.

195 *"A man was proud"*: *Outside the Magic Circle,* 30.

196 *He was a "wonderful influence"*: *Outside the Magic Circle,* 45.

196 *Hugo absolutely worshipped*: *Outside the Magic Circle,* 47.

196 *"I think if Sister"*: *Freedom Writer,* 38.

197 *The poor white children*: *Outside the Magic Circle,* 31.

197 *"the greatest adventure"*: *Outside the Magic Circle,* 56.

197 *"I went to the dining room"*: *Ibid.*

197 *"I just think you're crazy"*: *Outside the Magic Circle,* 57.

198 *the incident "may not have been crucial"*: *Outside the Magic Circle,* 59.

198 *"The boll weevil ate up"*: *Freedom Writer,* 5.

198 *"he was tall, blond, and blue-eyed"*: *Outside the Magic Circle,* 67.

198 *"I came back"*: Outside the Magic Circle, 73.

200 *As their daughter Lucy recalls*: author interview with Lucy Durr Hackney.

200 *"I began little by little"*: Outside the Magic Circle, 77.

200 *"I saw more accumulated misery"*: Outside the Magic Circle, 79.

201 *"I got so I wanted"*: Ibid.

201 *"That was a great word"*: Outside the Magic Circle, 89.

201 *"with a great big Adam's apple"*: Outside the Magic Circle, 105.

202 *"If I went in the car pool"*: Outside the Magic Circle, 151.

202 *"Hugo and Sister's dinner parties"*: Outside the Magic Circle, 163.

202 *"I thought she was absolutely lovely"*: Outside the Magic Circle, 99.

203 *voting rates in southern states*: George C. Stoney, "Suffrage in the South: Part I, The Poll Tax." Survey Graphic, 1 January 1940.

203 *An excerpt from*: Stoney, "The Poll Tax."

203 *Stoney wrote*: George C. Stoney, "Suffrage in the South: Part II, The One-Party System." Survey Graphic, 1 March 1940.

204 *Virginia recalled her own father*: Outside the Magic Circle, 102.

204 *caused "an absolute storm"*: Outside the Magic Circle, 103.

204 *We got in the most awful fight*: Outside the Magic Circle, 104.

205 *"blood of my blood"*: Freedom Writer, 31.

205 *Bethune was a teacher*: "Mary McLeod Bethune," The Columbia Encyclopedia, 6th ed. (New York: Columbia University Press, 2001–04), www.bartleby.com/65/ .(accessed 16 February 2005).

205 *"looked like an African queen"*: Outside the Magic Circle, 121.

205 *"You sweet Southern ladies"*: Lynne Olson, Freedom's Daughters: The Unsung Heroines of the Civil Rights Movement from 1830 to 1970 (New York: Scribner, 2001), 102.

205 *Terrell, born in Memphis*: Roberta Church and Ronald Walter, "Mary Church Terrell," Tennessee State University Electronic Library, http://www.tnstate.edu/library/digital/terrell.htm (accessed 16 February 2005).

206 *It was hot summer*: Outside the Magic Circle, 170.

206 *According to a study*: Cook v. 2, 426.

206 *These "nice-looking men with white hair"*: Outside the Magic Circle, 108.

207 *"I was terribly depressed"*: Outside the Magic Circle, 108.

207 *"these high-class gentlemen"*: Outside the Magic Circle, 110.

207 *"Killing pigs when people were hungry"*: Outside the Magic Circle, 112.

208 *All three conditions*: Disease and Distinctiveness in the American South, edited by Todd L. Savitt and James Harvey Young (Knoxville, TN: The Univ. of Tennessee Press, 1988), was fascinating and two essays were especially helpful here: "The South's Native Foreigners: Hookworm as a Factor in Southern Distinctiveness" by Alan I. Marcus, and "Pellagra: An Unappreciated Reminder of Southern Distinctiveness" by Elizabeth W. Etheridge. The following journal articles also were useful: "Pellagra in the United States: A Historical Perspective" by Kumaravel Rajakumar (*Southern Medical Journal* 3, 2000), and "Inventing the Tropical South: Race, Region, and the Colonial Model" by Natalie Ring (*Mississippi Quarterly* 4, 2003). I also relied on Ellis's and Carrigan's work on yellow fever, as noted in the Wells-Barnett chapter.

208 *"A child who's shaking"*: Outside the Magic Circle, 112.

208 *"Hugo encouraged me"*: Outside the Magic Circle, 176.

209 *As Blanche Weisen Cook writes*: Cook v. 2, 509.

209 *"The only hope"*: Cook v. 2, 510

210 *"But Gelders and other southerners"*: Diane McWhorter, *Carry Me Home: Birmingham, Alabama: The Climactic Battle of the Civil Rights Revolution* (New York: Simon and Schuster, 2001), 47.

210 *McWhorter recounts a joke*: McWhorter, 50.

210 *left Virginia "full of love and hope"*: Outside the Magic Circle, 120.

210 *"The black man is the primary test"*: McWhorter, 48.

211 *"she got a little folding chair"*: Outside the Magic Circle, 121.

211 *"All that stuff"*: McWhorter, 51.

211 *The* New York Times *account*: Winifred Mallon, "Sweeping Moves Urged to Aid South," *New York Times,* 23 November 1938.

211 *A very brief* Washington Post *article*: "'Jim Crow' Issue in Welfare Group," *Washington Post*, 23 November 1938.

211 *The next day's* New York Times: "Jim Crow Law Condemned," *New York Times*, 24 November 1938.

211 *"If the people of the South"*: quoted in Cook v. 2, 565.

211 *In March 1931*: summary from James Goodman, *Stories of Scottsboro* (New York: Pantheon Books, 1994).

212 *Virginia herself made a speech*: Mallon, "Sweeping Moves."

212 *"That sounds like a small thing"*: Outside the Magic Circle, 121.

213 *He described it as "a symbol"*: Winifred Mallon, "Black Hails Gain in Rights in South," *New York Times*, 24 November 1938.

213 *"I can see that meeting now"*: Outside the Magic Circle, 128.

213 *the conference's "chief achievement"*: McWhorter, 51.

213 *the Alabama Democratic Women's Club*: "Alabama Women Ask Inquiry on Parley," New York Times, 26 November 1938.

213 *"Of course, a lot of Republicans"*: Outside the Magic Circle, 161.

213 *"I've always been more personal"*: Outside the Magic Circle, 164.

214 *"a lovely man"*: Outside the Magic Circle, 128.

214 *"the epitome"*: Ibid.

214 *"I had no money"*: Outside the Magic Circle, 163.

214 *"He even called Shirley Temple"*: Outside the Magic Circle, 165.

214 *There were some Communists in SCHW*: A few unionists and civil-rights activists completely lost faith in the capitalist system, and they explored and even embraced communism as an alternative. There's a relevant quote commonly attributed to then-Senator Lyndon Johnson, someone not generally considered soft on Communism: "No member of our generation who wasn't a Communist or a dropout in the thirties is worth a damn." Even though most liberal activists never joined the party, their opponents condemned all unions and all integrationists as part and parcel of subversive Stalinism.

215 *My family's favorite political story*: Let the Glory Out, 78–79.

215 *"Well, McKellar got up"*: Outside the Magic Circle, 162.

215 *"When these red-baiters get out"*: Outside the Magic Circle, 155.

215 *Louis Burnham (a black activist)*: McWhorter, 77.

216 build a *"countervailing force"*: Freedom Writer, 97.

216 *"I have an invincible belief"*: Freedom Writer, 13.

216 *"from Dr. New Deal"*: Outside the Magic Circle, 158.

216 *"She had us out for tea"*: Ibid.

217 *There were six daughters*: summary from The Sisters: The Saga of the Mitford Family by Mary Lovell (New York: Norton Publishing, 2001).

217 *"They didn't have air-conditioning"*: Outside the Magic Circle, 139.

218 a *"bout of melancholia"*: Outside the Magic Circle, 145.

218 *"We had a strange household"*: Outside the Magic Circle, 146.

218 *"They were always two big dumb goofs"*: Outside the Magic Circle, 147.

218 *A favorite family story*: Freedom Writer, 15.

218 *Lucy wistfully recalls*: Hackney interview.

219 *I sat next to a tall southern woman*: Jessica Mitford, Hons and Rebels (London: Victor Gollancz Ltd., 1960), 199.

219 *"Why, I'm so absolutely delighted"*: Mitford, 201.

220 *"The poll tax committee"*: Outside the Magic Circle, 186.

220 *"We were always having"*: Outside the Magic Circle, 188.

221 *"My position on the Communists"*: Freedom Writer, 190.

221 *dwindled to "left-wing unions"*: Outside the Magic Circle, 191.

221 *He wrote his wife*: David McCullough, *Truman* (New York: Simon and Schuster, 1992), 533.

222 *According to Lewis*: George Lewis, *The White South and the Red Menace: Segregationists, Anticommunism, and Massive Resistance, 1943–1965* (Gainesville: Univ. Press of Florida, 2004), 16.

222 *"If the investigators found"*: Outside the Magic Circle ,193–194.

222 *"Cliff went to see Truman"*: Outside the Magic Circle, 217.

222 *Truman acknowledged*: McCullough, 533.

222 *"Uncle Hugo was sometimes anxious"*: Hackney interview.

223 *"A member of the committee asked"*: Outside the Magic Circle, 222.

223 *"Cliff would come home"*: Outside the Magic Circle, 224.

223 *"Hugo and Bill Douglas dissented"*: Ibid.

223 *In 1949 Clifford Durr became president*: Freedom Writer, 22.

224 *"I am frankly terrified"*: Freedom Writer, 3.

224 *"in the world of nature"*: Freedom Writer, 22.

224 *"It seemed to me"*: Outside the Magic Circle, 234.

225 *Dear Sir, In reply*: Ibid.

225 *The couple soon moved*: Freedom Writer, 59.

225 *"I was so glad to get back"*: Outside the Magic Circle, 218.

225 *"I will hear the sound of rain again"*: Freedom Writer, 23.

226 *"Even in a battle"*: Freedom Writer, 28.

226 *"He took one of those cases"*: Outside the Magic Circle, 250.

226 *"Every time Cliff got one"*: Outside the Magic Circle, 307.

226 *"I'm not basically an ideological person"*: Ibid.

226 *"When I called Mr. Nixon 'Ed'"*: Freedom Writer, 377.

227 *"We used to meet and pray"*: Outside the Magic Circle, 245.

227 *"That broke the group up"*: Ibid.

227 *"For so many years"*: Freedom Writer, 35.

227 *"Nobody thought I was a Communist"*: Outside the Magic Circle, 207.

228 *"It would not be far-fetched"*: Alfred Maund, "Battle of New Orleans: Eastland Meets His Match," *The Nation*, 3 April 1954.

228 *"Lyndon got on the phone"*: Outside the Magic Circle, 256.

228 *"I have the highest respect"*: Outside the Magic Circle, 259.

229 *Later he recalled: Outside the Magic Circle,* 260.

229 *Horton was a Tennessee native*: summary from John M. Glen, *Highlander: No Ordinary School* (The Univ. Press of Kentucky, 1996).

230 *"[Horton] was drawn to Niebuhr's attacks"*: Glen, 14.

230 *Finally Horton burst out*: Glen, 213.

231 *Taylor Branch describes this*: Taylor Branch, *Parting the Waters: America in the King Years, 1954–1963* (New York: Touchstone Books, 1989), 22. Branch added, "His wife was far less tolerant. She combined the background of a Southern belle with the sharp tongue of an early feminist, and had called Eastland a 'nasty polecat' long before the Highlander hearings."

231 *"We never had a big practice"*: Outside the Magic Circle 269

231 *"It was like being peed on"*: Freedom Writer, 17.

231 *"I was grateful that my cover"*: Outside the Magic Circle, 171.

231 *"I used to think it was funny"*: Outside the Magic Circle, 11.

232 *In more than thirty years*: The quotations from Black's opinions were found through the database of U.S. Supreme Court decisions at FedWorld.gov, http://www.fedworld.gov/supcourt/ (accessed 10 May 2005).

232 *At school the Durrs' three daughters: Outside the Magic Circle,* 269.

233 *"I have gotten a job"*: Freedom Writer, 64.

233 *"It was amazing"*: Freedom Writer, 278.

233 *"She had complained"*: Outside the Magic Circle, 279.

233 *she "had been destroyed"*: Septima Clark, *Ready from Within: Septima Clark and the Civil Rights Movement: A First Person Narrative,* edited by Cynthia Stokes Brown (Navarro, CA: Wild Trees Press, 1986), 17–18.

233 *"I could not help others"*: Ibid.

234 *"When [Rosa] came back"*: Freedom Writer, 103.

235 *"About six o'clock that night"*: Juan Williams, *Eyes on the Prize: America's Civil Rights Years, 1954–1965* (New York: Penguin Books, 2002), 67.

235 *As Taylor Branch describes it: Parting the Waters,* 129.

235 *"That was a terrible sight for me"*: Outside the Magic Circle, 280.

236 *"So that night it was decided"*: Outside the Magic Circle, 281.

236 *"If you will protest courageously"*: McWhorter, 94.

236 *"He started the movement"*: Outside the Magic Circle, 284.

237 *"The unity of the black people"*: Outside the Magic Circle, 283.

237 *"the first thing that happened"*: Williams, 82.

237 *Well, you have never heard: Outside the Magic Circle*, 282–283.

238 *They stay silent: Freedom Writer,* 11.

238 *"There was another kind of terror"*: Williams, 83.

239 *"He knew something was wrong": Freedom Writer,* 141.

239 *"I still think it is economic competition": Freedom Writer,* 186.

239 *"They accuse all the Marchers": Freedom Writer,* 235.

239 *"I sometimes feel": Freedom Writer,* 165.

239 *Upon his inauguration in January 1959: Freedom Writer,* 179–180.

240 *Southern Manifesto*: summary from Kyle Longley, *Senator Albert Gore, Sr.: Tennessee Maverick* (Baton Rouge, LA: Louisiana State Univ. Press, 2004).

240 *Just months before: Let the Glory Out,* 270–271.

240 *"If the Army and the Air Force": Freedom Writer,* 129.

241 *"The terrorization still goes on": Freedom Writer,* 180.

241 *"'Strom' troopers": Freedom Writer,* 265.

241 *"The idea was that if libraries": Outside the Magic Circle,* 233.

241 *"The funniest thing": Freedom Writer,* 239.

241 *"We live on a narrow edge": Freedom Writer,* 99.

242 *"The black people would leave"*: Hackney interview.

242 *"Montgomery goes on"* : *Freedom Writer,* 270.

242 *"Northern hit-and-run liberals": Freedom Writer,* 215.

242 *Joan Baez spoke up: Outside the Magic Circle,* 205.

243 *Three years later Virginia wrote: Freedom Writer,* 295–296.

243 *"I disagree completely": Freedom Writer,* 225.

243 *"O! That nasty Nixon!" Freedom Writer,* 415.

243 Freedom Rides: To describe the experiences of the riders, I drew on several accounts: Taylor Branch, *Parting the Waters*; John Lewis, *Walking with the Wind: A Memoir of the Movement* (New York: Harcourt Brace, 1999); Diane McWhorter, *Carry Me Home*; Juan Williams, *Eyes on the Prize*.

244 *The Congress of Racial Equality*: "The History of CORE," CORE Online, http://www.core-online.org/history/history.htm (accessed 10 May 2005).

245 *A reporter described*: Williams, 51.

245 *Diane Nash, the daughter of a middle-class family*: Olson, 151–160, 404.

245 *"If the Freedom Riders had been stopped"*: Williams, 55.

245 *"We went on singing"*: Lewis, 149.

246 *a Justice Department aide named John Siegenthaler*: Williams,

152. Siegenthaler remembered Patterson stating his position in these terms: "I'm going to tell you something. The people of this country are so goddamned tired of this mamby-pamby that's in Washington, it's a disgrace. There's nobody in the whole country that's got the spine to stand up to the goddamn niggers except me. And I'll tell you I've got more mail in the drawers of that desk over there congratulating me on the stand I've taken against Martin Luther King and these rabble-rousers. I'll tell you I believe I'm more popular in this country today than John Kennedy is. I want you to know if the schools in Alabama are integrated, blood's going to flow in the streets and you take that message back to the president and you tell the attorney general that." Williams, 150–153.

246 *"And then, all of a sudden"*: Williams, 60.

246 *his briefcase "was ripped"*: Lewis, 156.

246 *Lewis remembers coming to*: Lewis, 157.

247 *I felt absolute stark terror*: Outside the Magic Circle, 297.

247 *"We'd been cooling off"*: Williams, 62.

248 *He felt that as written*: Eye of the Storm, 134.

249 *The National Democratic Party of Alabama*: Freedom Writer, 400–401.

249 *"She still takes my breath away"*: Freedom Writer, 413.

249 *Lyndon Johnson wrote*: Ann Durr Lyon provided me with a photocopy of the letter, which is also archived in the president's papers at the LBJ Library in Austin, Texas.

250` *she told their daughters*: personal communication with Lucy Durr Hackney and Ann Durr Lyon.

250 *"I wish I could spend"*: Ibid.

250 *"Really, what they want to do"*: Freedom Writer, 413.

250 *We children were left*: Lucy Durr Hackney supplied a copy of her son's very funny and affectionate speech.

250 *She speaks in her murmurous soft voice*: William Styron, "Women We Love: Virginia Foster Durr," Esquire, September 1986, 73.

Septima Clark

Surprisingly, Septima Clark has not yet attracted the historical attention she deserves and so there's no full-scale biography available. *Echo in My Soul*, her 1962 autobiography, was written with the assistance of an editor, Blythe Legette; later, historian Cynthia Stokes Brown worked with Clark to produce a briefer and less formal memoir, *Ready from Within*, published in 1986. As with Virginia Durr, Lynne Olson's

Freedom's Daughters was very valuable. Other essentials: Taylor Branch's books, *Parting the Waters* and *Pillar of Fire*, and John Lewis's *Walking With the Wind*. I am grateful to Yvonne Clark, Alice Poinsette Frazier, and Maggie Sanders for granting me very interesting and helpful interviews.

252 *In teaching them*: Septima Poinsette Clark, with Blythe Legette, *Echo in My Soul* (New York: Dutton Books, 1962), 252.

252 *I am always very respectful*: Septima Clark, *Ready from Within*: *Septima Clark and the Civil Rights Movement: A First Person Narrative*, edited by Cynthia Stokes Brown (Navarro, CA: Wild Trees Press, 1986), 16–17.

252 *Her name might be*: Lewis, 81.

253 *The committee heard testimony*: Myles Horton with Judith Kohl and Herbert Kohl, *The Long Haul: An Autobiography* (New York: Doubleday, 1990), 105.

253 *"the center of communism in the South"*: Horton, 107.

253 *members "felt that the ultra-liberal positions"*: "Four at Highlander Arrested at Raid," *Chattanooga Sunday Times*, 2 August 1959.

253 *"found no evidence of subversion"*: Aimee Isgrig Horton, *Highlander Folk School: A History of Its Major Programs, 1932–1961*. (Brooklyn, NY: Carlson Publishing, 1989), 235.

253 *About ten minutes before 9 P.M.*: Clark herself describes the raid in both *Echo in My Soul* and *Ready from Within*. It's also recounted by John M. Glen in *Highlander: No Ordinary School* (The Univ. Press of Kentucky, 1996). Yvonne Clark's personal memories of the event were helpful as well.

254 *The* Times *was first published*: summary from *The Trust: The Private and Powerful Family Behind the* New York Times, by Susan E. Tifft and Alex S. Jones (New York: Little, Brown and Company, 1999).

254 *"I said to them"*: *Ready from Within*, 57.

254 *The old spiritual*: summary from David Halberstam, *The Children* (New York: Fawcett Books, 1999). His account of how "We Shall Overcome" came to be adopted by the movement appears on 231–233. These events also are described in Lewis, 108–111.

255 *"made the police feel nervous"*: *Ready From Within*, 57.

255 *Septima reported later*: Dan Wakefield, "The Siege at Highlander," *The Nation*, 7 November 1959.

255 *As Yvonne recalls*: author interview with Yvonne Clark.

255 *"a quart bottle containing some gin"*: "Highlander Raid Draws Protest," *Nashville Tennessean*, 2 August 1959.

255 *Sloan teased Septima*: Glen, 232.

255 *with "all the stuff"*: Ready From Within, 58.

255 *At about two-thirty* A.M.: Glen, 234.

255 *Yvonne remembers*: Clark interview.

256 *indicted it "mostly on integration and communism"*: "Highlander Raid Draws Protest," *Nashville Tennessean*, 2 August 1959.

256 *"Being with her"*: author interview with Maggie Sanders.

256 *"the underground things"*: author interview with Alice Poinsette Frazier.

256 *"a miraculous balance"*: Parting the Waters, 264.

257 *The summer before the raid*: Lewis, 80.

257 *The Student Nonviolent Coordinating Committee (SNCC)*: Robert C. Smith, "Student Nonviolent Coordinating Committee (SNCC)," *Encyclopedia of African-American Politics* (New York: Facts On File, Inc., 2003), www.fofweb.com (accessed 2 March 2005).

257 *What I loved about Clark*: Lewis, 81.

258 *Childhood*: Ready from Within, 87–102, and Echo in My Soul, 13–27.

259 *"I was supposed to be"*: Ready From Within, 91.

259 *"She wanted you to be able"*: Olson, 215.

259 *My mother said*: Ready From Within, 96.

260 *"a small thing happened"*: Echo in My Soul, 19.

260 *she found the world of knowledge*: Ready from Within, 100.

261 *According to one theory*: summary from several Mary A. Twining and Keith E. Baird, "Introduction to Sea Island Folklife," *Journal of Black Studies*, June 1980; Patricia Jones-Jackson, "Contemporary Gullah Speech: Some Persistent Linguistic Features, *Journal of Black Studies*, March 1983, 290. With increasing land development and mobility in the twentieth century, Gullah language and culture once seemed in danger of disappearing. Now several organizations work to preserve and promote Gullah, including one housed at the Avery Normal Institute building. This attention to a rich and complex culture helps African-Americans, and all Americans, appreciate our past, and demonstrates the wisdom of the Gullah proverb, *Mus tek cyear a de root fa heal de tree*—"Must take care of the root to heal the tree."

261 *"a mass of children"*: Echo in My Soul, 38.

262 *"On rainy days"*: Echo in My Soul, 36.

263 *When I taught reading*: Ready From Within, 106.

263 *Johns Island was "never boresome"*: Echo in My Soul, 54.

263 *"It was the Johns Island folk"*: Echo in My Soul, 52.

264 *"I volunteered and started visiting"*: Echo in My Soul, 61.

264 *"I kissed him so hard"*: Ready From Within, 111.

264 *Her "caste-conscious" mother*: Ready From Within, 112.

265 *"in time to say good-bye"*: Ready From Within, 113.

265 *Her granddaughter recalls*: Clark interview.

265 *"an industrious and courageous man"*: Echo in My Soul, 64.

265 *she "pieced together"*: Ready From Within, 113.

265 *"I would not have done that"*: Ibid.

266 *"the school's grounds"*: Echo in My Soul, 73.

266 *"Coughing, exhausted"*: Echo in My Soul, 74.

266 *"When the Negro doctors"*: Echo in My Soul, 80.

266 *"room for him to range about"*: Echo in My Soul, 84.

266 *"burst into uncontrollable tears"*: Olson, 216.

266 *The youngest of the six*: Clark interview.

267 *"my first radical job"*: Echo in My Soul, 85.

267 *Her salary immediately tripled*: Echo in My Soul, 87.

267 *"We Negroes felt"*: Echo in My Soul, 91.

268 *targeted by the "rougher boys"*: Ibid.

268 *The mayor had not known*: Echo in My Soul, 92.

268 *"But I refused"*: Echo in My Soul, 94.

268 *"including the virtue"*: Echo in My Soul, 92.

269 *"I am mentioning it now"*: Echo in My Soul, 94.

269 *Septima remembered him saying*: Ready From Within, 24.

269 *"red and swollen"*: Tinsley E. Yarbrough, *A Passion for Justice: J. Waties Waring and Civil Rights* (London and New York: Oxford Univ. Press, 1987), 48.

270 *Woodward responded*: Yarbrough, 50.

270 *to "put aside prejudice"*: Yarbrough, 52.

270 *"If Lynwood Shull is convicted"*: Ibid.

270 *As a result, Waring banned*: Judge Waring continued to break judicial ground in the South. In 1951, Waring was the dissenting vote on a three-judge panel ruling on a South Carolina school desegregation case, *Briggs v. Elliott*, later enfolded into *Brown v. Board of Education*. (The lawyers for the *Briggs* plaintiffs were Robert Carter, Spottswood Robinson, and Thurgood Marshall.) Two of the judges in *Briggs* concurred with the 1896 *Plessy v. Ferguson* ruling that "separate but equal" accommodations were constitutional, but Waring wrote in dissent: "I am of the opinion that all of the legal guideposts, expert testimony, common sense and reason point unerringly to the conclusion that the system of segregation in education adopted and practiced in the state

of South Carolina must go and go now. Segregation is per se inequality." From "Bitter Resistance: Clarendon County, South Carolina," *Separate Is Not Equal: Brown v. Board of Education*, National Museum of American History, Behring Center, http://americanhistory.si.edu/brown/history/4-five/clarendon-county–4.html (accessed 28 January 2005).

Waring resigned from the court in 1952; he and his wife moved to New York soon after. In *Ready from Within*, Clark notes the Warings' revenge: "They gave his retirement money to the College of Charleston, and it has to be used for a black student to live on campus. Of course, at that time the College of Charleston did not allow black people to go there. It took the college until 1976 to spend that money. Now black students can live on campus. That has come out of Judge Waring's will." *Ready from Within*, 29.

270 *Several days before the election*: Ready from Within, 24.
271 *Yvonne remembers*: Clark interview.
271 *"all hell broke forth"*: Echo in My Soul, 98.
271 *"because if the Klan comes in"*: Ready From Within, 26.
271 *Speaking of Charlestonians generally*: Echo in My Soul, 100.
272 *At one faculty meeting*: Ready From Within, 27–28.
272 *"Everyone is entitled"*: Poinsette Frazier interview.
273 *"It didn't matter whether you could carry a tune"*: Lewis, 81–82.
273 *The Highlander Folk School*: The Freedom of Information Act (FOIA), passed in 1966, opened up many previously secret government documents. The FBI file on Highlander is available online, in the FBI's Electronic Reading Room, http://foia.fbi.gov/foiaindex/hfschool/htm (accessed 22 April 2004).

The FBI file on the Highlander Folk School contains a great deal of information about the school itself but it reveals much more about the segregated South and Cold War paranoia.

Two letters in the file, both from 1958, illustrate the range of opposition to Highlander. The first, dated March 24, 1958, reads:

The members of Campbell Chapter, Daughters of the American Revolution, one hundred strong, wish to call your attention to the Highlander's [sic] School located in Monteagle, Tennessee and urge you to take steps to revoke it's [sic] charter. We are not familiar with the necessary technical procedure for such an act but have confidence in your knowledge and ability.

We feel that this school, though accomplishing some good, is influencing the mountain people of that area toward Communistic ideals.

We do not want such a school anywhere but certainly not in Tennessee.

We would like for you to know we stand firmly back of you in all such efforts.

The second is undated but the FBI stamp indicates it was received October 3, 1958. The penmanship sprawls over the page and is so hard to read that the office produced a typewritten true copy:

You Find inclosed Some Paper. There a lot of talk about this School Some of the Doctors and Preacher here are going down there making talks I think it ought to be look in to. it the only School of it Kind in Tenessie they Say and Preacher From other States are telling about it over the Radio Ark. Texas and other States. Saying Tenessie has a communist School I dont Know anything about it. You can tell more when you read this paper.

273 *"Highlander workshops"*: Echo in My Soul, 134.

274 *Clark "just moved through"*: Ready From Within, 17.

274 *"Myles Horton just washed away"*: Ibid.

274 *The one thing that struck me*: Poinsette Frazier interview.

275 *"People always say"*: Olson, 108.

276 *"When I heard the news"*: Ready From Within, 34.

276 *"the big failure"*: Ready From Within, 37.

276 *"I could just feel"*: Poinsette Frazier interview.

276 *"I felt then"*: Echo in My Soul, 118.

277 *Yvonne remembers*: Clark interview.

278 *During an evening session*: David Levine, "The Birth of the Citizenship Schools: Entwining the Struggles for Literacy and Freedom," *History of Education Quarterly* Vol. 44, Issue 3, http://www.historycoop-erative.org/journals/heq/44.3/levine.html (accessed 7 February 2005).

279 *"Bernice and her students"*: Ready From Within, 50.

279 *"People wanted"*: Frank Adams, "Highlander Folk School: Getting Information, Going Back and Teaching It," *Harvard Educational Review* 4 (1972), 224.

279 *Jenkins recalled telling him*: Levine.

279 *"You see, one thing spreading out"*: Echo in My Soul, 162. Reading a draft of this book, my father immediately thought of Sen. Robert F. Kennedy's beautiful speech at the University of Capetown on June 6, 1966: "Each time a man stands up for an ideal, or acts to improve the lot of others, or strikes out against injustice, he sends forth a tiny ripple of hope, and crossing each other from a million different centers of energy and daring those ripples build a current which can sweep down the

mightiest walls of oppression and resistance." Robert F. Kennedy, "Day of Affirmation" speech, the Robert F. Kennedy Memorial Web site, http://www.rfkmemorial.org/RFK/affirmation2.html (accessed 7 February 2005).

280 *"so the people of Georgia will know"*: "Negroes Accused of Agitation Plot," *New York Times*, 5 October 1957.

280 *Myles Horton responded*: John H. Popham, "Leaders Defend School in South," *New York Times*, 22 December 1957.

281 *"some people in Sewanee"*: Ibid.

281 *Sloan shook his finger*: Glen, 233.

281 *On September 16*: "Folk School Told to Shut a Building," *New York Times*, 17 September 1959.

281 *You can padlock a building*: Isgrig Horton, 237.

281 *Sloan dropped that request*: "Tennessee Seeks Folk-School Ban," *New York Times*, 4 November 1959.

281 *revoked the school's charter*: "Judge Revokes Highlander Charter," *Nashville Banner*, 16 February 1960.

281 *"I knew he was all stirred up inside"*: Dan Wakefield, "The Siege at Highlander." *The Nation*, 7 November 1959, 324.

282 *After the success of the Montgomery boycott*: *Parting the Waters*, 199.

282 *Ella Baker was a quiet but powerful presence*: Lawrie Balfour, "Ella Baker Biography," North Carolina State University, College of Humanities and Social Sciences, http://www.ncsu.edu/chass/mds/ellabio.html (accessed 7 May 2005).

282 *"one of the hallmarks"*: Lewis, 80.

282 *Other SCLC leaders*: *Parting the Waters*, 382.

283 Unless otherwise noted, all quoted material in the remainder of the chapter is taken from the Records of the Southern Christian Leadership Conference, 1954–1970, Part 4: Records of the Program Department, Series III, Subseries 3, Records of Septima Clark.

283 *bristled at what they saw*: Olson, 215.

284 *"The people who left Dorchester"*: *Ready From Within*, 62.

284 *"The cobwebs are moving"*: Olson, 214.

285 *"He ran up to put his arms around his mother"*: *Ready From Within*, 71.

285 *Ponder was Septima's teaching assistant*: Historian Kay Mills describes the beatings in Winona, MS, and the legal aftermath in *This Little Light of Mine: The Life of Fannie Lou Hamer* (New York: Plume Books, 1993). I also drew on Taylor Branch's account in *Parting the Waters*, 717–718 and 819–820; *Pillar of Fire*, 192–194.

286 *Hamer's summary of her motivations*: Mills, 93.

286 *Even the meals at Dorchester*: Parting the Waters, 819.

287 *Taylor Branch reports*: Parting the Waters, 820.

287 *Three white men*: Askia Muhammad, "Fannie Lou Hamer: Testimony before the Credentials Committee of the Democratic National Convention of 1964," *Mississippi Becomes a Democracy*, http://democracy.soundprint.org/FLHTestimony.php (accessed 7 February 2005).

287 *Septima Clark and Ella Baker*: Pillar of Fire, 192.

288 *Clark simply told him*: Pillar of Fire, 193

288 *"They asked me to move"*: Olson, 220–221.

288 *"She never let me see"*: Clark interview.

288 *Clark recalled*: Olson, 221.

281 *he should "develop leaders"*: Olson, 222.

291 *"Many states are losing"*: David J. Garrow, *Bearing the Cross: Martin Luther King, Jr., and the Southern Christian Leadership Conference* (New York: William Morrow and Company, 1986), 309.

291 *"If you can pay"*: Parting the Waters, 577.

292 *"the SCLC's mother conscience"*: Parting the Waters, 540.

292 *she "couldn't accept it"*: Parting the Waters, 899.

292 *"She had a real issue"*: Poinsette Frazier interview.

293 *It was funny to me*: Levine.

293 *King obliged but chose to focus*: Olson, 222.

294 *"Well, Stokely went right out"*: Ready From Within, 74.

294 *"There's Mrs. Clark"*: Ready From Within, 75.

294 *"I put a sign"*: Clark interview.

295 *NOW was formed*: summary from Barbara McGowan, "Betty Friedan and the National Organization of Women," in *Against the Tide: Women Reformers in American Society*, edited by Paul A. Cimbala and Randall M. Miller (Westport, CT: Praeger, 1997), 150.

295 *"I am all for women's liberation"*: Ready from Within, 82.

296 *told the* New York Times: "Some in Rights Council Fear Racial Polarization in Politics," *New York Times*, 19 November 1984.

296 *"From one end of the South to the other"*: Olson, 224.

296 *"I have a great belief"*: Ready From Within, 123.

Dolores Huerta

Much of the available material on the United Farm Workers focuses on César Chávez but inevitably, Dolores is included in the story. Jacques Levy's *César Chávez: Autobiography of* La Causa offers a contemporary picture of the movement and its leading figures, told largely in their own words. Daniel Rothenberg's *With These Hands: The Hidden World of Migrant Farmworkers Today* brings the story up to the present using a similar approach, interviewing many workers and growers. Personal interviews with Sarah Komer and Gloria Steinem were very helpful, and I'm profoundly grateful to Dolores Huerta for her insights and recollections.

297 *Anger is important:* Daniel Rothenberg, *With These Hands: The Hidden World of Migrant Farmworkers Today* (Berkeley and Los Angeles: Univ. of California Press, 1998), 242.

297 *"Dolores is absolutely fearless"*: Judith Coburn, "Dolores Huerta: *La Pasionaria* of the Farmworkers," *Ms. Magazine*, November 1976, 12–13.

297 *When we got to New York"*: Jacques Levy, *César Chávez: Autobiography of* La Causa (New York: W.W. Norton and Company, 1975), 267.

298 *"those hardened produce buyers: Ibid.*

298 *"I think we brought"*: Coburn, 14.

298 *She is an effective speaker*: Barbara L. Baer, "Stopping Traffic: One Woman's Cause," *The Progressive*, September 1975, 38.

299 *Her father, Juan Fernandez*: Levy, 94.

300 *"My first exposure to union action"*: Dolores Huerta email to the author.

300 *"a Mexican-American Horatio Alger type"*: Coburn, 12.

300 *she "knew the restaurant business"*: Huerta email.

300 *"At home, we all shared"*: Ibid.

301 *"My mother was always pushing me"*: Richard del Castillo and Richard A Garcia, *César Chávez: A Triumph of the Spirit* (Norman: Univ. of Oklahoma Press, 1995), 64.

301 *"There were all these guys"*: author interview with Dolores Huerta.

301 *The zoot suit*: "People and Events," *Zoot Suit Riots: The American Experience*, http://www.pbs.org/wgbh/amex/zoot/eng_people events/e_riots.html (accessed 2 May 2005).

301 *"When I got into high school"*: del Castillo, 65.

301 *"that really discouraged me"*: Ibid.

301 *"This is a common situation"*: Huerta email.

302 *"I felt I had all these frustrations"*: del Castillo, 66.

302 *"This trip opened my eyes"*: Huerta interview.

302 *Dolores stayed in touch*: Ibid.

302 *"He probably wasn't ready"*: Ibid.

302 *"I knew there was something"*: Baer, 39.

303 *as Huerta points out*: Huerta interview.

303 *The 1932 National Labor Relations Act*: Rothenberg, 213, Levy, 155.

303 *at the time she was criticized*: Karig, 22 October 1938, 50.

304 *the farm labor situation was tangled up*: summary from Kitty Calavita, *Inside the State: The Bracero Program, Immigration, and the INS* (New York: Routledge, 1992); Chávez discusses his family's experiences as farmworkers during this time in del Castillo, 10–13.

304 *The population of Mexican nationals*: Ibid.

304 *elicited nativist attacks*: del Castillo, 12.

304 *over 500,000 Mexicans*: Calavita, 217.

305 *In the driest regions*: summary from Donald Worster, *Dust Bowl: The Southern Plains in the 1930s* (New York: Oxford University Press, 2004). Worster describes several first-person accounts of "Black Sunday" in which the dust was so dense people were lost a few feet from their doorways, and one case of a small child swept away and suffocated by the storm.

305 *"The impact is like"*: Avis D. Carlson, "Dust," *The New Republic,* 1 May 1935.

305 *In a 1936 essay*: John Steinbeck, "Dubious Battle in California," *The Nation*, 12 September 1936, 303.

305 *On May 30 of that year*: summary from *Zoot Suit Riots: The American Experience*; Rodolfo Acuña, "The Sleepy Lagoon Case and the Zoot Suit Riots" in *The Mexicans*, edited by C. J. Shane (Farmington, MI: Greenhaven Press, 2005).

306 *known as the Bracero program*: summary from Calavita.

306 *As in the Colorado coal mines*: Rothenberg, 213.

306 *"Growers dehumanize"*: Rothenberg, 243.

307 *Ross himself had come to the cause*: Mark Arax, "UFW Memorial Honors Lifelong Activist Fred Ross," *Los Angeles Times*, 19 October 1992.

307 *"I thought Fred Ross was a communist"*: del Castillo, 65.

308 *"Fred showed me the proof"*: Huerta interview.

308 *Under Ross, the CSO opposed*: Coburn, 12; Baer, 39.

308 *The Los Angeles Police Department*: summary from Edward J. Escobar, "Bloody Christmas and the Irony of Police Professionalism: The Los Angeles Police Department, Mexican Americans, and Police Reform in the 1950s," *Pacific Historical Review*, May 2003.

308 *"All the Huerta kids"*: Coburn, 14.

309 *In the off season*: del Castillo, 18.

309 *the National Farm Labor Union*: The root of the NFLU was the Southern Tenant Farmers' Union (STFU), a biracial union of sharecroppers, tenant farmers, and small landowners formed in the cotton plantation country of Arkansas in July 1934, under the leadership of a group of socialists, including H. L. Mitchell and Howard Kester. Although locals were soon established in Missouri, Oklahoma, Texas, Mississippi, and Alabama, the union's base of operation remained in Arkansas until 1945. Farm mechanization and the impact of World War II shifted the union's focus from tenant farmers to migrant farm workers, whose numbers were rapidly increasing. The union also began supplying temporary cannery workers during the 1940s. From 1937 to 1939, the STFU was affiliated with the CIO through the United Cannery, Agricultural, Packing and Allied Workers of America (UCAPAWA) but ideological differences soon caused it to withdraw and the STFU remained independent until it secured direct affiliation with the American Federation of Labor (AFL) in 1946. At that time, the organization changed its name to the National Farm Labor Union (NFLU) and shifted its organizing efforts to farm workers in California. "Organizational History," *Guide to the Southern Tenant Farmers' Union Records, 1934–1970,* Kheel Center for Labor-Management Documentation and Archives, Cornell University Library Web site, http://rmc.library.cornell.edu/EAD/htmldocs/KCL05204-001.html (accessed 20 February 2005).

309 *Chávez recalled*: Levy, 90. Some Roman Catholic priests played an instrumental role in the effort to organize migrant workers, guided in part by liberation theology, which holds that the poor must be protected and defended here on earth and not simply prepared to receive a reward in heaven. While some clergy had long fought against the oppression and exploitation in Latin America, liberation theology as a movement took shape in the wake of the Second Vatican Council (1962–65). Vatican II, as it is known, was seen as modernizing and opening up the church in both doctrine and practice (for example, the priest was now allowed to face the congregation and recite mass in the local language instead of Latin). As this new doctrine took hold and spread in Latin America, it met violent resistance. Archbishop Oscar Romero, assassinated in 1980 after speaking out against the El Salvadoran government, is probably the best-known victim but hundreds of other members of the clergy were tortured and killed as well. Many conservatives in the church hierarchy have always suspicious of liberation

theology and John Paul II, who became pope in 1978, publicly condemned it. "Liberation theology." *The Columbia Encyclopedia,* 6th ed. New York: Columbia University Press, 2001–04, http://www.bartleby .com/65/ (accessed 20 February 2005).

310 *"I invited some of the rougher guys"*: Levy, 89.

310 *"César had always talked"*: Levy, 147.

310 *"Farmworkers work very hard"*: Rothenberg, 243–244.

310 *"Workers who have a union"*: Rothenberg, 246.

310 *In 1958, with the help of*: Levy, 145–146.

311 *"I made my husband"*: Levy, 145.

312 *"I heard a lot about him"*: del Castillo, 31.

312 *"I kept pushing"*: Huerta interview.

312 *"My mother was present"*: Ibid.

312 *"I knew I wasn't comfortable"*: Baer, 39.

312 *"It was difficult"*: Huerta interview.

313 *"He said I was a negligent mother"*: Ibid.

313 *to "lobby the legislators"*: Ibid.

313 *Her drive paid off*: Huerta email.

313 *"All these bills"*: Huerta interview.

314 *"They said CSO"*: Levy, 147.

314 *"One day, César called me over"*: Rothenberg, 242.

314 *"There was no disagreement"*: Huerta interview.

314 *"We wanted only people"*: Levy, 166.

315 *"The power of the growers"*: Levy, 151.

315 *As Huerta explains*: Huerta interview.

315 *"All of us have very exotic wardrobes"*: del Castillo, 68.

315 *"my relatives thought I was crazy"*: Huerta interview.

315 *"Our first office"*: Ibid.

316 *"People tend to forget"*: del Castillo, 70.

316 *"At first I wasn't"*: Rothenberg, 242.

316 *"César's dream"*: Ibid.

316 *"Our success is due"*: del Castillo, 72.

317 *"She always, from the time we were very little"*: Maria Martin, "Profile: Dolores Huerta's Struggles on Behalf of Immigrant Farm Workers," National Public Radio *Morning Edition,* 22 February 2000.

317 *César and Dolores was "symbiotic"*: del Castillo, 60.

317 *"César and I have"*: Levy, 264.

318 *"He knows I'll never quit"*: Coburn, 12.

318 *"I think we really built"*: Martin, "Profile: Dolores Huerta's Struggles on Behalf of Immigrant Farm Workers."

318 *"Chávez, a traditionalist"*: Coburn, 12.

318 *"Initially he felt our relationship"*: Huerta interview.

318 *"I know I have a terrible temper"*: Baer, 38.

319 *"I am a logical person"*: del Castillo, 73.

319 *"I could never go to a bar"*: Coburn, 13.

319 *"Poor people think"*: Coburn, 14–15.

320 *"Huerta's union activism"*: del Castillo, 62.

320 *"Women have one advantage"*: del Castillo, 67.

320 *"focused on motherhood kinds of things"*: Huerta interview.

320 *"A couple of weeks ago"*: Rothenberg, 244.

321 *"The participation of women"*: del Castillo, 71.

321 *"We had a pledge ceremony"*: Levy, 179.

321 *"Thinking that maybe"*: Levy, 180.

321 *"Everybody was angry"*: *Ibid.*

322 *"Dolores and Larry"*: Levy, 184.

322 *"This strike was begun"*: *Ibid.*

323 *"[Sergeant Gerald] Dodd"*: Levy, 192.

324 *"strong medicine"*: Levy, 195.

324 *"As brothers in the fight"*: Levy, 246.

325 *Kennedy asked Sheriff Leroy Gaylen*: Levy, 205.

325 *On August 11, 1965*: summary from Gerald Horne, *Fire This Time: The Watts Uprising and the 1960s* (Charlottesville, VA: Univ. Press of Virginia, 1995).

325 *"For the first time."*

326 *We had great difficulty*: Levy, 267.

327 *"I decided to start"*: Huerta interview.

327 *"We took the fight"*: Rothenberg, 242.

328 *"Growing grapes was never our problem"*: Rothenberg, 251.

328 *"The growers I was negotiating with"*: Huerta interview.

328 *"My speaking to workers"*: *Ibid.*

328 *"Huerta is a brave woman"*: Baer, 40.

328 *Chávez himself sometimes joked*: Coburn, 12.

328 *"Dolores Huerta is crazy"*: Baer, 40.

328 *"What the growers hated"*: Huerta interview.

328 *"We lost the PR battle"*: Rothenberg, 252.

329 *"Our workers earn higher wages"*: Rothenberg, 242–243.

329 *"Reagan was very much opposed"*: Laura Kurtzman, Dana Hull, and Mary Anne Ostrom, "For Critics, Death Resurrects Controversies, Bitterness," *San Jose Mercury News*, 11 June 2004.

330 *"The Teamsters became an alternative"*: Rothenberg, 251.

330 *"The Teamsters contracts"*: Huerta interview.

330 *At its peak, the UFW had 55,000 members*: Baer, 38.

330 *the union "antagonized their own members"*: Rothenberg, 252.

330 *"We know the work"*: Coburn, 12.

331 *"Farm workers kill themselves"*: *Ibid.*

331 *Dolores was so worried*: Levy, 335.

332 *picket captain Nagi Daifullah*: Levy, 421.

332 *"Just stand up"*: Susan Ferriss and Ricardo Sandoval, *The Fight in the Fields: César Chávez and the Farmworkers Movement* (New York: Harcourt Brace, 1997), 207.

333 *"a flat-out symbol"*: *Ibid.*

333 el cortito *was banned*: The UFW continued their push to extend the ban to hand-weeding as well. Finally, in September 2004, California banned hand-weeding in all non-organic farming operations. Forty-eight-year-old farmworker Jose Gazcon welcomed the new regulations: "When you're bending, it's nothing but pain," Gazcon told a reporter. "After three or four hours, you can't stand up. You're bent over like a question mark by the end of the day." John Ortiz, "Backbreaker Gets the Boot," *Sacramento Bee*, 25 September 2004.

333 *a "born-again commitment"*: Martin, "Profile: Dolores Huerta's Struggles on Behalf of Immigrant Farm Workers."

333 *Steinem recalls*: author interview with Gloria Steinem.

333 *Steinem helped*: *Ibid.*

334 *"She saw that adversaries"*: *Ibid.*

334 *"The women's movement has done a lot"*: Huerta interview.

335 *"We were in our board meeting"*: Martin, "Profile: Dolores Huerta's Struggles on Behalf of Immigrant Farm Workers."

335 *"I always made it a point"*: Huerta interview.

335 *"I have friends who were single parents"*: Susan Samuels Drake, "Dolores Huerta: A Role Model for Any Age," *Senior Women* Web site, http://www.seniorwomen.com/articles/articlesDrakeDolores.html (accessed 16 October 2004).

335 *"There's a long called 'El Rey'"*: "The Tavis Smiley Show," National Public Radio, 6 October 2003.

335 *"Mothers today often say"*: Dolores Huerta, "Engaging Kids in Society," *Miami Herald*, 7 May 2005.

336 *"Getting a union contract"*: "Farm Workers on the Front Lines: An Interview with Dolores Huerta," CorpWatch, 31 March 1997, http://www.corpwatch.org/issues/PID.jsp?articleid=893 (accessed 3 March 2004).

336 Earth in the Balance: He writes, "Even without the catastrophic side effects, harmful pests often quickly develop immunities
and encourage farmers to use larger, more deadly doses of pesticides.
And agricultural runoff carries the residue into groundwater reservoirs
and surface streams and into birds and fish. These hazards are not
news: Rachel Carson's epochal book, *Silent Spring*, eloquently warned
America and the world in 1962 of the dangers posed to migratory birds
and other elements of the natural environment by pesticide runoff. But
according to the National Coalition Against the Misuse of Pesticides,
we produce pesticides today [1992] at rates thirteen times faster than
we did when *Silent Spring* was published." (141)

336 *"The pesticide manufacturers"*: "Farm Workers on the Front
Lines."

336 *"God knows how many workers"*: *Ibid.* Recently some have argued that the ban on DDT increased malaria cases and deaths world-
wide. In fact, the ban applied only to the United States, and DDT use
continued in many regions where malaria is endemic. (The Stockholm
Convention on Persistent Organic Pollutants restricts DDT use to public health measures, excluding commercial and agricultural applications.) In areas where the insecticide was sprayed—the method that
causes the most widespread contamination—the mosquito that spreads
malaria often developed resistance. Currently the World Health Organization recommends applying DDT directly to interior walls, in a
concentration of two grams per square meter. In most regions with
year-round malaria transmission, two applications per year offer effective protection. *Frequently Asked Questions on DDT Use for Disease
Vector Control*, World Health Organization, 2005.

336 *pesticides remain a terrible worker hazard*: Margaret Reeves
and Kristin S. Schafer, "Greater Risks, Fewer Rights: U.S. Farmworkers and Pesticides," *International Journal of Occupational and Environmental Health*, January to March 2003, 30.

337 *In San Francisco in 1988*: Ferris and Sandoval, 257.

337 *"It was a totally unwarranted, brutal attack"*: Dan Morain,
"Police Batons Blamed as UFW Official Is Badly Hurt during Bush
S.F. Protest," *Los Angeles Times*, 16 September 1988.

337 *mayor Art Agnos*: *Ibid.*

337 *"Controversy gripped the city"*: Ferris and Sandoval, 257.

338 *Several years later*: According to the *Los Angeles Times*:
"Huerta, a leader of the United Farm Workers, suffered broken ribs and
a ruptured spleen when a police officer allegedly hit her with a night

stick at a demonstration protesting the presence of then-Vice President George Bush at a fund-raiser. The grand jury, while saying no laws were broken, recommended punishment for officers who deliberately removed the memo. [A memo about the incident was removed from the file turned over for the trial]. The Police Commission is the only agency that can decide whether to discipline the officers." "The State Jurors Clear S.F. Officers," *Los Angeles Times*, 24 July 1989.

In a later article about the use of police videotapes, the *Times* reported, "Dolores Huerta, co-founder and vice president of the United Farm Workers, filed a $23.7-million suit against the city Sept. 14, alleging that an officer broke five of her ribs and ruptured her spleen during a rally last year. The officer was reassigned after television videotapes showed him thrusting his wooden baton into a crowd outside a hotel where then-Vice President George Bush was holding a campaign fund-raiser. Huerta was distributing grape boycott literature. . . . [Police officer] Senkir complained that one crucial TV tape is 'somewhat deceptive' because it was edited to show two points of views of the incident, stretching 30 seconds of action into a minute of film. 'That's one of the reasons we do it,' he said of the police filming. 'Nobody can tamper with ours.' But Dianna C. Lyons, the attorney for the United Farm Workers, complained that the police tape, while showing Huerta in the crowd, missed the moment when she was struck. The police photographer 'immediately pans to the pavement when he notices anything questionable,' she said. 'It's amazing.'" Paul Lieberman, "Arrests, Lies and Videotape," *Los Angeles Times*, 11 October 1989.

338 *more than 35,000 mourners*: del Castillo, 174.

338 "I've always been comfortable": Huerta interview.

339 *"When Gray signed"*: Bill Bradley, "Growing Pains: What the Governor Sows, He Will Reap," *LA Weekly*, 30 August 2002.

339 *"Dolores has an incredibly strong"*: Lalo Lopez, "Si Se Puede," *Hispanic*, August (1996), 41.

340 *She proudly lists*: Huerta interview.

340 *"tough, political, responsible"*: del Castillo, 70.

340 *"We need to respect"*: Drake.

340 *"It's because of the Latinas"*: Huerta interview.

Helen Rodriguez-Trias

The material on Helen and her daughters in *The Conversation Begins* provides wonderful insights into Helen as a woman and a mother, while the interview in *For Women Only* does the same for her professional work. Many of Helen's friends and colleagues granted me personal interviews, including Marney Cowan, Marie Harvey, Sarah Kovner, Dorchen Lietholdt, Carol Marte, Esperanza Martell, Judy Norsigian, Cynthia Pearson, Elsa Rios, Barbara Seaman, and Gloria Steinem. I am especially indebted to Jo Ellen Brainin-Rodriguez, Laura Brainin-Rodriguez, David Brainin, Eddie Gonzalez, and the Center for Puerto Rican Studies at City University of New York, which houses Helen's papers.

341 *Individuals and leadership*: Laura Newman, "Helen Rodriguez-Trias," *British Medical Journal,* 26 January 2002, 242.

341 *construction workers in hard hats*: Homer Bigart, "War Foes Here Attacked by Construction Workers," *New York Times,* 9 May 1970.

341 *The New York rally featured*: Linda Charlton, "Women March Down Fifth in Equality Drive," *New York Times,* 27 August 1970.

342 *The Black Panther Party*: Jennifer Nelson, *Women of Color and the Reproductive Rights Movement* (New York and London: New York Univ. Press, 2003), 103–110. On the later years: "Black Panthers," *The Columbia Encyclopedia,* 6th ed. New York: Columbia University Press, 2001–2004. www.bartleby.com/65/ (accessed 20 March 2005).

342 *The Puerto Rican Young Lords*: Nelson, 115–116.

342 *"universally deplored"*: Michael T. Kaufman, "Lincoln Hospital: Case History of Dissention that Split the Staff," *New York Times,* 21 December 1970.

342 *"socially conscious"*: Ibid.

343 *"a pediatrician with impeccable credentials"*: Harry Schwarz, "Lincoln Hospital: Behind the Conflict over the Pediatric Post," *New York Times,* 29 November 1970.

343 *"I don't think they know"*: Kaufman, 21 December 1970.

343 *"So far as I'm concerned"*: John Sibley, "Pediatric Chief out at Lincoln Hospital, Puerto Rican Named," *New York Times,* 17 November 1970.

343 *A friend and colleague says*: author interview with Barbara Seaman.

344 *"When he drank"*: Christina Looper Baker and Christina Baker Kline, *The Conversation Begins*: *Mothers and Daughters Talk about Living Feminism* (New York: Bantam Books, 1996), 65.

344 *"most constant nurturer"*: Helen Rodriguez, "Caring for Pediatrics and Social Justice," photocopy of book chapter, title and publication date unknown, from the Helen Rodríguez Papers at the Center for Puerto Rican Studies, City University of New York, 104.

344 *"children could not learn"*: "Caring," 105.

344 *The Spanish-American War*: Edmund Morris, *Theodore Rex* (New York: Random House, 2001).

344 *During my sixth summer*: "Caring," 103.

345 *"It combined the things"*: Joyce Wilcox, "The Face of Women's Health: Helen Rodriguez-Trias," *American Journal of Public Health*, 4 (2002), 566.

345 *"My mother's people"*: "Caring," 104.

345 *"In second grade"*: "Caring," 105.

345 *"seeking a better life"*: Baker, 65.

345 *"I knew I would see"*: "Caring," 106.

346 *Helen recalls those first years*: "Caring," 107.

346 *"In Puerto Rico"*: Wilcox, 566.

346 *"One day I was called upon"*: Ibid.

347 *"I learned quickly to 'pass'"*: "Caring," 107.

347 *Helen was constantly reminded*: "Caring," 109.

348 *Every ocean wave*: "Caring," 110.

348 *"I was peripheral"*: "Caring," 111.

348 *He demanded that she stop*: "Caring," 112.

349 *"She always had leadership skills"*: author interview with David Brainin.

349 *A friend and protégé*: summary from Gerald Meyer, *Vito Marcantonio: Radical Politician, 1902–1954* (Albany, NY: State Univ. of New York Press, 1989).

349 *Helen was pregnant with Jo Ellen*: Brainin interview.

350 *"I was conveyed in a wheelchair"*: Helen Rodriguez-Trias, "Two Lectures: November 10 and 11, 1976," The Women's Center Reid Lectureship, (New York: The Women's Center, Barnard College, 1978), 2.

351 *"Having three children"*: Baker, 66.

351 *"The loneliness and isolation"*: "Caring," 113.

351 *"My decision arose"*: Baker, 66.

351 *"Dave came to Puerto Rico"*: Ibid.

352 *"I was not a great mom"*: Baker, 67.

352 *"a period of conformism"*: "Caring," 115.

352 *he "felt shortchanged"*: David Brainin Rodriguez, "In Celebration of My Mother's Physicality," unpublished eulogy, 28 February 2002, from the Helen Rodríguez Papers, Center for Puerto Rican Studies, City University of New York.

352 *her mother "studies and sleeps"* "Caring," 114.

352 *"One of the most troubling sensations"*: David Brainin Rodriguez.

353 *"my mother didn't graduate first"*: Baker, 73.

353 *"absolute chaos"*: "Caring," 118.

353 *I remember her coming home*: Jo Ellen Brainin-Rodriguez, untitled and unpublished eulogy, 28 February 2002, from the Helen Rodríguez Papers, Center for Puerto Rican Studies, City University of New York.

353 *"a sense of potential"*: Nora Zamichow, "How to Succeed: Dr. Helen Rodriguez-Trias," *Savvy*, September 1981, 41.

353 *"crucial in changing"*: "Caring," 119.

354 *"I could not stop"*: "Two Lectures," 4.

354 *"As an intern on the obstetrical service"*: Ibid.

355 *"You can't get a raise"*: Baker, 68.

355 *"When Daniel was five"*: Ibid.

355 *"I suspected I had"*: Ibid.

355 the island *"was not a happy place"*: "Caring," 119.

356 *Jo Ellen finally snapped*: Baker, 75.

356 *"He came from a large and apparently close"*: Baker, 67.

356 *"When I was twelve"*: Baker, 80.

357 *"During my third year"*: Baker, 67.

357 *"I regret not being"*: Baker, 71.

357 *"My mother has a wonderful"*: Baker, 75.

357 *"I last saw him"*: Baker, 70.

358 *"My mother is an incredible person"*: Baker, 76.

358 *"I am constantly approached"*: Baker, 79. Both daughters share their mother's passion for community outreach and public health. Jo Ellen is a psychiatrist with the UCSF School of Medicine and San Francisco General Hospital, where she has headed an inpatient unit with two specialized teams focusing on the needs of women and Latinos. Laura is a community nutritionist with the San Francisco Department of Public Health, where she develops programs to fight obesity and improve nutrition among low-income children.

358 *"the women's movement"*: Wilcox, 567.

358 *approximately 150,000 cases*: Jean Giles-Sims, "Current Knowledge about Child Abuse in Families," *Marriage & Family Review*, 3–4 (1997), 216.

359 *I found myself in the middle*: "Caring," 123.

359 *My first impression*: "Caring," 122.

360 *a meeting "with a group"*: Ibid.

360 *"I think my sense"*: Helen Rodriguez-Trias video transcript, *Changing the Face of Medicine*, National Library of Medicine Web

site, http://www.nlm.nih.gov/changingthefaceofmedicine/physicians/ biography_273.html (accessed 17 January 2005).

360 *"who determines who runs"*: "Caring," 125.

360 *"You have fumbled into a mess"*: *Ibid.*

360 *"It was a challenge"*: Tania Ketenjian, "Helen Rodriguez-Trias" [interview], in *For Women Only: Your Guide to Health Empowerment*, edited by Gary Null and Barbara Seaman (New York: Seven Stories Press, 1999), 1057.

360 *"irritating, fascinating"*: "Caring," 128.

360 *"precision and discipline"*: "Caring," 129.

360 *I said, "You can't give away"*: "Caring," 128.

361 *"My own orientation"*: "Caring," 130.

361 *As one activist*: author interview with Esperanza Martell.

361 *"I felt I had literally crossed"*: Zamichow, 41.

362 *"any delivery of an infant"*: Sidel, 111.

362 *"a poor woman"*: Wilcox, 567.

362 *"A decade after"*: Naomi Wolf, *Misconceptions: Truth, Lies, and the Unexpected on the Journey to Motherhood* (New York: Doubleday, 2001), 19.

363 *with a "surge of joy"*: Helen Rodriguez-Trias, "For the preface of the new *Our Bodies, Ourselves,*" draft document, from the Helen Rodríguez Papers, Center for Puerto Rican Studies, City University of New York.

363 *She attended many women's rights conferences*: Gloria Steinem recalls such discussions and meetings as catalytic for the women's movement. "I went to cover an abortion hearing when I was working for *New York* magazine in 1969 held in a church basement in the Village. [The government] was trying to decide whether or not to liberalize the state law and they had invited fourteen men and one nun to testify. So a group of early feminists organized this other hearing and it was like a light bulb went on: I realized I had never heard women telling the truth in public about this issue before." Author interview with Gloria Steinem.

363 *"I remember thinking"*: *Ibid.*

363 *"by far the most frequent"*: Sidel, 108.

363 *"in the context of"*: CWLU Archive, "A Young Woman's Death."

363 *"The same medical school"*: *Ibid.*

364 *As sociologist Leo Chávez has documented*: Leo R. Chávez, "A Glass Half Empty: Latina Reproduction and Public Discourse," *Human Organization* 2 (2004).

364 *the "intellectualization of sexism and racism:"* "Two Lectures," 12.

364 *Some male Young Lords*: Nelson 118–119.

364 *"She was giving us"*: Martell interview.

365 *The Peace Corps always denied*: James F. Siekmeir, "A Sacrificial Llama? The Expulsion of the Peace Corps from Bolivia in 1971," originally published in *Pacific Historical Review,* at the Peace Corps Web site, http://peacecorpsonline.org/messages/messages/467/6056.html (accessed 16 October 2004).

365 *"That was when"*: Ketenjian, 1054. Helen went on to describe welfare reform, launched by the 1996 Personal Responsibility and Work Opportunity Reconciliation Act (PRWORA) under the Clinton-Gore administration, as an example of non-explicit social policy. "No one actually said that women were going to be thrown off welfare and wouldn't have any health insurance, nor that they were going to be put into low-income jobs, be without child care, and there would be pressure on them not to have more children. Yet when we begin to examine the effects on women, it certainly seems that much of this happens to them."

366 *fully one-third*: Bonnie Mass, "Puerto Rico: A Case Study of Population Control," *Latin American Perspectives*. 4 (1977), 72; Betsy Hartmann, *Reproductive Rights and Wrongs: The Global Politics of Population Control* (Boston: South End Press, 1995), 248.

366 *"I was working"*: *Changing the Face of Medicine* transcript.

366 *"Women were usually asked"*: Ibid.

367 *"crowded, impoverished and ripe"*: Nelson, 124.

367 *a survey of 850 single Puerto Rican women*: Nelson, 122.

368 *In 1907 President Theodore Roosevelt*: Dennis Hodgson and Susan Cotts Watkins, "Feminists and Neo-Malthusians: Past and Present Alliances," *Population and Development Review*. 3 (1997). Eugenics was embraced by many prominent philanthropists and politicians in addition to Theodore Roosevelt. Mrs. E.H. Harriman and John D. Rockefeller supported eugenics studies. Dr. John Harvey Kellogg, who had organized the First Race Betterment Conference in Battle Creek, Michigan, went on to found a college devoted to eugenic education. In 1910, the Eugenics Record Office (ERO) was established at Cold Spring Harbor Laboratory, a prestigious center for biological research. For the next thirty years, ERO was the center of eugenics research and study. Much to their credit, the laboratory has taken steps to acknowledge their involvement in what they call "a dark period in American scientific

history." Through their Dolan DNA Learning Center, the Laboratory has set up a searchable online archive—www.eugenicsarchive.org—offering public access to over twelve hundred documents and photographs from the ERO files, along with essays providing historical context and pointing out the flaws and fallacies in the eugenics argument.

368 *"No doubt many"*: Malone Duggan, M.D., *The Surgical Solution of the Problem of Race Culture* (San Antonio, TX: Texas State Society of Social Hygiene, 1911), 6.

368 *"It is a reproach"*: quoted in Philip R Reilly, M.D., J.D., *The Surgical Solution: A History of Involuntary Sterilization in the United States* (Baltimore MD: Johns Hopkins Univ. Press, 1991), 45.

368 *From 1900 to 1920*: Reilly, 91.

368 *Between 1907 and 1960*: Reilly, 94.

368 *Goddard was invited*: J. A. Plucker (ed.), "The Kallikak Family," *Human Intelligence: Historical Influences, Current Controversies, Teaching Resources,* http://www.indiana.edu/~intell/kallikak.shtml (accessed 9 October 2004).

369 *"Our studies show"*: Ibid.

369 *"biological checks"*: Mariann S. Olden, *History of the Development of the First National Organization for Sterilization* (Gwynedd, PA: Self-published, ca. 1974), 15. Olden, the wife of a Princeton professor, was chairman of social hygiene for the League of Women Voters in 1934. She published pamphlets and often lectured in support of involuntary sterilization, and went on to found the Sterilization League of New Jersey and later Birthright. In each of these organizations, more moderate members ended up ousting her, but her writing reflects the mentality behind the sterilization movement in the thirties.

369 *After World War II*: Reilly, 112. Most surgeons were in the armed forces, which put limits on home-front sterilizations. There was also a growing awareness of the injustice and bad science of eugenics. In 1942, in *Skinner v. Oklahoma*, the United States Supreme Court struck down, on very narrow grounds, an Oklahoma state law that mandated sterilization for thrice-convicted felons. Justice William O. Douglas wrote the majority opinion, in which he pointed out that the statute applied to a three-time chicken thief but not a three-time embezzler. His conclusion: "We have not the slightest basis for inferring that . . . the inheritability of criminal traits follows the neat legal distinctions which the law has marked between those two offenses."

370 *the driving force*: author interview with Marney Cowan.

370 *From 1970–1974*: Antonia Hernandez, "Chicanas and the Issue of Involuntary Sterilization: Reforms Needed to Protect Informed Consent," *Latina Issues: Fragments of Historia(ella) (Herstory)*, (New York: Garland Publishing, 1995), 291.

370 *Sterilization was horrifically imposed*: Lisa J. Udel, "Revision and Resistance: The Politics of Native Women's Motherwork" *Frontiers* 2 (2001), 43.

370 *Bertha Medicine Bull*: Ibid.

371 *Hamer shared*: Nelson, 68.

371 *"The Southern Poverty Law Center"*: Ketenjian, 1055.

371 *"Although Congress has been"*: Helen Rodriguez-Trias, "Sterilization and Sterilization Abuse," in *The Reader's Companion to U.S. Women's History*, edited by Wilma Mankiller, *et al.* (Boston, New York: Houghton Mifflin Company, 1998), 272.

372 *The second important case*: Hernandez, 271–274. Maria Hurtado was given general anesthesia for a C-section and sterilized while unconscious. She did not remember signing a consent form and was not aware of the sterilization until her six-week check-up. Maria Figueroa was asked, during labor, whether she wanted her "tubes tied" and said no. After giving her anesthesia, the doctor asked her again and she said yes, but only if the baby was a boy. Her baby was a girl, but she was sterilized while under general anesthesia, never having signed a consent form. Georgina Hernandez, told she needed a C-section, signed a consent form she believed covered only that procedure. While in labor, she was asked if she wanted to be sterilized and said no. She was sterilized anyway and found out on her follow-up visit.

372 *"Most of the members were women"*: Helen Rodriguez-Trias, "Grit and Grace" in *Eliminating Health Disparities: Conversations with Latinos* (Santa Cruz, CA: ETR Associates, 2003), 20.

372 *"Helen modestly described"*: email from Barbara Seaman to the author.

373 *someone who "embodied"*: author interview with Elsa Rios.

373 *"celebrity status"*: author interview with Edward Gonzalez.

373 *"it was a trap"*: Ibid.

373 *A 1975 CESA publication*: "CESA Statement of Purpose," 1975. *The Chicago Women's Liberation Union Archive*, http://www.clwuher story.com/CWLUArchive/cesapurpose.html (accessed 9 October 2004).

373 *"More efficient means"*: "The Politics of Sterilization," ca. 1971. *The Chicago Women's Liberation Union Archive*, http://www.clwuher story.com/CWLUArchive/sterilpol.html (accessed 9 October 2004).

373 *"speaking to colleagues"*: Ketenjian, 1056.

373 *It wasn't about political analysis*: *Ibid.*

374 *went to "every single hospital"*: Ketenjian, 1057–1058.

375 *"She was soft-spoken but commanding"*: author interview with Judy Norsigian.

375 *"We were unprepared"*: "Two Lectures," 20.

375 *Some of the strongest opposition*: Ketenjian, 1053. The National Organization for Women initially opposed the proposed guidelines on sterilization as paternalistic. Helen was instrumental in the dialogue between NOW and CESA, and in the end NOW's positions on sterilization abuse were almost in accordance with CESA's. The 1970s NOW resolutions stated that "the women's movement must take the initiative to ensure a woman's right to reproductive choice and an end to sterilization abuse through education, legal and legislative programs" and endorsed all the tenets of CESA except the thirty-day waiting period, which it denounced as "paternalistic and a denial of women's reproductive choice."

Planned Parenthood also objected to the waiting period. When the New York city council was debating a bill to make CESA's guidelines apply to all city health facilities, they campaigned fiercely against it. As Councilman Carter Burden put it, "The principal, and certainly most effective lobbyist against this bill has been Planned Parenthood, a distinguished and dedicated organization which we all have reason to respect."

375 *"Perversely," according to Helen*: "Two Lectures," 22.

375 *Despite this powerful opposition*: As Helen wrote later, "Initially, the New York coalitions working to establish guidelines in the city hospitals brought together representatives of hospital community boards, health care professionals, civil rights groups, and women's groups involved in securing abortion rights. Such diverse groups as the National Black Feminist Organization, the Lower East Side Neighborhood Health Center, Healthright, Health-PAC, the Committee to End Sterilization Abuse, the Center for Constitutional Rights, the Family Planning Division of the Human Resources Administration, the Puerto Rico Socialist party, *Ms.* Magazine, the National Council of Negro Women, and the National Organization of Women ensured that many experiences, opinions and positions were shared."

376 *"I began to understand"*: "Grit and Grace," 23.

376 *"She had an ability to transcend"*: Martell interview.

376 *"The Third World Women"*: "Grit and Grace," 27.

376 *"Helen believed you could"*: Seaman interview.

377 *That was the year*: "Grit and Grace," 28–29.

377 *American Public Health Association*: summary from the American Public Health Association Web site, http://apha.org/ (accessed 2 February 2005).

378 *"There is no doubt"*: Helen Rodriguez-Trias, "A Young Woman's Death," 1974. *The Chicago Women's Liberation Union Archive*, http://www.cwluherstory.com/CWLUArchive/womansdeath.html (accessed 9 October 2004).

378 *"One of her greatest gifts"*: Wilcox, 569.

378 *"It's the slight inconvenience"*: Judy Klemesrud, "Complacency on Abortion: A Warning to Women," *New York Times*, 23 January 1978.

379 *Dr. Helen Rodriguez-Trias*: Zamichow, 40.

380 *"Racism is the hardest nut"*: Zamichow, 41.

380 *"Leadership means encountering"*: Ibid.

380 *"It is important to acknowledge"*: Ibid.

381 *"She had just gotten back from Cuba"*: author interview with Edward Gonzalez.

381 *"I try to emphasize"*: Ketenjian, 1051.

381 *The recognition of domestic violence*: Barbara Seaman, who has written many books on women's health and founded the National Women's Health Network, was herself a victim of domestic violence. She found help initially through an insightful and sympathetic emergency room nurse, and then through Sanctuary for Families, a nonprofit devoted to legal, clinical, and shelter services for domestic violence victims, on whose board I am privileged to serve.

381 *"deep understanding"*: author interview with Dorchen Lietholdt.

381 *Joint Commission on Accreditation of Healthcare Organizations*: The JCAHO regulations expect health care facilities to hold regular staff trainings, have written policies and procedures governing abuse victims, have personnel who take injured women aside, outside the listening distance of their escort, to conduct interviews and secure their immediate safety, have cameras and other tools to compile evidentiary records, and provide referrals to sources of help and support. (*The Lawyers Manual on Domestic Violence*, edited by Anne Lopatto and James C. Neely, introduction by Barbara Seaman, Albany NY: Supreme Court of the State of New York.) As Dr. David Axelrod and State Commissioner Karla Digirolamo wrote in the paper that introduced the protocols, "If domestic violence continues over time, there will often be an increase in the severity of the violence as well as

an increase in the victim's isolation and fear." In 1985, Surgeon General C. Everett Koop publicly acknowledged that more women were injured by battery than by rape, muggings, and accidents combined. Under Koop and his successor Antonia Novello, the federal government developed guidelines for combating domestic violence and by 1993, most health care facilities in the United States were subject to regulations requiring victims to receive the same attention and legal assistance that victims of rape and child abuse already did.

In the early nineties, there were many fronts fighting domestic violence and Helen was always eager to help. One example shows her pragmatic style. Elinor Guggenheimer, a civic activist and Linda Fairstein, author and sex-crimes prosecutor, formed a committee on domestic violence for the New York Women's Agenda and asked Barbara Seaman to co-chair it. The other women involved in the effort were, Seaman says, "astonished when I showed them the New York State, JCAHO, and other protocols Helen had already helped to finesse." With long-distance help from Helen, who was now living in California and about to become president of the APHA, the domestic violence movement fought back against what Seaman describes as a "wall of indifference." Seaman interview.

382 *"I might even say"*: email from Barbara Seaman to the author.

382 *In 1999 Helen coauthored*: Janet Nudelman and Helen Rodriguez-Trias, *Building Bridges between Domestic Violence Advocates and Health Care Providers*, sixth publication in the series Building Comprehensive Solutions to Domestic Violence (Washington, DC: National Resource Center on Domestic Violence, June 1999).

382 *"the women's movement is about survival"*: "Two Lectures," 22.

382 *In 1985, Rodriguez-Trias became director*: Helen Rodriguez-Trias, biographical sketch, undated, from the Helen Rodríguez Papers at the Center for Puerto Rican Studies, City University of New York.

383 *"She was very influential"*: author interview with Carol Marte.

383 *"The identification of HIV"*: Helen Rodriguez-Trias, "Candidate's Statement," undated, from the Helen Rodríguez Papers at the Center for Puerto Rican Studies, City University of New York.

383 *spur a "broad social reform movement*: Helen Rodriguez-Trias, M.D., "An Ethical Look at Minorities and AIDS," paper presented at a special session during the 117th Annual Meeting of the American Public Health Association, 25 October 1989. Draft document from the Helen Rodríguez Papers at the Center for Puerto Rican Studies, City University of New York.

383 *"She always carried two aspects"*: Gonzalez interview.

384 *"Her keen insight"*: Wilcox, 569.

384 *"At a time when"*: Newman, 242.

384 *"She was passionate"*: author interview with Marie Harvey.

384 *"I'm at a point that I don't talk"*: "Grit and Grace," 21.

385 *"During the recent election"*: Helen Rodriguez-Trias, "From Where I Sit," *FLEducator*, Spring 1997, 16.

386 *"women are not only the majority"*: "Two Lectures," 14.

386 *"I expressed the conviction"*: Helen Rodriguez-Trias, "Can Women Manage Managed Care? Notes from the Front Lines," *Newsletter of the Pacific Institute of Women's Health*, Spring/Summer 1998.

386 *"There are only three reasons"*: author interview with Cindy Pearson.

386 *"Nothing has the seeds of improvement"*: "Grace and Grit," 22.

387 *the "gaps between rich and poor"*: "Helen Rodríguez-Trias, APHA President Says Researchers Must Reach Out to Underserved," *Nation's Health*, October 1993, 8.

387 *Marie Harvey recalled*: Harvey interview.

388 *"Salient among [Latina cultural values]"*: Helen Rodriguez-Trias, *Gender Differences in Susceptibility to Environmental Factors: A Workshop Report*, edited by Valerie Petit Setlow, C. Elaine Lawson, and Nancy Fugate Woods (Washington, DC: National Academy Press, 1998), 58.

388 *be able to "look around"*: Ketenjian, 1055.

389 *"There has to be"*: Ibid.

389 *"the long arm of smoking"*: Gonzalez interview.

389 *"As we rush"*: Eddie Gonzalez and Helen Rodriguez-Trias, unpublished letter, from the Helen Rodríguez Papers, Center for Puerto Rican Studies, City University of New York.

Gretchen Buchenholz

Much of the material in this chapter was drawn from a long interview with Gretchen (for which I am grateful), as well as contemporary media coverage. I am also grateful to David Saltzman, Abigail Disney, David Dinkins, and Tom Styron for personal interviews.

390 *In this work*: Hilary Cosell, "We Love Children Back to Life," *Working Mother*, December 1988, 98.

390 *"there were three bare crib mattresses"*: Author interview with Gretchen Buchenholz. Unless otherwise indicated, direct quotes from Buchenholz were taken from author interviews.

391 *"I began to think"*: John Kasich, *Courage is Contagious: Ordinary People Doing Extraordinary Things to Change the Face of America* (New York: Doubleday, 1998), 188.

391 *"ABC is a response"*: "Gretchen Buchenholz: All Kids Deserve a Chance," *Sesame Street Parents*, July/August 1988, 28.

395 *"What's important to children"*: Cosell, 97.

395 *"Inclusion is the latest"*: Lisa Belkin, "Is There a Place in Class for Thomas?" *New York Times Magazine*, 12 September 2004, 41.

396 *"saintly and remarkable"*: Marian Wright Edelman. "The Association to Benefit Children," *New York Voice*, 28 May–3 June 1998.

396 *Perhaps best known*: "About CDF: Marian Wright Edelman," Children's Defense Fund Web site, http://www.childrensdefense.org/about/mwe.aspx (accessed 26 June 2005).

397 *homelessness*: When I was in elementary school, my mother responded to our questions about homelessness by bringing us to volunteer in homeless shelters. She also became an advocate, organizing several photography exhibits to raise awareness and founding Families for the Homeless to lobby for more low-income housing and other services.

397 *The growing gap between rich and poor*: This phenomenon and its consequences have been widely documented and studied. One of the early examinations was *The Politics of Rich and Poor: Wealth and the American Electorate in the Reagan Aftermath* (New York: Random House, 1990) by Kevin Phillips—who, ironically, was a chief architect of Richard Nixon's "Southern Strategy" of the late 1960s. More recently, in *The Reagan Effect: Economics and Presidential Leadership* (Lawrence, KS: Univ. Press of Kansas, 1999), John W. Sloan states, "Evidence from the Census Bureau, the Federal Regulatory Board, the Internal Revenue Service, the Congressional Budget Office, and numerous academic studies demonstrates that inequality is growing in the United States. Republican denials of this mountain of evidence are reminiscent of tobacco companies' denials that smoking constitutes a health threat." (250) Sloan also points out that while Reagan's economic policies may have influenced the extent and severity of this inequality, the trend began before Reagan took office and has continued, though at a slower pace, since. Sloan argues that beyond specific economic policies, one of the most significant changes that took place during the Reagan administration was a shift away from traditional ideals of fairness, which "[nullifies] one of the dynamic and progressive forces in our political culture—the quest for equality." (262) John Ehrman's study, *The Eighties: America in the Age of Reagan* (New Haven, CT: Yale Univ. Press,

2005), describes the decade as immensely transformative with significant shifts in all aspects of American life. Ehrman identifies one definitive aspect: "Not only did Reagan's economic policies do much to stimulate the wide range of changes that marked the 1980s, but reactions to them were a large part of what defined liberalism, both internally and in the popular mind, during the decade." (4) That redefinition, Ehrman points out, continued through the 1990s and into the contemporary political scene.

397 *There's no exact census*: summary from Heidi Sommer, *Homelessness in Urban America: A Review of the Literature* (Berkeley, CA: Institute of Governmental Studies Press, 2000). Sommer compiled and analyzed information from all available academic studies, and I've drawn on her work for the statistics in this paragraph. Sommer concludes that "structural factors and public policies create an 'at-risk population' and personal deficits or disabilities determine which at-risk individuals become homeless."

397 *The national poverty rate*: Robert Pear. "Middle Class Shrinks as Poverty Engulfs More Families, Two Studies Say," *New York Times*, 11 December 1983.

397 *Food stamp programs*: "Foxes, Chickens and Hunger," *New York Times*, 18 September 1983.

398 *While overall employment increased*: Anthony S. Campagna, *The Economy in the Reagan Years: The Economic Consequences of the Reagan Administrations* (Westport, CT: Greenwood Press, 1994), 116. As with income redistribution, this phenomenon has been widely documented. According to Ehrman: "Altogether some 2 million industrial jobs disappeared during the 1980s—employment in the steel industry, for example, fell by almost half from 1980 to 1988, a quarter of mining jobs disappeared, and automotive employment stagnated." (64)

398 *One study measured availability*: Sommer, 29–30.

399 *According to the original plan*: Joel E. Miller, "Cast Away: America's Abandonment of the Chronically Mentally Ill," National Alliance for the Mentally Ill, 6. More generally, Michael Givel examined the effects of funding policy shifts during this time in *The War on Poverty Revisited: The Community Services Block Grant Program in the Reagan Years* (Lanham, MD: Univ. Press of America, 1991). During the 1960s and '70s, community services block grants, or CSBGs, from the federal government to the states provided the foundation of many direct assistance programs. As a tenet of "new federalism," Reagan slashed federal funding for CSBGs. According to Givel, the states

"generated little or no budgeting resources to compensate for the federal budget cuts to the CSBG program. In addition, the reduced CSBG funds were allocated to more political jurisdictions in a larger geographic area, including some previous unserved political jurisdictions, thus reducing further the amount of funding provided any single jurisdiction. Those political jurisdictions that were served before the Reagan administration assumed office, who bore the brunt of the large budget cuts, probably were impacted even more by this trend." (214)

399 *From 1980 to 1989*: Campagna, 69. Similar results are documented in Peter H. Rossi (with the assistance of Eleanor Weber and Kathleen Morley), *Homelessness in America: Selected Topic*s (Amherst, MA: Social and Demographic Research Institute, University of Massachusetts, 1989) and James Wright and Beth Rubin, "Is Homelessness a Housing Problem?" *Housing Policy Debate* (vol. 2, issue 3), 948.

399 *Reagan sat down for an interview*: Steven V. Roberts, "Reagan on Homelessness: Many Choose to Live in the Streets," *New York Times*, 23 December 1988.

401 *"Their problems are not food"*: "Ron Doc: Who's Hungry?" *New York Daily News*, 26 August 1983.

401 *"Don't tell me"*: *Ibid*.

401 *"The greatest threat"*: "Hunger Panelists Are Criticized," *New York Times*, 26 August 1983.

401 *"wasteful and unneeded"*: *Ibid*.

401 no *"authoritative evidence"*: "What Meese Said to Reporters," *New York Times*, 15 December 1983.

401 *"because the food"*: *Ibid*.

401 *"the cruel joke"*: Bella English, "Ron Doc: Who's Hungry? We Are, Pros Here Say," *New York Daily News*, 26 August 1983.

402 *"That's when I realized"*: Kasich, 187.

402 *"There are so many"*: Sheila Rule, "Study Calls City Indifferent to Growing Crisis of Hunger," *New York Times*, 17 November 1983.

405 *"All of us have a vision"*: Marianne Arneberg, "Plea to Aid City Hungry," *New York Daily News*, 3 July 1985.

405 *"It made sense"*: Kasich, 188.

405 *Gretchen herself traveled*: Deirdre Carmody, "Delivering Dinner to Grand Central, Where the Hungry Homeless Wait," *New York Times*, 2 March 1985.

405 *A FEMA spokesperson explained*: Steven Waldman, "Aid for Homeless a Drop in the Pot," *New York Daily News*, 22 July 1985.

405 *"People should not walk"* by: "Home At Last," *Glamour*, April 1988, 195.

406 *"one-woman social agency"*: Madeline Weitsman, "The Women of '83," *New York Daily News*, 8 January 1984.

406 *"You were behind me"*: letter from Helen Palit to Gretchen Buchenholz, 31 August 2004.

406 *"In 1985, in affluent America"*: testimony before the U.S. House of Representatives Select Committee on Hunger, 8 November 1985.

407 *One woman, a thirty-year-old*: Ralph Blumenthal, "City Is Forced to Let 43 Homeless Stay the Night in Welfare Offices,' *New York Times*, 13 April 1985.

408 *In 1979 Robert Hayes*: Patrick Markee, "A History of Modern Homelessness in New York City," Coalition for the Homeless, March 2003, available at the Coalition Web site, www.coalitionforthehomeless .org/ downloads/callahanhistory2002.pdf, 2.

408 *One woman, Maria Vestres*: Bella English, "Mixing Despair with Disaster," *New York Daily News*, 1 June 1984

408 *"The thing that really haunted me"*: Ibid.

409 *The city government paid*: Victor Back and Renee Steinhagen, *Alternatives to the Welfare Hotel: Using Emergency Assistance to Provide Decent Transitional Shelter for Homeless Families* (Dept. of Research, Policy, and Program Development, Community Service Society of New York: 1987), 8.

409 *"intensified the atmosphere"*: Roy Grant, "No Place to Call Home," in *Working Together with Children and Families: Case Studies in Early Intervention*, edited by P.J. McWilliam and D. Bailey (Baltimore: Paul H. Brookes Publishing, 1993), reprinted by permission on the Case Method of Instruction—Outreach Project Web site, http://www .cmiproject.net/Stories/no_place_tocall_home.htm (accessed 22 May 2005).

409 *"I used to wake up"*: Bella English, "Home Sweet Home," *New York Daily News*, 8 March 1985.

410 *"unfamiliar and pungent"*: Grant, "No Place to Call Home."

410 *"One time we heard"*: Donald G. McNeil Jr., "As Welfare Hotels Return, Children Recall What Life Inside Was Once Like," *New York Times*, 1 June 1990.

410 *"There is a baby"*: Ibid.

411 *One of the roughly*: Sara Rimer, "'Hotel Kid' Becomes Symbol for the Homeless," *New York Times*, 16 March 1986.

411 *Hello. My name is David Bright*: testimony before the U.S. House of Representatives Select Committee on Hunger, 6 March 1986.

411 *"a kind of homeless everychild"*: Rimer.

412 *Association to Benefit Children (ABC)*: Other programs include the Graham School, which is a preschool and nursery for homeless children; the Jamie Rose House, a permanent supported-housing program for medically fragile families; the Keith Haring School, a nursery, day care, and preschool for the children of the Jamie Rose families; Echo Park, where after-school programs, early childhood education, mental health care services, job training, and family counseling are offered under one roof. These are located in East Harlem, one of the poorest neighborhoods in New York, just uptown from one of the wealthiest. Still another program is Cassidy's Place on East Eighty-sixth Street, whose mission since its opening in 1996 has been to help "100 children who are economically deprived and whose families need support—children with AIDS, children with cancer, children who are severely handicapped—and to provide for those children the educational and medical and social services support and the love and fun that will make their childhood happy." Most ABC programs also have physical therapy rooms for children with special needs and some include classrooms funded by Head Start, the federal program that began in the Great Society years, with the enthusiastic backing of President Johnson's friend Virginia Durr.

412 *"The stress of living"*: Felica R. Lee, "Poor and Rich Children Join in Novel Day-Care Center," *New York Times,* 23 January 1989, B1.

412 *The boy took one look*: Grant, "No Place to Call Home."

412 *"Every month is September"*: Ibid.

414 *the "Housing New York" initiative*: Markee, 7.

415 *David Saltzman*: In 1988 Saltzman established The Robin Hood Foundation, which fights poverty by focusing on underlying causes and seeking out programs, including ABC, that achieve measurable results. In 2003 Robin Hood spent $65 million to fund programs—93.8 percent of the money raised that year. "Robin Hood Foundation," Charity Navigator, http:/www.charitynavigator.org (accessed 20 February 2005).

415 *"look different so quickly"*: "Home at Last," *Glamour.*

415 *"Since Ruben went"*: Lee, "Poor and Rich Children."

416 *"Gretchen and ABC"*: Edelman.

416 *"She is such a good person"*: author interview with David Dinkins, 24 June 2005.

416 *Rosie and Harry's "got people"*: author interview with David Saltzman.

417 *the trading of (often unprotected) sex for crack*: Among women participating in an AIDS intervention/prevention project at

the University of Miami School of Medicine, 64.5 percent of crack users reported trading sex for money. The rate among women who were not crack users was 18.4 percent. The difference remained when women were asked about trading sex for drugs of any kind: 24.2 percent of the crack users versus 2.7 percent of non-users. James A. Inciardi, Dorothy Lockwood, and Anne E. Pottinger, *Women and Crack-Cocaine: Macmillan Criminal Justice Series* (New York: Macmillan Publishing, 1993), 102.

417 *In New York, the number of babies*: Peter Kerr, "Crack Addiction: The Tragic Toll on Women and Their Children," *New York Times*, 9 February 1987.

418 *"It was horrible"*: Kasich, 190–191

418 *The* New York Times *reported*: Crystal Nix, "Infants Linger in Hospitals, Awaiting Foster Homes," *New York Times*, 12 December 1986.

418 *"Unless the city makes children"*: Bruce Lambert, "Amid Tragedy, Concern for the City's Most Helpless," *New York Times*, 1 February 1987.

418 *"It was costing a million dollars"*: Saltzman interview.

418 *"It's cruel and foolish"*: Lambert, "'Boarder Babies.'"

419 *Now social workers*: Edelman.

419 *New Jersey was the only state*: Jennifer Preston, "In New Jersey, Infants Languish in Hospitals," *New York Times*, 16 September 1996.

419 *"Warehousing babies"*: Ibid.

419 *New Jersey agreed*: Jennifer Preston, "State Agrees to Speed Help For Infants Without Homes," *New York Times*, 21 December 1996.

420 *"We have a little boy in that crib"*: Robin Hood Foundation documentary, 1991.

420 *CBS News ran a story*: Mariah Blake, "The Damage Done: Crack Babies Talk Back," *Columbia Journalism Review* 5 (2004), at the Columbia Journalism Review Web site, <http://www.cjr.org/issues/2004/5/voices-blake.asp?printerfriendly=yes (accessed 2 November 2004).

420 *"blighted by chemical exposure"*: quoted in Deborah A. Frank, M.D.; Marilyn Augustin, M.D., Wanda Grant Knight, Ph.D.; Tripler Pell, M.Sc.; Barry Zuckerman, M.D.; "Growth, Development, and Behavior in Early Childhood Following Prenatal Cocaine Exposure: A Systematic Review," *Journal of the American Medical Association*, 28 March 2001, 1613.

420 *"interfer[ed] with the core"*: Blake.

420 *"A cohort of babies"*: Charles Krauthammer, "Children of Cocaine," *Washington Post*, 30 July 1989.

420 *A nonprofit organization called CRACK*: Frank, et al., 1613.

421 *It started in fourth grade*: Blake.

423 *We are looking*: Gretchen Buchenholz, "Mandatory AIDS Tests for Babies? Yes, for Babies' and Moms' Sake," *New York Daily News*, 17 March 1995.

423 *"Everyone agrees"*: *Charlie Rose Show*, episode 5103, 24 May 1995.

423 *One flier attacked*: ABC archive. Gretchen also recalled the events in an interview.

425 *New York City alone*: Mireya Navarro, "H.I.V. Testing For Children in Foster Care," *New York Times*, 7 June 1994.

425 *"In the case of foster children"*: Gretchen Buchenholz, "HIV Babies have Rights, Too," *New York Daily News*, 30 March 1995.

425 *"The balancing comes out"*: Navarro, "H.I.V. Testing"

426 *Since 1990, the number of U.S. infants*: Marc Santora, "U.S. Is Close to Eliminating AIDS in Infants, Officials Say," *New York Times*, 30 January 2005.

426 *"The newborn testing"*: Ibid.

426 *"It is very hard for us"*: Ibid.

426 *"A boy named Wilfredo"*: Kasich, 194.

428 *City officials estimate*: Robert Pear, "City and State to Give Free Asthma Care to Homeless Children," *New York Times*, 29 April 2003.

428 *Across the country*: "Childhood Asthma," Center for Children's Health and the Environment at Mount Sinai School of Medicine, http://www.child environment.org/factsheets/asthma.htm (accessed 15 February 2005).

428 *A 2004 study found*: Diane E. McLean, M.D., Ph.D., M.P.H.; Shawn Bowen, M.D.; Karen Drezner, Med.; Amy Rowe, P.N.P.; Peter Sherman, M.D.; Scott Schroeder, M.D.; Karen Redlener, M.S.; Irwin Redlener, M.D. "Asthma among Homeless Children: Undercounting and Undertreating the Underserved." *Archives of Pediatric and Adolescent Medicine*, 2004:159, 244.

428 *The homeless children were also more likely*: Ibid.

428 *In turn, lack of ongoing treatment*: Ann-Marie Brooks, M.D.; Robert S. Byrd, M.D., M.P.H.; Michael Weitzman, MD; Peggy Auinger, M.S.; John T. McBride, M.D. "Impact of Low Birth Weight on Early Childhood Asthma in the United States," *Archive of Pediatric and Adolescent Medicine*, 2001:155; 401–406.

429 *Homeless women show high rates*: Patrick Casey, Susan Goolsby, Carol Berkowitz, Deborah Frank, John Cook, Diana Cutts, Maureen M. Black, Nieves Zaldivar, Suzette Levenson, Tim Heeren, Alan Meyers, and the Children's Sentinel Nutritional Assessment Program Study Group, "Maternal Depression, Changing Public Assistance, Food Security, and Child Health Status," *Pediatrics*, 2004:113, 298.

429 *Gretchen knew one child, Dajour B.*: Pear, "City and State."

429 *"Over the years"*: Eve Bender, "Fast Break Team Brings Crisis Care Home," *Psychiatric News*, 3 September 2004, 13.

432 *"There is no finer public service"*: author interview with David Dinkins.

PERMISSIONS

Acknowledgements

Many thanks to: my editor JillEllyn Riley who helped me hone the idea for this book and shepherded it through from start to finish; researcher Jan Werner whose curiosity, intellect, and creativity were invaluable in finding sources off the beaten track and who also was a significant help in the editing process; photo researcher Amy Pastan, who unearthed such poignant images; Rob Weisbach, whose vision was so crucial in the final stages; Judy Hottensen who brought such insight and experience to the project; Kristin Powers, who produced the book with care; the rest of the team at Miramax Books especially Adrian Palacios, Dev Chatillon, and Richard Florest; Camille McDuffie for her skill and sensitivity in planning and executing the launch; and the inimitable Harvey Weinstein, a friend to my family who encouraged and supported me. I am also very grateful to my agent Andrew Wylie whose exceptional judgment was critical at many moments.

Three people edited several drafts of this book and shaped it profoundly: My friend Chloe Hooper who lent her keen novelist's eye for a good story and her particular savvy about tone and structure; my friend Ted Widmer, who shared his expertise on American political history; my father, Al Gore, generous and wise as always, who imparted his gifts for precision, clarity, and grounding complex subjects in timeless and essential moral imperatives. I also want to thank my mother for her advice and backing; my siblings Sarah, Albert, Kristin, my brother-in-law Paul Cusack; my uncle Frank Hunger, my grandfather Jack Aitcheson, his wife, Barbara, and the Schiff family: Lisa, David, Ashley, Dana, and Scott.

To the families of the women that I have written about, I appreciate your generosity in sharing their legacies. To those who have written about these subjects before, thank you for the doors you have opened. I am indebted to everyone who imparted their personal recollections and insights: Lucy Durr Hackney, Ann Durr Lyon, and Walter Lyon, Rose Styron, Yvonne Clark, Alice Poinsette Frazier; Maggie Sanders, Gloria Steinem, Sarah Kovner, Laura Brainin-Rodriguez, Jo Ellen Brainin-Rodriguez, Eddie Gonzalez, David Brainin, Marny Cowan, Barbara Seaman, Dorchen Lietholdt, Esperanza Martell, Elsa Rios, Marie Harvey, Cynthia Pearson, Judy Norsigian, David Saltzman, Tom Styron, David Dinkins.

I also want to thank the following friends for their contributions: Natalee Duning, Lisa Beattie Frelinghuysen, Jamie Miller, Keith Walton, Aubria Corbitt, Nader and Alexandra Mousavizadeh, Damien Miano, Lynn Sherr, Arthur Schlesinger, Jr., Walter Isaacson, and Trooper Sanders, Nancy Rhoda, Maya Lin, Daniel Wolf, Kate Solomon, Mark Roybal, and Megan Colligan. Many institutions were goldmines, but I want to single out the New York Public Library, Harvard University's Schlesinger Library, and the Hunter College Center for Puerto Rican Studies. Also, I am very thankful to those who put their archives online, making research from home possible.

Thanks to my children, Wyatt and Anna, and to those who care for them while I am working, Maria Vieira and Teresa Oliviera. Most important, I want to express my immeasurable gratitude and love for my husband, Drew Schiff, whose patience, humor, and intelligence enabled me to complete Lighting the Way.

Index